SENSATIONAL VICTORIAN

The Life & Fiction

of

Mary Elizabeth Braddon

ROBERT LEE WOLFF

Garland Publishing, Inc. • New York & London • 1979

Library of Congress Cataloging in Publication Data

Wolff, Robert Lee.
  Sensational Victorian.

  Includes bibliographical references and index.
  1. Maxwell, Mary Elizabeth Braddon, 1837–1915.
2. Novelists, English—19th century—Biography.
I. Title.
PR4989.M4Z96   823′.8   76-52717
ISBN 0-8240-1618-1

Printed in the United States of America

To Henry Maxwell, Esq., of Coddenham, Suffolk

and to the memory of
his father, W. B. Maxwell,
and of his grandmother
MEB

I dedicate this book

CONTENTS

ILLUSTRATIONS

Note: Unless otherwise specified, all photographs are from the Wolff Collection and were taken by Rosamond Wolff Purcell and Dennis Purcell.

PROLOGUE

"A Magnificent Benefactress to the Literary Estate": the Mystery of a Reputation

The background of the young woman's full-length portrait is largely dark and rich in texture: at her left a heavy brocade curtain is barely visible; behind her rises a somber crimson wall. She is dressed in voluminous black velvet, high at the neck, long at the sleeves, and so full and long in the skirt that it flows to and over nine-tenths of the lower edge of the canvas. Only a brilliant white collar and cuffs relieve her dress. Bare-handed, she loosely holds a white handkerchief in her left hand, and the long slender fingers of her right curve gently over it, in the center of the painting. The light strikes these, as it does her face: the crisp-curling short brown hair, low forehead, plump cheeks and rounded chin, the straight nose and faintly crooked mouth with a recognizably Irish expression about the lips.

To her right, the edge of a second curtain is looped back, revealing part of a deeply embrasured window, its upper portion covered by a dark valance or pelmet. Below, in the left windowframe, a lace curtain stirs in the breeze coming in through the half-revealed open central portion of the window, beyond which one barely catches sight of a green tree in a garden. From an elaborately carved plaster ornament in the ceiling of the bay hangs a chandelier, whose pendants almost merge with the fringe of the valance. Through this window a dramatic little second burst of light shines from behind the woman, illuminating the objects on a small table at her side: a little pile of calfbound books with brightly colored labels, a small folding writing-desk lined in dark velvet, with a sheet of white paper on the writing-surface, a glass inkwell, and, nearest the woman's right hand, a pen. Before the table stands an oval-backed chair.

The chiaroscuro forces the spectator to concentrate his attention upon the woman's face and hands, her pen, ink, and paper. Determination, even doggedness, can be seen in the steady look of her eyes and the firm set of her chin. Though standing in repose and not in the least pretty, or even handsome, she is buxom, healthy, tense with energy. She is no virgin, nor yet a sheltered cosseted matron: she has lost her innocence, known

I

betrayal, seen the world at its harshest. She has little patience with cant and she rather expects the worst. She is kindly but formidable; there is no nonsense about her. She is looking at you seriously above her velvet and out of the brocaded, fringed, and tasseled scenery behind her. The right-hand corner of her mouth looks as if she might smile at any moment or even laugh aloud at something ridiculous.

Amidst the gloom and the overpowering Victorian propriety of her surroundings—it is clearly the *best* velvet, the heaviest brocade, the most durable fringe to be had for money—she is at ease with herself and with the objects on her table, which are obviously the tools of her trade. She has temporarily laid down the pen so that it might produce for the painter its own highlight alongside the dark writing-desk, conveniently close to the slight glitter of the heavy crystal base of the inkwell, with the positive flash of that blank sheet just beyond, insistently demanding—as nature abhors a vacuum—to be filled with even-flowing cursive handwriting. When the sitting is finished, she has but to reach out her right hand, as important in the portrait as her face or the sheet of paper, grasp the pen once more, turn her back upon the painter and the observer, seat herself in her austere but comfortably upholstered chair, and resume her interrupted work.

It is a very fine Victorian portrait indeed, and so it ought to be: the artist was William Powell Frith (1819–1909), still celebrated for his "Derby Day," exhibited in 1858. He painted our picture seven years later, in 1865, at the height of his powers. The sitter was already a close personal friend, and so remained for the rest of his life. We may trust the view of her character that he has transmitted to us so subtly. When he painted her in 1865 she was thirty years old and already as famous for her novels as Frith for his painting, although her success was more recent than his. Her name was Mary Elizabeth Braddon, and she is to be our protagonist. Hereafter she will often appear as MEB.

"She is a part of England," wrote Arnold Bennett admiringly in 1901—MEB was by then sixty-six and still going strong—"she has woven herself into it; without her it would be different. This is no mere fanciful conceit." Reflecting on her celebrity, he remarked, "there are thousands of tolerably educated English people who have never heard of Meredith, Hardy, Ibsen, Maeterlinck, Kipling, Barrie . . . but you would travel far before you reached the zone where the name of Braddon failed of recognition." When she died in 1915, almost eighty, this was still true. Yet now she is totally forgotten.

So are many other Victorian novelists, once famous. Some of them deserve oblivion. But when I first began to read MEB's fiction and the comments of her contemporaries upon it, I was struck by a second irony: not only was she forgotten, but even at the height of her fame she had never been properly appreciated. She wrote famous tales of murder and bigamy—"sensation-novels." But unlike other sensation-novelists, she introduced into these novels of crime psychological subtleties and social commentary that went unnoticed. And she wrote many novels without a trace of mystery or crime, in which she explored social relationships with understanding, irony, and wit.

How had she learned so much about human nature? What had her life been? To seek the answers was to court frustration and mystification. A few affectionate paragraphs in the autobiography of her son, W. B. Maxwell, himself a novelist, a brief and unsatisfactory notice in the *DNB*, a charming and appreciative essay by Michael Sadleir: that was all. During the 1960's a series of fortunate encounters and discoveries enabled me to examine and often to acquire large numbers of unpublished Braddon letters, diaries, notebooks, and literary manuscripts. By the early seventies, it was possible to tell for the first time the story of her life, as sensational in its way and for its time as any novel she ever wrote. Only gradually could one appreciate the close relationship between her experience of life and her novels. The biographer's job and the critic's job proved to be the same job.

Mary Elizabeth Braddon's adventures and the thousands of pages of fiction that she wrote illuminate each other. Neither is understandable without the other. Looked at together, they help us recreate the lost age of the Victorians and Edwardians as a time for a woman to be alive. The standards and behavior of a departed society, the life of the theatre, the inside of the novel-writing industry, what it cost a woman to defy sexual conventions, the conflict between money-making and artistic integrity, the brutality of hostile critics, the delicious fruits of success: all these are brought to life once more in her experience and in her prose. Our exploration of social history and of literary criticism, our biographical detective work revive the complex character of a talented and sophisticated woman.

In 1862, three years before MEB sat for Frith and thirty-nine years before Arnold Bennett reached his judgment, she had published *Lady Audley's Secret*, the novel that rocketed her into celebrity. Its protagonist, Helen Maldon, a poor girl with magnificent wavy golden hair, marries George Talboys, a young dragoon of good family, whose father disowns him for marrying beneath his station. George goes off to seek his fortune in Australia; Helen changes her name to Lucy Graham and takes a post as governess in the family of a country surgeon. Here she meets Michael Audley, a rich widowed baronet with a splendid country estate. When Sir Michael proposes to her, she has not heard from George for several years and easily persuades herself that she is probably a widow. She becomes Lady Audley. Though Sir Michael already has a great white beard (he is fifty-six) his new wife makes him blissfully happy, and he indulges her by surrounding her with every luxury.

When George Talboys returns from Australia, having made twenty thousand pounds in the gold fields, Lady Audley inserts into the newspapers a notice of the death of Helen Talboys. But George Talboys had been a school friend of Sir Michael Audley's nephew, Robert Audley, a young barrister. So the bereft George meets his former wife now bigamously married. Lady Audley resourcefully takes him for a stroll. In a remote corner of the garden at the end of an avenue of lime trees is an old disused well. George makes the mistake of leaning on the windlass, whereupon Lady Audley pulls out the iron spindle and sees her real husband "sink with a horrible cry into the black mouth of the well."

Determined to find out what has happened to his friend, Robert Audley undertakes the arduous investigation that finally enables him to pin the crime upon his stepaunt. In order to thwart him, she tries to burn him alive in a locked bedroom at an inn. He manages to escape, but the fire kills the landlord. When Robert denounces Lady Audley to his uncle, Sir Michael, broken-hearted, has her immured in a Belgian *maison de santé*. Her crimes have been due to a hereditary taint of madness; this is Lady Audley's deepest secret. George Talboys has escaped alive from the well—arm broken and clothes covered with slime—and his bigamous wife and would-be murderess is allowed to die in the madhouse.

Unfortunately for her reputation, MEB all her life remained "the author of *Lady Audley's Secret*." Even today, when she is remembered at all, she is still associated with her artless and somewhat trashy first great success. Yet the novel reached the public almost by accident. *Robin Goodfellow*, a new weekly London sixpenny magazine, had published a first installment in its first number of July 6, 1861; but the magazine failed after thirteen issues. MEB abandoned *Lady Audley's Secret* incomplete and went to work immediately on her next novel, *Aurora Floyd*—"When I began her," she afterwards wrote of *Aurora Floyd*, "I did not mean to finish 'Lady A.'" But then came anxious letters of inquiry from the public, notably from the famous actor and writer of comedies J. B. Buckstone, who had known MEB, asking insistently how the story would have come out. So in January 1862, *Lady Audley's Secret* began serial publication all over again in Ward and Lock's *Sixpenny Magazine,* a monthly "for all classes and all seasons." This time Miss Braddon brought it triumphantly to a conclusion in twelve installments. Three months before it ended its serial run, the new firm of Tinsley Brothers published it in October 1862 in the three-volume form then conventional for the novel.

MEB dedicated it to Sir Edward Bulwer-Lytton, "in grateful acknowledgment of literary advice most generously given," and told him that she had written "the third and some of the second vol. of 'Lady A.' in less than a fortnight, & had the printer at me all the time." *Lady Audley's Secret* was off at once to enormous sales, requiring eight three-volume editions between October and December 1862. The Tinsleys made so large a fortune that the elder brother, Edward, called his new house "Audley Lodge" in appreciation.[1]

In *Lady Audley's Secret,* MEB was asking its readers to overlook a good many improbabilities. Could Robert Audley, the barrister whom Miss Braddon had described as too "lymphatic" to practice his profession, and who spent his time smoking and reading French novels, have summoned up the energy and determination to carry out his arduous inquiry? Would two servants who held Lady Audley in their power, because they knew what she had done with George Talboys, have limited their blackmail to a few pounds at a time? Would Sir Michael Audley, infatuated though he was, have married a governess without knowing anything about her personal background? And how was it that Lady Audley's fits of madness descended upon her only at the precise moments when it was necessary for her to commit a crime in order to obtain what she wanted or to prevent exposure?

In spite of all this, Robert Audley's prolonged duel with his beautiful stepaunt still retains its suspense and excitement. The two labels, pasted one above the other on a bonnet box, that first reveal Lady Audley's change of name from Helen Talboys to Lucy Graham; the letter in Helen Talboys' hand that is identical to Lady Audley's hand, proving that they are the same person; the interviews with the landlady of a run-down seaside boarding house or with the school mistress down on her luck—each damning episode that contributes to the growing case against Lady Audley whets one's interest and, incidentally, provides a vignette of England in the late fifties. These were literary techniques only recently invented by Wilkie Collins in his brilliant *Woman in White* (1860), and Mary Elizabeth Braddon now bade fair to become as skillful as he in their use.

Much indeed was new about the genre that Collins had invented and MEB was adapting: notably, the setting of a story of criminal suspense in everyday surroundings, and the invitation to the reader to unravel the mystery as the detective (whether amateur or professional) was unraveling it. But much was old, as *The Spectator* recognized when it said of *Lady Audley's Secret*: "People . . . nowadays . . . will not read about haughty barons, and virtuous bandits, and haunted castles, and innocent victims flying from an unintelligible pursuit to an incomprehensible rescue." But readers of the class who would once have read Mrs. Radcliffe "now pore over stories as absurd as hers." MEB had "appreciated the popular taste, and constructed a story as wild" as a Gothic novel, but "modern in its machinery, and in the language in which that machinery is described." The reviewer feared, however, that writers for the "classes who love the horrible and grotesque" would not be "content with their true place in literature, which is not above the basement,"[2] amongst the servants. Far kinder, the *Times* critic found it "really delightful to see how the evidence accumulates bit by bit, and each bit in its proper place and at the proper time, in the most logical order." Beauty and deformity had been skillfully combined. If MEB could have managed to reconcile the contradictions perfectly, she "would be entitled to rank as the first of lady novelists. . . . it is seldom that one sees a novel . . . showing such *even* excellence of passion, of character, and of diction."[3]

Neither reviewer commented on one striking aspect of Miss Braddon's writing: her effort to set her stage. Still the work of a beginner, her descriptions of Lady Audley's apartments and of her person showed an exuberant imagination and a sharp eye. Lady Audley's boudoir lay beyond

> a great drawing-room, rich in satin and ormolu, buhl and inlaid cabinets, bronzes, cameos, statuettes, and trinkets, . . . then . . . a morning-room, hung with proof-engravings of valuable pictures . . . [and] an ante-chamber . . . octagonal . . . hung with Claudes and Poussins, Wouvermans and Cuyps. . . .

In her dressing room, the atmosphere was

> almost oppressive from the rich odours of perfumes in bottles whose gold stoppers had not been replaced. A bunch of hothouse

flowers was withering away upon a tiny writing-table. Two or three handsome dresses lay in a heap upon the ground. . . . Jewellery, ivory-backed hairbrushes, and exquisite china were scattered here and there.

Though a novice, MEB was already more than a mere cataloguer. In Lady Audley's portrait, the painter "had spent a most unconscionable amount of time upon the accessories . . . my lady's crispy ringlets and the heavy folds of her crimson velvet dress." No one but "a pre-Raphaelite would have so exaggerated every attribute of that delicate face as to give a lurid lightness to the blonde complexion and a strange sinister light to the deep blue eyes . . . or could have given to that pretty mouth the hard and almost wicked look." Thinking, in her boudoir, Lady Audley sat in "half-recumbent attitude, with her elbow resting on one knee, and her perfect chin supported by her hand, the rich folds of drapery falling away in long undulating lines from the exquisite outlines of her figure, and the luminous rose-coloured fire-light enveloping her in a soft haze, only broken by the golden glitter of her yellow hair."[4] In time, MEB would acquire greater skill, but already she had clearly caught the eternal fascination aroused by the close conjunction of beauty, luxury, and wickedness. However old the formula might be, she had added new ingredients to it. As Percy Fitzgerald remarked, she had "exactly hit the public mood or humour of the moment."[5]

And for more than half a century she went on hitting it, year after year. *Lady Audley's Secret* was her third or fourth novel, the number depending on one's choice of serial or book-publication date; and from 1862 onward, a steady stream of novels poured from her pen, sometimes two or three a year. Her last, at least her eightieth, appeared posthumously in 1916. Besides all the novels that MEB acknowledged, in the early 1860's she also turned out anonymously or pseudonymously a good deal of still more lurid fiction, published in penny or halfpenny journals, written in a monosyllabic and repetitious style designed for a newly literate audience, and steeped in violence. Much of this still lies buried in the papers for which she wrote it. But two of these novels she rescued and published in the standard three-volume form. These penny-dreadfuls—resurrected in order to take advantage of her soaring reputation and to increase her large earnings—gave her enemies a chance to sneer at her.[6] For in the sixties even her acknowledged fiction aroused violent antipathy in some critics, who bitterly attacked her as a purveyor of immorality. Yet moral outrage, real or feigned—often combined with professional jealousy—fails to account for the virulence of the onslaught accompanied, at times, by obvious personal hatred. Only the mysterious circumstances of MEB's life can explain the venom of her hostile critics. She defended herself and found other defenders. By late 1868, the tempest, an important episode in the literary criticism of the 1860's, had died down.[7]

Her success and reputation bade fair to trap her in the genre she had invented. Although she was always careful to try to hold her original public, she quickly transcended *Lady Audley's Secret*, learning to make incident flow from character, to understand human motivations, to draw credible and sympathetic personages in the round. Unflaggingly inventive, an assiduous student of French models, she soon left far behind the somewhat mechanical devices of her first great success. Her sensation-novels became steadily more interesting, and she often wrote a novel wholly without "sensational" themes. Flaubert, Balzac, Zola, in turn taught her lessons. She suffered at the hands of Victorian society and loathed its hypocrisies and cruelties. These she taught herself to satirize so skillfully that her readers need not see her doing it. Even friendly critics failed to note that she was experimenting, innovating, developing, improving, changing. From time to time some discovered in her what they called "Miss Braddon's new manner," but they let it puzzle them and made no effort to analyze it. Her versatility escaped their notice.

Richly rewarded for her efforts from *Lady Audley* onward, possessed of almost superhuman energy, curious and ambitious, she became a cultivated woman of the world, at home in French, German, and Italian literature, as well as English, reading history and theology, looking at paintings, and listening to music. One cannot argue that each of her novels marked an advance over all its predecessors: there were, of course, potboilers and disappointments. But from the early sixties to the early nineties the trajectory of her writing was generally upward. Her masterpieces—wholly different from each other and each different from anything else she wrote—were *Joshua Haggard's Daughter* (1876) and *Ishmael* (1884). After a slump in the mid-nineties, she was off again to a wholly new career, no longer a Victorian but an Edwardian and—in the end—an early Georgian.

Among her eighty novels, a modern reader will find half a dozen of surprising excellence, all able to stand comparison with the achievements of novelists who are still idolized while she is forgotten. Immediately below her top level he will distinguish thirty or forty more novels that are unfailingly interesting and entertaining, full of expert character drawing and notable for their sardonic and up-to-date comment on the changing social scene. Although the rest of her novels are less memorable as literature, there are only three or four of the whole number that do not contribute to one's appreciation of Victorian social history. MEB was versatile, observant, satirical, both humorous and witty, sophisticated, and full of shrewd common sense.

When *Lady Audley's Secret* appeared in 1862, she was twenty-seven. She had deliberately decided in the late 1850's and early 1860's to flout Victorian convention and the Victorian proprieties. She had brought down upon herself bitter suffering and had incurred a degree of social ostracism. In the chapters that follow, the drama of her experience can be discussed freely for the first time. By the mid-1870's her time of trial was largely over. By then she had become—and remained until she died in 1915—an admired and beloved member of the London literary, theatrical, artistic, and social world. Befriended in her early days as a writer only by Bulwer-Lytton and Charles Reade, two men a generation older than she, she knew everybody worth knowing in the many decades of her success and prosperity. She led an exemplary, demanding, and joyous family life.

The acknowledged masters of English fiction enjoyed her books and paid her tribute. Dickens' daughter, Kate Perugini, remembered that her father's favorite Braddon novel had been *The Doctor's Wife* (1864), while Thackeray's daughter, Lady Ritchie, wrote that *her* father—who had died in 1863—especially admired *Lady Audley's Secret*. Three times in the same day he had walked to the railway station in Westgate to inquire for a parcel he was expecting from London. Finally he returned with it, calling out happily, " 'It has come; I have it here.' " It was MEB's latest novel. Bulwer was MEB's friend and mentor. He read her novels with relish and so did his son Robert, the poet "Owen Meredith." In conversation, Charles Reade, who knew her well, would declare, "Her fertility of invention is boundless, her industry phenomenal, her style sound and vigorous, and she has rare dramatic instincts."[8]

Before he died in 1894, Stevenson wrote MEB from Samoa: "I remember reading *Lady Audley's Secret* when I was fifteen, and I wish my days to be bound each to each by Miss Braddon's novels." Everywhere in the Pacific, he went on, when a new schooner came into port and the traders eagerly hoped to find aboard some novel that they had not read, there was always one that they already had: MEB's *Aurora Floyd* (1863): "It is something to be out and away greater than Scott, Shakespeare, Homer, in the South Seas, and to that you have attained."[9]

In his *Confessions* (1886), George Moore remembered his parents sitting in the "great family coach" as it lumbered along a narrow Irish road, "talking of a novel the world is reading. Did Lady Audley murder her husband? Lady Audley! What a beautiful name! and she, who is a slender, pale, fairy-like woman, killed her husband." Moore "took the first opportunity of stealing the novel. . . . I read it eagerly, passionately, vehemently. I read its successor, and its successor. . . . until I came to a book called *The Doctor's Wife*—a lady who loved Shelley and Byron. There was magic, revelation, in the name, and Shelley became my soul's divinity."[10] And in an autobiographical novel, "Rita" (Mrs. Desmond Humphries), a popular Irish novelist, recalled her childhood self at twelve confessing to a young aunt that she had read *Aurora Floyd*:

> "Mamma does not know—"
>
> "Good gracious! I hope not. A book like that isn't fit for a child of your years."
>
> "I thought it lovely," I said, "I would give anything to read the other one, 'Lady Somebody's Secret.' I heard people speaking about it. . . . They said that it was a new sort of novel, different from anything done before—sensational. There's a murder in it, isn't there?"
>
> "Yes," she said, "And many other things that little girls have no business to know anything about."[11]

Aged only twenty-one, the precocious Henry James reviewed *Aurora Floyd* at length in 1865 for *The Nation*, appreciating its skill and discussing the new genre's place in literature. "Miss Braddon," he said, "goes to work like an artist." Many years later, in 1911—long after they had come to know one another—when they were both old, and he had sent her a book, and she had thanked him, he wrote to her:

> It was delightful to me, at the end of so much time, to have the occasion to make you a small definite sign in respect to all the fond beguilement of other days that your gallant literary name calls up for me the memory of. I used to follow you ardently, and track you close, taking from your hands deep draughts of the happiest of anodynes. I wanted to sacrifice—so very easily—to that warm remembrance—which so many of the dear old associations and presences of our younger time are mingled with.

And a few weeks later, as she worked on a new book, he encouraged her in a memorable Jacobite sentence:

May your strain and stress over the terrible act of neat and not slobbery transfusion to which we are all condemned—transfusion from the perpetual and all so greasy *pot-au-feu* to the beautiful little painted and carefully wiped and smilingly-presented bowls in which we hawk the precious mixture—may that fond convulsion, I say, presently abate, and leave you resignedly conscious of—well let us call it so bravely—of being again, and for the hundredth time a magnificent benefactress to the literary estate.[12]

Ford Madox Ford admiringly remembered MEB as a writer "who took her work more seriously than herself." Just before the first World War, he had found her at home in her handsome house in Richmond, almost eighty, dressed like Queen Victoria, learning Greek. "She was then reading the 'Iliad.' I hope she finished the 'Odyssey' too before she died . . . there she sat, with her family . . . and with vicars and maids of honour" and notable actresses like Madge Kendal, "with her court and the Greek words running around in her mind. And her room even was perfection. There were long black velvet curtains with gold-edged scallopings a-top, and embroidered fire-shields like the pennants of knights, and a great Turkey carpet with a pile into which the feet sank as if into a Scotch lawn." And in the center was "the great ormolu drawing-room table. Upon it was a great album of Views of Venice; on that a slightly smaller Views of Rome; a still slightly smaller Views of Heidelberg, and so, on the top of the pyramid, an ivory model of the Taj Mahal." MEB talked about the Indian Mutiny and the first London appearance of Sir Henry Irving. "Her voice was low, soft, and, as it were, inexorable, as if some of the intolerant youth of the young woman who had ridden to hounds remained at the back of that acute brain. The good sea-coal fire shone on gleaming steel and gilt accoutrements. So there you had the clean fire, the clear hearth, and the vigour of the Victorian game."[13]

Nor was it only the novelists who found MEB's books absorbing. In the summer of 1868, when Tennyson was dining with the young Arthur Brookfield, then sixteen, the son of his old friend William Henry Brookfield, he was delighted to discover that Arthur had been reading Miss Braddon, and said, "Do you know that I am simply steeped in Miss Braddon? I'm reading every book she ever wrote." And in 1891 Gladstone declared himself "fairly launched" on her new novel, and wrote her that he would "promptly and with warm interest pursue my voyage to the close." He added,

All my life I have known, and a little fretted, yes wept, under the
knowledge that to construct a novel worthy of the name was for
me not difficult but impossible. The abundance and brightness of
your material, and the facility and skill with which you arrange it,
quicken this sense within me and make me feel, as when I stand
before a real picture, that some human beings have faculties which
are in others not merely inferior but absent.[14]

MEB, who had destroyed many of the admiring letters she received,
kept this one: how agreeable to have the great man—of whom she
had once painted a not wholly flattering portrait in a novel—not only paying tribute to her book, but confessing his frustration at not having
been able to challenge Disraeli in fiction as well as in Parliament. From an
elderly Englishman teaching English at the University of Bologna, MEB
in 1888 received within two days a letter addressed only "Miss Mary
Elizabeth Braddon, author of *Lady Audley's Secret*, London, Inghilterra."
He told her that he used her novels as first English books for his pupils:
"Your books are the best of all, both as to continued interest, construction, and fine effect on the spirits."[15]

When Arnold Bennett tried in 1901 to analyze the reasons for her success, he turned back to *Lady Audley's Secret*, then almost forty years old.
It already seemed old-fashioned in externals ("It refers to postillions and
chariots"), but "the essential vitality remained." The plot had been used a
thousand times since, but was

admirably adapted for broad and simple sensationalism. Take a
young and beautiful woman, golden-haired, amiable, exquisitely
feminine. Surround her with every circumstance of happiness—a
wealthy middle-aged husband, who worships her innocent
simplicity; a fine old English home; the universal adoration of
dependents. Then lift the edge of the curtain of the past, disclos-
ing behind it the monstrous shadow of a crime. Slowly raise the
curtain, and raise it, till the full history of this enchanting creature
. . . stands dreadfully clear.

Although the reader was early aware of Lady Audley's guilt, and
although the ending was not a happy one, the book was enormously successful because the crime was revealed slowly and ingeniously, but above
all because Miss Braddon, an artist, never let her invention flag.
Bennett had read *Lady Audley's Secret* prepared for the worst, with his

mind "hypersensitised to receive critical impressions." He was surprised "at its level excellence, its honesty, its fine disdain of trade tricks . . . the sound vigour of the writing. . . . Not infrequently she strikes the true lyric note:

> "He will do it," she said, between set teeth; "he will do it unless I get him into a lunatic asylum first; or unless—" She did not finish the thought in words. She did not even think out the sentence; but some new and unnatural pulse in her heart seemed to beat out each separate syllable against her will. The thought was this: "He will do it, unless some strange calamity befalls him, and silences him for ever." The red blood flashed up into my lady's face with as sudden and transient a blaze as the flickering flame of a fire, and died as suddenly away, leaving her paler than winter snow. Her hands, which had before been locked convulsively together, fell apart and dropped heavily at her sides. . . . Lady Audley stood still for about five minutes in that strangely statuesque attitude, her head erect, her eyes staring straight before her—staring far beyond the narrow boundary of her chamber wall, into dark distances of visionary horror.

"That is English," said Arnold Bennett. "Wilkie Collins could not have done it; . . . nor, I dare to say, sundry greater men whom to name in this connection would be to call forth a protest; nor any other living sensational writer. '*Staring far beyond the narrow boundary of her chamber wall, into dark distances of visionary horror!*' It is prose. It has the genuine vital impulse—the impulse which created *The Duchess of Malfi,* *Wuthering Heights,* and other masterpieces of dread."

But, for all his generous appreciation, Arnold Bennett altogether failed to recognize the complexity of Miss Braddon's case. He declared that *Lady Audley's Secret* "in some ways . . . remains unsurpassed by her later work," whereas he might more accurately have called it only a primitive prototype of her later sensation novels. Although perceiving that "she has developed in her middle and later periods a manner which is at once more elaborately skillful and more especially her own," he abandoned his analysis at that and so fell into the oversimplification of earlier critics. He praised her then recent novel *Rough Justice* (1898) : "She knows the ways of prosecuting counsel at Bow Street, how lodgers bang doors, what game is shot in South Africa and the Dutch name of it and the name of the gun, how a ship leaves port, and how a guttersheet [i.e., a scandalous newspaper] dies." But he failed to note that in *Rough Justice* the murderer is a philanthropist, who shoots his female cousin in order to inherit a fortune that he intends to use solely for the benefit of mankind. This fanatic has convinced himself that the life of a single individual does not matter when measured against the benefactions he intends to confer upon the lower orders. So *Rough Justice* provided a pungent comment both on late Victorian social work, and on the subtle relationship between wealth, the charitable impulse, and the lust for power. This Bennett missed.

It was, then, not only petty details she knew, like "how lodgers bang doors." She had also thought hard about larger social questions and she viewed the entire structure of Victorian and Edwardian plutocratic society with a jaundiced eye. For MEB, Bennett noted, "Sin must be punished; the future must pay for the past; but, this being granted, let us have riches and bright tempers, and eat and dress well, and live in glorious old mansions. The life of the English country house, with its luxurious solidity—with what unaffected satisfaction she describes it!"[16]

To which one must reply, "Yes, but . . ." Again and again MEB made the inhabitants of those country houses—ostensibly her heroes and heroines—selfish, snobbish, and smug, the men idle and lecherous, the women haughty and ignorant; and sometimes she contrasted with them explicitly or implicitly nobler human beings from a less exalted station in life. If Arnold Bennett, sympathetic critic though he was, failed to observe this in 1901, after MEB had written three-score novels, what wonder if her ordinary readers and reviewers seem never to have noticed it? We return to our paradox: although she had myriads of readers, nobody ever appears to have read her.

In the 1950's in France, the case of Georges Simenon was somewhat similar. Literary critics ignored him. Clerks in pretentious bookshops, when asked for his latest novel, would scornfully reply that they stocked no *romans policiers*. And if the customer protested that—in addition to the Maigret stories—Simenon wrote psychological novels in a wholly different genre, and that even his Maigret novels often dealt with much more than crime and detection, the protest met with pitying smiles. Only the general public inside and outside France could never get enough of Simenon, and eventually, toward the end of the decade, he won his first serious critical recognition. Like Simenon, MEB wrote novels of crime (sensation-novels) and novels without crime; and like him, she was sometimes a hack and more often a distinguished novelist. Unlike him, she has yet to be properly appreciated.

Recognition has been postponed by the total collapse of her popular reputation. In 1901 she was known not only—as Arnold Bennett wrote—throughout the English-speaking world, to people who knew not Hardy or Barrie, but also to Hardy and Barrie themselves, both of whom—like Dickens and Thackeray, Bulwer and Reade, Stevenson, Tennyson, Henry James, and George Moore, Ford Madox Ford, and Bennett himself—esteemed her novels highly. Nowadays Miss Braddon's name brings a flicker of recognition only to the face of an occasional Victorian specialist, and it is never more than a mere flicker. What happened? Lucy Clifford, novelist and woman of letters and the world, wrote MEB affectionately in 1911, after reading a reprint of her *Vixen* (1879), ". . . you have its absolute atmosphere, and the people all *live*. . . . it is precisely what *happened*—how it *was*. . . ."—but went on to say:

> you have always been such a masterly story-teller; that goes without saying. . . . Your stories are *all* admirable, *but* you have written too many—or rather . . . you have put your name on too many. You might have had three reputations. . . . People can't *believe* your work can all be on its highest level . . . because there is so much of it, so many good books, that they think it impossible that anyone could do so much that is *good*—though of course every book of yours . . . had only to appear to command its thousands of readers. It is a great triumph. In the far distant years (to come) you will be sifted down, probably, to a dozen or so, and live by those; no one in the more and more hurrying world will have time to read very *much* of anyone I expect. It is horrible to think of.[17]

But Mrs. Clifford's prediction proved too sanguine. Not even a dozen Braddon novels are now remembered, and MEB has been sifted not down but out. The exceptions prove the rule: in 1965 a burlesque revival of a dramatic version of *Lady Audley's Secret* was staged both in Edinburgh and in London, and in the 1970's a musical comedy based upon it played in America, but only to raise a laugh at the quaintness of our Victorian forebears.

Yet Miss Braddon epitomizes her age in a way no other novelist does. A modern reader, jaded with crime and its detection, mystery and its solution, still finds even her sensation-novels strong in the accuracy of her eye for detail, the sensitivity of her ear for speech. Her other novels, her other manners, provide a constantly rewarding exploration of the mores of the era. Complying, as she had to comply, with the Victorian code for novelists, she became a master of ambiguity. Insisting that her personages were behaving as Mrs. Grundy would have them behave, she nonetheless managed to convey her own skepticism.

She seems at times to be inviting a reader in the "more and more hurrying world" of the late twentieth century to reread her books and to make out at last what she had been unable to say aloud. Constricted in her own lifetime by the stubborn refusal of critics to recognize that she had early and often broken the mold into which they insisted on cramming her, she should now be rescued from an oblivion she never deserved. A modern reader can still experience again the joys that her contemporaries—including the most judicious—found in her fiction. And with the narrative of her life at last reconstructed and set down before him, he can go far beyond her contemporaries in forming a fair assessment of her as a writer and as a woman.

PART I

THE YEARS OF STRUGGLE, 1835–1875

CHAPTER I

"Before the Knowledge of Evil": an Early Victorian Girlhood (1835–1847)

1. The Braddons

In 1914, when MEB was almost eighty and had less than a year to live, she wrote a memoir of her girlhood which she called, significantly enough, *Before the Knowledge of Evil.* Found among her papers after her death, it has remained unpublished.[1] It provides a series of vivid childhood experiences. At important moments it echoes passages from one or another of her novels, often so precisely that the reader can confidently identify those particular novels as in part autobiographical. Except for her own, no testimony as to her childhood survives; so "the other side" of the family quarrel, for example, must remain unexplored.

MEB wrote that she had been born in "the year of Queen Victoria's accession," 1837, but about this she was mistaken, perhaps deliberately; her true birthdate was October 4, 1835, and she was baptized on March 21, 1836. Had she arrived a few days earlier, she would have been born in the Braddons' family house, Skisdon, at St. Kew, near Wadebridge, in Cornwall, the residence of her Braddon grandmother.[2] All her life MEB loved Skisdon for its warmth, and for the beauty and abundance of its gardens. Cornwall had a special place in her affections. She remembered with pride the Braddon who had sat in Parliament for Cornwall under Elizabeth, and the Lawrence Braddon, tried in 1686 by Judge Jeffreys on a charge of treason, who had escaped with his life, paying a fine of two thousand pounds.

But she was born in London at number 2 Frith Street, Soho Square, "a long dull street of substantial Georgian houses. . . . fashionable in the days of the Georgian Kings, . . . and . . . prim and respectable in . . . early Victorian days. In all its grey length I can recall only one shop—and that . . . refined and superior . . . its windows showing silks or velvets with an unobtrusive splendour." Here MEB spent her first four years. She remembered the cows in St. James's Park, the sight of her first fog, when she thought that the street "was filled with milk and water," and the beautiful view across the street into a room of the house opposite, where "the carpet was of vivid colouring, and seemed to me to go uphill, while the end of the perspective was one of those circular mirrors" so common then in furnished rooms. In this brilliant environment, "strange and remote," no living creature was ever to be seen.

She recalled affectionately the "quiet and safety of that shabby London where the muffin bell tinkled in the dusk at tea time, and where Punch could be heard two streets off." Besides Punch, there was an organ with "a row of gaily dressed figures on the top . . . that waltzed to the music underneath; and . . . lighted windows in Leicester Square where at intervals mailed knights on mailed coursers charged across the glass." At Covent Garden she saw goldfish swimming in a crystal bowl, and rabbits munching cabbage leaves behind wires, while she found the Soho Bazaar "a fairy palace of toys, which one might look at but not touch." Here sixpence lasted a long time: the best buy was a tiny four-poster bed "curtained with pink-glazed calico, and with a waxen baby inside, of which the wax was . . . so ethereal . . . that the baby perished if one took it out of bed, crumbled to atoms in his tiny muslin shirt." MEB bought dozens of these. "They were irresistible, but they did not last." At her first theatrical performance, of dogs and monkeys at the St. James's, she burst into tears with excitement at the music of the band and the sound of the drums, and had to be taken home.

MEB's sister Margaret—Maggie—was eleven years older than she, and spent the first four years of Mary's childhood in Cornwall with their grandmother and aunts. When the sisters first met, Maggie was "horribly grown up, fifteen at least," and MEB "had no use for her." Their brother Edward was five years younger than Maggie and six years older than Mary, and except during holidays lived at his preparatory school in the Fulham Road. During these earliest years, then, MEB was to all intents and purposes an only child, and, aside from her kind nurse, it was her mother on whom all her affection was concentrated.

Born Fanny White, Mrs. Braddon was the daughter of Patrick White, an Irish Catholic from County Limerick. She had been brought up largely by her Protestant mother, whose maiden name was Babington. Anne Babington had married Patrick White "against the will of her people," and her marriage was "almost ranked as an abduction in the good old Irish style." She soon separated from her husband ("not a satisfactory person"), but she had always been cared for "by friends who had wealth and power, and she had never known money troubles." She did not try to bring up her children as Catholics, but did treat Fanny with great severity. Fanny later told MEB "of long mornings when uninteresting lessons were followed by plain needle work as dry and severe as oakum-picking," and how Mrs. White would "observe in an awful voice 'You are *puckering*, Madam.'" Anne Babington White had told her children that *her* grandmother was a Macaulay, and Fanny White Braddon always hoped that the conjunction of the two names Babington and Macaulay meant that she might somehow be related to the great historian. But MEB in later life, after reading Trevelyan's *Life* of Macaulay, decided that the appearance of the two names was only coincidence. Occasionally she would use Babington White as a pseudonym.

Fanny White Braddon was unlike her dour mother, and MEB adored her then and always:

> Could it have been only in the course of two summers that I used to sit on the carpet by the massive mahogany leg of the Broadwood grand to hear my mother singing in the twilight? She had a sweet mezzo-soprano voice, and a perfect ear—and she had just a few songs that she played and sang in the summer dusk, and which have always been dearer to me than any other music. . . . *Portrait charmant* was one—a tender little ballad which I have never seen in print—and another was *Farewell, oh farewell to thee, Araby's daughter*; *Flow on, thou shining river* was a third. I had no need to know what the words meant—I loved to hear her sing, I loved to be with her, yet I know those gentle melodies and the sound of her low voice . . . filled me with inexpressible melancholy—the vague sadness of a child who does not know what sorrow means, and yet is sad.

She remembered a godfather and a male cousin who held his gold watch up for her to listen to. She also knew her mother's sister's family, the Delanes. William Frederick Augustus Delane, who had married the elder of the White sisters, had become in middle life business manager of the *Times*. From the Delanes' house Fanny White had married Henry Braddon in 1823, and with her Delane nephews, William and John, who refused to call her "aunt" because she was too near their own age, she always remained on affectionate terms. William became a partner in the Taversham Paper Mills in Norfolk, which supplied the *Times* with newsprint, while John became its famous editor.

But, MEB tells us, it was not until after her fourth birthday that she became conscious of

> another figure in the shape of an agreeable gentleman in spotless linen, who took snuff out of a silver box, and who was associated with brown paper bags of winter fruit, which he would seem to have carried from Covent Garden, and with Sunday morning leisure in empty offices, and Sunday evening dessert. This was Papa. The children of the lower classes had fathers and mothers, but in any house with a drawing room, and three servants, the heads of the family were Papa and Mamma.
>
> Papa had whiskers, and was always what is called nowadays well-groomed. I think he wore a blue, or perhaps bottle-green coat, with a suspicion of brass buttons, and some kind of buff waistcoat. As I was never downstairs after five o'clock I did not enjoy the privilege of seeing him in evening dress—but I know from Mamma that he was proud of his small foot and arched instep and very particular about his boots. I have even heard him called handsome—but never by Mamma, who said his large brown eyes were like the eyes of oxen. She was not a student of Homer, and did not mean this for praise. I liked Papa, he was always kind, and gave me sixpence when I showed him my new frock with my first pocket. It was in the empty offices [which Mr. Braddon as a solicitor maintained in the house] on a Sunday morning that I drew on Papa for that sixpence. I do not think he was often to be found there on a lawful day.
>
> Papa was nobody's enemy but his own. That was what I heard about Papa when I was old enough to be told things, a good many years after the drawing room . . . and the Broadwood grand had dropped into the great gulf that swallows our past years. "Mr. Braddon was his own enemy." Everybody liked him, so good-natured, so generous, a man who would give his last five-pound note to a hard-up friend although he had to leave his clerks without wages on Saturday, and to leave his wife to tell them their employer had gone out of town and would not be home until Monday. It was not altogether a blessing for Mamma, when, in those earliest years of my life, the office and the home were under the same roof; as they had been for a good many years before I was born. . . .

I liked to make incursions into Papa's room, and creep under the knee hole desk, and play at being a bear on the sheepskin rug, and to run about in the great empty rooms where clerks were supposed to be busy, but where I remember only Mr. Freeman, who was Papa's clerk for a long time. . . . Mr. Freeman was always kind, and would let me clamber in and out of great empty deal boxes, intended I believe for papers. There were rows of . . . dark tortoise-shell japanned boxes, with grand Cornish names upon them, which I read and wondered about often in later years, when Maggie and I used to make friendly calls upon Papa and ask him for largesse.

Maggie was an inveterate asker, and having asked for money, and having been told that, however well intentioned towards his family, a man could not pick up money in the streets to satisfy their cravings for gold, she would go on asking for anything else she could think of, for foolscap, for blotting paper, for quill pens, for sealing wax; till Papa would ask her in return if she wanted the teeth out of his head! He was never really cross. He would sit there behind the knee hole desk, trimming his superior nails. Papa had nice hands, and his nails were a source of amusement which never seemed to fail. He had not much conversation on these visits, and after he had asked us "How's your mother"—he called Mamma by that vulgar name—and if we had any news from the West, he had exhausted himself. He always spoke fondly of the West, poor prodigal, meaning the old house in the valley [Skisdon], and the little market town on the hill where his brother lived [Camelford]; but I do not think he ever went there or saw Grandma after his self-enmity became developed in fatal ways.

People said he was clever—and if he had not been his own enemy might have done well for himself, and his wife and children, but he had begun to be his own enemy very early in his career, very soon after my mother had married him with the approval of the Delanes, and a settlement of three hundred a year, of which only a rent of thirty to forty pounds from a small farm in Cornwall ever materialised—the rest of the three hundred seems to have been the dream of a sanguine mind. It is wonderful to think how Papa was able to humbug Mr. Delane and another substantial trustee.

Certainly Papa, with good abilities, good connections, and a

popular manner, might have done well. His mother bought him a
partnership in a superior firm of solicitors. . . . But after a year or
two the superior firm had begged to be allowed to return
Grandmamma's capital, and to wish Papa a long farewell. Clever
and agreeable as he might be in the bright years of his youth, he
did not suit the superior firm, . . . Mamma's first home with Papa . . .
collapsed suddenly in a house-quake that swallowed the nice new
furniture and all Mamma's wedding-presents, silver, jewellery,
china, everything except a set of Byron's poems beautifully bound
in white calf. . . . Mamma's life . . . was acquainted with such trouble as a wife endowed by nature with a delicate and scrupulous
honesty must indeed suffer when linked to a careless and happy-
go-lucky gentleman who is nobody's enemy but his own.

Written only a few weeks before MEB died, these passages strike a
note that alters the nostalgic feeling of her memoir. *Before the
Knowledge of Evil*, indeed! Once "his own enemy" intrudes into the
idyllic relationship between the little girl and her mother, the scene
darkens. Papa's delinquencies had aroused the fierce sympathy of the
child for her mother and had wounded her so severely that, when three-
quarters of a century later she ostensibly set out to tell a tale of infant innocence, his own enemy's shadow almost immediately fell across the
page. At once she began to remember wicked things that she could indeed
have known only vaguely at the age of four, and that, as she said, her
mother confided to her later.

Henry and Fanny Braddon for a time contributed articles to Pitman's
Sporting Magazine (under the names "Rough Robin" and "Gilbert
Forester"), in which Henry "provided vivid descriptions of clinking runs
or tremendous shoots," and Fanny "developed his crude notes in
magazine English" and "supplied flowing paragraphs and lavish quotations from Byron and [Thomas] Moore." The additional income that the
articles brought them was welcome, but eventually "there came an
unlucky bill transaction in which his own enemy offended the good lady
who was proprietor of the magazine, and never again appeared in her list
of contributors."[3] These things Mary learned as a girl, for her mother
"told me much that is not generally told to a girl before her Kenwiggs
pigtails are exchanged for a coil of plaits in a tortoise-shell comb," but it
was only after her mother's death that she learned of her father's un-
forgivable sin, infidelity: "However nobly a wife may pardon sin,
whatever dignified silence she may preserve, she hardly ever burns *les*

pièces de conviction, they remain among her papers—those sordid letters which tell the humiliating story of a husband's infidelity." Soho, then, was left behind. Drawing room and grand piano and Mary's nurse disappeared, and Mamma and Mary went in 1839 to live in St. Leonard's-on-Sea, Sussex.

These passages from the unpublished reminiscences of 1914 lend new meaning to a novel by MEB published in 1880, *The Story of Barbara.* Set in the years just before the Crimean War, the story tells of a mother and two daughters, named Trevornock, deserted by their Cornish husband and father, a solicitor. Mrs. Trevornock had been "Irish by birth, English by culture." Her husband, a younger son, "was beginning life brilliantly as the junior partner in a first-class firm of City solicitors," but "went utterly to the bad, and proved himself . . . the black sheep of his highly respectable family." Mrs. Trevornock does not even tell her elder daughter's suitor that her husband is still alive: she is " 'absurdly reserved about it.' "

" 'We might justly say we have no father,' " says Bab, " 'he has never done a father's duty.' " To which her younger sister, Flossie, answers,

"Nonsense, Bab; don't be hard upon the author of our being. I perfectly remember one Sunday, when I had my first frock with a pocket, papa gave me sixpence to put in that pocket. And he used to call me his little maid. I think those were two nice traits in his character, at any rate."

"It would have been nicer of him if he had paid his debts, and kept a roof over our heads, instead of squandering his money," said Bab with a touch of bitterness.

And when her suitor asks Barbara what kind of man her father is, she replies:

"I'll describe him as I've often heard him described—in five words, 'nobody's enemy but his own.' " . . .

"He is a most good-natured person," said Flossie. "You could hardly put him out of temper if you tried. He will swear at you occasionally, but not savagely. He has threatened to throw me downstairs or out of the window, but he doesn't mean it. I dare say he finds me rather trying."

When Trevornock's daughters visit him in his chambers, they find him among "tin boxes japanned the colour of tortoise-shell combs, with . . . names painted upon them in white letters," mostly of old Cornish clients. The visit is identical with Maggie's and MEB's visit to Mr. Braddon. Like Braddon, Trevornock trims his nails, asks for the "news from the West," and responds with protests to his daughters' demands for money and stationery. Twice in *The Story of Barbara* the scene is repeated with only minor variations.[4] As a novelist of forty-five, MEB was here remembering the scenes that still haunted her as an old woman of seventy-nine when she came to sketch her early life. In the novel she made the demanding sister, who moved aggressively from gold to silver to copper to sealing-wax, the younger instead of the elder. In life it had been, we know, Maggie, the elder, who made the demands of Papa; and MEB, the younger, who sat, no doubt twiddling her parasol and loathing every moment of it. Humiliating the extortion was, we can be sure, despite the rollicking Dickensian sentences in which Flossie hit off the interview which MEB would sketch again in *Before the Knowledge of Evil.*

In *The Story of Barbara* nothing is said directly about infidelity: " 'Ma left Pa,' " says Flossie,

> "when Bab and I were little. They had no vulgar quarrels, you know; but he never gave her any money for the housekeeping bills or the servants' wages, or anything, and there was usually an execution in the house. . . . Taxes meant one succession of sum- monses. . . . Of course I was not old enough to know anything about it then. . . . We always had dinner, and I had no idea we were on the brink of starvation. But the executions and the worry were killing poor ma. She is honest by nature, poor dear, and she could hardly breathe in an atmosphere of dishonesty. Pa used to go to his clubs, and to races and gambling houses, and enjoy himself, leaving his clerks without their salaries. The clerks used to come to ma—we lived over pa's offices in those days—and ask her for money on a Saturday afternoon, when Pa had made himself scarce. It was dreadfully trying, and at last ma felt she ought not to bear it any longer; so one day she packed her boxes, wrote pa a polite note, and came away with us to some lodgings in the Old Kent Road, which had been taken for her by an old nurse. And ma has toiled, and striven, and thought for us ever since, and educated us, and dressed us, and made us supremely happy, and if

we did not love her; which we do, thank God—we should be hard-hearted little wretches."

As the narrator of *The Story of Barbara*, MEB reflected on Mr. Trevornock as on the author of her own being:

When it is said of a man that he is nobody's enemy but his own, it may generally be taken as a solemn fact that . . . he has . . . begun by breaking his mother's heart; he has . . . reduced a virtuous father to bankruptcy; . . . he has brought his wife and family to the gutter; and he has degraded a good old name. Yet his own particular set speak indulgently of him to the last as a good-hearted well-meaning fellow, incapable of harming anyone but himself. . . . Thomas Trevornock, solicitor. . . . was the black sheep in an otherwise spotless and unblemished flock. His family had . . . propped him up when he lurched, and had picked him up and set him on his feet when he fell. But . . . Thomas Trevornock . . . had vices of which his daughters knew nothing. He had been a drunkard and a gambler. He had squandered his money amidst the lowest surroundings; he had wallowed in the gutter. He had been engaged in so many doubtful transactions that it was a marvel that he had escaped being struck off the rolls. That some few clients of seeming respectability and assured means still stuck to him was even a greater marvel. Yet he had clients, and contrived to maintain a reputable appearance in his neatly furnished office . . . much to the satisfaction of his kindred, who told each other complacently that Thomas seemed really to be doing well, and that it was a great pity that he and poor dear Flora were not living together comfortably.

So MEB put into *The Story of Barbara* some details she chose to omit from the autobiographical fragment. Virtually everything MEB said of the failed Cornish solicitor of good family, Thomas Trevornock, with his Irish wife and two daughters, she clearly believed to have been true about her own father, Henry Braddon, the failed Cornish solicitor of good family, with his Irish wife and two daughters. When Barbara's suitor calls upon Trevornock in his chambers and asks for his consent to their marriage, Trevornock replies that Barbara "might look high." Her lover "wondered inwardly where the girl was to look for a loftier suitor unless it were in the threepenny omnibuses or in the Camberwell highroad." Flossie asks Barbara's fiancé, " 'What did you think of the Author? . . . He always looks clean, his shirtfronts and wristbands are perfection. If anything could reconcile me to his manifold shortcomings, it would be his cleanliness. I could not respect a dirty father.' "5

Thomas Trevornock was the most photographic reproduction of the Henry Braddon of real life that MEB would ever put into her novels. But she repeatedly strove in her fiction, both before and after *Barbara* (1880), to deal with this central problem of her own girlhood: the feelings and behavior of daughters toward neglectful, dishonest, incapacitated, or unloving fathers. At the opening of *The Doctor's Wife* (1864), the heroine, Isabel Sleaford, a girl whom MEB drew as a kind of half-deprecatory, half-affectionate self-portrait, lives in a run-down household in Camberwell, where the abandoned Trevornock ladies and the aban doned Braddon ladies also lived. Unlike Braddon or Trevornock, Sleaford *père* lives with his family. He says he is a barrister, but is actually a forger, who murders a suitor of his daughter.6

Forty years after *The Doctor's Wife* and twenty-four after *Barbara*, MEB gave a new treatment to the same theme. Like *The Story of Barbara*, set in the early 1850's before the Crimean War, *A Lost Eden* (1904) once more centers about two daughters, the Sandford girls, living with their mother in Camberwell. Their father is a proud, embittered man, ruined through no fault of his own, who had once earned fifteen hundred pounds a year as an official of an insurance company and had a house in Russell Square, but now must live on an annual pittance of two hundred. He thinks his foolish, frivolous wife is trying to entrap a suitor for their beautiful elder daughter, and in a quarrel he strikes her. She falls, hits her head on the fender, and dies. Thus, again, the father is a killer. MEB's great sympathy with her mother's plight was here reflected, in however distorted a mirror.7

These three successive efforts—in 1864, 1880, and 1904—to deal in fiction with her father's character and behavior may well reflect MEB's changing attitude as she grew older. In 1864, newly launched on her successful career as a novelist, she was supporting her mother by her own earnings. Determined for the first time in *The Doctor's Wife* to write a genuine novel of character, she found her inspiration for Isabel and Mr. Sleaford in herself and her father, and struck savagely at the "author of her being" by making him a forger and murderer. In 1880, more than a decade after her mother had died, secure in middle life, and richly rewarded for all her literary efforts, MEB was able in *The Story of Barbara* to look at her own family history with sardonic detachment. So literally did she this time describe the actual facts that, when thirty-four years later still she turned to autobiography in *Before the Knowledge of Evil,* she selected the same incidents and described them in the same words. The fictional Trevornock and the historical Henry Braddon were not murderers but merely weak, vicious, indifferent fathers, and MEB's tone in dealing with them had become less vindictive and more ironical: "I could not respect a dirty father," says Flossie. By 1904 the father was a figure of pity. Mr. Sandford, in *A Lost Eden,* killed his wife, but only by accident—nor was his poverty his own fault. And the very title, *A Lost Eden,* would be echoed and reenforced in the title MEB gave to the autobiographical fragment of 1914, *Before the Knowledge of Evil.* Although she never forgave the wicked "author of her being," her youth now seemed to her an age of primal innocence.

2. Girlhood with Mamma

For Henry and Fanny Braddon, as people of small means, divorce was out of the question: "the best thing man and wife could do when the marriage vow had been broken, and circumstances financial and otherwise had made home life impossible, was to part without fuss or unkindness." Mrs. Braddon had never truly loved her husband, and MEB, whatever her own later resentments, believed that her mother lived out her life "without an evil feeling" about him. They occasionally met, "without any spurt of anger—met, one might say, as friends."

After an interlude at St. Leonard's-on-Sea, Mary and her mother returned to London, where Maggie, now sixteen, and Edward, now ten and much admired, joined them for the Christmas holidays. The two girls then went off to school together in Kensington at Scarsdale House, where Maggie was being "finished" and Mary was to "be begun." MEB disliked the big turnip radishes and thick bread and butter which she was given to eat, but enjoyed the lessons, which "included something rather difficult which I think must have been the multiplication table." As the youngest girl in the school, she was allowed to come to the end-of-term fancy-dress ball as a little Dutch Broom Girl, while Maggie was disguised as a gypsy. When school was over, she made her memorable first trip to Cornwall.

By railway to Southampton, thence by coach to Exeter, and on, the next morning, to Wadebridge, where Grandmamma's carriage would meet them, Mrs. Braddon and her two daughters traveled to Skisdon: two long days and a long night for Mary, impatient to see the house her mother and sister had talked of so much, with its five gardens, its old and faithful servants, and its generous meals. "There was nothing palatial about Skisdon," she remembered; its parlour was small compared to the great room at Scarsdale House or even the Georgian drawing-room in Soho. But tea the first afternoon was memorable for the "cold roast chickens, the tongue, . . . the apple pasty . . . and the glass bowl of Cornish clotted cream. . . . vastly superior to the cream clotted in adjacent Devon"; and for the old silver on the table, "a brace of Georgian teapots and the urn, whose handles were the heads of lions with dangling rings in their ferocious mouths." Next day, she discovered the five gardens:

> one on the slope of the hill behind the house with a long wall against which fruit grew with a luxuriance I have seldom seen anywhere else—egg plums as big as turkey's eggs, apricots and greengages that were sweeter than the finest fruit on Regent Street, [one] perhaps genteeler, . . . in front of the drawing-room windows, all lawn and pond, [one] full of dahlias, behind which was a terra incognita of shrubbery through which meandered a trout stream,

and two kitchen gardens, both walled.

And she met new, affectionate relatives: Grandmamma Braddon, almost ninety, a maiden aunt, a married aunt, Uncle John Braddon, "my father's eldest brother . . . the old fashioned family solicitor, . . . a squire . . . with farms and tenants of his own, and above all a sportsman," whose gaiters Mary knelt down and buttoned devotedly when he rode back to Camelford after a long Sunday with his mother. Soon Uncle William arrived; he had spent thirty years as a judge in Bengal and had now come home, well-to-do and generous, with his two daughters almost grown up. There were no other children, but Mary was used to playing alone.[8] She was bored at watching the brewing and displeased with the taste of the beer. Instead of waiting to see the cows milked, she ran away when they bellowed. But she savored every moment of her Cornish visit. Even her Spartan Braddon grandmamma treated her with warmth and indulgence.

Back in London, MEB's mother took furnished a "pretty little inconvenient house" in Hampstead—where there was a shower of frogs one morning—and Mary had a governess, Miss Parrot, who also served as chaperone for Maggie and who made reading and writing pleasant and

English history exciting. But then "came the work basket and endless strips of cambric which had to be neatly hemmed with a small needle and fine cotton, and a severe regularity in the stitches" for the cambric frilling which "in those simple Victorian years was considered a sufficient trimming for feminine under-linen." Miss Parrot gave MEB her "first idea of religion," without "fire and brimstone" and without the "tremendous pictures of lost souls in hell" that had terrified Mrs. Braddon in her own youth. Here in Hampstead Mary met for the first time the two Misses Green, highly educated young women, with radical views and a "dislike of the privileged classes from the Queen downwards. All that was generous and tender in their nature had been enlisted in the cause of the nameless poor against the titled rich," and they were often bitter in arguing their views. At the age of six, Mary could hardly yet have been deeply aware of these opinions, but the Misses Green became her lifelong friends, and their ideas may well have helped to shape her own when she later came to write of wealth, poverty, philanthropy, and religion.

Hampstead offered rural joys: playing in the sand on the Heath, and in the hayfield of a nearby farmer. But London was not far, and MEB remembered a day when her godfather gave her strawberry ice at Grange's in Piccadilly: "for two shillings Grange gave his patrons a soup plate filled with the finest strawberries in Covent Garden, a jug of cream, and pound cake *à discretion*." The first ice was served on the marble table in a deep cup-shaped glass "frosted with the intense cold of its contents, the pyramidal form of that creamy pinkness." Alas, Mary felt faint in church next morning, and the attack was attributed to the strawberry ice: she was never allowed another. When Uncle William appeared in London, he took his daughters and his niece to see a model of St. Peter's at Rome, "so elaborate, so complete in every detail of form and colour" that when MEB went to Rome half a century later she was not surprised by dome, colonnades, obelisk, or fountains. Uncle William ended his treat by giving Mary a present—not the doll that he proposed and that she would have welcomed, but "quite a nice victorine, lined with brown satin, and ... of a smooth shiny fur the colour of a dark bay horse." She soon became proud of it and wore it for years.

From Hampstead, Mrs. Braddon moved her daughters to a rented house on the Thames in Hammersmith, near Chiswick, with a small garden and an iron gate that led to a terrace on the river, delightful even in winter. Here there was a room for Edward, who was at school in Greenwich and divided his holidays between his separated parents. Once after his French master had hit him on the head "as hard as he could very well without cracking it," Edward, now thirteen, pleaded with his mother to ask that he be given a night at home. But she waited vainly for him to appear at the Elephant and Castle, where they were to meet: Mr. Smithers, the headmaster, had forbidden him to leave the school, as a punishment for having had a feast in his room. He wrote that he would be "happy as a king" if Mrs. Braddon called for him after a few days to take him home, and added an affectionate personal note to Mary urging her to "gain over the kind feelings of Mama" to let him come.[9]

The furniture in the Hammersmith house charmed Mary as a child and dwelt in her memory as an old woman, furniture that her mother had found here and there in secondhand shops at a bargain:

> the capacious sofa, long and broad and substantial . . . the rosewood circular table . . . the pretty Italian desk of rosewood inlaid with ivory... the old French armchairs with white enamelled oval backs and touches of pink, and roses at the top of the oval frame . . . covered with apple green damask . . . and all the pretty ornaments—the Dresden lady at her harpsichord, the Dresden gentleman whose occupation I forget, the old Dresden jug with a tiger on one side and a lion on the other. . . . once . . . a chocolate jug for some *petite maîtresse* who gave herself airs in a boudoir in the Faubourg Saint-Germain, but it had drifted to a broker's shop in Newport Market, where Mamma bought it for eighteenpence, and cherished it ever after, as I have done to this day; and . . . bits of old French china, cups and saucers and sugar basins with covers all white and gold.

Here the seven-year-old Mary found her first playmates, the Cayne sisters, aged four and five, who were eager to adopt her as their companion and respected her seniority. Every morning they appeared at the garden gate, shouting "Mary Braddon, Mary Braddon," until Mary ran out to join them. Now came "the delightful pretending games, the dinner parties, the long sea voyages, the sick dolls." The Caynes' cook had the children to tea in the kitchen, better than the real party tea in the dining-room, "where one generally spilt something on one's best frock, before going upstairs to dance the first set in the drawing-room where one was painfully conscious of the stain in setting to partners." The Caynes' cook made "Yorkshire 'fat rascals,' thick little pastry cakes, stuffed with currants and candied peel, hot and buttered, smothered with powdered sugar, . . . something to be remembered for a lifetime." And so they were.

Mr. Cayne daily rowed to and from work at Doctors' Commons. From the Thames to his garden gate there was a staircase that he could draw up at night, and he had made himself not only a causeway by which he could walk to his boat at low tide but a raft moored nearby, on which he kept the boat.

Mrs. Braddon and her daughters spent more than four years in this riverside house. Every Christmas came a great hamper from Cornwall, anxiously awaited and usually arriving as Edward and Mary were about to give up hope. Inside were a turkey, chickens, and ducks, and "in the interior of these birds there were new-laid eggs which had to be extracted gingerly, and the straw was full of apples that rolled about the room while the major operation of unpacking went on, to be collected by Edward and me afterwards." Grandmamma always sent one of her home-cured Skisdon hams, "which Mamma declared to be superior to the best York that was ever smoked." The cakes were "not rich cakes that would have to be kept for company, but cut-and-come-again dough cakes with plenty of plums and currants, and they were yellow, and tasted of saffron . . . and there was always a tin of clotted cream, the real Cornish cream."

Christmas itself was a quiet feast at home. The great amusement was "Snap-Dragon," the snatching of raisins from a dish of flaming alcohol. For MEB "the big dish of blue flame in the darkened room, the fearsome joy of snatching scorched raisins . . . and Mamma and Edward enjoying the fun with faces that looked strange in the blue light, was a delight that came each year with undiminished pleasure." As for the Christmas pudding, no matter how "faultless the compound that we had all stirred in the big yellow basin," what really mattered was the boiling, and "the perfect pudding was not to be counted upon every year. It might be feeble and sprawl . . . or it might be firm yet break, and appear in halves, or even the flavour might not satisfy Mamma, too sweet or not sweet enough, too much British brandy, or too much noyau, with the faint suggestion of prussic acid." But for MEB and for Edward it did not matter. They "ate it to the last valencia raisin, the last morsel of candied peel, in hot frizzling slabs powdered with sugar-snow, or, best of all, cold for lunch."

The first Christmas in Hammersmith (1843), Mary's godfather gave her her first writing-desk, with a stock of pretty notepaper and envelopes and "wafers, not such vulgar red ones as tradesmen used in those days but . . . gold or silver, that did not always stick on the envelope but at least indicated that a lady had written the letter. . . . a stick of sealing wax that looked like tortoiseshell, speckled with gold . . . with which it was rapture to seal a letter with my pretty glass seal—a ship in full sail—and the motto 'Such is life.' " Over the desk Mary sat every evening until bedtime, writing. In her first story, a "proud elder sister treated her younger sister cruelly, made a scrub of her," until a fairy came to the rescue. "I was not thinking of Maggie," MEB protested, "but Maggie was an elder sister, and the whole race of elder sisters from Cinderella's downwards was an evil, and though Maggie was not actually cruel to me, she sometimes sent me upstairs to fetch her handkerchief, a liberty which I resented."

In the spring, there were the masses of perennials to tend in the gardens, and walks in Chiswick, or a ride in a red omnibus to hear the military band play in Kensington Gardens, or a voyage for twopence across to the south bank of the Thames in a skiff belonging to one of the boatmen who frequented a waterside Chiswick tavern. It was sometimes impossible to make the boatmen hear a shout for a return trip, and when they did not, it meant a long weary walk back to Hammersmith Bridge. At Chiswick Parish Church, the Reverend Mr. Bowerbank gave dull sermons that seemed to go on interminably: nobody looked at his watch, however, because "the bracelet watch had not been invented." On a Sunday afternoon there was little to do except to disobey orders, descend Mr. Cayne's stairs into the river mud at low tide, and spoil "at the first wearing" a new muslin frock sent from India by Cousin William Braddon, Uncle William's son. Even the indulgent Mrs. Braddon grew angry when she saw the ruined dress.

When Mrs. Braddon went out of an evening, Mary was allowed to wait up for her until ten o'clock, talking to Sarah Hobbs, the "cook-general," a sturdy needlewoman and a great reader of the *Family Herald* and *Reynolds's Magazine*. She loaned Mary *The Last Days of Pompeii* in a condensed version published in a "little stunted duodecimo magazine," and so introduced her to the novelist whom in later life she would hail as her master, and treat with adoring respect until his death. MEB also remembered winding a rainbow-colored silk Indian shawl from Uncle William around her head as a turban "in which one looked in the glass and thought oneself lovely and fancied oneself Byron's Zuleika." Bulwer and Byron: MEB was launched on both before she was eight years old.

Sarah would recite "in a sing-song with a powerful twang" her two ballads, probably dating back to George III's time, each about a nobleman's daughter who wanted to marry, in the one case a sailor, in the other a soldier. True love conquered class distinctions in both affairs, despite many vicissitudes and adventures. Sarah had previously been in service with a butcher's family, where during the summer she had nothing to eat but meat: no bread was served. It made her strong and healthy. Sarah was also an "amateur of corpses," who always went to coroner's inquests in Chiswick. "She had fourteen corpses, and she would in the most good-natured way recite the whole list and in the same rotation . . . and I knew them all so well that I am sure I should have missed one if she had omitted him from her death roll." Perhaps MEB's own later matter-of-fact attitude toward violent death and her frequent use of it in her fiction derived from the "ghoulish gusto" she felt as a child at Sarah Hobbs's recital.

A pleasant nearby day school continued the formal education that Miss Parrot had begun, and Mrs. Braddon herself began to teach Mary French. Her first French book focused on "Charles," "in whom I was keenly interested, possibly because his life history opened at his dinner, and I became acquainted with knives and forks and vegetables, meat, and pudding." It was "a long long road to travel between Charles's turnips and potatoes and Pascal, Balzac, Flaubert, and Anatole France." But it was a road that MEB always loved. Arithmetic was far less pleasant. And music, which now began, proved to be a great deal more trouble than expected. Semibreves and minims, quavers, semiquavers, and demisemiquavers intervened between Mary and the piano itself, but "When I could play 'Ah, vous dirai-je, Maman?' and 'Woodman, spare that Tree' with the proper fingers, I was in the land of music without tears."

Soon Mrs. Braddon took over the whole process of education: "She never treated me as a child . . . but talked with me as if I were on the same plane." She did have a "quick temper, but . . . neither a sullen nor a sour temper . . . and those occasional boxed ears which were the *sauce piquante* of my education never diminished by one iota my affection. . . ." Mrs. Braddon's "Irish wit and Irish sense of humour" were accompanied by quickness of imagination and by a readiness to suspect others and impute motives to them that was "sometimes disconcerting." But she was generally right. Formal teaching never took more than two hours a day. MEB did not have to memorize, but took dictation and wrote "little bits" of history and geography. "For history, English, Roman, and Grecian," she read Pinnock and Goldsmith, and the "adorable Walter Scott's 'Tales of a Grandfather' which made Scotland the most interesting of all my histories, even more than that of Greece, which I had found so delightful after the dryness that was Rome."

Of course Mary had long been reading for pleasure. She once wrote: "The history of my life is for the most part the history of the books I have written and the books I have read," and remembered that Mrs. S. C.

Hall's *Marian* was her first three-volume novel, read at the age of seven, and the first book she managed to read altogether silently.[10] Odd numbers of *Ainsworth's Magazine*, to one of which Mrs. Braddon had contributed "a sprightly descriptive paper,"[11] enabled Mary to peruse Ainsworth's own account of "the disjointed adventures" of Henry VIII and Anne Boleyn. Before she could read, she had suffered the usual childhood horrors brought on by *Red Riding Hood*, and as an adult she believed that only the most cheerful stories should ever be told in the nursery. But in the Hammersmith house she had become an ardent reader, and enjoyed Maria Edgeworth's *Parent's Assistant* and Charles and Mary Lamb's *Mrs. Leicester's School*, besides old favorites: Aesop's *Fables* and *The Swiss Family Robinson*, "a fat octavo of open print with many engravings," much more interesting than *Robinson Crusoe*, "a forbidding little volume of small print, without a single picture. . . . I did not even want to know what became of Friday." Before Mary was nine, she was launched on Scott and Dickens. Though *Kenilworth* began by seeming "a little dry," she read every page conscientiously, "and soon the magician had woven his spell around me." And "in *Nicholas Nickleby* there was not a dry page. . . . The book seemed written for children"; but *Martin Chuzzlewit* was still too difficult.

Mamma, who had great ambitions for Mary as a musician, took her straight from the early pages of the instruction book into difficult treble and bass duet parts from operas, on which she had to labor two and a half hours every day, while listening to the "shrill voices of Polly and Charlie on the Terrace, and other happy backward children at play." But Mary had "playfellows and dolls and a swing," and Johnnie, "a devoted young slave in an Eton jacket who owned a dinghy" and could take her on the river.

> . . . here was the Hampton Court steamer forging up from the Suspension Bridge, and Johnnie wanted to row me into her wake, and in a minute we were down the steps and in the dinghy, and three minutes after that the dear boat was bobbing up and down on summer waves behind the Cardinal Wolsey or the Catherine Howard, and sometimes rude men would shout at Johnnie from the deck, and he would tell me he was liable to be taken in custody by the Thames Police, which gave the last delicious zest to the whole thing.

Each summer the three-day Regatta was

> our great festival . . . the quintessence of the year's delight, just
> the core of summer, the week when July was hottest and when a
> thunderstorm might be momentarily expected. Everybody had
> visitors . . . light talk and laughter floated out of all the open
> windows, strange young ladies in muslin dresses and their pret-
> tiest bonnets—drawn silk, white chip, leghorn, areophane . . .
> strange men who had been wet bobs at Eton . . . every kind of
> stranger congregated on the Terrace when the boats were coming,
> shepherded by the proud householders who felt that these races
> which did not cost them sixpence were *their* show.

Even piano practice was suspended. The other "and more exclusive treat"
of the summer was always a drive with friends to Hampton Court, in a
carriage specially rented by Mamma for the day, for a tour of the Palace
and a picnic in the Park. The first summer in the Terrace (1844) there
was even a long tedious wait in a large crowd to see Tsar Nicholas I, who
proved a great disappointment.

Miss Godfrey, an itinerant upholstery repairer who had been employed
for a month at Dartmouth Lodge, a boarding school for girls in Old
Brompton, filled Mary's ears with reports of the school's glories, and
inspired her to ask that she be sent there in spite of the delights of life at
home. So off she went at the age of nine, in January 1845, with a new
school outfit, to "a house of rural appearance, with a long verandah and a
spacious lawn approached by an avenue of two or three hundred yards"
that led from the Old Brompton Road. The entire drawing room was
furnished in papier-mâché, which "sparkled with inlaid work in mother-
of-pearl," and Miss Barnet, the principal, "middle-aged and very stout . . .
wore the smart lace cap trimmed with satin ribbon and artificial flowers.
. . . There never was a kinder or a more conscientious guardian of
childhood and youth." Assigned to Mary to "look after my clothes and do
everything for me that I was incapable of doing myself" was "a young
person of modest appearance too genteel for a servant, but not smart
enough for a pupil." With the first dancing lesson at Dartmouth Lodge,
and the first feelings of homesickness that Mary Braddon felt on her first
night at school, *Before the Knowledge of Evil* abruptly breaks off, its
author-heroine still under ten years of age.

She followed her childish fairy tale of the two sisters with other ex-
periments in fiction. "The interval between the ages of eight and twelve,"
she later wrote, "was a prolific period, fertile in unfinished MSS., . . . a
historical novel on the siege of Calais—an Eastern story suggested by a
passionate love of Miss Pardoe's Turkish Tales,[12] and Byron's 'Bride of
Abydos,' which my mother, a devoted Byron worshipper, allowed me to
read aloud to her—and doubtless murder in the reading—a story of the
Hartz Mountains, with audacious flights in German diablerie; and lastly,
very seriously undertaken, and very perseveringly worked upon, a
domestic story,"[13] called "The Old Arm Chair," the outline of which was
suggested by her mother, who may have read it in a newspaper, or
thought of it because of her own interest in hunting for Sheraton and
Chippendale furniture in secondhand shops.

An honest couple, in humble circumstances, possessed a good old
cushioned easy chair, the pride of a former generation. When they were
unable to pay their rent, and the landlord's agent seized their household
furniture, he taunted them with the bad condition of the chair, and dug
"his clasp-knife into the cushion . . . and lo! an avalanche of banknotes
fell out of the much maligned horsehair stuffing, and the family was lifted
from penury to wealth." Written while MEB was still at boarding school,
"The Old Arm Chair" was "abandoned unfinished" before her eleventh
birthday (October 4, 1846). Astonishingly enough, however, the
manuscript survives. Even at ten, MEB gave circumstantial detail and
wrote vivid dialogue. How did the old couple become poor?

> Old Martha used to support herself by making lace, and her hus-
> band was assistant to a gardener. But the winter of the first year in
> the new cottage coming on his business failed and what made it
> worse so much imitation lace being worn Martha could no longer
> get any employment. . . .
> It was about five o'clock on an afternoon in November that an
> old couple were seen plodding through one of the streets of the
> busy town in Buckminster having as their destination the cheapest
> pawn broker's shop. The husband thus began:
> "Here we could buy a few cheap things for the cottage," said he.
> "For instance this old deal table (addressing the broker) What is
> the price?"
> "Why, sir, as I know you are poor, you shall have it for a
> crown," said the man.

"Well, wife, I think that would do, what think you?" said old Robert Gray.

"We have ten shillings. We could buy that and something else," said his wife.

"Let's have it. With all my heart, we will have it, sir."

"What is the price of this armchair?" said his wife. "I think it will do for us if cheap, do you Robert?"

"It is the same as the table, Madam," replied the pawn broker.

"Oh we will have it if you please," said the husband, "and that will be all."[14]

This effort—surely it *preceded* the others she mentioned—gives the last available glimpse of MEB as a child at school, writing busily away, heedless of any interruption, to the bafflement of her schoolmates and the amusement of her teachers.

CHAPTER II

"Do You Think the British Public Would Pay to See *You* Act?" (1847–1860)

1. Overture in Camberwell

In 1847, Mrs. Braddon gave up the Hammersmith riverside house, and Edward—aged seventeen or eighteen—went out to India to join his elder cousin, William Braddon, Jr., in the family mercantile business. To supplement Edward's salary, a Cornish great-aunt paid his father, Henry Braddon, "an allowance for . . . board and lodging"; but one wonders how much of it ever reached India. "I doubt not," wrote the generous aunt, "that Edward will get on in the world"; and her hopes were not disappointed. He soon abandoned commercial life for a successful career in the Indian civil service. He married young and had five children. In a cheerful gossipy letter from Lucknow September 16 (1863), his first wife, "Georgie" (née Georgina Palmer), told Mrs. Braddon, her "dearest Mama," how greatly she hoped soon to find a good English nurse, because "Ayahs are worse than useless. . . . not to be trusted out of one's sight, and even when kind, . . . are injudicious and deceitful." Poor Georgina died in 1864, and ten years later Edward married again. He retired in 1878 and moved to Tasmania, where he entered political life and eventually became Prime Minister in 1894. Letters and visits to England would serve to keep him in touch with his sister Mary. But their "childhood intimacy" was forever ended in 1847.

Sometime thereafter, Maggie Braddon married an Italian named Antonio Cartighoni, who took her to Naples to live. Their only son, Nicolino, was in 1864 of an age to spend the entire day at school. Eleven years older than Mary, Maggie would have been thirty in 1854; so a date in the early fifties for her marriage seems most likely. Perhaps Mr. Trevornock's haughty attitude toward Barbara's suitor in *The Story of Barbara* reflected the line that Henry Braddon took with Maggie's suitor, Antonio, who came of a well-to-do family, but whose father held the purse-strings.[1] At any rate, after Edward had gone to India and Maggie to Italy, Mary and her mother were left alone.

But well before Maggie's marriage, Mrs. Braddon had felt the need to economize. Mary did not stay long at the expensive Brompton school. Probably as early as 1848, the three Braddon women had moved to Camberwell, south of the Thames, a far poorer suburb than any they had lived in previously. All three of MEB's novels which we have identified as in part autobiographical help us reconstruct the Camberwell years. In *The Story of Barbara* (1880), where the neglectful father, the deserted mother, and the two daughters of the Trevornock family are Braddon family portraits, MEB describes the Trevornock women, living in Camberwell before the Crimean War, as "poor, absolutely poor." Despite occasional windfalls that sometimes bring their annual income up to two hundred pounds, they can count on only about one hundred and fifty. Yet their poverty never degenerates into ugliness. They live in a "little semi-detached house . . . —rent, twenty-five pounds per annum," with "a dainty prettiness not always attainable by people of larger means." They are "always trying to surprise each other with some improvement in house or garden," if "only a shilling rose-bush planted in the border, or a penny bunch of violets in a vase on the mantel-piece." They are "industrious, ingenious, temperate." Mrs. Trevornock is constantly dusting away "those wandering atoms of solidified smoke which came floating on the wings of the wind from the tall chimneys of Lambeth and Bermondsey." By 1880, when *The Story of Barbara* appeared, new housing developments, as MEB remarks, would have overrun South Lane, Camberwell, but in the early fifties the land still has only agricultural value. Houses, villas, cottages, all stand in their own gardens with many trees. Camberwell is still rustic.

The Trevornock girls do the household marketing in the small shops in the Camberwell Road. They have a single maid-servant. They know only a few people, and those "not brilliant." If they are invited "to a tea-party once in six weeks, or to a friendly dinner once a quarter," they consider themselves lucky. To ease the financial burden, they rent a room to a lodger. So did Mrs. Braddon: in a letter of 1848 sending a present of ten pounds, an aunt wrote, "I hope you may succeed in the spring in filling your house to your satisfaction." The Trevornocks advertise: "A lady and her daughters, having a house larger than they require, are willing to receive a gentleman as partial boarder. Room large and airy, use of sitting room, dinner on Sundays." The lodger's room overlooks "half an acre of flower and vegetable garden, a canal, a stretch of open ground, and a con-glomeration of roofs, melting away into the thickness of London smoke." Full of flowers and boasting a vegetable garden with fruit trees, the garden is separated from the canal only by an old brick wall. The peace and cleanliness of the Trevornocks' humble Camberwell house reflect the contentment and happiness that MEB always felt in every dwelling that she shared with her mother. In *The Story of Barbara,* the man who answers the advertisement and rents the room falls in love with the elder Trevornock girl; perhaps Maggie's husband, Antonio Cartighoni, made his first appearance on the Braddon family scene as the Camberwell lodger.[2]

In *A Lost Eden* (1904), also set in the early fifties, a predatory artist jumps into the Camberwell omnibus to follow the elder Sandford girl, Marion, home, an "endless"-seeming journey. He finds the road from London "now respectable, now squalid, but less glaring and flaring, and offensively rampant than it has become. . . . The omnibus rolled steadily along, meeting very little traffic. . . . The shop-windows were like those of a country town, save where here and there a cheap butterman, or a cheap draper, displayed his flaunting pricecards." When Marion gets off at Camberwell Gate, her suitor follows her until she has "walked the length of Camberwell Grove, [and] turned into a road where there were only a few houses in gardens . . . of a rustic type, with white-washed walls and slate roofs, which arrogance called villas, while proud humility talked of them as cottages." Marion stops at the gate of one of these small do-mains, and tries but fails to ring the bell.

The Sandfords' Chestnut Lodge is larger than the Trevornock ladies' cottage and wholly detached rather than semidetached. Marion's younger sister, Flora—her name is the same as that of the younger Trevornock girl—with her arms full of parcels and a basket of groceries, has trouble with the bell because of its "awkward cranks and windings of wire." So the artist rings it for her and is soon inspecting in the Camberwell draw-ing-room the not very talented drawings of Flo herself, just like those that MEB made at the same age, "copies from engravings in books or in the *Illustrated London News,* some of them original, her own ideas of scenes in Scott or Bulwer," with many sketches of Napoleon. Chestnut Lodge rents for forty pounds a year; the garden is over two acres in size, "such . . . as no one could hope for nowadays [i.e., 1904] within five miles of London. Now it would be described as a 'residential estate, ripe for building.' "[3] On a summer's night the Sandfords give a party in their garden, to which come their neighbors in Camberwell, a wholesale corn merchant and a musically-minded chemist and their wives, with other members of a social class that the aristocratic painter has never met before.

In *The Doctor's Wife* (1864) the Sleafords also live in Camberwell in the early fifties, amidst "many convolutions of narrow streets and lanes, where there were pretty little villas and comfortable cottages nestling among trees," near the "stern-looking" church of St. George's and the Surrey Canal, "wild and sterile" country in the year 1852. Behind a high wall, with "straggling rows of cottages dwindling away into pigsties" on each side, stands the Sleafords' square brick house with "sickly ivy straggling here and there about it, and long narrow windows . . . obscured by dust and dirt," a contrast to "the trim white-walled villas . . . neat little mansions at five-and-thirty-pounds a year; . . . cosy little cottages with shining windows and . . . dazzling brass plates . . . like brazen shields upon the vivid green of newly painted front doors." Mr. Sleaford's bell is broken (like the Sandfords' and perhaps the Braddons'): the handle rattles "loosely in a kind of basin of burnished brass, so it was no use attempting to ring." The garden is untidy, though it had once been beautifully kept: "rare orchids" sprout "out of beds that were full of chick-weed, and lilies-of-the-valley" flourish "among the groundsel in a shady corner under the water-butt. . . . The odour of distant pigsties" mingles "faintly with the perfume of the roses."[4]

Here, in the garden in Camberwell, in 1852, readers of *The Doctor's Wife* first meet Isabel Sleaford, not yet eighteen, drawn in 1864 by MEB largely as a portrait of herself as she had been twelve years earlier in Camberwell, except that Isabel is beautiful and has dark hair, while MEB had light brown hair and was rather plain. Isabel had been "taught a smattering of everything. . . . a little Italian, enough French to serve for the reading of novels that she might have better left unread," and just enough modern history to enable her to pick out all the "romantic and horrible stories scattered amid the dry record of Magna Chartas and Reform Bills, clamorous third estates and beds of justice." Isabel plays the piano a little, and sings a little, and paints "wishy-washy looking flowers" on board "*from* nature but not at all *like* nature; for the passion-flowers... came out like blue muslin frills, and the fuchsias would have passed for prawns with short-sighted people." Having left school before she was sixteen, Isabel has got her real education from the novels in the nearby circulating library. Her favorites, from which she has copied extracts in penny account books and learned whole pages by heart, include Bulwer's *Ernest Maltravers* (1837), with its violet-eyed seducer; and *Eugene Aram*

(1832), with its gloomy and intellectual murderer; Thackeray's *Esmond* (1852); and Dickens' *David Copperfield* (1850), where Steerforth, the dashing seducer, not David himself, is naturally her hero.

Isabel yearns "to sit at the feet of a Byron, grand and gloomy and discontented, baring his white brow to the midnight blast, and raving against the baseness and ingratitude of mankind," or "to be the chosen slave of some scornful creature who should perhaps ill-treat her and neglect her." If Dickens' Sikes had only been an aristocrat, says MEB with gentle irony, Isabel would have been happy to have him kill her, not in a garret like Nancy but "in the ruined chamber of some gothic castle, by moonlight, with the distant Alps shimmering whitely. . . . And then the Count Guillaume de Syques would be sorry, and put up a wooden cross on a mountain pathway to the memory of *ananke* [inexorable necessity]; and he would be found some morning stretched at the foot of that mysterious memorial, with a long black mantle trailing over his king-like form, and an important blood-vessel broken."[5]

In her teens in Camberwell, MEB continued to write fiction. Her novels were now more ambitious than "The Old Arm Chair" and were modeled chiefly on *Jane Eyre*. One romantic story of the Restoration, *Master Anthony's Record,* she based on the account of Lord Grey's elopement with his sister-in-law, found among the State Trials in the British Museum Reading-room and written, she remembered, in "Esmondese." She left it unfinished, but she returned to the theme many years later in her *London Pride* (1893).[6]

But the reading and writing of fiction soon took second place. Like Isabel Sleaford, Mary Braddon was stagestruck. Sometimes Isabel "let down her . . . hair before the little looking-glass and acted to herself in a whisper. She saw her pale face, awful in the dusty glass, her lifted arms, her great black eyes [not blue like MEB's], and she fancied herself dominating a terror-stricken pit." With a five-pound note, she would go to a London theatrical manager and tell him that she wanted to act tragedy. "There might be a little difficulty at first, perhaps, and he would be rather inclined to be doubtful of her powers; but then she would take off her bonnet, and let down her hair, and would draw the long tresses wildly through her thin white fingers—so; she stopped to look at herself in the glass as she did it,—and would cry 'I am not mad; this hair I tear is mine!' [*King John,* III, iv, l.45] and the thing would be done." At once the manager would realize that nobody since Eliza O'Neill—the famous actress whom Thackeray portrayed in *Pendennis* as "the Fotheringay" and who had married the heir to a baronetcy—could have delivered

Constance's line so well. " 'Come tomorrow evening' " he would say " 'and play Constance. You don't want a rehearsal? No, of course not; you know every syllable of the part. I shall take the liberty of offering you fifty pounds a night to begin with, and I shall place one of my carriages at your disposal.' "

But Isabel does not fulfill her fantasy. Instead of becoming an actress, she marries a country doctor. MEB lamented that all Isabel's foolish daydreams "of a modern Byron, fever-stricken at Missolonghi and tended by you; a new Napoleon exiled to St. Helena, and followed, perhaps liberated by you" have now ended in "a commonplace square-built cottage," married to "a commonplace country surgeon." Isabel now would "never be Charlotte Corday and die for [her] country. . . . never wear ruby velvet and diamonds," like Edith Dombey and "lure some recreant" lover "to a foreign hostelry, there to denounce and scorn him." All the "mystic cloudland" of Isabel's dreams would "collapse and shrivel into"[7] a prosaic provincial marriage, in which she would be powerfully tempted by a dashing seducer. But unlike Isabel, MEB did not abandon her romantic aspirations and embark upon a respectable and stifling marriage. Instead, she sought and found adventure. She made Isabel's girlhood dream her reality and became an actress.

2. Mrs. Hector Sternhold and Others: the Evidence of the Documents

In 1857, when a young girl of good family went on the stage, it was, as MEB herself wrote more than half a century later, "a thing to be spoken of with bated breath, the lapse of a lost soul, the fall from Porchester Terrace to the bottomless pit." It "convulsed her family to the most distant cousin,"[8] and they begged her not to do it, or, if she must do it, at least to change her name. But MEB's mind was made up. She was determined to be self-supporting and to earn enough money to relieve her mother's financial worries, but she also wanted the adventure of acting. Her mother accompanied her on all her travels during her three years as an actress. And she decided on her own to take a stage name.

Writing his own memoirs late in life, MEB's son, W. B. Maxwell, paid tribute to his mother's courageous decision: he remembered her stage name as "Seaton" and added that "all records" of her stage career had disappeared, even from her novels. But several clues preserved by chance—a little note, some signed verses called "Islam" clipped from a newspaper and pasted in one of her notebooks, a scribbled address on the back of a manuscript page—show that MEB called herself Mary Seyton, not Seaton.[9] And when one searches the playbills of the late 1850's for the name of Mary Seyton, the record of MEB's stage career that her son believed had disappeared begins to reappear again.

Among her papers there has survived a rumpled piece of scribbling-paper folded into three. When unfolded and turned over, it proves to be a worn but perfectly legible playbill, printed in blue, advertising Friday, May 1, 1857, as the last night but one of a performance at the Assembly Rooms, Norwood, Beverley, Yorkshire: the three-act drama, *Still Waters Run Deep* and the "petite comedy," *The Wonderful Woman*. "Miss Seyton" appeared as Mrs. Hector Sternhold in the drama and as Hortense in the "petite comedy." Both pieces were performed in Beverley by the company of Messrs. Wolfenden and Melbourne, the lessees of the Queen's Theatre at the nearby city of Hull.

Still Waters Run Deep was the most celebrated play of an important dramatist, Tom Taylor (1817–1880). Charming, radical, the friend at Trinity College, Cambridge, of Thomas Hughes and Charles Kingsley (who portrayed him in his novel *Two Years Ago,* 1859), Taylor wrote both the famous play *Our American Cousin* (1858), which Abraham Lincoln was watching on the night of his assassination, and the verses in which *Punch* apologized after Lincoln's death for its past sneers at him. Most of Tom Taylor's seventy-four plays were "adapted"—which is to say, freely plagiarized—from French originals, according to the practice widespread among Victorian English playwrights. *Still Waters Run Deep* was based on *Le Gendre,* a novelette by Charles Bernard.

As Mrs. Hector Sternhold, MEB, still in her first season, had a fat part indeed. She appeared as the domineering aunt of a young wife who has embarked on a dangerous flirtation with a practiced rake. And she cannot warn her niece because she herself had once been the rake's mistress, and he still has indiscreet love-letters she had written him. But Mrs. Sternhold does teach her niece how to boss a husband: he has no " 'ridiculous pretentions to a will of his own. . . . You can do what you like with him if you'll only take the trouble,' " MEB declaimed in Act I. Confronted in Act II with her former lover, she ranted: " '. . . love drove me on to serve your ends—blindly—devotedly—to give countenance to your deceptions—credit to your lies: this is what I have done for you, and thus it is I am rewarded. My blind love has made me thus guilty, and you—you, for whose sake I have done these things—upbraid me with my weakness! Heaven is just! but 'tis bitter! very bitter.' " But her niece's meek husband—played by Wybert Rousby—confounds the seducer, regains his wife's love and respect, and recovers the incriminating letters of his aunt-in-law, who must abdicate in Act III. It was then MEB's turn to be meek, as the triumphant hero commanded Mrs. Hector Sternhold to "go and dress for dinner."

Still Waters Run Deep, which had had its première in London at the Olympic Theatre on May 14, 1855, was only a little more than two years old when MEB appeared in it. In spite of the play's admission—extraordinary for the 1850's—that illicit love was a fact of life, the Beverley playbill reminded potential ticket-buyers that Queen Victoria herself had already seen it twice and that it was a favorite in fashionable private theatrical performances. At various times Ellen Terry, Madge Kendal, and other prominent actresses played Mrs. Sternhold. Wybert Rousby remained MEB's friend. Born Edmund Boothby, son of a manager of a mill at Hull, he became a popular Shakespearian actor in the provinces and would later come up to London.

Once Mrs. Hector Sternhold had been discomfited, MEB returned after the intermission as *The Wonderful Woman* herself, in the comedy by Charles Dance (1794–1863), sometimes regarded as a feeble precursor of Bernard Shaw. MEB as the wealthy Parisian widow, Hortense Bernard, is so consumed with social ambition that she marries a penniless marquis and pays his debts just for the sake of being invited to court. The despatch with which she causes her new husband to sign a marriage contract that forbids him her house brings her recognition as a "wonderful woman." But even more wonderful is her eventual acceptance of the lesson in humility he later teaches her. Once he knows the terms of the contract, he humiliates her by going into partnership with a cobbler rather than accept any more of his bride's money. It was a trivial piece; but once more MEB had a leading part, and both lessees of the theatre themselves shared the limelight with her, Wolfenden as the marquis and Melbourne as the cobbler.[10]

Among the large collections of local playbills still preserved in Hull, only a single one from the season of 1857 includes the name "Miss Seyton." On May 11, ten days after the Beverley performance of *Still Waters Run Deep* and *The Wonderful Woman,* she appeared at Hull itself with the same Queen's Theatre Company as Olivia in *Evadne; or the Statue* by Richard Lalor Sheil (1791–1851), the Irish barrister and politician, who wrote dramas in his youth to earn money. *Evadne,* his fourth and most successful play, originally written for the famous Eliza O'Neill and William Macready, had opened at Covent Garden on February 10, 1819. A free adaptation of James Shirley's *Traytor* (1631), the drama reeked of the foulest villainy, and its language was full of bombast. An ambitious nobleman plots to bring about the murder of the king of Naples by involving him in the seduction of the pure and blameless Evadne, whose brother, Colonna, will surely avenge her. Evadne is already plighted to Vicentio, who loves her truly, but is quick to suspect her. And Olivia, for love of Vicentio, joins in the conspiracy to procure Evadne's seduction by the king. At Hull, a well-known actress, Miss Marriott, played Evadne, and Wybert Rousby, Colonna. MEB, as Olivia, driven—she said—by "unhappy passion, . . . meanly crept / Into Evadne's soft and trusting heart, / And coiled myself around her." By stealing a page of a letter and substituting one miniature for another, Olivia makes the plot machinery spin properly. But she appeared only in the first two of the five acts; it was a minor part.

The same evening, the company also performed Bulwer's famous *Lady of Lyons* (1838), with Miss Marriott as Pauline and Rousby as Claude Melnotte; but the surviving playbill is unfortunately defective: the names of the actresses who played Madame Deschappelles, Pauline's mother, and Madame Melnotte, Claude's mother, are torn away. It seems certain, however, that Miss Seyton acted one or the other, in a play she always greatly admired.[11]

For the season of 1858, the surviving Hull playbills give no indication that Miss Seyton played there. But on a single playbill from the Theatre Royal, Brighton, for Wednesday, November 17, 1858, Miss Mary Seyton appears on the program for the "Annual Military Bespeak," under the "immediate patronage of Col. Douglas, C.V. and the Officers of the 11th Hussars, on which occasion, by Permission, the Band of the Regiment will attend." The main drama was to be J. R. Planché's *Charles XII or, The Siege of Stralsund*, followed by an original farce, *Tit for Tat*, by Captain Horton Rhys. But MEB appeared only in the concluding attraction of what must have been a very full evening indeed, the "celebrated and original Haymarket Comedy, in Three Acts, by J. B. Buckstone, Esq. entitled *Leap-Year! Or The Ladies' Privilege*." Prolific author of melodramas, comedies, and farces, and well-known comic actor, Buckstone (1802–1879) had first staged *Leap-Year* on January 15, 1850, at the Haymarket, and it soon became a staple of the comic stage.

MEB played Mrs. Crisp, the housekeeper of a widow, who by the terms of her husband's will must remarry within a specified time or lose his fortune. Rejecting her eligible suitors, she prefers to make a love-match with her own manservant, who proves, naturally enough, to be the very heir who would have received her inheritance had she not married him. As Mrs. Crisp, MEB at first laments the prospect that her mistress may have to give up her house and servants if she does not remarry. But in the end, Mrs. Crisp and all her fellow maid-servants follow their mistress's example, each proposing—leap-year fashion—to her own male favorite.

The Theatre Royal, Brighton, was leased to H. Nye Chart, whose company played a season running from late July or early August until March, after which the actors had to seek employment elsewhere for the remainder of the year. *The Era* advertised on April 3, 1859, that the members of the Theatre Royal company were now available individually or collectively for new engagements. It listed the players according to their positions: "lead," "low comedian," and the like. Among them, Mary Seyton appeared merely as "walk." So even after two years on the stage, MEB in Brighton apparently did not often play speaking parts.[12]

Perhaps in response to the advertisement in *The Era,* the Theatre Royal in Hull, whose lessee was John Pritchard, engaged the Brighton company to appear there "for six nights only" beginning on Monday, May 30, 1859, and then extended their engagement for a second week. The entire Brighton company, said Pritchard in his playbill for May 30, were "Metropolitan artistes, and bring with them a London as well as a provincial reputation." There were seven actors, including H. Nye Chart himself, and eight actresses. Miss Mary Seyton was listed fourth among them, along with the later celebrated Florence Haydon, and immediately after the leading tragedienne and comedienne. Fortunately the Hull collections include the playbills for six of the twelve nights of the Brighton company's engagement there, and MEB's roles show how her career had progressed.[13]

On June 1, she played Mary O'More in the "comic drama" *Rory O'More* by the Irish poet, painter, and novelist Samuel Lover (1797–1868). Rory had begun as the hero of a ballad in 1826, continued as hero of a novel in 1837, and in the same year was played by Tyrone Power at the Adelphi in the enormously successful dramatic version. A thoroughly masculine adventure story, full of action (including the collapse of a stone wall on stage during a thunderstorm that precipitates a flood) *Rory O'More* gave neither of its two girl characters much to do. Kathleen, Rory's love, played by Florence Haydon, was a more important part than Rory's sister, Mary, played by MEB, beloved by a wounded French officer whom the O'Mores are sheltering illegally. Except for singing two songs: "Oh! come to the west, love, oh! come there with me/'Tis a land of green verdure that springs from the sea. . . ." and "The Hour before Day" (" 'Tis always the darkest the hour before day!"), Mary's main contribution is to scream when the villainous Shan Dhu fires a shot at Rory (he misses and kills a wicked Frenchman instead). Of all the parts we know MEB to have played, that of Mary O'More is one of only two that cast her in the role of a young girl with a lover. Usually she was middle-aged at least: an aunt, a widow, a spinster, or a wife.

The same night, for example, she appeared as Mrs. Popples, the wife of Peter Popples, *The Man of Many Friends*. This "celebrated comedy" by J. Sterling Coyne (1803–1868) had opened at the Haymarket on September 1, 1855, with J. B. Buckstone as Popples. In the Brighton company, H. Nye Chart himself took the part of the newly rich ex-manufacturer of dolls, unhappy that his beloved wife (MEB) has yearnings after fashionable life, and not at all deceived by the new "friends" who drink his wine and eat his food and try to sell him things he does not want. When Mrs. Popples protests that "Nature formed me for fashionable life," he rejoins, "Don't blame nature. Nature formed you for a good sensible little wife, but art has well-nigh spoiled you." A misplaced miniature (hackneyed device) leads to suspicions of her fidelity, and MEB must have enjoyed herself in the scenes in which the cries of "mamma" proceeding from a doll in a locked workshop are mistaken for those of a real baby, causing the most sinister conclusions to be drawn about poor Popples himself. Reconciliation and a determination to live more simply end the comedy, as the false friends are dismissed.[14]

The playbills for the second week of the Brighton company's appearance in Hull show that on Monday night, June 6, MEB once again, as she had two years earlier, played Mrs. Hector Sternhold in Tom Taylor's *Still Waters Run Deep*. This time it was followed by Buckstone's "operatic comedy" in two acts, *Rural Felicity*, in which two young girls (MEB and Florence Haydon), whose engagements have been disrupted by the malicious gossip of London, disguise themselves and pursue their ex-fiancés to the country in search of a reconciliation. But the country has the same vices as the town, and each of the men makes advances to the wrong girl. Florence Haydon had the more interesting female part, since her disguise at least included a Scotch accent, while MEB's part was far less taxing, as befitted an actress who had already played Mrs. Hector Sternhold on the same evening.

Tuesday night, June 7, 1859, was the most exacting occasion of all, "Miss Mary Seyton" appearing in every one of the company's three offerings. She began the evening as Lady Starchington, the leading female role in the "petite comedy," *The Last of the Pigtails*, a one-acter by Charles Selby (1802?–1863), who had himself played the male lead on opening night less than a year before on September 6, 1858, at the Strand Theatre. As the vivacious new wife of an old-fashioned gentleman with an old-fashioned household, Lady Starchington manages to reform not only the servants and her husband, but even her sister's husband, whose fault is vulgarity. Starchington's pepper-and-salt suit, his nankeen breeches, and—of course—his pigtail, "a remnant of barbarism," all must go, and MEB reigns triumphant at the end. Another one-acter followed, billed as a "laughable farce," *An Object of Interest* by Joachim Hayward Stocqueler (1800–1885), which had first been seen at the Lyceum on July 14, 1845. Here MEB played Mrs. Trevor Vernon, a handsome widow giving a dinner party; but the main female part was that of Fanny, Mrs. Vernon's maid, steeped in stories about crime and wishing to become an "object of interest," who contrives to become a suspect in the disappearance of her mistress's emerald ring.

The second play over, MEB had still to appear in another "straight" role in Tom Taylor's three-act comedy, *Victims*, which had opened at the Haymarket on July 8, 1857. The situation is much the same as that in Coyne's *Man of Many Friends*: a newly rich husband is unwillingly besieged by his wife's hangers-on. But in Taylor's play the satire is sharper: one of the fair-weather friends is Mr. F., a sentimental poet, the author of *Withered Leaves, Solitudes of the Soul,* and *Ruins of the Heart.* He has written the lines "Alas the banquet tempts not me,/I find no pleasures in the bowl," on which a poetic footman comments, "I think for all his gloomy language/Expressive of sich mental anguish/That Mr. F. enjoyed his sangwich." While gourmandizing at Mr. Merryweather's table and making love to Mrs. Merryweather (MEB), the poet is hiding the fact that he is married and that his own wife and child are living in poverty. His lovemaking causes Mrs. Merryweather to find her husband vulgar by comparison, to move out of the conjugal bedroom, to suffer from the megrims, and to admit to the poet that "Griefs I have never confided to human ears are laid bare in your verses," to which he replies, "How mysterious is the freemasonry of suffering." One of the female hangers-on is a militant feminist, who—owing to a comic confusion—receives as a present a parcel containing a pair of trousers. Of course, Mrs. Merryweather returns to her senses in the end, and—as in *Still Waters Run Deep*—the husband triumphs in his own house. Florence Haydon, as the poet's beautiful and neglected wife forced to give piano

recitals to earn her bread, had a fatter part than MEB, but the success of
the entire play would have depended on MEB's skill in convincing the audience of Mrs. Merryweather's plausibility.[15]

Although the company presented three plays again on the next night,
MEB, presumably given a light evening after her strenuous duties of June
7, appeared only in the second, the "screaming farce" of *Lend Me Five
Shillings* by J. Maddison Morton, in which Buckstone had opened at the
Haymarket on February 19, 1846. Its manifold complexities all derive
from the existence of *two* ladies named Mrs. Phobbs: Mrs. Major Phobbs,
a widow, and Mrs. Captain Phobbs, her sister-in-law, whose husband is
still alive. MEB played Mrs. Major Phobbs, pursued by the male lead, Mr.
Golightly (H. Nye Chart), who desperately needs five shillings to pay for
a cab to take her home from a dance, but who is also terrified that he may
have been paying court to a married woman all along. A modern reader
feels that the only hope for success would have depended upon playing
the farce at top speed.

On Thursday, June 9, the bill was the same as that of June 1, with MEB
reappearing as Mary O'More and as Mrs. Popples. And on June 10, the
final night for which a playbill is available, the company once again gave
three performances. In two of these (John Oxenford's comedy, *The
Porter's Knot*, which had opened at the Olympic on December 2, 1858,
and William Bayle Bernard's farce, *His Last Legs*, which had opened at
the Haymarket on October 15, 1839) MEB did not appear. The third piece
was again a John Maddison Morton farce, *Slasher and Crasher*, with a
new subtitle added for the Yorkshire audience: *A Mistake in the Beverley
Grand-Stand*. In the play, which had opened at the Adelphi on November
13, 1848, an old soldier breaks off the engagements of his niece (Florence
Haydon) and his sister (MEB) to two accepted suitors whom he regards
as cowards: one has been unprotestingly kicked while in the grandstand at
the local racecourse, and the other is the head of an antidueling society. A
spurious duel between them is finally brought about—although one is so
cowardly that he must be got drunk first—and the women recapture their
fiancés. MEB played Miss Dinah Blowhard, the elder and less attractive
girl, the very idea of whose marriage seems absurd to her brother. Her
niece calls her an "unfeeling middle-aged creature."[16]

The discovery of these playbills, preserved by chance, and a reading of
the plays in which Miss Seyton appeared strongly suggest that MEB was
a serious, hard-working, reliable actress, useful in farce, in comedy, and
in drama (*Evadne*), who would learn a long part or even several for the
same evening, but who was seldom cast in a truly romantic role. When

she died in 1915, a knowledgeable obituary writer for the *Daily Telegraph* wrote that MEB's very first appearance had been in the Brighton company as the Fairy Pineapple in Planché's pantomime called *The Prince of Happy Land*. The good Fairy Pineapple emerges at the end of the first act as the savior of the heroine, Princess Desiderata, transformed into a white fawn through the spell of the wicked Fairy Carabossa. Singing "Come with me to Fairy Land" and waving her magic wand, Pineapple reassures the audience that she will protect the bewitched princess until the evil spell is dissolved. In Act II, the Fairy Pineapple enables the princess to assume her own form during the hours of darkness, although by day she must revert to being a fawn. And at the finale, Pineapple reappears with Oberon's judgment freeing the princess from the spell and enabling her to marry the Prince of Happy Land. Full of the traditional puns and would-be comic songs of the English Christmas pantomime, *The Prince of Happy Land* had first been performed at the Lyceum on December 26, 1851. Though the Fairy Pineapple's part was critically important, it was also very small.

In Miss Braddon's first season, the *Telegraph* continued, she appeared in a farce by Thomas Egerton Wilks and in a drama by Mark Lemon, the celebrated editor of *Punch*, and acted Bianca in an adaptation of *The Taming of the Shrew*. In her second, she had appeared with Ira Aldridge, the "African Roscius," born on the West Coast of Africa, a famous black Othello. In her third and last season she played in a revival of Arthur Murphy's *All in the Wrong*, a talky eighteenth-century comedy of love and jealousy that dated back to 1761; and in two Shakespearian roles, the Queen in *Hamlet*, and Queen Eleanor in *King John*. Miss Braddon, said the *Daily Telegraph*, " 'rang down' " on her stage career in the early spring of 1860:

> To her "The Dumb Man of Manchester; or, The Orphan and the Outcast," "Perowrou, the Bellows-Mender," and "Phoebe Hessell; or Eighty Years of a Woman's Life," together with the numberless tragedy and pantomine queens became no more than a memory. "Miss M. A. Seyton of 26 Newtown Square, Brighton" gave up the footlights for literature, and the country was soon agog with the fate of the worthy man [George Talboys] a wicked woman [Lady Audley] had pushed down a well.

The paper recalled also that on the island of Jersey in August 1876, MEB again played Mrs. Sternhold in *Still Waters Run Deep*, for one night on-

ly, "as a compliment to Wybert Rousby, the manager with whom she had
been professionally associated in previous years."[17] On the same occasion, she also played Pauline in Charles Dance's comedy, *Delicate
Ground*, first staged in 1849, set in Paris in 1793. As Pauline, the wife of
citizen Sangfroid, she plans to elope with her former lover, who loses his
enthusiasm when Sangfroid offers to divorce her.[18]

MEB always retained her fondness for theatrical people. In 1864, four
years after she left the stage, she wrote an "Address" in blank verse for
the benefit of the widow and children of Sam Cowell, a celebrated comic
actor lately dead. H. Nye Chart and—after his death—his widow and son
remained intimate friends of MEB's. So did Florence Haydon. So did
J. B. Buckstone, whose anxious inquiry prompted her to complete *Lady
Audley's Secret* and to whom she dedicated her novel *Henry Dunbar* in
1864. MEB valued her friendship with Wybert Rousby and his wife so
highly that in 1873 she wrote a play for them, *Griselda*, which played in
the provinces and in London;[19] and in 1876, sixteen years after abandoning the theatre as a career, she even returned to the stage at the height
of her fame and powers as a novelist to play once more for Rousby's
benefit her old part of Mrs. Hector Sternhold.

But the outline of MEB's three-year stage career that reemerges from
detective work among scraps of paper and playbills and the titles and
texts of forgotten plays conveys only the faintest suggestion of the *flavor*
of the Victorian theatre in the late fifties. What was it really like? For an
answer we turn gratefully to MEB's novels, where, despite W. B. Maxwell's belief to the contrary, she left an abundant and vivid record of her
theatrical days.

3. The Stage Remembered: the Evidence of the Fiction

Just as Isabel Sleaford in *The Doctor's Wife* gives us our best view of
MEB as a romantic, novel-mad schoolgirl of eighteen, so Flora Sandford's
stage career in *A Lost Eden* (1904) surely reflects MEB's own. Flora has
not enough talent to become a professional artist, and decides to become
an actress. She had once played Mrs. Bounce in Maddison Morton's farce,
Box and Cox (1847), in private theatricals, and everybody had said she
would have a great professional career: " 'That's what Mrs. Keeling's

uncle, the house-agent said, a man who had seen Miss O'Neil [*sic*].' "

Flora's sister Marion is troubled because she has heard about "brilliant and beautiful creatures of light-hearted morals, left-handed queens, mistresses of princes and dukes, blown about the world of wealth and fashion like fallen leaves, then sinking into a sad obscurity, dying poor and forsaken at Boulogne or in Calais or in a debtors' prison." But Flora has thought of all this. "With solemn self-complacency," she reassures her sister: she realizes she cannot " 'walk on to the stage and play Juliet.' " She knows she must begin at the bottom and that her first salary will do no more than pay for her bus fare. In two or three months, she will be good enough for speaking parts.

At the Phoenix Theatre, where Flora knows a kind actress who can introduce her to the stage-manager, there are eight extra ladies, "who must be young, and ought to be pretty." They play harem girls in an Oriental burlesque, "guests in an adapted French comedy, . . . peeresses, peasants, pages, peris . . . sparkling, fascinating, all grace and movement, but speechless." Her friend, Miss Mandlebert, will help Flora to apply for one of these posts, which pays twelve shillings a week. Then Miss Mandlebert will find her a small part in a farce: " 'She'll get round the author and make him give it to me.' " And *then* there will come a good engagement in London or in the provinces.

In the Queen's Theatre company at Hull, there actually was an actress named Miss Mandlebert, whom MEB must have known. Half a century later, she described the fictional namesake as

the pink of respectability . . . in a tightly-fitting claret-coloured merino gown, which set off her sloping shoulders and slender waist, with a crimson velvet rose in her black velvet bonnet. She wore myrtle-green gloves, that for tightness might have been thumb-screws, and made a point of showing a kid boot with side-springs and a military heel . . . quite the most fashionable thing in boots. She wore neither paint nor powder, and had a commonplace manner which seemed reassuring. She had what theatrical agents called "a fine appearance," but was not beautiful. Her figure was her strong point; and she had played the young wives and dashing widows in one-act farces, of whom it was only required to look nice, and speak like a human being, for three or four years at various theatres without blame and without distinction; and in this unambitious walk, with occasional ambitious flights in provincial theatres, she was likely to continue until marriage with a man of means removed her from the boards, or until encroaching Time compelled her to take to spinster aunts and termagant mothers-in-law, instead of wives and widows.

At the Phoenix, she tells Flora, the manager teaches "his extra ladies dancing or singing or the broadsword exercise, or anything in the world he wanted them to do. To be bullied by him was better than elocution lessons at half a guinea." So well-behaved is the company that Miss Mandlebert describes them as " 'a parcel of slomigoes.' " But a kind male friend of the family reports that among the girls " 'there are two or three black sheep, or sheep suspected of blackness; and my friend Egerton, real name Green, will take care that they don't get thick with Miss Flora, even if she should have to dress in the same room with them.' " Although the manager swears, he is " 'not otherwise objectionable.' "

The Phoenix itself, the smallest theatre in London, "somehow managed to keep alive [by putting on] new and original comedies stolen from Scribe, or sentimental plays adapted from Frédéric Soulié [1800–1847]." Its programs are miscellaneous indeed, especially in summer, when you might find "a concert, and a young gentleman's first appearance on any stage in the third act of *Hamlet*, or a ventriloquist, or a young lady's *début* in the balcony scene from *Romeo & Juliet* followed by the Alabama minstrels. You might go . . . expecting a tragedy and find a conjuror cooking live pigeons in a brazen cylinder." The Phoenix would be more prosperous if the wife of the new lessee did not insist on being in every play herself. The manager tries to confine her to "a two-act comedietta in which the dash, the fun, the fire of the play would be in the hands of that inimitable comedian, Willoughby Tracy, who carried the audience with him from start to finish." In Willoughby Tracy, MEB was portraying the mentor and friend of her youth, Wybert Rousby.

Burley, the manager, pays his stars high salaries; so the lesser actors' salaries are small: the only reason they are being paid at all is that the stars are there. " 'Do you think the British public would pay to see *you* act?' " he enquires. When introduced to Flora, he says, " 'A d——d pretty name and a d——d pretty figure,' " and "runs his eye over the slender form as deliberately as if he had been looking at a horse in Tattersall's yard." The Phoenix has an awful smell, "compounded of a perennial escape of gas, charged with the quintessence of the London sewers." And by day, the stage looks drab indeed:

Could those shallow boards, that dirty canvas—where dingy blue and tarnished gold arches and pillars and latticed windows suggested a Moorish hall—could that be the same stage where she had seen the splendour of a Parisian duchess's boudoir . . . ? What became of the dust and grime and gloom at night, when love and murder, virtue and vice, joy and sorrow, thrilled the audience with an ebb and flow of poignant emotion, and made all the life outside the theatre seem as if it were not?

Once hired, Flora has to make and pay for her own costumes. She is yelled at and sworn at and bullied. But her friend Willoughby Tracy encourages her—as no doubt Wybert Rousby had encouraged MEB—by telling her that she is " 'young enough and pretty enough to make your way in the most diabolical profession that ever Satan put it into the heart of man to choose.' " Somewhat disconcertingly, Flora discovers that two of her seven fellow-chorus-girls are indeed black sheep. They " 'dress up to the nines, and pay the rent of a drawing-room floor in Norfolk Street out of twenty-four shillings a week; so . . . there must be somebody in the background.' " This was a discovery that a young actress in the fifties would naturally have made. But it could not then have been mentioned in a novel in such unequivocal language; so MEB waited until 1904 to report it in fiction.

When summer comes, Flora has an engagement as "second walking lady and general utility" at the Theatre Royal, Manchester. Here she plays Maria in *The School for Scandal*, the widow Melnotte in Bulwer's *Lady of Lyons*, and Lady Capulet, who "is always played by the youngest actress in the theatre. . . . Nobody expects you to make up old," a practice which "has given rise in the provinces to the fixed belief that in mediaeval Verona daughters were always ten years older than their mothers." Most of all—more than to play Juliet, or Cordelia, or Miranda, even more than to play Rosalind, "though the witchery of doublet and hose might have turned the scale"—Flora yearns to play Pauline in *The Lady of Lyons* (1838), Bulwer's enormously popular and successful drama. At Manchester, all the women in the company are of good character: " 'there is not a single black sheep. . . . the worst feature about black sheep is that they are dreadfully good-natured, always offering one chocolate, or to lend one sashes and jewellery for the stage.' "

MEB had originally planned to call this novel of Flora's adventures *The Suburbans,* in reference to the Sandfords' residence in Camberwell. But the change to *A Lost Eden* reflected MEB's vision of her own childhood as having taken place "before the knowledge of evil." The novel's time, place, and circumstances all strongly suggest that Flo's experiences as a neophyte and her gallery of stage acquaintances owed much to MEB's own memories, and that Flo herself—who also changed her name to go on the stage—represented the Mary Ann Seyton who in 1857 made her début in Brighton as the Fairy Pineapple in a Christmas pantomime.

And in a short story of 1884, called "Across the Footlights," MEB took Brighton itself as her setting, calling it "Helmstone" (the original name of the village having been Brighthelmstone), and nostalgically described the place as it had been in "those old days when 'Pam' was still a power, and the Indian Mutiny [1857] was still fresh in the minds of men, when Macaulay's History and Tennyson's Idylls were new books," and before the town had "grown a new pier, a grand hotel, an aquarium, a colossal and splendid swimming bath in place of a small and shabby one." In those days, there was "not a *table d'hôte* in the whole town [but] private sitting-rooms, stately little dinners, and wax candles, in the good old Georgian manner." The men were "grander and better-favoured . . . tall moustachioed youths . . . with golden lockets and fusee-boxes flashing on their waistcoats, clad in peg-top trousers and rough overcoats"; and "All the girls had golden hair shining under pork-pie hats, and dainty little seal-skin jackets, and flounced silk frocks, showing the neat little boot and slender ancle, just revealing at windy corners that portion of the feminine anatomy which the French novelists describe as 'the birth of a leg." In "this lesser Helmstone, at the old Theatre Royal—a smaller, shabbier building than the theatre of today, Miss Rosalie Morton appeared as the fairy queen in the pantomime of 'Gulliver and the Golden Goose, or Harlequin Little Boy Blue, and Mary, Mary, quite contrary, how does your garden grow?'—in the New Year of 1860." So a quarter-century after she had played the Fairy Pineapple at the Theatre Royal in Brighton, MEB took her readers back there and told them what it had been like.

"Now the role of the queen of the fairies, in a Christmas pantomime," she went on,

> is not the loftiest walk in the British drama. It does not rank among the Portias, and Juliets, and Lady Teazles. The fairy-queen is apt to be snubbed by the first singing chamber-maid who plays "Mary, Mary, quite contrary," and even to be looked down upon by the *première danseuse*; but still there is a certain dignity about the part which is respected by the gallery, and regarded kindly by

boxes and pit. Above all, the fairy-queen . . . must be young, and fair, and gracious-looking.

These qualities Rosalie Morton has, and so she has been engaged by Mr. de Courtenay of the Theatre Royal, Helmstone, "the kindest of men and of managers. His actors and actresses adored him. He was so thoroughly good, so friendly, so honourable, so conscientious, that it was impossible to grumble at anything he did." Surely this was MEB's affectionate tribute to H. Nye Chart. And as "Cerulia, the queen of the azure fairies in the hyacinthine dell," Rosalie Morton wears "a short frock of palest blue tulle, starred with silver, and a silver tissue bodice," and has "only about a hundred lines of doggrel [sic] . . . highly spiced with local and topical allusions . . . but she had to occupy the stage for a long time." The generous Mr. de Courtenay pays her thirty-five shillings a week instead of the usual thirty, the extra five shillings coming as "a godsend to Miss Morton and Miss Morton's mamma," because of course Rosalie, like MEB, lives with and supports her mother; and like MEB, "adored her, had never been separated from her for more than a week."

Bending the facts of her own life into fiction, MEB made the stagestruck Rosalie a Yorkshire girl, from a village between Hull and Beverley, who had seen her first plays there. But like MEB, Rosalie overcomes her mother's initial opposition to her stage career and changes her name before going on the stage, from Melford to Morton, as MEB had from Braddon to Seyton. Making her debut at the Theatre Royal, Ryde, at a salary of a pound a week, Rosalie had begun by playing

a round of the most humiliating parts in the British drama, Lady Capulet; a black girl in "Uncle Tom's Cabin;" Maria, in the "School for Scandal;" she had *walked on* in a cluster of five or six ballet-girls, supposed to represent a seething populace or a dazzling assembly in high life. But she had seen the footlights; she had heard the sound of her own voice—which was more than the gallery had done—and she had earned a golden sovereign.

Though Miss Boulderby, who "talked like a clown and sang like a nigger minstrel" and who, as Mary, Mary, quite contrary, wears "a very short red petticoat bedizened with silver bells, and a black velvet bodice garnished with cockle-shells, and very *décolletée*," still gets the loudest applause, Rosalie night after night attracts to the theatre Lieutenant Randolph Bosworth, handsome and rich.

It is here, presumably, that "Across the Footlights" leaves real life and becomes a standard late mid-Victorian Christmas story, in which the reader is asked to believe that Bosworth has determined to marry Rosalie even before he has met her, and that a worldly forty-year-old major who had known the Melford family stoutly refuses even to introduce Bosworth to the ladies until he has ascertained that Bosworth's intentions are honorable. That was fiction: but the queen of the fairies and the Brighton theatre were history, MEB's personal history. How Rosalie marries not the rich young Bosworth but the poorer older major, and how he dies, and how Bosworth returns unmarried after a twenty-year military career to find Rosalie once more in the Christmas pantomime at Brighton as "Diaphanosia, queen of the water-nymphs," as lovely at thirty-nine with two children as she had been at nineteen, and what happens when he meets her nineteen-year-old daughter—all this formed the substance of the little story. But MEB's memories of the Brighton stage transcend the froth. She even included a tribute to Mr. de Courtenay's widow—MEB's dear friend, Mrs. Chart—who was as kind to the widowed Rosalie Morton as her husband had been to the maiden.

MEB may well also have given her readers a brief glimpse of her stage career, and one perhaps closer to life—because she portrayed both Flora Sandford and Rosalie Morton as prettier than she was—in a short story called "Too Bright to Last," first published in 1871. Here the actress-narrator says of herself:

> "I played old women because my personal appearance was unattractive, my stage wardrobe somewhat scanty, and my aspirations of the humblest. . . . I was only two-and-twenty, but I had a grave old-fashioned way that suited the old women, people said; and I took to that line willingly enough. . . . I used to redden my nose night after night, until I scarcely knew what it was to appear with that feature of its natural colour; though I really don't know why it is that dramatic old age should always be distinguished by that particular infirmity; but if at any time I did venture to omit the reddening process, I was sure to be told that I had no real love for my profession, and no appreciation of character. . . . the stage-manager said to me. . . . 'There's nothing like a touch of vermillion at the end of the nose to give character.' "[20]

MEB peopled her novels with authentic personalities of the theatre. In *Eleanor's Victory* (1863), we meet the theatre violinist, Richard

Thornton, who usually comes late to rehearsal. "All the effect of a murder or an abduction depended upon the pizzicato twittering of the violins, and the introduction of explosive chords at particular crises" in the melodrama. Thornton complains bitterly when the stage-managers abolish the usual ten minutes' grace for the performers and post the "no ten minutes" notice, meaning that everybody must be on time. But he is also amazingly versatile, painting most of the scenery, writing in the music cues, accompanying "Mr. Grigsby in his new comic song, or Madam Rosalie in her latest cachuca," and "adapting" French dramas to add to his income.

His managers send him to Paris to "pick up the music, sketch the scenery and effects," and translate (i.e., steal) *Raoul l'Empoisonneur*, a "great drama in eight scenes and thirty-two tableaux" playing at the home of French melodrama, the Théâtre de la Porte Saint-Martin. " 'Such a scene, in the seventh act,' " he says enthusiastically: " 'The stage is divided into eight compartments with eight different actions going on simultaneously, and five murders before the fall of the curtain.' " When he gets home to London, his manager will pay him five pounds for the "adaptation" and claim for himself all the great scenes. But Thornton, the son of a gentleman, is the only man in the theatre who does not fear the managers. Indeed, he had once threatened to throw one of them into the pit in a dispute over "the unfair use of gold leaf on the Enchanted Caves of Azure Deep." Carpenters and gasmen touch their hats to Thornton despite his shabbiness. And the ballet girls come to him for consolation "when the stage manager . . . put their names down for shilling fines in a horrible old black book."

In Paris, Dick Thornton makes rough pencil sketches of all eight scenes in *Raoul l'Empoisonneur* and later copies them carefully in watercolor, while referring to "M. Michel Lévy's sixty-centimes edition": " 'Raoul's a doctor, and the house with the staircase is his. The house at the corner belongs to the comic barber, and the practicable lattice is Madeleine's. She'll come to her window . . . to talk to the doctor, who has been giving her mild doses of *aqua tofana* for the last three weeks.' " Soon, over the practicable bridge—a bridge that actually works—comes Catherine de Médicis disguised as a nun. " 'Did she ever do anything except poison people . . . when she was alive? She never does . . . at the Porte-St.-Martin or on the Surrey side of the Thames,' " the particular homes of melodrama in Paris and London. Charles the Ninth, who has " 'just finished reading the arsenicated manuscript of a treatise on hawking,' " feels his death pangs coming on and asks who has murdered him. " 'That woman, that sorceress, that fiend in human form,' " cries the light-comedy soldier, who is drunk at the time, tearing off Catherine's velvet mask. " 'Merciful Heaven, it is my mother!' " shrieks the king, falling dead, which " 'ought to be good for three rounds of applause at least.' "

Here MEB was satirizing not only the preposterous French melodrama designed to make so great a hit when pirated and transferred to the London stage, but also, by indirection, her own melodramatic fiction. In Richard Thornton she was clearly portraying an old friend, while revealing details of day-to-day theatrical management and of human relations in the theatre that could hardly be recaptured otherwise. Before leaving Paris, Richard has "a look at the Morgue" for a London playwright who has never crossed the channel but is "doing a great drama in which one half of the *dramatis personae* recognize the other half on the marble slabs." He has only foggy notions of the Morgue, which he believes is "about as big as Westminster Abbey . . . and he wants the governors to give him the whole depth of the stage for his great scene, and set it obliquely, like the Assyrian Hall in 'Sardanapalus,' so as to give the idea of illimitable extent. I'm to paint the scene for him. *'The Interior of the Morgue by lamplight. The meeting of the living and the dead.'* That'll be rather a strong line for the bill, at any rate."[21]

In MEB's *John Marchmont's Legacy* (1863), John Marchmont inherits a vast estate and great wealth only after plumbing the depths of misery as a supernumerary, whose fellow-performers—in 1838—call him "barking Jeremiah" because of his tubercular cough and his gloomy look. On the stage he

> appeared and reappeared; now as a well-dressed passenger carrying a parcel, which he deliberately sacrificed to the felonious propensities of the clown; now as a policeman, now as a barber, now as a chemist, now as a ghost; but always buffeted, or cajoled, or bonneted, or imposed upon; always piteous, miserable, and long-suffering; with arms that ached from carrying a banner through five acts of blank verse weariness, with a head that throbbed under the weight of a ponderous edifice of pasteboard and wicker, with eyes that were sore through the evil influence of blue-fire and gun-powder-smoke, with a throat that had been poisoned by sulphurous vapours, with bones that were stiff with the playful pummeling of clown and pantaloon; and all for—a shilling a night.[22]

In *Rupert Godwin* (1867), Violet Westford, out of a job, walks down Bow Street, the center of the theatrical world of London: "Here the theatrical wigmaker exhibits the flowing *chevelures* of roistering Charles Stuart . . . side by side with the oily locks of Tartuffe or the close-cropped poll of Jack Sheppard. There the theatrical hosier . . . treacherously reveals the means by which art and cotton wool can supply the deficiencies of nature. Next door the theatrical gold-lace maker . . . allows the vulgar eye to gloat upon the diadem of a Richard and the jewelled sword-hilt of a Romeo." Seeing an agent's brass doorplate, Violet asks herself why she should not be an actress. But never having acted in any theatre, she cannot say that she is either the "juvenile lead . . . or first walking lady," and the agent offers her only a month on trial without salary—which she cannot afford—or small parts in a country theatre, which she cannot accept. Then a stranger, who has been listening, suddenly says that Violet " 'is the very person we want . . . for the Queen of Beauty . . . in the new burlesque. What would you say,' " he asks her, " '. . . if I were to pay you eighteen shillings a week for sitting in a golden temple for ten minutes every night in one of the most splendid dresses that was ever made in a theatre? . . . You'll have nothing to do; but sit still and allow the audience to admire you.' "

Once inside the theatre, Violet smells that smell, "a perpetual escape of gas, mingled with that odour of corduroy and shoe-leather which the working-classes are apt to leave behind them, and which a very witty lady once spoke of as their *esprit de corps*." Among the supernumeraries, many of the girls "were dressed neatly and plainly, others were distinguished by a tawdry shabbiness . . . cheap finery . . . ; but there were some . . . lounging together in little groups [the black sheep, no doubt], whose attire would scarcely have seemed out of place upon women of rank and wealth." The wardrobe-mistress warns Violet not to "let any of the ballet ladies persuade you to plaster your face with *blanc de perle*, or *blanc Rosati*, or *blanc de* somethings, as most of them do until their faces have about as much expression as you'll see in a whitewashed wall.' " Her youngest daughter, she tells Violet, is to be one of the Cupids: " 'She went on in last year's pantomime as the Singing Oyster, and did *so* well, bless her dear little heart.' " Violet takes a false name and is assured that " 'Most actresses and ladies of the ballet . . . have . . . some relations or friends who . . . fancy that the stage-door is the entrance to a kind of Tophet.' " Even in one of MEB's poorest novels,[23] the stage scenes had an immediacy that could only come from experience.[24]

In *Dead Sea Fruit* (1868), one of the most ambitious and experimental of MEB's serious novels of the sixties, the charming Lucy Alford, daughter of a former Oxford scholar now down on his luck and a drunkard, goes on the stage as Miss St. Albans. Her father says: " 'Such an idea was to me, at the first blush, absolute HORROR; but when my sweet girl urged her predilection for the drama, and reminded me of the handsome fortunes realised by Garrick, Mrs. Siddons, Miss O'Neil [sic], . . . I relented.' " At nineteen, Lucy had already appeared at the Theatres Royal Stony Stratford, Market Deeping, Oswestry, and Stamford. Though she prefers tragedy to comedy, she had won applause as Lady Teazle in Oswestry "from an appreciative, though somewhat limited audience."

When people hear that Lucy is playing Pauline in Bulwer's *Lady of Lyons*, they all say, " 'My dear, I remember seeing Helen Faucit [celebrated actress, wife of Sir Theodore Martin]' " in the role. And Mrs. M'Grudder, who "plays old women on the Oswestry circuit," adds that if Lucy knew how Helen Faucit played the cottage-scene, she would go home and cut her throat. Mrs. M'Grudder herself is no great actress; she " 'speaks the broadest, broadest Scotch, and in Lady Macbeth the boys in the gallery laugh at her dreadfully.' " It is not the audience but her fellow-actors who frighten Lucy:

> "they come to the wings and watch me; and then they tell me what they think; and they give me advice; and somehow they contrive to make me miserable. . . . sometimes, when I have been playing Ophelia, and have been quite carried away by the part. . . . I have happened to look towards the prompt entrance, and see Mrs. M'Grudder standing there staring at me in her dreadful stony way, and have heard her say 'St-st-st' quite loud, and it has made me break down. . . . most actors . . . have a kind of prejudice against amateurs and novices, and try to put them down."

Lucy Alford is acting now in London at the Oxford Road Theatre, where the regular company is often strengthened by a visiting star such as "the famous transatlantic equestrienne, best known to fame as the divine Miss Godiva Jones, [who] pranced and galloped in her celebrated performances of Dick Turpin and Timour the Tartar," a clear reference to Adah Isaacs Menken, who appeared as Mazeppa in a costume that made her look naked. The lessee and leading man, Mr. de Mortemar (né Morris), believes he can surpass all the most celebrated actors in their most celebrated roles: Edmund Kean as Hamlet; Gustavus Brooke (a tragedian whose most famous part was Othello, and who died in a shipwreck in 1866) as Master Walter, the lead in Sheridan Knowles's *The Hunchback* (1832); W. C. Macready as Lear; Charles Mathews as Sir Charles Coldstream in Dion Boucicault's *Used Up* (1844); Alfred Wigan as John Mildmay in Tom Taylor's *Still Waters Run Deep* (1855); Dion Boucicault as the faithful Miles na Coppaleen in Boucicault's own *The Colleen Bawn* (1860); and Edward Wright as the inquisitive Paul in *Paul Pry*, by Douglas Jerrold (1827). "This much he felt he could do, and he had no greedy desire to outstep the limit which liberal Nature had set upon his genius." Mortemar has engaged Lucy "because she was very young and inexperienced and he could do as he liked with her; which means, in a dramatic sense, that he could keep her with her back to the audience, in an ignominious corner of the stage . . . and that he could take her up so sharply at the end of her most telling speeches as to deprive her of . . . applause."

When Lucy's lover visits the theatre, he finds

> the dress circle in occupation of two young women in scarlet Garibaldi jackets and black velvet headdresses; one fat elderly lady, in a cap which offered . . . a small museum of natural and artistic curiosities in the way of shells, feathers, beads, butterflies, and berries; three warm-looking young men, sprawling and lounging . . . in a corner box, and a scanty sprinkling of that class of spectators who come with free admissions. . . . a subdued crunching of apples and sucking of oranges went on round and about him.

Lucy spends much of her time on stage "half concealed by the stiff curve of Mr. de Mortemar's encircling arm." When she has her big scene—the play is Bulwer's *Lady of Lyons*—"she was only a timid young actress trying to act. She was not the Demoiselle [Pauline] Deschappelles—proud, loving, passionate, and maddened by the cheat that had been put upon her. . . . She was self-conscious, nervously anxious to please her audience." But, at nineteen she has had only a year's experience. Acting, after all, is "among the most difficult and exacting of all the arts." It "has no formulae," it "is rarely taught well, and very often taught badly." It "demands from its professors a real moral courage and an expenditure of physical energy, intellectual power, and emotional feeling demanded by no other art." Even when an actor achieves perfection, "he is spoken of in a patronizing tone as only an actor; and it is somewhat a matter of wonder that he should be 'received in society.' "

In the green-room, "a long narrow slip of a room underground, furnished with a few shabby chairs and benches, some flaring gas-lamps, and a cheval glass," de Mortemar expatiates on his own genius. Claude (Melnotte), he says, he does not consider as one of his *great* parts,

". . . though my friends are pleased to tell me that I have left William Charles Macready some distance behind. . . . you were no doubt struck by some points which are not only new to the stage, but which go a step or two beyond the original meaning of the author, as, for instance, at the close of the third act, where, instead of the ordinary, 'Ho, my mother!'—a mere commonplace summons to a parent who is desired to come downstairs, I have adopted the heavy sigh of despair: 'Oh, my mother!'—expressive of Claude's remorseful consciousness that he has disregarded the widow's very sensible advice in the first act. This reading opens up—if I may be permitted to say so—long vistas of thought, and also gives an importance and an elevation to the character of the widow Melnotte, for which the lady performing that part can scarcely be sufficiently grateful. 'Oh my mother! Oh, my second self, my counsellor by whose sustaining wisdom I might have escaped my present degradation and despair!' All that, I flatter myself, is implied in the sigh and gesture which I introduce at this point. Subtle, is it not?"

"Extremely subtle. . . . you must have studied the German critics. . . . There is a profundity in your ideas that reminds me of Schlegel."

"No, sir, I have studied *this*," replied the tragedian, thumping the breast of his . . . coat. [Upon which one of the other actors says:]

"That's a strong case of coals, a'nt it?"

"A case of coals?"

"Yes, coals, nuts, barcelonas. The gorger's awfully coaly on his own slumming, eh?" [which turns out to mean "The manager is rather sweet on his own acting."]

Lucy's admirer tries to get her a part by appealing to the manager of the Theatre Royal, Pall Mall, who has just received "a charming little adaptation of *Cotelettes Sautées chez Véfour.* . . ." It calls for "six young ladies . . . —*ces dames* of the Quartier Bréda . . . in the original"—but now transformed into "school-girls from a Peckham academy, who go to dine with a West-Indian uncle at Verey's." So the original French prostitutes have become English schoolgirls, and MEB has had a quiet ironical joke at the constant English plagiarism of plays written for the French stage, and at the contrasting moral codes of the two peoples. Lucy prefers to stay on with Mortemar and have speaking parts.

But she is deprived of her promised role as Julia in Sheridan Knowles's *Hunchback* (first produced in 1838) by the arrival of Ida Courtenay to play the part—" 'an amateur lady, who comes in a brougham with two horses, and whose dresses . . . cost hundreds of pounds.' " An amateur lady this kept woman surely is, and she insists on calling rehearsals at times to suit herself: "A mighty rushing sound as of a Niagara of moiré antique" heralds her arrival, as she bounces into the green-room, "with the air of a Semiramis in high-heeled boots." Tall, stalwart, thirty-five years old, she is "as handsome as rouge, pearl-powder, painted lips, painted nostrils, painted eyelids, painted eyebrows, and a liberal supply of false hair could make her." Only her fierce black eyes and her "fine" figure are all her own. "A white-lace burnous, and a bonnet from the Burlington Arcade" top her mauve moiré, which comes from "Madame Carabine Nourrisson of Paris." Eventually Ida is roundly denounced: " 'It is you and ladies of your class who bring discredit upon the profession which you condescend to take up for the amusement of your idle evenings.' "

Now Lucy has to take another engagement at Market Deeping, where she will play Gennaro, the son in a burlesque of Lucrezia Borgia. " 'He gets poisoned or something at the end. I have to sing parodies on "Sam Hall" and the "Cat's-meat Man"; and I have to do a—a—cellar-flap breakdown, I believe it's called. It is a very good part.' " She must leave for Market Deeping at quarter past five in the morning by the parliamentary train, much used by actors because it is so much cheaper:

"One meets most respectable people, generally with large families of children and canary-birds; and sometimes people even play cards, if one can get something flat—a tea-tray or a picture—to play on. One has to hide the cards, of course, when the guard comes round, unless he happens to be a very good-natured guard, who pretends not to see them. Oh, I assure you, it is not at all disagreeable to travel by the parliamentary train."[25]

In *A Strange World* (1875), MEB's readers met Matthew Elgood—

"heavy man" of a theatrical company at "Eborsham" (York), who plays the King in *Hamlet*, Iago, Friar Lawrence, and "the relentless father of ponderous top-hatted and pig-tailed comedy"—and his daughter, Justina, "general utility," at which she works "with the unrequited patience of an East-end shirtmaker." Matthew reproaches his daughter for "running down" the profession that had maintained her since babyhood, but Justina still hates it:

> "Hasn't it kept me ignorant and shabby, and looked down upon . . . since I was two years old, and went on as the child in 'Pizarro' [by R. B. Sheridan, 1799]? Hasn't it kept me hanging about in the wings till midnight from year's end to year's end, when other children were snug in bed with a mother to look after them? Haven't I been told often enough that I've no talents and no good looks to help me, and that I must be a drudge all my life? . . . If I'd been a young lady, now, . . . brought to the theatre for the first time to see 'Romeo and Juliet,' I could fancy myself wanting to play Juliet; but I've seen too much of the ladder Juliet stands on in the balcony scene, and the dirty-looking man who holds it steady for her, and the way she quarrels with Mrs. Wappers, the nurse, between the acts. . . . I've tried to fancy Juliet as a real living woman in Verona . . . but . . . I can only think of Miss Villeroy, in her whitey-brown satin and Mrs. Wappers, in her old green and yellow brocade—and the battered old garden scene, and the palace flats we use so often, and the scene-shifters in their dirty shirt-sleeves."

MEB herself, who also had no particular "talents" or "good looks to help" her, must often have had moments like this, when she dreaded a lifetime of drudgery.

The manager of the Elgoods' company has been forced by financial losses to make it a "commonwealth, . . . a body without a head," in which "the weekly funds are divided into shares, each share representing half a sovereign. The actor whose nominal salary is two pound ten takes five shares." One whose pay is fifteen shillings takes a share and a half. Then the shares fluctuate, depending on box-office receipts. Sometimes, says an experienced member of the commonwealth, he has known them to rise to fourteen and ninepence halfpenny, sometimes fall to one and seven pence. When a commonwealth is declared, " 'the little people are generally the first to fall away. . . . the second walking lady and chambermaid go home to their mothers; the second old man opens a sweet-stuff shop!' "

At York, the commonwealth's theatre green-room is "a small dingy chamber, carpetless, curtainless, uncleanly, . . . with narrow baize-covered benches, and . . . one cloudy looking-glass," with an unscreened gas-jet flaring on each side of it. The manager, himself a superb low-comedian (" 'You'll hear the people screaming at him in "The Spitalfields Weaver" [by Thomas Haines Bayley, 1838] by and bye. His business with the tea and bread and butter is the finest thing I ever saw.' "), eloquently laments the sad state of the theatre:

> "The provincial stage is in its decline, sir. Time was when this very theatre could be kept open for ten consecutive months in every year, to the profit of the manager, and when the good old comedies and the Shakespearian drama were acted week after week to an intelligent and approving audience. Now-a-days a man must rack his brains in order to cater for a frivolous and insatiable public, which has been taught to consider a house on fire or a railway smash, the end and aim of dramatic composition. I speak from bitter experience. My grandfather was manager of the Eborsham circuit, and retired with a competency. My father inherited the competency, and lost it in the Eborsham circuit. I have been cradled in the profession, and have failed as manager, with credit to my head and heart . . . some three or four times."

Two years later Justina Elgood's "art has grown out of the depths of her own feeling," and her "acting is the outcome of a rich and thoughtful mind rather than the hard and dry result of tuition and study of the mechanical art of imitation." She is now "as much at ease on the stage as in her own room," appearing in London at the Royal Albert Theatre, where the "bright and comfortable-looking" green-room has a "carpeted floor, looking-glasses over the chimney piece and console table, photographs and engraved portraits of popular actors and actresses upon the gaily papered walls, a cushioned divan all round the room, and nothing but the table . . . wanted to make it resemble a billiard-room in a pleasant unpretentious country-house." Justina now earns six guineas a week: wealth to her father, whose ideas of luxury are "bounded by a Bloomsbury lodging, a hot dinner every day, and his glass of gin and water mixed with a liberal hand." The girl who hated the "pro" has triumphed.

But success in the theatre, *A Strange World* proclaims, was now possible only in London. In MEB's favorite Cornwall, where the later action of the novel shifts to the little town of Seacombe (Wadebridge), the decay of the drama has gone even further than in York. Here the theatre has been turned into a Methodist chapel, and only the combination "tobacconist, hairdresser, and dealer in fancy and miscellaneous articles," whose shop is opposite, laments its passing. On his wall he cherishes a playbill of Edmund Kean's performance of *Othello* in Seacombe early in the century. He remembers Kean and Miss O'Neill and Macready and all the other great actors of the great past. As a boy he spent all his sixpences to go to the theatre twice a week and he still knows his Shakespeare by heart. The closing of the theatre had cut him to the heart.

As he says,

"the town had grown serious-minded . . . the great actors and actresses were dead . . . and the stars that were left did not care about coming to Seacombe. Managers had been doing worse and worse every year, business dwindling down to nothing, half salaries or no salaries toward the end of every season, . . . the actors and actresses . . . were sticks . . . they made up in rant what they wanted in talent. The county families left off coming . . . there were no Bespeaks, and the poor old theatre got to have a dilapidated woe-begone look. . . . The actors looked hungry and out at elbows. . . . Many a time I asked one of them in to share my one o'clock dinner, if it was but a potato pasty, or a squab pie made with scrag of mutton. The stage door used to be just opposite my shop. It's walled up now, but you may see an outline of it in the brickwork."

As consolation, he has collected copies of all the theatrical playbills for more than a decade, and bound them "in a ponderous marble-paper" volume, "a triumph in amateur bookbinding."[26] This passage rings so reportorially true that one is sure that MEB herself knew the Cornish barber and amateur of the theatre with his great file of old local playbills. The decline and closing of the local theatres were to her melancholy signs of the drying up of the cultural life in the provinces in the sixties and seventies.

Unlike Justina Elgood, MEB herself never graduated as an actress from the provincial stage to the prosperity of theatrical London. But she remained a devotee of the theatre all her life, and knew by observation if not by experience what Justina's moderate success at the Royal Albert Theatre would mean in terms of increased salary and modest comforts. Still ahead of Justina Elgood lay the luxury and elegance to be found at the very top of the theatrical ladder. And these too MEB put into her novels.

In *Hostages to Fortune* (1875), the popular leading lady Myra Brandreth manages her own company at the Frivolity, especially built for her by an admiring peer, who would far rather not collect the annual rent of twenty-five hundred pounds that Myra insists upon paying. The Frivolity is "like a bonbonnière, all quilted canary satin and gold, with a background of burgundy-coloured velvet," adorned with medallion portraits of Shakespeare's heroines, painted by Royal Academicians. A dome of gilded latticework screens the "sunburner" lamp, and large skylights above open to the fresh air in fine weather. Crystal girandoles with "clusters of parian candles in which a slender gas-tube is artfully inserted"; a "smoking divan, opening upon a wide stone balcony overlooking the street"; and the star's dressing-room, "upholstered in blue satin embroidered with butterflies and birds, . . . doors veneered with ivory, mantelpiece of Sèvres, . . . chair and couches of white enamelled wood and quilted blue satin, toilet-table . . . entirely of ivory and silver": everything at the Frivolity is quietly and ostentatiously splendid.

In this bijou theatre, the plays are modish and ephemeral. *Hemlock*, written especially for Miss Brandreth by a popular novelist and former suitor, is billed as "a classical comedy, suggested by Émile Augier [1820–1885]," but, as two habitués remark to each other on opening night, " 'Suggested' is a good word. Of course we know what it is, *La Ciguë* [by Augier, 1844] done into modern slang." *Hemlock* is followed by an "adaptation" of a play by Dumas, which has startled all Paris at the Gymnase. In London, its plot "cut clean away and its morality white-washed," it has been tortured into an "invertebrate domestic drama." As usual, all the prostitutes of the Paris version are schoolgirls in London, and somehow the adaptations are less interesting than the originals. London is not startled.

But Myra Brandreth is not content with Dumas. She goes to Paris herself to see a play called *L'Ange Déchu* that even the critics there have called " 'tant soit peu hasardée' " and recommended that " 'les jeunes demoiselles et même les jeunes mariées' " should stay away, adding, however: " 'C'est d'une audace magnifique! Cela va jusqu'au sublime. . . .

C'est d'une désinvolture à faire rougir Belot.' " Six nights running, Myra Brandreth studies "every turn" of the leading lady's head, "every look, every tone, every phase of agony in the great poisoning scene at the end, where this angel of corruption . . . poisons herself after having tried . . . to poison her rival, her husband, and one or two other personages who are obstacles in the broad path of passion." Back to London goes Miss Brandreth "with *L'Ange Déchu* in her pocket and the right to produce a literal translation of the same bought and paid for." It is to be "adapted" by "a clever young dramatist . . . who enjoys the advantage of being dramatic critic on three or four journals. . . ." He wants to make the leading lady the hero's sister instead of his wife, and her lover a bachelor, so that there would be " 'no harm in their love scenes. We might make some clause in the father's will the obstacle to the marriage.' " But Myra grumbles that this would be " '. . . purely English. . . . In order to escape the charge of immorality, we make our plots more improbable than the wildest fairy tale.' " After producing the highly successful uncensored version of *L'Ange Déchu*, Myra has a heart attack, to satisfy MEB's multitudes of middle-class readers that the wages of sin were still being properly paid, although MEB herself manifestly disbelieved it.

Like Ida Courtenay in *Dead Sea Fruit*, the beautiful Miss Belormond in *Hostages to Fortune* is a would-be actress. She discovers "all at once that she is dying to make her *début* as Juliet in white satin and silver passementerie," and "is happily endowed with a rich godfather, who seems to be a near relation of Cinderella's fairy godfather, . . . grey-moustached and in the sugar-baking trade, who kindly arranges everything, even to the neat single brougham which is indispensable to Miss Belormond's launch." But there is a limit. Although Miss Belormond wants her own theatre, "and actresses of her own to sneer at, as Mrs. Brandreth sneers at her," the fairy godfather "allows these hints to pass him by like the wind."[27]

In *The Cloven Foot* (1879) a French dancer plays an important part, as does an Italian opera-singer in *The Venetians* (1892). But—always excepting *A Lost Eden* (1904),—MEB's later novels seldom revisit the now vanished stage world of her youth. Occasionally she provides a rapidly-sketched macabre portrait, like that of the girl singer, whose specialty is two songs illustrating the DT's, "Rats" and "The Demon of Drink." As a theatrical agent admiringly says, " 'She can make their blood run cold one minute, and make 'em roar with laughter the next. Her father died with the horrors, and she's a first-class mimic. It ain't every girl would have the grit to do it.' "[28] Feeling the way she did about girls and their fathers, MEB would naturally have been amused and pleased by this particular display of grit. And in *The Green Curtain* (1911) she retold as fiction the dramatic career of Edmund Kean, a historical exercise that only underlined her passion for the stage. But in the main, it was into her novels of the sixties and seventies that she poured her theatrical memories.

MEB surely knew the down-at-heels manager in the provinces who had had to turn his company into a commonwealth; the brisk and sympathetic self-respecting professional actress, doomed to perform in minor roles until some kind man married her or she was reduced to playing old women; the actor with the paranoid conviction that he alone could achieve greatness and give new interpretations to classic parts; the totally inexperienced ambitious woman who owed her place on the stage only to the lover who subsidized her apprenticeship; the scene-painter who doubled as a second violinist and translator from the French; the tubercular super who earned a pittance by receiving buffets from the clown. She knew at first hand the shabby green-rooms, the look of the stage by day when the floodlights were off and the tinsel seemed tawdry, the smell of the gas and the sewer in the back passageways of the theatre. She had surely played cards on a tea-tray in the parliamentary train. And she supplemented the experiences of the three brief seasons of her own theatrical career through observation later on: she continued to go to the theatre with zest all her life. She had never played in the Frivolity, but she had often sat in its quilted satin seats. She continued to know Florence Haydon, the Charts, the Rousbys, the Buckstones, and the others she had first met between 1857 and 1860 when she was herself an actress; and she became intimate with Madge Kendal, Lady Monckton, the Squire Bancrofts, Sir Henry Irving, Bram Stoker, Pinero, Beerbohm Tree, and many other luminaries of the later Victorian and Edwardian stage.

She gave the readers of her fiction a personally conducted tour of the provincial and metropolitan playhouses, remembered and observed with wit and affection and sometimes with healthy anger. What hard work acting is! How seldom it is done well! How absurd to pretend that there is anything necessarily degraded or degrading about it! What extraordinary and delightful people one meets in the theatre! Accurate, revealing, amusing, sympathetic, MEB's picture of the Victorian stage is unique in fiction.

4. "Circumambulatory" and *The Loves of Arcadia:* the Curtain Rings Down

MEB's published novels only occasionally touch upon the pleasant camaraderie between the congenial men and women of a theatrical company. Rivalries, jealousies, ambitions, successes, and disappointments: these she naturally set down in profusion. But she was writing for an audience which would have regarded easy, natural friendships among actors and actresses as a sign of loose morals; so she usually passed over this part of their life. Some of it can be recovered from an unpublished short story, written very early, probably before 1860, called "Circumambulatory; or, The Adventures of Three Gentlemen and a Lady in Search of a British Public."[29] All four of MEB's characters are members of "a hybrid class, half actor, half author, half dramatic artist, half three halfpence a liner (we scorn the vulgar fiction of the penny), pressmen who dabbled with the stage, actors who dabbled with the press." They belong to a London company, their theatre is closed for a week, and they need money.

The lady, Hypatia, is the young wife of one of the three gentlemen. She is "only moderately given to crinoline, and has been seen with a bonnet on her head. . . . doesn't mind cigars in the drawing room. She never has headaches or hysterics. She can make an omelet, a dish of macaroni, an Irish stew, and rum punch. . . . she can correct a proof, and play the piano; and she has a soul not above buttons, *id est* the sewing of them on. She is a charming travelling-companion, a good sailor, and doesn't mind being chaffed." Her husband is called "Volage . . . from the eternal gaiety which made him alike indifferent to an empty purse, a bad dinner, a crying wife, or an angry creditor." The other two are a languid Scot who worships Carlyle, and a "talking jellyfish," nicknamed the "Zoophyte." The four lightheartedly decide to tour Sussex during their free week. In towns that have no theatre they will put on one-act farces such as *The Swiss Cottage* with Hypatia "in short petticoats, a black velvet necklace, and a gold cross, with a dreadful Swiss song in which she will make insane remarks ending in 'tra-la-la i-ou!' "

With much persiflage, no funnier to modern taste for the Dickensian polysyllables and circumlocutions that MEB so favored at the time, the four set off at dawn by train, encumbered by Hypatia's canary bird and pet dog, eating anchovy sandwiches and drinking whiskey from a bottle, with the canary's cage hung from a penknife stuck into the partition of the compartment. When they get to the Sussex station they have chosen and disembark with all their luggage, the place proves to be no town at all but merely "the villas and grounds of two or three gentlemen for whom the station has been made." Worse, there will be no return train for three hours. Hungry, thirsty, and thoroughly out of sorts, but teasing each other unremittingly, the four return to town and cheer up over a late dinner at Volage and Hypatia's lodgings in Camberwell. As "a theatrical speculation" their day had been a horrible failure, but "as an adventure it was an unprecedented success." While her husband and the Scotsman play dominoes, Hypatia accepts the gracious invitation of the Zoophyte to put him to sleep by reading aloud the *Idylls of the King*. Their day will make a comic article for one of the magazines.

"Circumambulatory" is probably that very article. For literary convenience, MEB married herself to one of the company. Apparently she had planned to go off with friends for a week's barnstorming tour of the Sussex countryside, and if they had got off at the right station she would have done so. Light hearted, Bohemian, innocent: this and similar memories she excluded from her novels: Victorian convention would have condemned them.

A relationship like those in "Circumambulatory" MEB enjoyed with a young man named William Sawyer, whom she met in Brighton while she was acting in the Theatre Royal Company there. Like Hypatia, MEB was "half actor, half author," and during her three Brighton theatre seasons filled her notebooks and covered all odd scraps of paper that came her way with bits of verse, dramatic dialogues—even entire acts for plays—and fragments of projected short stories. Sawyer, who was on the staff of the *Brighton Herald*, had some of her verse published in its columns.[30] By late 1859 or early 1860 she had completed a comedietta called *The Loves of Arcadia*, which was accepted for London production by Louise Swanborough, the lessee and leading lady at the Strand Theatre, where it opened on March 12, 1860. It was never published, but an enthusiastic review of the piece (from an unidentified newspaper) effectively describes it.

The reviewer reported that "the Arcadia to which we are introduced is . . . a forest in the neighborhood of Versailles," in the time of Louis XV. Miss Swanborough appeared as Mademoiselle de Launay, whom the king was proposing to marry to the Chevalier de Merrilac. As the two have never met, both object to the marriage and flee into the forest disguised as Narcissus and Daphne, a shepherd and shepherdess. Here they meet by chance, and fall madly in love with each other. Louis XV himself then encounters and falls in love with the shepherdess, causing Narcissus painful jealousy. Narcissus is "conveyed to the king's private apartments with a frame, behind which he takes his stand, still in pastoral dress, and there represents his own portrait." A courtier wafts some snuff to his nose and he sneezes, and is thus discovered. The king had not betrayed Daphne but defended her honor; Narcissus is placated, the lovers learn one another's identity, and all ends happily. The reviewer commented that

> Sticklers for historical accuracy might object to the character of Louis XV as portrayed by this drama, and to the romantic nature of some of the incidents introduced. But the audience were evidently satisfied, and paid no attention to these trifles. They applauded the opening decorations; they applauded a rustic dance at the end of the first act; they applauded when the curtain rose and when it fell. Nay, so great was their enthusiasm that they applauded the footman who arranged the carpet between the acts, and if the check-takers of the house and the box-keepers had appeared at the right time, they doubtless would have come in for an ovation also.[31]

Obviously, the piece, frothy and trivial as it clearly was and was intended to be, had scored a signal success.

The fortunate production of *The Loves of Arcadia* followed shortly upon the end of MEB's career as an actress, and her departure from Brighton, where she had made her headquarters since 1857. Early in March 1860, she and her mother went to live near Beverley, in Yorkshire. Remaining in Brighton, William Sawyer began to write to MEB. His letters show that they had shared ideas, opinions, and literary aspirations. Sawyer was youthful, exuberant, and given to bad puns. He was married to a girl named Bird, whom with would-be Dickensian wit he called "the Ornithological." Addressing MEB as "My dear Pollee," he asked whether "the extreme hilarity of your northern retreat has affected your mind?" What other reason could there be for her not having written? Recently, in a pub, Sawyer had met an actor named Clarke from the Strand Theatre. "We spoke of thee—of the loves of a cadger [a typical Sawyer pun: he meant her comedietta, *The Loves of Arcadia*] and he was pleased to say that Miss Swanborough had faith in it, great faith in it, and was disposed to think it will draw for many weeks. So now fortune smiles upon you—go in and win." From an actual member of Miss Swanborough's company, such a prediction about the comedietta that had not yet opened would be welcome news indeed. Sawyer was planning to publish in the *Brighton Herald* a poem by MEB, so that "the fame of your poetic powers may not willingly be let to die out."

Sawyer's mother shared one of his letters to MEB. Addressing her as "Miss Seyton" and signing herself "Yours affectionately," Mrs. Sawyer added, "You have always shown yourself so free of affectation or vanity as to success" that she was sure that MEB's own account of her play's fortunes would be completely fair. Having yielded the first page of the letter paper to his mother—"*Place au dam* of course as we say in Anglo-French circles,"—Sawyer told his "dear Pollee" how much he regretted that he could not come up to London to see the comedietta. Soon both Sawyers were congratulating MEB on her "recent triumphs, dramatic and plutonic," although "for any person to have money—real money—for that person's mere writings, is a personal insult, outrage, and disgust." The play had opened, and MEB was launched.

By October 1860, when the six-month period in Beverley had come to an end and MEB had moved to London, Sawyer received a "panto" she sent him, which he admitted was " 'dem'd clever' especially for a gal . . . the opening drags by reason of a superabundance of talky talky. . . . there must be songs, I fancy. . . . The deficiency of incident strikes me . . . but a good spirit-rapping scare will save it. . . . The dialogue is quite as brilliant as I could have hoped to render it. Isn't that magnanimous?" He thought it would be in better taste if the heroine were not threatened with corporal punishment, and sent: "Very best love to Madame Mère and accept ditto or seconds or thirds as you require for yourself, in which the ornithological unites." Ten days later (October 29, 1860), Sawyer reported that he had seen "Nye C. [hart] who from his tone I am sure will not accept the panto." He sent MEB verses of his own that he hoped she could get published for him.[32]

Sawyer's letters to MEB reflect an uninhibited, faintly Bohemian, and utterly innocent friendship. After MEB's death in 1915, the *Morning Post* reported that in 1859 she and Sawyer had made and carried out a compact to divide between them the proceeds of the first literary success that either should achieve, and the *Times* added that " . . . the curious but entirely literary friendship between the two went so far that they came up together to London, determined to try their fortunes."[33] But the original letters from Sawyer to MEB do not corroborate these fancies. Sawyer stayed in Brighton, and, so far from sharing in MEB's financial success, he teased her about it gently and not without a touch of jealousy.

During her three years on the stage did MEB encounter any man who meant more to her than Sawyer? Was there a real-life Volage to her Hypatia? No direct evidence survives, but it would be strange if, between the ages of twenty-one and twenty-four, she had not had a suitor. The experiences of her fictional actresses, even when professionally similar to her own, offer no reliable clues to MEB's intimate life. Perhaps she may have put into her unhappy romances of the theatre some now unidentifiable fragments of her own experience. The evidence is slim and indirect: only three years after she left the stage—when she was well-launched on her career as a novelist—we shall find her at just twenty-seven unaccountably skeptical in her worldly-wise views about the childishness of romantic love, the stupidity of lovers' jealousies, and the wastefulness and futility of passion. But the meaning of these attitudes for her own life remains enigmatic.

Only detective work among documents hitherto unknown will reveal how MEB found the means of abandoning her stage career and launching herself as an author, and will provide evidence for her stormy relationships with the two much older men who now entered her life. Perhaps these adventures were turbulent enough in themselves to account for her somewhat premature cynicism about love. But the nagging doubt will remain whether she may not during her years in the theatre have had an adventure that cannot now be recovered, fallen in love with somebody who cannot be identified, and experienced disappointment if not betrayal. If we cherish this doubt until the end of her long life, we shall find that posthumously she will reward us with a tantalizing suggestion that we may have been right all along.

CHAPTER III

The Secret of "The Author of
Lady Audley's Secret" (1860–1868)

1. What Charles Reade Really Said

Exhibit A, offering the first clue to MEB's history after the curtain rang down in Brighton in the spring of 1860, is a brief paean of praise to her by Charles Reade, twice published—undated—during the 1930's:

> As for M. E. Braddon, I don't know where to find a better woman. Industrious, self-denying, gentle, affectionate, talented, and utterly unassuming, a devoted daughter, faithful wife, loving mother, and kindly stepmother. Her first stories were masterpieces of narrative. She was a genuine *raconteur*. By and by her task-master drove her too hard, and, of late I fail to recognize the same hand all through, and think that much that goes by her name is done by understrappers.[1]

But this is only a fragment of what Reade actually wrote.

Exhibit B is the full text—except for one paragraph temporarily withheld—now published for the first time from Reade's four-page handwritten entry, headed "Braddon, Miss," in an alphabetized notebook for 1874, duly entered under the letter "B":

> Her first patron was a simple noble-minded Yorkshire squire, Gilby. He got her "trail of the serpent" published at 2d. a number to assure her wider circulation. Used also to come to London and consult F. G. about the works of a young man, his friend. He [i.e., Gilby] was father, lover, and friend. When she fell into the hands of M., he came up dejected, and put questions about M. G's [i.e., "F. G.'s"] answers, though guarded, made him [Gilby] sink back into his chair. He then said to tell you the truth, the young *man* is a young *woman* I have long loved, and would have asked her to marry me: but I am rich: she was poor. I wished her to have reputation. And everything; that it might be she who did me the

favor in marrying me. Ah! I fear I have waited too long. He went away. But presently came limping back. Let me ask you one question. Do you think he is capable—of—seducing her?

"I can't say."

He never came again, and the lady became the wife of a man, who had got a wife and children. . . . [paragraph omitted here]

The excessive delicacy of the Yorkshireman would have cost him almost any woman. Women do not appreciate feminine delicacy and restraint of passion in a man. They secretly despise it and openly praise it. Their conduct is literally a trap in this respect.

And only then, at the very end, came Reade's tribute of Exhibit A, beginning "As for M. E. Braddon . . ."[2]

In this melodramatic anecdote, the "F. G." whom Gilby consulted was, I believe, Frederick Greenwood, a prominent London journalist. But the "M" into whose hands MEB had fallen was certainly John Maxwell (1820–1895), an Irishman who had come to London as a youth in the late 1830's to arrange for the publication of the complete works of a fellow-countryman, the novelist and playwright Gerald Griffin, and who then became a publisher. Maxwell bought periodicals, experimented with them, combined them, sold them, and started new ones. He was always restless and often successful. Sometimes his magazines were shoddy little cheap ones: *Town Talk* (in which Edmund Yates published the notorious paragraphs about Thackeray that caused all the trouble at the Garrick Club), *The Welcome Guest* (at first a penny, and then a twopenny, weekly that ran from 1858 through 1861), the short-lived *Robin Goodfellow* (in which *Lady Audley's Secret* was born and died abruptly, only to be revived elsewhere), or the *Halfpenny Journal* (cheapest of all, running from 1861 to 1865, full of lurid fiction for the lower classes). Sometimes Maxwell's magazines were large and lavishly produced and designed to be read by the middle and upper classes: in the sixties, *The Saint James's Magazine*, *Temple Bar*, and *Belgravia* would prove the most successful. MEB herself would found the latter in 1866 and "conduct" it for a decade, all the while remaining its most important contributor. Outside the window of Maxwell's shabby little office in Shoe Lane, off Fleet Street, there stood in the late fifties half a dozen hungry young journalists, drawn up in a rank like cabs, eager for any commission. When Maxwell wanted one he would open the window and shout, and up would come George Augustus Sala or Edmund Yates or Percy Fitzgerald—whoever was at the head of the queue at the moment—and proceed to edit a new periodical, write a series of articles, or produce a guide book.[3]

Maxwell, then, according to Charles Reade, writing in 1874, took MEB as his wife, although he had a wife still living. She was, in fact, in a mental home. Maxwell was widely known as MEB's publisher and business adviser (Reade said her "task-master"), as her husband, and as the father of her children. But Gilby, the excessively delicate "father, lover, and friend," the Yorkshireman who waited too long, has hitherto been completely unknown. If we turn to Exhibit C, an essay that MEB published in the 1890's about her first novel, we shall catch a second glimpse of him.

In Beverley, MEB recalled more than thirty years later, she had found "a Maecenas . . . a learned gentleman who volunteered to foster my love of the Muses by buying the copyright of a volume of verses, and publishing the same at his own expense," losing money by his "noble patronage of Poet's Corner verse." It was he who chose the topic of the longest poem, "which was to sing—however feebly, Garibaldi's Sicilian campaign." Simultaneously, a "blindly enterprising" local printer, who had read some of MEB's verses in the *Beverley Recorder*, offered her ten pounds for a serial story—her first novel—to be printed in Beverley and published in London. The printer paid her two pounds ten—fifty shillings—in advance. It "seemed like the opening of . . . paradise." So she embarked on both literary projects at the same time.

The novel was to "combine, as far as my powers allowed, the human interest and genial humour of Dickens with the plot-weaving of G. W. M. Reynolds." She called it *Three Times Dead, or the Secret of the Heath*. The local printer was C. H. Empson, of Toll-Gavel, Beverley. After a few penny numbers, he begged MEB to cut the story in half and accept five pounds for it instead of ten; she agreed and finished the book, but Empson never paid her the second fifty shillings. While writing the novel and the poems, MEB lived with her mother in "farm-house lodgings in the neighbourhood of Beverley, where I spent, perhaps, the happiest half-year of my life,— . . . tranquil, studious days, . . . with the mother whose society was always sufficient for me, among level pastures, with unlimited books from the library in Hull, an old farm-horse to ride about the green lanes, the breath of summer, . . . all about us." The "one dark shadow" was "Garibaldi, . . . looming . . . as the hero of a lengthy narrative poem in the Spenserian metre."

For very practical reasons she regarded the completion of the book of verse, including "Garibaldi," as her most important job: " . . . my Yorkshire Maecenas, at that time a very rich man . . . paid me a much better price for my literary work than his townsman, the enterprising printer, and . . . had the first claim on my thought and time. With the

business-like punctuality of a salaried clerk, I went every morning to my
file of the *Times* and pored and puzzled over Neapolitan revolution and
Sicilian campaign." She had never been to Italy or studied Italian history; she hated Garibaldi, she hated Edmund Spenser as the inventor
of her stanza-form, and she fell back upon Byron's *Childe Harold* as her
model. Money, she wrote, was at the heart of the matter: "My Beverley Maecenas . . . looked upon the matter from a purely commercial
stand-point." He thought her poetry would pay, although she "honestly
strove to combat" his delusions before accepting his handsome offer.

The weekly numbers of *Three Times Dead* were "thrown off in brief
intervals of rest from my *magnum opus.*" It was "an infinite relief to turn
from Garibaldi and his brothers in arms to the angels and monsters which
my own brain had engendered, and which to me seemed more alive." And
so, she remembered, "In that peaceful summer I finished my first novel,
knocked Garibaldi on the head with a closing rhapsody, saw the York
spring and summer races in hopelessly wet weather, learnt to love the
Yorkshire people, and left Yorkshire almost broken-heartedly on a dull
gray October morning, to travel Londonwards through a landscape that
was mostly under water."

The "Beverley Maecenas," who had commissioned the book of poems,
who paid far better than the publisher of the first novel with its
"melodramatic poisoners and ubiquitous detectives,"[4] and who selected
Garibaldi's Sicilian campaign as the subject for MEB's Spenserian
stanzas, we can now recognize as Charles Reade's "simple noble-minded
Yorkshire squire, Gilby," MEB's "first patron." But Reade was wrong in
thinking that Gilby had sponsored the publication of her novel: it was
only her verse that he subsidized. And since Garibaldi's campaign took
place during 1860, and she left Beverley "in October," and her book—
Garibaldi and Other Poems—did indeed appear in February 1861, it is
clear that the "half-year" MEB spent in the Beverley farmhouse, simultaneously engaged in writing *Garibaldi* and *Three Times Dead,* was
the spring and summer of 1860.[5]

Exhibit D is an orange printed paper mailing-label, reading "J. Gilby
Esq. Beverley, Yorkshire." It is pasted on the back of the first leaf of the
holograph manuscript, folded for mailing, of MEB's unfinished and
unpublished story called "The Kingdom of Boredom." The postmark
reads only "Brighton, Sp. 14" without indication of a year, but 1859
would not be an unlikely guess.[6] She was sending Gilby work in
progress. And Exhibit E is a letter from Louise Swanborough, purchaser,

producer, and leading lady of MEB's comedietta, *The Loves of Arcadia*. Written from London on March 18, 1860, only six days after the piece's opening, it begins, "Dear Sir, I think we may congratulate ourselves upon the success accorded to the 'Loves of Arcadia' by the public" during Lent. After Easter the season would be still more favorable. Miss Swanborough proposed to buy for twenty pounds the right of acting the play in London for a period of three years, instead of abiding by an earlier agreement whereby she would pay a nightly fee for each performance. Because her health would not permit her to act more than four or five times a week, she thought the flat fee would be more profitable for MEB than the nightly fee. But she would keep to the first agreement if that should be preferred. She also gave the name and address of Sterling Coyne, Secretary of the Dramatic Authors' Society, so that Miss Braddon might apply for membership, and promised to support her application. If MEB did not join, Miss Swanborough pointed out, she would have "little chance of obtaining any remuneration for her pieces from *country* managers," who apparently felt free simply to pirate a play by a nonmember. Miss Swanborough completed her kindly and meticulous business letter by "Trusting that Miss Braddon will continue to prosper in her career."

Although the letter itself nowhere names the addressee, it is preserved in its original envelope which is addressed to J. Gilby, Esq., Beverley, Yorkshire.[7] So, less than a week after *The Loves of Arcadia* had opened and before MEB had settled down in Beverley to work simultaneously on *Garibaldi* and *Three Times Dead*, J. Gilby—whom Charles Reade called "her first patron" and whom she herself would call her "Beverley Maecenas"—was busying himself with the intimate financial and professional details of her career as a playwright. So much is established by the full text of the Reade notebook, the selective memories of Beverley that MEB put into her article, and the mailing-label and Swanborough letter both addressed to Gilby. But the drama of Reade's hastily recorded anecdote has not yet been recovered. Was Gilby the "simple, noble-minded" squire of "excessive delicacy" that Reade called him? The discovery of Exhibits F through V—seventeen original letters from Gilby himself to MEB, in which he speaks in his own voice—has made it possible to answer that question.

2. The Beverley Maecenas

"I have just been to church, and I hope I am not angry, but I wish I could show you how you often try to make me so," Gilby began abruptly. "Here are my 2 letters back by the dead letter office that (I thought) you said you had received—*Business habits these!*" So the first surviving letter—written from Beverley on March 11, 1860, the day before the first performance of *The Loves of Arcadia*, to MEB in London—opened with a scolding. He had addressed two letters to her as Miss Braddon, but they had been returned because she was still calling herself Miss Seyton. Gilby grumbled that "you utterly hate & detest yr own name, showing the profound love that you are not even conscious of from its profundity, for your old [name, i.e., "Seyton"]. . . . Ah! what is the use of writing."

He went on to reproach MEB for not having gone to Kew Gardens or the natural history exhibits at the South Kensington Museum: "What a task shall I have if I try to guide your studies. You know best whether you will be guided or not, but it is the only thing that gives me misgivings and pain. Will you please me by going to see these objects of history & creation many of which lead us to thoughts far transcending anything human?" And he added with underlinings, "*I don't want you* until you go to the gardens & to the Museum." Obviously, Gilby already considered himself MEB's tutor at least; their intimacy was far advanced.

He also considered himself in charge of her business affairs. "*You may see* Miss Swanborough," he told her, adding that a letter from Miss Swanborough setting forth her conditions for the staging of *The Loves of Arcadia* was written "in a most decisive and peremptory manner" and had frightened him. But he had accepted the terms at MEB's urging and now expected that she would receive between ten and twenty pounds, "I hope the latter." Miss Swanborough had "dwelt upon your being an unknown authoress," and Gilby thought her "slippery. I advise you not to go into any business dealing with her." But Gilby was writing the day before the comedietta opened and a week before he would receive the second letter from Miss Swanborough, already quoted, in which she expressed her pleasure with MEB's success. He and his solicitor had been carrying on the negotiations, and MEB had not even seen some of the letters exchanged, but he would show them to her when she came to Yorkshire. Gilby told her he would visit her as soon as possible after she arrived in Hull and asked "Is your Mamma coming to Hull or not?"

Although Gilby had been negotiating on MEB's behalf, he had yielded to her request and bargained no further with Miss Swanborough. He obviously had more than a paternal interest in MEB's financial success: "Don't be nervous," he cautioned her in giving her permission to see Miss Swanborough, "there is no reason whatever." He was expecting her imminent arrival in Yorkshire and indeed there were no more letters for a period of six months. That interval, between March and late September, 1860, MEB spent in Beverley, no doubt seeing Gilby frequently, busily writing *Garibaldi* and *Three Times Dead*.

"Perhaps the happiest half-year of my life," she long afterwards said of the interval in Beverley, despite the strain of her double task in writing. But about the town she had deep reservations, which appear in her novel *Dead Men's Shoes* (1875), written in a mood of disillusionment. Here Beverley is "Redcastle," a country town, "not . . . designed to be of . . . use to society. It exists for itself alone, and is exclusive to a fault. . . . Erase it from the map of England tomorrow, and nobody but its inhabitants would be the worse off. . . . It produces nothing but elderly people with limited incomes and scandal." Though not a bad place to rest in, it would be dreadful to live there, regulated by "its petty proprieties and narrow creed." Redcastle is clean: "A rainy day, which makes mud and slush in busier places, only washes down and renovates Redcastle." It boasts only "the one wide street, with its massive old brick houses, . . . the historic gateway, which divides the one street into two, Below Bar and Above Bar—and the fine old Coach and Horses Inn . . . all . . . the pink of cleanliness." The minster, "architecturally perfect," looks "as if it were kept under a glass shade." The marketplace is "spotless," the turnpike "one of the best in Yorkshire," the "Wesleyan Chapel, the Independent Chapel, and the masonic temple, the Athena Lodge," all of "whitest freestone with shining windows and . . . classic porticoes."

Although very few rich people live in Redcastle, there is "perhaps no town in England in which respect for wealth is more deeply implanted." The rich all live in red-brick Georgian houses just below Bar and in larger, more modern stone houses just above Bar. The biggest of all is owned by "Colonel Stormont . . . his wife and family . . . who . . . are at one in the opinion that Redcastle was called into being for [them]. . . . Their names are at the head of the croquet and archery club, which blackballs everyone . . . suspected of having once had a cousin connected with trade." They patronize the assize and masonic balls and "the more chaste and classic of the Redcastle concerts." Nearby, a rich Hull shipbuilder and his wife live in solitary splendor: " . . . their names grace the subscription list of no local charity. . . . and will be remembered when they are dead for the

many noble deeds they have not done." Below Bar are the successful professional men and "On the outskirts of the town . . . three or four
gentlemen who derive their income from houses or land, are more rustic
in their bearing and attire than the inhabitants of the citadel, and in a
general way give themselves airs, as affecting to belong to the county
families." And the county families themselves live "far off, in their
various fastnesses, isolated, inaccessible, unapproachable." A few of them
are on visiting terms with the richer townsfolk and the clergy,

> but they regard the town otherwise as a depot for groceries and
> draperies and a centre of Radicalism for the lower classes. Their
> big family landaus, with tall slab-sided horses and brass harness,
> pervade the street on fine afternoons; their sons trot briskly
> through the quiet town on hunting mornings in well-worn pink.
> They turn out occasionally for a concert, and take care to testify
> by loud talk and laughter among themselves, and a supercilious
> contemplation of the rest of the audience through eye-glasses, that
> they hold themselves as people apart.

In *Dead Men's Shoes,* MEB was paying off a few old scores. In
recollecting those anonymous gentlemen who pretended to be county
gentry, she was perhaps thinking fifteen years later of Gilby. She actually
wrote the drafts of the poems in the *Garibaldi* volume and of some of her
earliest stories in a green morocco ledger with the name of the Beverley
Archery Society stamped in gold on its cover and the former records of
the Society cut out. Perhaps she had been a member of the Society;
perhaps she was blackballed and acquired the volume in some other way.
Surely this exchange in *Dead Men's Shoes* between a girl of a county
family and a "Redcastle" girl came from recollection and not from
imagination:

> "You have a croquet club or something of that sort in Redcastle.
> . . . I rather think my sister and I are honorary members, but
> we've never been."
> "Yes, there is a club for croquet and archery. They meet in Sir
> John Boldero's park."
> "Very nice for you I dare say," remarks Miss Cardonnell, as
> much as to say, "People of your class must be provided with
> amusements of some kind."[8]

When the six months in Beverley were over, MEB had completed both *Garibaldi* and *Three Times Dead*. She left Beverley for London, and Gilby's letters resumed on September 29, 1860, coming at brief intervals until the correspondence reached a resounding end on February 20, 1861. Occasionally he went to London and saw MEB there. He wrote her about his visits to race meetings and about his betting gains and losses, but concentrated chiefly upon the details of publishing *Garibaldi*. One publisher, Moxon, had said that his firm had already declined a poem on Garibaldi by a Frenchman (September 28 and 29, 1860). Gilby asked that MEB revise and send to him in Beverley any manuscript not yet ready for the printer, and that she and her Mamma correct the proofs, which were being printed by a London printer named Strangeways: "I wish you would make one or two 'melodies' from Isaiah or elsewhere," he added, "but they must be *tip-top* or I shall make *spills* of [i.e., light the fire with] them [October 7, 1860]." Expecting to see her in about a fortnight, he would "have something to talk over about yr writing & other matters, if you do not give me *generalizations* instead of answers as you sometimes do. I have never asked your opinion of things in general yet [October 11, 1860]."

Fussily and fretfully, Gilby interspersed his instructions with demands that MEB write more poems and not be idle: "I have forwarded to the printers the copy they sent me with both your own and my corrections—you had missed some important ones. These bad grammars will be your plague when you have your own MS. to correct. You must try and do better for yourself. It strikes me you must be pretty idle now having no peice [*sic*] of work cut out, & London to amuse you. . . . When will you write a Shakespearian play? [October 13, 1860]"; and again, "I wish you would write one or two more powerful poems of about 50 to 100 lines on anything that will go down, Italy for instance [October 18, 1860]." Soon he was deeply irritated because the printing of the long poem about Garibaldi had been held up for a week to allow MEB time to supply footnotes: "It will really be hardly of any use to publish at all, in the present way of going on. I am so much annoyed that I can hardly write with much patience." MEB had a sore foot and could not go out, but Gilby urged her to take a cab to the printers and get them started again, "a most important thing so far as any chance for profit is concerned from Garibaldi. Of course it has deranged my whole plans. . . . P.S. It is not very flattering to me that you agreed to the notes &c. *at Mr. M's suggestion* [italics mine] without writing to me by first post? [October 21, 1860]."

Why was Gilby, rich as he was, apparently so eager for profit on *Garibaldi*? ("I have but faint hope," he wrote a week later, "of the book coming out in time to pay me much [October 28, 1860].") If we recall Reade's notebook entry to the effect that Gilby was anxious to see MEB financially successful before proposing to her and if we imagine him as very much in love and trying not to show it, we can understand his angry and sometimes almost frenzied reproaches. A week's delay to allow for the compilation of some footnotes, hitherto unplanned, would not otherwise have been so hard to bear. Moreover, the appearance in Gilby's postscript of "Mr. M.," the man who has suggested the notes, suggests that Gilby was already worrying about John Maxwell as a rival.

Once again, the preservation of a key document among MEB's own papers provides confirmation for this supposition. On March 26, 1860, Andrew Halliday, well-known journalist, author, member of the Savage Club of authors and artists, and editor of its papers, wrote to Louise Swanborough, "I have much pleasure in forwarding a letter of introduction for Miss Braddon to the proprietor of the 'Welcome Guest.' She had better call some morning about 11 at the address and take any M.S.S. she may have with her." The proprietor of *The Welcome Guest* was John Maxwell. Miss Swanborough now wrote MEB, "Dear Madam, Until this moment I have been unable through press of business to forward the enclosed to you."[9] The "enclosed" was clearly Halliday's actual letter of introduction for MEB to John Maxwell—a fateful document which has disappeared: no doubt she presented it when she called at the office of *The Welcome Guest*. But Halliday's note to Miss Swanborough and Miss Swanborough's note to MEB tell us how MEB first met Maxwell, and through whom she met him, and even *when* she met him: late March 1860. Even before returning to Beverley, then, to undertake the pleasurable task of writing *Three Times Dead* for Empson and the *corvée* of writing *Garibaldi* for Gilby, she had already had at least one interview with the man who was to be the great love of her life.

By September, 1860—five months after MEB had met Maxwell—she had had a short story accepted and printed in his *Welcome Guest*: "Captain Thomas," told in the first person by a young man in love. He grows deeply jealous of his young woman's warm public expressions of affection for a certain Captain Thomas, whose whiskers she praises, whose absence she mourns, and whom—she is heard to say—she has warmly kissed on his return. Captain Thomas proves to be no rival, but the young lady's cat. Next, *The Welcome Guest* of September 29, 1860, carried her grim little short story called "The Cold Embrace," in which a German student who had been faithless to his betrothed while traveling abroad returns to find that she has committed suicide and is then haunted to his death by her spirit. On October 20 appeared her essay, "My Daughters," a pleasantly cheerful series of reflections on the agony for a parent of watching his daughters respond to the impact of *Adam Bede*, the *Idylls of the King*, *A Tale of Two Cities*, and *John Halifax, Gentleman*, the most popular recent fiction and poetry, together with the works of Carlyle and Froude.[10] A few days later, on October 29, 1860, William Sawyer sent MEB a poem of his own for *The Welcome Guest*, asking if there would be a Christmas number to which he might send a "long Christmas carol" in verse. "I suppose," he added, "there is no chance of the enclosed going to the Temple Bar M? Of course I should *prefaire* that." *Temple Bar*, a monthly—the newest and most lavish of the Maxwell periodicals—paid better and attracted more attention than the more modest twopenny weekiy *Welcome Guest*.

So the Mr. M. who in October 1860 had been advising MEB about footnotes to *Garibaldi*, and whom Gilby had already begun to resent, was John Maxwell. As October and November passed, Gilby grew more and more impatient: "If you are the *least* nearer getting some more proof ready, send me some by return. But my feelings are now in the state represented by the name a friend of mine has given his horse, 'Smallhopes' [from Newmarket, October 8, 1860]." Once he praised MEB's corrections, but added that he did not want her to delay the printers by correcting "Olivia," a second long poem written for the *Garibaldi* volume: "I revised her most thoroughly, and fancy there is very little to complain of. I made very few alterations. . . . I do not think Olivia requires any notes at all. . . . I have the other poems revised and about ready for the printers [October 30, 1860]." Gilby was scrutinizing all details as if he had written the poems himself: "I write . . . to ask if the word guerill*os* in Garibaldi is right, or should it be guerill*as*? I do not know anything of Italian [!]." There was an American Indian maiden in MEB's short poem, "Under the Sycamores," and Gilby asked, "Have you any objection to Menamen*ie* being spelt Menamen*ee*? The latter is more Indian."

Soon Gilby was instructing MEB "to make no engagement for *time* with the Guest people. If your poetry were to pay, a few lines of it would be worth all they wd give you in a year." The "Guest people," which is to say Maxwell, had apparently been dangling before MEB the prospect of some regular employment. Gilby was manifestly worried—and with reason—about the dangers to MEB that might arise from such an association, but couched his warning in purely financial terms. He begged her now to call on Miss Swanborough, whom he had a few months earlier so disliked, and on his own friend and adviser, Oakey (November 5, 1860).

Maxwell in fact seems to have promised MEB that she would be the editor of *The Welcome Guest* and then reneged. William Sawyer's sister in Brighton wrote her on the same day, "Naturally we feel disappointed at the result of your labour, when to us it appeared to promise success. . . . I . . . only hope you wriggle something out of the Wraxwell—surely perseverance like yours shall somewhere gain its true right."[11] "Wriggle something out of the Wraxwell" needs explanation: the editor of *The Welcome Guest* from January 1860 to March 1861 was Captain Frederic Charles Lascelles Wraxall (1828–1865), one of Maxwell's stable of impecunious novelists and hack-writers, who would succeed his uncle as third baronet in 1863.[12] So "Wraxwell" is a portmanteau-word: Wraxall + Maxwell = Wraxwell. Sawyer's sister was obviously consoling MEB for a severe disappointment: the loss of the editorship itself, as a letter to MEB from Sawyer demonstrates:

What you tell me of the W[elcome] G[uest] is news indeed, only Maxwell is a humbug of the first water—quite a solid gem of "purest ray serene" in the humbug line and therefore all his vows are to be taken *cum grano salis*—rather say a good large lump—a handful at least.

" 'Tis better to have nurtured in your breast
A vision of the ever *Welcome Guest*
Bearing your name and under your control [italics mine]
Than to have sunk in bitterness of soul
To the conclusion that your revolutions
Of pen and brain are doomed (a good rhyme's Proosians)
Always to be rejected contributions [December 3, 1860]."[13]

So Maxwell had held out to MEB the hope that she would be sole editor ("Bearing your name and under your control") of the magazine when Wraxall left (as he would do in another three months). Maxwell had not only withdrawn his offer, but had rejected some of MEB's writing. Yet, said Sawyer reassuringly, the very fact that she had been thought of as editor meant that her future contributions would probably be accepted. Sawyer was consoling her, but, like Gilby, was also warning her against Maxwell.

Disappointed by the "Guest people," MEB had asked Gilby for further financial support and found him acquiescent: "I was much pleased with your letter received today. I shall be *very happy to re-engage you* [italics mine] on as good terms as yr writing warrants, if yr book is well received." Still worried about the printing, and still without a publisher, Gilby now pressed MEB "to earn a more lasting claim on the public by taking up some subject of history, some sustained matter of interest not soon exhausted. . . . There might be some tale running through it to give interest to light readers &c. It should be what you can write on at length without lack of matter, and in short give you material for writing a poem that may rank with others of standard merit"—fumbling, maundering suggestions that illustrate how rudimentary were his notions of literature. "Have you given up the idea of a Shakespearian play?" he asked (November 10, 1860).

So Gilby had not merely undertaken to have *Garibaldi and Other Poems* printed and published at his own expense—with the profits to be his. He had also been paying MEB a retaining fee while the book was being written: the words, "I shall be very happy to re-engage you," can hardly bear any other interpretation. He still wanted her to feel no indebtedness to him beyond the merely business obligation ("on as good terms as your writing warrants"), but to consider that she was earning her own way.

Coming thick and fast during November 1860, the letters only heighten one's impression of Gilby. He found the printed advance sheets "*very pale* in the ink. . . . I think it ought to be a better black. I think you have been careless with the type. How could you put insouciant*e* in the feminine & there were clerical errors too—& as for stops you have a pepper box full to make me sneeze over." He was full of ideas for MEB's improvement: "You must learn Astronomy if you are to be any good. I'll take you to a lecture if you like. Read the article in Vol. 29 of the Quarterly Review & you will glean some crumbs of information to strew over your *green* damask ideas." And he was anxious to fill her time, no doubt to keep her away from Maxwell: "I fear you are a little idle now, are you not? Ask Mr. O[akey] about the various publishers. Can you not write to Miss Swanborough & see her when she is better. Is there a bus? [November 15, 1860]" Whose book was it? one asks, as two days later Gilby demanded to select the smaller poems—"the fugitives," he called them—for the volume: "I have other views than yours. I want to catch one or two classes of tastes that we have not catered for yet," while reiterating his advice about astronomy. "I have bought you a nice easy

Astronomical book, & you *must get it up.* You want this most, as you are always bringing the stars in, sometimes as if they were so many farthing candles [November 20, 1860]."

Sometimes he grew shrill and querulous ("I am *very anxious* to get the whole into the printer's hands. It scarcely seems kind of you to have sent the peice [*sic*] on Isaiah to them without showing it to me. Consider how you increase my letters & trouble. Now I have to send for it from them & return it. 2 more letters!"), while remaining didactic and possessive ("In poetry, however paradoxical it may seem, words of inferior power sometimes come home to us the best. I do wish you would read Greek & Latin & you would see this. . . . I am arranging all your remaining poems."). MEB had obviously resisted his pressure to call on Miss Swanborough and Mr. Oakey, and now Gilby said: "Do as you like. . . . This, and many other requests I have made only from a desire *for yr own good.* But whether it is your nature or your mamma's wish, I don't know—but anything out of the immediate line of writing poetry you seem to do unwillingly." Literary talent alone was not enough. MEB needed

the power to turn everything *to use* and advantage and never lose a chance that Providence throws in our way. You know the proverb about a certain place that is paved with good *intentions.* Now I consider that in wishing you to see those sort of people, I am urging the most disinterested and desirable request that I can make. This sort of pushing yourself forward (next to the elements of various scientific and literary information) is the most necessary and indispensable for you. Mr. O[akey] has in his time known *all* the London publishers & both from good feeling and interest (& gratitude to me) he would give you advice & instruction at any time.

Blaming Mrs. Braddon as well as MEB herself for her obvious unwillingness to consult and see Oakey, who may possibly have served as a kind of spy upon her other associations, Gilby preached like an anxious authoritarian father. He went on to tell MEB about a Miss Blythe, also a young writer, perhaps from Beverley, who had pushed ahead in the way he would have liked MEB to push. His words reveal his fantasies:

Mr. Brereton has just been in, & has been describing to me how Miss Blythe got introduced to Mr. Macmillan's family [the publisher, no doubt], then asked to his house, then got him to sell her works among his friends, & so on, till she told him her fairy tales & got a permanent engagement! But then she had such a good dear father! he used to have a cane for her *special* use in his study (besides those for his school) and when she didn't please him, of course he applied it effectively.

How *I* should like to cane *you*, my dear, Gilby was saying, in his frustration.

Yet he protested that he was not at all irritated and was simply trying to convince her how much she needed "a better knowledge of what every one is supposed to know" and how she ought "to get introductions to & to make acquaintance with every one who will be of use to you [November 20, 1860]." Before coming to London to see MEB, Gilby made one more effort on the very next day to round up all the poems she had written, as within a week the printer needed much more copy. "You must not talk of time" he wrote, "or you'll put me in a rage, but sit up all night till they are done. I think Lord B[yron] is your idol. If you don't send me 500 lines of fair copy in a day or two, I must put some of your 'prose' in. Three times dead? [her novel]. [November 21, 1860]"[14]

Nagging, hectoring, demanding instant responses and poems written and revised to order—and that grammatically; enjoining upon MEB the immediate acquisition of astronomy, Latin, and Greek; worrying lest she be idle; asking for a Shakespearian play and in the next breath for a "poem of sustained historical interest"; raging at slight grammatical slips as if they were fundamental to the literary quality of the verse itself; rebuking every carelessness or fancied oversight; attempting to dictate to MEB who her associates should be; taking every advantage of the hold that his financial aid had given him over her; giving her the crassest sort of go-getter advice; and openly expressing his wish to give her a paternal caning—Gilby painted a vivid portrait of himself in these surviving letters. Yet one wonders whether he may have been a man with more bark than bite. What his relationship with MEB may have been when they were in each other's company one can only surmise; but behind all the gruffness and bossiness one can perhaps at times detect a hint of humor, a hint of jolliness, a suggestion that she will know he does not really mean half of what he says. From these letters alone, however, we could not recognize Gilby as Charles Reade's "simple noble-minded Yorkshire squire," while from Reade's notebook entry alone we could never have imagined the captious, domineering, insistent bully who emerges from the letters. Yet they do confirm Charles Reade's story: Gilby loved MEB and wanted to put her on her feet financially before he began—on even terms—what, we can now safely conclude from the letters, would have been a hopeless courtship.

Not much more can be learned about Gilby. His first name was John. He was probably the son of the Reverend William Robinson Gilby (1784–1848)—Fellow of Trinity College, Cambridge, in 1811 and Vicar between 1823 and 1833 of the beautiful church of St. Mary's in Beverley—by his wife Harriet, whose maiden name was also Gilby and whose family lived in Clifton, a suburb of Bristol. They were married in 1820; so John Gilby must have been under forty when he fell in love with MEB. He had a brother named William, who was baptized in 1824 and took his B.A. at St. John's College, Cambridge, in 1842. In 1857, John Gilby lived in Newbegin (sometimes spelled "Newbiggin"), a street in Beverley long the preserve of the leading inhabitants, where his house was listed as one of the twenty-two "principal residences" of the town. He supported the Beverley races, and had wins there and in the East Riding handicap in 1859 with his horse, Flash in the Pan, a three-year-old.

The most startling bit of information is that both Gilby's legs were paralyzed. He used a specially constructed saddle with grips in front, which enabled him to ride to hounds, and to retain his seat while jumping. But he did not ride his own race horses. If he was paralyzed from birth or boyhood, this probably accounts for the fact that he did not, like his father and brother, attend Shrewsbury School or Cambridge. Moreover, Charles Reade's words describing Gilby after he had learned from Greenwood of MEB's involvement with Maxwell—he "presently came limping back"—should perhaps be interpreted literally. In any case, had his paralysis been his only handicap as a suitor, it would not have kept MEB from loving him: indeed, it might have aroused her affection for him instead. But there seems to have been no real question of that.[15]

By December 15, 1860, after a hiatus of almost two months marked by editorial rejection and professional disappointment, contributions by MEB began again to appear in *The Welcome Guest*. In an essay called "London on Four Feet" she contrasted the sad lot of the omnibus horse and other horses in London with the splendid treatment horses received from their worshipers in Yorkshire. The special Christmas number for 1860, twice as large as the usual twenty-page issue, carried her short story, "My First Happy Christmas," about a group of lonely schoolboys invited for Christmas dinner by a retired naval officer.[16] This story Edmund Yates long afterward remembered as his own discovery. He had been editing contributions for the Christmas number, and when John Maxwell asked him whether he had discovered anything especially prom- ising he selected MEB's offering, submitted anonymously, "clearly told" and "full of new and genuine fun." Yates preened himself on having had "sufficient editorial sagacity to detect latent genius in the first production of Miss Braddon's ever submitted to my notice."[17]

Early in the new year 1861, MEB's contributions became ever more regular. So whatever misunderstanding may have arisen between her and Maxwell had been cleared up. Now Gilby made his anxious inquiries about John Maxwell. Charles Reade noted that Gilby learned the bad news by consulting "F. G." An "F. G." obviously in a position to give Gilby information about Maxwell was Frederick Greenwood, who, with his brother James, had in 1859 published anonymously in *The Welcome Guest* a novel, *Under a Cloud*, and alone and under his own name a se- cond, *Looking Back*.[18] He continued to write occasionally for the *Guest* in 1860 and 1861. His later bitter public hostility to Maxwell and MEB makes still more plausible the suggestion that he was Gilby's "F. G."

On February 20, 1861, Gilby wrote from Beverley his last letter to MEB. It must be read in full:

For several reasons, Miss Braddon, I have not replied to your last letter sooner. You have so often acknowledged your deficiency in punctuation that I attach not much importance to your opinion of my corrections. The criticisms on your work [*Garibaldi* was by now published] have been on the whole, very much what, you will remember, I had anticipated. My enquiries respecting Mr. Maxwell were conducted in a strictly business manner, and so given to you—and it was natural for me to infer, from your having so frequently consulted me on your literary affairs, that you would thank me for making them—I need therefore scarcely notice the sneering language in which you tell me that my information is "vague and undefined, not to say absurd." A contrast no doubt it is to the hundred fulsome and varied expressions of gratitude in the letters which I have in my desk from you (continued as long as you imagined I could be of any service to you) and to your "promise on your honour" to consult me in seeking literary employment, and to take none without my permission!

But my mistake in taking you from your legitimate profession may afford me a not unprofitable lesson—gratitude! why you hard- ly know the meaning of the word. Honour! Your code of Honour?

You have become such an actress that you cannot speak without acting—I have worked as hard and done as much for you as it was possible for a gentleman to do for a woman in your position. But you never can forgive anyone to whom you are under obligations. And I think I shall be the last person that you will forgive! The only return (title-page of your novel) that I ever asked of you, if return it could be called, has not been granted. It matters not now—I can only feel a pity for you not unmingled with contempt, and wonder if you have one redeeming trait in your character. You will probably not object to return (marked as mine) to Mr. D. F. Oakey, 2 Bridge Street, Westminster, S. W., such books of my own property as are still in your possession—Byron, Admiral Rous, and (if any) others—I am etc., J. Gilby.[19]

With this bombshell of a letter, Gilby vanished from MEB's life. His words confirm beyond question that he had "taken" MEB from her "legitimate profession." It was Gilby's money that had enabled her to leave the stage and embark upon a literary career. No doubt he had seen her act in Hull or in Beverley itself and had made her acquaintance. Nothing in his letters suggests that there could ever have been a liaison between them. Moreover, MEB's mother accompanied her everywhere during her years on the stage. But by early 1860, when that third Brighton season was over, Gilby and MEB had reached their arrangement: he supported her at least in part, and in exchange for his money he had—and there is no reason to doubt him—a "hundred fulsome expressions of gratitude" from her in his desk. He thought he also had the right to treat her book of verse virtually as his own. It is clear that in the end she had rebelled, told him how little she thought of his niggling corrections, and perhaps insisted on writing as she chose. Gilby had also asked for some favor or other with regard to the title page of *Three Times Dead*—the only novel she had published by February 20, 1861—perhaps having his name mentioned as her benefactor—but this she had refused or at least had not granted: his name did not appear on the title page.

But surely the nub of his letter and the cause of the final quarrel was the question of Mr. Maxwell. "In a strictly business manner," Gilby had made inquiries about Maxwell, just as Reade recorded in his notebook, and the distressing information he had discovered, he had imparted to MEB, thinking—so he pretended—that she would be grateful to him. But instead she said that what he had told her about Maxwell was "vague and undefined, not to say absurd." Perhaps Gilby had learned only that Maxwell had a doubtful reputation; but it is far more likely that "F. G.," his informant, had told him—as Charles Reade recorded—that Maxwell was married and living apart from his wife. Whether Gilby had then passed this fact on to MEB is not clear; but had he done so, it might have been difficult to avoid an insulting suggestion that she was somehow already involved with Maxwell. Moreover, had he done so, MEB could hardly have dismissed the charges against Maxwell as she did. There was nothing "vague" or "undefined" or "absurd" about receiving attentions from a married man with children. On balance, then, it seems probable that Gilby only warned MEB in a general way against Maxwell, and elicited a scornful ("sneering") reply from her, which in turn convinced him that the game was up; his own chance to win her was destroyed. Perhaps Gilby thought—with "F. G."—that Maxwell had already seduced her. Perhaps they were right. In anger and despair—both are visible in his final letter—Gilby broke off their relationship violently.

It seems extraordinary that MEB—who at least twice in the diaries of her later years referred to burning letters and papers—should have retained these letters from Gilby. It is hardly possible that she never knew that Gilby was in his own way in love with her and had hoped to marry her, hardly possible that she thought of him only as the "learned and rich Yorkshire Maecenas." Perhaps she kept the letters as her own mother had kept the letters that revealed Henry Braddon's adultery, those *"pièces de conviction"* which, MEB declared in *Before the Knowledge of Evil*, no woman throws away. In any case, Gilby played a major part in her life. His money—and the stifled but genuine love that accompanied it—had made it possible for her to leave the stage, perhaps to sell and see produced her comedietta, and certainly to write both the book of verses about which he had become so heated and the first in the long series of novels that would make her reputation and her fortune.

3. "A Big Burly Florid-faced Loud-spoken Irishman"

As for John Maxwell, only three letters from him to MEB have survived from the entire thirty-four years of their close association. On December 25, 1895, the first Christmas after his death in March, she wrote in her diary, "Burning M[ax]'s letters afternoon." But the three that she kept were written within forty-eight hours of Gilby's scornful farewell. MEB had gone off to Brighton for a brief visit, and Maxwell wrote her on three successive days, each time on the letter-paper of the Editor's Office, *The Welcome Guest*, 122 Fleet Street. "My dear Polly," he began, on February 20, 1861,

> Lonely, sad, and very full of thought, I obey your wish that I should write to you this evening. But, oh! how I feel the want of words to express the weariness of soul that arises when, after an arduous day's work—one of unceasing toil—the heart wakes up to find itself *All Alone! All Alone!!* No kind voice to utter the sweet sounds of sympathy or a soft glance that talks of feelings the lips could only fail in attempting to voice. Well, I am alone! Alone in every sense tonight. And yet no one ever desired loneliness less than I do! but so it is; and to the ordinance of fate I bow with all the resignation I can muster. Most fearfully egotistic and selfish all this sounds. What else could you expect? Asking me to write fresh on the loss of your society, how else can I do but declare the void your absence causes? Of course you will be ready with a toss of the head, curl of the lip, and gentle nervous twitch in an organ that has a natural inclination to turn upwards (horrid impertinence) and with all those graceful accomplishments you will say "It's all very fair Mr. M. but Brighton air is to be preferred to the fetid heated atmosphere of a Turkish bathroom. Moreover, Sir, green-room associations [many of her former fellow-members of the Royal Theatre Company would have been in Brighton in February] and gossip are somewhat livelier than your dull-pated conversation." Even this can't be helped. Go forth, then, and may every step you take be one of pleasure, every word you hear one of joy, and every acquaintance you meet a friend who can appreciate without loving you, yet love you without offending Ever faithfully yours, John Maxwell.

Very Victorian, very Irish, very banal, this is unmistakably a love letter from a man already certain of his conquest.

The next day he was more concerned with business. He had heard from MEB, which gave him a "bright spark of true pleasure." He told her that, as proprietor of the *St. James's Magazine*, he had just concluded a formal agreement with his new editor, Anna Maria Hall, a well-known novelist, and her husband, the journalist and spiritualist Samuel Carter Hall, thought to have been the original of Dickens' Pecksniff. Mrs. Hall, Maxwell reported proudly, "spoke in the kindliest manner of your gentleness and most unpresuming demeanour. She is well inclined to act matronly towards you and I have encouraged the idea that you are most anxious to profit by her experience and counsel." MEB was expected to work for the magazine one day a week under Mrs. Hall's supervision. And Maxwell had been "most of all gratified by the candid admission that dear Polly is brimful of unconscious and almost wholly undeveloped power! Think of that coming from such folk."

John Maxwell had got hold of a very good thing indeed and he was fully aware of it. He had just taken MEB's first novel, *Three Times Dead*, so obscurely published at Beverley, and reissued it under its new title, *The Trail of the Serpent*. Now, he wrote triumphantly in his third letter: "One thousand copies of 'The Trail of the Serpent' sold in *seven days*. Pleasant news! I have just sent it out for review."[20] After a week in its new incarnation, it was already a bestseller.

So the only remaining letters from Maxwell to MEB close on the note of business that was always his major interest. Despite his clumsiness at writing love letters, it is clear that he loved this vivacious, talented, and charming young woman, and there can be no particular mystery why. But it is harder to understand why she should have fallen in love with him. Maxwell was handsome and likeable, but people often found him overbearing and difficult to deal with.

Robert Buchanan (1841–1901), for example, novelist, dramatist, and poet, later recalled that in the early sixties he had been contributing to *Temple Bar* and the *St. James's Magazine*, both of which belonged to Maxwell, "a big, burly, florid-faced loud-spoken Irishman." Maxwell was "far from unkindly by disposition" and believed in Buchanan when few other people did. But he "had the knack" of making Buchanan feel like the pauper he was. Proud and sensitive, Buchanan resented the way in which Maxwell weighed in his hand the bundles of manuscript he brought him and estimated their value without ever reading them. Sometimes he kept Buchanan waiting, sometimes he refused to buy the manuscript. One morning Buchanan announced to his fellow-lodger and "companion in wretchedness," Charles Gibbon—who later also became a successful novelist—that he had bought a thick cudgel and intended to beat Maxwell's brains out if he were "as offensive as usual." As it happened, all went well, and Maxwell never knew how narrowly he had missed being assaulted. Buchanan wryly reflected that by failing to murder a publisher he had forfeited the "worship" of future generations of impecunious authors.[21]

W. B. Maxwell in 1937 remembered his father as "a big strong creature, deep-chested, broad-shouldered, and possessed of very great vitality." Strikingly handsome in his youth, he coarsened and grew heavier with age, but always had presence. By temperament he was "courageous, sanguine, open-hearted, and exuberantly good-humoured. He sometimes made so much noise in joyous welcome of a friend that at a very little distance it sounded as if he was violently quarreling. But he scarcely ever quarreled." When he did, his son thought it was "because he felt that he had been wilfully injured and then he was quite unappeasable." Perhaps W. B. Maxwell underestimated his father's bellicosity. Isabella Mayo, novelist and journalist, reported that a lady she knew had actually seen Maxwell and J. Hain Friswell, journalist and essayist, come to blows in Maxwell's office.

John Maxwell had characteristically Irish "queer ups and downs of mood. Breaking off an enthusiastically hopeful narration of some new project, he would suddenly fall into darkest pessimism, giving as he sank a forlorn gesture that expressed his almost complete despair. Then as suddenly, after a few minutes, he would rise from the black depths and again be all hope, energy, and good humour." He seemed to have the gift of second sight, sensing in advance misfortunes that would happen even to total strangers. Everywhere he slept, he insisted that his bed have its head pointed north, and to the chagrin of his children would refuse hotel accommodations if the beds could not be "properly polarised." Generous, he would always give his children money from his pocket when they needed it; but he would also always offer them his purse, which never had anything in it but a few coppers and a key or two, and invariably make the same joke, " 'There. See! Who steals my purse steals trash,' " with an uproarious laugh.

W. B. Maxwell felt that he and his brothers and sisters had ill repaid their father's kindness:

> We took all that he had to give and gave scarcely anything in return. When he wanted our company we often withheld it. When we saw him coming towards us we often avoided meeting him. Growing older we made a mock of sayings that were characteristic because of a portentous weightiness with which he delivered them. They were usually very sensible, although we chose to consider them ridiculous.

And in the Maxwell family, there still survives a tradition that none of

MEB's five children by John Maxwell ever liked their father.[22] So Robert Buchanan and W. B. Maxwell amplify, but do not much modify, the view of John Maxwell's personality that his three love letters to MEB suggest. And yet, however limited his attractions, she remained devoted to him until his death in 1895. She always called him "Max."

In his last years, he was often ill for long periods, and MEB's diaries record the hours she spent every day reading aloud to him and her pleasure when he particularly enjoyed the book she had chosen. Her heavy schedule of writing and editing, her innumerable family and household duties, took second place, although she managed never to neglect them. About three weeks after John Maxwell died, she wrote to Mrs. Cordy Jeaffreson:

> To me he was the best and most unselfish of husbands—and never shirked a domestic duty, however difficult and painful. I feel his loss keenly, for though he had long been dependent on the help of others, and his life had been sadly narrowed, he was very happy, & I was happy with him—and ventured to hope that this quiet life—sheltered and secluded—might go on yet for some placid uneventful years. A three days illness, influenza, ended that hope [March 30, 1895].

"Never shirked a domestic duty": in that apparently conventional Victorian laudatory phrase may lie an important key to a union otherwise hard to understand. Over MEB's childhood there had lowered the shadow of her father, a man who had shirked every domestic duty. Henry Braddon had been unscrupulous about money, unreliable in his profession, and unfaithful to his wife. He had made MEB's beloved mother miserable by his irresponsibility, not even telling his own clerks that he could not pay them their wages, but leaving that delicate task to Mrs. Braddon. For the girl who had wanted to love her father but instead was forced to hate him, the quality of devotion to domestic duty may well have ranked very high among those to be sought, whether consciously or unconsciously, in a husband. Perhaps Maxwell, more than forty years old, gave MEB at twenty-five a sense that he would always be dependable.

Nor was she disappointed. About 1912, for example, she wrote to her friend Lady Monckton the details of a tragi-comic household difference of opinion with her daughter-in-law, Mrs. W. B. Maxwell: a cook whom MEB liked was discharged because the younger Mrs. Maxwell was dissatisfied with her, and MEB, now an old woman, wrote an angry letter, headed "Private and Confidential," saying "One thing I cannot do, and that is to go on with the daily grind of ordering meals to please everybody. The only bad blood between my poor Max and me was warmed to fever heat over the dinner-table."[23] Even fifteen years and more after her husband's death, and in a moment of temporary ill temper, MEB remembered that they had quarreled only when he did not like his dinner.

Calling her "My dear Polly" and writing her love letters in February 1861, Maxwell was obviously a serious suitor. Did he tell her that he was already married? Since Gilby learned of the marriage from his conversations with "F. G.," the fact must have been generally known. Moreover, Maxwell had five children, and even if he had wanted to, he could hardly have hoped to conceal from MEB the fact that his wife was still alive. Perhaps still less could he have deceived Mrs. Braddon, who accompanied MEB everywhere, from whom she had no secrets, and who was quick to suspect people's motives.

In 1956, the daughter of a former servant who had been kitchenmaid, cook, and housekeeper for the Maxwells between 1866 and 1889 remembered that her mother had told her that Miss Braddon in her youth had gone to Brighton to recuperate from an illness:

> She was sitting on the front one day when a tall, fine-looking young man—John Maxwell—got into conversation with her. She told him she was having difficulty in getting her books published, and eventually he fell in love with her and told her he would help her to have her novels published if she would marry him. She agreed, only to discover that he was already married with several children and a wife in a mental home in Dublin, from whom he was separated. This must have been about 1860, and it seems that some form of marriage was gone through.

This anecdote, recorded almost a century after the events, reflects belowstairs gossip inflated over the years into a kind of legend. It was just the sort of story a Victorian kitchenmaid would have invented to explain the equivocal nature of her mistress's relationship with her master. After three years on the stage, MEB knew the world too well to let herself be duped into going through an illegal "form of marriage." Nor, if by any chance she had done so, would she have continued to live in harmony with her seducer afterwards. Mrs. Braddon was even less likely to have been deceived or to have joined the deceiver's household and lived contentedly as a member of it. Before MEB began her affair with Maxwell, then, she almost surely knew that he was not free to marry her and decided to live with him anyhow.

John Maxwell needed MEB as a stepmother for his five children, whose own incapacitated mother could not look after them. Since his wife was in Dublin, he may somehow have persuaded himself that scandal could be avoided. No doubt he recognized MEB's talent, but in 1861 he could hardly have foreseen the extent of her success. Despite the servant's anecdote, MEB hardly needed Maxwell as a publisher; there would have been others—and she must already have known it from the success of her comedietta—who would have been glad to buy or market her fiction. Had she wanted only security, she could have married Gilby. Perhaps some younger and more obviously romantic suitor had left her disappointed with passion and eager for stability. Perhaps she felt affection but not youth's first love for Maxwell. Or perhaps Maxwell *did* actually sweep her off her feet, a "plump, fair-haired, unassuming" girl, as Robert Buchanan noted, but a very clever one, full of wit and energy, and delighted to have found a lover—so delighted that she was ready to link her future with his, despite his inability to marry her and the social ordeals she would need to face. About the state of her feelings we cannot be certain. But about her enormous courage there can be no doubt.

Her first child, Gerald, was born on March 19, 1862; so the liaison cannot have begun later than June 1861. By then, if not sooner, MEB would have had to face spiteful, wounding gossip—all too true—and social ostracism. For some time she and Maxwell tried to conceal their true relationship. Mrs. Hall, editor of Maxwell's *St. James's Magazine*, told her friend, Isabella Fyvie Mayo, that one day she asked after the health of Maxwell's Irish wife, whom she had known: "Maxwell coolly replied 'She is defunct.' Mrs. Hall could not believe her ears and repeated the question, only to receive again the reply: 'She is defunct.' 'Mr. Maxwell,' she cried, 'surely you do not mean to say that your wife is dead?' 'Madam,' he returned, with a sardonic smile, 'She is de—funct.' The poor lady, broken in mind and body, was alive for years afterwards."[24]

Apparently Mrs. Mayo did not stop to wonder whether the initial question might not have been malicious, and its triple repetition triply malicious. Since Mrs. Hall was receiving MEB's help one day a week in the offices of the *St. James's Magazine*, she had no doubt observed something going on between her young assistant and her publisher, and would have been entirely capable of trying to bring Maxwell back to the path of duty by a pointed question about his wife: indeed Mrs. Hall, true wife of the original of Dickens' Pecksniff, would have considered herself derelict in her duty had she not done so. Maxwell brazened out her impertinent question; but no wonder his smile was sardonic.

Had there been no children, perhaps Maxwell and MEB might have concealed their liaison. But Gerald's birth was followed by that of Fanny in 1863 and—in 1864 or 1865—by that of a son, whose death in the summer of 1866 almost broke his mother's heart.[25] Still there could be no legal marriage, and people in the know, like Mrs. Hall, must have gossiped furiously. Presumably in an effort to undo the damage, Maxwell early in 1864 did allow word to get into the newspapers that he and MEB had been married. On January 16 the *Court Journal*, on January 18 the *Sun*, the next day the *Morning Advertiser*, and on January 23 *Public Opinion* told their readers that "Miss Braddon, the novelist, was recently married to Mr. Maxwell, the publisher."

But the trial balloon thus unobtrusively launched was quickly shot down. Maxwell's first wife, née Mary Anne Crowley, had a sister, Eliza Mary, married since 1845 to a journalist named Richard Brinsley Knowles (1820–1882) and living in London. Knowles now took it upon himself to deny the report of John Maxwell's new marriage in every paper that printed it. He had first seen the news, he wrote, in the *Morning Advertiser,* and "knowing that Mr. Maxwell was already married, I looked anxiously to see him or Miss Braddon contradict a report which was not and could not be true." But neither of them had done so; so Knowles himself, "as Mrs. Maxwell's brother-in-law," wrote in to declare the report of MEB's marriage "utterly without foundation." He pointed out that Mary Anne Crowley Maxwell—sister of the late N. J. Crowley, a well-known painter—had "borne her husband a large family" and was herself still living.

Charles Reade recorded this episode in his notebook immediately after he had described Gilby's discomfiture at the discovery that MEB "had become the wife of a man who had got a wife and children." Maxwell, Reade said, in the paragraph we omitted above, "was so unwise as to advertise in some way Miss Braddon as Mrs. Maxwell. Then a brother of the real Mrs. Maxwell advertised in a newspaper saying that Miss Braddon could not be married to Mr. Maxwell the publisher, as Mrs. Maxwell his sister was still alive." Reade's only mistake was in thinking that the man who exposed John Maxwell's bluff was Mary Anne Crowley Maxwell's brother instead of her brother-in-law.

Son of the popular playwright, James Sheridan Knowles (1784–1862) —a first cousin once removed of the great Richard Brinsley Sheridan—

Richard Brinsley Knowles had reacted against the strong anti-Catholic views of his father and had been converted to Catholicism. His chief occupation was the editing of historical manuscripts belonging to noble Catholic families. No doubt his religion, his sense of family pride, and pressure from his wife combined to inspire him to do justice to his unfortunate sister-in-law, Mary Anne Crowley Maxwell. Married to John Maxwell in a Catholic ceremony in 1848, she had had seven children by him, of whom five had survived. She went mad sometime after the birth of the seventh, and entered an asylum near Dublin at a date which cannot have been very long before 1860, when Maxwell and MEB first met. Knowles contradicted the story of MEB's marriage not only in print, but wherever he "heard it repeated in private conversation."[26] The impact on MEB, in the London social and literary world of 1864, must have been agonizing.

MEB and John Maxwell could not answer Knowles by publicly reaffirming that they were married. This could have led only to even more unhappy publicity. So the ambiguity and the social strain persisted. Even close friends did not appreciate the situation. Sometimes Maxwell would set one of them right by implying or asserting that MEB was his wife. In March 1865, for example, Charles Mathews, the celebrated actor, and his second wife, the American actress, Lucy Davenport, invited both Maxwell and MEB to a party but sent them separate invitations. Maxwell protested, dating his protest from 26 Mecklenburgh Square, Soho, where MEB and her mother had been living since 1862. Mathews replied that Maxwell's letter, "though most kindly and courteously worded, seems to administer a reproof. Being dated from '26 Mecklenburgh Square' and speaking of 'your wife' it of course conveys a hint that in addressing her separately as 'Miss Braddon' I had committed an error which had to be corrected, and I stand corrected accordingly." But, said Mathews,

> we had not the slightest idea when thus dividing our invitation that we were separating man and wife. The Fates forbid! Pray pardon a poor devil who is shut up in a theatre morning noon and night and who really knows nothing of what is going on out of it, but who on bended knee craves your joint forgiveness for his error, and who, with kindest wishes from *husband* to *husband* and *wife* to *wife*, subscribes himself Faithfully yours.

Few friends would have been so graciously tolerant as the Mathews. And the fact that Maxwell had "rebuked" them for a slight they did not intend testifies to the tension within his own household.

So reluctant were Maxwell and MEB to advertise themselves as married that even MEB's own sister, Maggie Cartighoni, did not hear the news in Naples until the spring of 1866, when a man named Piccirillo brought her some presents from her mother in England. But he did not know who MEB's "husband" was. "Piccirillo says Mary is married," wrote Maggie to Mrs. Braddon on April 3, "Fancy your never telling me! I had long guessed it, but as you did not mention the subject I never said anything about it. But now as the public knows, you don't mind my knowing it also. I suppose Mr. Maxwell is the gentleman. He is an extremely nice good-hearted man and I am sure Mary must be very happy in having him for her husband. I liked him so much in England. [This is all that is known of a visit to England by Maggie.] I am quite glad to think he is my brother-in-law." She added that she would send MEB a wedding present when she could afford one.[27] Maggie obviously relished the situation she had discovered: Mary, the younger sister; Mary, always their mother's favorite and now very successful, who always sent presents—money and, most recently, a watch—to young Nicolino Cartighoni; Mary had come a cropper. She was "married," and to that nice Mr. Maxwell, as Maggie had long guessed; but Maggie had not mentioned the subject, and Maggie was not told until after the "public" already knew. MEB knew, and Mrs. Braddon knew, and Maggie knew, and we know that the "marriage" between her sister and John Maxwell was irregular indeed.

On June 4, 1866, MEB's fourth child, William Babington (W. B.) Maxwell was born. And that September, for the first time in their correspondence she hinted broadly to Bulwer that she was married: "If you should happen to speak to C[harles] R[eade] of so small a personage as *me*," she wrote, "he may tell you something which may surprise you. I have never presumed to bore you about my affairs—or any change in my life—I plague you enough with my doubts and difficulties about literary matters—and I have kept my domestic personality in the background." Charles Reade, who was himself living in an irregular ménage with the former actress, Laura Seymour, and whom MEB and Maxwell saw a good deal socially, obviously knew of their "marriage." Despite his regular exchange of letters with MEB, Bulwer had not seen her since 1854. Even now, MEB gave Bulwer only a hint. It was more than a year (October 10, 1867) before she mentioned it to him again, still indirectly but far more precisely, saying "I think I told you that great changes had taken place in my domestic position. I am now the head of a grown-up family—who I think love me almost as well as if I were indeed their mother."

Of the "grown-up family," Maxwell's five surviving children by his first wife, the eldest, Nicholas, was perhaps in his late teens in 1867. John and Robert were at a boys' school near Totteridge, and Elizabeth (Bessie) and Mary (Polly) at a convent school. Beginning in the winter of 1866–1867, they returned for their holidays to Lichfield House, the early Georgian mansion that John Maxwell and MEB had just bought and occupied in Richmond, Surrey, a beautiful Thames-side London suburb. Maxwell's children did indeed love MEB, and she loved them. They had been brought up as Catholics, and although MEB herself was a member of the Church of England, she was deeply tolerant of "the older faith" and its observances. Her third child having died during the summer of 1866, she now had three living children of her own, and was in 1867 responsible for eight in all.

She closed the letter in which she first mentioned her new "grown-up family": "I will sign myself by a name which I have for some time borne, but which for very powerful commercial reasons I have refrained from assuming in any public manner," and, for only the second time in the twenty-nine letters so far written to Bulwer, she signed herself "Mary Maxwell."[28] No doubt she had had "commercial" reasons for not calling herself Maxwell's wife publicly: as we shall see, his creditors had at least once tried to collect his debts to them by attaching some of her earnings. But surely there was also a legal reason for not doing so: simply, that she was not Maxwell's wife in the eyes of the law. And there were also "very powerful" social reasons: Richard Brinsley Knowles was always ready to contradict any published reference to MEB as Maxwell's wife and thereby proclaim aloud the illegitimacy of her children. A few years later Knowles would strike at her again. She had to live in fear of his obvious determination to persecute her.

Reconstructed, the story of MEB's youth proves as melodramatic as any novel she ever wrote. When Mrs. Braddon's money ran low in 1857, MEB went on the stage to keep them from poverty. After three years, a rich and high-minded but pompous and bossy Yorkshireman, who recognized her literary talent and had fallen in love with her, took her off the stage, and gave her money enough to enable her to write uninterruptedly for about six months. He was determined not to propose to her until she became financially independent. But before she could enjoy the success for which he had been hoping, she had fallen in love with a married man, living apart from an insane wife and with five children. Soon she was living with him, writing busily to earn money for their household and acting as loving mother to his children and to theirs.

The eldest of her own five children was born while she was still writing *Lady Audley's Secret* and *Aurora Floyd*, "my pair of bigamy novels" as she once called them in a letter to Bulwer.[29] A specialist in literary bigamy, she was herself involved in a liaison with a married man. This is the reason why in later years she was unwilling to discuss the details of her early life with John Maxwell.[30] The indiscreet attempt in 1864 to publicize their "marriage" led to Knowles's damaging denials. The truth became widely known, and MEB now encountered the sneering disapproval and cruel snubs of the self-righteous Victorian social world. Her sufferings permanently affected her attitudes toward society and would be manifest in her writing for the remainder of her days.

CHAPTER IV

"The Amount of Crime, Treachery, Murder, Slow Poisoning, and General Infamy Is Something Terrible" (1861–1868)

In the interlude between MEB's quitting the stage in March 1860 and the appearance of *Lady Audley's Secret* in October 1862, everything she wrote—whether verse or prose, published or unpublished—bore the marks of the apprentice hand. Rapidly she abandoned her false starts, developed her skills, tested her market, and ingratiated herself with editors. Poetry she soon abandoned. But even in the fiction she never finished, she left some important clues to her later interests. In her second published novel, *The Lady Lisle*, she rose at times above hackwork. And beginning in mid-1861, Maxwell's new *Halfpenny Journal* gave her for four years a natural outlet for all the hackwork she could produce, enabling her to devote her abundant remaining energies to more serious fiction, still in these years almost wholly "sensational."

She herself keenly felt the difference between her halfpenny fiction and her other work, despite two ill-starred efforts—in 1867 and 1868—to pass off the inferior as the superior article. Into *The Doctor's Wife* (1864) she introduced a character named Sigismund Smith, a writer exactly like herself, whose hilarious comments on the fiction-writing trade reflected her own views on what she was doing. Like Sigismund, MEB wrote prodigiously, spurred by her need for money: at first to support her mother and herself, then to render them financially secure, and then for the ever-growing Maxwell family. During the years 1862–1866 she published nine three-volume novels: in 1862, *Lady Audley's Secret*; in 1863, *Aurora Floyd*, *Eleanor's Victory*, and *John Marchmont's Legacy*; in 1864, *Henry Dunbar* and *The Doctor's Wife*; in 1865, *Only a Clod* and *Sir Jasper's Tenant*; and in 1866, *The Lady's Mile*.[1] While revealing in some detail how much she earned and for which novels, her correspondence also discloses her business worries. It sheds much new light not only on the relationships between novelists and publishers but between novelists and the pirates who stole their plots and made plays of them, a particularly annoying practice against which MEB's publishers won a historic, if incomplete, legal victory. The record of her experience introduces us to the innermost workings of the Victorian bestseller industry.

1. The 'Prentice Hand

Despite Gilby's worries, *Garibaldi and Other Poems* appeared in February 1861, neatly published in a little volume made to look antique by the odd choice of a font with elongated eighteenth-century s's. The long title poem ended on a high nationalist note, calling for the reuniting of all Italian territory: "While Austria holds a rood, a stain/Sullies the lustre of th' Italian shield./Emanuel, thine the glory to regain./The sceptre an Augustus sighed to wield." MEB sent a copy to Garibaldi himself, but he never acknowledged it; apparently it never reached him.[2] Though the verses were sometimes well made, the poem reflected MEB's own frustrations in writing it. It had never been more than an unwelcome assignment.

William Sawyer, himself a poet, thought "Garibaldi" powerful but boring and regretted that MEB had not published it by itself "while the Garibaldi fire rages." Had she done so, he argued, public attention could have been focused on "Olivia," the second poem in the volume, MEB's "chef d'oeuvre and no mistake," as good a poem as any that had appeared in recent years. If "Olivia" had been published accompanied by minor poems only, MEB "would, like Byron (no not in quite such a hurry perhaps) awake to find herself famous." In his Dickensian vein, Sawyer added that everybody in Brighton was "overwhelmed with the power and passion of the whole book, and wonder how they can permit you to walk about in the inflammatory state of mind which it denotes, which they wouldn't do but only they know no better at present."[3]

Byronism indeed saturated "Olivia," in which a disillusioned English nobleman hands over his wicked Neapolitan wife to the Duke she has ensnared: "Take her! worst hatred scarce could wish you worse:/In having her your Grace has every curse!"[4] By the standards of the early sixties, the shorter poems—the "fugitives"—were workmanlike and respectable, perhaps better. The review that Robert Buchanan published in the *Athenaeum* at Maxwell's prompting called "Garibaldi" a "rhythmical paraphrase" of the London *Times* correspondent's account of the campaign. In "Olivia" he found "passages of great beauty." MEB, said Buchanan, had only to "prune her fancy and cultivate her judgment" to become a poet of character, passion, and originality.[5]

After *Garibaldi*, MEB occasionally published a single poem, for example, she mourned the death of the Prince Consort in verse[6]—but she never again produced another volume of poetry. In her notebooks, however, with the drafts of her published poems,[7] there survive portions of two long poems that remained incomplete and unpublished. One of these told of the love affair between an opera-singer named De Grammont Grayham and a beautiful young marchioness. Tone, theme, verse were all Byronic. Probably dashed off in 1860, it serves to show MEB, with something of Isabel Sleaford still about her, imitating the master and occasionally achieving a genuine echo. Two specimen stanzas may suffice:

> De Grammont sang in English or Italian
> Or French or German, if it was required.
> He was a reckless, clever wild rapscallion
> And learning came to him, tho' scarce desired.
> Not one the classics he to set a value on
> But sometimes with a sudden freak inspired
> He Ovidisms would in Latin speak
> Or mildly curse a bit in Attic Greek.

> All life was changed, one long wild unrest
> Her nights were madness and all her days were fever.
> A demon made its home within her breast,
> Miscalled a god, and would not, would not leave her.
> Like true love-bird that broods upon the nest,
> So she upon his image. Oh, retrieve her,
> Spare her, Oh God, the stormy sighs and tears,
> Days that are centuries, moments that are years.[8]

And in two stanzas from the second long poem, MEB portrayed her heroine, Madeline, as exemplifying her own lifelong hatred for the charity of the smug and pious evangelical, and her admiration for true Christian generosity to the poor:

With liberal hand from liberal store she gives,
And never dreams that she can give enough.
There is no creature, suffering, that lives,
However loathsome, vulgar-mannered, rough
That cannot move her. Argumentative
Philanthropy and other showy stuff
She does not shine in; in her wealth, she knows
A better panacea for their woes.

She does not think that tracts keep out the cold
Nor offer good advice instead of food.
She does not think the sick, infirm, and old
Ere they be succoured must be *first* made good:
That is, made to the pattern they are told
Is the one pattern. If the peasant's mood
Rebelling fierce, makes him forget his station,
And shoot the game, she thinks of his starvation.[9]

MEB's own verdict that she seldom rose above "Poet's Corner" verse was surely closer to the mark than Sawyer's enthusiasm. Even in the earliest days of her career, she preferred the "angels and monsters" that her fiction-writing brain engendered.

Her incomplete and unpublished story, "The Kingdom of Boredom," foreshadows some of her later characteristics as a novelist. At first, it seems to be an allegory:

The land of Boredom! It was a kingdom of which Ennui was the King and Indifference the Queen; in which fashions were the prime ministers that came and went . . . in which the highest of high treasons was to think or to feel or to act; and the worst of traitors were men of genius, agitators, philanthropists, and poets, who were generally cast forth for their disloyalty. It was a bore to be born, and a worse bore to have to die; but the worst bore of all was to live . . . the life of Boredom . . . which had neither action, nor aim, nor end, nor hope. It was champaigne [sic] with the effervescence gone down . . . the morning after a carouse, a race course after the races . . . a fire with the gas burned out . . . London in September. . . . The women never loved; the men never hated . . . there was no jealousy . . . no despair . . . no hate, no crime.

But the Kingdom of Boredom, it soon appears, is in England. The London Coach runs, and the continent of Europe lies across the Channel, where it belongs. The Kingdom of Boredom is the social region inhabited by the nobility and gentry.

Sir Douglas Astrandell, rich and noble, and so a "senior wrangler in that great science of the land of Boredom," is the elder of twins. The younger twin, Philip—not so elegant but more intelligent—had missed the succession by two hours and was born blind besides. The twins' fashionable mother dislikes him. At Douglas' twenty-first birthday fête she arranges for him a suitable marriage with a Duke's daughter, while the guests and tenantry are "happy and drunk and disorderly . . . in their own good old English way." The party over, Philip Astrandell announces his departure: he too is now twenty-one, though nobody has noticed it, and will now use his small income for high purposes. The family doctor promises to send him money whenever he may need it. Twenty-five years later, Sir Douglas is a widower, "a cynical hypochondriac passing his life at a German Spa." His heir is an even more accomplished scientist of boredom than his father. Philip has died, leaving a son and daughter, who as the fragment ends are invited to visit the ancestral house.

It is a safe guess that the blind twin Philip was actually the elder and therefore the lawful heir, and that his mother had conspired with the doctor to substitute the healthy but younger twin. Presumably Philip's son is returning to wreak his overdue vengeance upon his uncle and cousin. It was sensible of MEB never to finish "The Kingdom of Boredom." Yet even in this crude early effort, as so often in MEB's later fiction, the mainspring was provided by a crime committed long before the story had begun. The harsh and repetitious attack upon the rich and noble prefigured the more gentle and far more devastating satire that MEB, when fully the professional master of her art, would skillfully direct—often unobserved—at the mores and the self-satisfaction of the Victorian upper classes. In time she would learn to show her characters behaving like subjects of the Kingdom of Boredom without blatantly insisting that they were so. But her belief in that Kingdom and her scorn for it would remain constant.[10]

Of her first published novel, *Three Times Dead*, virtually stillborn at Beverley in 1860, and cut by about ten thousand words but otherwise very little changed in its London revival in 1861 as *The Trail of the Serpent*, MEB herself indulgently wrote thirty-two years later that she had let herself go: "Death stalked in ghastliest form across my pages; and villainy reigned triumphant till the Nemesis of the last chapter. I wrote with all the freedom of one who feared not the face of a critic." Indeed, because of its obscure appearance and "its re-issue as the ordinary two-shilling railway novel," it "has almost entirely escaped the critical lash, and has pursued its way as a chartered libertine. People buy it, and read it, and its faults and follies are forgiven."

When the original publisher, Empson of Beverley, objected to Ward, Lock, and Tyler's republication of the novel, John Maxwell declared himself "wholly taken by surprise" and assured Empson that he had bought the copyright from MEB herself. He apparently silenced Empson's protest by inviting him to "forward to a friend of your own in London any documents sustaining your position." And when Empson went bankrupt a few years later, the judge in the bankruptcy court remarked that "as Miss Braddon was now making a good deal of money" she ought to "come to the relief of her first publisher." Since Empson had never even paid her the second fifty shillings he owed her, MEB felt that this was "rather hard lines."[11]

For the Dickensian element in this "compound of Dickens and G. W. M. Reynolds" that Empson had originally ordered, one need only turn to the opening paragraph of *Three Times Dead*:

I don't suppose it rained harder in the good town of Muddleton-on-the-Sloshy than it rained anywhere else. But it did rain. There was scarcely an umbrella in Muddleton that could hold its own against the rain that came pouring down that November afternoon. . . . Every gutter in High Street, Muddleton; every gutter in Broad Street (which was of course the narrowest street) ; in New Street (which by the same rule was the oldest street) ; in East Street, West Street, Blue Dragon Street, and Windmill Street; every gutter . . . was a little Niagara, with a maelstrom at the corner, down which such small craft as bits of orange peel, old boots and shoes, scraps of paper, and fragments of rag were absorbed. . . . That rather dingy stream, the Sloshy, was swollen into a kind of dirty Mississippi, and the graceful coal barges which adorned its bosom were stripped of the clotheslines and fluttering linen which were usually to be seen on their decks. A bad, determined, black-minded November day. A day on which the fog shaped itself into a demon, and lurked behind men's shoulders, whispering into their ears, "Cut your throat! You know you've got a razor, and can't shave with it, because you've been drinking and your hand shakes; one little gash under the left ear and the business is done. It's the best thing you can do. It is, really." A day on which the

rain ... says "Don't you think you could go melancholy mad? ..."
Then again the wind. What does the wind say, ... ? Why it
whistles in your ear a reminder of the little bottle of laudanum
you've got upstairs, which you had for your toothache last week,
and never used. A foggy wet windy November day. A bad day—a
dangerous day. Keep us from bad thoughts today, and keep us out
of the Police Reports next week.

The master himself would have been delighted with this.

As for G. W. M. Reynolds, the villainies of *Three Times Dead* were
villainous indeed. Ephraim East (for some reason he became Jabez North
in the revision), at the age of nineteen an usher in a school, murders one
of his young charges before the third chapter is over, and continues in the
fourth by cutting the throat of an elderly gentleman. From then on, he
never looks back. In the preface, MEB solemnly said that Ephraim was
"one of those characters of which unfortunately there are too many in
the present state of society." She had shown him "in his true colours,"
stripped off "the mask of assumed piety behind which he had so long
sheltered," and exposed "his vices in all their hideous deformity to the ex-
ecrations of the well-thinking members of the community." His fate
should "serve as a warning to the vicious."[12] But obviously she believed
none of this. *Three Times Dead* bears little discernible relationship to
MEB's later serious novels, but it was the immediate forerunner of the
blood-and-thunder contributions that she would soon begin to write each
week for Maxwell's new *Halfpenny Journal*.

Just as *Garibaldi* was appearing, the great George Augustus
Sala—journalist, novelist, Bohemian, man-about-town, recently appointed
editor of Maxwell's ambitious new monthly, *Temple Bar*—could be heard
inquiring who the devil Mary Braddon was.[13] No doubt, Maxwell ini-
tially recommended her to Sala, and by early spring, 1861, she was
demonstrating how little she had needed Gilby's advice about pushing
herself forward. She closed her first letter requesting an appointment
with Sala by saying conventionally that she "had the honour to be his
obedient servant"; and when he fixed a date for their meeting he asked
her not to be so formal. To this MEB responded archly, with jocular and
admiring references to Sala's many writings and to his new country
house. How could she be anything "but obedient" to so busy a man, who
had nonetheless allowed her to "chivy" him with "stupid letters, vilely
written, ... in the midst of your Temple Bar editorship, your Seven Sons
of Mammon, your nine leaders, all that immense and varied labour?" But

she was now awaiting the day "upon which I am to be so happy (see how neatly I avoid having the honour) as to see you."[14]

What would MEB write for *Temple Bar*? Together, she and Sala explored two possibilities: either a tale to be set in "the dark ages before George the Fourth," or one to be based on Balzac's *La Peau de chagrin*, which MEB preferred. But first, she had to fulfill two existing obligations: her "St. James's business"—*Ralph the Bailiff*, a novelette in which a weak-spirited Lincolnshire farmer who has murdered his elder brother is black-mailed by his ubiquitous servant[15]—and "a story for the Guest," a longer novel called *The Lady Lisle*. In mid-June she sent Sala two sample chapters of a historical romance, "Tommy and Harry: the History of a Bad and a Good Boy." In this she planned to give a reverse twist to the old "spelling-book" story by punishing her good boy and rewarding her bad boy. She made him a Jacobite agent and intended him to win the girl and the fortune in the end.[16]

Apparently Sala kept "Tommy and Harry" for fifteen months, only in October 1862 writing to John Maxwell, "Tommy and Harry with Miss Aurora No. It is the same confounded old pigtail and squared toe business . . . in which all one's reading and research go for nothing, and for which the public do not care one damn." But if MEB had ever been disappointed by the delay, she would long since have got over it, since as early as November 1861 she had been admitted to the sacred pages of *Temple Bar*. Already billing her as the "Author of [the still uncompleted] *Lady Audley's Secret*," Sala had published her two-part "Mystery at Fernwood," in which a homicidal lunatic, unwittingly freed, murders his twin brother. And by January 1862, *Aurora Floyd* itself—to which she owed the long lasting nickname "Miss Aurora" that Sala gave her—had begun its triumphal run in his magazine.

Although Sala rejected the idea of "Tommy and Harry," he had a grandiose plan for collaborating with MEB. If John Maxwell wanted "to resuscitate *Temple Bar* and make a tremendous hit, let Miss Aurora buckle to, and do with *me* my long contemplated and gigantic *duel* [*sic*] romance of *Dr. Forster*." This, said Sala, would be "the legend of Faust and Mephistopheles adapted to modern life, but with a concurrent legendary setting in Germany." He declared that "the *Misérables* would be the model and Goethe's *Faust* the plot," and predicted that "Aurora would be tremendous at dialogue and love-making, and the painting and decorations would belong to me. Done together in Fleet Street, the copy would never be late. . . . Will you talk to Miss Floyd about Forster and let me know?" The scheme never came off, but many years later MEB and

Sala each wrote a novel based upon the Faust legend. When Sala promised John Maxwell that copy for the projected *Dr. Forster* would "never be late," he was suffering from a bad conscience: he was behindhand with the story he was writing for *Temple Bar, The Adventures of Captain Dangerous,* of which he said he was "heartily sick." If Maxwell would only employ J. Hain Friswell to finish the remaining instalments, Sala promised that he would "wind Captain Dangerous up like a clockwork mouse."[17]

While corresponding with Sala in 1861 and waiting for *Temple Bar* to open its pages to her, MEB had remained largely bound to the demands of *The Welcome Guest,* which published her short story, "Samuel Low-good's Revenge"—about a forged check and the blunting effect of time upon the wish for vengeance—and her first serial story, "The Lawyer's Secret," in which a young woman is left a large inheritance by her uncle on condition that she marry within a year the young man her uncle has adopted. She and her lawyer are in love, but he advises her to take her uncle's money and the husband he has nominated. In fact, the lawyer has embezzled his client's fortune, but her new husband hushes up the matter, to his own cost.[18] The essential element of this plot—a testator who binds his legatee to a marriage dictated in the will—MEB would use again many years later in *The Cloven Foot* (1879).

The *Guest* also ran MEB's second full-length novel, *The Lady Lisle,* in which a smiling handsome officer of the East India Company's Service successfully plots to kidnap the rightful heir to a baronetcy and substitute an impostor. The false heir is the vicious son of a former gamekeeper, a murderer with a grudge against society. The relatives of a gypsy girl, whom the fraudulent baronet has seduced and killed, eventually kill him; while his father, the gamekeeper, bilked of his money, kills the master-plotter. The rightful heir returns in the end to his title and estates.

Somber and sharp throughout, *The Lady Lisle* produces no satisfaction at the triumph of virtue. The true baronet is an unattractive weakling; his mother a woman of little character, easily swayed. Major Varney, the villain—with blond hair, whiskers, and mustachios, and with gold chains strung across his yellow waistcoat—flashes through the pages with a smooth glittering radiance, a forerunner of Long John Silver. Gilbert Arnold, the revolutionary-minded gamekeeper, is an unmitigated scoundrel, yet MEB apparently sympathized with him as the victim of society. For the first time she was trying to portray genuine character, although within the framework of a conventional thriller.

And, for the first time, she displayed both fluency and wit. Sir Rupert's mother as a girl is only "a pretty, pink and white, blue-eyed, flaxen-haired waxen image." Yet "people who didn't care an atom for her were dying to marry her. She became as fashionable . . . as a man who had written a novel about the working classes, or been tried for murder." Gilbert Arnold, the hardened murderer, likes to read tracts, "because they generally go pretty hard against the rich, the handsome, the prosperous, the powerful, and the happy, whom he hated with a . . . fury that almost touched upon . . . madness." On first acquaintance, Varney recognizes Arnold as a man who " 'has done bad things in his youth, and . . . hates himself so much that he hates everybody else for not being like himself. A dangerous, treacherous, thieving, sneaking, cold-blooded coward, I'll be sworn; and yet . . . I like to look at him.' " And Varney himself, late in the novel, describes his own temperament: " 'I defy anybody to say that they have ever seen me in a passion . . . I am not a good man, but I am a good-tempered man. This gives me some influence over the rest of the world. A good-tempered man is always mistaken for a good man.' "19 These are genuine Braddonisms, appearing at a time when MEB was still uncertain of her gifts, or, indeed, of her goals as a writer.

2. Sows' Ears and Silk Purses: Halfpenny Fiction, 1861–1868

Despite the quality of *The Lady Lisle*, *The Welcome Guest* was "moribund," as its editor Robert Buchanan later noted. Its last issue, of August 14, 1861, bore the announcement that the staff was being transferred to a new weekly magazine—*Robin Goodfellow*—under the editorship of Charles Mackay, a prominent journalist, occasional novelist, author of *The Delusions of Crowds*, whose illegitimate daughter born in 1864 would become the famous sentimental novelist, Marie Corelli. *Robin Goodfellow* had already begun publication on July 6, 1861, with the first instalment of *Lady Audley's Secret* and it lasted, as we know, only thirteen weeks. It was designed to continue the more genteel fiction of *The Welcome Guest*.

But, the last issue of the *Guest* declared, "The tradesman's wife, the hard-working girl, and the shopboy want a stronger class of fiction for their halfpenny than we have ever cared to give them at twopence."20 To meet this demand, Maxwell launched on July 1, 1861, another new weekly, *The Halfpenny Journal*. MEB did most of the work, and in *The Halfpenny Journal* it was subliterary hackwork. In the four years between July 1861 and June 1865, she contributed anonymously seven novels and perhaps an eighth to *The Halfpenny Journal*. She surely wrote *The Black Band; or, The Mysteries of Midnight*, whose first eleven instalments were published under the pseudonym of "Lady Caroline Lascelles." Without explanation the twelfth instalment dropped the pen name, but its use would eventually cause trouble. MEB's *The Octoroon; or, The Lily of Louisiana* was based without acknowledgment on Dion Boucicault's successful play. *White Phantom* was hers, as was *The Factory Girl; or, All Is Not Gold That Glitters. A Romance of Real Life*, advertised as "founded on actualities," an obvious effort to bring in the halfpennies of the factory girls who were imagined to make up a large portion of the *Journal's* public. *Oscar Bertrand; or, The Idiot of the Mountain* was a sequel to *The Black Band*. "The Idiot of the Mountain" was the title of the first portion of the story, while the second was called "The Coil of the Snake." "Most attractive window-boards, posters, and handbills," said the *Journal*, were available to advertise *Oscar Bertrand*.

When *Oscar Bertrand* came to an end on June 13, 1864, there was, for the first time since the *Journal's* foundation, a hiatus of six weeks without any contribution by MEB. And when her "new" work began on August 1, it was a mere re-issue of her first novel, triumphantly reprinted now for the second time, under a combination of its former titles, as *Three Times Dead; or, The Trail of the Serpent*, "by one of the most eminent writers of the Age." In later years MEB conveniently forgot this extraordinary incarnation of her "chartered libertine." Her last *Halfpenny Journal* contribution was *The Banker's Secret*. Possibly she also wrote an anonymously published novel of Restoration England, called *Woman's Revenge; or, The Captain of the Guard*.[21] MEB's *Halfpenny Journal* novels achieved immediate book publication in pirated, crudely printed paperback form in America.

But in 1877, when she was at the height of her successful career, the London firm of George Vickers reissued *The Black Band*,[22] cleverly quoting on the title page from a recent speech of Disraeli, then Prime Minister: "There are the Secret Societies, an element which we must take into account, and which at the last moment may baffle all our arrangements; Societies, which have regular agents everywhere, which countenance assassination, and which, if necessary, could produce a massacre." From Dumas' *Mémoires d'un Médecin* (1846–1848), in which Cagliostro presides over the revolutionaries in their secret mountain headquarters, down to any one of John Buchan's thrillers, in which Sandy Arbuthnot and his friends frustrate a sinister plot to subvert world order, the novel about mysterious societies has flourished. Like many such novels, MEB's *Black Band* was blood-curdling claptrap.

At a masked ball at the Drury Lane Theatre, Lord Lionel Montfort—younger brother of Angus, Marquis of Willoughby—asks Lady Edith Vandeleur—daughter of the Earl of Hocton—

> in suppressed but impassioned accents, "Once more, and for the last time, do you love me?"
>
> "Once more, and for the last time, yes," she answered with a scornful laugh.
>
> "And yet you refuse to marry me," . . . The lady lifted her haughty white eyelids, and raising her flashing eyes to his face, said defiantly—
>
> "Lionel Montfort, I refuse to marry you because you are a ruined man; because you are fettered with debts you cannot pay; because you are hourly in danger of disgrace and of a prison; because you are, in short, a penniless younger son, with no chance of ever becoming anything better, unless. . . ."

Lionel's brother should die. Edith will not marry Lionel until he is rich. Behind a pillar, listening to this conversation, stands Colonel Oscar Bertrand—thought to be of the Austrian army—laughing "softly to himself": he had suborned Lady Edith's maid and learned of her plans for the evening; and so he has come, with a strip of black crepe around his left wrist fastened with a slipknot. He takes advantage of Montfort's despair and, by promising him wealth and Lady Edith within a year, recruits him at once into the Order of the Black Band.

Mortal man has never known "who and what" Colonel Bertrand is:

> Mention my name in London, Paris, Vienna, Rome, St. Petersburg, Constantinople, and they will tell you of my reckless expenditure, my horses, my carriages, my inexhaustible wealth, my fabulous generosity. . . . I am the center of a system so vast in its operations that it extends to the greater part of civilized Europe. I am the captain of a company so large that there are men in it upon whose faces I have never looked, and never expect to

look. It is a company, which, though continually at war with society, can yet . . . afford to defy society year after year.

Initiation into the masked band of brethren follows promptly, and
Montfort becomes its "blind and pitiless instrument." The crepe noose
around his wrist represents the Order's defiance of the hangman and is
the weapon they use to execute their enemies.

How Lionel and Colonel Bertrand lure Lionel's elder brother, the Marquis of Willoughby, flushed with wine, into a gambling hell, where
Colonel Bertrand so cheats him at *écarté* that a duel naturally follows, and
the Colonel kills the Marquis, so that Lionel succeeds to the title; how
Edith Vandeleur, unaware as yet of Lionel's succession, is persuaded to
marry in haste and secretly the good-hearted Manchester millionaire to
whom she has become engaged, but who is anxious—and with
cause—about her loyalty to him; how Lionel curses her when he finds out
(". . . may your soul be racked with the agonies that now consume
mine—may your days be wretched and your nights restless—may remorse
haunt you as a hideous phantom . . . —and may every coin of the filthy
gold . . . become a separate . . . torment to you!") ; how Colonel Bertrand
persuades Edith to poison her husband and provides her with "twenty
drops of that mysterious essence of which only the science of the east
holds the fatal secret," enclosed in a "tiny phial of emerald crystal and
filigree gold"; how Lionel—wishing to be saved from the society—begs his
new love, the generous-hearted Spanish première ballerina, Lolota
Vizzini, to "fly with him," but is thwarted by Colonel Bertrand's claims;
how Edith's attempt to poison her husband is foiled when he sees her in a
mirror as she pours the drops into his wine; and how he repudiates her
and has her father lock her up for life as a madwoman in a Scotch castle
"far from all human habitation": all these things the reader of *The Black
Band* might learn, while absorbing several equally gripping subplots, and
all before the story was one-quarter finished. Readers of the *Halfpenny
Journal* got their money's worth.

The Black Band must serve us here as an example of MEB's penny-
dreadfuls. A reader of her other fiction will ask himself whether the same
woman could have written these diffuse, pedestrian, primitive efforts to
entertain the nearly illiterate. Or, if she was responsible for them, did she
not perhaps dictate them, or entrust large portions of the work to what
Charles Reade called "understrappers"? The answer, however, must be

"probably not," since there still survives a single leaf of the original manuscript of *Oscar Bertrand* in MEB's own hand.[23] It is likely that she scribbled these potboilers herself. Had she written nothing but these, she would have little claim on our attention. Had she never written them, she would have been far less of a drudge, and could have devoted more time to her serious writing.

The last of her *Halfpenny Journal* novels, *The Banker's Secret*, was not allowed to die a decent death in the pages of that paper. In 1867, two years after it had completed its serial run there, MEB published it as a three-volume novel under the title *Rupert Godwin*. A prefatory note declared that from "a cheap Weekly Journal . . . the tale was translated into . . . French . . . and ran . . . in the *Journal pour Tous*. It was there discovered by an American, who retranslated the matter back into English, and . . . obtained an outlet . . . in the columns of the *New-York* [*sic*] *Sunday Mercury*." So the author, who had had no reward from these ("and other [unspecified] versions") had "revised the original," and now defensively offered the result as "a Tale of Incident written to amuse the short intervals of leisure which the readers of popular periodicals can snatch from their daily avocations, and also as a work that has not been published in England except in . . . crude and fragmentary shape."[24]

Crude the *Halfpenny Journal* version of *Rupert Godwin* surely had been, but the suggestion that MEB had done substantial revising was hardly warranted: the heroine is still the victim of the villainous banker who murders her father, obtains control of her property, forces her to go on the stage, and has her kidnapped for the delectation of a stupid and profligate marquis. Illegitimacy, brain fever, immurement in a private asylum, a runaway horse: all play their part in a preposterous plot. Maxwell and MEB were trying the experiment of pushing into the full light of day one of her novels that had never been designed to reach it. By 1867 she had published nine three-volume novels. So far below the quality of these was *Rupert Godwin*—with its bumbling multiple recapitulations of each episode and its shameless use of every Gothic cliché—that the true Braddon addict could hardly fail to realize that he was reading something quite different and far shoddier. By issuing *Rupert Godwin* in the three-volume form sanctified for the novels of the middle and upper classes, Maxwell and MEB were violating contemporary publishing practices, and thereby inviting retaliation.

In the next year, 1868, they repeated the offense with a novel first called *Diavola; or, The Woman's Battle* while it was appearing in *The*

London Journal (1866–1867), which ascribed it to "The Author of *The Black Band,*" a work never acknowledged by MEB. Determined not to lose money as he had with *The Banker's Secret,* Maxwell this time *sold* the sheets of *Diavola* to the *New York Sunday Mercury,* which promptly published it as *Nobody's Daughter; or, the Ballad-Singer of Wapping* "by M. E. Braddon." Triumphantly they advertised, "Two Worlds have endorsed Miss E. Braddon [*sic*] as a novelist of transcendent power. . . . The English reviews have carped at her works—probably because they had not soul enough to appreciate them, but she queens it today in the department of *Sensational Romance* wherever the English language is spoken."

The *Athenaeum* sneered at this advertisement, and with a careful show of innocence inquired whether *Nobody's Daughter* could possibly be by Miss Braddon, since it was obviously the same book as *Diavola,* which was appearing as "by the author of 'The Black Band': . . . either Miss Braddon is the author of 'The Black Band' or . . . she is not the writer of 'Nobody's Daughter.' Which of these two?" Last year, they went on, Miss Braddon had "indignantly denied" the authorship of *The Black Band* when it had been republished in New York by the Messrs. Hilton under the new title *What Is This Mystery?* The *New York Sunday Mercury* had "exhibited" Miss Braddon's receipts for one hundred and fifty pounds, instalments on the total sum of two hundred and fifty pounds that it had paid for *Nobody's Daughter,* as well as letters by "Mr. Maxwell of London" about the sale of the sheets. It was all a "Grub-Street tempest," said the *Athenaeum,* but MEB should "lose no time in giving her explanation of facts that may be unfairly used to her disadvantage [February 26, 1867]."[25]

The *Athenaeum,* indeed, had started its own tempest. A correspondent wrote in to say that, when *The Black Band* had first appeared in the *Halfpenny Journal* in 1861, the "name of the authoress was given as Lady Caroline Lascelles."[26] And the next week a certain Hugh Morgan pointed out that Maxwell had owned the *Halfpenny Journal,* had sold the sheets of *Diavola,* and was now the owner of *Belgravia*: "Surely . . . the Lady Caroline Lascelles of the *Halfpenny Journal* is the Miss Braddon of *Belgravia*; and . . . in the interests of literature . . . Mr. Maxwell . . . should lose no time in giving his explanation of this scandal, which may be used to Miss Braddon's disadvantage."[27] But Hugh Morgan's tone belied his professed anxiety for MEB's advantage. Why was it so scandalous for her to have written anonymously or under a pseudonym fiction that she preferred not to acknowledge? Goaded into entering the controversy,

Maxwell replied that the interests of literature were not involved in a disclosure of "who suggested, who planned, and who wrote" *The Black Band* and the other *Halfpenny Journal* serials. Otherwise he would be happy to name the authors if he could obtain their permission. Mr. Morgan, a complete stranger to him, had displayed "an unaccountable intimacy with my name and business affairs," and had displayed bad taste in threatening MEB with "disadvantage."[28]

The *Athenaeum* itself now attacked MEB and other novelists for "reproducing old works under new titles," a practice which inconvenienced readers, caused losses to the book trade, and in the end would be disadvantageous for authors. It sneered at Maxwell, who had now given "an instructive peep into a factory of novels for the halfpenny press," and was himself the "master of the mill." And it crushingly agreed with him that the whole process, which it called the "manufacture" of novels, had nothing to do with literature.[29] Maxwell rejoined that the *New York Sunday Mercury* had "honestly paid" him, whereas other American publishers—such as the Messrs. Hilton—"live upon the policy of stealing as much literature as they can. [They] announce 'What is this Mystery?' [i.e., *The Black Band*] as reprinted from Miss Braddon's advance sheets, when it was nothing of the kind; and they advertise the work as being 'Miss Braddon's latest and best,' when they well knew it was neither the one nor the other." Naturally MEB, who had never received any communication from the Hiltons, had protested. And as for the *nom de plume*, "Lady Caroline Lascelles," it had been suggested by Maxwell's "late literary colleague . . . poor Sir C. F. [*sic* for F. C.] Lascelles Wraxall, Bart. He claimed a family right in the names. For five weeks [actually eleven] the *nom de plume* was adopted. At the end of that time it was discarded, for it was found that 'fine words butter no parsnips.' " What was wrong with that? The *Athenaeum* had certainly been gratuitously disagreeable, but Maxwell had been disingenuous in suggesting that a team of writers had produced the *Halfpenny Journal* stories, and in attributing to Wraxall, now deceased, the idea for the pen name that had been abandoned in all probability because the real Lady Caroline Lascelles had protested.[30]

Six weeks later, the Hiltons, referring to Maxwell as "the immaculate trader in Miss Braddon's productions," pointed out unashamedly that their actions were perfectly legal in the absence of an international copyright law and that it was a lot cheaper to print books without paying for them. They had "affixed" MEB's name to their version of *The Black Band* "to maintain identity as to authorship," and MEB had protested;

but when the link was made manifest by the publication of *Diavola* in the *New York Sunday Mercury,* she had "reluctantly acknowledged" authorship of both romances. "We regret," they concluded nastily, "that Miss Braddon or her friend should be compelled to protest against our critical judgment as to the work represented by us as being 'her latest and best'; but . . . a declaration to the contrary might prove detrimental to the fair authoress, and decidedly inimical to her future chance of disposing of 'advance sheets.' "[31] "Adding insult to injury," said Maxwell in reply: the Hiltons had sold eighteen thousand copies of their pirated *What Is This Mystery?* in its first week of publication, and were now insulting their victim, MEB.[32]

This ended the exchange. Unpleasant though the attack had been, it was, as we shall see, mild compared with the assault being leveled against MEB elsewhere on literary and moral grounds. The *Athenaeum* and its correspondents had not criticized *The Black Band—What Is This Mystery?* or *Diavola—Nobody's Daughter* from the literary point of view, where they were most vulnerable. Nor, in all the fuss about "manufacturing" novels, had anybody even mentioned the republication in England of *The Banker's Daughter* as *Rupert Godwin.* If it hurt readers and the book trade to have a novel appearing under different titles in England and America, how much more offensive might it not have been made to seem to give the same story two different titles in England alone? Yet this point the critics missed.

And in 1868, unregenerate, MEB and Maxwell took the offending English *Diavola* and American *Nobody's Daughter* and turned it into a three-volume novel under a third title, *Run to Earth,* thus compounding the misdemeanor they had committed with *Rupert Godwin.*[33] More than any of MEB's other books, *Run to Earth* was thus a "manufactured" novel in the *Athenaeum's* sense of the term, and the atrocity was perpetrated within a few months of its attack. Yet, with the inconsistency that for decades distinguished its criticism of MEB, the *Athenaeum* in reviewing *Run to Earth* altogether failed to identify it as that very *Diavola— Nobody's Daughter,* about which they had protested so violently when it had only two incarnations instead of three. They did not like the book because of its sensationalism,[34] but they missed their chance to condemn it as wholly inferior to MEB's other novels, and as a "manufactured" novel par excellence. With *Rupert Godwin* and *Run to Earth,* MEB had twice in two years dragged an inferior romance out of the obscurity to which most of her penny-dreadful fiction had been consigned, dressed it up in the form of its superiors, and fobbed it off on the public as if it were of the same genre as her true novels. *Rupert Godwin* and *Run to Earth* were her only cheap novels to attain three-deckerdom, and indeed they were her last penny (or halfpenny) fiction.

It was probably these two efforts to palm off works in one genre as genuine works in another that had led Charles Reade to speculate that MEB's "task-master" was driving her too hard, and that "much that goes by her name is done by understrappers." Reade was wrong about the books' authorship: the first portion of the original manuscript of *Run to Earth* survives, in MEB's own hand.[35] But they were written for a different audience, in a different manner. They were denizens of the literary deep that surfaced in a form far too good for them. Had her enemies addressed themselves to their undoubted shoddiness, they could have made her squirm. She herself was uneasy about resurrecting them. And she had no illusions about them.

3. The Voice of Sigismund Smith

While *Lady Audley* was enjoying its first boom, MEB told Bulwer that she was doing "an immense deal of work that nobody ever hears of for half penny and penny periodicals, . . . most piratical stuff, and would make your hair stand on end. . . . The amount of crime, treachery, murder, slow poisoning, and general infamy required by the halfpenny reader is something terrible. I am just going to do a little parracide [*sic*] for this week's supply."[36] In the pages of *The Doctor's Wife* (1864), her own creation, Sigismund Smith, a writer of serial penny fiction who has changed his first name from Sam, serves as her own mouthpiece.

His latest work, *The Smuggler's Bride,* Sigismund explains, " '. . . teems with suicides. There's the Duke of Port St. Martin's, who walls himself up alive in his own cellar; and there's Leonie de Pasdebasque, the ballet dancer who throws herself out of Count Caesar Marischetti's private balloon, and there's Lilla, the dumb girl—the penny public likes dumb girls—who sets fire to herself to escape from the—in fact there's lots of them. . . . ' " For the Duke's own dukedom—Port St. Martin's—Sigismund had chosen the name of the Paris theatre, the Porte Saint-Martin, that specialized in melodrama. Smith's half-dozen novels "enjoyed an immense popularity among the classes who like their literature as they like their tobacco—very strong." He had never appeared before the public "in a complete form," but "in weekly numbers at a penny . . . and except on one occasion when he found himself, very greasy and dog's-eared at the edges, and not exactly pleasant to the sense of smell—on the shelf of a humble librarian and news vendor, who dealt in tobacco and sweet stuff as well as literature—Sigismund had never known what it was to be bound." Although his work paid well, he yearned "to write a great novel," whose "archetype was the dream which he carried about with him wherever he went, and fondly nursed by night and day."

A "very mild young man [who] could not have hit anyone if he had tried," and who would not have minded much if you had hit him, Sigismund was not what his public expected. Could he really be "the author of *Colonel Montefiasco; or, The Brand upon the Shoulder Blade?*" He ought to have been a Byronic hero, "half magician, half brigand, [with] a bare white throat, a long black velvet dressing-gown, and thin tapering hands with queer agate and onyx rings coiling up the flexible fingers," living in "an oak-panelled chamber . . . with grotesque and diabolical carvings . . . a crystal globe upon a porphyry pedestal; a mysterious picture, with a curtain drawn before it—certain death being the fate of him who dared to raise that curtain by so much as a corner. A mantel-piece of black marble, and a collection of pistols and scymetars, swords and yataghans—especially yataghans—glimmering and flashing in the firelight. A little show of eccentricity in the way of household pets: a bear under the sofa and a tame cobra di capella coiled upon the hearth-rug." Instead, he was a mild young man "with perennial ink-smudges upon his face," and in his rooms "nothing more romantic than a waste-paper basket, a litter of old letters and crumpled proofs, and a cracked teapot simmering upon the hob." And this, despite the fact that in his stories "there were more masked doors, and hidden staircases, and revolving picture-frames and sliding panels than in all the old houses in Great Britain; and a greater length of vaulted passages than would make an underground railway from the Scottish border to the Land's End."

" 'What the penny public want,' " says Sigismund,

"is plot, and plenty of it; surprises and plenty of 'em; mystery as thick as a November fog. Don't you know the sort of thing? 'The clock of St. Paul's had just sounded eleven hours;'—it's generally a translation, you know, and St. Paul's stands for Notre Dame;—'A man came to a pier upon the quay which extends itself all the length between the bridges of Waterloo and London. . . . This man—who had a true head of vulture, the nose pointed, sharp, terrible; all that there is of the most ferocious; the eyes cavernous and full of a sombre fire—carried a bag upon his back. Presently he stops himself.. He regards with all his eyes the quay nearly deserted, the water, black and slimy, which stretches itself at his feet. He listens, but there is nothing. He bends himself upon the borders of the quay. He puts aside the bag from his shoulders, and something of dull, heavy, slides slowly downwards and falls into the water. At the instant that the heavy burden sinks with a dull noise to the bottom of the river, there is a voice, loud and piercing, which seems to elevate itself out of the darkness: "Philip Launay, what doest thou do there with the corpse of thy victim?" ' That's the sort of thing for the penny public."[37]

" 'It's generally a translation, you know, and St. Paul's stands for Notre Dame,' " says Sigismund and there can be no doubt, as he proceeds, that it is a literal translation from the French that MEB was guying. Just as it was the theatre of the Porte Saint-Martin that staged so many of the melodramas that inspired English playwrights to emulation, plagiarism, or even outright theft, so it was French fiction that provided an inexhaustible well of inspiration for the harassed English writer of penny-romance who was as fluent in the language as MEB. In one of the two letters that survive from Bulwer to MEB, he asked her, "Have you read Soulié's novels? They are worth studying for the sake of their extraordinary ingenuity in plot. They used to interest me much in spite of improbabilities [December 13, 1864]." And within a few days, she replied: "I have read Soulié, at least many of his stories, and have helped myself very freely to some of them for my anonymous work. He is certainly magnificent for continuous flow of invention—incident arising out of incident."

Frédéric Soulié (1800–1847), now almost forgotten, wrote "tales of impossible adventure and gruesome mystery; stories of first loves and virginal emotions and stories that are *grivois*; stories about day-laborers, nobles, blacksmiths, brokers, priests, prostitutes, bankers, planters, notaries, soldiers, actresses, murderers, public officials, thieves," and dozens of plays as well as novels. His most famous work was the eight-volume *Mémoires du Diable* (1836–1838). He hammered out his sensation fiction for the rich financial rewards it brought him, but commanded such an "ironic twist" that he "made it almost sincere." His sensationalism was both "physical and moral. Blood, corpses, ghastly murders, ghoulishness, revolting details of disease, or torture, or decomposition" enlivened his descriptions of "unusual crimes . . . such as rape, incest, illegal sequestration, treacheries."³⁸ Soulié's fluent narrative, keen psychological insights, cynicism, and hatred of hypocrisy made him enormously popular in his own day; he launched a whole new school of "satanic" fiction and drama. Perhaps a bold future student will one day read all of MEB's *Halfpenny Journal* contributions and all of Soulié and discover exactly how and where she "helped" herself "pretty freely" to his materials. At any rate, she cheerfully admitted to Bulwer that she had done so; for her, as for Sigismund, writing for English audiences, it would not have been easy to clean up Soulié's plots.

If Sigismund could not get inspiration from the French, he tried what he called a " 'good strong combination story.' "

". . . the best thing you can do, if you haven't got ideas of your own, is to steal other people's ideas in an impartial manner. Don't empty one man's pocket, but take a little bit all around. . . . I'm doing a combination novel now—'The Heart of Midlothian' and 'The Wandering Jew'. You've no idea how admirably the two stories blend. . . . I throw my period back to the Middle Ages. . . . what is there that isn't possible if you go back to the days of the Plantagenets? I make Jeannie Deans a dumb girl—there's twice the interest in her if you make her dumb—and I give her a goat and a tambourine, because . . . the artist likes that sort of thing for his illustrations. . . . I call my Jeannie 'Aureola,' rather a fine name, isn't it? and entirely my own invention. [N. B. *The Doctor's Wife* appeared more than a year before *Alice in Wonderland*] . . . I make her walk from London to ROME to get a papal bull for the release of her sister from the Tower of London . . . over the Alps—which admits of Aureola's getting buried in the snow, and dug out again by a Mount St. Bernard's dog; and then walled up alive by the monks because they suspect her of being friendly to the Lollards; and dug out again by Caesar Borgia, who happens to be travelling that way, and asks a night's lodging, and hears Aureola's tambourine behind the stone wall in his bedroom, and digs her out and falls in love with her; and she escapes from his persecution out of a window, and lets herself down the side of a mountain by means of her gauze scarf, and dances her way to ROME, and obtains an audience of the Pope, and gets mixed up with the Jesuits—and that's where I work into the Wandering Jew."

When Sigismund is reminded that the Jesuits did not exist in the days of the Plantagenets, he admits it, but adds: " 'If you tie me down to facts . . . I can't write at all.' " As things are, he maintains, he has " 'very much improved upon Sir Walter Scott—a delightful writer— . . . but decidedly a failure in penny numbers.' "

The trouble with the otherwise pleasant pastime of writing for the penny public, says Sigismund, is that it calls for so many dead bodies, " 'and when you've once had recourse to the stimulant of bodies, you are like a man who is accustomed to strong liquors, . . . it isn't so easy to turn teetotaller.' " When Sigismund waxes eloquent about popular writing and great writing, the voice we are listening to is unmistakably MEB's own:

> " . . . I would rather be the author of 'Box and Cox' [by J. Maddison Morton, 1847], and hear my audience screaming with laughter from the rise of the curtain to the fall . . . than write a dull five-act tragedy. I should like to have been Guilbert de Pixérécourt [René Charles Guilbert de Pixérécourt (1773–1844), prolific playwright], the father and prince of melodrama, the man whose dramas were acted 30,000 times in France before he died (and how many times in England?) ; the man who reigned supreme over the play-goers of the time, and has not yet ceased to reign. Whoever quotes any passage from the works of Guilbert de Pixérécourt, or remembers his name? But his dramas are acted in every country's theatre; his persecuted heroines weep and tremble; his murderous scoundrels run their two hours' career of villany, to be dragged off scowling to subterranean dungeons, or to die impenitent and groaning at the feet of triumphant Virtue. . . . Guilbert de Pixérécourt was never a great man; he was only popular. If a man can't have a niche in the Walhalla, isn't it something to have his name in big letters on the boulevard?"

Admitting that he would rather have written *The Vicar of Wakefield* than his own *Colonel Montefiasco*, Sigismund proclaims that in fact he could write *The Vicar*, but it would not be Oliver Goldsmith's *Vicar*. His would be done

> " . . . in the detective pre-Raphaelite style. Moses knows the secret of his father's—forged accommodation-bills, or something of that kind; sets out to go to the fair on a drowsy summer morning. Not a leaf stirring in the vicarage windows. . . . and Miss Primrose walks

slowly back to the house and says 'Papa, it's very warm;' and you know there's something going to happen. Then the second chapter comes, and Mr. Primrose has his dinner, . . . and the two girls walk about . . . watching for Moses, who NEVER COMES BACK. And then the serious business of the story begins, . . . one night, when the curtains are drawn, and the girls are sitting at their work, and dear Mrs. Primrose is cutting out comfortable flannels for the poor, the Vicar opens his desk, and begins to write a letter. You hear the faint sound of the ashes falling on the hearth, the slow ticking of an eight-day clock in the hall outside the drawing-room door, the sharp snap of Mrs. Primrose's scissors as they close upon the flannel. Sophia asks Burchell to fetch a volume from the bookcase behind the Vicar's chair. He is a long time choosing the book, and his eye looks over the Vicar's shoulder. He . . . sees . . . a glove, a green kid glove sewn with white, which he distinctly remembers to have seen worn by Moses when he started on that pleasant journey from which he never returned."

And so the Vicar is shown up as Moses' murderer. " 'That's how *I* should do the 'Vicar of Wakefield,' " says Sigismund. " 'But I don't suppose the clergy would take to murdering their sons by reason of my fiction.' "[39]

This brilliant scenario of the *Vicar* as it would be written by a writer of sensation-fiction reflects MEB's estimate of her own powers: she wished to be great, but consoled herself by remembering that she was popular, and that greatness might perhaps lie ahead. She was also trying to disarm her critics by gently denying their charges of immorality: a fictional murder, even by the gentle Mr. Primrose himself, would not lead others—not even the clergy!—to follow his example.

One of Sigismund's adventures had actually happened to MEB herself: he "would visit a pleasant country house, and receive hospitable entertainment, and . . . would stroll out into some peaceful garden, . . . and plan a diabolical murder, to be carried out in seventy-five penny numbers. Sometimes he was honourable enough to ask permission . . . and when, on one occasion, after admiring . . . a dear old place . . . he ventured to remark that the spot was so peaceful it reminded him of slow poisoning, and demanded whether there would be any objection to his making the quiet grange the scene of his next fiction," his host cheerfully answered " '. . . You are welcome to people the place with fiends, as far as I'm concerned.' " When Percy Fitzgerald wrote to ask MEB whether the plot of

Lady Audley's Secret had been inspired by events that had taken place in any actual mansion, she told him of "a long avenue of limes, very quiet, very secluded, and aloof from the garden of a dear old oak-panelled grange in Essex, and it seemed to me one summer evening, walking with the master of the house, that this lime-walk suggested something uncanny in the history of domestic crime." Would her host mind, she asked, if she " 'were to take this house as the scene of a novel,' " and make " 'the inhabitants a rather bad set of people?' 'Mind! People it with fiends, if you like, my dear!' said he. Now that is a verbatim report of a brief question and answer spoken thirty years ago."[40]

Again like MEB, Sigismund Smith soon produces his first three-volume novel. His *Lady Audley's Secret* he calls *The Mystery of Mowbray Manor*, "a legitimate three-volume romance, with all the interest concentrated upon one body." When he visits a friend's country house, he finds that its cellar has " 'accommodation for a perfect regiment of bodies; which would be a consideration if I was going to do the story in penny numbers.' " But he is determined instead to write a second three-volume novel about " 'twin brothers hating each other from infancy, and both in love with the same woman, and one of them—the darkest twin, with a scar on his forehead—walling up the young female in a deserted room, while the more amiable twin without a scar devotes his life to searching for her in foreign climes accompanied by a detective officer and a bloodhound. It's only a rough idea at present. . . .' "[41]

When satirizing herself, MEB pretended to see very little difference between a penny-dreadful and a three-decker, except for the number of murders needed: for a three-decker, one was enough; for a penny-dreadful there was no limit. And so far was she from despising the melodramatic elements she ridiculed, that as late as 1887 in her novel *Like and Unlike* she actually utilized Sigismund's theme of the twin brothers who love the same girl. No scar distinguishes the less amiable brother who marries her, nor does the more amiable brother search all his life for her in foreign climes: he does not need to, because he catches his twin red-handed immediately after he has killed the lady; and he connives at the hiding of the body—not in a deserted room but at the bottom of a stream. In 1864, as Sigismund had said, it was only a rough idea. By 1887 MEB had perfected it and used it skillfully.[42]

Like MEB again, Sigismund continued to write penny-dreadfuls after his success in three volumes. At the very end of *The Doctor's Wife*, "Telegrams from infuriated proprietors of penny journals pursue him . . .

and a lively gentleman in a white hat has been known to arrive per express train, vaguely declaring his intention of 'standing over' Mr. Smith during the production of an urgently required chapter of *The Bride of the Bosphorus; or, the Fourteen Corpses of the Caspian Sea*." Sigismund has just finished off " 'Bella the Ballet Girl,' (one of Bickers' [ie., Vickers'] serial touch-and-go romances; the first five numbers and a magnificent engraving of one of Landseer's best pictures for a penny). . . . she poisoned herself with insect powder in ·a garret near Drury Lane, after setting fire to the house and grounds of her destroyer; she ran through a hundred and thirteen numbers, and Bickers has some idea of getting me to write a sequel. You see there *might* be an antidote to the insect-powder.' "[43]

For Smith the novelist, MEB cherished a genuine affection. Except for a certain detective Faunce who appeared in two of her later novels (*Rough Justice* [1898] and *His Darling Sin* [1900]), Smith was the only one of her characters whom she ever introduced into a second book. Having already in *The Doctor's Wife* (1864) changed his first name from Sam to Sigismund and progressed from penny numbers to his first three-volume novel, he reappears in *The Lady's Mile* (1866)—MEB's first novel without even a single murder—and has changed his last name to Smyth. Already he has written two dozen three-volume novels, many more than even his creatrix and alter ego was ever able to manage in a period of two years. He is married now and in jovial fashion he lays down to his new wife the law about reading his novels: " 'If you read my books, you'll make suggestions, and if you make suggestions, I shall hate you, and the better your suggestions are the more I shall hate you. . . . The critics inform me that my fictions are demoralizing. As a writer and a rate-payer, I believe in my fictions, but as a husband I defer to the critics, and forbid my wife to read my novels.' "[44] Samuel-Sigismund Smith-Smyth, though created in a light-hearted mood, had his purpose. He is "a sensation author. That bitter term of reproach, sensation, had not been invented for the terror of romancers in the fifty-second year of this present century [in which, like *The Story of Barbara* and *A Lost Eden*, *The Doctor's Wife* was set]; but the thing existed nevertheless in divers forms, and people wrote sensation novels as unconsciously as Monsieur Jourdain talked prose."[45] For Sigismund, as for MEB, there were two classes of sensation-novel. Long before she abandoned her labors in the lower depths of penny-fiction, she had, like Sigismund, been "bound" and had achieved a series of spectacular successes in three volumes.

4. "The Highest Rate to Be Screwed Out of a Publisher"

"I have never written a line that has not been written against time," MEB told her confidant and mentor, Bulwer, in December 1862, after *Lady Audley* had appeared but before *Aurora Floyd* was finished. Sometimes the printer's boy was waiting outside her door. "Serial writing and hand to mouth composition" was a curse and accounted for the "errors, absurdities, contradictions, and inconsistencies," for which she felt apologetic. But it was all profitable. With "delicacy and kindness," Bulwer had advised MEB to be "prudent in money matters," and she undertook to follow his advice to the letter: "*I hope to save all I have received for my copyrights; as my serial work pays all current expenses and then leaves a margin for saving* [Italics mine]." She told him she had "very little inclination for spending money, & positively no time to be extravagant, if I wished to be so. I go nowhere where I require fine dress—I can't drink wine. I am not able to stir from London, or would spend my money in travelling; but am altogether bound hand and foot by hard work."[46]

How much money was MEB actually earning? While *Lady Audley's Secret* was appearing in Ward and Lock's *Sixpenny Magazine,* the Tinsley brothers bought the book publication rights for two hundred and fifty pounds, with the promise of an additional fifty pounds if the *Times* should review it.[47] But as the book took off, Edward, the elder Tinsley brother, wrote to MEB within a few days of its publication, on October 17, 1862, " 'Lady Audley' is a great success." Already a third edition had sold better than the first. If she would accept his terms "for 'Aurora Floyd' for a thousand pounds, and 'Lady Audley' is reviewed in the 'Times,' " he would pay "two hundred and fifty pounds beyond the fifty" he had "already promised to pay when the review appears." The *Times* review (could it have been managed through the Delane family connection?) did not appear until November 18, when it called *Lady Audley's Secret* "a galloping good novel . . . full of rapid incident, well put together. . . . it is seldom that one sees a novel so well balanced in the display of plot, of passion, of character, and of diction."[48]

But on October 20, well before the review appeared, indeed only three days after the letter from Edward Tinsley, MEB and Tinsley signed the contract for *Aurora Floyd,* which had been running serially in *Temple Bar* since January 1862 and was also clearly marked for immediate success. Tinsley was to pay her one thousand pounds for the sole right to publish *Aurora Floyd* as a book for a period of two years: one hundred pounds down and the remainder in three equal instalments of three hundred pounds after two, four, and six months. Signed by MEB and Edward Tinsley, the contract was witnessed by John Maxwell.[49]

But instead of the total bonus of three hundred pounds that Tinsley had promised her for *Lady Audley's Secret*, he actually paid her five hundred. On March 3, 1863, he wrote her, "We have this day much pleasure in handing you our acceptances at two months for £250 and at 6 months for £250," or five hundred pounds. Maxwell had obtained the extra money for her: " . . . we beg you will regard these payments as given to you in performance of our promise to Mr. Maxwell that you should derive benefit beyond our agreement in proportion to whatever success was achieved by your 'Lady Audley's Secret.' We have much pleasure in declaring that the success of that work has far exceeded all expectation, and . . . fully justifies" the additional payment. Four days later MEB formally acknowledged that she regarded the five hundred pounds as "a discharge of your promise to recompense me in proportion to the success of Lady Audley's Secret."[50] Over and above her earnings from serial publication, then, she had received from the Tinsleys by March 1863 a total of eight hundred pounds for the book publication of *Lady Audley's Secret*, and had with them a contract for one thousand pounds for *Aurora Floyd*, the copyright of which would revert to her after two years, so that she alone would receive the very high proceeds from all subsequent editions.

On April 13, 1863, she wrote to Bulwer, "I shall take good care to avail myself of your kind offer of advice as to the commercial value of my next novel." But the two on which she was at work, *Eleanor's Victory* and *John Marchmont's Legacy*, both still appearing as serials, were already sold, "I think at the highest rate to be screwed out of a publisher for the class of book I can write, *but if I live to complete these two I shall have earned enough to keep me & my mother for the rest of our lives* [italics mine], & I will then try & write for Fame & do something more worthy to be laid upon your altar. The Messrs Tinsley, who are young people quite new in the trade, are to give me £2000 for a two years *license to print* each of the novels, after which time the copyrights are to revert to me. I don't think they *could* give me more with any chance of obtaining a profit themselves."[51] So book publication of these two new novels alone would net MEB four thousand pounds during the year 1863, and after two years the enormously lucrative copyrights would revert to her. Since she regarded all of this as pure capital accumulation—her serial earnings produced enough income to support her and her mother—it is understandable that she already saw them both as secure for life.

The Tinsleys, we know, wanted to publish her next novel, *Henry Dunbar,* first serialized under the title of *The Outcasts.* On January 12, 1864, MEB wrote Edward Tinsley that a recent criticism in the *Times,* which disapproved of her hasty writing, "has made me very cautious with regard to 'The Outcasts.' " She intended now "to cut away the entire underplot . . . rewrite at least a third of the story, and very carefully revise and polish the rest." The novel would therefore not be ready until May. "I cannot sell the right of publication for less than two thousand pounds, and I shall take more trouble with it than with anything else I have done. You may recollect having offered this sum on the last occasion I was at Audley Lodge. Then the sum of twenty-two fifty pounds was asked and I should expect this sum from anyone else."[52] No doubt coached by Maxwell, MEB had first asked Tinsley for two thousand two hundred and fifty pounds for a two-year lease on *Henry Dunbar,* an advance of two hundred and fifty pounds over the two thousand pounds apiece she had received for the leases on *Eleanor's Victory* and *John Marchmont's Legacy.* Instead, Tinsley had offered the same figure of two thousand pounds, and MEB now declared her willingness to accept the lesser sum.

But the Tinsleys apparently jibbed. Their huge profits on *Lady Audley's Secret* and *Aurora Floyd* had flowed in large part from the orders placed by a new enterprise calling itself "the Library Company Limited." Founded as a rival to Mudie's and the other circulating libraries, the Library Company had bought many copies of MEB's first two three-deckers. But it charged borrowers such low fees that thieves began to enter multiple subscriptions and steal the books they were ostensibly borrowing. So the Library Company failed, and the Tinsleys found themselves deprived of their largest single customer just when they were paying MEB two thousand pounds apiece for the two-year leases on *Eleanor's Victory* and *John Marchmont's Legacy,* which William Tinsley, Edward's younger brother, recalled in 1900 as "no very good bargain."[53]

Perhaps the Tinsleys simply refused to come to terms for *Henry Dunbar* or perhaps Maxwell now thought that he could make more money by publishing MEB's novels himself. In any case, he published *Henry Dunbar* under his own imprint later in 1864. The "underplot" that MEB had excised from the original *Outcasts* she thriftily saved and later published separately as a short story called "Lost and Found."[54] And in

1864 and 1865 Maxwell also published MEB's next three novels, *Only a Clod, The Doctor's Wife,* and *Sir Jasper's Tenant,* after they had appeared serially. Perhaps because the business arrangements were now between ostensible husband and wife, no financial details have survived.

But the books were all financial successes. To Bulwer, who was always urging her to take more time and try something loftier and more poetic, MEB wrote, late in 1863, "I have tried to rise & already the 'Dweller on the Threshold' appears to me, in the form of a very friendly and kindly meant letter from Edmund Yates the editor of 'T. Bar' which I will enclose with this. I know that I . . . can scarcely hope to improve while my work is so close that I dare not throw away a page of copy, though it may be the veriest bosh."[55] The original "Dweller on the Threshold" was the dreadful apparition in Bulwer's *Zanoni* (1842), which terrified a neophyte too impatient to undergo the full course of prescribed occult training before exploring the spirit world;[56] but here MEB used the term as an equivalent for "temptation." Yates, who had succeeded Sala as editor, had been offering her much money for a contribution to *Temple Bar.* She accepted, and *Sir Jasper's Tenant* began its run there in February 1865.

In what was probably her letter of acceptance, MEB wrote Yates:

The Balzac-morbid-anatomy school is my especial delight, but it seems you want the downright sensational: floppings at the end of chapters, and bits of paper hidden in secret drawers, bank-notes and title-deeds under the carpet, and a part of the body putrefying in a coal-scuttle. By the bye, what a splendid novel, *à la* Wilkie Collins, one might write on a protracted search for the missing members of a murdered man, dividing the tale not into *books* but *bits*! "BIT THE FIRST: The leg in the gray stocking found at Deptford." "BIT THE SECOND: The white hand and the onyx ring with half an initial letter (unknown) and crest, skull with a coronet, found in an Alpine *crevasse*!"

Seriously, though, you want a sensational fiction. . . . I cannot promise you anything new, when . . . everything on this earth seems to have been done, and done, and done again! . . . I will give the kaleidoscope (which I cannot spell) another turn, and will do my very best with the bits of old glass and pins and rubbish.

There they all are—the young lady who has married a burglar, and who does not want to introduce him to her friends; the duke . . . who comes into the world with six and thirty pages of graphic detail, and goes out of it without having said "bo!" to a goose; the

two brothers who are perpetually taken for one another; the twin
sisters ditto, ditto; the high-bred and conscientious banker, who
has made away with everybody's title-deeds. Any novel combination of the well-known figures is completely at your service,
workmanship careful, delivery prompt.[57]

Even when working now at the three-decker, though simultaneously continuing with the penny-number novel, MEB had the same ironical view of
her own writing that she gave to her alter ego Sigismund Smith.

In January 1864, she told Bulwer that she had been "sharply urged to
produce 'The Mayfair Magazine.' "[58] The project was temporarily shelved,
but obviously MEB was eager to make still more money. In June 1864,
she reported that in France *Henry Dunbar* was her greatest success yet,
and that the translator had doubled his charges "(which even when
doubled are very small) on the strength of its success,"[59] a reminder that
such translations were also bringing her income. Late in 1864 she referred
to *Only a Clod*, then appearing in the *St. James's Magazine*, as "quite a
hand-to-mouth affair, & done to keep my hand in & earn money."[60] And
on December 9, she wrote, "every day the inexorable printer's devil . . .
comes to loll with his greasy little back against the wall, & to demand
'more copy.' " So she walked the treadmill, and the respite she had been
promising herself did not come. Moreover, the public did not seem to care
how much she tried to improve her books. They demanded "strong
meat." *Henry Dunbar* "which I wrote off the reel for the 'London
Journal' " sold just as well as *The Doctor's Wife* "to which I gave my best
thoughts—such as they are."[61]

Early in 1865, MEB bought a house, "freehold, with a tiny garden on
part of the site of Pope's villa" in Twickenham. It was small and compact,
and for the moment she intended to let it, "as London suits me best
while I write against time" and she wanted to be near the British
Museum.[62] Although she never lived in this house, she obviously had
capital to invest. Later in the year she reported that *Only a Clod* was
"more successful in a pecuniary sense" than *The Doctor's Wife*. *Sir
Jasper's Tenant*, by then out in three-volume form, bade fair to sell better
than *Only a Clod*. "But" she told Bulwer "I want to please you as well as
to 'put money in my purse.' "[63] Her inferior novels were selling better
than *The Doctor's Wife*, which she rightly thought her best to date.

Early in 1866 MEB reported that she had been worried for a month,
and her Christmas spoiled "by a most dishonorable attempt of a rich firm
holding a mortgage—or having lent money to the *actual* proprietor of the

[*Temple Bar*] Magazine published in the name of Maxwell & Co. to rob me of a large sum of money (large at least for me £1,000) or at any rate to impound or detain the money under a flimsy technical pretext until they can ascertain whether it rightly belongs to me—which *they know* as well as I know that my hand is now writing these words." MEB found herself obliged to appeal to the Court of Chancery, and "the worry . . . is more painful to me than the possibility of losing my '*thou*'—which is the balance of the proceeds of 'Sir Jasper's Tenant'—published by the firm of Maxwell & Co. for me & at my own risk. The Mr. Maxwell who represented that firm has no hand in this proceeding, which is partly prompted by a malicious feeling against him—as my agent and intermediary in the matter—as well as by the desire to stick as long as possible to the money." The "rich firm" was almost surely Richard Bentley and Son, who—we know—acquired *Temple Bar* from John Maxwell in January, 1866.[64]

Bulwer promptly advised MEB to have the matter arbitrated, and she took his advice. In reporting that she had consented to refer the dispute "to some respectable publisher," she described her opponents' action as a "most dishonest claim made against me for a publisher's commission on my last four novels—contrary to an understanding generally known & acted upon by all parties for a period of nearly two years." So Maxwell's creditors—Bentley, in all probability—were trying to collect part of his debt to them by withholding money due MEB from *Sir Jasper's Tenant*, on the ground that the Maxwell publishing firm should have been collecting a publisher's commission for this and MEB's previous three novels: *Henry Dunbar*, *The Doctor's Wife*, and *Only a Clod*. Until the case should be settled, she complained, "I am most unjustly kept out of eleven hundred pounds, to my serious inconvenience—as I have had to sell out of Consols at a top of 5 per cent, to pay for a purchase at Richmond, and the use of the 'Sir Jasper' money would have saved me some part of the loss."[65]

The purchase at Richmond was Lichfield House, a splendid early Georgian mansion into which she and Maxwell would soon be moving their large family and where they would live the rest of their lives. It was a large investment; eleven hundred pounds was only a fraction of the purchase price. If this temporary loss had created a major financial crisis, the Maxwells could not have purchased Lichfield House at all. So MEB had experienced severe annoyance and inconvenience, but no indebtedness or ensuing financial bondage, a point worth emphasizing in view of the fact that her remarks to Bulwer have been misinterpreted.

No doubt, John Maxwell's affairs were embarrassed: he had mortgaged *Temple Bar* to a new *"actual* proprietor," while it continued to be "published in the name of Maxwell & Co." The "rich firm" that held the mortgage were apparently receiving all of Maxwell & Company's income until Maxwell's debt was settled. Among these moneys were the last one thousand (or eleven hundred) pounds owing to MEB for *Sir Jasper's Tenant,* also published by Maxwell & Company. This they kept back, on the pretense that it belonged to the firm ("a flimsy technical pretext until they can ascertain whether it rightly belongs to me"). MEB thought that their withholding of her money was "partly prompted by a malicious feeling against" Maxwell, although what they withheld was a small sum compared with her total earnings. No doubt the creditors knew of the relationship between Maxwell and MEB, and of their need to keep it as private as possible.

At the same time, MEB also told Bulwer that she was "on the look out for a publisher" and hoped "if possible to make permanent arrangements for the production of my books, past, present, and to come. Messrs. Chapman and Hall are to make me an offer, I believe in the course of the next week." They wanted "to buy a permanent third share in my novels—and to publish them for me—subject to this third share and commission. Do you think I should do wisely in making such an arrangement?"[66] Whatever Maxwell's debts, MEB was clearly altogether free to find her own publisher and to make the most advantageous arrangements possible. Bulwer advised her to hold out for a better offer than Chapman and Hall were making; she promised to take his advice, though fearing that he "put a higher value on my past books than the publishers will do—but—*nous verrons.*"[67] Chapman and Hall lost out, and Ward, Lock and Tyler became her publishers. Perhaps Maxwell had a financial interest in the firm. He may even have been able to avoid paying some of his debts by publishing MEB's books over their imprint rather than his own.

Soon after, MEB reported that she had "been working very little for the last six months, during which time I have done nothing but the Lady's Mile, a wonderful falling off from the four separate romances upon which I have been wont to work alternately."[68] So she was feeling no financial stringency. By September, she told Bulwer on the letter paper of her newly founded magazine *Belgravia* (the originally projected *Mayfair Magazine* rechristened) that she had been "compelled for the last three years to preserve a certain secresy [*sic*] with regard to my position—on account of certain commercial entanglements which might have stripped me of very hardly earned possessions—and I am not chivalrous enough to make any such sacrifice"[69]—a remark which fits in with the hypothesis that Maxwell's financial embarrassments and his illicit union with MEB made her property vulnerable to attack. Perhaps if he and she had been legally married, his creditors could have treated her property as his; so for business reasons she had to act as if she were not married to him, while for social reasons it was in the highest degree desirable that she should be thought of as his wife. The details of the complexities are unlikely to be discovered. But MEB was prosperous. Maxwell, as her companion, whatever his personal financial difficulties may have been, was living in luxurious comfort. And she was less driven to overproduce than at any earlier time in her life.[70]

On August 9, 1866, the arrangements had been concluded for the purchase of Lichfield House, "a big red brick house built by some Bishop of Lichfield & with a rare old fashioned garden." MEB would take possession during the winter, and wrote Bulwer, "I think I am now pretty nearly arrived at Swift's ideal of Happiness. 'Ah, yet—& yet—& yet!' as your son [Robert Lytton, the poet "Owen Meredith"] says." Perhaps the great house seemed less attractive once it had been acquired. Perhaps the tensions of the irregular ménage were increasing. Perhaps MEB was posing. But she could afford luxuries. She offered Bulwer as a present a pair of "small full length portraits" of the Earl and Countess of Clarendon, into whose family Robert Lytton had married in 1864.[71]

A year later, in October 1867, pressing Bulwer to visit at her "large old fashioned house," which she badly wanted to show him, she wrote him, "Such as it is, it all came out of my own head, but that head would never have earned me a living if it had not been for the strong business like brain and clear perception that have assisted me in every step of my literary career."[72] So she paid tribute to Maxwell as her adviser in the enterprise of marketing her novels. At the same time, she was proud that she had earned the money that paid for Lichfield House.

By then she had also bought Skisdon, "my grandmother's old house near Wadebridge—a nest in one of the most fertile valleys of Cornwall—mild as Madeira—myrtles & roses climbing to the chimney-pots, tulip trees growing high on the lawn," and she hoped "daringly" that some winter Bulwer would bring his "pipes & papers to that calm sunny haven" and "smoke & muse undisturbed save when it is your royal pleasure to admit worshippers to yr shrine."[73] Bulwer never came to Skisdon, and since MEB was never able to use the house she soon resold it to a Braddon cousin. But she had nonetheless stepped in and bought the beloved ancestral home with her own earnings and so kept it from going out of the family,[74] a second important purchase reflecting her prosperity.

In November 1868, MEB suffered a nervous collapse from which recovery was slow but complete. Thereafter, in the early seventies all went smoothly at Lichfield House: in December 1872, for example, she told Bulwer of "the largest party it has ever been my good—or evil fortune—to receive in this capacious old house." Seventy to eighty people had come to see the private theatricals, and danced afterwards till five the next morning, "much to the satisfaction of my stepdaughters, & much to my own delight—when they went away!"[75] So the literary and business partnership of MEB and Maxwell moved from strength to strength. Affluence was at hand, literary hackwork abandoned, and the future rendered secure, all within five years after the first appearance of *Lady Audley's Secret*. The financial trouble of 1866 was only a momentary and minor irritation involving a relatively unimportant sum of money.

There remained the question of the dramatic pirates. In 1874, after MEB had published twenty-four novels, many of which had been dramatized, she wrote, "I have never received the slightest pecuniary advantage from any of these adaptations, nor does the law of copyright in any way assist me to protect what appears to be a valuable portion of my copyright, the exclusive right to dramatize my own creations." Indeed, the law to which she objected was generally execrated. A Royal Commission in 1887 called it "bad . . . totally destitute of any sort of arrangement, incomplete, often obscure, and even where . . . intelligible after long study . . . so ill-expressed that no one who does not give such study can expect to understand it." But it was still unreformed in 1887. Anybody might steal a novel and "adapt" it for the stage without payment, often adding or subtracting characters or episodes, and so distorting the original.[76]

To protect himself, the author of a published novel had to take three steps. First, he had to write a play based on his own novel, before any pirate could do so. Second, he had to stage at least a single performance of that play in the presence of witnesses who could later swear that they had seen it performed on the stage. Third, he had to enter (i.e., register) his dramatic version at Stationers' Hall. Most novelists did not know this law, and of those who did, no doubt most found it too cumbrous. On one occasion Charles Reade complied with it by first writing a play, called *Gold*, which was successfully staged, and then transforming *Gold* into his novel, *It Is Never Too Late to Mend* (1857), thus putting himself in a position gleefully to sue the dramatic pirates of that novel when they tried to stage their own version. Few authors were as energetic or as litigious as Reade.

Far from resenting it, however, in the early days when *Lady Audley's Secret* was first being turned into a play at no benefit to herself, MEB was delighted. She wrote to the adapter, Robert Walters (his pen name was George Roberts), that she was "flattered and gratified by the promptitude and earnestness" that he and Frank Matthews, the manager of the St. James's Theatre, had shown. She was as eager as they for the play's success, saying "it must be the fault of the story itself" if it failed. She praised the scenery; she praised the casting of Louisa Herbert as Lady Audley; she agreed to come to rehearsals, but "would not for a moment dream of offering any suggestions," knowing that Mr. Matthews' artistic taste and Walters' dramatic experience "will get the greatest possible effect out of my story."[77] She was also pleased that Leicester Buckingham's "adaptation" of the recent French play, *Jeanne qui pleure et Jeanne qui rit,* would continue to be acted under its London title of *The Merry Widow* along with *Lady Audley's Secret*: Miss Herbert would be "Angel and Demon in the same night," and the contrast between the two heroines would be "very piquant."[78] And after the play opened (February 28, 1863), MEB wrote Bulwer that Miss Herbert was very good, and offered him a box for any night he might choose: "They would all be so honoured by your going."[79] So MEB raised no question of payment for this adaptation of *Lady Audley's Secret*.

But "George Roberts" himself was suffering at the hands of pirates. Soon he was forced to claim in print that his was "The Original Version" of *Lady Audley's Secret*, and "the only one in use at the West End Theatres and adopted by Artists of celebrity." He explained that "This notice is found necessary, various versions being in circulation, containing direct imitations of constructive peculiarities and situations invented and introduced by Mr. Roberts into his Drama, and not existing in the Novel."[80] Indeed there were at least two other "adaptations" in the field: one by C. H. Hazlewood, published by Thomas Hailes Lacy, of which no performance is recorded, and one by William E. Suter, "Adapted from Miss Braddon's popular work . . . ;" which was performed at the Queen's Theatre a week before the St. James's production, on February 21, 1863, and was also published by Lacy.[81]

Aurora Floyd also promptly appeared in at least four different dramatic versions. Early in March 1863, Henry Morley, who kept a journal of his visits to the theatre, saw George Belmore (whose real name was George

Garstin) act the dimwitted murderer in a production at the Princess's Theatre, which took two and a half hours to play. And only a few days later, Morley saw another version "adapted" by the celebrated Benjamin Webster, the actor-manager, who played the same part. This one took four and a half hours. Webster assured the public that "Miss Braddon had nothing whatever to do with the construction of the drama" and that it was his object "rather to make up a good piece than to simply put the novel upon the stage." Although Morley found in Webster's acting "a terrible energy" and "diabolical" greed, cunning, and malice, he lamented that the "best new plays of a creditable sort" had proved so unpopular that producers had been driven to fill their theatres by staging such dramas as *Lady Audley's Secret* and *Aurora Floyd*: "The lowest form of literary taste in the uneducated having been forced into fashion among readers who have better fare at their command, the players, who seek only to please the palate of the town, will cook the garbage that is in demand." Like the literary critics who found that MEB's novels posed a threat to public morality, Morley predicted the degradation of the stage if such "stimulants" were to continue.

A third *Aurora Floyd*, by the same William E. Suter who had already adapted *Lady Audley's Secret*, opened at the same Queen's Theatre on April 4, 1863, and the same T. H. Lacy published this version. And a fourth by C. H. Hazlewood opened at the Britannia Theatre in Hoxton on April 21.[82]

The Lacy publication of Suter's adaptations of MEB's two novels became the subject of an important lawsuit. Indeed, they alone made the lawsuit possible. In the case of *Lady Audley's Secret*, William Tinsley long afterwards remembered that ". . . as soon as the work became popular, several of the dramatic pirates made dramatic versions of it, and we gained an important injunction against Mr. Lacy, the then theatrical bookseller, to restrain him from printing and publishing dramatic versions of the book." Lacy fought the case very hard, but Sir William Page Wood, Vice-Chancellor, found for the Tinsley brothers, remarking "that the custom relied upon was a very bad one; for if any number of compilers or dramatic authors were allowed to make printed versions of a book, the author would ultimately have little or no property in the work at all." But Wood said that, "As the authoress had not protected the 'playing' right of her book," by writing, staging, and registering her own dramatic version, he would "only restrain Mr. Lacy, or anyone else, from printing and publishing plays made from it."[83]

Tinsley's account is supported by the manuscript notes in the actual copy of *Lady Audley's Secret* used by his counsel, Sir John Rolt, who fought the case. In 1869 Rolt noted that "as I best remember this was the first case in which it was insisted that turning a novel into a drama was an infringement of copyright. Tho' the decision was in my favour, I am not quite satisfied that it was right. There was a substantial amount of mental labour in writing the drama."[84] But writing six years later, Rolt had forgotten how narrow a point had actually been at issue.

The lawsuit was directed against Lacy's printing Suter's adaptations of both *Lady Audley's Secret* and *Aurora Floyd*. In the High Court of Chancery on June 30, 1863, Vice-Chancellor Wood actually held that "It is no infringement of copyright to represent a play dramatised from a novel written by another author; but it is an infringement to print and publish a play so constructed," and he granted "perpetual injunction against the printing and publishing of such a play without any preliminary inquiry as to damages." Mr. Rolt, Q. C., and his associate Mr. Martindale, for Tinsley, had complained that "the published drama is a mere compilation from the novel, with the same leading characters and same incidents and in great part the same actual language," and that "certain ridiculous characters have been introduced which have no connection with the plot or action of the piece, but which mar the effect of the work as a work of genius." They were presumably alluding, for example, to a drunken butler and a drunken footman called Bibbles and Bubbles invented by Suter and introduced into *Lady Audley's Secret*. Counsel quoted Lord Eldon's opinion that to be a legal abridgment the compilation must show "a fair exercise of a mental operation, deserving the character of an original work."

In rebuttal, counsel for Lacy argued that "this case is merely intended as an advertisement. The profit on these two little books [i.e., the printed versions of the Suter plays] amounted to exactly twenty shillings each," and went on to urge: "From the time of Shakespeare it has been the practice for dramatic authors to borrow their plots from published novels. Many of Sir Walter Scott's novels were dramatised, without complaint on his part; and it is obvious that the original author is rather benefitted than injured. . . . These books [i.e., Lacy's printed texts] are sold for the purposes of the theatre and to enable the audience to follow the performance." It was obvious that the play could not "interfere improperly with the sale of the novel."

Giving judgment, the Vice-Chancellor noted that Parliament had not

seen fit "to provide that the works of an author should not be dramatised.
. . . The only way in which an author can prevent other persons from
reciting or presenting as a dramatic performance the whole or any portion
of a work of his composition is himself to publish his work in the form of
a drama." But "it could scarcely be said" that an adapter

> would be at liberty, on the occasion of his recitation or perform-
> ance, to distribute copies of the work for sale among the audience,
> nor could it be any excuse to say that the copies were intended
> merely to assist the audience. . . . Miss Braddon is the author of
> two works of fiction which have proved very interesting from the
> incidents contained in them, and from the manner in which they
> are narrated, and of which a number of editions have been deman-
> ded by the public. These novels being thus popular, Mr. Suter
> took—not, indeed, the whole—but a very large portion of them, or
> at any rate constructed a very large portion of his own dramas out
> of passages taken word for word from the novels. . . . It is no
> answer to say that similar infringements have often been com-
> mitted. Although Sir Walter Scott and other authors did not
> choose to assert any claim of this kind, this does not affect the
> rights of the Plaintiff.

The abridgment arguments were invalid, since "these plays do not pro-
fess to be abridgments of the works of any other author. Still less is there
any analogy to the use which Shakespeare made of the writings of Boc-
cacio [sic] and others."[85]

Yet, despite the importance that Tinsley attributed to the decision (and
John Maxwell too, who many years later referred W. F. Tillotson, the
newspaper proprietor, to it as establishing the law on the subject), the
perpetual injunction gained was more of a moral than a financial victory.
Tinsley's counsel waived the accounting: no damages were sought or
awarded; and, most important of all, the right of pirates to adapt and
stage dramatic versions of a novelist's work was not even at issue.

Even in the smaller area affected—the right to publish such
versions—the decision was apparently not wholly effective. Some
dramatic versions of MEB's novels circulated, as "Privately Printed, not
Published." Though probably illegal, these seem to have gone unchallenged. And in 1865, Lacy printed and published a dramatic version
of MEB's *Henry Dunbar* by Tom Taylor himself, the author of *Still*

Waters Run Deep and the creator of Mrs. Hector Sternhold. The Taylor version of *Henry Dunbar*—which had already been staged at the Ambigu in Paris as *L'Ouvrière de Londres*—was produced at the Royal Olympia Theatre on December 9, 1865.[86] Apparently MEB and Maxwell decided that it was hardly worthwhile to try to prevent the publication of such dramatizations. And so, despite Vice-Chancellor Wood's decision of 1863, MEB was no doubt representing the facts accurately when she said in 1874 that she had never received any money for plays made from her novels.

CHAPTER V

"Can the Sensational Be Elevated by Art, and Redeemed from All Its Coarseness?" (1863–1868)

Could MEB get rich, keeping her public, with its demand for "strong meat," and at the same time become a great novelist, scaling the heights of "poetry" and "truth"? In the wake of the success of *Aurora Floyd*, she came to grips with the problem for the first time. Asking herself why the "sensation" in her novels did not more nearly approach high art, she reluctantly answered that her personal disillusionment with human emotions and her consequent tendency to laugh at the jealousies of disappointed lovers might have rendered her incapable of writing a great romantic novel. Subjectively, she related her own feelings to her powers as an artist.

But for the next three years—1863, 1864, 1865—writing two novels a year, she each time relegated one to the class of pure sensation fiction, content to turn it out as neatly as possible, while giving to the other her best artistic effort. In the second year particularly—1864—she strove anxiously and mightily in *The Doctor's Wife* to achieve high art. When the result proved to some degree disappointing—perhaps because she had set herself too difficult a task in trying to adapt Flaubert's *Madame Bovary* for her prudish readers—she found herself incapable in 1865 of repeating the exercise so intensely. In the six novels of the years 1863–1865 and in her letters to her mentor, Bulwer, about them one can follow this struggle in her artistic life.

In 1866, she tried a new experiment, for the first time abandoning sensation altogether. In *The Lady's Mile* she produced a social novel, full of powerful insights into the world she lived in and illuminating anew—she was still highly subjective—her views about art and about herself. This was the literary high-water mark of her early career.

With the founding of *Belgravia* in 1866 came the heavy new responsibility of editing a popular magazine. She herself was responsible for most of its fictional content. So she reverted to the sensation-novel, successfully challenging Wilkie Collins and for the first time revealing the influence of Balzac. In *Dead Sea Fruit* (1868), she drew upon another—unidentifiable—French source for a story rich in the social ambiguities she had begun to enjoy. But the productive period of the sixties came to an end in November 1868 with a grave illness. The search for its complex causes will lead us into the enemy territory inhabited by the critics of the sensation-novel.

1. *Aurora Floyd,* Henry James, and Bulwer: Art and the Passions

Aurora Floyd has "masses of ebon hair, uncoiled and falling about her shoulders in serpentine tresses that looked like shining blue-black snakes." It is as raven black as Lady Audley's had been golden blonde. And Aurora is a horsey girl. Dazzlingly beautiful in her ball-dress at eighteen, she opens her first conversation with a would-be suitor by asking whether " 'Thunderbolt won the Leger.' " He confesses that he knows " 'no more of Thunderbolt than of King Cheops,' " to which she answers, " 'Cheops wasn't much. He won the Liverpool Autumn Cup in Blink Bonny's year; but most people said it was a fluke.' " Indeed, as a girl Aurora had spent far too much time riding with a groom named Conyers, chosen by her rich banker father "on account of his good looks for Aurora's special service."

Naturally enough this proves to be a mistake. Sent off to finishing school in Paris, Aurora runs away and marries Conyers, leaves him, and falsely assures her father that her husband is dead; and later—upon reading of Conyers' death in a racing accident—accepts the proposal of Bulstrode, a proud aristocrat. When Bulstrode fails to obtain an explanation for Aurora's Paris escapade, he sorrowfully breaks the engagement, and she marries his rival, Mellish, a hearty sporting squire. Conyers had not been killed, only been injured in the accident. He reappears to train Mellish's horses while blackmailing Aurora. At night in Mellish Park, Aurora delivers two thousand pounds in cash to her true husband. A few moments later he is shot dead, and suspicion falls upon her. Her former governess and present housekeeper, jealous of her wealth, tries to ruin her.

But the crime is eventually brought home to one of the most notorious of all the murderers of Victorian fiction, the Softy, a half-witted hanger-on in Mellish's stables, whom Aurora had once—in a celebrated episode—chastised for being cruel to her dog. She

> sprang upon him like a beautiful tigress, and catching the collar of his fustian jacket in her slight hand, rooted him to the spot. . . . Taller than the stableman by a foot and a half, she towered above him, her cheeks white with rage, her eyes flashing fury, her hat fallen off, and her black hair tumbling about her shoulders, sublime in her passion. The man cowered beneath the grasp of the imperious creature.
> "Let me go!" he gasped. . . .
> "How dared you!" cried Aurora. . . . My poor dog! . . . You cowardly dastard! You ————."
> She . . . rained a shower of blows upon his clumsy shoulders with her slender whip; a mere toy, with emeralds set in its golden head, but stinging like a rod of flexible steel in that little hand.
> "How dared you!" she repeated again and again, her cheeks changing from white to scarlet in the effort to hold the man with one hand. Her tangled hair had fallen to her waist by this time, and the whip was broken in half a dozen places.[1]

Having seen Aurora pay off Conyers, the Softy had killed him for the money. After a suitable legal remarriage and a trip abroad to forget, the Mellishes resume their happy married life.

Begun at a moment when MEB had thought she would never return to the interrupted career of Lady Audley, *Aurora Floyd* made similar use of an inconvenient reappearing first husband. But there was nothing in *Lady Audley's Secret* to compare with the scene in which the loose-tressed, passionate, panting, strapping female furiously lashed her cowering male victim with the emerald-studded, gold-headed, flexible steel rod. Probably MEB shared the fantasies of her contemporaries so thoroughly that she could write the scene with comparative innocence. But Wilkie Collins, founder of the sensation-novel, would have been quite incapable of it.

The pages of *Aurora Floyd* are studded with references to *Othello*: even Conyers refers to the pleasure of revenge as what Iago, " 'the chap in the play got for his trouble when the blackamoor murders his wife.' " Like Othello, both Bulstrode and Mellish feel the pangs of jealousy, while the housekeeper plays the part of Iago with thoughts and lines much like his. But Othello succumbs to jealousy and becomes a murderer; Mellish conquers jealousy and remains a happy husband. Iago triumphs; the housekeeper meets defeat. Most important, Desdemona is innocent and yet is killed; Aurora is guilty but gets away scot-free. MEB, we shall see, scorned Othello because he took his suffering so hard, and this cold-eyed view underlay the melodrama of *Aurora Floyd*.

At times MEB allowed Aurora to plead her case: " 'I had only a school-girl's sentimental fancy for his dashing manner, only a school-girl's frivolous admiration of his handsome face. I married him because he had dark-blue eyes, and long eye-lashes, and white teeth, and brown hair. He had insinuated himself into a kind of intimacy with me by bringing all the empty gossip of the race-course. . . . he was always my companion in my rides.' " Mr. Floyd had been reckless in exposing an impetuous young girl to constant association with a groom who "sprang from the mire of the streets like some male Aphrodite rising from the mud . . . a blackleg in the gutter at four years of age, and a 'welsher' in the matter of marbles and hardbake before his fifth birthday." But at other times MEB judged her heroine harshly: when Aurora writes to Conyers to make an assignation to give him the money, she ends the letter: " 'Above all, *express no surprise*——A.' " And MEB added, in a sentence that had an entire paragraph to itself and that ended the chapter, "There was no ordinary conclusion to the letter; no other signature than this big capital A." This was a direct allusion to *The Scarlet Letter*: like Hester Prynne, Aurora is an adulteress. MEB would have enjoyed the realization that few of her readers would catch the reference.

Had she damned Aurora to an early death—the wages of sin—or separated her from her husband and forced her to spend the rest of her life in good works, or even visited upon her continued unhappiness, MEB might have disarmed her critics. But Aurora is not punished. She manages not to have a child by Conyers, or even by Mellish until a suitable time *after* her legal remarriage. With her handsome black-haired baby boy, she continues despite her sins triumphantly to enjoy the good things of this world. Moreover, Aurora, who would have liked to become a missionary in Africa with Dr. Livingstone, is a girl of properly charitable impulses, like Madeline in MEB's unpublished poem or like MEB herself: " 'I have no doubt I assist many people who ought by rights to die in a work-house or on the high-road; but . . . if I stopped to question their deserts, they might die of starvation . . . so perhaps it's better to throw away a few shillings upon some unhappy creature who is wicked enough to be hungry, and not good enough to deserve to have anything given him to eat.' "2

As in Sigismund Smith's first "bound" three-volume novel, the number of corpses in *Lady Audley's Secret* and *Aurora Floyd* was down to one, and the characters were interesting in their own right. MEB's preoccupation with bigamy is at least piquant when one considers the irregularity of her own relationship with John Maxwell. The *Saturday Review* praised "the make of the sentences and the choice of words, the easiness with which the sense is conveyed . . . and the absence of all that is awkward and ponderous" and found that the story aroused a reader's pity and terror, according to Aristotle's formula. "We are kept at the topmost pitch as long as possible; . . . We have a heroine marrying a groom; we have two lovers accepted by the same woman in two successive chapters; and both in the most honourable way and on the highest principles. We have bigamy, murder, divorce, . . . a lady whipping her stableman, criminal trials and horse-racing." Although Miss Braddon "knows all about men and their ways . . . sporting, horses, dog-carts, tobacco, the signs of intoxication, and betting," the critic credited her with "a vein of feeling higher than the world of brandy and water."3

When a new American edition of *Aurora Floyd* appeared in 1865, Henry James, then only twenty-one, reviewed it in *The Nation,* calling MEB "an uncommonly clever person," whose novels were "distinguished by a quality for which we can find no better name than 'pluck.' " Should not "pluck have its reward wherever found?" She had sought "at any hazard to make a hit, to catch the public ear. It was a difficult task, but audacity could accomplish it. Miss Braddon accordingly resorted to extreme measures, and created the sensation novel." By keeping up with "the subtle innovations to which her art, like all others, is subject," and "the equally delicate fluctuations of the public taste," she had steadily improved her style. Wilkie Collins, James wrote, "whose 'Woman in White' . . . was a kind of nineteenth-century version of 'Clarissa Harlowe,' " had first introduced into fiction "those most mysterious of mysteries, the mysteries which are at our own doors. Instead of the terrors of 'Udolpho,' we were treated to the terrors of the cheerful country-house and the busy London lodgings. And there is no doubt that these were infinitely the more terrible." Although crime "has always been a theme for dramatic poets, . . . with the old poets its dramatic interest lay in the fact that it compromised the criminal's moral repose. Where else is the interest of *Orestes* and *Macbeth?*" However, with "Mr. Collins and Miss Braddon (our modern Euripides and Shakespeare) the interest of crime is that it compromises the criminal's personal safety," and "an admirable organization of police detectives" has replaced the "avenging deity." Of course, the nearer the criminal and the detective are brought home to the reader, the more lively his sensation. Both Collins and MEB employed "thorough-going realism."

But Henry James contrasted Wilkie Collins with MEB. Collins had produced "massive and elaborate constructions—monuments of mosaic-work. . . . not so much works of art as works of science. To read 'The Woman in White' requires very much the same intellectual effort as to read Motley or Froude." Wilkie Collins bore the same relationship to Miss Braddon as Samuel Richardson to Jane Austen. Jane Austen founded the novel of "domestic tranquillity," MEB the novel of "domestic mystery." She had begun with

> a skillful combination of bigamy, arson, murder, and insanity . . . all represented in the deeds of Lady Audley, . . . a nonentity, without a heart, a soul, a reason. But . . . her eyes, her hair, her mouth, her dresses, her bedroom furniture, her little words and deeds—are so lavishly bestowed that she successfully maintains a kind of half illusion. Lady Audley was diabolically wicked; Aurora Floyd, her successor, was simply foolish, or indiscreet, or indelicate—or anything you please to say of a young lady who runs off with a hostler.

MEB owed her increasing popularity to novel-readers' constant search for something new and exceptional: "Bigamy, murder, and arson are exceptional. Miss Braddon distributes these materials with a generous hand, and attracts the attention of her public." But to hold the public attention, MEB had to write better than other authors of tales of crime: "Miss Braddon, accordingly, goes to work like an artist." She had read the best writers and had profited by her reading. She had "shrewd observation, and wide experience . . . a turn for colour." She knew well "that disorderly half of society which becomes every day a greater object of interest to the orderly half." MEB

> deals familiarly with gamblers, and betting-men, and flashy reprobates of every description. She knows much that ladies are not accustomed to know, but that they are apparently very glad to learn. The names of drinks, the technicalities of the faro-table,

the lingo of the turf, the talk natural to a crowd of fast men at supper, when there are no ladies present but Miss Braddon, the way
one gentleman knocks another down. These things are the incidents of vice; and vice has its romance. Of this romance Miss
Braddon has taken advantage, and the secret of her success is,
simply, that she has done her work better than her predecessors.
That is, she has done it with a woman's *finesse* and a strict regard
to morality. If one of her heroines elopes with a handsome stable-
boy, she saves the proprieties by marrying him. This may be indecent, if you like, but it is not immoral.

The young Henry James thus produced a friendlier and more
perceptive serious appreciation of MEB than any of her own coun-
trymen.[4] She probably never saw this cleverly analytical tribute, but as
we know, James almost half a century later emphasized his affectionate
recollection of his own youthful addiction to her novels. MEB was
thoroughly aware that many of her characters were what James had called
Lady Audley: "a nonentity, without a heart, a soul, a reason," despite the
lavish detail in which she had "painted" them and their "belongings."
Often, in fact, she took a far harsher view of her writing than he. And she
remained determined to find time to write something better.

When she told Bulwer that she hoped he would consider *Aurora Floyd*
"more boldly written and less artificial" than *Lady Audley's Secret,* she
emphasized his own great influence upon her: "I have never forgotten a
word you said to me, and the hints dropped so kindly for my benefit, but I
daresay forgotten by yourself, have been my guiding principle in almost
everything I have written."[5] After he had congratulated her on *Aurora
Floyd,* she reminded him that he had once told her "that the strongest &
safest point in a story or a play is domestic interest—that is the position
of a man & wife as compared to lovers—. . . every story I have hitherto
written has been built more or less with this idea in my mind." She had
no illusions about her recent good fortune: "Believe me, I feel very little
elated by the superficial success of my pair of Bigamy novels, & the
hardest things the critics say of me never strike me as unjust. I know I
have *everything* to do yet; but it has been my good, or bad, fortune to be
flung into a very rapid market, & to have every thing printed & published
almost before the ink with which it was written was dry." But she
thought perhaps that this had spurred her on, "for my temperament is
unfortunately so terribly lymphatic that I doubt if I should ever write at

all but for the pressure of what racing men call 'heavy engagements.' "
MEB can hardly have believed in her own indolence.

With each successive novel, MEB's letters grew more apprehensive and apologetic: "I doubt if you will like 'Aurora Floyd' any better than her predecessor. . . . but I venture to hope you will think 'John Marchmont's Legacy,' the novel now running in Temple Bar, better written than the other two. . . . I fear I shall never write a *genial* novel. The minute I abandon melodrama, a strong coarse painting in blacks and whites, I am quite lost & at sea." Serial-writing, she said, forced her "into over-strained action in the desire to sustain the interest."[6] And when Bulwer apparently urged her to strive for higher art, she thanked him effusively but without much confidence: "I think when I first knew you I was far nearer the artistic, that is a far worthier pupil for so great a master than I am now. *Then* I could have sat at yr feet for ever, content to waste years upon patient work which should never have seen the light, with the far-away hope of yr saying some day as the great music-master said to his pupil 'Go, my son, I can teach you no more. You can now write a great novel.' "

MEB's very choice of words—"waste years upon patient work"—showed how unwilling she was to strive for a distant perfection instead of capitalizing on the instant success that was at hand. Disillusionment had set in: "I have learned to look at everything in a mercantile sense, & to write solely for the circulating library reader whose palette [sic for palate] requires strong meat, and is not very particular as to the quality." But the old inner conflict had now resumed: "Now *your* kind interest arouses an ambition which was . . . utterly dead . . . I want to be artistic & to please *you*. I want to be sensational, & to please Mudie's subscribers. . . . Can the sensational be elevated by art, & redeemed from all its coarseness?"

Bulwer himself, MEB went on, had answered the question in his own "glorious" series of sensation-novels written many years earlier, including the first of the "Newgate novels," *Paul Clifford* (1830), and *Lucretia* (1846), a fictionalized version of a celebrated poisoning case. These—she did not remind him—had brought down upon him charges of immorality in a torrent of hostile criticism, exactly like that which she herself had already begun to experience. Bulwer's keen interest in MEB's work was surely kept alive not only by his gratification at her almost fawning adulation, but by his pleasure at seeing her in the early sixties revive a genre that he had launched in the early thirties. She acknowledged herself his disciple, hoping to please an elderly man, always prickly, who had now begun to outlive his own enormous popularity. She was beginning to compare her own work with his.

But MEB continued to protest that his achievements were beyond her; by the term a "genial" novel she meant Bulwer's *Caxtons* (1849), a quiet domestic story, which she called "a book to be read forever and for ever, like the New Testament and Shakespeare." This, she was sure, Bulwer himself valued more highly than his own sensational fiction. And soon—perhaps with *The Caxtons* as a distant goal—she declared that she would vary her current reading of Balzac and Soulié by "another and strong pull at the Pierian spring" of Bulwer's own work, beginning with his series of essays then appearing in *Blackwood's Magazine,* soon to be published as *Caxtoniana*. For the moment, she did not even dare to have an appealing book in the house: "I go on grinding and grinding until I feel as if there were nothing left in me but the stalest and most hackneyed of ideas."[7]

The "beautiful letter" from Bulwer suggesting to MEB new principles upon which to base her next novel is lost. But her self-doubts suggest that in it he preached his favorite doctrine of the superiority of the ideal in art to the merely realistic or photographic, the Greek school of sculpture to the Dutch school of painting. "I am a patcher up of sham antiquities as compared to a Grecian sculptor," she replied after having pondered his letter for another month, "a dauber of pantomime scenes, all Dutch metal, glue, and spangles, as compared with a great painter." He had surely also criticized her specifically for not taking seriously enough the jealous torments of Aurora's disappointed lover Bulstrode and her deceived husband Mellish. In responding to this point, MEB—in the most respectful way—reminded Bulwer that he himself had often made his own characters behave without lofty emotion in their love affairs, although she quickly sugar-coated the pill by admiring Eugene Aram and Zanoni for their constancy in love. But even with respect to those two lovers MEB's cynicism won out: it was, she feared, "the halter and the guillotine" that had kept them faithful: Aram was hanged and Zanoni beheaded; so they died before they could grow jaded.

In "trying to explain why" she had "failed to reach a higher tone in Bulstrode and in Mellish," and why she found herself "compelled to get *sensation* in lieu of *poetry* and *truth*," MEB turned inward to her own emotions, and wrote to Bulwer some of the most intimate lines in her surviving correspondence. "I have begun to question the expediency of very deep emotion," she told him, and this state of mind had caused "the flippancy of tone which jars upon your sense of the dignity of art. I can't help looking down upon my heroes when they suffer, because I always have in mind the memory of wasted sufferings of my own." She looked down on Othello for all his anguish, "when by packing his portmanteau and writing a few lines to Desdemona . . . that he had reason to believe her a very wicked woman, and that he had sold his commission, and made his arrangements . . . for the payment of an adequate income to her through the hands of her solicitors, he might have avoided all the bolster and pillow and subsequent dagger business, and lived down his sorrow, . . . perhaps to wonder what he had ever seen in her." As for writing a love story, "We cease to believe in the God when we find he is not immortal," and the art of writing a convincing romance "must die out with the first death of love." This, said MEB flatly, was her own case.

It would perhaps be risky to read too much into this letter: surely it contained an element of self-pity and of MEB's natural wish to excuse her falling short of Bulwer's ideals. But it is tempting to think of it as a personal confession. When passion dies, a novelist can no longer convincingly describe it. When one has "the memory of wasted sufferings" of one's own, it is hard to take seriously the sufferings of one's characters. "Happy the Amy Robsarts and the Haidees who die before their first illusions are worn threadbare,"[8] wrote MEB to a man as intimately familiar with Scott's *Kenilworth* and Byron's *Don Juan* as she.

Perhaps MEB's relationship with John Maxwell had become clouded by some disillusionment. He was a practical man of affairs, not a poet or a romantic lover. If one takes them seriously, the clues in this letter lead to the conjecture that MEB's undoubted attachment for Maxwell sprang primarily from womanly duty and wifely respect rather than from girlish passion. The wasted sufferings to which she refers cannot, therefore, have been those created by the snubs inflicted upon her for her liaison with Maxwell, but must have stemmed from some earlier passionate love affair. Who her lover was and what the circumstances we cannot know. We can be sure it was not Gilby or Sawyer. Nor could she have been thinking of those early indignities inflicted upon her by her delinquent father, Henry Braddon, "his own worst enemy." At twenty-seven, already the mother of two children by Maxwell, MEB felt that deep emotion was no longer expedient. The letter to Bulwer suggests that her past may have been even stormier than one could otherwise have guessed.

2. "That Archetype Is a Perfect Eel": the Struggle for Excellence in Three Pairs of Novels

In each of the successive years 1863, 1864, and 1865, MEB wrote two three-volume novels, deprecating one of the pair and pinning on the other her hope for literary recognition. She told Bulwer that she had "always felt a kind of depression in writing" *Eleanor's Victory* (1863), the first of the three novels that she put into the lower category: "I couldn't rise to the archetype hovering distantly before me."[9] In 1864, she called *Henry Dunbar* "the sloppily-told story of a murderer's adventure," and sent it to Bulwer "only as tribute to the Great Master of my art, quite reconciled to its being cast . . . into limbo." When he enjoyed it, she was surprised and delighted; this proved, she said, that his mind was still boyish.[10] And in 1865, she spoke of *Only a Clod* as a "hand-to-mouth affair."[11] She never asked Bulwer for advice while she was writing any of these three novels, as she often did about the ones she rated more highly.

Of the three, *Only a Clod* warrants no higher appraisal than MEB gave it.[12] *Eleanor's Victory,* however, was hailed by the *Saturday Review* as MEB's best novel, deserting "the familiar field of bigamy" and superior to Wilkie Collins' fiction because it lacked "those solemn announcements . . . by which Mr. Collins compels his reader to understand that the secret which he has invented is unfathomable." Although MEB "could talk of gussets and seams and dress"—woman's things—like a woman, she could also talk of "theatricals, and little Paris dinners, and brandy-and-water, and grisettes, and horses, and dogs"—men's things—like a man.[13] But this favorable notice in a journal which "every tyro dreaded" MEB later discovered she owed to chance: Douglas Cook of the *Saturday* and her Cornish uncle John Braddon were old friends and fishing companions.[14] The novel itself told an improbable story about a girl bent on vengeance, who marries a man she does not love only in order to be certain that she will live near the villain she holds responsible for her father's suicide. Eleanor's victory is her triumph over herself: eventually she abandons the idea of revenge.

Henry Dunbar, one of MEB's greatest financial successes, hinges on a question of identity: an ex-valet, who has had to assume full blame for a forgery committed long before the novel opens, murders his former master, who had passed the forged check. The valet then pretends to be the man he has murdered. Blackmail and a long tense pursuit by detectives render the proceeds of the murder worthless to the criminal. His struggle to keep up the deception, his inability to meet his own daughter, his purchase of a huge fortune in diamonds, which are eventually spilt into the sea, all lend the story an interest transcending its mystery and keep it readable today.[15] But MEB had not yet learned to make action spring from character.

This necessary step in her development as a genuine novelist she first consciously took in *John Marchmont's Legacy*, her preferred novel of 1863. She told Bulwer that she had been pondering deeply his remarks "with regard to a novel in which the story rises naturally out of the characters of the actors in it, as contrasted with a novel in which the actors are only marionettes, the slaves of the story." She had "fancied" that in *John Marchmont's Legacy*, which had just appeared, she had made "the story . . . subordinate to the characters," but the reviewers were denying it.[16]

Yet her efforts had begun to bear fruit. John Marchmont himself, at first the wretched stage "super," inherits a great gloomy country house and a vast fortune. Widowed, tubercular, expecting to die, he marries Olivia Arundel to provide a mother for his daughter Mary. But after Marchmont's death, Mary falls in love with and marries Olivia's cousin, Edward Arundel, whom Olivia had wanted for herself. So the jealous stepmother and the next heir to the property conspire against Mary's life and sanity, and succeed in separating the young couple and in temporarily convincing Edward that Mary is dead. When their plot fails, the frustrated heir burns down Marchmont Towers, with himself and his art collection inside.

The wicked Olivia is the sort of philanthropist that MEB despised. She has "trodden underfoot and trampled out" every "natural womanly vanity" or "simple girlish fancy. . . . The poor people. . . . rheumatic men and women, crippled and bed-ridden," know that "the blankets which covered them had been bought out of money that would have purchased silk dresses." They are "grateful . . . and submissive" but they do not love Olivia: there is "something chilling in the full monotony of her benevolence." Olivia has no favorites, is never "foolishly indulgent or extravagantly cordial." Unchanging, she is "Church of England charity personified; meting out all mercies by line and rule; doing good with a note-book and pencil in her hand; looking on every side with calm, scrutinising eyes, rigidly just, terribly perfect." If only she "could have gone to America, and entered herself among the feminine professors of law or medicine—if she could have turned preacher, and cried to the lost souls wandering in darkness, if she could have set up a printing press in

Bloomsbury, or even written a novel," Olivia would have found an outlet for her repressions. Instead, they explode into passion and savagery. Unlike any of MEB's previous female characters, Olivia Marchmont rings true.

And Edward Arundel, whom Olivia loves and Mary marries, handsome, with a fine military record in India, would have seemed an acceptable hero to MEB's romantic readers. But he often acts recklessly, failing to tell anyone about his marriage to Mary, or to conduct an energetic search for her after she has been kidnapped. He wrings his hands instead, rightly attributing his troubles to " 'my own folly, my own pro-crastination.' " This too MEB credibly made to derive from character. Just before marrying Mary, Edward has said to her: " 'You must never grow older or more womanly, Polly. . . . Remember that I always love you best when I think of you as the little girl in the shabby pinafore [she had been eight years old at the time] who poured out my tea for me one bleak December morning.' " Edward Arundel, soldier-hero, prefers a little girl to a grown woman. MEB was for the first time portraying male sexual inadequacy, a phenomenon to which she would often later return.

In *John Marchmont's Legacy*, the reader encounters no identical twins, no forged wills, few stock properties, and only an incidental corpse. Though the villainy is black indeed, behind it there lies convincing human motivation, to say nothing of eleven thousand pounds a year and Marchmont Towers, a heritage that brings happiness to nobody, that leads to criminal actions, and that finally goes up in flames. Here the hallmarks of future Braddon novels are clearly discernible. Yet MEB's girlhood love of Dickens is still manifest, and Marchmont Towers, deep in Lincolnshire like Chesney Wold, Sir Leicester Dedlock's place in *Bleak House,* enjoys pure Bleak House weather:

> The rain beat down upon the battlemented roof of Marchmont
> Towers . . . as if it had a mind to flood the old mansion. The flat
> waste of grass, and the lonely clumps of trees were almost blotted
> out. . . . The low grey sky shut out the distance. This part of
> Lincolnshire—fenny, misty, and flat always—seemed flatter and
> mistier than usual today. The rain beat hopelessly upon the leaves
> in the wood behind Marchmont Towers, and splashed into great
> pools beneath the trees, until the ground was almost hidden by the
> falling water, and the trees seemed to be growing out of a black
> lake.[17]

Even while she was writing it, *John Marchmont's Legacy* had begun to seem inadequate to MEB. She told Bulwer she was "terribly apt to take a disgust" to the novel in hand, and to concentrate on "a novel I *mean* to write. . . . This unfinished novel always seems to me destined to become my *magnum opus. Je le couve,* as Michelet would say. I can *see* the scenes. I compose the dialogue . . . such lovely passionate outbreaks. I can never write anything half so good, for that Archetype is a perfect eel. . . . There he goes gliding through the turbid waters of the brain, and he is gone."[18] And, when *John Marchmont's Legacy* was finished and work on the next pair of novels only begun, she added: "All the poetry has gone out of my life within the last five or six years, and I fear when I try to call it back for my next story, it will scarcely come." Once again she struck the note of personal disillusionment: she felt that she herself had grown too prosaic to put into her novels the "poetry" that Bulwer was demanding of her. But the elusive "archetype" she now pursued more earnestly than ever before. Into *The Doctor's Wife,* produced simultaneously in 1864 with the little-regarded *Henry Dunbar,* she poured her real energies.

It was scarcely underway in January 1864 when she confided in Bulwer that "for the first time I am going to infuse a touch of poetry into my hero." She was "going in a little for the subjective"[19] and she thought that he would like the novel better than anything she had done yet. By June, she was promising it to Bulwer in October. It was still "unutterably far from what I want to do," although she was giving it more thought and working harder at "character painting" than ever before.[20] She was too anxious now to wait until October for his verdict and during the summer sent him the instalments of *The Doctor's Wife* that had so far appeared serially in *Temple Bar,* and begged him to read it and give his opinion before she completed it. As she said, "I would not ask this favour for any novel, written carelessly, but I have done my best with *this* book."[21]

Even before sending him her incomplete novel, MEB had twice mentioned Flaubert to Bulwer, inquiring whether he had read *Salambbô,* and confessing herself "wonderfully fascinated by that extraordinary pre-Raphaelite style." Professedly striving to "infuse" Bulwerian poetry into *The Doctor's Wife,* she regretfully supposed that Flaubert's "unvarnished realism" was the "very reverse" of what she had been aiming at.[22] But it was Flaubertian realism that triumphed. Bulwer promptly read what she sent him, liked it, and immediately recognized that it was derived from *Madame Bovary,* then only seven years old, and still a scandal in France, while hardly known in England. Deeply grateful for his encouragement, MEB felt "more pleasure and inspired . . . with more earnestness" than she could express.

She admitted her borrowing from Flaubert: "The idea of the Doctor's Wife *is* founded on 'Madame Bovary,' the style of which struck me immensely in spite of its hideous immorality." Flaubert had a power—she again called it "pre-Raphaelite"—to "make manifest a scene and an atmosphere in a few lines—almost a few words" unequalled by other writers, and "even a kind of grim humour equal to Balzac."[23] So this cherished novel—in which she put her memories of the Braddons' hard-pressed life in Camberwell, pictured her own girlhood romanticism in Isabel Sleaford, and commented in the voice of Sigismund Smith on her own writing—she primarily intended as an anglified *Bovary,* a novel of character rather than a novel of sensation, although there was a murder in it.

After Isabel's criminal father has vanished, and she has become a governess, Sigismund Smith's friend, the country doctor, George Gilbert, falls in love with her. Instead of some Byronic lover, she marries George, only to find him stodgy and unimaginative, contented with a drab provincial existence, and unwilling even to give her the money to buy new drawing-room furniture. Soon she encounters Roland Lansdell, a rich young squire and poet, well traveled, a man of many love affairs, slightly jaded. Lansdell is just what the innocent and bored young Isabel has been yearning for. They fall in love, meet clandestinely, exchange books, but nothing illicit occurs between them. Unable to give her up, Lansdell begs her to run away with him. All surprise, Isabel refuses. George Gilbert eventually catches typhoid and dies, without ever having suspected his wife's attachment. But by then Lansdell begins to wonder about Isabel: she borrows money from him, and he sees her talking to a mysterious stranger, who kisses her. It is her father, Sleaford, now a fugitive from justice, for whom she had needed the money. Sleaford recognizes Lansdell as the man whose testimony had sent him to jail and kills him. Isabel inherits Lansdell's fortune and is left to a life of good works, even more oppressive, perhaps, than marriage to the virtuous dull George Gilbert.

Adapting *Madame Bovary* for the middle-class English reader of 1864 presented great opportunities and correspondingly great dangers. Emma Bovary's plight aroused sympathetic vibrations in the heart of every romantic young woman condemned to provincial respectability and deprived of romantic adventure. But Victorian English convention made it impossible for Isabel to follow Emma's example, to run off with Lansdell, or to have an affair with him. This forced MEB into inconsistencies, as she labored so conscientiously to portray real character.

At first, Isabel seems a credibly appealing romantic girl, but after she had fallen in love with Lansdell MEB had to make her simple enough to believe that he would continue to love her indefinitely without expecting any sexual return. She had to be appalled at the discovery that he wanted her to run off with him. So, although she had been steeped in Byron and Bulwer since childhood, Isabel had to become—and after marriage at that—preternaturally innocent and bland. At first, George Gilbert seems intelligent, agreeable, and attractive enough to gain Isabel for his wife. But the *Bovary* plot forced MEB to transform him after marriage into a dull, unresponsive, and insensitive provincial. As for Lansdell, a practiced rake, MEB had to make him at times so respectful of Isabel's chastity that he seems either ready to give her up or to confine himself to mawkish expressions of admiration. The evidence on which he begins to suspect her virtue and loyalty would have been quite inadequate for so experienced a man.

Unlike Emma Bovary, Isabel could commit no adultery, yet her mere romantic affection for a man not her husband had necessarily to bring down upon her a dreadful punishment. To write a novel of character that would satisfy herself and please Bulwer, while simultaneously telling Flaubert's story without offending the moral sensibilities of the English critics, posed an almost impossible dilemma for MEB: "I do dread the things that will be said of 'The Doctor's Wife,' but I can most solemnly vouch for the purity of my own intention," she told Bulwer when sending him the still unfinished novel. She wanted to show "the fatal error" of a marriage too hastily entered upon. In Roland Lansdell, she was portraying "the utter uselessness or barrenness of all gifts that are not supported by the power of truth." But she felt this to be beyond her, and she seemed "to stop short on the threshold of it." She had made Lansdell "weak & vacillating—always oscillating between good and evil, because a better man would not suit my purpose as well." The critics who "have pelted me with the word 'sensational,' & who will gird at me so long as I write a line" would attack her in any case; so she was not thinking of them as she wrote.

It was the forthcoming August 1864 instalment of the novel as it would appear in *Temple Bar* in which MEB said that "my story gets very critical, and the scenes which should be the best and most powerful are I fear weak."[24] In this number Roland, unable to stay away from Isabel, returns to pursue her, and Isabel fails to realize that "the blossoming pathway along which she wandered hand in hand with Roland Lansdell was all downhill, and that there was a black and hideous goal hidden below in the farthermost valley." He is preparing to carry her off, but she cannot understand what he intends, and is inexpressibly shocked to hear that he wants her to become his "——mistress!"[25] Of course she refuses, and Roland is astonished at her naiveté and unhappy at her decision.

A fan letter from an Irish lady reassured MEB that her public approved of this moral but inartistic dénouement. "I am so *sorry* for Roland and Isabel but I am sure you are right, and it would never do to sacrifice public opinion for the sake of ideal [i.e., imaginary] characters, though you make them so *real*, one feels sure they are living and loving and suffering somewhere." If Isabel and Roland "may not be happy together," she went on, "I only trust Roland doesn't marry [his jealous cousin] Lady Gwendoline, that would be *too much*. May I thank you very gratefully for all the pleasant hours and great enjoyment you have given me. . . . I only hope you won't leave off writing for many years to come."[26]

So despite our modern doubts, MEB's own readers deeply believed that Roland and Isabel were "*real*." Yet she worried greatly about both of them. "I am so afraid," she told Bulwer, "of making Roland Lansdell unmanly, or ungentlemanly. I want him to be a gentleman whatever he is—but I want also to show the wide difference between a man's love & a woman's sentimental fancy, which is utterly out of the region of a man's comprehension," except for Bulwer himself and Dickens, who, she hastily added, had never "described a purely sentimental woman" as Bulwer had in *Zanoni*. MEB said that Isabel's past reading had been "all in the region of romance, and, unbalanced by *graver* books," it had "produced the exaltation which poetry must always produce." Reminding Bulwer of an episode in his own *Caxtons*, where the father sends his son to read biography, MEB said that "Isabel has been revelling in light, & colour & music, & it is the calm gray twilight of biography & history, & philosophy that I fancy lulling that eager sentimental nature to repose."[27]

She had wrestled seriously with the task of making her characters ring true. Bulwer reassured her, and she soon responded that she was:

> especially anxious about this novel; as it seems to me a kind of
> turning point in my life, on the issue of which it must depend

whether I sink or swim. I am not a bit tired of writing, & feel rather as if I had scarcely begun yet in real earnest, but have been only squaring my elbows—very inelegant by the bye—and trying my pens, with just a few false starts. But I feel every day more ignorant & life seems so short, & literature so long. And again I am always divided between a noble desire to attain something like excellence—and a very ignoble wish to earn plenty of money.[28]

So far, of course, Bulwer had not seen the end of *The Doctor's Wife,* which indeed had not yet even been written.

But when it appeared in book form in October 1864, he did not like the ending and apparently suggested that it would have been better had MEB not killed off Isabel's husband, George Gilbert. She accepted his criticism gracefully:

> I most entirely agree with what you say about the close of the "D. W." I was cruelly hurried in writing it, and only towards the last decided upon what I should do with George and Isabel. I always meant Sleaford to kill Roland, but to the last I was uncertain what to do with George. My original intention was to have left him alive, & Isabel reconciled to a commonplace life doing her duty bravely, and suppressing all outward evidence of her deep grief for Roland. Thus the love story would have been an episode in a woman's life, succeeded by an after-existence of quiet work and duty. I think now it is too late. I might have done much better with the story in this way, but I am so apt to be influenced by little scraps of newspaper criticism, & by what people say to me. And I sometimes fancy I am like one of those unprofitable racehorses that "shut up at the finish."

In general, Bulwer recommended that MEB should draft the third and last volume of a novel immediately after finishing the first, in order to avoid haste and fatigue at the dénouement, and then return to fill in the middle and less dramatic second volume. This MEB called a "most valuable hint . . . I saw at once what an advantage it would be to write a novel in that manner, and if I can *possibly* get time in advance for the work, I will write my very next story in that way." He also seems to have objected to George Gilbert having died of typhoid, a mere accident not arising from any element in the character of any of the personages in the novel. To this MEB rejoined, "That question about the inadmissibility of accident in art is always terribly perplexing to me. Why not admit accident in a story, when almost all the great tragedies of real life hinge upon accident?" Her uncle, William Braddon, the Bengal merchant and judge, she told Bulwer, "was murdered in his bed because he refused to give a false character to a Swiss butler . . . the merest accident. I know of so many tragedies that seem to have arisen out of accident, & yet I feel that you are right, and that art must be something above the experience of real life."

While writing *The Doctor's Wife,* MEB had been "nervous" and "anxious," hoping desperately that it would be a "turning point" in her career. Now the "master of her craft," who had praised the novel when it was in progress, found the ending faulty. It must have been especially daunting that he should *now* have advised her to write a "novel of character," when this was exactly what she thought she had been doing, and had indeed actually done. Yet even to this she only responded that she felt "especially flattered" by the suggestion.[29] In her answer to Bulwer's criticisms, she showed herself modest, cool, and thoroughly professional, betraying no sign of the disappointment she must have felt. With no discouragement or rancor, she was looking forward to the next attempt.

Two of the important reviewers were kind, the *Saturday* thanking MEB for her "indefatigable efforts" to amuse the public. Like an "acrobat upon the high rope," her feats caused "far more giddiness to the breathless spectator beneath than to the cool and practiced performer overhead." And *The Doctor's Wife* was, the reviewer declared, "in the fullest sense a novel of character," a "path of art new and comparatively untried" for MEB. The critic found Isabel "wholly consistent from first to last," and rejoiced that MEB's talents were now being "applied in a . . . more wholesome direction, and reaching a point of moral elevation which . . . shows her . . . capable of real excellence in the highest and purest walks of art."[30] When she read this article, MEB must have felt the irony of having an anonymous stranger find in *The Doctor's Wife* exactly what she had vainly hoped Bulwer would find; yet she must also have realized that she had succeeded in her efforts to bowdlerize Flaubert.

The *Spectator,* so often hostile, also declared that *The Doctor's Wife* was indeed a novel of character, whose "whole interest"—despite the presence of a criminal and of a murder—centered in "the inner life of a girl gifted with a romantic imagination, but whose outer surroundings are of the most ordinary kind." MEB had "displayed quite unexpected power." There was "some beauty in the dowdy figure" of Isabel Sleaford, "and a kind of poetry lurking in the over-heated silly imagination." The scene in which she decided *not* to flee with Roland is "one of the ablest we ever read . . . Miss Braddon has at last contributed something to fiction which will be remembered." MEB would now be introduced "into houses where her novels have not hitherto been seen." Only a "little more pains, a little more time, a little more of the lovingness with which the author has painted single scenes, and Isabel might have" joined those heroines of English literature who—like Scott's Flora in *Rob Roy*, Jane Austen's Emma, and Thackeray's Becky Sharp—had become "real figures" instead of mere characters in fiction.[31]

Despite its great debt to Flaubert—unrecognized by these reviewers— *The Doctor's Wife* was by far the best novel MEB had yet written. George Moore portrayed Kate Ede, heroine of his second novel, *A Mummer's Wife* (1885), reading *The Doctor's Wife* ("a novel in which the lady with the oval face used to read Shelley to the handsome baronet, while her husband was away doctoring the country folk"), and in his *Confessions of a Young Man* Moore told of his own early enthusiasm for it. *The Doctor's Wife* may have suggested to Thomas Hardy some characteristics of Eustacia Vye in *The Return of the Native* (1878), and even, it has been argued, "both major plots" of George Eliot's *Middlemarch* (1872).[32] MEB must have known that she had come closer to capturing the eel-like "archetype" than ever before. But was the anguish worth the effort, especially as it seemed to make no difference to her sales, and as Bulwer had not been "satisfied"? She showed her discouragement by continuing to work against time, not giving her work the "little more lovingness" for which the *Spectator* had asked.

She virtually admitted as much when she accepted Edmund Yates's invitation to contribute *Sir Jasper's Tenant*, the more important novel of her 1865 pair, to *Temple Bar*, semijocularly offering him, as we saw, a mere collection of "bits of old glass and pins and rubbish." So even this novel,[33] on which she lavished far more attention than she ever thought of devoting to the lightly regarded *Only a Clod*, was never intended primarily as a novel of character like *The Doctor's Wife*. MEB now felt herself directly competing with Wilkie Collins, whose *Armadale* was simultaneously appearing in *The Cornhill Magazine*, "a most powerful opponent," whom she could only "fight with his own weapons, mystery, crime, etc." She apologized to Bulwer that she was "obliged to sink her own inclinations in deference to the interests of *Temple Bar*," but one senses that her regret was rather perfunctory. Although she promised to give herself a three-month course in Bulwer and Balzac, "and it will go hard with me if I do not make some progress,"[34] there is no evidence of their influence in *Sir Jasper's Tenant*. She said she wanted "to make the story one of character—and incident also—" but protested that she had to consider her public, "which demands strong meat." With "very little leisure for the concoction" of her plot, she would simply do her best "to build a decent house out of second-hand bricks."[35]

Clearly on the defensive and edgy after her disappointment in *The Doctor's Wife*, she commented to Bulwer rather cattily on *Armadale* that Wilkie Collins was "too openly and inartistically sensational." He was "telling his story too rapidly" instead of letting his plot develop gradually, had not introduced any "female interest," and was falling far short of that "delicious puzzle," *The Woman in White*.[36] She was also keeping a wary eye on Dickens, whose *Our Mutual Friend* was appearing in monthly parts. She thought he was "getting into a muddle" with it, and that it would not be as good as *Little Dorrit* or *Great Expectations*: "We cannot believe in any of the characters, and I can perceive . . . the force of what you said about the very wealth of Dickens' imagination sometimes carrying him too far."

Probably the wish to flatter Bulwer, vain, aging, and sensitive to his own loss of public favor, in part at least underlay MEB's deprecation of Collins and Dickens—she also told him, for example, that "in construction, poetry, the whole art of story-telling," Balzac was "entirely deficient, where you are so eminently great"—but her own anxiety over improving the circulation of Maxwell's *Temple Bar* against such formidable rivals was clear enough, as was her fatigue and depressed resignation to haste and mediocrity:

> I am working very hard, and have just finished the first 30 pages of my eighth three-volume novel, "Sir Jasper's Tenant." . . . It is to be all the old sort of thing—mystery—and murder & so on—written with a view to the popular market. . . . I shall try to observe your canon as to the exclusion of all accidental agency. . . . When one has two sets of Dramatis Personae [the other being those of *Only a Clod*] to keep moving from month to month, the mind is apt to get rather foggy.[37]

Not surprisingly, *Sir Jasper's Tenant* depends on identical wicked twin sisters, one of whom dies, while the other assumes her identity in order to collect an allowance from her twin's estranged husband. This unfortunate man, George Pauncefort, believing that his wife is still alive, cannot marry the girl he loves. He does write her a long letter—filling one hundred and thirty-five pages of the second volume—telling the tragic story of his early entrapment by the twin he had unluckily married. Parallel to the hackneyed plot in high life there runs an unlikely one, packed with comic incident, in the servants' hall. In *Sir Jasper's Tenant,* MEB's efforts to portray character were limited to Sir Jasper Denison himself, a fractious self-indulgent semi-invalid and esthete, reminiscent of Wilkie Collins's hypochondriacal Mr. Fairlie in *The Woman in White,* a stock figure derived from the tradition of comedy.

Its prose full of "bits of bombast which actors thirty years ago delighted in,"[38] MEB's novel elicited from Bulwer a severe criticism of the long interpolated letter from Pauncefort. In self-abasement, MEB agreed that the letter had been "an entire mistake from the first word to the last." Having intended at first that Pauncefort should "*tell* his story in a few broken sentences," she had changed her mind in order to throw some light on his past. It was "inexcusable carelessness"; her hand was "too weak to hold" the character of Pauncefort; she had hoped he would please Bulwer, but now feared that she could "never describe, much less create, a great or good man," but just keep on writing "by the mile" about villains "or villainesses." She had come to "doubt if I shall ever write an artistic novel—or a novel that will *satisfy* you," but still hoped to do better, and at least "succeed in pleasing you."[39] So despite the real excellence of *The Doctor's Wife,* MEB's high hopes were temporarily dashed, and in *Sir Jasper's Tenant* she failed to rise above mechanical ingenuity.

3. "Your Ideal Artist Is Above Envy and Above Despair": *The Lady's Mile* (1866)

Yet MEB quickly rebounded from her defeat and from her relapse into her old ways. The year 1866 she devoted largely to *The Lady's Mile,* in which she abandoned murder and mystery and produced her first purely social novel. Without even a single corpse, it owed nothing to Flaubert or to any other great master. And while her plot, which consisted simply of three interrelated love stories, may have been derivative and is certainly not noteworthy, for the first time plot in itself had little importance. She broke away from the genre she had invented, and in her first attempt at a new one she achieved a signal success. The theme, and the characters she invented to play upon its variations, were arrestingly and convincingly presented. Moreover, she used it in an unprecedented way as a vehicle for her ideas about her own life, about society, and about art.

While she was writing *The Lady's Mile*, she said little about it to Bulwer, and when she did mention it, she did so deprecatingly. It was a "light social life novel," and though she would "try to bring to bear upon it all the force of" his "kind advice," the subject was "flimsy, and can only be elevated by touches of majestic pathos, which I fear may prove beyond my reach."[40] She said that Tinsley, her former publisher, had once commented on a novel he had published, that it was " 'about a parcel of people who ain't worth putting into a novel!' and I really am afraid you will think the characters of my 'Lady's Mile' a 'parcel of people.' " She doubted whether Bulwer would much like the book.[41]

The Lady's Mile itself was the celebrated carriage and bridle-path in Hyde Park. MEB used it in part to symbolize the treadmill of fashionable gaieties, in their unvarying recurring round from A to B and back again. Her unfashionable readers might console themselves with the thought that the wealth and social success they had been longing for would bring them only boredom, while her fashionable ones might be prodded into admitting that the luxuries and lavish parties they took for granted were after all frightfully dull. Beyond this, she explicitly used the Lady's Mile to represent the restricted lives of Victorian women. She put the comparison into the mouth of Sigismund Smith (now Smyth), her fictional recreation of her professional self, now reappearing two years after his first incarnation in *The Doctor's Wife*:

> "The lives of women of the present day are like this drive which they call the Lady's Mile. They go as far as they can, and then go back again. See how mechanically the horses wheel when they reach the prescribed turning-point. If they went any farther, I suppose they would be lost in some impenetrable forest depth in Kensington Gardens. In the drive the rule has no exception; because, you see, the barrier that divides the park from the gardens is a palpable iron railing, which the stoutest hunter might refuse. But on the highway of life the boundary-line is not so clearly defined. There are women who lose themselves in some unknown region beyond the Lady's Mile, and whom we never hear of more. . . . let us pity those benighted wanderers whose dismal stories are to be found amongst the chronicles of the

Divorce Court, whose tarnished names are only whispered by scandal-loving dowagers between the acts of an opera or in the pauses of a rubber. On this side, the barrier they pass seems so slight a one—a hedge of thorns that are half hidden by the gaudy tropical flowers that hang about them—a few scratches and the boundary is passed: but when the desperate wanderer pauses for a moment on the other side to look backward, behold! the thorny hedge-row is transformed into a wall of brass that rises to the very skies, and shuts out earth and heaven."[42]

Sigismund's powerful metaphor about the rigid limits that social convention imposed upon the lives of mid-nineteenth-century women was immediately applicable to MEB herself. Nobody knew better than she how slight seemed the barrier a woman had to pass on the highway of life in order to find her name bandied about by scandal-mongers. She was experiencing at the time the consequences of Richard Brinsley Knowles's denials that her marriage was valid. These had been publicized well beyond the small circle which already knew that the first Mrs. Maxwell was alive and that MEB's own three children were illegitimate. Having passed the tenuous barrier in her own life, MEB herself had seen the "thorny hedge-row . . . transformed into a wall of brass." Into the poetic and tragic speech of her male alter ego she put something of her own agonizing experience.

But even if a woman dutifully stuck to the prescribed paths she could only go to the end and then come back again. " 'See how mechanically the horses wheel when they reach the prescribed turning-point,' " said Sigismund. A woman was damned if she did and damned if she didn't. MEB was thus doubly damned: having incurred social ostracism, she found herself in her moods of depression still bound to the treadmill of her writing schedule, kept up to the mark by her "taskmaster" John Maxwell, unable to take the necessary time for the novels she wanted to write. The "poetry had gone out" of her life, and *The Lady's Mile* can plausibly be read as voicing her indignation at her own predicament.

Of the three women in the novel, two narrowly miss crossing the barrier. Lady Cecil Chudleigh, married on the rebound to a kind-hearted successful barrister, whose "crimson bag" full of legal papers accompanies him everywhere and whose conversation deals only with the law courts,[43] agrees to run away with her former lover, an army officer, now widowed. Only a lecture—ostensibly about a friend of his—delivered by the barrister to the would-be elopers, expatiating vividly on the impossibly isolated life that faces those who have established an illicit connection, drives the seducer away and saves the marriage. But Cecil is back on the Lady's Mile again: in the very last sentence of the novel, her husband has returned to his legal briefs, as uncommunicative and unsatisfactory a lover as ever.

Cecil's friend, Florence Crawford, a hard-bitten girl who cares only for fashionable elegance, daughter of a successful painter, refuses the hardworking young artist whom she loves, in order to marry the son of a Manchester millionaire. Her husband, a sullen boor, keeps a mistress and hires a detective to procure the evidence that will enable him to divorce his wife. Florence escapes social death only because of her husband's sudden financial ruin and suicide. The third heroine, a rich young widow, once sold into a hateful marriage, does not wish to sacrifice her freedom a second time by marrying William Crawford, the great painter, Florence's father. She relents only when he is threatened by blindness, the result of overwork undertaken to deaden his pain at her refusal to marry him.

MEB's fashionable people live in luxury. One of Florence's dresses is "dark-grey poplin . . . looped up on each side, revealing a glimpse of a scarlet-cloth petticoat, a pair of miraculous boots, and the faintest scintillation of grey-silk stockings. Her hair was tied in a clustering knot, . . . the perfection of artistic carelessness, and one little bit of turquoise-blue ribbon peeped from among the gold-coloured tresses." Another girl's hat " 'cost two guineas and a half. . . . A ruche of peacock's feathers, you know dear; and the sweetest mother-of-pearl butterfly, and a tiny, tiny green chenille birds-nest, with three gold eggs in it, at the side.' " It is almost worth selling one's self for a wardrobe that included such marvels. And as *her* price, the rich young widow now proudly possesses a house near the park, "the maximum of earthly bliss. . . . a long glazed corridor, where there were hot-house flowers whose waxen petals glimmered whitely amidst foliage of dark shining green; . . . at the extreme end two marble figures seemed to keep guard over a pair of dark-green velvet doors, which divided the corridor from the inner sanctuary." One of the statues is "the Genius of Night, with starry veil and extinguished torch; the other, a Silence, with lifted fingers pressed upon closed lips." In the rather small entrance hall "a Persian carpet . . . covered the centre of the floor. . . . yet more pale exotics and antique bronzes loomed duskily through the shade. Curtains of soft-grey silk shrouded a doorway . . . into the drawing room, where there were again dark foliage and starry-white blossoms in the shade of the grey-silk curtains lined with a pale-rose colour, and where two white Angora cats were sleeping peacefully amidst the fleecy fur of a huge polar-bearskin spread upon the hearth."[44]

Subtly but decisively, MEB in *The Lady's Mile* rejected the conventional heroes of Victorian fiction: her brave officer sells his commission and leaves the army in order to pursue another man's wife; her learned barrister is a loud-mouthed, shop-talking slave to his profession, her manufacturer a loutish animal despite his Eton education. Only the painters—William Crawford, the accomplished man who is Florence's father, and Philip Foley, the beginner who is Florence's rejected suitor—emerge with honor for their high professional standards and their high moral character. It is they who are the real heroes of *The Lady's Mile*. And into her account of them MEB put her ideas not only about painting but about the life of the artist and its trials, including the agonies caused by the attacks of ignorant and prejudiced critics. These passages surely portray her own ordeals as a writer.

Often before *The Lady's Mile* MEB had introduced paintings into her novels: the "pre-Raphaelite" portrait of Lady Audley, Dick Thornton's scenery in *Eleanor's Victory*. Once—also in *Eleanor's Victory*—intending a sardonic commentary on public taste, she had described at length a pre-Raphaelite painting "called 'The Earl's Death,' from a poem of Tennyson's, with the motto, 'Oh, the Earl was fair to see.' " It shows a "preternaturally ugly man lying at the feet of a preternaturally hideous woman, in a turret chamber lighted by Lucifer matches, the blue and green light of the Lucifers on the face of the ugly woman, and a pre-Raphaelite cypress seen through the window." Ugly though it is, "people went to see it again and again, and liked it, and . . . talked of it perpetually all that season; one faction declaring that the lucifer-match effect was the most delicious moonlight, and the murderess of the Earl the most lovely of womanhood, till the faction who thought the very reverse of this became afraid to declare their opinions, and thus everybody was satisfied."[45]

And in *Henry Dunbar,* an old-fashioned English painter, whose own son is a pre-Raphaelite, attacks the new school briskly:

> "No pre-Raphaelite theories in those days, sir; no figures cut out of coloured paste-board and glued on to the canvas; no green trees and vermillion draperies, and chocolate-coloured streaks across the ultramarine background, sir; and I'm told the young people call that a sky. No pointed chins and angular knees and elbows and frizzy red hair, sir, and as frizzy as a blackamoor's—and I'm

told the young people call that female beauty. No, sir, nothing of that sort in my day. There was a French painter in my day, sir, called David, and there was an English painter in my day called Lawrence, and they painted ladies and gentlemen, sir; and they instituted a gentlemanly school, sir. And you put a crimson curtain behind your subject, sir, and you put a brand-new hat or a roll of paper, in his right hand, and you thrust his left hand in his waistcoat pocket—the best black satin sir, with a strong light on the texture—and you made your subject look like a gentleman. Yes sir, if he was a chimney-sweep when he went into your studio, he went out of it a gentleman. . . . I am told there is a young man called Millais, sir, and another young man called Holman Hunt, sir, positive boys, sir; actually very little more than boys, sir;—and I'm given to understand that when these young men's works are exhibited in the Royal Academy . . . people crowd around them, and go raving mad about them; while a gentlemanly portrait of a country member, with a Corinthian pillar and a crimson curtain gets no more attention than if it was a bishop's half-length of black canvas."[46]

One of the best touches in *Sir Jasper's Tenant* is the elderly Sir Jasper's "painterly" appreciation of female charms in terms of Etty and Rubens. He makes what must have seemed risqué references to the luscious villainess: her "flesh tints are finer than Etty's. I should give five or six hundred pounds for an example of Etty without the dress!" The educated reader instantly sees the lady naked; MEB had already dwelt upon her voluptuous figure, bare arms, and "demi-toilette." When he has to give her up, Sir Jasper comments resignedly that her " 'flesh lately has not been quite up to the mark. There has been a woolliness about the cheeks and a want of feeling in her chin which considerably deteriorated my enjoyment of her society.' "[47]

But never before *The Lady's Mile* had MEB made painters and painting play the central roles in one of her novels. By 1866, she had become a close personal friend of Frith, who had painted her the year before, and who jocularly called her "Lady Audley" or "Aurora" or "Doctor's Wife" in their correspondence. As the portrait neared completion, he begged her for one more sitting so that he might give it the finishing touches that his own teacher had called " 'the little more or less imperceptible to your eyes.' " After all, he and she were "to go hand in hand to posterity." Without naming him, she had referred to him in *John Marchmont's*

Legacy in 1863 as the "greatest painter of the time, [who] lived in a miserable lodging in Chelsea. It was before the days of . . . 'Derby Day.' " And in *Circe,* which she would publish pseudonymously in 1867, Frith appears as "Mr. Skith, R. A. with his handsome wife and daughters," a "popular painter" who is also a "genial and pleasant man." MEB dedicated *The Lady's Mile* itself to Landseer, as a "humble tribute to his genius."[48]

William Crawford, "a painter in the highest and grandest sense," has struggled long for his success: "Year after year . . . his pictures came back . . . from the Academy . . . rejected! rejected! rejected! . . . then appeared a gorgeous Rubens-like canvas, wheron Pericles reclined at the feet of Aspasia: and in a day, in an hour, . . . the world knew that William Crawford was a great painter. . . . He had no secret except his genius . . . unremitting industry, undeviating temperance." He has designed his own house in Kensington, "a dazzling white palace," with a pair of Roman marble fountains, an "Italian façade," and an "Alhambra-like colonnade at the back." His "noble tapestried painting-room" is "rich . . . in black oak cabinets and stamped-leather cushioned chairs, coloured marbles and mediaeval armour, majolica vases, and Venetian glass." Even the fashionable now ask him to dinner: " 'Mr. Crawford is a nice sort of person to have, you know. . . . for there is such a rage about these painter people just now, and I hear the prices he gets for his pictures are *something fabulous.*' "

In describing Crawford's mistreatment at the hands of his hostile critics, MEB was really writing about herself. Some of them had been "besotted enough" to accuse Crawford of "sensualism," a charge often leveled against MEB. Other "funny little writers . . . wrote facetious little criticisms upon the great man's pictures. His Cupid had the mumps, his Psyche was in the last stages of scarlet fever, his Alcibiades was a butcher's boy, his Timandra a scorbutic shrew, his Boadicea a prize-fighter disguised in female raiment." These were men "who could not have sketched the outline of a pumphandle correctly." But Crawford meekly accepts "just" criticism from people who know their subject. He is "not too proud to believe that he could have done better if he had 'taken more pains.' " This sort of criticism is a fine "tonic for the true worker."

When encouraging his disciple Foley, Crawford reminds him of Bulwer's novel, *Zanoni,* in which the student who seeks to become an initiate in the occult is " 'arrested at the outset by a hideous spectre that haunted the threshold of the shadowy temple.' " For Crawford, the "Dweller on the Threshold" had been " 'toil and poverty, failure and humiliation. He has dressed himself in the clothes of the hanging-committee, and has rejected my pictures; he has made himself an art-critic, and has demolished me in a malevolent criticism. In every form I have encountered him, and have mastered him—only because I loved my art better than I loved myself.' " Crawford recalls that Benjamin Robert Haydon, the painter who had gone mad and in 1846 committed suicide, had rejoiced, " 'With an execution in his house, and a cook dunning him for her wages, that there was one person left in the world to paint big classical unsaleable pictures.' " That " 'poor fellow was a real artist. . . . Your ideal artist is above envy and above despair.' " Admonishing Foley, Crawford urges him to persevere.

So MEB pilloried the critics who persistently accused her of sensualism and scoffed at her; but she welcomed the helpful adverse critic—Bulwer—who suggested that she take "more pains." When MEB made Crawford mention *Zanoni*, Bulwer's own favorite among his earlier novels, she was trying to please Bulwer himself. Moreover, the aesthetic theory of the ideal that Crawford was urging upon Foley echoed one of *Zanoni*'s chief themes. And the relationship between Crawford and Foley was parallel to the relationship between Bulwer and herself. He had encouraged her and sustained her, and she sometimes signed her letters to him as his "humble disciple." The initial harsh critical rejection that painters like Crawford and Foley must experience and overcome was also the fate of writers like MEB, whose critics in 1866 were growing ever more savage. Her Dweller on the Threshold was there to be wrestled with and conquered.

In *The Lady's Mile*, MEB took a conservative aesthetic position, reserving her admiration for Crawford's great paintings. There is nothing pre-Raphaelite about his "Dido and Aeneas." Dido is "no beautiful doll, but a living, breathing woman, sublimely lovely in her womanly anguish." MEB liked a painting that reproduced things exactly as they were. In this one, "the atmosphere was not of Kensington but of Carthage. It was evening; and athwart barbaric pillars you saw the sun going redly down behind a waveless sea, while far above, dim stars glimmered in an opal-tinted sky. A faint, languorous mist crept over the purple distance; . . . . The tesselated pavement upon which [Dido] knelt was inlaid with mother-of-pearl and gold, ... The gaudy plumage of strange birds made a confusion of colours amidst the purple cushions. . . ." And as for the "Cupid and Psyche," over which Crawford had so toiled that he almost went blind, the two "lay asleep . . . divinely innocent. . . . A crowd of zephyrs holding one another by the hand, have come to peep. . . . They float on a wandering ray of moonlight, they hover in aerial circles . . . ethereal beings, transparent as waterdrops against a moonlit sky, with sweet arch faces and gauzy wings."[49]

These were pieces of fashionable "word-painting" of the sort that could be counted on to win the approval of Victorian readers and literary critics, but one cannot help conjecturing that the down-to-earth MEB had her tongue firmly in her cheek. If, however, she was serious, she totally failed to see that the very pictures whose triumph she was proclaiming were the natural adjunct, and indeed the reflection, of precisely the society whose false, new-rich standards she was simultaneously denouncing. Such obtuseness in her would be hard to credit; it seems more plausible that, while she was eager enough to show the faults of Victorian social attitudes to those readers who might be interested in something more than her plot, she was very careful not to embrace aesthetic values more advanced than those of her public.

Bulwer broke a social engagement and gave up "a whole Sunday evening" to read *The Lady's Mile*. MEB told him that she was delighted "to think you should have read my flimsy story, and that it should have amused you." But he had obviously gone on to comment on her "want of earnestness." By now he was sixty-three, and perhaps he saw in the thirty-year-old MEB the flippancy of one of the younger generation. She said she could explain it in many ways. For the past five years, she had "lived chiefly among practical people—very clever but entirely unpoetic." When she read a book of Bulwer's or a poem of Shelley's, "sentiment" returned to her mind "for a few moments"; but otherwise she was struck by "the ridiculous side of things" rather than the poetic. When she had recently listened to some of the best of Racine read aloud, "the tragedy seemed to touch the borders of caricature": she was more inclined than not to laugh. And then too, she never had time to get herself "in *tone*" for her work. "Tormented by all sorts of petty cares, and always impressed by the ever-present idea that I ought to write so many pages before I dine," she sat down each day to her desk. Greatness, she feared, depended on loneliness, and even if she could, she would not pay that price.[50]

Surely, by the "practical," "clever," and "entirely unpoetic" people surrounding her MEB meant pre-eminently John Maxwell. Bulwer as yet knew nothing of her circumstances, her five stepchildren, her three children, her multitude of domestic duties, her ambiguous social position. Earlier, she had freely told him of her past "wasted sufferings" and her distrust of passion, perhaps reflections of an occasional mood of disillusionment with her choice of a partner. Now she ascribed her failure to rise to poetic heights, her lack of "earnestness," and her inclination to laugh at circumstances and speeches designed to be tragic, to the same unpoetic, workaday, practical "people."

In her excuses to Bulwer, as in her repeated declarations of her wish to achieve greater artistry in her writing, the lady may have been protesting too much. While she did want to keep the interest and support of the great man, she may never have been quite as determined to follow his advice as she kept on assuring him that she was. Yet however strong may have been the element of self-exculpation or even of deception in MEB's letters to him, there was surely also a large element of truth in what she said of her feelings about her career and her private life. John Maxwell was not the most sympathetic yokefellow imaginable for an aspiring artist. Yet *The Lady's Mile*—MEB's first "social life novel"—proved neither "light" nor "flimsy." It was her best novel so far and contained in embryo many elements of her "new manner" that would later puzzle the critics whenever she abandoned the sensation stories that they insisted were all that she could write.

4. "This Fellow Balzac Knows Better": *Belgravia* and the Return to Sensation (1867–1868)

For some years, *The Lady's Mile* was destined to remain a unique experiment, because by the summer of 1866 John Maxwell—who had sold *Temple Bar* in January—had decided to found a new monthly magazine, *Belgravia*, with MEB as its "conductor." During the next decade she usually had at least one novel appearing serially in its pages, sometimes under her pseudonym, "Babington White." About this clear triumph of the practical money-making spirit over "poetry" and "art" she told Bulwer defensively that she would have preferred her life to be "a quiet daze rather than a fever, but *some people* [italics mine] will have the fever, and I find there is nothing more difficult than to live one's own life." Now her name would soon be "blazoned on hoardings and railway stations," and she fancied that it was really not herself "but some bolder and busier spirit which worketh *for* me," which she would "at times fain to lull to temporary rest." As before, MEB's "some people" could only be John Maxwell. Perhaps there was something specious in her high-flown Bulwerian prose, apologizing—after all her protestations—for another chiefly commercial decision.

She begged Bulwer not to laugh "at the snobbery of the title. 'Belgravia' is the best bait for the shillings of Brixton and Bow." Although *Belgravia* was only the latest in a series of successful magazines named for a London region or landmark—like *Cornhill* or *Temple Bar*—it was the first to make to the lower-middle-class reader (from Brixton or Bow) the direct snobbish suggestion that when he opened its pages he would be moving into the fashionable world of the aristocratic rich. A decade later, Swinburne called it a "damned shopboy sort of title," and added, "Belgravia *stinks*." His fellow-aristocrat Bulwer would surely have felt the same way, as MEB sensed. She begged him for even "the smallest fragment of verse, the merest chip from your quarry of gems," but he never sent her a contribution.[51]

And about her own new writing she said only that she was "going in for a strong sensation story for 'Belgravia' not because I particularly believe in 'sensation,' but because I think the public shilling can only be extracted by strong measures."[52] Before it was finished, her story would consist of two entire three-volume novels: *Birds of Prey* and its sequel, *Charlotte's Inheritance*.[53] Intended to be read together, they made up her longest sustained narrative, comparable in suspense and intricacy of plot to Wilkie Collins at his very best. Occasionally MEB gibed at Collins' wordiness, once declaring that he could not have told the story of Bulwer's *My Novel* "rich alike in character and incident," in "under five and twenty volumes of mystery & diary."[54] So it is ironical that she herself was busily writing a six-decker: Collins always managed to bring even his most elaborate plot safely within the compass of three volumes.

The Birds of Prey are a sinister trio: a dentist, who poisons the husband of his own former sweetheart, thus acquiring his victim's wife and daughter, Charlotte, together with his life insurance; the poisoner's brother, "a hunter of genealogies, a grubber-up of forgotten facts, a joiner of broken links, a kind of legal resurrectionist," who seeks for lost heirs and reaps the reward when he finds them; and a Regency rake and blackleg, who has "joined the vultures . . . a promoter of joint stock companies that never saw the light, . . . treasurer of loan offices where money was never lent, . . . a gentleman with capital, about to introduce a novel article of manufacture from the sale of which a profit of five thousand a year would infallibly be realised, and desirous of meeting a gentleman of equal capital." All three become rivals in an effort to find the heir to a large estate, which requires them first to search for an eighteenth-century marriage certificate and then to trace the descendants of the marriage.

Told in the first person by one of the investigators, as Wilkie Collins would have told it, the dramatic narrative—whose plot, MEB told Charles Reade, she "got" at dinner at his house[55]—provides vivid genre scenes in remote Yorkshire villages and in the London establishments of carpet-makers and frame-gilders. Aged men are interviewed in almshouses, the records of parish churches combed, old letters discovered in unlikely hands. And when the heir appears to be Charlotte herself, she and the reader must face together the likelihood that her stepfather will kill her for the money, as he had killed her father. Ruined by a bear market, a process knowingly described by MEB, the murderer begins to poison Charlotte gradually. Her lover's efforts to gain access to her sickroom before she succumbs provide the suspense on which the sequel depends. By skillful twists of her kaleidoscopic plot MEB deprived Charlotte of her inheritance but saved her life. She left the punishment of the poisoner and his shady associates to the judgment of heaven—an oversight unusual for her.

Beyond the influence of Wilkie Collins, *Birds of Prey* and *Charlotte's Inheritance* reveal that of Balzac. As early as 1864, MEB, who thought he was the greatest French stylist of all time, had asked Bulwer's opinion of him,[56] and must have received a detailed answer, whose drift can be inferred from her response. "Enlightened by your criticism," MEB wrote, "I seem to see the false flash and glitter," the "impossibly elegant" Madame de Beauséant (who appears chiefly in Balzac's *La Femme abandonnée* [1832], *Le Père Goriot* [1834–1835], and *Albert Savarus* [1842]), and "the incredibly supine husbands." She compared Balzac's novels to "so many studies in morbid anatomy," declared herself "excruciated" by Père Goriot's twisting his silver plate before selling it in order to get more money for his rapacious daughters, and called him "what King Lear . . . must have been had destiny made him a City tradesman instead of an early British King." Balzac, she said, "seems to have been always peering into the most hideous sores in the social body." She also mentioned the horror of Baroness Hulot in *La Cousine Bette* (1846) and her perpetual trembling, and the "galling insolence" of Cousin Pons's relations (1847) who grudged him a dinner. But she saw Balzac as "unrivalled for a certain grim and ghastly humour, almost Shakespearean." Bulwer agreed with her comments in general, but observed that Balzac "is disagreeable because he is cynical, and that fault prevents one's reading him again and again. But . . . he is a very great novelist in his best books. He owes much to his patience in detail."[57]

It was surely her reading of Balzac that suggested to MEB the raffish group, Birds of Prey, around whom her big double novel of 1867–1868 revolved. She even introduced him directly into its dialogue. Until the poisoner read Balzac, for example, he had looked upon fiction as " 'the high-flown prosings of impossibly virtuous inanities,' " totally unlike real life, and scorned his wife for liking novels. But now he found himself "rivetted by the hideous cynicism, the supreme power of penetration into the vilest corners of wicked hearts," and he developed for Balzac an "unmitigated admiration." Balzac, said the murderer, " 'knows his fellows, and is not hypocrite enough to conceal his knowledge or to trick out his puppets in the tinsel and rags of false sentiment. . . . This Frenchman is an artist, and is not afraid to face the difficulties of his art.' " After Philippe Bridau—who appears in Balzac's *La Rabouilleuse* (1841–1843) and *Illusions Perdues* III (1843) and briefly in *Splendeurs et Misères des courtisanes* (1838–1847)—has " 'wallowed in the gutter, he lives to bespatter his virtuous brother with the mud from his carriage-wheels. That is *real* life. Your English novelist would have made his villain hang himself with the string of his waistcoat in a condemned cell, while his amiable hero was declared heir to a dukedom and forty thousand a year. But this fellow Balzac knows better than that.' " This could easily be taken as MEB's own opinion; yet if a critic had reproached her for immorality or cynicism, she could easily have retorted that she had put the words into the mouth of a murderer, and that they were intended to represent his opinion, not hers.

And by way of contrast she made Charlotte's sweetheart say that he was sick of all Balzac's characters: " 'the German Jews and the patrician beauties, and the Israelitish circles of the Rue Taitbout, and the sickly self-sacrificing provincial angels, and the ghastly *vieilles filles*.' " About his novels there hung " 'an odour of the dissecting-room.' " He could never have known a woman like Charlotte, " 'an angel who can be angelic without being *poitrinaire*, and whose amiability never degenerates into debility.' " And he could never have created a heroine like Lucy Ashton, Scott's Bride of Lammermoor. Balzac was " 'the greatest and grandest of painters of the terrible school; but the time comes when a man sighs for something brighter and better' " than his women.[58] But this contrary opinion she put in only to appease her romantic English readers. MEB herself had for some time found her girlhood favorite Lucy Ashton "tame and poor" and Scott himself "a trifle dull and commonplace,"[59] and even in his great scenes "little above the writing of a first-class newspaper reporter." In Scott, she missed the "fiery glow" of Byron and of Bulwer himself, of Dickens' account of Jonas Chuzzlewit's journey or Carlyle's of Louis XVI's last drive through Paris. Her "dear old" *Bride of Lam-*

mermoor she now found only "a very exquisite story told by a dear sensible, high-minded . . . elderly gentleman." It was the realism of Balzac that she now preferred, and she declared that Thackeray owed much to him, including Becky Sharp, who was only Valerie de Marneffe of *La Cousine Bette* "in English dress."[60]

So great indeed was MEB's preoccupation with Balzac at the time of writing *Birds of Prey* that she had even contemplated a return to her old idea of somehow "adapting" *La Peau de chagrin*. It was to be "a semi-supernatural novel, a humble and popularized . . . imitation" of that book and Bulwer's *Zanoni*, and she had planned to "steep" her mind in "supernatural and diabolical" literature, a new field to her. She had read *Faust* in a French translation—almost surely that of Gérard de Nerval—and Lewes's life of Goethe, and she intended to read Michelet's *La Sorcière*. But she asked Bulwer to suggest other reading, and he did recommend some books, including his own *Strange Story*—which she had read hastily and without much liking on its first appearance in 1862—and works on the occult, the "most valuable" of which he offered to lend her. She declined the loan, preferring to use the British Museum, but she did accept an invitation to visit his library. The whole project, however, obviously seemed too difficult, and she dropped it. It was six years before she even re-read *A Strange Story,* over which she promptly rhapsodized.[61] But her own *Peau de chagrin* she abandoned until 1891, when it appeared as *Gerard.*

What took the place of the supernatural story was a wholly different project, *Dead Sea Fruit,*[62] which MEB characterized as "rather a critical" subject. A blasé man of fifty, a cynical dilettante, "a *vieux garçon* of unnumbered successes in the past" falls in love—after a long interval of disbelief in love—and "finds a rival in his own unknown son." She declared that the "idea is taken from the French stage," but she did not identify the play, and she feared she might not have the power to "handle" it properly.[63]

MEB's "*vieux garçon,*" rich and worldly, is separated amicably from his wife, whom he had discovered exchanging innocent letters with her former suitor, the editor of an influential newspaper. The "rival" and "unknown son"—a bastard—is determined to find his father and avenge his mother's honor. But before he can identify his father, they fall in love with the same girl. After recognition comes reconciliation, and the elder man leaves the younger a clear field in his courtship. The father's past cruelties are the "dead sea fruit," which can produce only a taste of ashes in the mouth.

The cold-hearted upper-class seducer is a stock figure, whose finicking dismissal of his wife for merely keeping up a correspondence with the editor is quite in character for a past rake. But *Dead Sea Fruit* has certain ambiguities: is the wife's relationship with her old lover really as pure as MEB asserted? If so, why then should she describe her status as having "all the charm of widowhood without its danger"? There was "even the faintest flavour of Bohemianism about her position," MEB went on, "spotless though her reputation might be":

> She was a saint and martyr who gave nice little dinners, and drove the most perfectly appointed of pony-phaetons. It was only by an indescribable something—a tranquil grace of bearing, a subdued ease of manner, a pervading harmony in every detail of her surroundings, from the unobtrusive colouring of her costume to the irreproachable livery of her servants—that strangers could distinguish her from other unprotected women of a very different class.

This is vintage Braddonism, an early example of a practice that later became one of MEB's specialties: the ability to suggest exactly the opposite of what she was affirming. Was not the reader, despite all protestations, encouraged to think of this woman as a high-grade whore?

And her admirer, the editor (whose paper, the *Areopagus*, was certainly intended for the *Athenaeum*, the major critical journal which had recently attacked MEB for "manufacturing" novels), is fiercely envied by his fellow journalists, who "would have rejoiced infinitely to catch him tripping . . . so that they might band together and rend him in pieces." When they hear of his attachment, "the literary Bohemians, the 'Cherokees' [i.e., the Savage Club] . . . set up their malicious chatter," and men who have never even seen the lady speculate upon her conduct, and gloat "over the anticipation of some tremendous scandal" that would ruin them both.

Into the ambiguous relationship between a handsome Irish magazine editor and a woman he could not marry, MEB—whether consciously or not—perhaps put something of her own relationship to Maxwell. Certainly she had felt at first hand the sting of the malicious gossip of the London literary world. If one could identify the French play that MEB had used as her inspiration for *Dead Sea Fruit*, one could more easily determine how much of the novel was her own, and how much was "adapted"—in the light-hearted larcenous fashion of the London stage, of

Tom Taylor, and of her own Dick Thornton and Sigismund Smith. She had already borrowed, without being detected, from Soulié in her penny fiction, from Flaubert in *The Doctor's Wife*, and, far more indirectly, from Balzac in *Birds of Prey* and its sequel. Soon she would be in deep trouble for what looked like gross plagiarism from Octave Feuillet. Fifteen years later it would be Zola who thoroughly captivated her and on whom she would draw for inspiration. No matter which French drama underlay *Dead Sea Fruit*, MEB would have had to censor with care its attitudes toward the sexual relationships between its characters in the piquant Gallic situation in which a middle-aged roué and his hitherto unknown illegitimate son compete for a young girl's love.

One character in *Dead Sea Fruit* was surely MEB's creation: her first full-length portrait of a living celebrity, whom she called "Daniel Mayfield." A journalist, between forty and fifty, and "very remarkable looking," Mayfield "had once been handsome . . . but the flower of his youth had faded in some pernicious atmosphere. . . . He had a fiery red nose, and fiery black eyes, and dark hair, which he wore longer than was authorised by the fashion of the day." He had some gray hairs, and his moustache "had that tinge of Tyrian purple which betrays the handiwork of the chemist." Tall and stalwart, "he lacked the conventional graces of a modern gentleman," but "was not without a certain style and dash of his own." Daniel Mayfield's

> genius had been of much use to other people, but of little to himself, and [he] contemplated the visage of his deadliest foe whenever he looked in the glass. . . . Everybody liked him. He was your true Bohemian. . . . Money ran between his fingers like water. He had been more successful, and had worked harder, than men whose industry had won for them houses and land, horses and carriages, plate and linen and Sèvres china. His acquaintances were always calculating his income, and wondering what he did with it. Did he gamble? Did he speculate on the Stock Exchange? Did he consume fifteen-hundred a year in tavern parlours? Daniel himself . . . wondered as much as anyone. . . . He had never known how he spent his money. It went, somehow, and there came an end to it. Jack borrowed a few pounds; and there was a night's card-playing, through which the luck went against poor Dan; and there was a Greenwich dinner on Tom's birthday; and he took a fancy to a rare old copy of the *Diable Boîteux* [by René Le Sage], on large paper . . . and there were occasional periods of famine, during

which Dan had recourse to a friendly usurer, for whose succour he ultimately paid something like one hundred and fifty per cent. . . . When his pockets were empty, he called for pen, ink, and paper, and set himself to fill them.

And when it came to his writing, though "genial and good-natured," Mayfield was at the same time "the most ferocious and acrimonious of critics." He

> smote right and left, cleaving friend and foe indiscriminately asunder; and if it was on a woman's head that the blow descended, so much the better. The woman should have been at home, studying her cookery-book, or working . . . the sewing machine. . . .
> "Hark forward, tantivy!" cried Daniel, the critic, "run her down, trample her in the mud, make an end of her! She would quote Greek, would she? Why, the creature can barely spell plain English! She would prate of gods and goddesses, whose names she picks haphazard from a cheap abridgement of Lemprière. She would discourse of fashion and splendour, forsooth, who was 'Born in a garret, in a kitchen bred.' "[64]

Now this was a wholly recognizable sketch of George Augustus Sala, who looked like Daniel Mayfield, behaved like Daniel Mayfield, and wrote like Daniel Mayfield. The seven-year-old friendship between Sala and MEB had greatly transformed itself since the days when she had been an arch and determined young woman seeking to crash the pages of *Temple Bar*, and he had been the august monarch of the world of letters to whom she was laying siege. At the very moment when *Dead Sea Fruit*, with its all-too-realistic portrait of Sala, was running in *Belgravia* (November 1867), Sala himself was defending MEB in the same magazine against her critics. Although she could take care of herself, he said, he felt "a kind of pleasure, mingled with sadness, in assailing her detractors in a magazine which she conducts" because

> it was in a magazine which *I* conducted—in *Temple Bar*—that she reached her first station in the highway of Fame. She very soon shouldered *me* out of the way, I can assure you, and the conductor was quite trampled under foot by the youngest and least experienced of his lady-passengers. . . . I often think with a droll kind of ruefulness of the young lady who came coolly and con-

fidently out of the multitude . . . and took her place on the topmost step of the daïs of fiction.[65]

MEB was therefore *not* the unfortunate female whom Sala had lambasted for bad Greek and ordered back to her kitchen.

The Salas and the Maxwells saw much of one another socially. When Frith was painting MEB's portrait in 1865, he was especially pleased with Sala's favorable verdict.[66] And when Sala passed through one of his "occasional periods of famine" in 1866, MEB told Bulwer that his "goods and chattels have been scattered to the winds," and she had acquired his set of Voltaire. She called him an "amusing scapegrace."[67] It was the Friths who gave the dinner party from which Sala stormed out rather than sit at table with Bret Harte. And when John Maxwell tried to persuade Sala not to quarrel with his publisher, Sala quarreled with Maxwell.[68] But nobody could hope to remain always on good terms with Sala, and the quarrel with Maxwell was only a brief interruption in a close friendship that lasted to the end of Sala's life. Just before he died, in 1895, Sala recalled in his *Life and Adventures* his affection for MEB dating back into her girlhood, praised *Lady Audley's Secret* as "one of the most powerful romances" since Godwin's *Caleb Williams,* and hailed her continuing power of "invention and dramatic energy," which had prevented "even the most malevolent" of critics from ever declaring that she had "written herself out." Once, he said, he and MEB and some other writers had gone to Downing Street to discuss with Disraeli some question of the copyright laws, and the Prime Minister, whom he had never previously met, introduced himself to Sala for the sole purpose of getting Sala to introduce him to MEB.[69]

So, when Sala read *Dead Sea Fruit* and recognized himself in Daniel Mayfield, he was probably less offended than amused at MEB's accuracy and effrontery. It is, however, reasonable to ask whether she may not also have been displaying gross ingratitude when she hit off her former editor and present friend as "lacking the conventional graces of a modern gentleman" and rather more than hinted at the reasons for his "fiery red nose." Sala was a leading member of the Savage Club—MEB's "Cherokees"—where men's gossip destroyed the reputation of women they had never seen. Perhaps he gave further currency in the cruel world of literary Bohemia to the scandal of John Maxwell's irregular ménage and so caused MEB pain for which she was taking a literary revenge: her novels were read everywhere, and any reader in the know would have recognized Sala. It is also possible that she simply could not resist the temptation to portray so picturesque and celebrated a figure. She may even have asked his permission: "Would you mind very much if I were to put you into *Dead Sea Fruit?*"—and obtained his consent, just as she had got permission from the owner of Ingatestone to "people it with fiends."

Ever since the appearance of *Aurora Floyd*, MEB's success had been soured by a variety of frustrations. Some were due to overwork: she could not, she felt, give enough careful attention to any one novel to produce a work of art. Some were due, no doubt, to the daily snubs and slights inflicted upon her for living in an irregular ménage. Still others were due to the critics. Some of their wounding slights she satirized, we saw, in *The Lady's Mile* by reporting the ludicrous comments of the art-critics on Crawford's paintings. Others she could not answer or satirize because they were too violent and too personal. The literary criticism of the sixties directed at the sensation-novel in general and at MEB in particular is little known. To trace the hostile barrage from its first guns through the heat of the bombardment and into its ultimate silence must be our next job. Its impact on MEB's life and work was of the utmost importance. In November 1868—with her new novel, *Bound to John Company*, just getting under way in *Belgravia*—she suffered a complete physical and nervous collapse. In precipitating it the hectoring of the merciless critics played a major part.

CHAPTER VI

"The Right to Choose My Subjects from the Tragic, Criminal, and Exceptional Situations of Life": MEB and Her Hostile Critics (1863–1868)

When MEB had exhumed *Rupert Godwin* and *Run to Earth,* some critics had accused her of "manfacturing" novels. Others had "girded" at her no matter what she wrote, and in *The Lady's Mile* she had denounced them—thinly disguised as critics of William Crawford's paintings—for accusing a genuine artist of sensuality or writing "little carping" criticisms that taught him nothing. She was not referring to the occasional strictures of the daily press or even of the more or less censorious weekly journals—the *Athenaeum,* the *Spectator,* the *Saturday Review*—that reviewed her individual novels as they appeared.

What hurt her most was the sustained barrage of the more weighty "quarterlies" and other periodicals, which began soon after the appearance of *Aurora Floyd* in 1863, grew in volume and in severity until it reached a climax in 1867, and rumbled to a silence only in 1868. In long serious essays that purported to analyze the sensation-novel as a new genre, one anonymous critic after another—identifiable only now after more than a century—unlimbered his batteries against MEB personally, accusing her of immorality: at first in her writing and, as time went on, by less and less veiled innuendo, in her personal life as well. When Henry James spoke of Aurora Floyd's behavior as "indecent if you like, but not immoral," he was indirectly alluding to such criticisms as these. It was possible to answer the charges that her writings were immoral, and staunch defenders arose to do so. The personal innuendo, however, was the more painful because it was impossible to refute. Occasionally—and notably in the autumn of 1867—she was also accused of plagiarism, in a bitter and bruising encounter with the *Pall Mall Gazette.*

These attacks on the sensation-novel and on MEB form a little-known and significant chapter of Victorian literary criticism. They also constituted an agonizing episode in her life.

1. Preliminary Skirmishing, 1863–1864

Shortly after the publication of *Aurora Floyd*, a novelist named S. W. Fullom wrote to *The Standard* (March 25 and 26, 1863), accusing MEB of plagiarism. "A great sensation," he said, had been produced by *Lady Audley's Secret* and *Aurora Floyd*, and he had been "startled" to find many "points of resemblance" between them and his own novel, *The Man of the World* (1856). He listed twenty-seven in *Lady Audley's Secret* and eleven in *Aurora Floyd*, calling them "links in a chain which is at least very curious." Both his *Man of the World* and *Lady Audley's Secret*, he declared, included a marriage for money between a young girl and a much older baronet with a young daughter. In his novel, the girl had jilted a suitor she preferred who was not so rich; in *Lady Audley's Secret* she had "thrown over" her first husband; in both novels the other man later caused the girl embarrassment. In both novels there were clandestine departures of a girl from her father's house, great fires, luxurious apartments, portraits, secret passageways, large dogs, drunkards, murders, paragraphs in newspapers, more or less bigamous goings-on, girls who rode well and enjoyed hunting. As for *Aurora Floyd*, both it and *The Man of the World*, Fullom charged, included a rich banker who married a lady first seen at the theatre, a secret marriage, a deserted lodge, a turnstile, an inquest, the recovery of stolen money, and, again, a large dog. There were also close verbal parallels. In both *The Man of the World* and *Lady Audley's Secret* a woman had "pearly" teeth, and her lady's maid "effected a transformation"; in both *The Man of the World* and *Aurora Floyd*, someone at an inquest said that he could "throw no light upon" the inquiry. And so on.[1]

Clearly, anybody might write of "pearly" teeth or "throwing light upon" an inquiry without necessarily copying anybody else. But what about the long list of parallel incidents? MEB had been accustomed to the loose standards of the theatre with regard to literary "adaptation"; but even the most desultory examination of Fullom's novel convinces a modern reader at once that her two immensely successful novels were not in the least plagiarized from *The Man of the World*. Fullom's charges were clever but paranoid. *The Man of the World; or, Vanities of the Day* was hardly a novel at all. Partly satirical, partly social—the Chartists played a large part in it—it had no plot, no mystery, and no structure.[2] MEB wrote to *The Standard*, saying that her novels were "entirely and thoroughly original, and not derived in the slightest degree from Mr.

Fullom's book," of which she had never previously heard.[3] But she was particularly concerned lest Bulwer, to whom she had dedicated *Lady Audley's Secret,* might believe that he "had by that act of generosity become the receiver of stolen goods." She promised to send him a copy of Fullom's novel, so that he might see for himself how "mischievous and absurd" the charges were. Nothing, she rightly declared, "could be more unlike 'Lady Audley's Secret,' . . . in plot, plan, and treatment." By pointing to the presence of dogs, turnstiles, and portraits in both books, Fullom appeared to be claiming "copyright to the English language."[4] No more was heard of his charges.

But within a few days, there appeared in the *Quarterly Review* for April 1863 a long review article called "Sensation Novels," the first sustained notice to be given to the genre in the serious quarterly magazines. Though published anonymously, the article was written by a learned Oxford philosopher, the Reverend Henry Longueville Mansel (1820–1871), later Dean of St. Paul's, who ominously noted that he had been "called from more wholesome studies to survey the wide field of sensational literature." He dealt at length with two dozen novels, all published since 1858. *Lady Audley's Secret* and *Aurora Floyd* were numbers one and two on his list.[5] MEB had never before received attention like this, but soon other similar journals were following the *Quarterly's* example.

Whether intentionally or not, Mansel declared, sensation-novels usurp "a portion of the preacher's office, moulding the minds and forming the habits and tastes of its generation." The method is " 'preaching to the nerves.' . . . Excitement and excitement alone seems to be their chief purpose." This means morbidity: sensation-novels belong "to the morbid phenomena of literature—indications of a widespread corruption . . . called into existence to supply the cravings of a diseased appetite." The novels themselves "foster the disease, and . . . stimulate the want which they supply." Moreover, about the sensation-novel there floats "a commercial atmosphere . . . redolent of the manufactory and the shop. The public want novels, and novels must be made—so many yards of printed stuff, sensation-pattern." The three chief stimuli for the new genre are periodicals, full of ephemeral materials, mostly borrowed by the public and not bought; circulating libraries—"chief hotbed for forcing a crop of writers without talent and readers without discrimination"—; and railway bookstalls, full of novels with "tawdry" covers, "hung out like a signboard to give promise of the entertainment to be had within. . . . a pale young lady in a white dress with a dagger in her hand . . . or a Red

Indian in his war-paint; or . . . a priest persuading a dying man to sign a paper."

Mansel compared himself to "the man of sound health and regular appetites," who could hardly understand "the perpetual cravings of the dram-drinker or the valetudinarian for spirits or physic." He found it hard to realize that a large public read nothing else: "Unhappily there is too much evidence that the public appetite can . . . descend from trash to garbage." Sensation-novels usually consist only of incident. They would be hindered rather than helped if they showed "deep knowledge of human nature, graphic delineations of individual character, vivid representations of the aspects of Nature or the workings of the soul—all the higher features of the creative art." Yet among them, "some . . . gently stimulate a particular feeling, and others . . . carry the whole nervous system by storm . . . some . . . tickle the vanity of the reader . . . others" are simply nauseating. Those written purely for amusement are better than those with a didactic purpose: better to forget all about a sensation-novel after one has read it than have a residue of "shallow dogmatism and flippant conceit." Dickens himself is a "grievous offender" when he uses fiction as a vehicle to attack some institution he happens not to like, and many lesser writers have imitated Dickens. Mansel acknowledged but condemned the excitement that came from the "thought that such things may be going on around us and among us," and from the readiness of the novelist to fictionalize contemporary scandal.

Eight of his twenty-four chosen novels hinged upon bigamy, among them of course MEB's *Lady Audley's Secret* and *Aurora Floyd*. Mansel called her books "exaggerated specimens of the sensational type," but conceded that "they are the works of an author of real power, who is capable of better things. . . ." He compared Lady Audley to Vittoria Corombona in John Webster's *White Divel* of 1612, whose "romantic wickedness" suffers by being "transplanted" into a nineteenth-century English drawing-room. Lady Audley, however, is "more than the rival of her prototype in boldness and guilt. She does with her own hand what Vittoria does by means of others." Mansel, one notes with a smile, was hooked: drawn from his "more wholesome studies," he honestly admitted that

. . . notwithstanding all the horrors of the story . . . the glaring improbability of the incidents, the superhuman wickedness of the principal character and the incongruities of others; not-withstanding the transparent nature of the "secret" from the very beginning, the author has succeeded in constructing a narrative the interest of which is sustained to the end. The skill of the builder deserves to be employed on better materials.

Compared with Lady Audley, the beautiful fiend, Aurora Floyd is only a fast young lady, "inferior to Lady Audley as a pick-pocket is inferior to a thug." But while Lady Audley "ends her days in a madhouse," Aurora Floyd, a happy wife, "bends over the cradle of her first-born." Morally more questionable, *Aurora Floyd* does show MEB's improvement in the drawing of real characters. Mansel quoted in full the scene in which Aurora whips the Softy. By reviewing MEB first, and letting her off easily, Mansel showed that he preferred her to the other twenty-two novelists, whom he proceeded to excoriate. So thorough a study had he made of his subject that he even realized that "cheap publications in penny and halfpenny numbers . . . are to the full-grown sensation novel what the bud is to the flower."[6]

Despite Mansel's attack on the sensation-novel for "morbidity, commercialism," and questionable morality, he did not denounce MEB personally, and he did praise her talents. On the whole, she would have thanked her stars that the review had been no harsher. It is less likely that she saw *The Medical Critic and Psychological Journal* for October 1863, with its anonymous leading article, entitled "Baits for Suicide—'Lady Audley's Secret' and 'Aurora Floyd.'" Extracting all references to suicide from the text of the two novels, the critic concluded that "for a parallel . . . recourse must be had to the most debased works of French novelists. Suicide . . . is intruded into the brightest as the darkest aspect of the stories, . . . it serves as the foil to happiness, the legitimate accompaniment of wretchedness, folly, or wickedness. . . . Admitting the "rare power of expression and observation" displayed by MEB, the author wished she had used her gifts better.

The French fiction from which her own novels stem, he declared, is notable for "pseudo-scientific scepticism . . . the elevation of sensuality to the dignity of the highest virtue, and the degradation of continence to the station of a pitiful vice . . . the tricking out of immorality in a garb of religious phraseology, and . . . the uplifting of suicide as a legitimate panacea against all ills."[7] The French had derived these attitudes from *Werther*, and the current English fascination with them could be seen in the popularity of the opera of *La Traviata* and in the tendency of contemporary English artists to paint suicidal subjects. Collecting all the references to French fiction in MEB's two novels, the critic triumphantly concluded that this was the source of her contamination. He adduced and analyzed Maria de Fos's novel *Gaëte*, which was indeed an apology for suicide. But he did not even try to show that MEB had ever read it.

By December 1863, still another anonymous critic had *Eleanor's Victory* and *John Marchmont's Legacy*, in addition to the earlier novels, to discuss in the quarterly *New Review*. MEB, he said, does not write "novels of character"; so her success cannot be due either to intellectual power or to "close observation of human nature." Her heroines owe their interest to "that half-serious, half-smiling curiosity with which the world is at present watching the efforts of the female sex to take up a stronger position" in society: "Woman standing alone . . . carrying out some strong purpose . . . showing herself independent of mankind and superior to" the softer passions: that is how "Miss Braddon loves best to depict her pretty darlings." And "another authoress of the same class" had claimed for women "as full a right to be a libertine" as bad custom accords to men.

In MEB's novels "there is not a single scene . . . which . . . you thoroughly 'enter into,'" and this defect alone "is sufficient to exclude" her from the ranks of the best novelists. Her characters are not lifelike; she lacks "knowledge of life"; she does not know how the inhabitants of the Inns of Court really lived. Robert Audley of the Inner Temple would never dine, as she made him dine, on a pint of sherry and a mutton chop, when he could go out to any one of the nearby restaurants, all excellent. In describing a hunt-breakfast in *John Marchmont's Legacy*, MEB shows that she does not know how people usually behave in county circles: her country gentlemen drink too much and are less intelligent than they ought to be. Trivial and patronizing, this critic was chiefly concerned with feminism, to which he reverted at the end with a fine series of nervous blasts:

> When we hear . . . so much about employment for young women, and so much scorn cast upon the old-fashioned theory, according to which they are intended as help-meets for man . . . are we not driven to ask ourselves whether woman's character is of a kind to *bear* . . . emancipation from male control and influence? . . . Honestly intended as a remedy for that sore of modern life, called the "social evil [prostitution]," is not the system which these reformers would establish calculated indirectly to promote it? . . .

such women as are many of Miss Braddon's heroines would have become mistresses, just as soon as bigamists.[8]

Baits for suicide, signs of the new immorality to be expected when women were emancipated: MEB's novels loaned themselves readily to the private phobias of her male readers. Amidst such humorless criticism, she must have been relieved to open *Beeton's Christmas Annual* for 1864 and find Thomas Hood poking amiable fun at her in two "sensation-novels" in the form of cartoon-strips, entitled "Quintilia the Quadrigamist; or, the Heir and the Hounds," and "Maurora Maudely; or, Bigamy and Buttons."[9] To the critics like Mansel who had attacked the sensation-novel as somehow in itself immoral, MEB replied indirectly on behalf of the genre in her preface to *Henry Dunbar*, quoting Daniel Defoe:

> "Throughout this book this fundamental is most strictly adhered to: there is not a wicked action in any part of it, but it is, first and last, rendered unhappy and unfortunate; there is not a superlative villain brought upon the stage, but he is either brought to an unhappy end, or brought to be a penitent; there is not an ill thing mentioned, but it is condemned even in the relation; nor a virtuous, just thing, but it carries its praises along with it."[10]

But even the *New Review* critic, hostile though he was, had not written *ad feminam*. MEB had made herself independent, had been on the stage, wrote for money, and was living in sin with a married man; but these early reviewers gave her only an occasional snobbish personal dig, and chiefly directed their often foolish remarks against her writings. Such restraint was now to disappear.

2. The Barrage Opens, 1865

The critical view of MEB hardened and a new kind of unpleasantness manifested itself in September 1865, when an important Scotch quarterly, the *North British Review*, published a long anonymous article entitled "Sensation Novelists—Miss Braddon." In fact, the author was W. Fraser Rae (1835–1905), journalist and traveler, and much later in life a novelist and the biographer of R. B. Sheridan.[11] If success and "fertility in invention" were the test of genius, Rae began, MEB would rank "very high on the list of our great novelists. Three years ago her name was unknown to the reading public. Now it is nearly as familiar to every novel-reader as that of Bulwer-Lytton or Charles Dickens." The critics, even those writing for newspapers which "habitually neglected, or carped at works that fell short of a very high standard of excellence," have paid her "exceptional compliments. Her triumph has been nearly complete. By the unthinking crowd she is regarded as a woman of genius. . . . She has bewitched so many persons that those who have the misfortune to be blind to her charms have had small chance" of a hearing.

Rae declared that he would not apply a moral test, but would judge MEB by "purely literary" standards, because what "is bad in taste is usually bad in morals." But Rae's purported literary criticism largely resolved itself into petty carping. How, he asked, could the well in *Lady Audley's Secret* be said to have "hid itself away," or the rope that had held the pail be called "lazy" and "rotten"? Did not the rapturous descriptions of Lady Audley's hair sound like advertisements? Was it not strange that she should have described lightning as "playing fitfully round the razors" in an open dressing-case, when this was "a phenomenon of which we never heard before"? These things show "how thoroughly ignorant Miss Braddon is of the ways of the world and the motive springs of the heart." Her people are not like living beings: *"With the exception of . . . the lady's maid, not a single personage has any resemblance to the people we meet with in the flesh* [italics mine]."

Lady Audley—who acts like Lady Macbeth—is portrayed as timid and gentle. This is "exciting but . . . unnatural. The artistic faults of this novel are as grave as the ethical ones. Combined, they render it one of the most noxious books of modern times." MEB had "misemployed her undoubted talents." An authoress "who could make one of her sex play the chief part in such a scene" as the whipping of the Softy in *Aurora Floyd* is *"evidently acquainted with a very low type of female character* [italics mine]." In *John Marchmont's Legacy*, Olivia Marchmont talks so melodramatically that Rae doubted "if *even at the Surrey theatre* [italics mine]" there had ever been anything like it. "Few other novelists could have invented anything so 'diabolical' " as the murder in *Henry Dunbar*. How could MEB "seriously consider a tale of crime as fitted for the 'amusement' of anybody?"

The Doctor's Wife, however, did show "how very nearly Miss Braddon has missed being a novelist whom we might respect and praise without reserve. But it also proves how she is a slave . . . to the style . . . she created. 'Sensation' is her Frankenstein." As to *Only a Clod*, "almost a moral treatise" compared with the others, how is it that "a lady should be able to describe" London night life resorts which she "designates as 'remote and inapproachable regions, whose very names were only to be spoken over the fourth bottle of Chambertin or Clos Vougeot at a bachelor's' "? Nor does she know how gentlemen behave when angry, as shown by a scene in which the hero hurls the villain to the floor. Not one of Miss Braddon's "personages . . . thoroughly amuses or interests us" or can be taken "as a model"; she is a "creator of unnatural monstrosities," who can "group her materials" and deal with "revolting topics" with a skill that prevents "the startled reader from tossing her volume away in sheer disgust."

Proponents of the sensation-novel, Rae continued, would argue that Scott or Bulwer or George Eliot wrote them too. True, "*The Heart of Midlothian* and *Eugene Aram, Adam Bede* and *The Mill on the Floss* are unquestionably novels wherein there are incidents as highly coloured as in *Lady Audley's Secret* or *Henry Dunbar*. The difference, however, is far greater than the resemblance. These works are truthful taken as wholes," and even the startling episodes do not seem impossible. But for MEB crime is "the business of life. . . . the chief end of man is to commit a murder, and his highest merit to escape punishment; . . . women are born to attempt to commit murders, and to succeed in committing bigamy." She teaches us to "sympathize with murderers and reverence detectives," and her principles are just like those "by which the Thugs used to regulate their lives." Having delivered this "purely literary" judgment, Rae concluded:

> We should act unfairly if we left on our readers' minds the impression that we do not regard Miss Braddon as an authoress of originality and merit. In her own branch of literature we hold that she is without a living rival. The notoriety she has acquired is her due reward for having woven tales which are as fascinating to ill-regulated minds as police reports and divorce cases. . . . Others before her have written stories of blood and lust, of atrocious crimes and hardened criminals. But the class that welcomed them was the lowest in the social scale, as well as in mental capacity. To Miss Braddon belongs the credit of having penned similar stories in easy and correct English, and published them in three volumes in place of issuing them in penny numbers. She may boast, without fear of contradiction, of having temporarily succeeded in

making the literature of the Kitchen the favourite reading of the Drawing room.[12]

The "purely literary" judgments that Rae had promised at the outset proved all to be ancient charges: MEB had "insufficient knowledge," her stories were improbable and her characters not fully developed. Had Rae said these things in a measured way, he would only have been echoing MEB's own private opinion of her novels. But instead of abstaining from moral judgment, he demonstrated by the fierceness of his tone that it was the moral indictment he was chiefly concerned to make. When Rae anticipated the likelihood that defenders of MEB would point to Scott, Bulwer, and George Eliot as authors of sensation-novels, and described their books as "truthful taken as wholes," it was especially ironic that he singled out *Eugene Aram* (1832), a novel which seemed to approve of murder and which had brought down on Bulwer violent disapproval like Rae's own attack on MEB.

Rae accompanied his condemnation by sneering personal digs: in *Lady Audley's Secret* only the lady's maid was convincing; MEB must be acquainted with low types of female character; not even at the Surrey Theatre (the home of melodrama in London) would such speeches as she wrote be delivered; MEB obviously knew too much about late-night bachelor haunts; she believed in bigamy; and she had moved kitchen literature upstairs to the drawing-room. Rae was implying that MEB was lower class, a former actress, and a woman of doubtful acquaintance and behavior. His sneering allusions would have struck a responsive chord in any reader of Knowles's attack on her "marriage" with Maxwell. Although Rae had criticized MEB for no purely literary defect that earlier adverse critics had not already cited, he had succeeded in being far more unpleasant.

She found a defender in Charles Kent (1823–1902), editor of *The Sun,* an important evening newspaper, who published in his issue for Tuesday, September 12, 1865, an anonymous article called "The North British v. Miss Braddon." He called Rae's anonymous article "extremely unfair throughout," protested "its appearance . . . in the interests of fair criticism," and saw in it "a singularly perverse disingenuousness." Though called "Sensation Novelists," it dealt with Miss Braddon alone, and therein lay "its coarse, and almost vulgar ungraciousness!" MEB—whom Kent knew only through her books—had, he said, in her seven three-volume novels "built up a wide and brilliant reputation." All her books had been "read and thumbed and circulated through all the circulating libraries of the United Kingdom!" The *North British Review* critic "with cold-blooded deliberation" intended to cut "Miss Braddon and her writings up piecemeal in the course of what is vulgarly called a slashing criticism." But he had overdone it: "The animus is too apparent throughout—and whenever that animus is recognised, as it is at every turn, [the criticism] proves to be . . . distressingly little."

MEB, Kent said, was sometimes guilty of over-rapid composition, of slips, of forgetfulness, as in *Henry Dunbar,* when the hero, "midway in the story, meets, apparently for the first time in his life, one of the partners in the great banking firm, of which he . . . is supposed to be the head partner." Although this kind of blunder could be found "scattered over the radiant pages of Miss Braddon's seven very brilliant Romances," it was a petty matter. As for the *North British* reviewer's sneering reference to the well that "hid itself" in *Lady Audley's Secret,* what would the critic make of Coleridge's "silly buckets on the dock"? Poets and novelists—Balzac, Scott, Dickens, and Bulwer—all exercised the right to idealize, individualize, and sensitize inanimate objects. The "onslaught" had been futile. Though "manifestly designed by the reviewer to be completely destructive in its effect upon her reputation," it really amounted to "a highly elaborated panegyric on her genius as a Novelist."[13]

MEB wrote immediately, thanking Kent for his "most kind, most disinterested, and able defense of me against the furious onslaught of 'The North British Review.' " She had been, she said, too busy finishing *Sir Jasper's Tenant* "to send for the Review, or to trouble my head with an attack at once so virulent and malignant." People had told her that the author was "a novelist whose failure to excite public attention should at least have made him more charitable to a fellow-labourer."[14] But W. Fraser Rae, the actual author of the attack, had in 1865 not yet written a novel; so MEB had been misinformed. Perhaps she thought that the "onslaught" was by Frederick Greenwood (Gilby's "F. G.") who had indeed recently written a novel called *Margaret Denzil's History,* which had been—deservedly—a failure, and who, as editor of the *Pall Mall Gazette,* would in 1867 show himself exceedingly hostile to MEB and to John Maxwell.[15]

A month after his first defense of MEB, Kent reviewed *Sir Jasper's Tenant* admiringly (October 17, 1865): "Another Novel in Three Volumes by Miss Braddon! An eighth elaborate fiction in less than half as many years!" Kent found her writing "evidence . . . of extraordinary industry" and "remarkable" intellectual achievement. Her books were "in their very nature and treatment, highly original." Dwelling on their enormous popularity ("they have been bespoken, ever-so-many deep as soon as the London book-box has brought them newly down to the seaside librarian's"), Kent declared that "they have held their own" with the novels of Scott, Bulwer, Dickens, Fielding, Richardson, and Thackeray. Of course one might ask how long their popularity would last. Perhaps no novelist would long retain his fame; yet think of Apuleius' *Golden Ass,* the earliest novel of all. Survival power aside, MEB's place was "clearly defined and signally conspicuous. Critics may snarl. . . . instance only the other day a very one-sided and even spiteful diatribe . . . in the *North British Review. . . .* for the life of us, having thoroughly enjoyed [her novels] . . . we can't find that we are one bit the worse for it." How absurd to call her the "originator of Sensational Fiction." What about Godwin's *Caleb Williams* (1794), Maturin's *Melmoth the Wanderer* (1820), Scott's *Guy Mannering* (1815)? Had there been no sensation-fiction before *Lady Audley's Secret,* had such "dull and ponderous specimens of sensationless" fiction as the works of Henry Mackenzie or R. Plumer Ward been the only novels available, it would have been a boring world. MEB's eight novels were "thoroughly and delightfully readable. . . . she has yet to write her first dull chapter." *Sir Jasper's Tenant* Kent found somewhat below her highest standard, but he particularly praised her humor, which the unfair *North British Review* article had denied her.[16]

Such a friend—arising spontaneously and unexpectedly to defend and praise her—was a most welcome acquisition. MEB appreciated deeply Kent's "unfailing kindness . . . hearty and chivalrous championship," and told him that an earlier editor of *The Sun,* Richard Martyn—now dead—had been a friend of hers: "however chequered my career has been, 'The Sun' has shone on me through it all. May it never cease to shine, and may I become more worthy." Kent continued to notice her books always fairly, and often enthusiastically. By 1866 they had met: he was no longer "Dear Sir," but "Dear Mr. Kent." When he saluted *Belgravia* on its first appearance, MEB wrote, "you have been so good to me that I have really begun to accept your kindness almost as a matter of course," and he and his wife in later years often dined at Lichfield House. After *The Sun* had failed in 1871, Kent for seven years (1874–1881) edited the Catholic *Weekly Register,* and here too he would continue to sing MEB's praises: "If I wrote a book you could not find it in your heart to praise," she wrote him in February 1878, "you would let the offending volumes pass unnoticed, for you could not find it in your heart to blame," although, she assured him in October 1879, she did not take his approval for granted.

Friend of Dickens, of Bulwer, and of Charles Reade, and later of the Earl of Lytton, editor of Bulwer's complete novels, and author of the biography of Charles Reade in the *DNB*, Charles Kent was a man naturally congenial to MEB.[17] She might never have met him had it not been for his prompt and gratifying response to the *North British Review*'s attack. Others too thought it brutal and did not hesitate to say so in print. A Dublin newspaper called *Saunders's News Letter and Daily Advertiser* saluted MEB's "genius," imagination, exuberance, brilliance, the "intricacy of design and mystery characteristic of the French styles of fiction," and "certain admirable character-sketches, perfectly English." It praised her to the skies as an entertaining novelist, who thoroughly deserved her popularity, and called the *North British Review* unfair. When MEB learned that this defense had been written by a man named Reynolds, she expressed her gratitude for it and for "the kindness with which my writings have been noticed in the columns of S[aunders's] N[ews] L[etter] . . . a paper I deem a credit to British journalism."[18]

Her letters to Kent and Reynolds provide our only evidence of MEB's response to the *North British Review*'s blast. They show her in a mood of resignation, toughly unwilling—so she said—to turn aside from her writing to worry about Rae's "virulence" and "malignance." Yet however ready she was to acknowledge the faults in her novels, she must have been bitterly stung by the scarcely veiled aspersions on her life and character. There was worse to come.

3. The Height of the Bombardment, 1867

Eighteen sixty-seven proved to be the climactic year for the enemies of the sensation-novel in general and of MEB in particular. During the spring had come the controversy over the *Athenaeum*'s accusation that MEB had "manufactured" novels. Far more devastating was the savage personal criticism leveled at her anonymously in September in the pages of *Blackwood's Magazine*. Called simply "Novels," the article was actually written by the prolific novelist Margaret Oliphant, whose anonymity MEB probably never penetrated.

Ever since Scott, said Mrs. Oliphant, the English novel had gained a reputation "for a certain sanity, wholesomeness, and cleanliness

unknown to other literature of the same class," kept "pure from all noxious topics" in contrast to the French, which had been "fatally injured" by
"corruption." But while the French hide their novels from their young,
nowadays English youth read sensation-novels, "with all their unseemly
references and exhibitions of forbidden knowledge, of young women,
moved either by the wild foolhardiness of inexperience, or by ignorance
of everything that is natural and becoming to their situation. . . . all these
stories of bigamy and seduction, these *soi-disant* revelations of things
that live below the surface of life." These days all English "minor
novelists" belong to the sensational school. "Writers who have no genius
and little talent make up for it by displaying their acquaintance with the
accessories and surroundings of vice, with the means of seduction, and
with . . . the secret tendencies of the heart . . . which . . . all point the one
way."

It all began with Charlotte Brontë, when *Jane Eyre* "made what advanced critics call her 'protest' against . . . conventionalities," and when
the curate's daughter in *Shirley* complained that there was no husband
for her to marry. And by now the heroines of English novels included:

> Women driven wild with love for the man who leads them on to
> desperation before he accords that word of encouragement that
> carries them into the seventh heaven; women who marry their
> grooms in fits of sensual passion; women who pray their lovers to
> carry them off from the husbands and homes they hate; women
> . . . who give and receive burning kisses and frantic embraces, and
> live in a voluptuous dream. . . . the dreaming maiden . . . waits now
> for flesh and muscles, for strong arms that seize her, and warm
> breath that thrills her through, and a host of other physical at-
> tractions which she indicates to the world with a charming
> frankness. On the other side of the picture, it is, of course, the am-
> ber hair and undulating form, the warm flesh and glowing colour,
> for which the youth sighs. . . . this eagerness for physical sensa-
> tion is represented as the natural sentiment of English girls.

Experts in the novels of MEB would recognize a Braddonian original
here and there: she did write about bigamy; Aurora Floyd married her
groom, not, however, in a "fit of sensual passion," but rather in girlish
fondness for his good looks and for his knowledge of the sporting world.
The girls whom Mrs. Oliphant knows, she went on, "are very nice girls."
They like men's company when it is to be had, but they do not "pant for

indiscriminate kisses or go mad for unattainable men."[19] Yet "it is thus that Miss Braddon" and Annie Thomas—Mrs. Pender Cudlip, author of many novels[20]—"and a host of other writers explain their feelings. . . . These ladies might not know, it is quite possible, any better. *They might not be aware how young women of good blood and good training feel* [italics mine]." Nobody now pays as much attention to Mr. Trollope's "nice girls . . . as to the Aurora Floyds." English women do not protest against MEB's depiction of their behavior. The *Times* and other critical journals do not denounce it. Mudie's objections are too faint. The French regard these writers as the most important English novelists. At least in France a wicked novel "may be very disgusting, but it is generally clever." But in England such novels are "the poorest of literary drivel—sentiments that are adapted to the atmosphere of a Surrey Theatre [note Mrs. Oliphant repeating Rae's personal dig at MEB as a former actress]—descriptions of society which show the writer's ignorance of society." They "are not literature at all." The construction shows "a certain rude skill . . . a certain clever faculty for theft," but no inventive genius, no good taste, no perception of character.

"Miss Braddon," Mrs. Oliphant conceded, had "certain literary claims. 'Aurora Floyd' . . . is . . . well knit together, thoroughly interesting, . . . full of life. The life is certainly not of a high description, but it is genuine in its way; and few people with any appreciation of fiction could refuse to be attracted by a tale so well defined." It is hard to see what Mrs. Oliphant meant by "life . . . certainly not of a high description," since *Aurora Floyd* is just as much the story of a banker's daughter and a Yorkshire landowner, as of a girl and a groom. If MEB were so overpoweringly sensual, how was it that "few people with any appreciation of fiction" could fail to be attracted by her books? Mrs. Oliphant let fall a few more words of grudging praise: "The 'Doctor's Wife' strikes even a higher note. It is true that it is to some extent plagiarised . . . from a French story," but at any rate it did not exceed "the amount of licence permitted by English taste."

But Mrs. Oliphant was only preparing for her shrewdest blows. Lady Audley has

> brought in the reign of bigamy as an interesting and fashionable crime, which no doubt shows a certain deference to the British relish for law and order. It goes against the seventh commandment, no doubt, but it does it in a legitimate sort of way, *and is an invention which could only have been possible to an*

*Englishwoman knowing the attraction of impropriety, and yet lov-
ing the shelter of law* [italics mine].

Here was the scarcely veiled insinuation that MEB knew too much about
bigamy for her own good. Concentrating her attack on *Rupert Godwin*,
the resurrected *Halfpenny Journal* novel, and mockingly quoting MEB's
prefatory account of its earlier incarnation, Mrs. Oliphant accused her of
stealing the plot from Charles Reade's *Hard Cash*, but added:

> there is something in 'Rupert Godwin' which *is Miss Braddon's
> own. When the poor widow's virtuous and lovely daughter earns
> her scanty living on the stage, she is made the victim of one of
> those romantic abductions which used to be so frequent in novels.
> . . . it does her no harm either in reputation or anything else, . . .
> but it is purely original and not copied* [italics mine].

Here the insinuation is not even veiled. MEB *was* a poor woman's
daughter, who *had* earned a scanty living upon the stage. She *was* in a
sense the victim of a romantic abduction, and in a sense it had done her
no harm. By singling out an utterly trite episode from *Rupert Godwin* and
pretending to think it "Miss Braddon's own," Mrs. Oliphant had struck
at her victim's most vulnerable points. Having accused her of plagiarism
and of foul-mindedness, Mrs. Oliphant then made fun of her for not
being foul-minded enough: the Duke in *Rupert Godwin* gives an actress a
house, jewels, and horses, but maintains with her only "relations of the
purest character."[21] Inconsistent, but powerful and charged with innuendo about MEB's private life, carefully composed to sting and elicit
sneers from those in the know, this article was the most painful critical
blow she had ever received.

For the first time, she wrote in anguish to Bulwer about a hostile
review, quoting in full Mrs. Oliphant's suggestion that MEB "*might not
be aware how young women of good blood & good training feel* [italics
are MEB's]. Now can anything exceed the covert insolence of this? Who
is this writer who dares to tell me that I do not know how a virtuous
woman feels? Does he judge by the evidence of my books? I can say boldly, No." MEB conceded that *Aurora Floyd* was "the story of a foolish
girl who eloped with her father's groom. But I declare that Aurora Floyd
is not *a woman who marries her groom in a fit of sensual passion.*"
Assuming that her tormentor was a man, MEB asked, "Is this gentleman
one of the 'nice men,' who are always nasty men, I wonder?" The charge

of sensuality "stung" her "to the quick." *The Doctor's Wife* did indeed "describe the sentimental fancy of a young married woman for a man who seems to her the ideal of all her girlish dreams." And while it was "not a story which I would care to place in the hands of 'the young person,' . . . I defy the critic—however nice, or however nasty—to point to one page or one paragraph in that book—or in any other book of mine which contains the lurking poison of sensuality." Of all "horrors" sensuality was the most abhorrent to her. She even told Bulwer, himself a phrenologist, "that all those who have examined my head phrenologically know that this sin is one utterly foreign to my organization, that, indeed, the great weakness of my brain is the want of that animal power which, as I am told, gives force and activity to the higher organs."

MEB said nothing of the critic's attack on *Rupert Godwin,* perhaps because she herself felt the novel's weakness; if, however, we had her letters to Charles Reade, we should probably find her denying Mrs. Oliphant's accusation that she had stolen the plot from his *Hard Cash.* Nor did she mention the digs at her as an actress and as an apologist for bigamy: these were matters too personal even for Bulwer, although these hidden unanswerable slurs no doubt wounded her most deeply. Others had accused her of immoral writing without upsetting her nearly so much. Yet that charge, so difficult to refute, offered her the sole ground on which she could fight back publicly.

She begged for Bulwer's help. His influence with Blackwood (publisher of his two most recent books) "must be supreme." Could he perhaps "cause the writer of the article in question to be awakened to the fact that he has done me—I hope ignorantly—a very great injustice, and that it would be only the act of a gentleman to make some *amende* for this wrong?" He might "condemn" her novels "as rubbish & twaddle," but he should "consider what I have written & say whether I have ever dwelt on the physical or raved about 'thrilling kisses,' and 'warm breath' and 'column-like throats' or in any way sinned the sin" of Annie Thomas or Miss Florence Marryat. "Pardon this long tiresome letter, dear Lord Lytton," MEB concluded, "and help me if you can. I am most deeply stung by this uncalled-for, unjustifiable charge."[22]

Bulwer immediately offered to write in her defense, and praised her "genius." "Believe me," she replied, "I . . . can only smile at the word 'genius' when uttered by you to me." She would find him "a magazine or journal that he could approve," whenever he could find time "to write an article about" her. His offer to do so had filled her with pleasure. But she was still dreadfully upset. For "six years of literary drudgery," she had "never written a line" designed to wound anybody's feelings. Why should she be singled out "as the scape-goat for this generation of second- and third-rate novelists, and made the target for every scribbler's venomous shafts?" Like Crawford, the artist in *The Lady's Mile*, she was struggling "against the disgust and depression occasioned by little carping criticisms which *teach* me nothing, and indeed seem intended only to wound and annoy." She found herself "stung"—it was the fourth time she had used the word—"into a most savage state of mind." Since the article had appeared, three weeks earlier, she had "lived in a perpetual fever." Only Bulwer's kindness and that of Charles Reade had prevented her from thinking herself "a kind of literary pariah." Reade too, then, had come to her support, no doubt ridiculing Mrs. Oliphant's charge that MEB had stolen from *Hard Cash*.

Now she had commissioned an article for *Belgravia* on "The Cant of Modern Criticism," to be written by Sala, "a brilliant essayist." MEB had expected him to "defend the right of the imaginative writer to choose his subjects" from the same field as all the great writers of the past: "the tragic, criminal, and exceptional situations of life." But she soon took alarm because Sala, in defending her, had pinned the label of "sensation-author" on Bulwer himself. Though MEB had begged Sala to "suppress" this passage, he had refused, "and dares me to tamper with his proof. What shall I do?"[23] Protesting that she would rather offend Sala than Bulwer, she enclosed a footnote she had drafted and offered to publish with Sala's article, dissenting "from the opinion of her brilliant ally" about Bulwer, "that great master of imaginative literature, from whose works" she had derived so much inspiration to persevere in the face of criticism.[24]

Probably Bulwer assured MEB that he would not be offended at anything Sala might say of his early works. It was many years since he himself had suffered, and recovered from, attacks made in the same spirit and sometimes in the same words as those now leveled against MEB, and a *tu quoque* argument from Sala could hardly have troubled him very much at this late date, especially since his own defense of his Newgate fiction had always taken the line that Sala was taking in MEB's behalf. Sala's article appeared in *Belgravia* in November 1867 without MEB's footnote; so she did not have to enter any dissent from the article of her "brilliant ally."

And indeed Sala was at his lively best. As a boy, he said, his favorite reading had included *Blackwood's*, then the "grandest repository of wit, learning, and eloquence the world had ever seen." But it had become "desperately dull" and old-fashioned. "Who are the people who buy it," Sala asked, "do they wear pigtails and hair-powder and Hessian boots?" The recent anonymous article on novels was "eminently unjust, mischievous, and disingenuous," offensively exemplifying "the prevalence of the worst kind of cant, hypocrisy, and sophistry, as applied to literary criticism." English novels are far from being the "sane, wholesome cleanly" works that the critic had imagined: Scott had encouraged Ainsworth, whose *Rookwood* (1834) displays "sensationalism . . . wilder, ghastlier and more immoral than . . . the craziest screed of Monk Lewis"; *Rockwood's* successor, *Jack Sheppard* (1839) is even wilder, "a drama of the gaol and lupanar." As for Bulwer, Sala continued, in the passage that had worried MEB, his *Eugene Aram* is

> the apotheosis of a bloodthirsty Yorkshire schoolmaster, who, actuated by the paltriest motives, murdered a barber and hid his body in a hole, and, after telling innumerable lies in the dock, was hanged. As the murderer was a good classical scholar, and had even some acquaintance with the Oriental tongues, the noble novelist—then Mr. Edward Lytton Bulwer—made him a hero, made him the lover of a beautiful and virtuous maiden, and implied that the detestable crime for which he was duly gibbeted had been inspired by his craving for learning and his desire to buy more Greek and Hebrew dictionaries.

And so with *Paul Clifford* (whose "hero was a highwayman, the bastard son of a judge"), *Ernest Maltravers*, and *Alice* ("the whole burden of the first was seduction; the pervading refrain of the other was concubinage"), and *Night and Morning* ("abduction and seduction went hand-in-hand with adultery and secret marriage, a torn parish-registry, murder, and the coinage of bad five-franc pieces"), to say nothing of *Lucretia*, the romance of the poisoner.

Theodore Hook, Mrs. Gore, Mrs. Trollope ("revoltingly coarse in tone"), Disraeli: none of them lived up to the standards piously proclaimed by *Blackwood's* critic. So the more modern novels, beginning with *Jane Eyre* and *Adam Bede*, and continuing with the whole range of MEB's novels, were indeed sensational. But MEB's characters act "like dwellers in the actual breathing world in which we live." Nobody who reads the newspapers would be harmed by these tales. The *Blackwood's* author is a "prurient prude." As for the danger to the young, novels are written for grown people. Naturally one should exercise proper care over a child's reading, but, said Sala, "there will come a time when our children will know quite as much as we do, and more too; and when they will read all our novels, and, it may be, write novels themselves." Moreover, "Our daughters will . . . grow up to be wives and mothers quite as admirable as their grandmothers were before them." Meanwhile, "we men and women . . . want novels about That which Is. . . . We don't want pap, or spoon-meat, or milk-and-water, or curds-and-whey, or Robb's biscuits, or boiled whiting, or cold boiled beef without salt. We want meat; and this is a strong age, and we can digest it." The "poor canting creature" in *Blackwood's* had shown "hatred and jealousy and spite towards one of the most successful novelists of the age . . . because she rose so rapidly by her pluck and perseverance . . . because her pen shows no sign of feebleness. . . . To abuse people they have never seen . . . to throw dirt, to accuse their betters of irreverence and immorality": these were the practices of a "Canting Critic." So Sala mopped the floor with Mrs. Oliphant.[25]

4. An Old Enemy Enters the Battle, 1867

But there was to be no respite for MEB. Between March and September her short novel, *Circe*, had been appearing serially in *Belgravia* under the pseudonym "Babington White," which she occasionally used for some of her lesser contributions. In these years there was never a number without its instalment of one of her major novels, written under her own name; so she resorted to the pseudonym in order to avoid giving the impression that M. E. Braddon was writing virtually the entire contents of the magazine. As its *Belgravia* run was nearing an end, *Circe* appeared—still pseudonymously—in two volumes published by Ward, Lock, & Tyler.

"No sooner have I recovered in some measure from the fever of rage inspired by Blackwood," MEB wrote to Bulwer early in October 1867, "than the Pall Mall Gazette falls afoul of a novelette written by a certain Babington White and founded on a French drama. Away they go at it, hammer and tongs, forge a letter from me . . . and then call names, Fagin, Sikes, larceny, theft, tout ce que vous voulez."[26] *Circe* told the story of a brilliant young painter, forbidden by a greedy patron and picture dealer to marry, for fear that marriage would extinguish the flame of his genius. It was indeed solidly "founded" on Octave Feuillet's *Dalila*, the great hit of the Paris theatrical season of 1857, itself drawn from his earlier unsuccessful novel. An enchantress—Circe—the patron's own former fiancée, leads the painter on and then abandons him, driving him mad. He destroys her portrait and shoots her before he dies. Feuillet's protagonist was a musician, his enchantress no mere ex-fiancée of the patron but a former mistress, who took the musician as one of her lovers; but except for such modifications necessary for an English audience, *Circe* took its theme and many details directly from *Dalila*.

Feuillet was arguing that, far from stifling genius—as Georges Sand, Alfred de Vigny, and Alfred de Musset maintained—marriage and a settled bourgeois domestic life alone permit an artist to do his best work. A Victorian Englishwoman with no such literary opponents to combat, MEB diluted and paraphrased Feuillet's message by emphasizing only that "sensuousness" is the enemy of art, a highly ironical theme in view of the charges of sensuality that Mrs. Oliphant was leveling against her in *Blackwood's* while *Circe* was actually appearing in *Belgravia*. Such striking lines as the siren's heartless remark when her admirer for the first time sees blood on his handkerchief—"Tous les artistes crachent le sang."—MEB took over verbatim from Feuillet. The original name Delilah—the hair-clipping, castrating female—was perhaps more appropriate for the wicked woman of the story than that of Circe, who merely turned her victims into swine; but even Circe's name MEB found in Feuillet's line, "Omphale, Circé, Dalila, ces noms de magiciennes."[27]

In an article of September 16, 1867, called "*Dalila* and *Circe*," the *Pall Mall Gazette* writer spotted the "almost identical plot" of the two works, apparently without realizing that Feuillet's play had ever been acted (". . . representation on the stage, without much modification, would scarcely be practicable"). He gloried in Babington White's occasional word-for-word translation (" 'I tell you that a genius married and settled is a genius flat-ironed into a nonentity' ") ; declared that the only original matter in *Circe* was the tasteless occasional introduction of "living persons under silly disguises and silly pseudonyms"—as when Frith appeared as "Mr. Skith"—; and blasted *Circe* for "its absolute dishonesty. Its adapter is simply trying to palm off upon the English public as an original novel a book stolen from the French. . . . We . . . protest against a proceeding so fraudulent. . . . obligation to the original author should be publicly acknowledged and formally placed upon record." And in passing, the writer mentioned MEB's earlier adaptation of *The Doctor's Wife* from *Madame Bovary*.[28]

On the next day, September 17, the *Pall Mall Gazette* published the following letter:

With the deepest regret I have perused your severe criticism of
"Circe." . . . The discovery of the theft from M. Octave Feuillet
has fallen like a thunderbolt upon my senses. Let me at once assure
. . . subscribers to *Belgravia*, that I was unconscious of Mr. Babington White's deception, he having undertaken to contribute an
original novel. . . . I should wish at once to publish my willingness
to return the amounts paid by my subscribers for those numbers
of *Belgravia* in which "Circe" has usurped a place.[29]

The letter was signed "M. E. Braddon," but of course she had not written
it. Next day, a letter signed "Chesterton Smith" asked Miss Braddon to
inform the writer of the "full name and address of Mr. Babington White.
I am an original author who cannot find readers or . . . a publisher. Not
being able to translate from the French . . . I should be very glad to combine with one who can turn French into English as skillfully as the author
of Circe.' " Also, would Miss Braddon's publisher kindly explain how it
was that the *Edinburgh Review* had published a special number in which
Circe is called " 'an extraordinary book,' " and where that number might
be obtained? Postponing for the moment any explanation of this new
query by (the non-existent) Chesterton Smith, we next find "A Man's
Man" sarcastically suggesting that if Miss Braddon had recovered "from
the shock of the 'discovery of the theft from M. Octave Feuillet,' " she
would perhaps "be good enough to tell us who committed the theft." He
could find nobody who had ever met Babington White. "Several persons
. . . have assured me that, as Mrs. Prig remarked of Mrs. Harris 'there
never was no such person' [Dickens, *Martin Chuzzlewit*], and that 'Circe'
was really written by a certain lady novelist of considerable popularity.
However, Miss Braddon must know," and should clear up the mystery.[30]

MEB did now write in: "Miss Braddon presents her compliments to the
Editor of the *Pall Mall Gazette*, and begs to inform him that the letter
purporting to be written by her, which appears in his paper for the 17th
inst., is a forgery." Immediately below, in square brackets, appeared the
following editorial comment: "The forged letter was one in which Miss
Braddon was made to express an honourable regret that the readers of
Belgravia should have been imposed upon by a novel stolen from the
French,"[31] which certainly implied that the forged letter, if genuine,
would have done MEB credit. The point was made explicit the next day in
a letter signed only "T. T.": "Of the two letters with the signature of M.
E. Braddon, most people, I am sure, will very much prefer the one that is
said to be forged to that which purports to be genuine." And where, T. T.

wanted to know, was Mr. Babington White, about whose existence there was so much doubt? Miss Braddon had no cause for complaint, since the "story which, as M. Feydeau wrote it, was called 'Madame Bovary,' and which as Miss Braddon wrote it, was called the 'Doctor's Wife' proved" that she did not mind taking French authors' work as her own.[32] T. T.'s own acquaintance with French literature must have been severely limited, or he could hardly have supposed that Flaubert was Feydeau. But the charges against MEB were essentially true and deeply embarrassing.

Two days later the *Pall Mall Gazette* said that Miss Braddon had invited them "to discover the author of the 'forged' letter . . . and to offer a reward for his apprehension," to which she would herself add one hundred guineas. They hoped she might find out who "unwarrantably used her name, though the 'forged' letter did not discredit her; quite the contrary." And if she found the forger, they hoped she would "be encouraged to offer another reward for the discovery of a far more reprehensible person—Mr. Babbington [sic] White."[33] They were now annoyingly and intentionally inserting a second "b" in Babington. Of course the *Pall Mall Gazette* itself did not accept MEB's "invitation," since its editor, Gilby's old friend Frederick Greenwood, was himself the forger. He had also written the original attack, and the letters from "Chesterton Smith," "A Man's Man," and "T. T." The joke was beginning to wear thin. But Greenwood was not prepared to call a halt. When the author of a column in the *Morning Star*, who signed himself "Jacques," protested at the insistent demand of the *Pall Mall Gazette* that Babington White identify himself, and asked why Babington White should not enjoy anonymity if he chose, the *Pall Mall Gazette* replied:

> The anonymous is for people who work honestly; when they work dishonestly, they ought to be stripped of the mask under which the work is done. Nobody would dream of asserting for Mr. Fagan [sic] and Mr. Sykes [sic] the privilege of concealment and anonymity, and the writer who is called Mr. Babbington [sic] White is simply a literary thief. Perhaps there is no harm in . . . stealing a novel from the French, and then advertising falsely (the advertisement lies before us) that it has been praised by the *Edinburgh Review*; that, however, is a matter of opinion, and our own view of it happens to be a strong one.[34]

Here, for the second time, the *Pall Mall Gazette* referred to an alleged false claim that the *Edinburgh Review* had praised *Circe*. With his usual mistaken insistence on brazening matters out, John Maxwell, who was of course responsible for advertising *Circe*, now did exactly what Greenwood must have hoped he would do: he wrote to the *Morning Star*, affirming that in borrowing from *Dalila* Babington White had done no more wrong than Tom Taylor, who so frequently borrowed his plays from French originals. Maxwell added that it had been the "Edinburgh *Daily* Review" that had praised *Circe*, and that in some of the advertisements, to "save a line," the printer had deleted the word "Daily." Gleefully, Greenwood returned to the attack: the *Edinburgh Daily Review* was "a very different authority" from the *Edinburgh Review*. Not even to save sixpence (a blow at Maxwell's penuriousness) would "any respectable publisher represent that the opinion of an obscure daily print is the opinion of the *Edinburgh Review*; he would see that . . . it is a dishonest trick." Worse: Greenwood reprinted the original advertisement from the *Times*, using identical type, and demonstrating to even the least practiced eye that "it was not to 'save a line' that the word 'Daily' was struck out here . . . there is room for printing 'Daily' . . . three times over." And there was. In fact the name of the paper in which the favorable notice of *Circe* appeared was *not* even the *Edinburgh Daily Review* since no such paper existed. The paper that had given *Circe* its boost ("This is an extraordinary book. It is a story of character, not of incident, and is fraught with a terrible moral") was the *Daily Review*. The word "Edinburgh" had been invented, and "Daily" omitted. If the publisher had wanted to save space, he could have done so by being honest instead of faking praise from a great journal for "the poor little bundle of stolen goods called 'Circe.' "[35] Maxwell had been effectively demolished.

In his very next issue Greenwood printed—in Dutch—an advertisement from a Dutch newspaper announcing (he considerately translated) *Circe* as " 'A new novel of Miss Braddon's derived from the French of Octave Feuillet by Babington or Babbington White. . . .' " "What authority," Greenwood wanted to know, "has the Dutch publisher for announcing that the new romance, which is not new, is 'van Ms. Braddon?' "[36] MEB replied that she believed "this advertisement to be maliciously concocted" and inquired the title, date, and place of publication of the Dutch newspaper. Of course the *Pall Mall Gazette* of the 28th could have published the Dutch advertisement of the 26th only if Greenwood himself had "concocted" and inserted it. Greenwood answered: "Miss Braddon believes too much, and explains too little." The Dutch newspaper was the *Nieuwe Utrechtsche Courant* and "the original lies at the office of the *Pall Mall Gazette* for the inspection of any one who chooses to take the trouble." But in the text of her letter, which the *Pall Mall Gazette* had not published in full, and which she had sent to the *Morning Star* as a precaution, MEB had called the advertisement "quite as wicked in intention as the forged letter," and expressed her "surprise at seeing a paper professing to be written 'by gentlemen for gentlemen' carrying on a crusade" against her.[37]

At this juncture, the *Saturday Review* and *Spectator* entered the lists. The *Saturday Review* conceded that "the practise of palming off sham pieces under sham names . . . has a tendency to reduce literature . . . to the level of horse-coping and thimblerig," but asked why Miss Braddon, "wearied with the glitter of fame and name," should not "mix with the crowd in disguise" if she wanted to. Already, they said ironically, she "had covered the name of Braddon with immortal glory." Now she had created Babington White "in her own image," and they "should be as Isis and Osiris, twin deities worshipped of all the readers of shilling magazines." As for *Circe*, it was "the trumpery adaptation of a poorish play, spoilt in the process," and the real fault lay with critics who praised such slipshod work.

The *Spectator* took a not very different line: possibly MEB was guilty of "literary dishonesty," but why was she "more deserving of censure than scores of similar offenders?" Despite all the puffs, few had heard of *Circe* until the *Pall Mall Gazette* attacked it, and so made "the chief part of its reputation." *Belgravia* was "chiefly . . . a vehicle for the publication of Miss Braddon's numerous novels; the padding furnished to fill up the interval between" them was usually flimsy. Most readers would have left "the second serial unread," until the *Pall Mall Gazette,* "which, amongst its numerous antipathies, nourishes a special dislike to novels of the *Lady Audley* school," discovered that *Circe* had been taken from Feuillet. Although the English author had used Feuillet's plot, and had translated a few passages directly, he had also "filled up the requisite number of pages with genuine and self-inspired twaddle. He did, in fact, what is done every day upon the English stage, and what is not infrequently done in English literature." Yet the *Pall Mall Gazette* chose to treat the offense "as of unparalleled enormity." The matter of the allegedly forged letter from MEB should be cleared up. The *Spectator* would be as "loath to believe that an authoress of reputation and considerable talent could descend to a willful and deliberate misstatement of facts" as that "a journal of such standing as our respected contemporary would make an unjustifiable use of a woman's name in order to gratify a literary animosity."

Yet the very phraseology indicates that the *Spectator* did believe that the *Pall Mall Gazette* had made just such an unjustifiable use of a woman's name. The plagiarism itself was "of comparatively small importance." Without literary borrowing, "there would be an end of bookwriting." Shakespeare had done it; Sir Walter Scott took the dumb girl in *Peveril of the Peak* from Goethe. "Miss Braddon herself would never have written the *Doctor's Wife* unless she had read *Madame Bovary*; yet . . . it would be utterly unjust to call the *Doctor's Wife*—the ablest, we think, of her stories—a mere translation of Flaubert's novel." Plagiarism was "entirely a question of degree. . . . No code has yet been invented to define what is, and what is not, literary larceny." But "to write a letter and then declare you did not write it, or to sign anybody's name to a forged composition, are acts of clear dishonesty; and . . . before we give judgement on . . . Babington White, we should be glad to see the authorship of the alleged Braddon letter in the *Pall Mall* cleared up satisfactorily."[38] In this way, one of the most respected and feared critical journals unmistakably intervened on MEB's side.

And so Greenwood felt it. On October 3, the *Pall Mall Gazette* gave an entire page to his reply. It was such good-natured critics, he said, who encouraged the kind of literary theft exemplified in *Circe*. In fact, *Circe* had plagiarized not only Feuillet but—the paper now charged for the first time—Balzac's *Le Chef d'Oeuvre inconnu* (1831); and indeed the destruction of the portrait in *Circe* paralleled that of Frenhofer's masterpiece in Balzac's tale. Even the *Spectator*, Greenwood lamented, now objected to any "asperity" in making such offenses known: "To go into your neighbour's field and steal his cow is clearly wrong; but every gentleman is at liberty to decide for himself how much of her milk he can honestly press into his own pail." When the *Pall Mall Gazette* some months earlier had denounced MEB for "selling old books"—*Rupert Godwin* and *Run to Earth*—as new ones, the *Spectator* had intervened to say that the practice involved no moral wrong. Now "all the Babbington [*sic*] Whites in England will say that while [the *Spectator*] does object to their want of brains, it has decided that there is nothing to carp at in their want of honesty." Tolerating such offenders endangers "an already enfeebled literature."[39]

To this the *Spectator* replied disarmingly that it hoped the *Pall Mall* would "set about discovering the authorship of the forged letter" and Miss Braddon that "of the stolen novel."[40] Greenwood complained that "what Miss Braddon is asked to do she can do at the stroke of the pen. What we are asked to do is scarcely within the bounds of possibility. We have absolutely no clue whatsoever." He went so far as to reprint the letter, and to say that "As a forgery, this letter was no doubt very reprehensible, and we are very sorry it imposed upon us." But, he added again, "in publishing it no harm could have been intended, because it is such a letter as would have reflected great credit upon Miss Braddon had it been genuine."[41] He also said he hoped it would be the last word on the subject. But it was not, quite. On October 8, in an article called "Favourable Notices," he quoted two separate reviews of *Circe* from the *Morning Star*, which had helped Maxwell and MEB throughout the controversy. On *Circe*'s first appearance, the *Star* (August 12, 1867) had called it "a wild race of words," and had said that "To speak of it at greater length would be a sheer waste of space." But by October 3, the *Star* said it was "a story of considerable originality and power, and not at all deserving of the wholesale charges of plagiarism made against it." Greenwood did not add that the *Star* had also attributed to "diffidence" (!) rather than to dishonesty Babington White's failure to acknowledge his indebtedness to Feuillet.[42]

What wonder that MEB was agonized by the sharpness and venom with which Greenwood had pressed this new attack? "I have cruel need of kindness," she wrote Bulwer the day after the *Pall Mall*'s final thrust, "for my enemies are many, and their arrows stick fast in me."[43] An enemy of Maxwell's since *Welcome Guest* days, and of MEB's because of his friendship with the disappointed Gilby, Greenwood was indeed brutally persistent and, in "forging" her letter, he was also highly unethical. Yet his main point was both irrefutable and important. MEB had taken most of *Circe* from Feuillet and one episode from Balzac, and she had no real defense.

The *Spectator*'s remark that such plagiarism was "done every day upon the English stage" provides the most generous and most plausible explanation of her action. As Clement Scott wrote in 1899 about the playwrights of the mid-sixties: "if anyone wanted to reproduce D'Ennery or Octave Feuillet or Dumas or Sardou, all he had to do was to send over to Paris for the book, which cost a couple of francs."[44] Thoroughly familiar with the practice of "adapting" French plays for the English theatre—often referred to in her novels—, equally willing to "borrow" from Soulié the materials for her own pot-boilers and to "adapt" Flaubert without acknowledgment in *The Doctor's Wife*, MEB had probably thought little of her latest transgression until it was discovered. But no return that *Circe* may have brought her could compensate for the pain it cost her. And John Maxwell's fake claim and unsatisfactory explanation with regard to the *Edinburgh Review* had only made matters worse.

MEB herself replied to the *Pall Mall Gazette* in the same issue of *Belgravia* that carried Sala's answer to *Blackwood's*. She reminded her readers that the original name of the *Pall Mall Gazette* had been invented by Thackeray in *Pendennis* (1849–1850) for a new paper to be founded by his Captain Shandon—then in the Fleet Prison for debt—whom he drew as a portrait of the brilliant and dissolute journalist, William Maginn (1793–1842). Captain Shandon's prospectus for the fictional *Pall Mall Gazette* in *Pendennis* had described it as to be "written by gentlemen for gentlemen."[45] So MEB cleverly wrote her protest against the actual *Pall Mall Gazette,* founded fifteen years after Thackeray's fictional prototype, in the form of a letter from Captain Shandon in Hades to the real paper's present editor.

In *his* day, MEB made Shandon say to Greenwood, the *Pall Mall Gazette* "rarely outstepped the limits which a gentleman prescribes for himself even when he is most acrimonious." But look at the paper now! "A bundle of cuttings from other papers, garnished with flippant and frivolous comment; and little, carping, spiteful paragraphs; and prurient harpings on subjects that decency best reprobates by decent avoidance; and sham letters from sham correspondents, all breathing the same malignant feeling against some one or something respected by other people; and, to give spice to the whole, an occasional forgery." Say what you like about Mr. Babington White's book. But to "carry on a crusade . . . against the Lady" who conducted *Belgravia* was "cowardly and paltry." Reviewing the entire controversy in fine Maginnian prose, MEB's "Remonstrance" blasted the *Pall Mall Gazette* for its overblown attack on *Circe,* for publishing a letter over MEB's forged signature and presenting it as genuine, and for making no effort to find the forger. Were his own name to be forged, "with the same malicious intent to injure the magazine you conduct," Greenwood would "find some machinery to trace out the wrong-doer." Babington White "derived the characters in his story from a French drama, and did not consider himself bound to blazon that fact upon his title page any more than William Makepeace Thackeray [founder of Greenwood's own *Cornhill Magazine*] considered himself bound to tell the world that he derived the broad idea of his wonderful Becky Sharp . . . from the Madame de Marneffe of Honoré de Balzac." Anne Thackeray got her "word-painting" from Flaubert; LeSage borrowed from the Spanish, Sterne from Rabelais and Burton, Bulwer-Lytton from Sterne.

MEB ended angrily: "A journal written by gentlemen for gentlemen! . . . Is it the part of a gentleman to war against a woman, or to give ridiculous prominence to an insignificant matter in order to injure a trade rival? . . . Go to school, Mr. Editor, and learn what it is to be a gentleman. Miss Braddon," she concluded, "I imagine, has no higher aspiration than to please [the] novel-reading public," which will not "withdraw their support from her because she has been made the subject of a most unmanly attack . . . more characteristic of the disappointed author of two or three unappreciated novels than of the gentleman editor who writes for gentlemen readers."[46] So MEB attacked her tormentor by name, and called him publicly—as she had privately called the anonymous author of the *North British Review* attack of 1865—a failure as a novelist.[47]

5. Last Exchanges: the Smoke Clears (1868)

In a second, more general *Belgravia* article, "On the Sensational in Literature and Art," Sala returned early in 1868 to the counter-attack. Just as the Scots had once denounced the "Cockney school" of Leigh Hunt and Hazlitt, he said, just as Southey and others had denounced Byron as a leader of the "Satanic school," just as "classicists" had fought "romanticists" in literature and painting, so now, Sala maintained, there was a cry against "sensationalism." The howls of distaste at Delacroix voiced by the followers of David provided an exact parallel in the arts. Dickens was a sensationalist; so was Shakespeare, as Voltaire had complained when he called him "un barbare grotesque."

> In the opinion of dolts, and dullards, and envious backbiters, everything is "sensational" that is vivid, and nervous, and forcible, and graphic, and true. . . . Fuseli . . . Hogarth . . . Goya. . . . Casanova. . . . Wedgwood. . . . Mr. Millais . . . Mr. Holman Hunt. . . . Mr. Woolner . . . Mr. Ruskin. . . . Dr. Newman . . . Professor Maurice. . . . Mr. Kingsley. . . . *Belgravia* is a sensational magazine, and Miss Braddon is a dreadfully sensational novelist. . . . Napoleon III . . . Bismarck. . . . Garibaldi . . . General Grant.

To give up the sensational, as the dullards and dolts want to do, would be to

> go back to the calmly dull, to the tranquilly inane, to the timorously decorous, to the sweetly stupid. . . . Let our Royal

Academicians turn coach-painters, or cut out profiles in black sticking-plaster . . . and the Bishop of London, in a wig like a bird's-nest, preach a sermon in St. Paul's against photography and the electric telegraph. Don't let us move, don't let us travel, don't let us hear or see anything; but let us write sonnets to Chloe, and play madrigals on the spinet, and dance minuets, and pray to Heaven against Sensationalism, the Pope, the Devil, and the Pretender; and then let Dulness reign triumphant, and Universal Darkness cover all.[48]

This resounding peroration from Sala brought the great "sensationalism" controversy virtually to its natural close. The enemy was silenced. Five years later, writing to Bulwer about a trip to Scotland, MEB commented, "I saw young Mr. Blackwood, who was very gracious—which considering how his Mag. had flayed me alive some years ago, he had need to be."[49]

MEB herself, still defiantly writing as "Babington White," contributed to *Belgravia*'s pages in March and April 1868 two instalments of what she called "The Mudie Classics," with a sardonic preface:

The critical contempt for all stories of a sensational character has of late become a fact so notorious that the Conductor of this Magazine would be wanting in deference to those great Teachers who preside over the Literary Journals of this country, if she failed to recognize the necessity for an immediate reform in the class of fiction provided for the indulgent readers of BELGRAVIA. She is thus compelled to consider the sensational element in fiction as an entirely modern innovation, devised by ignorant and reckless writers, whose only hope of creating interest lies in the employment of those exceptional situations which should properly be excluded from all romance.

So she had commissioned a "series of short stories," conscientiously adapted from "those models . . . the dramatists and epic poets of ancient Greece . . . modernised in accordance with the prevailing taste of the novel-reading public." The first, "Sir Alk Mayonn [Alcmaeon], or the Seven against the Elector," was an adaptation of *The Seven Against Thebes* into the period of Bonnie Prince Charlie, told in Scott-like style, and including every sensational episode imaginable: bribery, adultery, assassination, matricide, bigamy, and mere murder. MEB proved her point: indeed, she may have overproved it, since "The Mudie Classics" stopped short after two instalments.[50]

As a kind of coda to the anti-sensationalist symphony, there appeared anonymously in 1868 a book called *Lucretia; or, the Heroine of the Nineteenth Century. A Correspondence Sensational and Sentimental.* The author was the Reverend F. E. Paget, a clever Tractarian satirist, who usually dealt with clerical subjects. At school, his heroine, Lucretia Beverley (real name: Lucky Frummage) put "one volume of 'Aurora Floyd' into a brown paper cover, and marked [it] 'Télémaque,' and another 'Simpson's Euclid,' and . . . Priscilla Compton sat on the third volume without ever moving an inch . . . though a wasp had stung her ankle, and she felt it creeping up her leg." Aurora Floyd herself is "the very jolliest female I ever came across. . . . a shade too fast and horsey, and of course it was a mistake marrying the groom. . . . I do envy her those grand sensational scenes which . . . culminated in her being a suspected murderess. And great big brawny . . . John Mellish, was there ever such a devoted, petting jewel of a husband! . . . I wish I could stumble on his duplicate."

Lucky runs off with her uncle's cowherd, who tells her that he is a nobleman in disguise named Marmion de Mowbray, but is in fact a burglar whose sobriquet is "Brummagem Brittles." He rescues her from her bed, when she has set it on fire by falling asleep reading *Jane Eyre*, and from then on their courtship is rapid. But Lucky's intimacy with him—a direct outcome of her fondness for sensation-novels—brings her nothing but distress. He gives her a bracelet, which she proudly wears until it is identified as part of the loot from a burglary. In her desk he hides the money he had stolen in a bank robbery. People now begin to mistrust Lucky. But she runs off with her suitor, and just after they have been solemnly married in church, the detectives arrest the bridegroom. Lucky is eventually cured of sensational literature, which she abjures forever.

All this gentle satire would have amused MEB, who would have agreed that sensation-novels should not be taken too seriously by the young and excitable. But Paget ended his book by dropping his story and addressing to the reader a sermon against the sensation-novel, in which he proved himself as much of a "canting" critic as Mrs. Oliphant, though not so hostile personally to MEB. He declared "the teaching of the sensation novels of the day to be . . . so infamous; the principles contained in . . . them so utterly demoralising; the conversations . . . so revolting for their looseness, wickedness, and blasphemy; the scenes . . . so licentious or so horrible" that he must try to protect the purity of the young against them. "Profligacy," "moral depravity," "irreligion," "crimes against civilised society," these he declared were not exaggerated charges: he himself had been contaminated and polluted by reading these works. And the upper and middle classes "through their insatiate perusal, for years past, of all this pernicious nonsense," have suffered "incalculable mischief." Worse: these books have passed "from the parlour to the kitchen," and the lower classes are likely to be turned into revolutionaries by them. It is especially distasteful that women should have written such books.[51] Paget here outdid even the most virulent of MEB's other critics in his vituperation. Even the *Spectator* rebuked him mildly: MEB's books, they said, were not immoral, and it was wrong of Paget to concentrate his fire on *Aurora Floyd*, when it was other writers who actually were the immoral ones.[52]

As the storm died away, a short-lived but entertaining satirical periodical called *The Mask* published a generous, almost affectionate, treatment of MEB's work, with a drawing—herewith reproduced—showing her as a circus-rider, tiptoe on Pegasus' back (his collar reads "Belgravia"), while John Maxwell as ringmaster holds up the last of the hoops through which she is to pass: it is labeled *Dead Sea Fruit*, and in the background are some of the others she has already traversed: *Trail of the Serpent, Lady Audley's Secret, Aurora Floyd*. A clown holds the more recent ones: *The Lady's Mile, Birds of Prey*, and *Charlotte's Inheritance*. The clown's sleeve is labeled "Circe" and his jacket "Nobody's Child," the first a reference to the Babington White novel that had stirred up such a tempest, and the second presumably to the American version of *Run to Earth* (actually called *Nobody's Daughter*), for which she had also been sharply criticized. On her winged steed MEB is drawn as serene, poised, determined. She flies through the air with the greatest of ease.

The Mask said that many of MEB's readers would expect to learn how

> as a babe she was found attached by a gold thread to the knocker of a convent in Mount Athos; how, having at an early age been brought up by the nuns in a secret drawer till her growth rendered concealment impossible, her education was continued at a ladies' school near Paris until the discovery of a modern mummy in the melon-frame of the *pension* kitchen-garden caused a break-up of the seminary and necessitated the return of our heroine to the Levant. . . . how she was stopped on the Simplon by a gentleman who had married his second wife's sister before his spouse departed this life, and who, on the eve of bankruptcy, had chosen

the profession of brigand . . . how [he] would have forced his
victim into untimely trigamy, had it not been for the succour op-
portunely offered by a noble duke . . . travelling under the name of
John Smith.

and so on, for quite a distance. Sigismund Smith knew better how to
parody MEB's love of incident, but at least *The Mask* was good-humored.
And its brief appended serious biography of her was wholly admiring:

> Novel after novel has appeared, attracting fresh readers into the
> magic circle of her talent. . . . even the French . . . have read most
> of her novels in their own tongue, and seen dramatized versions of
> more than one of them. . . . No Englishwoman has written with
> such male power and skill. She draws on her powerful imagination
> for incidents, and shows great penetration and judgment of
> character. . . . Those who object to sensation . . . cannot deny her
> power of description and her faculty of giving life to the images of
> her brain. . . . We candidly admit that the sensational in works of
> fiction seems to us as allowable as any other effort of the imagina-
> tion, and most of the great writers of romance have made copious
> use of it,[53]

notably Victor Hugo and Dickens. This was the tone that critics in subsequent years would almost uniformly adopt in reviewing her books individually or considering them in groups. The controversy, by mid-1868,
was over.[54]

Yet MEB could not have known this. The half-dozen years since the
triumph of *Lady Audley's Secret* had been years of intense labor and of
occasional bitter disappointment. Though she was now financially secure,
each of her efforts to transcend literary mediocrity had met with only
partial success. When Bulwer had failed to approve *The Doctor's Wife*
whole-heartedly; when nobody seemed to notice that *The Lady's Mile*
constituted a new and promising experiment; when, just as partial libera-
tion from the treadmill seemed to be in view, the founding of *Belgravia*
made it impossible and forced a return to the over rapid production of
sensation fiction, MEB became emotionally depressed and professionally
cynical, if not disheartened.

The chorus of voices denouncing her for immoral writing was hard
enough to bear, even though she knew that charge was absurd. But when
to this her critics subtly added the charge of living an immoral life, and of

not knowing what it was to be a lady, the lash stung, and stung the harder because, as the result of Knowles's publicity, the charge was impossible to refute. MEB knew, and her friends knew, that despite her liaison with Maxwell she was indeed a lady. And friends like Kent and Sala and others rose to the defense of her novels.

But the new charges of plagiarism leveled against Babington White could not be refuted either, despite the best efforts of MEB and her allies. Under the pressure of heavy commitments she had yielded to the Victorian playwright's temptation to "help herself pretty freely" to Feuillet's ideas; so she could not convincingly protest against the charge itself, but only against the peculiar personal malice with which it had been pressed, and against the unethical forging of her name. She had indeed acquired many enemies: they were jealous of her success; they were friends of Gilby, who felt she had betrayed him ("Gratitude!" he had written, "why you hardly know the meaning of the word") ; they resented John Maxwell's real or fancied past ungenerous treatment of them; they sided with the family of his unfortunate wife. For any or all of these reasons the enemies took their revenge during the five years between 1863 and 1868, by attacking MEB at her most vulnerable points. What slurs she had to face in her daily life we can only guess. Her sensibilities were made raw by the critical onslaught. It left her both tense and weak in the face of grim personal troubles that the latter months of 1868 had in store.

CHAPTER VII

"Over All There Hung a Shadow and a Fear" (1868–1875)

The series of domestic griefs that struck MEB in rapid succession at the end of October 1868 found her without her usual resilience. They precipitated a nervous collapse, complicated by an attack of puerperal fever. Madness seemed to hover over her, as the surrounding world grew shadowy. She was forced to lay down her pen for more than a year. During her illness John Maxwell was deeply worried and even after she was well he hated to have her refer to it. Early in 1870, she began to write again, hesitantly and feebly at first, then with gradually returning strength and self-confidence. By 1871, with *The Lovels of Arden*, her second domestic novel, she had completely recovered. She confided to Bulwer the details of her illness and continued to consult him about her work until his death early in 1873, after which she paid public tribute to him.

Although she returned to writing for the stage in 1873, her plays brought her little success. For that she continued to depend upon her novels, finding in an enterprising Lancashire newspaper publisher, W. F. Tillotson, an additional outlet for their appearance in serial form. For two years she stuck close to her proven formulas, but experimented with a new and stiff admixture of "cant," striving to compete with her popular rival, Mrs. Henry Wood, by making her characters adopt a solemn piety and an often hypocritical lip service to evangelical Christianity, while at the same time subjecting them for her own pleasure to dead pan satire. When scolded for this "new manner" by one unusually perceptive critic, she apparently decided with some reluctance to abandon it, but not before she had produced some of her most effective—if unpleasant—comments on a stuffy censorious society.

And in 1874, with the death of John Maxwell's wife, that society in the person of Richard Brinsley Knowles once again and in a most painful way advertised the fact that she and Maxwell were not man and wife. They were married as soon as it was legally possible. But the new publicity forced them temporarily to leave their beloved Lichfield House. MEB's bitter resentment of the cruelty and hypocrisy surrounding her was mirrored in the cynical and reprehensible characters of her next two novels. Her marriage, however, finally closed the long era of social ambiguity initiated by her decision to become an actress in 1857 and made ever more difficult during the thirteen long years of her liaison with Maxwell and the births of their children. In 1875, at the age of forty, MEB had lived exactly half her life and had reached its major turning point.

1. Family Tragedy and Nervous Collapse (1868–1869)

The troubles began at Naples, where Maggie Braddon Cartighoni had gradually become a virtual invalid, while sharing her husband's financial anxieties. In her letters to her mother, she reported one affliction after another. In August 1864 it was the heat and flies of the Neapolitan summer that she found unbearable; at Christmas 1865 she came down with "a malady called 'chiodo solale,' " an agonizing "complaint in the head," increasing each day in violence as the sun rose and not abating until sunset. Maggie thought she was going mad, and two doctors had told her that quinine was the only cure. The illness lasted four months. In January 1867, her husband Antonio dislocated his foot, and a man-servant robbed them of a thousand franc bank note, a terrible blow "particularly in these times."

And Maggie was ill again, this time with an eye complaint. She had "passed three months in agony," and three successive doctors had attended her. The last had almost cured her, but said he could have done so more quickly had she not been in such delicate health. He found, she wrote, that she was threatened with "a consumption. What I have suffered no mortal can tell." MEB had offered to assist Antonio in England, but he could not leave Naples because his entire future depended upon his father, at whose death he would be "anything but badly off." Grateful for the money that Mary had sometimes sent her, Maggie protested that she had not asked for it, although at the time of the robbery she would have done so if she had had "more confidence" in her mother. "But I have never taken that liberty with you, though so near a relative. . . . you have always told me how much Mary has to do for strangers. Consequently I could not imagine she could assist *me*."

The rather spiteful irony of Maggie's words echoed her phrasing in the earlier letter in which she had complained that, "now that the public knew" of MEB's "marriage," her mother no longer minded her knowing of it too. In view of her distance from home, her domestic worries and painful illness, and her jealousy of Mary's success, her tone is perhaps understandable. How much money MEB had actually sent her sister over the years cannot be estimated. Maggie's letters regularly include thanks for presents, among them a gold watch for her son, young Nicolino. It was certainly true that MEB helped other relatives. She rescued a Braddon cousin from bankruptcy, incurred, he admitted in a long letter of self-abasement, by his own recklessness. With a clean slate he set off to make a new career abroad. MEB loaned money to aged aunts in Devon and refused to accept interest for it. But these were hardly "strangers." Perhaps by "strangers" Maggie meant John Maxwell's children by his first marriage. From the little sheaf of her letters that Mrs. Braddon retained, there still breathes the resentment of an elder and less fortunate, less talented and less cherished sister against the younger, happier favorite of their mother.

And Maggie's illnesses were all too real. In July 1868, heartily acknowledging a present of money from MEB, she reported that she had been compelled to leave Naples for a nearby mountaintop village, because she had been growing steadily weaker from dysentery. The doctor feared that this too would "end in consumption." Antonio was as solicitous of her as he could possibly be even if he had been richer. Now he would like to take her to England to see if "native air" would improve her health. But as his income came from editing a newspaper and giving private lessons (in English perhaps?) he could not leave Naples without the prospect of a job in England. "Do you think Mary could get him anything there in whatever way? as he can do all things." With an English job he would abandon everything in Italy to give Maggie a chance of recovery. Antonio's "dreadfully tyrannical father" would do nothing for him: his late mother had been an angel but his father was "the contrary." It was the recent change of government, Maggie said, that had ruined Antonio. Before then they had got on "pretty well with only Antonio's exertions."

Perhaps spurred on by the hope that MEB would finance a trip to England, perhaps newly resigned to her ill-health, Maggie now showed none of her former bitterness. Mrs. Braddon asked her sisters-in-law in Devon whether they could take Maggie in if she were to come to England; it seems clear that MEB was willing to pay the Cartighonis' travel expenses. But the aunts were old and unwilling or unable to undertake so grave a responsibility; moreover, they were sure that after Naples the English climate would be fatal to their niece and they may well have been right. Distressed at her illness, they wrote that she was young (she was forty-four) and they hoped she might soon recover. Only some ten days after her inquiry about a job in England for Antonio, however, Maggie reported that she was worse. Her legs and feet had swollen so that she could hardly leave her bed: "I thank you a thousand times for . . . all . . . kind expressions of affection from you and Mary. . . . believe me I deeply feel your kindness, but I don't think I shall be long here to trouble you. . . . For poor Nicolino I feel grieved for he will never find anyone like a mother, tho' I must say that a better father than Antonio never lived." At the end, she sent "my repeated thanks to you and Mary and praying that I may see you once again."[1]

Despite the inability of the aunts in Devon to receive the Cartighonis, Mrs. Braddon and MEB apparently went ahead with plans for the visit. Antonio, MEB wrote later to Bulwer, was determined to bring Maggie "home to us to be restored by her native air, and this reunion my mother had looked forward to with much tenderness." But on October 20, 1868, Mrs. Braddon learned that Maggie had died in Naples. MEB had been planning that night to see Bulwer's new play, *The Rightful Heir*, which had been running a little over two weeks, and her mother kept the news from her so that she would not miss the performance. She went to the theatre all unknowing. Next morning, Mrs. Braddon came sad-faced to her with the news that Maggie was dead.[2] Though Maggie had for so many years lived far apart from her mother and sister, and though they had never managed to visit Naples despite repeated invitations—presumably because MEB was working too hard to take the time to go—, her death surely revived those days in Camberwell—only fifteen years earlier—when the mother and the two sisters had faced the world together courageously and cheerfully on one hundred and fifty pounds a year.

The blow, MEB told Bulwer, had struck Mrs. Braddon hard, "but another and more cruel blow was inflicted by the hand of him who should most have cherished her—her only son." This was an extraordinary confidence for MEB to make even to her old friend and adviser. What could Edward have done that hurt Mrs. Braddon even more than Maggie's death? The only clue comes from Maggie Cartighoni's last letter of the previous July, in which she told her mother that Edward had suddenly and unexpectedly appeared in Naples from India. They had not met for more than twenty years, since 1847, when he had gone out to Calcutta, and they did not at first recognize each other. But, said Maggie, "he looks young and *good-looking*. He has got your face precisely, every feature." Edward and Antonio had been to the top of Vesuvius together, and were walking "all over Naples." The next day he was leaving for Rome, and thence for Germany to see his children, who were presumably at school there. But he was planning to be in England about the end of August.[3]

Edward Braddon, we know, had always remained in touch with his father. Had he perhaps sided with him in some family dispute? Unlikely, since MEB herself wrote, in *Before the Knowledge of Evil*, that after their separation her parents met "almost as friends," that there was in fact nothing left to quarrel about. Had Edward found it necessary to disappoint his mother and MEB by not coming to England after all? But even though she had not seen him for twenty-one years, Mrs. Braddon could hardly have regarded that as a worse blow than Maggie's death. A Braddon family tradition in the next generation held that Edward—nicknamed "His Dryness" because of his haughty carriage and behavior—once cut MEB at a family wedding because of her ambiguous social position. But there is no record of a Braddon family wedding in the few days between Maggie's death and Edward's cruel behavior to his mother. Nor, if such a wedding had taken place then, would Mrs. Braddon or MEB have attended it, since they were in mourning for Maggie.

Yet the tradition that Edward disliked or would not accept his sister's irregular union with Maxwell probably holds the kernel of the truth. Quite possibly he did come to England in October 1868 but refused to stay under John Maxwell's roof at Lichfield House or even to call upon Mrs. Braddon while she was living there. Such an affront from her only son—which would of course have deeply wounded his sister MEB as well—suggests itself as a plausible hypothesis. Whatever Edward may have done, MEB believed that it killed her mother. "From that hour," she continued her letter of November 3 to Bulwer, "she faded, and a long-standing chronic disease—of the heart & lungs—became suddenly acute. For ten days she kept her bed, the first time in her life illness so long imprisoned her." MEB never left her for more than half an hour at a time, and "by the merciful deception" of the doctor did not realize for several days that her mother's life was in danger. Even then, the doctor said that there was hope, and "on this poor comfort I held out all through the night, ministering to my beloved, who took the repugnant stimulants I was told to give her *hourly* with an angelic meekness, she who so hated all medicine & messes, & who never would see a doctor while she could hold out against my entreaties to do so." But at midnight on November 1, after a nine-hour struggle, Mrs. Braddon died, "in a sweet & placid slumber, with her hand clasped in mine."

To Bulwer, MEB now poured out her grief: "She is gone. I cannot tell you how I loved her; but I know your own devotion as a son, the spirit of which breathes in every page of your last poetic drama, and I feel assured of your sympathy. Thus ends thirty years of the most perfect union, I believe, that ever existed between two human beings of the same sex. I told her every thing, for no act or feeling of mine was complete without her sympathy & I have rather endured her reproaches or her anger than lock one secret in my heart." Mrs. Braddon had "died a Protestant with all holy administrations from our Vicar," but MEB's Catholic stepdaughters burned candles at the head and foot of the coffin and watched around the clock. MEB would not deny them "the privilege of administering to her in the more poetic spirit of the older faith." Mrs. Braddon would be buried in Hendon Churchyard, where MEB's own dead child lay and where she hoped to join them. MEB wrote that her mother had been altogether without "thought of self—a most beautiful woman, much admired & courted, but sorely tried in the battle of life."

Even though Bulwer had never met Mrs. Braddon, MEB felt "perfectly assured" of his sympathy. She thanked God that she had moved out of the London her mother had hated and had taken her to Richmond to give her the garden she had always wanted. Here Mrs. Braddon "found much happiness in the devotion of my stepdaughters, who came home from their convent school to this house, and who have tended her with watchful & devoted affection ever since, and now lament her loss with a grief second only to mine." As for John Maxwell, the girls' father, he "ever fulfilled every duty of a son—to her who had no son." The last three words MEB triply underlined. Maxwell mourned Mrs. Braddon's death and "studies every wish of mine in reference to the end."[4]

At the saddest moment of her life, MEB wrote to Bulwer almost without reserve. Her words at such a time demonstrate how strong were the bonds that united the Maxwells as a family. Mrs. Braddon and John Maxwell's daughters by his first wife had been deeply attached to one another. And to John Maxwell MEB affirmed her deepest loyalty and gratitude. She felt that he had proved himself a true son to her beloved mother. Such filial devotion had obviously not begun only when Mrs.

Braddon was on her death bed. MEB believed that he had exhibited it for all the seven years since MEB had decided to add him to the ménage she shared with her mother.

"I have rather endured her reproaches or anger than lock one secret in my heart," MEB now wrote. It was a moment of truth. She had always told her mother everything, and her mother could not have very much liked (at least in the beginning) her beloved daughter's liaison with Maxwell. With her Irish short temper and her ready suspicion of other people's motives, Mrs. Braddon could not always have been easy to live with. Yet whether at Mecklenburgh Square or at Lichfield House, Maxwell "fulfilled every duty of a son." MEB's anger at Edward, idol of her childhood, would vanish in later years, no doubt assuaged or removed by the passage of time or by explanations. But her deep regard for John Maxwell remained unshaken always, despite her occasional disillusionment with romantic young love, or her inability to pursue poetry and high art in his prosaic and worldly company.

MEB did not tell Bulwer that she was expecting another child within a few weeks. Her fifth—and fourth surviving—child, Winifred Rosalie, always called Rosie, was born on December 14, 1868, some six weeks after Mrs. Braddon's death.[5] By that time MEB was very ill indeed. It was three and a half years—June 13, 1872—before she wrote again to Bulwer and told him what had happened to her immediately after her mother died, "the bitterest hour of my life." For more than six months, she said,

> life was a blank or something worse than a blank, an interval in which imagination ran riot, and I was surrounded by shadows—*one* towering above all the rest, and always appearing to me with gravely gracious aspect, as protector, counsellor, friend. When that unreal world faded the actual world seemed strangely dull and empty—and my own brain utterly emptied out—swept clean of every thought.

She had suffered a complete collapse. While her mind was unhinged, it was Bulwer she saw as the "gravely gracious" shadow who was always her "protector, counsellor, friend." She did not tell him that after Rosie's birth her illness had been compounded by an attack of puerperal fever, but this is remembered in the present generation of the Maxwell family. Poor John Maxwell feared that MEB, like his first wife, might become permanently mad. MEB cautioned Bulwer not to mention her illness when replying, "as that is a point on which my husband is sensitive—and he is so good to me that I feel bound to consider his feelings on every sub-ject."[6]

By MEB's own account, then, she dwelt in the unreal world of shadows for more than six months after November 1868. Her return to the actual world may have begun about June of 1869, and her gradual convalescence took at least another six months. She turned for comfort to her second son, Willie, just over two years old when Mrs. Braddon died, and found in this little boy a love and devotion that helped restore her strength. When he grew older she told him that she had counted on him in her trouble and that he had sustained her; and he inwardly vowed that he would always do so.[7]

2. The Revival of Imagination, and the Death of the Master (1870–1873)

For the first time since she had left the stage in 1860, MEB wrote nothing for an entire year. When she began again, she found her first efforts "beyond measure feeble, and I thought imagination was dead."[8] The immediate impact of her illness was to interrupt *Bound to John Company* after five instalments in *Belgravia*. Saying nothing to her readers, Maxwell used up whatever copy she had completed before her mother's death, and when that was gone called in another writer to bring the story to an end: as MEB said, it was "finished for my magazine by a stranger's hand." By dint of cutting each instalment as short as he dared, Maxwell kept it running until October 1869. Three years later, MEB wrote a new third volume for it and published it as *Robert Ainsleigh*. A historical romance of the early days of the East India Company, written in what MEB called "Esmondese," the novel never recovered from its early mishaps. MEB herself admitted that "neither the characters nor plot" had much interest, and that the hero was "a profound spoon."[9]

Her earliest new efforts were two unimportant short stories, appearing in *Belgravia* in February and March 1870. Next, in the April issue MEB published the opening number of her first novel since her illness, *Fenton's Quest*, to which her own words "beyond measure feeble" fully apply.[10] But while it was still running, what she self-deprecatingly called "the knack of copy-spinning at least . . . returned" in two further short stories of September and October 1870. In "On the Brink," a handsome young factory owner sends off his honest foreman, like Uriah the Hittite, to do an errand, while he persuades the foreman's young wife to run off with him. She is "on the brink" of yielding when the husband returns to defeat his master in fair fight. In "The Sins of the Fathers," an elderly nobleman at the court of Charles II kills his young wife and a man she is kissing, to discover that the man was not only her priest but her half-brother.[11]

Better still was *Milly Darrell*, a short novel that ran in *Belgravia* from November 1870 through January 1871. Deprived in her girlhood of her true love by a conspiracy between her father and the lover's mother, Milly Darrell marries an elderly squire. When her former lover pays court to Milly's new stepdaughter, Milly is so jealous that she tries to poison the girl. MEB skillfully contrasted the peacefulness of a slow-paced country life, amidst all the comforts that wealth could provide, with the violence of her characters' passions. Too many overheard conversations were all that marred a narrative of which Wilkie Collins would not have been ashamed, and it was now clear that MEB could once again spin a successful sensation-yarn.[12] The recovery of her powers was proceeding well, especially in view of the fact that during most of 1870 she was pregnant again. Her fifth surviving and last child, Edward Henry Harrington Maxwell—Ted—was born on December 20.[13] So her household now included ten members of the younger generation.

MEB's next novel, *The Lovels of Arden*, a purely domestic story in the genre of *The Lady's Mile*, carried further her growing interest in exploring an irregular relationship between a man and woman of the upper class. Daughter of an impoverished and coldly selfish widowed father, Clarissa Lovel, while still hardly more than a school girl, is persuaded to give up the man she loves and marry the middle-aged millionaire who has bought the beloved family estate. Until he realizes how his daughter "might render him the greatest service" possible, Mr. Lovel has been only "perfectly civil" to her; but thereafter he becomes kinder, and contemplates her "with a meditative air now and then." After she has refused the millionaire once, Mr. Lovel declares that he will probably not live very long anyhow. "After that one bitter speech and that one dreary sigh, Mr. Lovel made no overt attempt to influence his daughter's decision. He had a more scientific game to play, and he knew how to play it. Mr. Lovel neither complained nor threatened; he simply collapsed . . . meekness pervaded all his words and actions, but it was the meekness of despair." Of course, Clarissa gives in.

But marriage to the man she did love would have brought its own misery. George Fairfax had been a rake, "wild and unsteady," with "unacknowledged attachments." Obviously idleness lies at the root of his dissipation. Like so many Victorian gentlemen, he has no occupation and no need of one. He himself is perfectly conscious of this, but sees no cure for it. And once Clarissa is married, he lays long and skillful siege to her. He is a calculating, determined, and redoubtable seducer, and when he has her alone in a locked flat in Paris, and is pressing her to run away with him, she almost faints, totters "ever so slightly," and is falling into his arms when her husband appears, knocks Fairfax down, and believes the worst. Fairfax's heated lovemaking reminds a modern reader of the inexorable Walter in the now famous Victorian pornographic autobiography, *My Secret Life*. As the nursemaid for Clarissa's baby says, " 'That Fairfax is a villain. . . . I don't forget the day he kissed baby in Arden Park. I never see any good come of a single gentleman kissing a lady's baby voluntary. It isn't in their nature to do it unless they've a hankering for the mar.' "

The irony—which MEB surely intended—was that her sensation-novels were less sensational than her two purely social novels. Lady Audley and Aurora Floyd both commit bigamy by accident, each thinking her first husband dead before marrying her second. But in *The Lady's Mile* and in *The Lovels of Arden* young married women wish to embark upon adultery and are saved only by circumstance. Of course, Clarissa must endure separation from her husband, poverty, and brain fever before she can resume her married life at Arden.

MEB's thousands of readers could find in *The Lovels of Arden* a story that ostensibly deviated not at all from the strictest Victorian moral requirements. It offered repeated enchanting glimpses of the accessories of an opulent life. When George Fairfax first encounters the beautiful Clarissa traveling alone in a compartment on the night train, for example, he scrapes acquaintance with her by offering her some magazines. Then he unlocks one of his traveling bags, the interior of which glitters "like a miniature arsenal," and takes out a lamp, which he lights "in a rapid dextrous manner" and fixes "with a brass apparatus of screws and bolts to the arm of Clarissa's seat." A lady's sitting-room is "furnished with chairs and tables and cabinets of satinwood, with oval medallions of pale-blue Wedgwood china let into the panelled doors . . . and a narrow beading of lustreless gold here and there; . . . with pale blue silken hangings and a carpet of white wool anemones scattered on a turquoise-coloured ground. . . . no pictures . . . only . . . a few choice bronzes and a pair of Venetian mirrors." In Clarissa's own new dressing-room at Arden there stands a "dressing-table . . . a marvel of art and splendour, the looking-glass in a frame of oxydized silver, between two monster jewel-cases of ebony and malachite with oxydized silver mouldings," and one entire wall is occupied by the wardrobe with seven doors and Clarissa's monogram on each, "a receptacle that might have held all the . . . costumes of a Princess Metternich."[14] A sophisticated reader, on the other hand, might read the book as a tense narrative emphasizing the sufferings of the rich, the hopeless lot of a beautiful but not very intelligent girl whose family is down on its luck, the cold calculations of a predatory seducer, and the triumph—not of virtue—but of one form of misery over another. It was MEB's most worldly novel yet and perhaps her most serious.

She followed it with *To the Bitter End*, the story of another seducer, a barrister who pays court to the charming well-educated daughter of a farmer in whose house he is recuperating from overwork. He tells her of his engagement to another girl, but returns to persuade her to elope with him. She does so, believing that he will marry her. But when she discovers that he merely intends to make her his mistress, she collapses and dies of a heart attack in the bijou residence he has prepared for them, amidst the fine new clothes he has bought her. "I really had no option but to kill that poor young woman," MEB told Bulwer, who had liked the novel, "(though all my young lady friends said what a shame, and hoped she was coming to life again in the 3d vol)." MEB had, however, wanted "to make her a shade different from the rest of my heroines—who have been a long-lived race." She might have added that her other heroines—Lady Audley, Aurora Floyd—had sometimes lived in illicit union with their lovers and had thereby brought her so much critical abuse that it was easier and just as sensational to preserve the conventions. The victim in *To the Bitter End* dies at the last possible moment: still untouched and unaware of her lover's intentions, she has fatally compromised herself by the elopement alone. It is time for her to die.

Though wretchedly unhappy, the barrister goes ahead with his marriage to a cold worldly woman of a rich City family, whose formal, vacuous, and stultifying life MEB by implication contrasted with the simple rural joys of the yeoman family whose daughter he has destroyed. His father-in-law lives in a stucco mansion in "Acropolis Square," where

> the dining-room curtains . . . were of the deepest and darkest shade of claret—no gaudy obtrusive crimson or ruby—and of a material so thick that the massive folds seemed hewn out of stone. . . . The drawing room was . . . a howling wilderness of gorgeous furniture. . . . bronze statuettes, and monster vases of purple-and-gold Oriental china. . . . opening by means of a vast archway into a

smaller desert, where a grand piano stood in the center of a barren waste of Axminster carpet. Everything . . . was of the solid school—no nonsense about it—and . . . costly to the last degree. Ebony cabinets, decorated with clusters of fruit in carnelian and agate; Hercules and the Bull in bronze, on a stand of verde antique. . . . a pair of carved-oak stands, for engravings, supporting elephantine portfolios of Albrecht Dürer's and Rembrandt's etchings, and early impressions from plates of Hogarth's own engraving.

And when the family rents a house at Eastbourne for a seaside holiday, "It looked almost as if the Acropolis Square mansion had been brought down by rail, and set up here with its face to the sea."

MEB had always thought that if "well-handled" *To the Bitter End* would "make a fair domestic drama." Eventually the victim's father tracks the guilty man down. But the final shooting is complicated by a case of mistaken identity: the avenger kills the right man by accident during a boisterous party for the tenantry on a great country estate. This would have made a fine bit of melodramatic "business."[15] Condescendingly, the *Athenaeum* found the novel "as good a piece of work" as any of MEB's, "less stagey, less melodramatic" than usual and written in "as near an approach to English as her readers have any right to expect."[16]

To the Bitter End was the last of MEB's novels that Bulwer would read and criticize for her. During the few months before he died in January 1873, she wrote to him that John Maxwell had "been making himself a power" in Richmond by his speeches at Ratepayers' meetings and in the Vestry. "He has to a large degree that peculiarly Irish—or Celtic—attribute, the gift of words, and is generally able to carry all before him." But, she went on, perhaps his "eloquence" would "hardly bear critical dissection." She wished he might have "a wider and worthier field," and hoped that "some day when we have made our fortune on a small scale, he will get into the House, and hold forth there."[17] She sent Bulwer "a rose painted from nature" by her favorite son, Will, "a little fellow of six—who I think will be a painter, please God, if he lives." With an earlier generation's belief in phrenology, MEB reported that "an old friend, a physician," had told her that Will had "one of the finest brains ever vouchsafed to a child, and must make himself heard if he reaches manhood."[18] Bulwer was pleased to hear of Will's promise and said that he "would keep your little boy's early flower."[19] Sometimes she told him an anecdote she had liked: in an Irish tragedy she had read, for example, Manlius, when pushed from the Tarpeian Rock, calls out "Sweet Jesus, where am I going?" which, MEB reported, was so Irish that it had made her "laugh for half an hour."[20]

She still confided in Bulwer her anxieties about her work. Should she worry about Rhoda Broughton and Ouida as literary rivals? From John Maxwell's knowledge of the book trade, she wrote, she had learned to take "rather a sordid view of things," and these two lady-novelists sold almost if not quite as well in three-volume form as she, though she doubted if "their after and permanent sale in cheap form" was as good. On reading Rhoda Broughton's latest, *Goodbye, Sweetheart*, MEB had found "a certain order of genius . . . a peculiar gift" in the "utter fearlessness and abandon of the dialogue," in which the story was almost entirely told. Bulwer reassured MEB, who was "cheered" to think that Rhoda Broughton's "meteoric light" would not make her own "poor little candle" invisible. Though genuine enough, Rhoda Broughton's talent was a lesser one than MEB's; it did not reach its peak until the nineties, when she had learned to limit herself to one volume, and the faint note of impropriety that had titillated her earlier readers had ceased to vibrate. "When I was young I was Zola," she once said punningly, "and now that I'm older I'm Yonge." Later in life she and MEB would become close friends.

As for Ouida's rivalry MEB was only feigning alarm: she found in Ouida "a gaudiness, a tinsel—or Dutch metal coating. . . . a perpetual gilding of roses and bedaubing of lilies . . . cloying and wearisome." She had mentioned Ouida chiefly in order to tease Bulwer—who had never accepted any of MEB's own repeated invitations to visit her at Richmond and to let her show him her house and garden and children—for having gone to one of Ouida's notorious parties at the fashionable Hotel Langham, male guests only, and all particularly requested to smoke cigars.[21]

For eleven years now, MEB had always outspokenly voiced to Bulwer her opinions of other writers: Scott and Balzac (giants but not above criticism), Georges Sand ("spooney when virtuous and unnecessarily immoral at other times"), Lamartine ("sickly sweet"), Fanny Burney (a childhood "bugbear"). Charlotte Brontë was "the only *genius* the weaker sex can point to in literature," George Eliot "somewhat passionless" although "a fine mind cultured to the highest point." Dickens had "something essentially feminine" in his nature, while the triumph of Trollope and the realistic school was regrettable.[22] Bulwer helped MEB get up a petition of authors to the Prime Minister, Lord Derby, to increase the pension of the novelist Emma Robinson.[23] Charles Reade also participated: "He is one of your most earnest admirers," MEB assured the touchy Bulwer and told him how Reade had "flung a shilling on our old-fashioned round dining-room table . . . and said 'Bulwer is to the men who criticise him in the proportion of that table to that shilling.' " The two men renewed their friendship.[24] MEB saw to it that Bulwer's poems in a new edition were favorably reviewed in Maxwell's *St. James's Magazine*.[25]

She continued to admire her girlhood favorites among Bulwer's own novels, and—on a second reading in 1872—abandoned her earlier doubts about his *Strange Story*, which she now pronounced "almost the loftiest and most wonder-striking" of his books. Not even Shakespeare (!) was so versatile as he. She begged him not to think she was rhapsodizing, but of course she was. Pleased, the old man wrote the next day that he had always felt reviewers ("I don't call them critics") had always misunderstood *A Strange Story*.[26] Her letters—now available in print—reflect her admiration for his Caxton novels,[27] for his poetry, his essays, his plays, and even his historical work. She begged him for a new novel, and he told her about *Kenelm Chillingley*, which would achieve publication only after his death.[28]

One can easily imagine her pleasure at receiving—only two weeks after Bulwer died on January 18, 1873, an extraordinary letter from his old friend, Julian Young, Rector of Ilmingston, Warwickshire, and a fellow-habitué of Torquay in the winter, "a courtly cleric, a great diner-out and giver of dinners to the great, a raconteur of the first order, a very complete re-embodiment of the spirit of Sydney Smith." Young had seen Bulwer daily at Torquay, winter after winter. "He invariably spoke . . . of your writings with a warmth akin to enthusiasm," Young wrote to MEB, "many a time at dinner when some dry matter-of-fact person has inveighed against the sensation novel . . . I have heard him warm to your vindication." And when the two old men exchanged the novels they had been borrowing from circulating libraries, Bulwer had "over and over again" said to him, " 'After all, Young, . . . if one needs relaxation from work, if one needs cheering when depressed, if one needs weaning from selfish and morbid introspection, what is so efficacious . . . as a good novel? And of all novels of the present day what others to compare with (pardon the language of propriation) our dear Miss Braddon's?' " On their last drive together before Bulwer died, he had said this again, and his son Robert had "cordially" agreed. Young hoped that John Maxwell would not challenge him to a duel for "writing with such freedom to his lady," and that, if he did, MEB would shield Young "from his vengeance."[29] For the woman who sometimes signed herself, "your devoted disciple" or "your reverential disciple" when she wrote to Bulwer, the news that he had praised her almost with his dying words would have been deeply moving.

Soon she paid formal tribute to him in *Belgravia,* in a fine critical essay. " 'He is dead,' " she began, quoting Sir Philip Francis' praise of the elder Pitt, " 'and has left nothing in this world that resembles him.' " He had inherited Scott's mantle and he himself had no heir. The hero of *Pelham*— "surely the most wonderful book ever written at three-and-twenty"—was "Chesterfield put into action. . . . His placid impertinence," his delightful aphorisms ("It is a very high mind to which gratitude is not a painful sensation") should make him a textbook model for young men entering the world. For MEB's own public she now summarized reflectively the admiring view of Bulwer's manifold achievements that she had so often dashed down informally in her letters to him. Among the novels, *The Caxtons* marked "the full flush of his power," and won him "a new reputation," while his plays even now were "more certain to draw a full house" in the English provinces (and here MEB was writing from experience) than those of Shakespeare. The thought and labor expended on every book, the charm and spirituality of his romances, his "knowledge of the human heart" made Bulwer unique.[30]

Nor did this essay represent MEB's final payment of her ancient debt. Soon, Bulwer's son Robert—"Owen Meredith"—was receiving from her what he called "many valuable hints" for the completion, casting, and production of *Darnley,* an unfinished early drawing-room play of his father's, which eventually did reach the stage. In one of her novels, MEB declared that Bulwer's fiction reflected, "as in a magic mirror, all the varieties of life from the age of Pliny [*The Last Days of Pompeii*] to the eve of the Franco-Prussian War [*The Parisians*]." As late as 1881, when her old friend Charles Kent misread a press notice and thought MEB had appeared in a play, she wrote him that long ago, "when encouraged by the generous advice of that great Master of his Art whom I revere as the first cause of all I have ever done in literature," she became a novelist, "there was no looking back at the more fascinating profession which I surrendered."[31] By 1873, when Bulwer died, MEB had long since stopped thinking of herself merely as his pupil. But hers was "a very high mind," of the sort to which, in Pelham's own words, "gratitude is not a painful sensation."

In severing her from the counselor who had from the beginning commented on each of her books as she wrote them, Bulwer's death marked a turning point in her professional life. For MEB's biographer, it marks the end of eleven key years during which she had set down freely her own views of her life and her writings. She seldom afterwards revealed her literary intentions or hopes or aims, or commented on her satisfactions and her disappointments. Henceforth we are deprived of these insights and must usually let the texts of her many novels speak for themselves.

3. "The Nice Adjustment of Murder and Morality" (1873–1874)

For the first time since *The Loves of Arcadia* had launched her as a writer thirteen years earlier, MEB in 1873 wrote a play and saw it staged. The drama, she said, was now "the only line which pays largely, and anyone who *can* write a play does wrong to write anything else." She was good-naturedly envious of the young W. S. Gilbert, who, she heard, was "coining money" from his *Pygmalion*, a "charming little piece," and from *The Palace of Truth*.[32] But her own *Griselda* was "pursued by every kind of ill luck" and had come into being "under some unholy ban." It was based upon the story of the patient wife, told by Petrarch, by Boccaccio, and by Chaucer in his *Clerk's Tale*. The audience, she said, wept satisfactorily "when the good old English sentiment of domesticity" was appealed to. But she feared the legend itself was "a weak fabric for a play. One must make Gualtiero"—Griselda's cruel husband—"either a brute or a fool," and MEB had chosen the latter course. Much as she "execrated" the critics, she thought them right in objecting.[33]

She had written the play for her old friend Wybert Rousby and his beautiful young wife, Clara Dowse Rousby, who had scored her first triumph three years earlier in Tom Taylor's *'Twixt Axe and Crown* and was now the rage. The public were buying "Rousby bonnets, Rousby gloves, and Rousby dresses." George Augustus Sala thought that Clara Rousby's Griselda was a "thoroughly womanly woman, who can and will bear a great deal, but will not forget to tell you . . . how much she has borne. . . . a worm . . . who will turn." In "dresses à *queue* long enough to reach from the Oxford Circus to Hanway-yard, seal-skin mantles, sable muffs, point-lace parasols and three-guinea bonnets," she was "beautiful, graceful, and accomplished" and could go mad "without being absurd and scream without splitting" one's ears. The play was apparently never published, despite the fact that William Longman, of the publishing house, thought it "perfectly charming." Poor Mrs. Rousby's head was soon turned by her popularity; she took to drink and bad company. Dissipation cost her her looks, her popularity, and in 1879—at the age of twenty-seven—her life. So when MEB played Mrs. Hector Sternhold for poor Wybert Rousby on Jersey in 1876, she was doing a kind favor for the unfortunate old friend of her own theatrical days.[34] MEB's next play, *Genevieve; or, The Missing Witness*, fared even less well than *Griselda*. It did achieve production in 1874, but never got beyond Liverpool despite an avalanche that took place on stage as the climax of Act III.[35]

MEB, then, remained primarily a novelist. For two of her five new novels in 1873 and 1874 she made wholly new publishing arrangements. Since the founding of *Belgravia* in 1866, all eight of the novels she had written had appeared serially in its pages before book publication. But in 1873 she sold the serial rights of *Lucius Davoren* to William Francis Tillotson, an enterprising newspaper proprietor of Bolton, Lancashire, whose weekly *Bolton Journal and Guardian* (1871)—one of a string of six Tillotson Lancashire papers—published fiction in instalments. A "keen and persistent businessman," Tillotson overcame the suspicions of established writers by offering them a flat sum ranging from ten pounds to one thousand pounds for serial newspaper publication only. The author retained all rights to book publication and so "lost none of his readers and gained hosts of new ones," his fiction coming into thousands of homes where he would otherwise have been unknown. The more famous he got, the better terms he could make for his next book with Tillotson and with the book publishers. Tillotson "persisted and prevailed," making a good many personal friends among his authors and "retaining" them even when they became very expensive.[36]

So advantageous an arrangement commended itself to Maxwell and MEB. *Belgravia* had been founded largely to give her fiction serial circulation and had always paid other contributors very little. Tillotson was offering her a large sum for the serial rights to her new novels and, in addition, the certainty that any subscriber who read his first Braddon novel in the *Bolton Journal* and thus became an addict had every incentive to buy all the cheap reprints of all her earlier works. In 1873, there were already two dozen such Braddon novels available everywhere, both as clothbound reprints and as two-shilling "yellowbacks" sold at the newsagents' on the platform of every railway station in Great Britain. MEB was the first established novelist to join the ranks of Tillotson authors and for four years contributed one novel a year to *Belgravia* and at least one to Tillotson. By 1876 she was ready to phase out *Belgravia* altogether. Maxwell then sold it to Chatto and Windus, and MEB ceased to be its editor.

It was Tillotson's practice to form a syndicate—he called it a "coterie"—of newspapers in England and elsewhere in the English-speaking world, whose members bought from him for a flat fee the right to publish MEB's fiction serially. In the surviving Tillotson files, the long series of business letters and telegrams from John Maxwell begins only in 1879, but the connection formed in 1873 lasted uninterruptedly until 1887. MEB liked Tillotson personally so well that she dedicated her second Tillotson novel, *Taken at the Flood*, to him "and to the other newspaper proprietors for whom the work was written."[37]

The first Tillotson novel, *Lucius Davoren*, moves from a prologue in the Canadian Arctic—where the young protagonist finds himself isolated in winter and almost starves—to his new surgical practice near the docks of the East End of London. Here—within "a heavily buttressed wall" and behind a rusty iron gate with "florid scroll-work and forgotten coat of arms"—stands a dark, square, red-brick mansion with an older "wing of grey moss-discoloured stone," in which one of his patients, a retired antiques dealer, lives with a granddaughter and the remains of a huge collection. The house has "nothing in common with the shabby rows and shops and skimpy terraces and bulkheads and low-roofed disreputable" dwellings nearby, and its gate—"like one of the outworks of a fortification"—is not to be opened by a latch-key. The owner pulls on an iron ring, "suspended beyond the reach of the gutter children of the district, and a remote bell" rings within the fastness. Here amidst the threat of robbery and murder from a renegade son of the household, begins the love affair between the surgeon and the young girl.

Coincidence runs wild in *Lucius Davoren*, but the reader willingly suspends his disbeliefs and relishes the contrast between the lone grim mansion, still standing among the London dockland slums, and the High Street of "Stilmington"—Leamington Spa—lined with handsome red-brick middle-class houses, "whose windows shine resplendent . . . on whose spotless doorstep no foot seems to have trodden, whose green balconies are filled with geraniums more scarlet than other geraniums. . . . whose sacred interior—archtemple of those homelike British virtues, ready-money and soapsuds—is shrouded . . . by starched muslin curtains." Here the "tax-gatherer never calls twice"; those "shining knockers have never trembled in the rude grasp of a dun."

The antique dealer's house—like a view from the famous Doré folio volume on London that had just appeared with text by MEB's friend Blanchard Jerrold—possesses the same solid reality as the Leamington hotel, "of the fine old English expensive and exclusive school, where people ate and drank in the splendid solitude of their private apartments, and stared at one another superciliously when they met in the corridors or on the staircases, instead of herding together at stated intervals to gorge themselves" publicly, like passengers aboard a steamer. Here MEB had stayed with her mother in order to write uninterruptedly and had emerged into the High Street to wonder how the elderly solicitors or bankers behind the muslin curtains "had borne the burden of their days" in such a town. The woman whose girlhood had so often been disturbed by the arrival of a dun on the doorstep and who was now secure cared nothing for the paradise of "soapsuds and ready money" where the geraniums were more scarlet than other geraniums and there was no worry about cash, but where life was deadly dull.[38]

Taken at the Flood, the Tillotson novel for 1874, gave the old *Lady Audley* plot a new twist: this time, the worldly young wife wants to rid herself of her rich elderly baronet, not to keep him. So she cleverly relegates him to a private asylum and announces his death. She then bigamously tries to marry a former suitor, but is stopped in time. As with Lady Audley, a hereditary weakness of character explains her action: her father had been an embezzler, her mother had run off with another man and actually gone on the stage! Nothing that the daughter of such parents might do would surprise MEB's middle-class readers. The *Athenaeum* praised the novel as "thoroughly good" if not great. By 1874, it heartily approved of a story that was only a variant of those it had censured so bitterly as late as 1868. MEB now sardonically made the necessary concessions to Victorian morality. Bigamy yearned for but thwarted would pass muster. Bigamy committed, even inadvertently, aroused censure.[39]

The fatal result of marrying for money without love is brought home even more vigorously in *Strangers and Pilgrims*, whose heroine is not a hard calculating beauty of dubious origin but the rather lazy and unintelligent daughter of a Devonshire clergyman. She falls in love with her father's curate and abandons her previous neglect of the parish poor only in order to captivate him. In the mistaken belief that he cannot love her, she spends a season in London society—she has always been taught to think in worldly terms—and accepts the attentions of a horsy and empty-headed young Devonshire nobleman. She is seen on his four-in-hand at the Derby and acts with him in amateur theatricals. Her curate sees the play, is profoundly shocked, and renounces her. So she marries the peer and reaps a harvest of misfortune: her child dies, her husband tires of her, she catches the plague, loses her intellect, and is immured in a madhouse. After her husband's death, the curate rescues her, only to preside over her deathbed and then to inherit half her huge fortune for a mission in Africa.

MEB's middle-class readers would have found this edifying: serve the girl right! She had got her due reward for her indiscretion and her failure to cling to her proud and pious clergyman, who had loved her all the time. But immediately beneath the varnished evangelical surface of *Strangers and Pilgrims* lay quite another, far less obvious story. The curate is in fact rigid, pompous, and prissy, has no sense of humor, and sets wholly unrealistic standards for a young woman's behavior. She has been adequately chaperoned every moment, as he could easily have discovered had he not preferred to treat her frivolities as sins. He and his remote African mission become in the end the sole gainers by her misfortunes.

Moreover, it was the heroine's devout and canting elder sister who had written the curate an anonymous letter that brought him rushing to see the offending play and so precipitated the entire catastrophe. Had it not been for her malicious intervention, he would never have known about the episode, and nobody would have been any the worse. Even the *Athenaeum*—which found the novel "the best piece of work" that MEB had done, "but at the same time one of the saddest stories we have ever read"—partly penetrated to the second level of meaning: "We have met with those who fancy that Miss Braddon meant" the curate "for an ideally perfect man. That he is not, for he is eaten up with vanity in its most disagreeable form: but we are convinced that Miss Braddon meant him to be exactly what she has drawn him."[40]

If—by indirection and for her own pleasure—MEB was satirizing the hypocrisy of middle-class Low-church values while seeming to espouse them, she openly handed out a full measure of punishment to the fashionable. When the rackety nouveau-riche couple who "take up" the heroine during her London season stage the fatal amateur theatricals "for the benefit of the widows of indigent stockbrokers," the hostess herself calls her guests " 'not hall-marked, only electro-plated.' " Her husband has remodeled their Thames-side house, "The Rancho," in the style of a Mexican farmhouse, surrounding it with a wooden verandah ten feet wide paved in blue and cream tiles, and furnishing it "in the purest rustic fashion—with light woods; pastoral chintzes scattered with violets and primroses; no draperies to the windows, . . . shaded by Venetian blinds within and Spanish hoods without. . . . few carpets, but oak floors polished to distraction, and Indian matting in the passages." Whenever anybody asks who the owners are, people plunge "at once into a glowing description of the Rancho."

When the heroine's worldly London aunt tries to entertain the parsimonious Devonshire dowager mother of the young peer—not, of course, with "virulent vulgar slander," but with "good-natured genial . . . gossip, touching lightly upon the failings and errors of one's acquaintance, deploring their little infirmities and mistaken courses with a friendly compassionate spirit, essentially Christian,"—the dowager refuses to acknowledge acquaintance with any of the people or to take "the faintest interest in those public characters, the shining lights of the great world, about whose private life every well-regulated British mind is supposed to be curious. 'I don't know her,' " says this "impracticable old woman, 'I never met him; I'm not acquainted with 'em,' " until the aunt's soul sinks in despair.

And the meals the dowager serves match her disposition. At lunch, the beef is

> gaunt . . . bony and angular, as of an ox that had known hard times, . . . a melancholy roast fowl, with huge scaly legs, whose advanced age ought to have held him sacred from the assassin. [He] seemed to feel his isolated position on a very large dish, with a distant border of sliced tongue, lemon, and parsley. There were two dishes of potatoes, fried and boiled; there was a little glass dish of marmalade, that was made quite a feature of on one side of the board; and a similar dish containing six anchovies reposing in a grove of parsley, which enlivened the other side. There was an artistic preparation of beetroot and endive on a centre-dish, and two ponderous diamond-cut celery glasses scantily supplied with celery; these with a pickle-stand or two and a good deal of splendour in the way of cruets, gave the table an air of being quite liberally furnished.

And dinner is "like the pale wraith of some decent dinner that had died and been buried a long while ago."[41]

In *Strangers and Pilgrims*, MEB had on one level appeased her middle-class readers by strictly observing all their rules, while on another level she had satirized them, if only faintly. In her two novels for 1874, *A Strange World* and *Lost for Love*,[42] she struck the satirical chord far more insistently, with a new, barely concealed note of distaste for the very

1. Mary Elizabeth Braddon, aged 29. Portrait by W. P. Frith, 1865. (National Portrait Gallery, London)

2. Lady Audley's Crime. Sketch by MEB herself, found in one of her notebooks. (Harvard College Library)

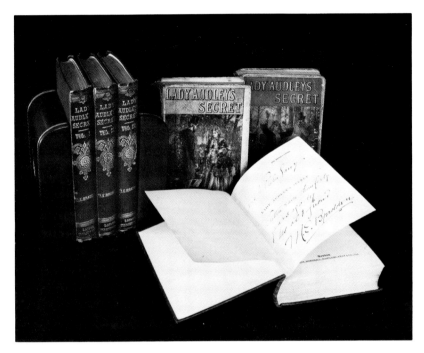

3. *Lady Audley's Secret*: the original three-volume edition; two cheap yellow-back reprints; another reprint with a presentation inscription by MEB.

4. "I used to follow you ardently and track you close. . . ." Henry James to MEB, August 2, 1911.

5. ". . . some human beings have faculties which are in others not merely inferior but absent." W. E. Gladstone to MEB, October 24, 1891.

6. Fanny White Braddon, MEB's mother.

7. Skisdon, the family house at St. Kew, Cornwall. Engraved for MEB's grandmother and published in 1820. The Braddon coat of arms (*sable*: a bend lozengy, *argent*), with those of Clode superimposed. Gilbert, *Historical and Topographical Survey of Cornwall*, II, p. 610.

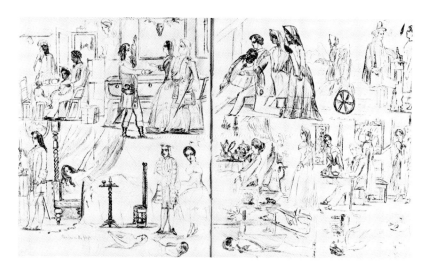

8. "She brought him . . . pen and ink drawings . . . her own idea of scenes in Scott or Bulwer" (*A Lost Eden* [1904], p. 29). A leaf from MEB's girlhood sketchbooks.

9. Another leaf with a profile of Bulwer and his initials "E.G.E.L.B.L.," for Edward George Earle Lytton Bulwer-Lytton, and a sketch of the "Dweller on the Threshold," the horrifying and depressing spirit in *Zanoni*.

10. "Mary Seyton": leaf from MEB's sketchbook on which she has signed her stage name.

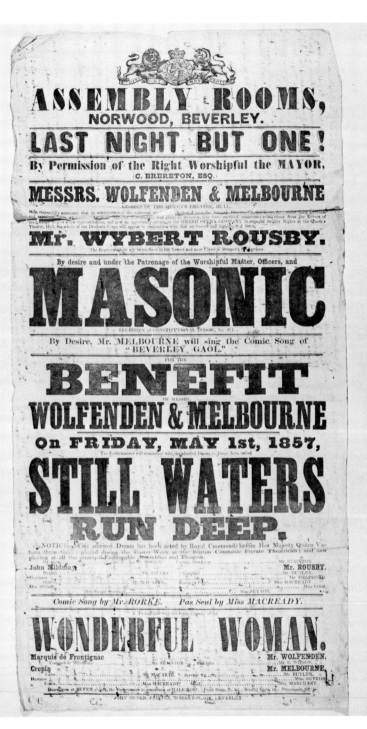

11. Miss Seyton: The Beverley playbill, showing the parts played by MEB on May 1, 1857.

ROYAL
STRAND THEATRE,

SOLE LESSEE, ... MISS SWANBOROUGH.

UNDER THE MANAGEMENT OF
MISS SWANBOROUGH.

On MONDAY, March 12th, 1860, and during the Week,

The Performances will commence at Seven, with the highly successful and Laughable New and Original
Farce, by THOMAS HIGGIE, Esq., Author of " *House Dog,*" " *Wilful Murder,*"&c., entitled

FRIGHTFUL ACCIDENT.

Mr. Fernandez Scroggie	...	... ...	Mr. J. CLARKE,
Sidney Kynaston	...	...	Mr. W. MOWBRAY,
Orlando Chromio Flobbers	...	... ...	Mr. E. DANVERS,
Policemen ...	...	Messrs. EDGE, and IRVING,	
Mrs. Isidora Scroggie	...	...	Miss ELEANOR BUFTON,
Karoline	...	...	Miss E. TURTLE,
Sally Shudders ...	...	... ...	Miss CHARLOTTE SAUNDERS.

Scene.—A Boarding School at Hastings.

After which every Evening, Saturday excepted, at 8 o'clock, (Never Acted) an entirely New and Original
Comedietta, in Two Acts, written expressly for this Theatre by Miss M. E. BRADDON, entitled the

LOVES OF ARCADIA.

Louis XV.	...	Mr. JAMES BLAND,	
Duke de Richelieu	...	... ...	Mr. POYNTER,
Chevalier de Merrilac	...	...	Mr. PARSELLE,
M. de Villefroi	...	Mr. E. DANVERS,	
M. de Charlori	...	...	Mr. W. MOWBRAY.
Leon ...	...	... ...	Mr. CHATER,
Victoire	...	... ...	Mr. J. IRVING,
Zamore	...	Miss E. TURTLE,	
Fabian	...	...	Mr. EDGE,
Désirée de Launnay ...	...	... ...	Miss SWANBOROUGH,
Lucie ...		...	Miss LESTER,
Jacquette ...	...	Mrs. CHARLES MELVILLE,	

On Saturday, at Eight o'Clock, the highly successful New and Original Comedietta, in One Act, by
J. P. WOOLER, Esq., entitled

SISTERLY SERVICE.

Count Delacour	...	...	Mr. JAMES BLAND.
Adolphe de Valmont		...	Mr. W. H. SWANBOROUGH.
Victor	...	..	Mr. PARSELLE.
Frederick	...	.. ...	Mr. W. MOWBRAY.
Officer	...	Mr. EDGE.	
Rosalie de Valmont	...	... ...	Miss MARIA SIMPSON.
Marie Lelacour	...	...	Miss E. TURTLE.

APARTMENT IN THE HOUSE OF CAPT. DE VALMONT.
Grand Corridor in the Palace of Louis the Thirteenth. W. BROADFOOT.

12. *The Loves of Arcadia*: Playbill announcing the opening of MEB's "comedietta," March 12, 1860. (Harvard College Library)

Your code of Honour? You have become such an actress that you cannot speak without acting —
I have worked as hard and done as much (for you) as it was possible for a gentleman to do for a woman in your position — But you never can forgive any one to whom you are under Obligations — And I think I shall be the last person that you will forgive! The only return (title page of yr novel) that I ever asked of you, if return it could be called, has not been granted — It matters not now —
I can only feel a pity for you not unmingled with contempt, and wonder if you have one redeeming trait in your character

13. "I can only feel a pity for you not unmingled with contempt." John Gilby to MEB, February 20, 1861.

A Guest that best becomes the table"—*Shakspeare.*

THE WELCOME GUEST.

EDITOR'S OFFICE :—122, FLEET STREET, E.C.

LONDON *Feb. 20th 1861*

My Dear Polly,

Lonely, sad, and very full of thought I obey your wish that I should write to you this evening. But, ah! how I feel the want of words to express the weariness of soul that arises when, after an arduous days work, — one of unceasing toil —, the heart wakes up to find itself All alone! all alone..!! No kind voice to utter the

14. "All alone! all alone!!": John Maxwell to MEB, February 20, 1861.

CORRESPONDENCE.

It is distinctly to be borne in mind that we do not, by inserting letters, convey any opinion favourable to their contents. We open our columns to all, without leaning to any; and thus supply a channel for the publication of opinions of all shades, to be found in no other journal in England.

No notice whatever will be taken of anonymous communications.

We cannot undertake to return rejected communications.

CAPITAL PUNISHMENTS.
TO THE EDITOR OF "PUBLIC OPINION."

Sir,—Will you kindly assist in drawing the attention of all who are interested in the weal of mankind to the fact that the present time is highly favourable for agitating the abolition of capital punishment?

It is a stain upon our national Christianity, and degrading to our vaunted civilization, that this relic of the dark ages should still survive —this law of blood still defile our statute-books. Surely the signs of dissatisfaction lately evinced at the execution of the law cry aloud for its repeal. The arguments advanced in support of this extreme measure have long since given way before the logic of truth; and it would greatly tend to increase the value of human life in the eyes of all men if the State were to show that, though a reckless man in his frenzy might take away another's life, she considered even that murderer's life far too sacred to be taken away from him.

I remain, Sir, faithfully yours,   ERNAN.

MISS BRADDON, THE NOVELIST, AND MR. MAXWELL.
TO THE EDITOR OF "PUBLIC OPINION."

Sir,—In the last number of PUBLIC OPINION I find the following paragraph quoted from the *Court Journal* :—

" Miss Braddon, the novelist, was recently married to Mr. Maxwell, the publisher."

I first saw this paragraph in the *Morning Advertiser* of the 19th inst.; and knowing that Mr. Maxwell was already married, I looked anxiously to see him or Miss Braddon contradict a report which was not and could not be true. Neither of them has done so.

In the presence of this extraordinary rumour, and still more extraordinary silence, I ask your permission, as Mrs. Maxwell's brother-in-law, to say that the above report is utterly without foundation. Mr. Maxwell was married, some years ago, to Miss Mary Anne Crowley, sister of the late N. J. Crowley, of the Royal Hibernian Academy—an artist well known in Dublin and in London. This lady, who has borne her husband a large family, is still living.

Therefore it is not and it cannot be true, that " Miss Braddon, the novelist, was recently married to Mr. Maxwell, the publisher."

I am, Sir, your obedient servant,

Jan. 25, 1864.   R. B. KNOWLES.

15. "... it is not and it cannot be true. ..." R. B. Knowles publishes his denial of MEB's marriage. (*Public Opinion*, January 30, 1864)

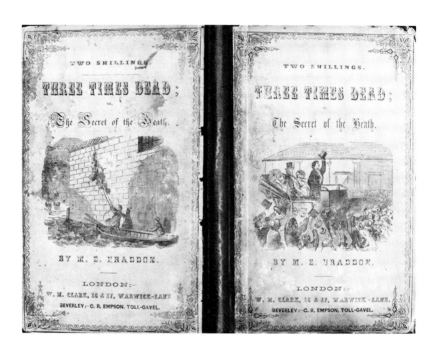

16. *Three Times Dead*. MEB's first novel in its first incarnation. One of two surviving copies in original boards, 1860.

17. "They were close to the pillar behind which the masked stranger stood. . . ." The first page of the first number of the *Halfpenny Journal*, with the opening chapter of MEB's *The Black Band*, under the pseudonym of Lady Caroline Lascelles, July 1, 1861.

18. *The Black Band*, revived as an 8vo yellowback in 1877. The only copy known.

19. Only surviving leaf of the original manuscript of *Oscar Bertrand*.

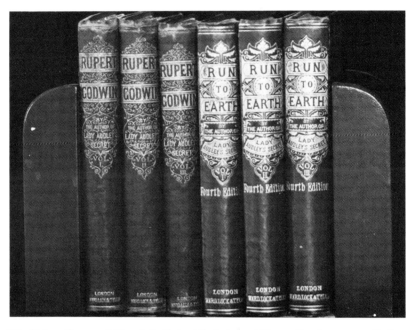

20. "Manufactured Novels": *Rupert Godwin* and *Run to Earth*—penny-fiction masquerading in three-volume form.

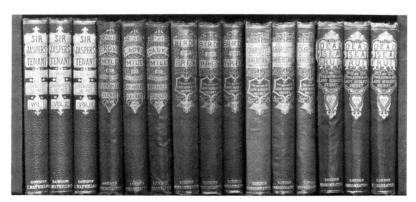

21. Braddon novels, 1863–1868.

22. *Belgravia*: the invitation to the launching of MEB's new magazine, illuminated in gold, violet, and vermillion.

23. *Belgravia*, Volume One, Publisher's binding. "Catching the Shillings of Brixton and Bow."

24. "Quintilia the Quadrigamist," Christmas 1864.

25. MEB about to leap through the latest of John Maxwell's hoops: *The Mask*,
June 1868.

26. After Recovery: Ramsgate Sands, probably summer of 1872. MEB and John Maxwell seated on the bench; standing behind them, John Maxwell, Jr. ("Jack"), and Polly Maxwell; seated on sands from left to right, Will, aged about six, Gerald about ten, Fanny about nine; on John Maxwell's knee, Rosie, about three and a half. Teddy, at one and a half, was presumably too young for outdoor photography. (Original in the possession of Henry Maxwell, Esq.)

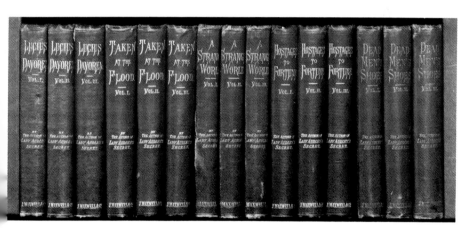

27. Braddon Novels, 1871–1875.

28. Avalanche on stage: MEB's sketch for Act III of her play *Genevieve;
or the Missing Witness*, 1874.

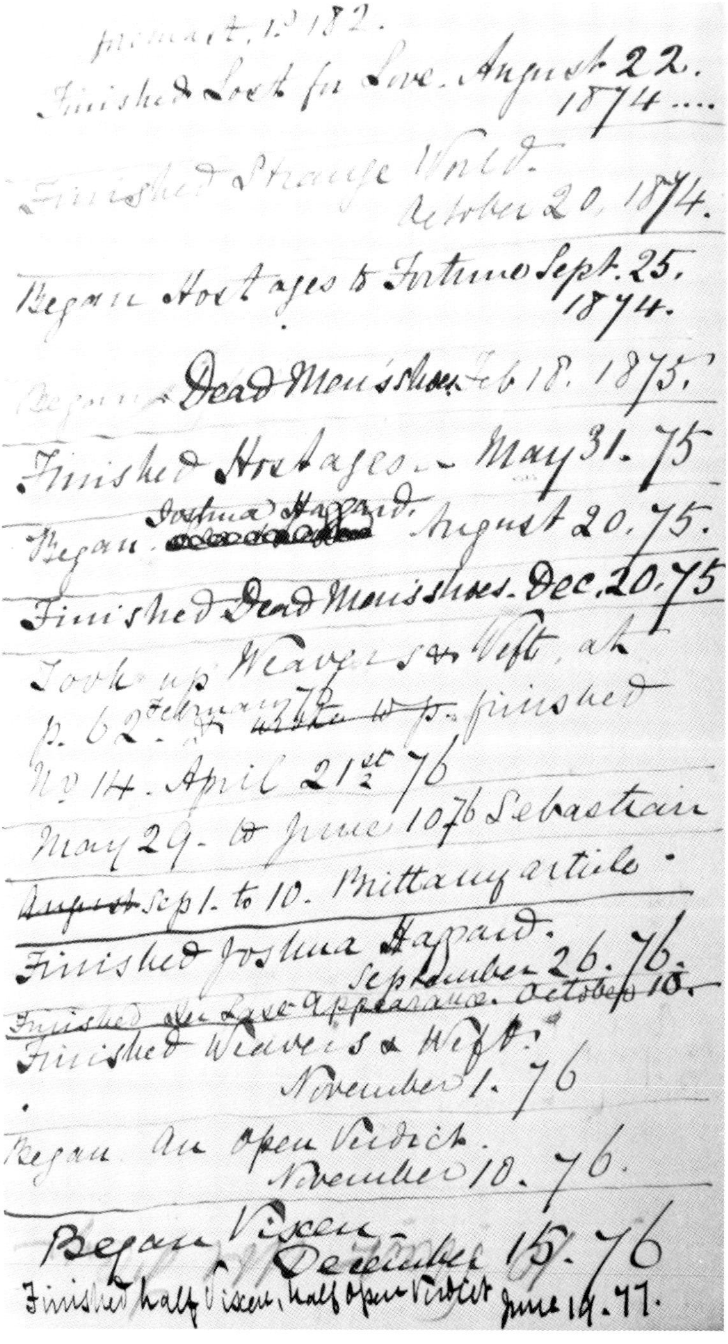

[illegible]

Finished Lost for Love. August 22. 1874....

Finished Strange World. October 20, 1874.

Began Hostages to Fortune Sept. 25. 1874.

Began Dead Men's Shoes Feb 18. 1875.

Finished Hostages — May 31. 75

Began Joshua Haggard. August 20. 75.

Finished Dead Men's Shoes. Dec. 20. 75

Took up Weavers & Weft, at p. 62. February 76. ~~[illegible]~~ finished No 14. April 21st 76

May 29 – to June 10 76 Sebastian

~~August~~ Sep 1. to 10. Brittany article.

Finished Joshua Haggard. September 26. 76.

~~Finished [illegible] October 10.~~

Finished Weavers & Weft. November 1. 76

Began An Open Verdict. November 10. 76.

Began Vixen December 15. 76

Finished half Vixen, half Open Verdict June 14. 77.

29. MEB's "schedule" of writing, 1874–1885 (see Appendix, 7).

29 and 30, NORTH BANK, N.W.
September 28th, 1874.

SIR,

ON the 10th inst. I published in the *Times, Daily News, Standard*, and *Pall Mall Gazette* the following announcement of the death of my Sister-in-law, Mrs. MAXWELL :—

"On the 5th September, at Mountain View, Kimmage Road, Dublin, "after a long and severe illness, MARY ANNE, wife of JOHN MAXWELL, Esq., "of Lichfield House, Richmond, Surrey, and of 4, Shoe Lane, Fleet Street, E.C., "Publisher, aged 48.—R.I.P."

This announcement was repeated in the *Times* of the 11th and 15th, and it also appeared in the *Morning Post, Daily Telegraph*, the *Weekly Register*, and the *Tablet* on the 12th.

With this tribute of respect to my relative's memory, the matter, so far as I am concerned, would have ended ; but I have discovered, by the merest accident, that though Mr. Maxwell did not dare publicly to deny the truth of my Advertisement—which he ought to have done, and undoubtedly would have done had he been able—he has privately distributed the following Circular, obviously with the intention of discrediting it altogether :—

"Mr. and Mrs. Maxwell present their Compliments to "and beg to disclaim any knowledge of the maliciously-intentioned announce-"ment of a death on the 5th inst."

LICHFIELD HOUSE, RICHMOND, S.W.
September 10, 1874.

It is therefore due to the name and memory of Mr. Maxwell's deceased Wife, to the feelings of her surviving friends, and to my own character, that some further evidence should be afforded to those whom an attempt has been made to mystify and mislead.

30, 31, 32. R. B. Knowles's "Counter-circular," September 28, 1874.

Mr. Maxwell married Miss Mary Anne Crowley, my wife's sister, and the sister also of the late N. J. Crowley, R.H.A., on the 7th of March, 1848. The marriage was solemnized at Saint Aloysius's Chapel, Somers Town, in the district of St. Pancras, the Rev. J. Holdstock being the officiating clergyman ; N. J. Crowley, of 13, Upper Fitzroy Street, and Peter Sarsfield, 11, Grenville Street, Somers Town, the witnesses ; and William Henry Matthews the Registrar. Of this marriage there were seven children, five of whom survive. Some time after the birth of the youngest a separation took place between the parents, and Mrs. Maxwell' resided thenceforth with her family in the neighbourhood of Dublin. Later on there appeared a paragraph in some of the newspapers to the effect that Miss Braddon, the novelist, had been married to Mr. Maxwell, the publisher. This statement I publicly contradicted in the journals in which I found it—the *Guardian*, the *Morning Advertiser*, *Public Opinion*, and the Dublin *Freeman's Journal*. It was also contradicted at my instance in the *London Review* and the *Court Journal;* and wherever I have since heard it repeated in private society I have contradicted it again.

Mrs. Maxwell died on the 5th inst., at Mountain View, Kimmage Road, near Dublin. In the entry in the Register Book of Deaths for the district of Rathfarnham, she is described as "wife of John Maxwell, Publisher, 4, Shoe " Lane, off Fleet Street, London, E.C." The informant, "present at death," is John Crowley, Mrs. Maxwell's brother, and the Registrar, Henry Croly, M.D., F.R.C.S.I. The news of his wife's death was at once telegraphed to Mr. Maxwell by Mr. Crowley. On the 7th, two days afterwards, Mr. Crowley received three telegrams from Mr. Maxwell, to none of which did he reply. Mr. Maxwell wrote subsequently to have them returned to him; but instead of doing so, Mr. Crowley has sent them to me.

The first, from Ludgate Circus, was handed in at 10.45 a.m., addressed, " From John Maxwell, 4, Shoe Lane, Fleet Street, London, to John Crowley, " Mountain View, Kimmage Road, Harold's Cross, Dublin." It runs as follows :—

"This moment (half-past ten), received melancholy telegram, delivered " after closing Saturday. Maintain courage. Expect money, probably myself " to-morrow morning. Order funeral same as sister's. Register death forth- " with. Get certificate. I shall provide for you. Neither advertise nor " telegraph anybody."

The second, from Ludgate Circus, was handed in at 2.20 p.m., from the same to the same :—

"Far from feeling well. Can you arrange without me? Five pounds "posted, more shall follow as required. Do things quietly, funeral should be "strictly private."

The third, from Temple Bar, handed in at 3.2 p.m., from the same to the same, runs :—

"If you have written your sister [my wife], telegraph requesting her not "to advertise death, as I shall do whatever is necessary."

These telegrams, as I have said, bear date September the 7th. On the 10th Mr. Maxwell issued his Circular above quoted. I leave these facts to the appreciation of all whom it concerns to know them.

I have the honour to be,

Your obedient Servant,

RICHARD BRINSLEY KNOWLES.

characters whom she was ostensibly applauding. In *A Strange World,* once the reader leaves the immediate company of the theatre people—the aspiring actress Justina Elgood, her father, and the members of the "commonwealth" at York, whom we have already encountered—he seems to be launched on a straightforward Braddonian murder novel: Justina's lover, heir to a large fortune and a Cornish manor house, is brutally shot from ambush by the next heir, Churchill Penwyn, who needs the inheritance to marry the girl he loves. But the murderer is blackmailed by an old gypsy woman who has seen the shooting and demands that he make her his lodgekeeper.

And one day when those untidy gypsies at the lodge have tried Mrs. Penwyn's patience, and she pleads with her husband to oust them, largely because they never go to church, she is deeply shocked to hear him say that there are indeed many respectable people who never go to church. He adds that in his bachelor days he rarely went himself. Suddenly she realizes what a gulf has opened between them. "Their life had been so glad, so bright, so busy, so full of action and occupation, that they had seldom spoken of serious things. Never till this moment" had she asked him "that simple solemn question, 'But you call yourself a Christian, Churchill?'" Alas, all he can say is that he hates "theological argumentation," and when she insistently maintains that "'a man is or is not a follower of Christ,'" he answers, "'Then I am not.'" The blow is "too sudden, too heavy"; she shrinks from him as if he had struck her; she "went away to her own room and shut herself in, and wept for him and prayed for him."

So, though she loves him, she is hardly surprised when the gypsy reveals to her that Churchill is a murderer and that they owe their wealth and position to his crime. She has already recognized him as an infidel, and what, after all, could be expected of a man who had not regularly gone to church in his youth? She quickly forgives him and persuades him not to make a legal effort to keep the property away from the legitimate heir—the actress Justina Elgood. But before they can emigrate to Australia, Mrs. Penwyn dies of a wasting disease, and her husband the murderer rides his horse over the cliffs and kills himself. The wages of sin have duly been paid. MEB's devout readers could accept her evangelical cant at face value, and her skeptical ones might join her in a cynical smile. Those who read her for her story alone were rewarded with one of her very best Wilkie Collins-style investigations, leading the sleuth into lodgings in a former Cornish manor house—now a simple farm—into the shop of the Cornish village tobacconist-hairdresser with his file of ancient playbills—one of which provides a major clue—and into the London house of a music teacher, where the Berlin-work chair-covers, "fluffy and beady mats on the tables and chiffoniers, and alabaster baskets of wax fruit and flowers . . . under glass shades"[43] offer instant proof that this must be the dwelling of a retired schoolmistress. MEB's eye had never been keener or her pen more lapidary than in the descriptions of the persons and places, the exteriors and interiors, theatrical and nontheatrical, of *A Strange World*.

In *Lost for Love*, however, she grew too careless in covering her tracks. Here a widower, who has made his fortune raising sheep in Australia, returns to England with a beautiful daughter of seventeen. She is soon courted both by her father's old friend, a successful doctor whom she refuses, and by a rich young amateur artist whom she accepts after her father has forced him to propose. The artist has been slow to come forward because he is already deeply involved with another girl, Louisa, beautiful daughter of a Dickensian lower-middle-class family: the grandmother keeps a genteel secondhand clothes shop (" 'no counter, no scales and weights, nothing humbling to the spirits,' " to which the girl retorts, " 'No; and no till, and no profits mostly' ") ; the father, a hard-drinking picture restorer not above larceny; and Louisa, who sits to the painter. He quickly teaches her to abandon penny numbers and read Keats and Byron, and—after she has been locked out of her own house—he secretly places her in a school so exceedingly proper that the head-mistress recoils in horror at her request for a volume of Shakespeare (" 'Until they expurgate the subjects of . . . the plays, no edition . . . shall ever enter any domestic circle where I keep watch and ward.' "). Yet this proper headmistress admits Louisa to her school without asking any questions, for the sake of the fees that the young artist will pay, and even gives the young pair time alone together to say good-bye, blinking at the probability that they are lovers. (Of course, nothing untoward has passed between them.)

When the rejected doctor learns that his successful rival, the artist, is involved with another girl, he knocks him off a cliff. Believing his victim dead, he becomes a far more regular churchgoer than hitherto, at the same time hypocritically participating in a search for the missing man. Soon he proceeds without compunction to marry the sheeprancher's daughter, whom he keeps in ignorance of his part in her fiancé's disappearance. Louisa's shady father then blackmails the doctor, whose wife leaves him when she discovers that he is a murderer. But since the victim has only had a concussion and has recovered to marry Louisa without notifying the doctor of his survival, all the guilty doctor must endure is a brief illness, after which his wife forgives him. The old proprietress of the secondhand shop proves to be the grandmother of *both* girls. Quite aware of the fact, she has refrained from identifying herself to the rich young lady in order to spare her embarrassment.

So the daughter of a shady blackmailer blossoms into a cultivated lady, a far more interesting woman than the bird-brained daughter of the rancher. The poor girl marries the rich gentleman artist, who "felt as Pygmalion the sculptor might have felt if his animated statue had been a clever woman,"[44] while the rich girl, who loves the same man, loses him. Yet the girls are first cousins. The churchgoing would-be assassin escapes almost without suffering. The blackmailer is eventually rewarded with a house (in Camberwell) and a large allowance from his son-in-law. The painter virtually seduces one girl, proposes to the second, and returns to his first without telling his true fiancée or his prospective father-in-law or his ostensible murderer even that he is alive. Hitherto, MEB's espousal of Low-Church values had at least led to an outcome desirable by Low-Church standards. But in this novel, she let cant take over, rather as if she were trying to see how far she could go. Was she saying that all levels of the middle class were equally admirable or equally detestable?

At any rate, the *Spectator*—which had ignored her novels for seven years—now took her sharply to task. Their critic flatly declared that he preferred MEB's "first or blue-eyed murderess manner, when her women were fascinating fiends, and her men were ennuyés . . . when she was great in upholstery, knowing in horse-flesh, cunning in *coulisses*, and before she developed her present knowledge of classical literature, European languages, Indian history, the fine arts, medical science, and Holy Scripture." At least in those days, she did not write about "grave, inscrutable physicians, whom she converts from free-thinking, and an evil tendency to stay away from church, by a process so uniform, that we look for saving grace in her later as confidently as we looked for bigamy in her earlier novels." MEB had been "more readable" before she had abandoned Bohemia and "the race-course, the music-hall, the behind-the-scenes, the lodging-house life". The real trouble, the *Spectator* shrewdly decided, was that MEB was now trying to compete with Mrs. Henry Wood, author of *East Lynne* (1861) and—by 1874—of twenty-three other novels, "the leading manufacturer" of fiction "for readers of the lower-middle class, whether 'Church' or 'Chapel' in their sympathies."

For several reasons, the *Spectator* critic believed, MEB had no chance to win. First of all, she could not "touch her veteran rival in gorgeous common-place, the nice adjustment of murder and morality, servants-hall episodes, the romance of the apothecary and the green-grocer, funeral etiquette and expenses, the gossip of the backshop, and pulpit eloquence." She lacked "the direct, bold, entirely confident philistinism" of Mrs. Henry Wood. Second, MEB had a past. The three or four novels she had written since "she finally adopted, after a brief transition-stage, her present lecture-room-plus tabernacle manner," were "heavily handicapped by the evil repute (among her new clients) of Lady Audley and Aurora Floyd," while "no such clouds" obscured "the lambent lustre of Mrs. Wood's fame." Even Mrs. Wood's worst enemies could never accuse her of dealing with any but solid British institutions: "the modest coroner's inquest, the homely justice-room, the unassuming smuggler's cave." Consistently adding no garnish to her plain English fare, Mrs. Wood served up "murders and mutton, suicides and rice-pudding, stolen cheques and thick bread-and-butter; and, as she never fails to say an emphatic grace over each heavy meal, she satisfies alike the appetite, the taste, and the conscience of her readers." Miss Braddon "says grace too, but she admits 'kickshaws.' . . . The people who read her novels in her second manner . . . not only do not like French verses, bits of German philosophy, scraps of art criticism," and all her learning "but . . . regard them with suspicion, not to be appeased by any amount of Biblical texts."

So by trying "to combine solidity and piety with learned elegance," MEB had made *Lost for Love* "a heterogeneous performance, which may be aptly compared to the contents of the old clothes-shop . . . where the rich and lovely heroine finds a grandmother nicely calculated to soothe the democratic breast," and a criminal uncle "whose conversion to a clear perception of the charms of labour and the beauty of holiness reads like a lost page from the report of the Brick-Lane Branch." When the "fine-minded, high-souled" doctor has knocked his rival over the cliff and then strolls home calmly reflecting on the violence of nature and of man (" 'Nature will indulge her bad passions just like the weakest of us' "), the reader may expect—and he gets—any amount of inconsistent behavior. The *Spectator* advised MEB to drop both "sensation" and "cant," and concentrate instead upon developing "a third manner," of which they professed to see early signs in the "good, true, and lovable" rancher's daughter. If she took this advice she might yet do "an admirable study of the quiet sort."[45]

The *Spectator* had not detected MEB satirizing the values of the lower-middle-class reader (whether "Church" or "Chapel" in his sympathies), but regarded with disbelief and distaste what it took to be her serious

effort to adopt them. The reviewer, who had obviously read her with hor-
rified attention and intelligent appreciation, was no doubt right: she
always liked to go her competitors one better if she could; and—perhaps
especially because so many of her new readers in the Tillotson
newspapers were Lancashire workingmen's or farmers' families—she was
now trying to outdo Mrs. Henry Wood at her own game, meanwhile enjoying her own deadpan satire, which the *Spectator* critic chose to regard
as hypocrisy.

MEB found an original and spirited way to reply to the review. She
made the leading character of her new novel, *Hostages to Fortune*—which
she was writing when the *Spectator* review of *Lost for Love* appeared—a
successful novelist, whose latest book, *His Last Love,* is attacked in a
paper called "The Censor":

> "Extract the acid cynicism and the half-veiled immorality from
> Mr. Westray's style, and the result is about as palatable as
> lemonade without lemon or sugar. . . . *His Last Love* is a novel
> which a schoolgirl might be proud to have written, for the gram-
> mar is faultless and the French quotations in no case misspelt. It is
> a work which Mr. [Martin Farquhar] Tupper [the epitome of
> evangelical mid-Victorian conventionality] might father without
> fear of lessening his hold upon the middle-class intellect, and it is
> a curious illustration of the depth of bathos to which a really
> clever writer may descend when he tries to dazzle his admirers in a
> line of art for which he lacks every element of success. Only to a
> Balzac is it given to create two such types as Valerie de Marneffe
> and Eugenie Grandet. Mr. Westray's sympathies are obviously
> with the former class, and his portraiture of *ces espèces* is not
> without merit. Let him stick to tinsel, with which he has achieved
> some rather brilliant effects, and not waste his labour in deep-
> sinking operations upon an imagination which does not abound in
> gold."[46]

Her pastiche of the *Spectator*'s comments on her own *Lost for Love* was
clever enough, but failed—as she must have realized—to meet the critic's
charges. She apparently decided that the game she had been playing was
no longer worth the candle. She could not satirize cant any more visibly
than she had done without giving the game away and offending the
canters; yet she could no longer pretend to present cant sympathetically
without irritating her less straitlaced readers into the cry of hypocrisy. It

had been an amusing experiment; it had been in part at least a failure. Cant in its more blatant forms would now gradually fade from her pages. But mid-Victorian values were not safe from MEB: she and they would remain at war.

4. "On the Highway of Life, the Boundary-line Is Not So Clearly Defined" (1874–1875)

While MEB was writing *Lost for Love*, she and John Maxwell went to Ireland for the first two weeks of June 1874, giving Dublin a wide berth, but traveling rapidly and happily as tourists through much of the south and west. At Cork, they stopped at the monastery of the Christian Brothers, on a hill above the city, to pay a reverential visit to the tomb of Gerald Griffin, the celebrated Irish novelist and poet. Thirty-five years before, not long before he died, Griffin had sent John Maxwell, then a penniless Limerick boy of nineteen, off to London on a salary to supervise the publication of the collected edition of his works. In her account of their travels of 1874, MEB made no mention of this episode, but she did pay tribute to Griffin as the Scott of Ireland and expressed her wonder that Dion Boucicault, who had made so great a fortune from turning Griffin's novel, *The Collegians*, into the successful play, *The Colleen Bawn*, had not erected to his memory some "costlier" monument than the simple headstone in the monastery graveyard. Once before, in 1866, Maxwell and MEB had visited Ireland; between the lines of her journalist's account of the 1874 journey one can detect how much pleasure it gave her to revisit with the man she loved the scenes of his impoverished youth in Limerick. Now they were staying at the luxurious George Hotel in a suite whose spacious drawing-room had three long windows and its own balcony, and whose bedrooms were "palatial in size and elevation."[47]

Less than three months later, only a few days after finishing *Lost for Love* on August 22, 1874, and while she was writing the last pages of *A Strange World*, MEB found herself once again at the center of a storm of scandalous publicity. By 1874 the memory of Richard Brinsley Knowles's denials of her marriage published ten years earlier had probably dimmed in the mind of the public. But now John Maxwell's unfortunate first wife finally died.

For the last time we return to Charles Reade's 1874 notebook entry on "Braddon, Miss" to read the few remaining lines hitherto withheld:

> At last Mrs M[axwell] died, and then came an obituary notice stating whose wife she was. Instead of keeping quiet, this foolish Irishman [John Maxwell] sends a printed notice to all the people at Richmond casting a sort of half doubt on the matter. Thereupon the brother or one of his party sends counter-notices with copies of the telegrams sent by M.[axwell] to Ireland expressing sympathy, saying spare no expense I will come over, and ending with his not going but sending a fiver.[48]

One of these "counter-notices" survives, as printed, signed, and circulated by Richard Brinsley Knowles. Dated September 28, 1874, it was deliberately calculated to shatter whatever peace of mind MEB and John Maxwell might have achieved.

On the fifth of September, Knowles wrote, his sister-in-law, Mrs. Maxwell, had died; and on the tenth he had published in the London newspapers an announcement to the effect that "after a long and severe illness," there had died in Dublin—aged 48—"Mary Anne, wife of John Maxwell, Esq., publisher, of Lichfield House, Richmond Surrey, and of 4, Shoe Lane, Fleet Street." This would have ended the matter, said Knowles, but "by the merest accident" he had discovered that on September 12 Maxwell had privately distributed a printed circular, dated "Lichfield House," and saying: "Mr. and Mrs. Maxwell present their compliments to ——————————, and beg to disclaim any knowledge of the maliciously-intended announcement of a death of the 5th inst."

Therefore, Knowles maintained, he was now obliged to tell the entire story. On March 7, 1848, John Maxwell had married Mary Anne Crowley, sister of Knowles's own wife. The Maxwells had seven children, of whom five were living. Some time after the birth of the youngest "a separation took place between the parents, and Mrs. Maxwell resided henceforth with her family in the neighbourhood of Dublin." After rehearsing his earlier efforts to deny the published statements that Miss Braddon and Maxwell were married, Knowles reported that on September 5, when the true Mrs. Maxwell had died, her brother, John

Crowley, had telegraphed the news to John Maxwell. On September 7, two days later, Crowley had received three successive telegrams from Maxwell, but had not replied to any. When Maxwell later wrote and asked that they be returned, Crowley sent them to Knowles instead, and Knowles now published them.

The first—sent at 10:30 A.M.—acknowledged the receipt of Crowley's "melancholy telegram," and said "Maintain courage. Expect money, probably myself tomorrow morning. Order funeral same as sister's. Register death forthwith. Get certificate. I shall provide for you. Neither advertise nor telegraph anybody." Four hours later, at 2:20 P.M., Maxwell telegraphed, "Far from feeling well. Can you manage without me? Five pounds posted, more shall follow as required. Do things quietly, funeral should be strictly private." An hour later he sent the third, to say that if Crowley had written Mrs. Knowles, he should now wire her "not to advertise" the death, "as I shall do whatever is necessary."

Having given the texts of John Maxwell's panic-stricken telegrams of September 7, Knowles reminded his readers that on the twelfth Maxwell had, with MEB, issued the circular begging "to disclaim any knowledge of the maliciously-intended announcement of a death." And, Knowles concluded, "I leave these facts to the appreciation of all whom it concerns to know them."[49]

It was clearly this dreadful episode of September 1874 that prompted Charles Reade to write down in his notebook for that year his whole account of "Braddon, Miss." The affair was fresh in his mind, and his brief summary of the Knowles counter-notice was accurate. His final words of tribute to MEB—"I don't know where to find a better woman. Industrious, self-denying, gentle, affectionate, talented, and utterly unassuming, a devoted daughter, faithful wife, loving mother, and kindly step-mother"—committed to the pages of a private ledger where nobody else would see them, testify to Reade's honest sense of outrage at the pain inflicted on her by the latest publicity given to her unhappy position. When his new book, The Wandering Heir, appeared in hard covers for the first time in 1875, he let the public know how he felt by dedicating it "to my friend M. E. Braddon, as a slight mark of respect for her private virtues and public talents."

As the first Mrs. Maxwell was now dead, one can hardly see the necessity for Knowles to insert in the London newspapers a prominent death-notice, phrased in such a way as once again gratuitously to underline the fact that the woman with whom John Maxwell, publisher, of Lichfield House and Shoe Lane had been living for thirteen years was not his wife. One must agree that Knowles's announcement was, as Maxwell's disingenuous circular called it, "maliciously-intended." The very texts of Maxwell's telegrams make it clear that he had hoped the relatives in Ireland—especially if they were offered money—would not inform the implacable publishing Knowleses in London. And perhaps if he had been more generous they would not have done so. But even in Dublin in 1874, after paying for a quiet funeral, one would not have had enough left over from a five-pound note to salve one's conscience. And so John Crowley told Knowles, and the fat was in the fire. After the death-notice had appeared, Maxwell compounded his folly by disclaiming in print all knowledge of it. Retribution promptly followed in the form of Knowles's counter-notice.

The impact must have been devastating. When the domestic staff at Lichfield House discovered that MEB and Maxwell were not legally married, they all gave notice and left, except for Eliza Pryke, whose daughter remembered in 1956 that her mother had told her how Maxwell asked, " 'Are you leaving us too, Eliza?' . . . Eliza answered, 'No, Sir, I mean to stay on with you,' to which 'You're a good girl, Eliza,' he said with his Irish brogue, 'you will never regret your decision.' And she never did," leaving the Maxwells' service only to be married in 1889.[50]

On October 2, 1874—as soon as the law allowed—John Maxwell and MEB were married at St. Bride's Church, Fleet Street, not far from his publishing offices. The Reverend Charles Procter, Vicar of St. John's Church, Richmond, officiated. But the Knowles bombshell had driven the Maxwells from Lichfield House. W. B. Maxwell long afterwards recalled that for a year in his childhood, "for reasons I never understood," his parents had lived in Chelsea, where he had known some of the soldiers in the barracks. The year in question he named as forty-five years before his return to those barracks in a parade after the first World War, in 1919.[51] So it must have been the year 1874. Presumably the Maxwells left Richmond in order to allow the gossip to die down for a year or so before they returned, and perhaps incidentally to recruit a new batch of servants. Although they legalized their relationship some thirteen years after it had begun, their six children, five of whom survived, had all been born before the first Mrs. Maxwell died. And it was this fact—as R. B. Knowles well knew—that his counter-notice would most forcefully call to public attention, even though he made no mention of Maxwell's second family of children.

Only three days before the Knowles "counter-notice" was published, MEB had begun a new novel, *Hostages to Fortune,* and, well before it was finished, in accordance with her practice, she embarked on its successor, *Dead Men's Shoes*, which she did not complete until the very end of 1875.[52] Much of the writing must have been done in Chelsea, after Lichfield House had been temporarily abandoned. Both novels clearly reflected her bitter frame of mind. The people of *Hostages to Fortune* were the most disagreeable lot that she had yet put into a novel, without even the redeeming interest of the shady gang of crooks that had gathered in *Birds of Prey*; but in *Dead Men's Shoes* she managed an additional turn of the screw, creating "from first to last . . . not a single person or incident capable of kindling a spark of sympathy."[53]

The theatrical actress-manageress of *Hostages to Fortune* is a villainess, although she looks "like a picture by Whistler," sitting in a low and graceful Louis quinze chair, in "her favourite black velvet and rosepoint," with the square-cut bodice revealing her graceful throat, and the lace giving "a madonna-like purity to the dress. Small diamond ear-drops and a yellow rosebud" in her bosom are her only ornaments; a "large black fan . . . painted with pale yellow roses," dangles from her wrist by a pale yellow ribbon. She is so jealous of the new wife of her rejected former suitor, the playwright, that she joins a dissolute rake in a squalid conspiracy to compromise her. But the reader hardly cares, because the wife is a strong-minded sabbatarian so stupid that when she reads some of her husband's verse—"the complaint of a soul ill at ease"—she decides that " 'No happy husband, no Christian gentleman, could have thought those thoughts or written those words' "—and so joins the most offensive of MEB's canting characters. One rather regrets that the rake—who for some obscure reason regards her as infinitely desirable, " 'the one, fresh, fair, unspotted and perfect woman whom it has been my lot to meet' "—does not succeed in overcoming her scruples when he has trapped her in a hotel room by means of a false telegram, if only because it would have served her smug and detestable husband entirely right. But the rake has a timely heart attack instead. It is not clear whether the stroke suffered by the wicked actress is due to her involvement in this plot or to her having produced the uncensored version of the risqué French play that we earlier watched her adapting. [54]

In *Dead Men's Shoes*, pure greed animates the young woman who leaves her husband—a gentleman down on his luck—and turns her infant son over to someone else, in order to live with a rich uncle in "Redcastle" (Beverley) while she waits for him to die and leave her his money. Her pretense that she is unmarried brings her unwelcome proposals, but she manages to avoid exposure, although at one moment she reaches a peak of infamy when she falsely tells her husband, who has tracked her down, that their son is dead. She fully deserves to be abandoned to the poverty from which she has fled and to which she must return in flight when under suspicion of murdering her uncle; but her husband gets her off the murder charge and resumes married life with her. The uncle, a reprobate ex-slave-trader, in fact had never had the money she was expecting, but luckily her husband has earned one fortune and come into a second. She wonders why love is not dead in him, and so does the reader.

Only the brilliantly realized scenes in which the characters of these two novels move: the fashionable London theatre, the back-biting Beverley small-town social world, the writer's new-built house with all its fashionable classical details ("the very beer-jugs are Etrurian"), the sordid Chelsea lodging house with its grim landlady, remain to convince the reader that they are indeed by MEB, so contemptible have all the personages become. But the period of complete disillusionment was brief. It marked the end of her years of struggle and the beginning of a new era.

PART II

THE YEARS OF FULFILLMENT, 1875–1915

CHAPTER VIII

"There Is Exuberant Life, not a Trace
of Fatigue or Distaste, or Decline
of Fancy"
(1875–1885)

MEB's marriage and return to Lichfield House—exactly midway in her life—meant that henceforth she could relax and expand in the comfortable environment and amidst the congenial friends that her personal warmth and talent and success had won her, and could occupy without challenge her rightful place as a *grande dame* in her own circles. As the years of struggle ended and the years of fulfillment began, she managed effortlessly to keep in balance the heavy claims of her large family and her growing circle of friends with those of her demanding profession.

Her first novel written in her new security, *Joshua Haggard's Daughter* (1876), the thirty-first of her career, is a masterpiece, a deceptively simple rural tragedy, its melodrama held well within bounds by a classic dignity of theme and treatment. The critics largely missed the point.

In its nine immediate successors, between 1876 and 1882, MEB attempted no similar experiment, nor did she recapture the extraordinary power of *Joshua Haggard*; but she sounded an ever more insistent radical note. Safe at last, abandoning all cant—even for satirical purposes—she rebuked the English rich in increasingly strident tones for their opulent display and their lack of social conscience, explicitly contrasting them, to their great disadvantage, with the poor. The critics missed the point.

As early as 1879, she began to experiment with Zolaesque episodes. But she no longer merely pirated from the French. In each of two successive novels in 1883 she transformed a major theme from Zola into a convincing English version. The critics missed the point.

Next, she crossed the Channel for her subject matter and in 1883 produced an arresting novelette of the Paris Commune of 1871, in which she demonstrated not only her accurate historical knowledge of the episode but her ability to transmute it into fiction. She showed the limits of her radicalism, denouncing revolutionary excesses. The decade culminated in 1884 with her second masterpiece, *Ishmael*, a brilliant and dense, original and innovative novel of the Second Empire, emerging out of and revealing her intimate acquaintance with the politics, social and economic life, literature, and *moeurs* of the period. These were furnished only to a very limited degree by Zola himself, from whom she took method rather than substance. As different from *Joshua Haggard's Daughter* as one novel could well be from another, written virtually in another genre, *Ishmael* testified to the depth and variety of MEB's talents. The critics largely missed the point.

When *Ishmael* was finished, she cobbled some excellent unused French bits and pieces into the otherwise undistinguished *Wyllard's Weird* (1885). And in March 1885, as if closing her own Second Empire period, she wrote a long, clever, and balanced critical essay on Zola, which was apparently never published. From its manuscript one learns at first hand her sophisticated appreciation of his naturalism and her accurate estimate of his place in the history of the French novel.

In *Joshua Haggard's Daughter* and *Ishmael*, MEB displayed her usual keen observation of persons and places. But except for this, neither novel had anything in common with the sensation-novels with which she had begun her career and which had made her famous. With the exception of one Edwardian novel of 1907, *Dead Love Has Chains*, she would never again achieve quite such distinguished fiction. The decade 1875–1885, therefore, marked the double peak of her Victorian career.

1. "A Solid Unchanging Environment"

In the autumn of 1875, after the year's exile in London, MEB and Maxwell returned with their children to life at Lichfield House. Legally married, they might still expect an occasional snub from those who did not choose to forget the past. But the Maxwells had too many loyal friends to permit this to cloud their days. In some affectionate recollections of his childhood, their son Will—eight years old when his parents were married—gives us a view of their family life in the five years before MEB's own diaries begin on January 1, 1880.

Lichfield House itself Will remembered as a splendid place to live, with its paneled walls, its carved doorways and mantelpieces, and its "lofty drawing-room with five high windows and a bay that all the world admired." Behind the house, a terrace looked down across a lawn to a "Broadwalk" leading between herbaceous borders to an orangery. There were stables with "capacious lofts" above, a stable-yard with the coachman's cottage at the far end, out-buildings, large grounds, and a paddock, where cows or horses ran loose. The trees were delightful: a Spanish chestnut's "drooping branches . . . formed a shady tent; a huge cedar was almost absurdly easy to climb; a gravel pit gaped invitingly." In the kitchen gardens, peaches and nectarines, great yellow pears, green figs "ripened on the sun-baked walls against a suburban sky as yet un-polluted by London smoke." It was, as Will enthusiastically recalled, "an ideal home for young children."

And here, at the moment when his reminiscences begin, there still lived all ten children: Maxwell's elder five—Nicholas, John, Robert, Bessie, and Polly—"almost grown up and presently to disappear one after another for wedlock and independence," and "the second brood," MEB's and Max-well's—Gerald, Fanny, Will, Rosie and Ted—to whom the elder step-brothers and sisters were kind, "submitting to our company, entertaining us, filling the cheerful hours for us." Miss Browne, an old woman who had been generous to MEB in her youth, was a permanent resident, and often there were also "staying visitors," as many as three or four at a time. There was Nurse Campbell, "old-fashioned in her ways even at that remote date," who could barely read. Her one book was *The Pilgrim's Progress* ("most boring"), and her one game was cribbage. But she was loyal and affectionate to her charges, the three youngest, all of whom fitted when necessary into the huge perambulator. Gerald and Fanny had "floated themselves free of nursery control." Poor Nurse Campbell was improbably lured into concubinage and drudgery by a local tavern-keeper and was replaced by the genteel and proper Mrs. Addington, who enforced strict rules of table manners and forbade exhibitionism when the children dressed or undressed. But after Mrs. Addington stayed out all night at a dance, she too had to go. Among the favorite visitors to the nursery was "Aunt O'Donnell," John Maxwell's elder sister, who played a wonderful game with the children, pretending to be the proprietor of a sweetshop.

Will remembered the excitement of lodgings at Broadstairs, where the landlady's husband owned a windmill and visits to Brighton with all its celebrities. At the age of ten or eleven, he and Harry Chart—the son of his mother's old friends and one-time employers, the managers of the Theatre Royal, Brighton—would pretend to be attending church at Rich-mond with MEB on Sunday, but instead of climbing to the gallery would steal away for a walk beside the river, getting back just in time to meet her when the service was over and so avoiding detection. Will remembered the stream of visitors to Lichfield House and of course he remembered how at fourteen (in 1880, the year MEB's diaries begin) he was allowed to leave school to study to be an artist.

Sometime in the mid-seventies, on a driving tour, the Maxwells found and fell in love with the Hampshire village of Bank, or Annesley Bank, near Lyndhurst in the New Forest. For three consecutive years thereafter they went there in the spring. John Maxwell and MEB stayed in a large cottage where the whole family had its meals, while for sleeping-places the children "were 'potted out' " in nearby cottages, "all . . . scrupulously clean." Then John Maxwell bought a large meadow and its surrounding cottages, and—sometime in the late seventies—built a new house for the family to live in. The countryside was beautiful, the country children wonderfully good companions.

When the son of a notorious local poacher broke his leg, John Maxwell discovered that the family was often hungry, and ordered that the baker deliver bread to them daily. Immediately, representatives of the local gentry asked him to stop, "lest it should appear that he was defending an outlaw . . . as against themselves." Maxwell refused to withdraw the free bread, and MEB suggested to Will that he go and read to the bedridden boy. Will braved the "intolerable odour of the cottage . . . that came floating out from the heavy and stagnant air within," interested the patient in the tales of Hans Christian Andersen, made friends with the family, and even got a window opened.

Gradually the Maxwells added to their own new house. By 1880, at least one sojourn at Bank was an important part of every year. In 1882, Maxwell wrote W. F. Tillotson that he was "over head and ears in debt for land, etc. bought in the New Forest" and asked him for the money owing for one of MEB's novels. The local pack of deerhounds afforded great sport, in which MEB herself twice a week eagerly participated, on her "magnificent grey mare called Vixen" or her "less interesting brown mare called Peggy," as they "plunged down into the noble old woods, clambered steep hill-sides clothed with heather, galloped in openness and freedom over the wide moorland, and plunged again to the low ground and a sylvan stream."

Almost from infancy, Will Maxwell recognized that "the true source of happiness in the house was its gentle unselfish mistress." She "could banish querulousness, anger, and all evil humours," and Will always adored her: "I talked to her about everything that concerned me deeply. I think I must already have understood that our love for each other was infinitely the biggest thing in my life. It was always developing, always growing finer and stronger," fortified by his discovery that at two he had helped assuage her grief for her own mother. "We became real companions. . . . I vowed to myself that I would never fail her." Naturally happy, MEB "rejoiced in laughter, and taught us young children to love innocent mirth. She used to read to us; she walked with us, played with us, and took us out for drives." It was a long time before Will "noticed that the name of a Miss Braddon was . . . often heard. Soon it seemed to have a glamour and a mystery." The very sound of the name was stirring. "People addressed her by it. 'Forgive me, dear Mrs. Maxwell, I can't help calling you Miss Braddon.' . . . We saw letters for Miss Braddon on the hall table. And then my father showed us a new book, with the name on the title-page—'By M. E. Braddon, Author of *Lady Audley's Secret*.'" MEB, Will remembered,

> got through her immense amount of work as if by magic. She never seemed to be given any time in which to do it. She had no stated hours, no part of the day to be held secure from disturbances and intrusions. She was never inaccessible. Everybody went uninvited to her library, we children, the servants, importunate visitors. I don't remember that she ever refused to come away from the quiet dignified room if we asked her. And she never failed to be available as a companion to my father when he wanted her, and no matter for how long.[1]

Occasionally there was a moment of emergency, as in October 1876, when MEB and her children were out for a drive at midday, and a steamroller at work on the road frightened the horses, causing them to bolt. MEB "fully thought" they "were taking me and mine to instant death—but thank God *we* were all saved at the cost of the near horse, which fell against a lamp post and stopped the carriage." Or we catch a glimpse of a single festive moment, as at Christmas 1876, when Mr. Venables, director of the firm from which the Maxwell publishing house bought its paper, sent MEB his usual present of a brace of turkeys. They were so good, MEB wrote, that "I only wish I could write a book as popular as Uncle Tom's Cabin, & use all the paper in Queenhithe." A few months later, she invited Mrs. Sala and "your inimitable—unapproachable—etc. etc. Lord and Master" to dinner, exuberantly promising them "quite a small party, no Philistines" and thanking the "great man" for having come only a few days previously to a "rustic tea-fight—but a dinner of herbs where love is" was "better than the finest American beef without it." MEB's own letters reflect the happiness and security that Will remembered.

Her old friend, Edmund Yates, described her in 1877 as "sweeping along at a hand-gallop" on Kaiser, her white-footed golden bay, whom she rewarded with a slice of bread when the ride was over; or as hard at work, huddled in a "low uncomfortable chair" in her study, seldom stopping to correct her manuscript. She wrote, he said, only two hours a day, with a tailor's thimble on the middle finger of her right hand to protect it from the ink. Each of her novels began as a "skeleton"—MEB herself called it a "charpente"—of a few pages. In her study she still preserved—in 1877—the "pleasant epistles" in which Bulwer had given her "severe but salutary criticism," while mingling flattery with useful hints. To Yates she praised *Adam Bede* with particular enthusiasm. Although Hetty Sorrel is "vain, silly, and almost heartless," MEB, in a dozen readings, had always wept for her. Yates found MEB spirited and vivacious, quickly responsive to beauty, her gray eyes bright, her voice earnest and full of contrast.[2]

In these years before 1880, Will remembered, "wedlock and independence" claimed three of the five stepchildren. About Nicholas' marriage and subsequent life no evidence remains. Robert married a girl named Lydia and remained close to his father's publishing business and family. Elizabeth—"Bessie"—married a man named Rumble, perhaps against her father's wishes: in 1878 he altered his will by revoking a previous bequest to her of one thousand pounds. MEB's diary for April 21, 1883, records tersely, "Mr. Rumble died at Bonchurch," and in 1886 John Maxwell altered his will again, leaving Bessie the income from one thousand pounds. Although she never is mentioned by name in MEB's diaries, the initials "E.R." and "B.R." appearing at quarterly intervals and frequent notations of change of address for "Rumble" suggest that in these later years MEB regularly sent money to her elder stepdaughter, whose life was probably an unhappy one. But the serenity of MEB's own existence in the late seventies and early eighties was virtually unclouded.

Yet serenity—as her manuscript diaries abundantly show—is in many ways an ill-chosen word. The diaries extend—with only the loss of 1889 and of part of 1887—from 1880 through 1914; the last entry was written only five weeks before she died. They are diaries, however, only in a limited sense: she seldom wrote in them anything she was thinking or feeling. Each little annual volume was designed as an engagement book with a space for every day of the year, in which MEB often entered her engagements in advance. At the end of every day she usually also jotted down a brief summary of her activities. The diaries record where she was and what she was doing, what people she had seen, what books read, what theatres attended almost every day for thirty-five years.[3] For her biographer they mean the virtual end of detective work on such questions. Yet neither the diaries nor MEB's surviving letters reveal as much about her inner feelings and her literary aspirations in the years after 1880 as the letters to Bulwer revealed in the years before 1873. So the need arises for detective work of a different order.

Almost every day included one or more time-consuming engagements at one of MEB's own houses or at the house of some friend, or at a restaurant or public function. Lunches, teas, dinners, balls, receptions, banquets, theatre parties, exchanges of visits, long informal sojourns with old friends or members of the family, shorter formal calls paid upon acquaintances or received from them succeeded each other in an unending procession. MEB frequently noted who was present at some party, but almost never wrote down what anyone said or did, although she sometimes commented favorably or unfavorably on the food, the music, or the company. Sometimes her hosts, her fellow-guests or her own guests at home were celebrated people: Robert Browning, Oscar Wilde and his wife, Whistler, the du Mauriers, the Laboucheres, Henry Irving, Bram Stoker, Lord and Lady Lytton, the Earl and Countess of Londesborough, Lady Dorothy Nevill, Sir Charles Dilke, the Salas, the Yateses. When MEB gave a dinner party, she occasionally noted that she "looked out" the plate and the wine, and she enjoyed polishing furniture. But of course she had a large staff of servants. Nor when the Maxwells migrated to Hampshire did their social life diminish in intensity. Married children and their spouses and *their* children, house guests for a single night or many nights, other visitors and callers—sometimes residents in the New Forest, sometimes Londoners—poured into and out of "Bank Cottage."

At Richmond, MEB rode regularly at least twice a week, and in Hampshire she hunted during the season at least as often with the local packs of deerhounds and foxhounds, usually recording the general outlines of a day's run and the kill, if any. If the weather or the season were not right for hunting, she walked or drove. The family and Miss Browne, grooms and horses migrated by rail from Richmond to Lyndhurst and from Lyndhurst back to Richmond, as did cook, housemaids, and other servants. No sooner had the move from one house to the other been accomplished than dinners began again immediately. Each year MEB and Maxwell also took several shorter trips, in the early eighties mostly in England, although sometimes to the Continent. During the sojourns at hotels the social life went on without a break. Friends appeared at the table d'hôte, and invited the Maxwells for an excursion. There were old acquaintances in the countryside nearby who must be called upon. The Maxwells might be at the "Granville," an enormous seaside hotel at Ramsgate in Kent, or at St. Malo, or in Cornwall: people they knew always turned up to lunch and dine and have tea.

When MEB went to Bournemouth in 1882 to visit a stepson and his wife, she walked on the pier and met Thomas Hardy, whom she had first encountered in Frith's studio two or three years earlier. He had always liked her, and once remarked that she had "a broad thought-creased, world-beaten face—a most amiable woman." In 1883, when the Maxwells went to Paramé in Brittany, there with a new wife was Wybert Rousby,[4] MEB's mentor in her theatrical days, for whom she had written *Griselda* in 1873; for whose benefit in 1876 she had returned to the stage for a one-night stand; and whom she would portray as Willoughby Tracy in *A Lost Eden* (1904). When friends or relatives were absent, MEB wrote letters to them, and an endless stream of letters flowed out from wherever she might be staying, as another endless stream flowed in.

In the early eighties, the pattern of her years varied only in detail. In 1880 the Maxwells went from Richmond to Hampshire on April 5 and returned to Richmond on May 10; in 1881 they went on April 14—"All things at Bank bright and pretty as ever," MEB noted—and returned on May 31; in 1882 they went on March 24 and returned on May 12. In 1883, they undertook an extensive remodeling and rebuilding of the house at Bank, buying fields, cottages, and stables. They spent shorter periods there while supervising the work; by November, tiling had begun; by January 1, 1884, the repairs were well underway; by February 21, the windows were glazed, the flooring in the drawing-room and the walls and floors in the bedrooms were finished. In London on March 6 MEB and Max selected the stoves for the house and by May 3 these were all in, new stabling was rising, and the lawns were being sown. July 16 saw the purchase of new bedding, carpets, and china, all in London. On July 21 a van called for the furniture and two days later delivered it in Bank, under the supervision of both Maxwells, who spent the whole summer there and most of October.

In 1880, MEB stayed for five days at Stratford-upon-Avon, absorbing local color for her novel *Asphodel*, then in progress. In August, the family went to Weymouth, took the channel boat to Cherbourg for a weekend, returned to spend several more days touring Dorset, and then went on to

Devon and Cornwall for ten days more. In the antique shops MEB bought old silver—a Charles II salver, a George II tankard. She passed a week in November at Brighton, going to the theatres and seeing old friends, including the Charts. During the summer of 1881, she stayed for a month at Broadstairs, Kent, once Dickens' favorite seaside place, and in October for two weeks in Bath and in Devon. A January week in Brighton, a week at the Granville at two separate times, and ten days in the Lake Country varied the longer sojourns in Richmond and at Annesley Bank. In 1883 the Maxwells spent most of August in Brittany: St. Malo, Dinard, Paramé, and Mont-St-Michel, all providing local color for *Ishmael*. Four days in Norwich and Lincoln in September, and another week at the Granville early in November completed the time away from home. In 1884 and 1885, perhaps because of the extensive remodeling at Annesley Bank, the Maxwells went nowhere else.

Family life was absorbing. On September 2, 1880, Maxwell's son, John Jr. ("Jack"), was married to Alice Wyndham, whose family were close friends of the Maxwells. By August 1, 1881, the young couple had a son, "Baby John," later always called Jackie, and the following year a second son, Reginald. John Maxwell, Jr., was gradually taking over some of his father's tasks in the publishing house, and he and his wife continued to visit often in Richmond and in Hampshire. Only seven months after Jack Maxwell's marriage his sister Mary ("Polly"), the last of MEB's step-children at home, was married on April 6, 1881, to "Joe" Christmas. Their first daughter, Katie, arrived promptly on February 22, 1882, and their second, Sybil, on October 18, 1883. Polly and her husband also re-mained close to MEB and John Maxwell. Of MEB's own children, Gerald spent the year 1881 at Trinity College, Cambridge. Rosie went to boarding school in 1882. Fanny and Will and Ted were at home. Everybody except MEB had illnesses and had to see the doctor. Together the family went to the boat races, the theatre, the London shops. On December 29, 1884, MEB noted in her diary that "Max weighed 16/2/4" or 226 pounds and a quarter. It was too much.

Long ago, MEB had told Bulwer, "as to religion, . . . I cling to the simplest faith," and we have seen how little doctrinaire she was when she allowed her stepdaughters to mourn her own mother according to the Catholic practice. On Sundays, despite her frenetic life, she usually went to church at St. John's at Richmond or at the Emery Down village church when she was in Hampshire. But there was nothing compulsive about her church-going; if the weather was too bad or if something important interfered, she would stay at home. When she went to church, one or more of the children usually accompanied her. Will was confirmed on March 29, 1881; Rosie on April 2, 1884, by the Bishop of Winchester. MEB was a sensible, no-fuss-about-it, Church-of-England Christian, with distaste for the evangelical Low-Church fervor with which she endowed some of the characters in her novels, and no interest in the ritualistic Catholic practices fashionable among High-Church people.

Amidst the mundane entries recording the ordinary day-to-day episodes in the life of a mother ("Dr. Anderson to prescribe for Fanny's rheumatic shoulder"; "Gerald bought top hat and ordered dress trousers and waistcoat, two shirts, four collars"; "Teddy at home with cough"), one finds interspersed the record of the weather ("Thermometer at freezing point in bathroom"), of visits to the exhibitions at the Royal Academy and the Old Water Colour Society, of banquets at the Mansion House (Lord Mayor of London) or at Ironmonger's Hall, and of theatre parties: to the opening of the Haymarket under the management of the Squire Bancrofts; with three of the children and MEB's former colleague in the Brighton company, Florence Haydon (Mrs. Waugh), now celebrated, and Bram Stoker, Henry Irving's manager, to occupy Irving's own box at the Lyceum for a matinée ("Tea sent in to us. Let out by private entrance"). We can follow MEB on a day's shopping in London ("Bought nightshirts etc. Peter Robinson's. Took brocade and black satin to Mrs. Jones") or on a day's hunt in Hampshire ("Deer-hounds met at Markway Bridge and rode to the other side of Brackenhurst Road, crossed and re-crossed road, a capital run, but short, through the old woods, ending by the deer—a fine buck—being taken on the water in Queenshead").

Occasionally the diaries record the death of a friend, usually in this decade one of an older generation. "Eheu fugaces," MEB wrote on January 28, 1880, when Mrs. Frith died; she would remain close to the widowed painter for the remainder of his long life and to his daughter Fanny for the remainder of her days. The diary does not record the death of Charles Reade on April 11, 1884, after a long period of physical and emotional illness, but MEB paid tribute to him promptly, as she had to Bulwer, writing a personal reminiscence which Reade's son and brother included verbatim in their *Memoir*: "Would that in return we could reproduce the hundred and one kind words he had always on the tip of his tongue for her!" they wrote. Emotionally MEB recalled how Reade had sought her out "at the outset of my career." She praised his chivalrous attitude towards women and the weak, contrasting his fierce partisanship in public with his gentle Christian spirit in private.

Remembering his and Mrs. Seymour's hospitality, his love of animals—he once "tried to acclimatize a small antelope in his back garden"—and the delights of a long evening's tête-à-tête discussion with him, she described him ending the evening at the piano, playing and singing "some old world ballad." Once she had told him that she seldom read newspapers, since she found too little time to read the books she loved. " 'You should read the papers,' " Reade had replied, " 'and leave books alone.' "[5]

But this advice—so typical of the "matter-of-fact" novelist—MEB ignored. She read widely: in English, Swinburne's essays on Dryden, Pope, and Prior, Carlyle's *Heroes and Hero Worship*, Macaulay's *Life*, Plato's *Protagoras*, Grote, Jeremy Taylor, Hugh Miller's *Testimony of the Rocks*, and of course some fiction, including *The Virginians*, *Middlemarch*, Rhoda Broughton's *Joan*, Ouida's *In Maremma*, and Mrs. Lynn Linton's *Under Which Lord*; in French, Labiche's comedy *Le Chapeau de paille d'Italie*, Pascal, Georges Sand's *Jeanne*, several novels by Zola, four by Daudet, Hugo's *Les Misérables*, and Gaboriau's *L'Affaire Lerouge*; in German, half a dozen current novels by writers now obscure, in addition to Goethe's *Wilhelm Meister*. Between a dozen and two dozen times a year, she went to the theatre: to the opening of Tennyson's tragedy *The Cup* ("Great house, Gladstone and family, Lady Londesborough etc.") ; to Shakespearian plays, including occasional recitals in the Hall of the Middle Temple ("brilliant gathering" at *Twelfth Night* in 1880; "splendid entertainment" at *Midsummer Night's Dream* in 1881) ; and to a wide variety of new plays. Sometimes she wrote a terse and professional comment on a performance: "Well-written play, oldest possible materials"; "Very pretty girl with easy, bright style, perfectly natural"; "All the critics; grand night."

If somehow one were to read only the diary entries recording such activities as these, ignoring those about her work, one would conclude that MEB was a full-time housekeeper, wife, mother, stepmother, stepmother-in-law, stepgrandmother, hostess, and social butterfly and would marvel how she managed to avoid collapse. Yet of course she was also one of the most prolific novelists of her day. And her work accompanied her everywhere, to Hampshire and back to Richmond, on all the excursions in the British Isles or across the Channel. The numbers for Tillotson's newspaper or other serial publication of each new novel came off her pen on schedule. As each neared the end of its serial run, Maxwell would publish it in three volumes and would "subscribe" it, soliciting the orders in person from the chief circulating libraries. Translation rights would be sold. And afterwards would come the reprintings in one-volume form, at first in handsome six-shilling single volumes, with frontispiece and title-page vignette, and then in a variety of cheaper editions, the least expensive being the gaudy yellow-back railway novel at two shillings. All her past novels and each new one as it came out were kept in print, each continuing to sell and sell and sell. After 1880 MEB's diaries record in detail the progress toward completion of each of her novels, short stories, articles, and plays.

Correspondence between John Maxwell and Tillotson was spirited and breathless: "Hold up your head, Sir, and open your mouth wide when you speak about the advance sheets of a Braddon novel. That is something to offer!" Maxwell wrote Tillotson in October 1882, for example, urging him to drive a hard bargain with the other newspapers who wanted to buy the rights to publish MEB's next novel serially. "Joking apart," he went on, "there is only one Braddon novelist in the whole world, but there are plenty of needy and greedy newspaper-proprietors." But before Tillotson himself could count on possession, he had to negotiate with Maxwell over each detail. Maxwell would sell him newspaper rights only, and those only for a year after the appearance of the first instalment. But Tillotson on his own could sell abroad advance proofs of his newspaper issues: in March 1882, after jibbing at first, Maxwell jocularly added to America and Europe (except for Tauchnitz) "Australia, Australasia, New Zealand, Queensland, and the Polyponnesian Islands."

For Maxwell, Tillotson's contribution of four hundred pounds to twelve hundred pounds was one-quarter or less of each novel's ultimate value. He fretted constantly during serial publication, lest English copyright be lost through the failure of some foreign newspaper to wait at least a day after each instalment had appeared in England. Tillotson's "craze for simultaneous publication in America," Maxwell once moaned, might cost him two thousand two hundred and fifty pounds. He did approve of Tillotson's circulars offering advance proofs to American newspaper publishers and proclaiming that "Experience has shown us that no author can write stories of such absorbing interest to the reading public as MISS BRADDON." But he often argued over the schedule of payments to MEB:

> Authors do not give credit any more than do Physicians or Barristers. . . . My wife does not participate either in your risks or gains; she does not like to wait while you gather in your harvest. . . . I am anxious to prevent its being said . . . that . . . at the height of her fame and with a publisher-husband to help her, the Author

of Lady Audley's Secret could only obtain a credit commission full twenty years after her reputation was made.

Letters and telegrams flew between London and Bolton: "I am in a terrible state of uneasiness," wrote Maxwell again about losing English copyright, "When you stand in jeopardy for £2,000 you will realise my agony." But then calm was restored: "As our past relations worked well and pleasantly, so should our future relations," until the time came for a new round of negotiations for a new novel, when the scenario would be played out once more.[6]

After the sale of *Belgravia* in 1876 to Chatto and Windus, MEB never again edited a magazine. But the *Belgravia* Christmas *Annual* had apparently been particularly lucrative; so in 1878 she founded a new Christmas annual, called *The Mistletoe Bough*, usually a typical collection of mid-Victorian Christmas stories and verse: "Sprig the First," "Sprig the Second," and so on. The last number appeared in 1892. For each of those fifteen years MEB herself (sometimes anonymously) wrote one or more contributions and until 1887, when Will Maxwell took over, she collected and edited the rest. Proofs were due before the end of October. Twice, in 1882 and 1883, she wrote an entire short novel that—exceptionally—made up the whole issue: *Flower and Weed* in 1882 and *Under the Red Flag* in 1883. Her diary entry for November 22, 1883, reads: "Report MB [*Mistletoe Bough*] Received 27,300. On hand 1,611. Sold 25,689. Published November 5, 1883." In seventeen days, almost the whole huge printing had been sold out, and, since in this case MEB had written the entire number, she alone received the proceeds.

Like the social entries in the diaries, the professional entries alone would have made up a full and exhausting life for anyone else. But MEB led both lives. And in 1875, freed at last from the anguish caused her by her ambiguous social position and no longer under attack for personal or literary immorality, her immediate resentments abated. While she would never forget her sufferings, she was not of a temperament to remain bitter for long, or to allow her indictment of society to grow in stridency. In her novels, rascals of every stamp would constantly reappear, and smug hypocrites inflict their petty social cruelties upon the helpless: these were part of her stock-in-trade and reflected her own view of the Victorian world. But never again would she lavish her energies upon so unredeemable a set of money-grubbers and cheats as had filled the pages of *Dead Men's Shoes*. The skies cleared, her talents had a free rein, her energies were altogether undiminished, and *Joshua Haggard's Daughter*, her first novel of the decade, though altogether different from any book she had yet written, demonstrates beyond question what she could do when at last she had a chance once again to pursue the archetype unencumbered.

2. MEB as a Classical Tragedian: *Joshua Haggard's Daughter* (1876)

MEB concentrated more directly on *Joshua Haggard's Daughter* and took longer over writing it than she had been able to do with any of her novels since *The Lady's Mile* a decade earlier.[7] Set in a North Devon fishing village in the 1820's, this dramatic narrative of the passions of a few villagers—including the squire and his two sons—reminds the modern reader of a novel by Hardy, although in 1876 *Far from the Madding Crowd* (1874) was the only one he had yet written that was as powerful. *Joshua Haggard's Daughter* is comparable to *The Mayor of Casterbridge* and *Tess of the d'Urbervilles*. The mature Hardy would have been proud of it. Without in any self-conscious way "transferring" the scenes and characters of a Euripidean tragedy into her Devonshire setting, MEB succeeded in telling a tragic tale with strong Euripidean overtones.

Tall and broad-shouldered, the widowed Joshua Haggard is the Methodist preacher of the Little Bethel, the most important church in the village. He has intellect and power in his face and the bearing of a man accustomed to command. Though he reads the Puritan divines—Bunyan, Baxter, and Low—he is also the village shopkeeper, having inherited a combination grocer's and draper's shop from his father. He enjoys "plenty of capital, shrewd judgment, long experience, unflinching industry, and the special protection of Providence. Who should prevail against these?" In a squall, he saves the life of the squire's son, Oswald Pentreath, bearing him off unconscious to his house, as the villagers remind one another that " '. . . no good ever come o' reskying a drownding man.' " All along the coast, people know the saying, " 'Save a stranger from the sea, And he'll turn your enemy.' " So at the outset, Joshua has doomed himself. The man he has rescued is "bound" to do him an injury.

Oswald recovers under the care of Joshua's maiden sister, Judith, in the Haggards' spare bedroom, lying in the four-poster with its curly posts, its "elaborate cornice, with a good deal of white fringe and dimity festooning," and its "counterpane and watch-pockets of silken patchwork"

—opposite the green-painted and once gilded dressing-table, and the fireplace with brass fender and fire-irons and the Swansea teacups and saucers on the mantelshelf above. He finds Joshua ruling the household "by a far-off affection and a pride which admitted of no familiarity" and is overpowered by the hour-long sermon that follows the prayers after supper. He has never known people like the Haggards before. His own father, the squire, having "raised money upon mortgage and wasted it on midnight orgies, in drink, in play," Oswald has nothing to do—now that his boat has been lost in the storm—but wait for his father to die.

He admires Joshua's daughter, Naomi, though Joshua reminds him of the social distance that separates them. Aunt Judith warns Naomi against Oswald: " 'I never could abide a pretty man,' " she says, remembering one of her own suitors, " 'with a complexion like a girl, and always on the simper. . . . I used to come over as if I'd been eating too much treacle at the mere sight of him.' " Had she accepted that " 'poor pink-and-white thing . . . lolloping about the place and making believe to be a man' " she would have led him a life indeed. But Naomi will not listen, accepts Oswald, and bows to Joshua's decree that there must be a two-year wait without lovemaking before they marry. With the promise of a five-thousand-pound settlement from Joshua, the wicked squire, a "disciple of Tom Paine," assents to the engagement.

Joshua himself, however, now falls in love with a beautiful waif, Cynthia, whom he encounters on a pastoral visit in Cornwall, an orphan who has run away from the strolling players who have brought her up. He prevails upon two spinster sisters in a distant village to take her as their servant, and soon proposes to her. Full of gratitude toward him and wanting to be his servant, she accepts him and his kiss, "fatherly in its protecting gentleness, lover-like in its suppressed passion." Keeping his plans a secret, Joshua now consents to an earlier marriage between Naomi and Oswald, who are also "very happy, but with a more quiet joy than Joshua's. The bloom of novelty had been worn off their joys by this time." So MEB's young couple in their late teens, strictly forbidden to engage in lovemaking, are less eager for their approaching marriage than a man in his late forties! In Oswald Pentreath MEB was portraying one of those unvirile men she had noticed long ago in *John Marchmont's Legacy* and to whom she would later return with the new frankness that the early twentieth century would make available to her.

When Haggard brings Cynthia home as his new wife, everyone is thunderstruck. Naomi and she make friends, but Aunt Judith proves difficult, and tensions mount both in the Haggard family and in Joshua's congregation. As external circumstances delay Oswald's marriage to Naomi, he falls hopelessly in love with Cynthia, his innocent stepmother-in-law to be. And when he reads *Werther* aloud to Naomi and Cynthia, it proves to be the "fatal book that told them what was amiss in their lives," introducing Cynthia for the first time to the thought of unhappy passion. To her alone Oswald reads the end, and when she weeps, he confesses his love for her and begs her to take pity on him. This Aunt Judith overhears, but not Cynthia's quick rebuff. Naturally, Judith says nothing to Cynthia but does tell Joshua, whose first response is: " 'Lies! Lies! . . . You see my happiness and envy me. You hate my wife because she is lovely, as you never were—passionately loved, as you never were.' "

Still confident of Cynthia's innocence, Joshua forces Naomi to break her engagement to the faithless Oswald, without telling her why. Then Joshua himself reads *Werther* for the first time and begins to doubt his wife. And when Naomi intercepts and gives to her father a letter from Oswald asking Cynthia for a farewell interview before he goes off to America, Joshua in despair leaves the letter for Cynthia to find in the copy of *Werther*, that "accursed book that taught them to sin." Cynthia finds it; she grants Oswald the interview, but only to urge him to return to his proper love for Naomi. He says farewell and kisses her on the forehead, with a passion not "base or sensual" but "the passion of a great love and a deep despair."[8] But to Joshua, watching from a distance and unable to hear what is being said, the kiss sets the seal on Cynthia's guilt.

It may seem improbable that in a remote Devon village in the 1820's *Werther* should have played for Cynthia the "fatal" role played by the romance of Lancelot for Francesca da Rimini: MEB was obviously thinking of Dante's dramatic lines at the end of Canto V of the *Inferno*. But *Werther's* enormous reputation as a mischief-making book made it a more likely candidate than any other for the part of Galeotto the pander that MEB assigned to it. We do not really know if Cynthia loved Oswald, or if *Werther* had simply unsettled her mind and taught her to look with a new discontent on her far older husband. As a married woman, Cynthia could hardly have been as innocent as MEB made her, especially after a girlhood spent in a traveling circus. Nor is it entirely likely that the effete Oswald would have fallen so desperately in love with Cynthia. But the very simplicity of life in the Devon village and its remoteness in place and time—half a century before the novel appeared in 1876—help the reader accept the improbabilities.

Joshua's preaching now dwells more and more upon the avenging God; more and more he neglects his shop. When no news comes from America, he suggests to Naomi that Oswald has killed himself, but she refuses to believe it. Oswald's brother, investigating, discovers that Oswald had never sailed, and in Oswald's journals he finds sketches of Cynthia's face. Cynthia tells him the true story of her farewell to Oswald. But Joshua, who has been watching this meeting too, fears that the brother will be Cynthia's new lover and, with a torrent of reproaches couched in biblical language, declares that Oswald is dead and drives Cynthia away. Empty-handed and penniless, she sets out on foot for Cornwall. Amidst ominous rumblings from the members of his congregation, reminding one another that to rescue a stranger from the sea can bring nothing but evil upon the rescuer, Joshua is confronted in his chapel by Oswald's brother, who has now found Oswald's body and denounces Joshua as a murderer. The coroner's jury brings in an open verdict; so Joshua is free, but his tragic fate cannot be averted.

Naomi bitterly blames herself for having shown her father Oswald's letter asking Cynthia for a rendezvous. And in pleading with her father to pray with her now, Naomi reveals the true motives for her action: " 'I told you then, as I tell you now, you were always first and dearest, always the object of my highest reverence and love. That could never change in me. No act of yours could lessen my love, no affliction Heaven could bring upon you could lower you in my esteem.' " It was not resentment of her lover's defection that had prompted Naomi to show her father the letter: her love affair with Oswald, as MEB had carefully shown, had been no real love affair. It had been Naomi's jealousy *of Cynthia*, who had married her all-too-well-beloved father, that had moved her to make trouble for Cynthia by revealing the rendezvous. Before the reader learns how Joshua had killed Oswald, he knows that it had been Naomi who had in effect done the deed herself, because she loved her father with a jealous love.

Joshua Haggard's Daughter has turned before our eyes into Greek tragedy, and Naomi has become Electra. Presumably it was no accident that, when the novel was reprinted for its cheap editions, MEB changed the title to *Joshua Haggard*. He is, of course, the most important character. Yet the first title, *Joshua Haggard's Daughter*, was the more fitting, because Naomi is the true mainspring of the action, a quiet girl who loves her father so well that she does not know how well she loves him—even after he has married another girl, just about her own age—until the opportunity for revenge presents itself. Nor has Naomi consciously blamed her father for his marriage ("'No act of yours could lessen my love'") ; she merely wrecks it by arousing his suspicions of Cynthia. She hardly knows what she has done, until, forced to face the truth by the charge of murder against her father, she realizes her own full responsibility and recognizes that her love for him lies behind it. To continue to call the novel *Joshua Haggard's Daughter* might possibly help a reader realize that MEB was writing about something very close to incest. So the more ambiguous title was preferred in the end. Readers of the novel must decide for themselves how far MEB's bitter disappointment in her own father had been daughterly love turned inside out; and whether *Joshua Haggard's Daughter,* the most daring and moving and convincing of all her explorations of the relationships between fathers and daughters, was an effort to deal with this central problem of her own life.

Left with his conscience as his only tormentor, Joshua slowly goes mad. He reproaches himself for having taken his father's fortune and the shop, for not having devoted himself exclusively to preaching, for having fallen in love with Cynthia. But he *had* loved Cynthia, and he no longer believes her guilty. Hearing a message from the Lord to go to Cynthia in Cornwall, Joshua leaves behind a letter for Naomi: he had shot Oswald Pentreath, but in a fair duel. " 'I met him with my wife's kiss still warm upon his lips,' " he writes, and Naomi feels exultant to discover that her father had done no murder. She prevails upon Oswald's brother, who has fallen in love with her, not to persist in his own intention of fighting a duel with Joshua. She tells him that Oswald's death had been caused only by her jealousy, as indeed it had; but she does not tell him that she was jealous of her stepmother not for having met secretly with her fiancé but for having married her father. She consents to marry her new admirer and is glad he loves her, but only for her father's sake: "She felt that her father was secure from any violence. . . . the vengeful spirit which had threatened Joshua with ruin and death would be calmed and appeased."[9] But Joshua cannot be saved. When he reaches Cornwall and finds that Cynthia has died, he has a stroke. On his deathbed he confesses to Naomi that, although he had indeed fought a duel with Oswald Pentreath, Oswald had fired in the air, after which Joshua had shot him. So he had committed murder after all, and though he dies repentant and sure of resurrection, he has had to pay the penalty.

The *Athenaeum* said enthusiastically: "There is a marvellous freshness about Miss Braddon. . . . she ought long ago to have written herself out," but in fact "her work seems . . . to improve." *Joshua Haggard's Daughter* depended "upon analysis of character rather than upon complication of incident" and only just fell "short of being a really powerful story." But the critic failed to see how powerful the novel really was or to realize the true relationship of its characters to one another. For reasons he did not explain, he saw the influence of *Middlemarch* at work, but *Joshua Haggard's Daughter* was not in the least like a George Eliot novel.[10] Even the *Spectator* grudgingly found in *Joshua Haggard's Daughter* a "power of an unusual though incomplete kind, . . . which suggests a young and inexperienced mind, rather than a practiced and slightly worn novelist." All the way through, the reviewer said, "Joshua Haggard is a figure such as it is not given to Mr. Mudie's fodder-providers to create, or perhaps to refined persons wholly to understand. They do not often see a small dissenting minister who makes money as a grocer and draper, and is also the kind of person possessed of high spiritual gifts." The creation of Joshua Haggard was "the best work" MEB had done. But Miss Braddon had exaggerated Cynthia's innocence to "absurdity." Yet in *Oliver Twist* Dickens had managed to reconcile the world to "an improbability just as great," the virtue of Nancy the prostitute. Like the others, the *Spectator*'s critic failed to realize that Naomi's jealousy was not for Oswald but for her father. He also found many of MEB's characters "insufferably vulgar people."[11]

It is only when one remembers the Victorian reviewers' scorn for Hardy's Dorsetshire personages that one sees as not untypical of the period the *Spectator*'s toplofty and insensitive attitude toward MEB's rustics. To us they seem wonderfully vivid and well realized. The two spinster sisters in the Cornish village have a precious silver teapot which they produce from its hiding-place in the bedroom before they serve tea to Joshua: in such families a silver teapot "took the place of a pedigree." Their tea-things are "blue willow-pattern cups and saucers, shallow cups with high handles," and a "white and gold covered bowl for the sugar, oval with coloured landscapes on each side." Here forks are called "prongs." And when the sisters take an afternoon nap while awaiting Joshua, they lie down side by side "upon the coverlet, the *County Chronicle* spread beneath their feet to guard the spotless counterpane, their hair repapered, lest the corkscrew curls" should work themselves out in sleep. Hearing that Joshua has arrived, they rush together to the looking-glass, take their hair out of the papers, smooth their "ample muslin collars . . . and . . . adjust the velvet bands upon their foreheads." Then they wash their hands "with sisterly familiarity in the same basin, not forgetting to expectorate gently in the water lest it should lead to unsisterly tiffs," and descend the winding staircase.

And among Joshua's congregation when he preaches about "the frivolity and extravagance of an unregenerate race, Mrs. Pycroft thinks of Mrs. Spradger's last bonnet, . . . clearly a superfluous and culpable outlay," which should not have been bought until Advent, but which is now being "flaunted . . . before the disapproving eye of the flock early in October." When Joshua denounces "sensuality and the vile indulgence of earthly desires, Mrs. Pentelow's thoughts flew at once to the Polwhele family, who were known to have hot suppers—squab pies and other savoury meats—every night in the week." On warm Sunday afternoons "you could see the grease oozing out of their complexions as if digestion as well as respiration were a function of the skin." So each good Christian takes the warnings of the preacher as applying to his neighbors, and not to himself.

Joshua's house MEB described outside and in with vivid realism: garden, orchard, and stable; kitchen shining with copper and brass; cool best parlour smelling of dried rose-leaves, spices, and lavender, with the Bow china busts of Whitefield and Wesley on the mantelpiece; and Joshua's bedroom, where his father's silver watch ticks away on its mahogany stand "with as lusty a beat" as when the old grocer had carried it in "his ample drab-cloth fob." On the wall are the samplers made by Joshua's mother and his first wife, "the pyramidal apple-tree innocent of leaves, the angular figures of Adam and Eve in the garden, with a curly serpent standing on tip-tail between them."[12]

Even MEB's old friend and champion, Charles Kent, who praised *Joshua Haggard's Daughter* to the skies in his weekly Catholic newspaper, comparing the book to *Adam Bede* and the character of Cynthia to a drawing by Greuze, altogether failed to see its meaning, and made the astounding suggestion that MEB had been arguing for a celibate clergy. Taken by surprise, MEB was not prepared to dispute him: "I think you have hit the right nail on the head, . . . the only critic who has noticed the point—. . . . A man who has the souls of his fellow men in his keeping should keep his own soul unclouded by passion."[13] But the idea surely had not been in her own mind while she was writing.

So MEB had written a novel that baffled the critics without their realizing it. They liked *Joshua Haggard's Daughter* but did not understand it. Yet to a modern reader it displays a sureness of touch that MEB had often hitherto lacked and that even in her best novels she had usually lost from time to time. Now, in portraying her minor as well as her major characters, it never failed her. She had explored the minds and hearts of genuine and appealing men and women, set convincingly in an environment and period that the reader eagerly accepts and enjoys. She had written a starkly simple Greek tragedy, taking into account all the human complexities that make real simplicity in fact impossible. Her use of the village fishermen as a Greek chorus to warn the reader at intervals of the dark consequences of saving a man from the sea only made the Euripidean realities of Naomi's emotions and Joshua's fate the more classical. There was no posturing, no dropping of references, *Mourning Becomes Electra* style, to alert the reader. MEB hid her scattered clues so well that nobody in the century since her novel was published has ever before picked them up.

3. MEB as a Crypto-Radical (1877–1882)

When a rich and disagreeable man jilts the handsome woman he has long been attached to, telling her that she is " 'as exacting as a wife, more jealous than a mistress,' " she joins forces with his money-lending solicitor, whom he has also insulted (" 'The county people wouldn't associate with you. They're very fond of money but they don't like money-lenders.' "), in a heartless conspiracy to kidnap their tormentor's daughter and arrange for her ostensible drowning. MEB had begun *Weavers and Weft* (1877), the novelette in which these unpleasant events occur, before Mrs. Maxwell's death and her own marriage, and although she returned to finish it only after *Joshua Haggard's Daughter* was almost completed, it belongs in spirit to the earlier period of her unhappiness and disillusionment.[14]

In *An Open Verdict* (1878), a priggish curate fails to stand by the girl to whom he is engaged when she is suspected of her father's murder, even though the coroner's jury has brought in an open verdict. Though he does not doubt her himself, he declares that a parson's wife must be above suspicion. Not until a jealous woman confesses the theft of the dead man's letter announcing his intention to commit suicide does the curate finally marry his true love. The *Athenaeum* thought one of the other characters had been right in calling the curate a "mean hound," and Charles Kent found in him an excuse to ride one of his favorite hobbies: "Better, a million times better, a celibate clergy than a minister" who acted like that. And MEB herself agreed: "My High Church curate is a cur—and yet I meant him to be all that is staunch and noble. Only he went askew somehow in the working out." But surely she intended him to be exactly what she made him: undersexed and disloyal. Among a varied and wonderfully well-drawn cast of minor characters is the wife of the *nouveau-riche* manufacturer, who has reluctantly abandoned chapel for church when they acquire a big house and seven indoor servants. " 'Church is very nice,' " she says mournfully, " 'and I don't deny that the bonnets and general appearance of the congregation has a higher stamp, but chapel is the place to make a sinner comfortable in his mind.' "[15]

Vixen (1879) MEB herself called "a simple easy-going love-story with a frank high-spirited girlish heroine." The Maxwell children, notably Gerald, aged fifteen or sixteen, and Will, more than four years younger, "helped" her produce it by printing its title with their toy printing press on the blank sheets of paper she used. She "sweetly encouraged our pretence," Will Maxwell remembered, "and would come into the nursery asking for further supplies." The boys "doled them out to her two or three sheets at a time," but did not mention the large number of sheets they ruined in their press. Her innocent-appearing tale about Violet Tempest ("Vixen"), a self-willed hoydenish outdoor girl—with an unaccomplished but attractive suitor, an aristocratic widowed mother, and a penny-pinching stepfather—MEB used as a vehicle for vigorous radical social satire.

In *Vixen*, country drawing-room conversation is far less innocent than it seems:

> "There has been a great deal of sickness . . . and want of work. The winter began early, and we have had some severe weather. James Parsons is in prison again for rabbit-snaring. I'm really afraid James is incorrigible. Mrs. Roper's eldest son, Tom—I daresay you remember Tom, an idle bitter ruffian who was always birdnesting—has managed to get himself run over by a pair of Lord Ellangowan's waggon-horses, and now Lady Ellangowan is keeping the whole family. An aunt came from Salisbury to sit up with the boy, and was quite angry because Lady Ellangowan did not pay her for nursing him."
>
> "That's the worst of the poor," said Mrs. Tempest languidly, the firelight playing upon her diamond rings, as she took her fan from the velvet table, and slowly unfolded it to protect her cheek from the glare, "they are never satisfied."
>
> "Isn't it odd that they are not," cried Vixen . . . "when they have everything that can make their life delightful?"
>
> "I don't know about everything, Violet; but really, when they have such nice cottages as your papa built for them, so well-drained and ventilated, they ought to be more contented."

"What a comfort good drainage and ventilation must be, when there is no bread in the larder!" said Violet.

"My dear, it's ridiculous to talk in that way just in the style of those horrid radical newspapers. I am sure the poor have an immense deal done for them."

In the talk of Vixen's mother, MEB was no doubt echoing the very language of those among the neighboring New Forest gentry who had objected to John Maxwell's sending bread to the poacher's family.

When an Irish peer describes his native land to Vixen, she says " 'Poor things' once or twice" when he dilates "on the wrongs of oppressed people." Apparently she imagines Ireland as "a vast expanse of bog chiefly inhabited by pigs," and she asks, not so innocently, " 'But people don't live there, do they?' " So when he answers, " 'If you were to see the outskirts of Waterford in the hills above Cork, you would find almost as many fine mansions as in England,' " she makes him admit that he himself only goes there each year " 'for the fishing.' " This enables her to crush him: " 'And then you go into the House of Commons and rave about Ireland. . . . I think all this wild enthusiasm . . . is the silliest thing in the world when it comes from the lips of landowners who won't pay their beloved country the compliment of six months' residence out of the twelve.' "

Vixen's own heart is clearly in the right place. Her fellow-members of the upper class, however, live in wicked extravagance. When her stepfather scrutinizes her mother's dressmaker's bill, the reader shares his astonishment:

"A dinner dress, *pain brûlé* brocade, mixed *poult de soie, marteau de cour,* lined ivory satin, trimmed with hand-worked embroidery of flowers on Brussels net, sixty-three pounds. What in the name of all that's reasonable is *pain brûlé?*"

"It's the colour, Conrad. One of the delicate tertiaries that have been so much worn lately. . . ."

"French cambric *peignoir,* trimmed with real Valenciennes, turquoise ribbon, nineteen guineas. . . . Surely you would never give twenty pounds for the gown you wear when you are having your hair dressed?"

"That's only the name dear. It's really a breakfast dress."

"Shooting dress, superfine silk corduroy, trimmed with cardinal *poult de soie,* oxydized silver buttons, engraved hunting subject, twenty-seven guineas. . . ."

Yet the woman who has ordered all these dresses leads only a

languid drawing-room life, dawdling away long slow days that left no more impression behind than the drift of rose-leaves across the velvet lawn. . . . A little point-lace, deftly worked . . . a little Tennyson; a little Owen Meredith; a little Browning; . . . a great deal of scandal; a great deal of orange pekoe . . . an hour's letter-writing on the last fashionable note-paper, elegantly worded inanities, delicately penned in a flowing Italian hand with long loops to the Y's and G's and a serpentine curve at the end of every word.

Penmanship is crucially important: Vixen is criticized for hers: " 'If you would slope more . . . and make your up-strokes finer, and not cross your T's so undeviatingly. . . . A lady's T ought to be less pronounced. There's something too assertive in your consonants.' "

The presents displayed at a fashionable wedding include

" 'silver candelabra presented by Sir Ponto's workpeople, so much more serviceable than a bracelet. . . . sweetly mythological—a goat and a dear little chubby boy and ever so many savage-looking persons with cymbals. . . . this liqueur cabinet . . . the most exquisite thing from the servants at Southminster. . . . And this lovely, lovely screen in crewels by the Ladies Ringwood, after Alma Tadema. . . . to think that our poor mothers worked staring roses and gigantic lilies in Berlin wool and glass beads, and imagined themselves artistic!' "

It is, we notice, the "workpeople" and the servants who have given the expensive presents, the Ladies Ringwood remaining content to offer their own handiwork. But there are also "Brussels point, oxydized silver glove-boxes, malachite blotting-books, pearls, opals, ormolu, antique tankards and candlesticks, Queen Anne teapots, diamond stars, combs, tiaras, prayer-books and 'Christian Years,' " and "the special presents" which stand out "from the chaos of commonplace [!]," which include

a rivière of diamonds from the Earl of Southminster, a cashmere shawl from Her Majesty, a basket of orchids, valued at five hundred guineas, from Lady Ellangowan, a pair of priceless crackle jars, a Sèvres dinner-service of the old *bleu du roi*, a set of knives of which all the handles had been taken from the stags slaughtered by the Southminster hounds.

MEB's criticism of the selfish rich surrounding themselves with opulence while denouncing or ignoring the poor passed unnoticed, as did her sardonic account of the book written by Vixen's cousin, a bluestocking Duke's daughter, *Tragedy of a Sceptic Soul,* lavishly produced in a gray linen binding with silver lettering and red edges, and destroyed by its reviewers, who discovered its "petty plagiarisms." Even Lucy Clifford, herself a novelist and an astute critic, made no mention of these things when she wrote to MEB about *Vixen*:

> It is so extraordinarily *vivid*. I feel that you know that country, let us say *county*, life so well, you have its absolute atmosphere, and the people all *live* (but your characters always do). . . . it is precisely what *happened*—how it *was*. But, dear Mrs. Maxwell, you have always been such a masterly story-teller that goes without saying. . . . Vixen is such a dear minx in the beginning. I feel that you must have known her. She is so full of youth, youth, youth, one sees her and in the end one loves her even more.[16]

Presumably MEB was not anxious to have her distaste for her fashionable characters and their lack of social consciousness made a subject for critical comment, or even to have it widely observed. Such behavior on the part of the rich and wellborn was, as Mrs. Clifford had perhaps implied, an integral part of MEB's knowing that *"county* life so well," of her being able to tell "precisely what *happened*—how it *was*." Yet for her own amusement and satisfaction at least, she enjoyed experimenting. How insufferably smug and callous could she make her characters, and still have her public fail to see them as anything other than ideal upper-class heroes and heroines? It would not do to make such themes a major part of each successive novel, or in any given novel to let them take the reader's attention away from the story. Even in *Vixen* MEB struck her satirical notes only occasionally and tentatively; to obtain their full impact one must assemble the passages as we have done here, and look at them outside the framework of the story as a whole.

MEB therefore gave radical themes an almost complete holiday in her next two novels, *The Cloven Foot* (1879) and *The Story of Barbara* (1880). In *The Cloven Foot*, it is true, a beautiful, docile, and ostensibly disinterested young woman marries the man designated in the will of her adoptive father. But only upon reflection does one realize that, far from being indifferent to the great legacy she will share only if she accepts this husband, she is hard-headedly determined to get the money. The faithful Victorian reader could see in her a true romantic heroine; but the skeptic could enjoy her meek acquiescence in the suit of a man she hardly knows well enough to marry: the estate and fourteen thousand pounds a year are too good to lose. Only in a brief description of the conversation around the Devonshire squire's dinner-table can one hear even the muffled sound of the radical note. Here, the guests denounce "the farming parson of a neighbouring parish for having treacherously trapped and slain four cub foxes." They voice their "cordial approval of a magistrate who had sent a lad of nine to jail for stealing three turnips, and who had been maligned . . . by the radical newspapers." For the rest, they discuss "the prospects of the hunting season . . . horses and dogs, and a little about the outside world, and its chances of peace or war, famine or plenty."[17] And in *The Story of Barbara* (1880), once past the idyllic scenes of the Trevornock/Braddon household in Camberwell before the Crimean War, the reader is plunged into a conventional Braddonian melodrama, rather less convincing than usual.[18]

But MEB returned with a new vigor to her radical message in *Just As I Am* (1880). Twenty years before the story opens, a rich man, son of a self-made inventor, had been dragged from his horse during a hunt and bludgeoned to death, at the very moment when the wife of a neighboring baronet had died in giving birth to a daughter. Now the baronet's daughter is engaged—much to her father's distaste—to marry the murdered man's son. Suddenly there reappears in the village an aged tramp, who confesses to the baronet—the local magistrate—that he had committed the murder and stolen the purse of his victim, who had turned him out of his cottage for poaching, at a time when his wife was pregnant. She had died in childbirth. The baronet says he disbelieves the story. Largely because the murdered man's son is eager to see the murderer hanged, however, the tramp is tried, found guilty, and sentenced. But the murdered man and the baronet's lady had been in love, a fact which, as judge at the trial, the baronet effectively prevents the tramp's counsel from bringing out. Moreover, the tramp inaccurately describes the murder weapon. When the baronet circulates a petition calling for the commutation of the tramp's sentence, suspicions are aroused. And indeed, the baronet himself had been the murderer. He admits his crime to his victim's son and goes off to a Trappist monastery to die.

The tramp's death-sentence is commuted to life imprisonment, the penalty for having stolen the dead man's purse and money. Perhaps the real reason for the baronet's opposition to his daughter's marriage is his belief that she is in fact the daughter of the man he has murdered, and so her fiancé's half-sister. MEB could easily have denied this, however, if any critic had accused her of immorality. Quite possibly MEB took the plot from some French play or novel and reworked it sufficiently to pass muster in England.

But this time she hardly bothered to conceal her radicalism. The county people of Daleshire are cruel snobs. They treat dogs and horses far better than human beings. The tramp's wife had died because she and her husband had been forced to leave their cottage for the petty crime of poaching; twenty years later this has been all but forgotten. A rich county lady, remarking that she " 'had no idea that the trial of a poor common creature could be made so interesting,' " reveals that to her the tramp's ordeal is sheer entertainment. And the accused man's daughter, a handsome, decent woman, who had emigrated to America and married a prosperous shopkeeper, returns to England to help clear her father's name, but finds the members of the lower classes in the village reluctant to stir up trouble by helping her discover the truth.

MEB portrayed the young engaged couple—Dulcie and Morton—as typical members of their class. The baronet—Sir Everard—

> gave his arm to his daughter, and Morton followed to the snug lit-tle dining-room, where the round table was bright with flowers and ferns and quaint Venetian glass, and artistic old silver. . . . Sir Everard . . . [left] the young people to talk of the things they cared about most—the church—the choir—the last penny reading at the school-house—the New Year ball at Highclere—the At Home early in January, for which Miss Aspinall had issued cards with the agreeable announcement "Dancing" in the left-hand corner....
>
> "Papa does not approve of public balls," said Dulcie. . . .
>
> "I approve of them immensely in the abstract as a pleasant impetus to the trade of a quiet little county town, but I don't want to see my daughter spinning around a public assembly room in the arms of any counter-jumper whom the master of ceremonies may introduce to her."

"Oh, papa, there's a formidable list of patronesses; tickets only by voucher. There's no possibility of a counter-jumper at the Highclere ball."

"Then there may be something worse than counter-jumpers—raffish hunting men perhaps, who come from heaven knows where, and get their living heaven knows how. Any man who comes . . . with three horses and a servant takes brevet rank as a gentleman."

"Very well," said Morton, "We will none of us go to the ball. I suppose you have accepted for Mrs. Aspinall's 'At Home?' "

"Yes, papa has no objection to that."[19]

The man who is so concerned about raffish hunting men dancing with his daughter at a well-chaperoned public ball is himself a murderer who had committed his crime while out hunting, and the daughter is quite possibly not his own. MEB's social satire was pungent indeed, although the baronet's sentiments would have seemed unexceptionable to many of her readers.

Morton eventually marries a girl whom his sisters have snubbed because her grandfather had been a fellow-workman with their own grandfather. Though now an M.P., Morton intends to remain on good terms with his wife's vulgar but warm-hearted family: the granddaughter of an honest workingman is thus a better match for him than Dulcie. The tramp and his loyal decent daughter are to be preferred to the snobbish murderer and his empty-headed daughter. The members of the upper classes are fools, knaves, and sometimes murderers; the honest workingmen whom they starve, beat, evict, and scorn are, with the clergy, the only decent human beings. MEB had always viewed the upper classes with healthy skepticism, but never before with such hatred. Moreover, in her novels of the sixties, her tramps and vagabonds had been tramps and vagabonds, to be suspected or properly kept down. The Softy had deserved the lashing that Aurora Floyd gave him, while Conyers was only a handsome guttersnipe. Now for the first time MEB was coupling her scorn for upper-class snobbery and hypocrisy with an explicit partisanship for the downtrodden.

After *Just As I Am*, MEB gave overt radicalism another temporary respite in her next two novels, *Asphodel* (1881) and *Mount Royal* (1882). She planned *Asphodel* as "intensely sentimental," and destined to "end in tragedy," and she fulfilled her plan. But she skillfully concealed—far below the surface this time—a pungent comment on the rich. A younger half sister discovers that an English artist she had met abroad and come to love is the fiancé of her elder half sister in England. She accepts another man, but finds that her half-sister's lover wants to make love to her too. Unwilling to break her sister's heart by running off with him, unable to allow him to continue courting her without her sister's guessing the truth, she drowns herself while all four young people are on holiday together in Switzerland; and the philanderer commits suicide also, by cutting his rope while climbing the Matterhorn.

By showing us the two engaged couples in a constant round of simple luxurious country pleasures—tennis, billiards, dancing, and boating on the Avon in a specially-ordered and manufactured craft—MEB painted with skill and deliberation what most of her readers would have regarded as a blissful, lazy, idyllic summer. Yet one can be sure that she thought it all as intensely dull as the things that the young people in *Just As I Am* "cared about most—the church—the choir—the last penny reading at the school-house—the New Year ball." Frivolous and not very intelligent, the younger half sister is a nice child forced to deal with a problem too difficult for her. And her suitor—who is thirty but acts more like a self-indulgent boy of nineteen—is a charming weakling who cannot bear to deny himself any of his pleasures. Had he ever considered anything so degrading as work of some sort, his dilemma might not have arisen. MEB was indirectly calling attention to the kind of artificial problem the rich and idle create for themselves by their very wealth and idleness. She was dwelling upon the despair to which they may be brought, upon the deaths they may die, because they lack self-discipline, restraint, and the need to think of anybody but themselves. Because their tragedy might so easily have been avoided, it is no less tragic.[20]

MEB did not begin to write *Mount Royal* until almost ten months after she had finished *Asphodel*. The interval without a novel on the stocks was unprecedented for her since her illness of 1868–1869. She spent the time on various smaller chores: a novel in French for *Le Figaro*, an abridged version of Scott's novels, to be published by Maxwell and sold "to the humblest" for a penny a volume, several essays, a *Mistletoe Bough* short story called "His Secret," and three plays, *Married Beneath Him*, *Dross*, and *Margery Daw*, of which the first was never published and has disappeared.[21] In *Mount Royal* itself (1882), MEB retold the Tristram story in modern dress, setting her scene in the Cornwall of the original which she knew so well, and making her characters talk constantly of their Arthurian prototypes. Her Iseult and her Tristram were perhaps less convincing than her Mark, a tough and inarticulate man unable to talk as glibly as his rival about Shakespeare and the musical glasses. Here the radical note is muted and sounds only occasionally in a new key, as when a brutal and vulgar army officer declares that " 'dueling is never out of fashion among gentlemen' " and eagerly poses as a newspaper-reporter in order to see a hanging for pleasure: " 'We've got an order to view, as the house-agents call it.' "

It was perhaps in her personages' conversations in which she straightforwardly reproduced the doubts characteristic of the early 1880's that MEB let her own thinking emerge, as in this interchange:

> "My idea of the close of the nineteenth century is that it will be a period of dire poverty . . . an age of pauperism already heralded by the sale of noble old mansions, the breaking-up of great estates, the destruction of famous collections, galleries, libraries, the pious hoards of generations of connoisseurs and bookworms, scattered to the four winds by the stroke of the auctioneer's hammer. The landed interest and the commercial classes are going down the hill together. Suez has ruined our shipping interests; an un-reciprocated free trade is ruining our commerce. . . . After a period of reckless extravagance there will come an era of dearth. Those are wisest who will anticipate the change, simplify their habits, reduce their luxuries . . . and thus break their fall."

To which came the answer:

> "I daresay the deluge will come, . . . but I think the dry land will last our time. And in the meantime, was there ever a pleasanter world than that we live in, an entirely rebuilt and revivified London—clubs, theatres, restaurants . . . ? If our amusements are frivolous, at least they are hearty. If our friendships are transient, at least they are pleasant while they last. We know people today, and cut them tomorrow; that is one of the first conditions of good society. The people who are cut understand the force of circumstances, and are just as ready to take up the running a year or two hence, when we can afford to know them."[22]

These open predictions of social catastrophe MEB put into the mouths of characters whose opinions were not necessarily her own. But in *Flower and Weed*, her novelette that made up the whole issue of the *Mistletoe Bough* for 1882, she gave the most sweeping and forthright expression

yet to the radicalism that she certainly did feel. The *Flower* of the title is
Lady Lucille, only daughter of a widowed Earl, living a luxurious life
in a grand ancestral house. The *Weed* is Bess, a seventeen-year-old waif,
whom Lucille finds asleep in the nearby woods abandoned, famished, and
ill and brings home in her father's absence. To a chorus of disapproval
from the servants—" '. . . the Union is too good for such a creature. Look at
her feet; she must have tramped for days. She must be a professional
beggar,' " she is probably a criminal, she is a tramp, she is "offal"—
Lucille insists on keeping the girl, on giving her food and drink and the
Gospels. Bess had been a flower-seller in London and had been given tracts
before; the ladies who had come down her alley had told her " 'I must
read 'em if I wanted to save my soul alive; but when I came in of a night,
after tramping half over London with a basket of violets or moss-rose buds,
I hadn't the strength left in me to tackle one of them there tracks, which
allus led off by tellin' me I was goin' to hell.' "

Now she learns needlework, the Lord's Prayer, the Psalms. Indeed, she
is launched on precisely the same trajectory that another flower-girl, Eliza
Doolittle, would one day follow. Told not to refer to a young man as a
"chap" because that is a vulgar word, Bess remarks that she " 'knows a
many that's a good deal vulgarer. . . . I could say words as would make
your hair stand on end.' " So her benefactress must first eradicate "a form
of English language . . . acquired in Whitechapel, . . . enriched with the
copious slang of London low life." Then, with an "intellect keen as a
razor," Bess embarks on a course of reading. Immensely adaptable, she
manages to "acquire all at once the graciousness of a lady, the low and
musical tones of voice, the quiet measured movement, the tranquil beauty
of educated girlhood. . . . Pygmalion's animated statue could hardly have
begun life more newly."

But trouble begins when Lady Lucille becomes engaged to her handsome
cousin, who has an eye for Bess. Bess jealously objects to being treated as
a plaything now that her mistress is devoting all her attention to her
fiancé, and is even discovered by Lucille late one moonlight night, weeping in despair to the sympathetic young cousin, who has his hand on her
shoulder. Suspicion of Bess is fed by Lucille's aunt (" 'I always begin by
thinking badly of persons of that class; and I have never been disappointed
in the result' "), who cannot understand how her niece can have as her
maid " 'a creature rescued from the gutter, . . . utterly without experience!
What could she do for your figure or your complexion if either were to give
way suddenly?' " So Bess is destined to be sent out as nursery governess,
" 'the most honourable career open to a woman . . . the one profession a

lady can enter without a blush. The governess can pass through life without over-stepping the bounds of maidenly modesty. She need never come in contact with the ruder sex. She is a nun without the restraint of the convent,' " a prospect that Bess finds less than enchanting.

In fact, Bess is married to a man who had mistreated and deserted her; but she has never told her new friends about him. When he tries to reclaim her against her will, she leaves the interview in tears, and her mistress's fiancé takes advantage of her emotional distress to embrace her: she responds, but quickly disengages herself. Told of her marriage, he promises not to repeat his indiscretion. He struggles with and overcomes "that fatal fancy . . . that strange and unhealthy fascination." This, surely, was designed to appease MEB's readers. Neither she nor we can take his reform at face value. He is one of her idle Victorian gentlemen, ready at any moment to seduce a pretty servant if he can. Though Bess catches consumption brought on by her hopeless love, she does not die of it, but of a stab wound inflicted by her own husband, who tries vainly to burgle the castle on Christmas night after a grand old-fashioned Christmas party, with a tree and presents for all. Lucille marries her cousin; he tells her how nearly he had been "lured away," and she forgives him. The flower flourishes. But the weed has perished, and on her tombstone her noble patrons put the inscription, " 'Valued Much and Lamented Much.' "23

Read at Christmastime, 1882, as a sentimental Victorian Christmas story, *Flower and Weed* barely conceals its bitter social commentary on the behavior of the upper classes. Even when they strive according to their lights to be generous to a waif from the gutter, they destroy her heedlessly, arrogant in their possession of all the world's desirable things. It was too early in the social history of England for Eliza to catch Professor Higgins. Bess, the weed, MEB had made so much more interesting and valuable a plant than Lucille, the flower, that the title itself took on deep overtones of savage irony. Which was truly the flower, which the weed? The victim in her young womanhood of social cruelty, MEB, in her own rich and powerful middle age, when she could write to please herself, was striking back at her early enemies and the harsh principles they represented, and so subtly that they could not catch her at it. Even as late as 1901, Arnold Bennett would still think of her as celebrating the comforts of aristocratic country-house life because her satire on its mores had escaped his notice. That nobody seemed to realize what she was doing must have given her the most sardonic pleasure of all.

4. MEB as a Student of Zola (1879–1883)

Rolandi's was the French circulating library in London, and MEB had a subscription. She often noted in her diaries that she had "changed books" there, but did not always record the titles. She regularly read the *Revue des Deux Mondes* and other French journals and effortlessly kept abreast of French literature, which she had loved ever since her mother had introduced her as a little girl to "Charles" and the food he ate. Penny fiction and Soulié now lay far in the past; the experiment with "adapting" Flaubert had not been a complete success; the "adaptation" of Feuillet had proved a disaster. Balzac had greatly impressed her and had had a certain impact on her writing, but by the late 1870's she was moving on. It was Zola and naturalism that she now found fascinating. She now abandoned the form of adaptation that at times had amounted virtually to plagiarism: it had served its purpose in the sixties when the pressure had been great and her standards the free and easy ones of the theatre. In any case, Zola was still so unacceptable to an English Victorian public that in order to "adapt" him in her former fashion she would have had to turn all the prostitutes into schoolgirls, as the playwrights she had so often mocked were forced to do. Neither her sense of fitness nor her sense of humor would have enabled her to do this. So she allowed Zola to influence her in more subtle ways.

In *The Cloven Foot* (1879)—the story of the young woman who too readily marries the man who has been left the large legacy on condition that he marry her—one catches the first faint whiff of Zola. The real impediment to the marriage is that the heir is already married, to a famous French ballet-dancer, La Chicot, whom he had met in Paris when he had been a young artist making a scanty living from caricatures and satirical drawings. He has even taken her name, signing his drawings "Jack Chicot," and when she becomes the rage in London he keeps it, though they grow apart as she begins to drink. When she is injured by a piece of stage-machinery and expected to die, he goes through a bigamous marriage under his real name, in order to gain the legacy.

Paris teaches La Chicot, a simple Breton girl of nineteen, that she is beautiful, that it is pleasanter "to whirl and bound among serried ranks of other Chicots in . . . 'The Sleeping Beauty,' or the 'Hart with the Golden Collar,' clad in the scantiest drapery, but sparkling with gold and spangles, with hair flowing wild as a Maenad's, and satin boots at two Napoleons the pair, than to toil among laundresses on the quay."

Although she is only one member of the *corps de ballet*, her "superb eyes and luxuriant hair, . . . statuesque figure and youthful freshness" attract much notice. The ballet-master gives her a solo dance now and then, and at his advice she migrates from the large house "where she was nobody, to a smaller house in the students' quarter . . . where she soon became everybody. *'C'était le plus gentil de mes rats,'* cried the ballet-master regretfully. *'Cette petite ira loin,'* said the manager. . . . *'elle a du chien.'* "

> She was fond of money, but only of money to spend in the im-
> mediate present; money for fine dresses, good dinners, wine that
> foamed and sparkled, and plenty of promenading in hired car-
> riages in the Bois de Boulogne. . . . To have a handsome young
> man . . . for her lover and slave . . . this was La Chicot's notion of
> happiness. . . . She did not expect him to work for her, or support
> her; she was quite resigned to the idea that she was to be the
> breadwinner. . . . This child of the people set a curious value upon
> the name gentleman. The fact that her husband belonged to a
> superior race made up . . . for a great many shortcomings. . . . It
> was an odd kind of life which these two led in their meagerly
> furnished rooms on the third floor of a dingy house, in a dingy
> street of the students' quarter; an odd, improvident, dissipated
> life, in which night was turned into day, and money spent like
> water, and nothing desired or obtained out of existence except
> pleasure, the gross, sensual pleasure of dining and drinking; the
> wilder pleasure of play, and moonlight drives in the Bois; the Sab-
> bath delights of free and easy rambles . . . beside the silvery Seine,
> on the long summer days, when a luxurious idler could rise at
> noon without feeling the effort too hard a trial; winding up always
> with a dinner at some rustic house of entertainment, where there
> was a vine-curtained arbour that one could dine in, and where one
> could see the dinner being cooked in a kitchen with a wide
> window opening on yard and garden, and hear the balls clicking in
> the low-ceiled billiard-room.

La Chicot

> earned her money gaily, and spent it royally; domineered over her
> husband on the strength of her superb beauty; basked in the
> sunshine of temporary prosperity; drank more champagne than
> was good for her constitution or her womanhood; grew a shade

coarser every year; never opened a book or cultivated her mind in the slightest degree; scorned all the refinements of life; looked upon picturesque scenes and rustic landscapes as a fitting background for the riot and drunkenness of a Bohemian picnic, and as good for nothing else; never crossed the threshold of a church, or held out her hand in charity; lived for herself and her own pleasure; and had no more conscience than the butterflies, and less sense of duty than the birds.

Her dancing grows more and more wild; she is a true Bacchante, and everybody is worried about her drinking; soon she begins to go out of style:

> "C'est connue comme une tartine de journal, ... C'est connu comme le dôme des Invalides, ... Cela fatigue; on commence à se désillusioner sur La Chicot."[24]

These brief Parisian passages cannot have been suggested by *Nana*, which only began to appear serially six months after MEB had finished *The Cloven Foot*. Nor do they derive from any identifiable Zola original. Yet they echo Zolaesque themes, however faintly.

In *The Golden Calf* (1883), the echo becomes fully resonant. Ida Palliser, daughter of a poor army officer, talented pupil-teacher at a London boarding school, is invited by a schoolfriend to the country for the holidays. Here she hears much talk of the family's two absent cousins, the "rich Brian," possessor of a magnificent old house and great fortune, and the "poor Brian," a briefless barrister. At a family party, she is introduced to an agreeable young man, the "rich Brian," who afterwards pays court to her—she is dismissed from school for having kissed him once—and persuades her to marry him. Not until the marriage service has been read does she discover that she has married not the "rich" but the "poor" Brian: she has been the victim of a practical joke that began innocently enough at the party, but that her husband has dishonestly prolonged. At first she repudiates him, but, after an interval—during which she meets and falls in love with the "rich Brian"—she begins to live with her husband. And when her father inherits a large country estate, they go to live there with her family, including her young half-brother. Here Brian gradually becomes a hopeless drunkard. Eventually he sets the house on fire and dies in the blaze.

MEB gave her readers a detailed description of his degeneration. His drinking begins when Ida's father dies and she inherits seven hundred and fifty pounds a year, while her younger half-brother gets the title and most of the property. Keeping his chambers in London but still briefless, Brian cannot help thinking how much richer he would be if his young half-brother-in-law, whom he actually likes very well, were to die. As for his wife, he knows that she is "good and loyal"; but he cannot forgive her "for that . . . strength of character which accentuated his own weakness." Brian's love for Ida wears to "a very thin thread indeed." In London, where he stays much of the time, he sits with his friends, "smoking . . . cigarettes, and sipping . . . Apollinaris slightly coloured with brandy—a very modest form of entertainment surely, and yet the cigarettes and the super-fine cognac . . . always on tap" cost him large sums of money.

When he does return to Ida in the country, he is "invalided and wanting rest and care," but will not consult the family doctor and protests that his only problem is " 'nervous exhaustion, and over-worked brain, and that kind of thing.' " Lacking appetite, suffering from insomnia, Brian has given himself over not "to riot and drunkenness, but to the half-unconscious consumption of much brandy and soda." His hands shake. The doctor has "strictly forbidden any stimulant except one glass of stout with his mutton chop at luncheon," but Brian, "quite unable to eat the chop," finds it "impossible to lunch without plenty of dry sherry, or to dine without champagne, and after dinner . . . a good deal of . . . fine old port." Ida is kind to him and takes him for drives, but he smokes two or three dozen cigarettes a day instead of the two or three to which he has been limited. She tells him that " 'every man is his own master—he can mould his life as he likes,' " to which he answers: " 'There is the question of temperament—hereditary instinct.' "

Brian cannot go for walks; he is morbidly jealous of Ida's half-brother; he hates the country and misses the good times he had had in London with his friends. Ida realizes "that this mysterious malady of his, which had at first seemed to her sheer hypochondriasis," is only too real. He is mentally as well as physically ill: "He who had been of old so easy-tempered, so lively, was now melancholy and irascible, at times garrulous to a degree that was painful to his hearers, keenly resentful of trifles, always fancying himself neglected or slighted." He is only twenty-nine, but he hates both law and literature, saying " 'all the professions are played out. Europe is over-crowded with educated men.' " He blames Ida: " 'I have known all along that . . . you despise me, detest me, perhaps; and that knowledge has made me . . . a broken, blighted man, a wreck at nine-and-twenty.' " He knows he had been pre-destined to damnation. When Ida steels herself to remonstrate with him about his drink-ing, he abuses her in "such language as she had never heard from mortal lips until that hour."

Sheepish when next they meet, Brian turns crafty; he no longer keeps "a brandy bottle on the table beside his bed, on the pretence that a little weak brandy and water" helps him to sleep, nor does the "decanter adorn one of the tables in his study; but more than once" his wife meets him "creeping to the dining-room with a stealthy air to supply himself from the sideboard." Gradually his clothes seem to smell of alcohol. Then he becomes paranoid, talking "mysteriously of some trouble which menaced him which gradually took the shape of a criminal prosecution overhang-ing him." He has been "falsely accused of some awful crime," presumably the murder of his young brother-in-law. "He was innocent, but his enemies were legion." One evening he has the illusion that one of the footmen is a detective in disguise. He attacks the footman and later apologizes: " 'You don't know what devils those detectives are . . . they can make themselves look like anybody.' " Brian will not take medical advice. He already knows exactly how to cure himself. Ida, who had thought that " 'Nobody drank nowadays,' " learns from the doctor that Brian is on the downward path toward *delirium tremens.* She tries to cut off supplies: overcoming her shame, she orders the butler not to produce any more brandy. But it does not work.

The delusions grow worse: Brian thinks he sees a snowstorm on a sum-mer night; he wildly plans additions to the house, believing Ida's brother dead; he tries to find imaginary lost coins on the carpet; he thinks he has been blinded by lightning; he has a fearful philosophical talking-jag. A male nurse must be brought in to look after him; the London doctor tells him that " 'There are men who can drink with impunity—go on drinking hard through a long life; but you are not one of those. Drink for you means death.' " In spite of the attendant's vigilance, Brian hides brandy bottles amidst the pipes in the wooden casing of his bathtub; his fits of the horrors grow worse; he makes a frightful scene in church. He becomes " 'very bad; pulse small and thready—a hundred and forty to the minute; violent throbbing in the temporal and carotid arteries; profuse perspira-tion.' " And we learn exactly what drugs are prescribed. Before the final catastrophe, he hunts for serpents in the bed-curtains and raves about flames.

So grim, so precise, so realistic, so photographic, so deliberate, and so unrelenting a study of the development of alcoholism represented a wholly new departure for MEB. Observant she had always been; she knew what drinks people generally took and at what hours, what the rich drank and what the poor. She had always been "up" on drink, as she had been up on sport or architecture or painting or women's fashions. But Brian's clinical case history was precisely a clinical case history, and in that respect it was new. We have fancied we saw the influence of Zola manifesting itself briefly in *The Cloven Foot* in MEB's account of the early career of La Chicot. Here, in *The Golden Calf*, we can be certain. The case of Coupeau in *L'Assommoir* (published as a book in 1877) provides the closest parallel in Zola's novels before 1883 to that of Brian. MEB had read and enormously admired *L'Assommoir*. She had probably seen Charles Reade's dramatic adaptation of it—*Drink*—which opened in London on June 2, 1879.[25] But of course Coupeau is a French roofer and zinc-worker, Brian an English gentleman. MEB did not imitate Zola slavishly. She simply transferred the stages of progressive alcoholic degradation from France to England and from a workman to a gentleman, and produced a totally convincing—far more than plausible—account of a young barrister's ruin by drink.

Brian's own attribution of his illness to "temperament—hereditary instinct" was pure Zolaism: this was the underlying theme of the entire Rougon-Macquart series of novels, as all the descendants participated in the wretched heritage of the grandmother and great-grandmother, Adelaide Fouque, the *nevrose originelle*. That MEB attributed this idea to Brian—and it was very much in the air in the seventies and early eighties—did not mean that she accepted it at its face value. Not at all: she provided for Brian a perfectly acceptable set of psychological and physiological conditions that might reasonably lead to alcoholism. He has a beautiful and now a rich wife, who had never loved him and whom he had been able to marry only by cruelly deceiving her as to his identity, so that he feels guilty every time he thinks of it. He feels still more guilty as he thinks of killing the little boy who stands between him and a great fortune, at times fearing that he may actually have done so. Brian is a failure in his profession and has no real incentive to work harder; he has the ease of bachelor life in London with its fatal easy drinking; he even has what we would call an "allergy" to drink: some natures can take it, but his cannot. What came direct from Zola, then, was only the theory of inherited neurotic disease that Brian accepted as applying to his own case, together with the symptoms of his downward progress into the pit. In *The Golden Calf*, MEB showed not only how hard she had studied Zola but also what a good psychologist she was on her own.

In her next novel, *Phantom Fortune* (1883), MEB did it again. The orphaned heroine, the beautiful Lady Lesbia—brought up in the country by her iron-willed grandmother, whose husband had disgraced himself in India in their younger days—is sent off to London to be introduced to society and to find a suitable husband. In London she is sponsored by an elderly woman, once a friend of her grandmother but now a leader in a set of fast people. Lesbia spends too much money on clothes and jewels, and having lost her true love—an Earl—to her sister, agrees to marry a commoner, an enormously rich self-made man. Instead of contenting herself with her catch, Lesbia disgraces herself by trying to elope on his yacht with a Cuban adventurer, already married, who has made his fortune in the slave trade. She is broken by her experiences and is driven from London.

For the first time, MEB mentions Zola openly. When Lesbia moves into artistic and intellectual society, she feels "as an Englishman may feel who has made himself master of Academical French, and who takes up one of Zola's novels . . . and finds that there is another French, of which he knows not a word," a point about Zola's French later made by André Gide and Harry Levin, among others. Moreover, when Lesbia is asked, " 'And now you read everything, I suppose—including Zola?' " she replies, " 'The books are lying around, and I dip into them sometimes when I am having my hair brushed.' " Her worldly chaperone announces that on a yachting holiday she will be " 'too deliciously idle even to read the last horrid thing of Zola's.' " And in the library of the rich man's country house, "one large round table was consecrated to Mudie, another to Rolandi"—the leading circulating libraries for English and French fiction—: "On the one side, you had Mrs. Oliphant, on the other Zola, exemplifying the genius of the two nations." (The sharp dig at the prissy Mrs. Oliphant almost leads one to wonder whether MEB had somehow identified her as the critic who had "flayed" her so unmercifully for sensuality back in 1867.) Lesbia's brother, worried that he may suffer for his grandfather's crimes in India, voices the Zola theory of heredity in more detail than the alcoholic Brian in *The Golden Calf*: " 'Hereditary genius is one of our modern vogues. When a man's grandfather was a rogue, there must be a taint in the blood. . . . Typhoid breeds typhoid, and typhus breeds typhus, just as dog breeds dog; and who will believe that a cheat and a liar can be the father of an honest man?' "

The entire episode of Lesbia's life in London—the extravagance of her clothes, her dressmaker, her engagement and her elopement—was a Braddonian version of Zola's *La Curée* (1871–1872). Of course, MEB could not make Lesbia a married woman committing not only adultery but incest, the sins of Renée in *La Curée*. Instead of being married to her financier—like Renée in *La Curée*—Lesbia is merely engaged. Whereas Renée fornicates with her lover, Lesbia merely gives her Cuban a few indiscreet kisses and encourages him to hijack her fiancé's yacht in order to run off with her: her chaperone is perforce below in the cabin the entire time. Always fond of vivid detail, MEB found in Zola a writer who believed in the same techniques and could give her pointers, a writer with whose methods she was comfortable, a writer who stimulated her to do more of what she had always tried to do.

While Lesbia's grandmother at nearly seventy, in red brocade with bands of sable at the wrists and throat and a few diamonds on her fingers, looks like "a picture in the Escorial," her old friend, Lesbia's chaperone, looks like "a caricature in *La Vie Parisienne*. . . . Plush, brocade, peacock's feathers, golden bangles, mousquetaire gloves, a bonnet of purple plumage set off by ornaments of filigree gold, an infantine little muff of lace and wild flowers, buttercups and daisies, eye-brows and complexion as artificial as the flowers on the muff." The London dressmaker who supplies these marvels is the French Jewess, Séraphine, with whom this lady has been quarreling and making it up again for thirty years and to whom she is always in debt. When they are on good terms, Séraphine is her *cher ange*, her *bonne chatte*, her *chère vieille sotte*. And when Lesbia's chaperone is made-up for a party by Séraphine, "with her little morocco bag of washes and creams, and brushes and sponges," she peers at herself in the mirror and sees a "dazzling image of rouge and bismuth, carmined lips, diamonds, and frizzy yellow hair; 'I verily believe I look under thirty—but do not you think this gown is a thought too *décolletée—un peu trop de peau, hein?*' " to which Séraphine answers: " 'Not for you . . . with your fine shoulders. Shoulders are of no age—*les épaules sont la vraie fontaine de jouvence pour les jolies femmes.*' " After that the two have another glass of chartreuse together before it is time for the party. Having been brought up in the country, Lesbia " 'has no figure,' " according to Séraphine, who soon fits her with corsets three inches too small for her waist and six inches too large for her "shoulders." Shoulders, MEB knew as well as her audience, had nothing to do with corsets or with décolletage, but she could not directly imitate Zola's preoccupation with female breasts.

Zola would thoroughly have approved, and would himself have been capable of creating, Lesbia's costumes. The one made to wear at the Henley regatta (" 'something of the most original—*tant soi peu risqué*—for 'Enley,' " as Séraphine calls it) is derived directly from a " 'watare dress,' " for a boating party at Bougival, worn by an actress in the brand-new play, *Une Faute dans le passé*—suggestive title: Lesbia's *faute* still lies ahead—" 'a toilet of the most new, striking, écrasant, what you English call a screamer' ":

> An exquisite combination of simplicity with vlan. . . . A skin-tight indigo jersey-silk bodice, closely studded with dark blue beads, a flounced petticoat of indigo and amber foulard, an amber scarf drawn tightly around the hips, and a dark blue toque with a large bunch of amber poppies. Tan-coloured mousquetaire gloves, and Hessian boots of tan-coloured kid.

The toilette has the success that was intended: the rich suitor proposes for the second time and is accepted.

Zolaesque too, but adapted to the English condition, is Lesbia's chaperone's response to a suggestion that Dumas' play, *Le Demi-monde*, was

> "rather strong meat for babes, eh? Not *exactly* the play one would take a young lady to see."
>
> "Why should a young lady be forbidden to see a fine play because there are some hard and bitter truths in it? . . . Lesbia sees Madame d'Ange and all her sisterhood in the Park and about London every day of her life. Why should she not see them on the stage, and hear their history, and understand how cruel their fate is, and learn to pity them if she can? I really think this play is a lesson in Christian charity."

Unlike Renée in *La Curée*, Lesbia could hardly wish to *be* a courtesan, a *demi-mondaine*, or explore their haunts with impunity—and disappointment; but in 1883, under the right—or the wrong—chaperonage, she might *see* the sisterhood on the stage, as she saw them—and one must not blink that—every day "in the Park and about London."

Fashionable things are *chic* or *chien* or *zinc* or even *tout ce qu'il y a de plus pschutt*. And of all the fashionable things in *Phantom Fortune* nothing comes up to Lesbia's fiancé's house in London, an English version of Saccard's Parc Monceau mansion in *La Curée*. Here money has been spent like water: "Painters, decorators, cabinet-makers had a merry time of it. Royal Academicians were impressed into service . . . and the final result" is an Italian Renaissance palace with "frescoed ceilings, painted panels, a staircase of sculptured marble, . . . a conservatory as exquisite as a jewel casket by Benvenuto Cellini," a picture gallery that is "the admiration of all London." Breakfast is served in the "smallest snuggery" of the three "apartments given up to feasting," where the walls are "upholstered in old gold silk, the curtains a tawny velvet of deeper tone, the cabinets and buffet of dark Italian walnut inlaid with lapis-lazuli and amber, the fire-place a masterpiece of cabinet-work with high narrow shelves, and curious recesses holding priceless jars of Oriental enamel—the deep hearth filled up with arum lilies and azaleas like a font at Easter." The pictures are mostly French, and among them were some

> of that new school which is called Impressionist, in which ballet dancers and jockeys, burlesque actresses, masked balls are represented with the sublime audacity of an art which disdains finish, and relies on *chic, fougue, chien, flou*, the inspiration of the moment. Lesbia blushed as she looked at the ballet girls, the maskers in their scanty raiment, the *demi-mondaines* lolling out of their open boxes, and half out of their gowns, with false smiles and frizzled hair.

Still conservative in her taste in paintings, MEB was up-to-the-minute just the same. In 1883, she was fully aware of Degas and Manet, and singled out for comment the décolletage that Zola himself always emphasized.

More MEB's own was the satirical glimpse of a Swinburnian sort of poet, shown "caressing" an "absinthe-coloured" jade cup and exclaiming " 'Great heaven, can anything be lovelier than this shadowy tint which is neither yellow nor green; faint, faint as the dawn of newly-awakened day? I have seen such a tinge in the sky going home from parties.' " Braddonian also is the millionaire's yacht, though Zola would have approved his delicate sentiments in redecorating his own cabins for Lesbia's use, and the resulting triumph of décor:

> The dark velvet and morocco which suited a masculine occupant would not have harmonised with girlhood and beauty; and Mr. Smithson's saloon, as originally designed, had something of the

air of a *tabagie*. The Bond Street man stripped away all the velvet and morocco, plucked up the Turkey carpet, draped the scuttle-ports with pale yellow cretonne garnished with orange pompoms, subdued the glare of the skylight by a blind of oriental silk, covered the divans with Persian saddlebags, the floor with a delicate India matting, and furnished the saloon with all that was most feminine in the way of bamboo chairs and tea-tables, Japanese screens and fans of gorgeous colouring. Here and there against the fluted yellow drapery he fastened a large Rhodes plate; and the thing was done. Lady Lesbia's cabin was all bamboo and embroidered India muslin. An oval glass, framed in Dresden biscuit, adorned the side, a large white bearskin covered the floor. The berth was pretty enough for the cradle of a duchess's first baby. Even Lesbia . . . gave a little cry of pleasure. . . . "Really Mr. Smithson is immensely kind," she exclaimed.

So to *The Golden Calf* and *Phantom Fortune, L'Assommoir* and *La Curée* respectively made important contributions, while Zola's practice of detailed description in depth re-enforced MEB's own long-standing inclinations as a writer. In its brief notice of *Phantom Fortune,* the *Athenaeum* did comment that MEB had portrayed "The very latest and worst development of . . . present day. . . . society given up to frivolity, sham admiration of art, and the worship of wealth, . . . in which there is absolute freedom of manners and an absence of principle."[26] But the critic did not speculate whether the impulse was entirely MEB's or whether she had found inspiration elsewhere, and, if so, where. Not yet translated into English in 1883, Zola was still an exotic import. That MEB had steeped herself in his novels only she knew, and what she had taken from him she had so thoroughly made her own that nobody now could call her to account, as they had done long ago when she had used large elements of *Madame Bovary* in writing *The Doctor's Wife,* or had virtually plagiarized the whole of Octave Feuillet's *Dalila* in scribbling "Babington White's" *Circe.*

5. MEB as Zola (1883–1885)

A Victorian Christmas story might be a ghost story—with or without an explanation that rendered the supernatural natural after all—as frightening as one liked, to be read before the fire. Or it might be a story of poverty and misery alleviated in the nick of time by the power of the spirit of Christmas. It might be both of these simultaneously, like *A Christmas Carol*. Or it might tell of sheer good fellowship—usually between gentry and peasantry—before the tree in the great hall and at the dance that followed, when the squire stepped out with the cook and her ladyship with the butler, after the village children had each had a present. It might be a tale of wild winter adventure: in the Arctic fastnesses, in a lonely railway signalman's hut, even in India or some other barbarous place where it was hot instead of cold in December. It might take the form of reminiscences from an elderly clown, or the housekeeper of an uninhabited mansion, or the landlady of a London lodging house, or the captain of a ship at sea, or the abbess of a convent in Belgium. The variety was almost endless, as indeed it had to be, since scores of Christmas stories were written every year for dozens of periodical publications whose sole purpose was to publish them. The public's appetite for them was apparently insatiable. The writing and purveying of Christmas stories was an industry, and the rules were elastic, but rules there were and everybody understood them: a Christmas story might be happy or sad—there could be deathbeds but they ought to be edifying; it might be funny or serious, but it ought in principle to have something to do with Christmas and it ought not to have too serious a social purpose. There was a place for everything, and a Christmas story was not the place to recapitulate in fictional form a grim chapter of recent history (in another country at that) and to leave out Christmas altogether.

Nobody knew these rules better than MEB, whose first Christmas story went back to 1860 and *The Welcome Guest*, and who for a decade after 1866 had "conducted" *Belgravia* with its yearly Christmas *Annual*, and since 1877 had edited *The Mistletoe Bough*, which appeared only at Christmas. And as a usual thing nobody followed the rules with better grace than MEB. Even *Flower and Weed*, with its radical lesson that one might transform a beggar girl—mere offal—into a lady, though she might die of it, had culminated in a grand Christmas party. But now, in 1883, for the second consecutive year, MEB was writing the whole of *The Mistletoe Bough* and this time she broke all the rules.

Under the Red Flag, her "commune story" (once tentatively called *Girt with Fire*), tells of two poor Irish orphan sisters, Rose and Kathleen O'Hara, who at eighteen and eleven escape from their convent in Bruges (like Criquette in Halévy's novel, which MEB was reading in June 1883[27]) and make their way to Paris, where Rose works as an artificial flower-maker, supporting them both, until Kathleen too is old enough to make flowers. By 1870 Rose has become engaged to a rising young journeyman cabinetmaker, and Kathleen to a young journalist who writes for the socialist paper, *Le Drapeau rouge*, and who has relinquished his earlier mild flirtation with the jealous proprietress of a *crêmerie*. As war with Prussia threatens, the two happy engaged couples dance at the Closerie des Lilas, attend a play by Dumas the younger at the Ambigu, and are married at Notre Dame, with a wedding breakfast afterwards. They spend the afternoon at the new Buttes Chaumont, "the wonderful gardens, the green valleys and Alpine crags, the blue lakes and Swiss summer-houses, and Grecian temples of the old, old quarries" that Napoleon III had made into a park for the people of Paris, "surely the gayest, prettiest most picturesque playground that ever a tyrant gave to his slaves." But by the end of their idyllic wedding day, the first news of a French victory is known to have been false, and in the months that follow, the Prussian triumphs speed the fall of the Empire and Paris awaits the invaders.

The young socialist, Gaston, who comes of the decayed aristocracy and has been educated by the Dominicans, hates " 'the insolent *roturier* brood that have battened in the sunshine of imperial favour; the stock-jobbers and gamblers, corrupt . . . and swelling with pride in their dirty gold.' " His paper, *Le Drapeau rouge*, has all along "told how France was being misgoverned, and called upon the supreme sovereign people" to seize power and "steer the . . . ship to . . . the smooth roadstead of Communism, Collectivism, Karl Marxism, . . . every man his own master, no hereditary nobility, no landowners, no millionaires, a universal level of blue blouses and cheap wines." The paper praises Blanqui and the Blanquists, "rivalling Félix Pyat's paper, *Le Combat*, and Blanqui's *Patrie en Danger*." Kathleen adores Gaston, fears that his " 'grand glowing words . . . may . . . lead to an explosion in which we may all perish,' " since so many of the workers are dangerous men. But Gaston, who predicts that " 'In the age that is coming there will be no . . . Gobelins tapestries, no Sèvres porcelain. There will be a bit of beef in every man's *pot-au-feu*, a roof over every man's head, food and shelter, light and air, and cleanliness and comfort, and a free education for all,' " wants no repetition of '93; he preaches " 'Communism, not Revolution.' " Symbolic of their discussion is a splendid sideboard that Rose's husband has been making. In the new France, his brother-in-law declares, nobody will buy it, and Kathleen, despite her loyalty, secretly thinks such a world will be a dreary place.

The socialist doctrine sounds reasonable in October 1870, during the strange interlude before the scarcities or the siege have begun. But by

January 1871 food and fuel have almost vanished and misery has set in; Paris surrenders, the Germans enter, and the respectable classes leave the city. In March, when the mob takes over, Gaston expresses his revulsion at their excesses, and his paper is suppressed. Penniless and suspect, he begins to write anonymous satirical political ballads, sold by hawkers in the streets. Fearing that danger threatens his old teachers, the Dominicans, he tries to prevent their arrest and is taken prisoner with them. When the brutal General Sérizier orders the monastery pillaged and the monks massacred, Gaston too is shot. Among the executioners is his former love, the proprietress of the *crêmerie*, who recognizes his body among the corpses.

During the defeat of the Commune and the violent revenge of its enemies, Kathleen begins to search for her husband's executioner through "butt-ends of muskets, fragments of belts, tails of coats, strips of blouses, caps, cartouche-boxes, shoes," piles of corpses and streams of blood. Knowing that Sérizier had once been a currier, she obtains a list of the hundreds of curriers' establishments in Paris and systematically goes hunting for him. As the reprisals for the Commune take place, as Paris gradually returns to peaceful life, with foreign tourists coming in to stare at the ruins, and theatres and cafés reopening, through June and July and August and half of September 1871, Kathleen, with a map and a photograph of Sérizier, doggedly goes from currier to currier in Paris, until on September 16 she spots him. She denounces him to the authorities, he is arrested, and—because "the law's delays are tedious"—he is not shot until February 1872.

Her frantic effort over and her vengeance accomplished, Kathleen is dying of exhaustion and grief when in November 1871 the proprietress of the *crêmerie* returns to reopen it. Hearing of Kathleen's heroism, she takes her to Gaston, whom she had rescued, still alive. His recovery is hastened by the reunion and he is soon writing for his old newspaper, now "resuscitated . . . as *The Friend of Freedom*," and even embarking upon the novel that he had always planned to write:

> a love story, full of passion and fire, and Kathleen felt that it must make a mad, a furious success. Nor was she far out in her reckoning. When a man, whose pen has grown bold and brilliant in the work of a literary journeyman, whose memory has garnered the experience of a youth and manhood spent in the very whirlpool of metropolitan life, and who has read and dreamed and thought superabundantly in his leisure hours and his wanderings to and

fro—when such a man girds up his loins and says, "Enough of the hard facts of life—now I will give myself full play in the garden of fancy," the chances are that he will write a grand novel.

When published, the novel "obtains a more brilliant success than any book since *Madame Bovary*." The splendid carved oak sideboard is bought by Sir Richard Wallace.

MEB's knowledge of the Franco-Prussian War and the Commune was detailed and accurate. She noted in her diary for March 30, 1884, that she had read "Beaumont-Vassy"—presumably the Vicomte de Beaumont-Vassy's *Histoire Authentique de la commune de Paris* of 1871;[28] but by March 1884 *Under the Red Flag* had long since been completed. Wherever she studied her history, she knew that it was not history she was writing. She used the grim events of 1870 and 1871 as a backdrop, against which the drama of her four attractive young people was acted out. All were agreeably sketched, but Gaston was far the most arresting.

For in Gaston, the well-meaning, mild, idealistic, socialistic newspaperman, who had lived life fully enough to make a great success as a novelist, MEB was surely presenting her own idea of Émile Zola, disguised barely enough to prevent instant recognition. After May 1868, when the imperial regime liberalized its press laws, Zola had joined the staff of the socialist *La Tribune*. For it and for *La Cloche*, a similar paper, he had written articles just like those of Gaston for *Le Drapeau rouge*. But, as MEB knew well, Zola had written five novels before the war; nor did his great success come with his first post-war novel of 1871, but in 1877, with *L'Assommoir*, his twelfth novel and seventh after the war, which was hardly a passionate love story in the sense that MEB's readers would have understood the term. When the success did come, however, it was indeed the greatest since Flaubert's in 1857.

Despite her admiration for Gaston, MEB did not disguise her conviction that his political beliefs and writings were naive and dangerous in the extreme, and that they had directly contributed to the horrors of the Commune. With Kathleen, MEB was quite sure that it would be a dreary world in which there was nobody to buy the beautiful sideboard. Indeed, by making its purchaser Sir Richard Wallace (1818–1890), the illegitimate son of the fourth Marquess of Hertford—Thackeray's Lord Steyne in *Vanity Fair*—whose splendid collection of paintings and furniture, including perhaps the sideboard itself, is still to be seen in Manchester Square, MEB was strongly asserting her own belief that we would have the rich always with us, and that this might be no very bad thing. In her novels set in England she often showed the contempt of a radical for them, but she thought that perhaps they could be educated up to their responsibilities. She was no revolutionary, but she was prepared to present the ideas of revolutionaries as fairly as she could until the blood started to flow. Then revulsion set in, and in the Commune she could see nothing but evil. All in all, as Tiny Tim did not remark, there never *was* such a Christmas story.

Having viewed the collapse of the Second Empire in *Under the Red Flag*, MEB in *Ishmael*[29] took her readers back before the advent of Louis Napoleon, but set most of her novel well within his reign. Like Melville's Ishmael, MEB's is self-christened. His real name is Sébastien Caradec, born about 1833, the son of a Breton country gentleman whose wife had run off with one of his friends, taking their young son with her. Caradec had pursued them to Mauritius, killed his wife's seducer, and returned to France without inquiring further about the child. Abandoned in the midst of the Indian Ocean, his wife had taken a new lover, who had brought her and her child and her maid to Paris. Here she had taken to drink, quarreled with her lover, and gone downhill fast, leaving the chief care of her son to the maid, whom she had joined as an entertainer in a *café chantant*. When his wife dies, Caradec reclaims his son, now about ten. But he never loves him, and at seventeen Sébastien is so unjustly treated by father and stepmother that he leaves home, abandoning his name as a symbolic gesture and calling himself Ishmael. He makes his way to Paris in October 1850 after Louis Napoleon has been elected president.

Ishmael finds work as a bricklayer's apprentice, a *garçon* or *gâcheur*. Paid two and a half francs a day, he has to give one franc to the foreman in recompense for taking him on. Stirring lime and sand, he makes a living, respected by the foreman because of his steady work and because he lives as the other men live. Among his fellow-workers Ishmael finds political feeling running high: Most feel the new republic is not "republican enough." Some are die-hard Bonapartists; some mourn the closing of the national workshops; others blame Louis Blanc for having made promises he could not keep. These impatiently regard presidents as kings in disguise, and want France governed by "a great confederation of working-men" together with a few intellectuals.

On a Sunday excursion, Ishmael meets Pâquerette, granddaughter of a cabinetmaker of the squalid rue Sombreuil in the Faubourg St.-Antoine, who makes beautiful furniture in the intervals when he is not drinking at his favorite *brasserie*, "The Faithful Pig." His agent, the shrewd *charabia*, sells his furniture and cheats him of his commissions. Pâquerette's mother, an apprentice in a laundry, had long ago run off with a plausible stranger and had come home to die, leaving the two-year-old Pâquerette to the tender mercies of her grandparents. They had soon turned her into a drudge, dressed her in rags, and allowed her no pleasures. Kind working girls of the neighborhood had taken pity upon her and occasionally loaned her clothes so that she might go along on their Sunday outings. It is thus that she meets Ishmael, a sober-sided young man who sympathizes with Pâquerette's plight, though he doubts if he could marry anybody from such low surroundings.

Promoted, living in a better lodging and studying mathematics, Ishmael is soon deeply involved in politics, "as ardent a republican as any . . . who helped make the Revolution of 1789. He had sat at the feet of such teachers as Victor Hugo and Louis Blanc. . . . he believed in the divine right of the people, as against the right of kings." In this mood, he participates in the dramatic violence of the *coup d'état* of December 1851, casting in his lot with the Reds; he is on the barricades at the very moment when Baudin the deputy is killed. Pâquerette's grandfather also is killed, and Ishmael himself wounded. Before the police can arrest him, he finds himself hauled up on a rope to the window of a young man who shelters him for a few days until his wound is healed and the *coup* is over. The rescuer, a young poet named Hector de Valnois, has "that half-boyish, half *petit-maître* vanity, which is prouder of small vices than other men are of great virtues. . . . the true type of Parisian dandy, Bohemian, very indifferent as to the company he kept, but very particular as to the cut of his coat, the colour and quality of his gloves." He works while other men sleep and sleeps while they work. He abandons himself "to long intervals of absolute idleness . . . his periods of incubation. And then, when the purse" is "empty, and hunger" begins to pinch he will "take out a quire of paper and write for twenty hours at a stretch, like a maniac, producing . . . a one-act farce, an article for the 'Revue des deux Mondes,' a *feuilleton* for the 'Figaro,' criticism, verse, sentiment, satire." The only son of a nobleman, he is heir to "a much impoverished estate in the vicinity of Nîmes." Valnois admires both the working man and the aristocrat. He detests "your middle class—your *épicier*—your Philistine." Ishmael is astonished at his new friend, who is "steeped in German philosophy and poetry," who can "read Cervantes and Lope de Vega in Spanish," and who has "the gems of the Divine Comedy on the tip of his tongue."

The *coup* over, Ishmael is promoted to the rank of foreman at twice the pay. Visiting the theatre where his mother and her maid had performed in his childhood, he finds it rechristened "Le Palais de Cristal," after the

Crystal Palace built in Hyde Park for the London Exposition of 1851. He instantly recognizes one of the *chanteuses* as his old friend and nurse, his mother's maid, Lisette. Her song, an enchanting ballad of the young man whose sweetheart has a perpetual cold in the head, is the audience's favorite. Braving the initial jealousy of Lisette's husband, a *charcutier*, Ishmael re-introduces himself to her, and is invited back to their rooms over the shop "with . . . new mahogany furniture and bright yellow damask curtains, clock and candelabra in alabaster and gold, all paid for out of Lisette's salary."[30]

At five o'clock one morning, Ishmael finds Pâquerette sitting on the landing outside his apartment. She has fled from home, where her grandmother has been trying to force her to marry the *charabia*. With some difficulty Ishmael persuades Lisette to take her in. Even the single day that Pâquerette must pass alone in his apartment she finds intolerably dull: she can barely read, and Ishmael's books mean nothing to her: she has nothing to do but think and wonder, "vaguely, disjointedly, like a child." In reluctantly accepting responsibility for this waif, Ishmael has doomed his own life. Should Pâquerette be sent to a convent? Or should she go with Lisette on the stage—an idea that Ishmael opposes, although—or because—his own mother had done so long ago. Valnois advises Ishmael against a convent: the girl would be physically wretched and emotionally starved. He and Lisette argue for the *Palais de Cristal*. Once Pâquerette has made a hit, she will instantly be offered an engagement at a boulevard theatre. Already far too deeply interested in Pâquerette, Valnois writes songs for her to practice, raises her hopes for a career, and then, with five hundred francs and a copy of *Faust*, goes off to "his beloved Rhineland, . . . in which his student-life had been spent . . . which he pretended to love ever so much better than the soil from which his race had sprung." Unreconciled to the idea of Pâquerette's exposing herself in public, Ishmael discovers that her grandmother has been evicted from her hovel and has become a rag-picker, in a "settlement on the boulevard de la Révolte, near Clichy, a kind of fastness of the dangerous classes, known as the Cité du Soleil." After a happy day at the great gingerbread fair at Vincennes, in a moment of high emotion he offers to marry Pâquerette. His father will consent only on condition that his son renounce the name and estates of Caradec.

Proud of her new status as a housewife with a comfortable apartment, a piano, and music lessons, Pâquerette is, however, full of romantic ideas absorbed from novels—"George Sand, Feydeau, Sue, Dumas father and son." After their child has died, Ishmael's matter-of-fact abilities—he studies every night and is on his way to a partnership—pale before the brilliance of de Valnois, back from Germany, who cleverly feeds Pâquerette's discontent. He is selling off his lands and, as "Samson junior," is writing brilliant reviews. Moreover, his short poems, *Mes Nuits blanches*—the passionate cries of the young unchastened heart, singing of "Love, unbelief, the sickly envy of the poor and the badly placed against the rich and the renowned"—make a great critical stir. Two of them are "quoted in almost every review. One—Gethsemane—was blasphemous to audacity. The other—Cleopatra . . . ought to be burned by the public hangman." But both have "a certain weird power," and are "perfect in versification." So Valnois wins a reputation as one of the coming men. He now has a lavishly furnished *entresol* in a grand house:

> The chairs . . . covered with crimson satin, the gueridons . . . of that graceful Louis Seize style which the Empress had lately brought into fashion by her quest of Marie Antoinette relics, Barbedienne bronzes and Oriental jars, choice books in still choicer bindings, miniatures set in turquoise velvet, rare etchings of doubtful subjects.

Here, he is near the scenes of his early dissipations:

> The wildest nights of his wild youth had been spent in some of those underground dens, those haunts where the music was as vile as the liquor, the company viler than either. . . . Les Ecossaises, or . . . the Salamander, alias Crocodile . . . the Bas-Rhin, which a few years later was to be made famous by the feat of *Nini la Démocrate*, who, for a wager with a rival celebrity, *Hélène la Sévère,* drank fifty-five *bocks* in a single evening.

At the opera with Valnois, Pâquerette gazes at the Empress and at the leading *demi-mondaine,* Zanita, who, Valnois says, " 'has slain more people than any assassin . . . ruined more families than any fraudulent banker in England, where they grow that kind of thing to perfection. . . . She has peopled the Morgue. . . . She is a pestilence. . . . like absinthe, which everybody drinks nowadays.' " Valnois makes love to Pâquerette; she has stopped loving Ishmael—who, indeed, has never deeply loved her—and she is almost ready to be seduced.

Ishmael is still a member of proscribed "democratic" clubs, whose members cherish the dream of a Republic, but he has begun to be converted into a supporter of the regime: "He saw great works inaugurated, houses built for the labouring classes, hospitals, charitable institutions of all kinds, arising in the outskirts of Paris. He saw the city prosperous, beloved of the world. . . . If there were rottenness under this seeming prosperity, Ishmael had not found it out." The years of 1852–1854

> had been a time of golden harvests, of wonderful fortunes, wonderfully and fearfully made. It was a day of speculation, of estates and reputations staked upon the hazards of the Stock Exchange. . . . Workmen sold their furniture, wives robbed their husbands, clerks embezzled their employers' money. . . . From . . . quiet towns and villages, the people brought their savings of long years. . . . Of those who lost their all in this wild game, Paris heard very little . . . but she could point triumphantly to the men who had made their fortunes . . . whose spotless primrose gloves covered hands which had lately known no cover save the pockets of a shabby overcoat. Varnished boots shone upon feet that had but now been slipshod; whitest cuffs were worn by some with whom a shirt had once been an uncertainty; overcoats broke out into collars and linings of velvet or satin; and the unknown citizen of yesterday was to-day the patron of the arts.

This is the "honeymoon of France and the Emperor," amidst the enthusiasm for the new war in the Crimea and the first outbreaks of cholera in 1854, while the "ribald jesters . . . cried 'À ta santé, Morbus!' as they tossed off their *cogne* or their *pétrole* at the wineshops on the road to the overcrowded cemetery."

When cholera wipes out Ishmael's family, he comes into his inheritance after all, and begins to invest his capital in Paris real estate, profiting by his special knowledge. Just before Ishmael's father dies, he mistakes his son for the seducer of his first wife, whom he had killed so long ago in the duel on Mauritius. Nor is this error of a dying man's clouded brain a chance one. In Ishmael, the Zola theory of hereditary destiny was at work: like the father many years before, the son loses his wife to a seducer; Pâquerette runs off with Valnois, just as her own mother had run off. When Ishmael discovers the elopement, he rushes to Valnois's rooms and kicks over "the slender marquetry toilet-table, all smiling with loves and graces, and comedy masks, and garlands of roses, and cloven-footed satyrs lurking among Cupids . . . the fragile *bonheur du jour* in amber-tinted satin and ormolu, lined with sky-blue moiré, stuffed with love-letters,

loaded with bibelots in porcelain, gold, and ivory." Then he scrawls a challenge: " 'My father killed the man who stole his wife. I am a stronger
man than my father, and I have less to lose. If it is in our race—an
hereditary doom—to be unhappy in our wives, it is also in our race to
revenge our wrongs.' " When Ishmael vows that he will kill Pâquerette,
Lisette answers only: " 'Life is troublesome enough . . . one does not want
to cut it short by spitting in the basket' " which is slang for being guil-
lotined.[31] With the disappearance of Valnois and Pâquerette in 1854, the
curtain comes down on the novel for thirteen years.

When it rises again, at the Paris International Exhibition of 1867, the
great Frenchmen and foreigners of the Empire's early days—Morny,
Palmerston, Cavour, King Leopold—have all died. Paris has been made
over, its "broad boulevards piercing east and west and north and south, . . .
mighty theatres, and newly-erected churches . . . as gaudy in colour as a
mediaeval chasse or an Indian tomb, . . . new bridges . . . parks and palaces,
fountains and gardens, villas and avenues," and new suburbs, "dotted
about with Swiss châlets, Norman châteaux, Italian villas." In this
opulent new Paris, "city of dissipation, pleasure, luxury, extravagance,
and ruin—a gulf for men's fortunes, a pest-house for men's health, a grave
for intellect, honour, manhood, religion—and quite the most delightful city
in the world," even the *demi-monde* has changed. Cora Pearl, the
celebrated *cocotte*, has taught "the women of Paris to enamel their faces,
to paint their eyebrows and eyelids, to draw blue veins upon their
alabaster foreheads, to wear a cascade of somebody else's hair flowing
down their backs like a horse's tail. . . . invented short petticoats, Polish
boots, chaînes Benoîtons." And the ladies of the imperial court have *"lived
. . . rubbed shoulders"* with Cora and her sisterhood. Though the Empress
is "lovely, graceful, gracious, a woman of exquisite taste," Cora has
"chic," and her influence extends even more widely.

Ishmael, many times a millionaire, falls in love with the widowed Lady
Constance Danetree, beautiful and rich, living at twenty-six a "life of
perfect independence" but irreproachable morally, as she moves among
these doubtful ladies of the court. He has a house in the Place Royale
(Place des Vosges) and a fine library. As a philanthropist he has founded a
home for poor children. But even now he does not know what has happened to Pâquerette; so he tells Constance that he cannot marry. Despite
his new affluence, he is still a member of his old workmen's secret society,
giving the password in a "low dark wineshop" at the corner of the rue St.
Honoré and the rue Pirouette: " 'Es tu solide?' " asks the lookout, and
" 'Jusqu'à la rue de Jérusalem' " is Ishmael's answer. It admits him into the

company of the Cercle du Prolo, founded in 1831 as the Société de la Loque, "now about to be affiliated with the International . . . to bring about the socialist millennium of equal fortunes, of direct legislation by the people, of which French workmen have been thinking ever since they learned how to think." A "capitalist," a "bourgeois," and "hated one," Ishmael attends his first meeting in seven years, to "protest against the amalgamation of this little honest-hearted society with the most pernicious and fatal association which ever threatened the peace of civilised Europe." He opposes the "iron discipline, the mechanical drill involved in the Karl-Marxian theory of Socialism." Behind it he sees "the working of one mind, . . . the mind of a dangerous visionary . . . the shadow of German despotism, a despotism of the socialist as perilous as the despotism of the monarch." He denounces "Karl Marx and his theories, . . . the dangers they involve, . . . their falsehood, their impossibility." But the majority of the audience is against him: he is the *patron*, the enemy.

To trace Pâquerette, Ishmael employs an unscrupulous private investigator, who interrogates de Valnois, now back in Paris rewriting other people's plays and ghost-writing decadent verses, "short detached lyrics—brief flights in the fashion of Heine—spasmodic, inconsecutive," which are published as his own by the latest fashionable poet. Valnois says that Pâquerette had long since left him after a quarrel and he does not know where she is. So the detective forges evidence that she is dead, whereupon Ishmael proposes to Constance and is accepted. He foregoes his vengeance and even sends Valnois money.

Near Clichy, "a region as little known to the ordinary Parisian as the North Pole itself," in the settlement of the rag-pickers, the Cité du Soleil, so-called because sunflowers grow around the squalid hovels of the rag-pickers, Pâquerette is actually living with her aged grandmother.

> The narrow alleys . . . are mere muddy channels, in which children, dogs, and swine crawl and grovel, fighting with each other for the bones, the stale cabbage stumps, the putrid lobster-shells, which fall from the rag-picker's baskets. The fronts of the rotten old hovels are decorated with skeletons of cats, skulls of dogs, foxes' brushes. The sickening stench of the place overpowers the passer-by at ten yards distance.

Pâquerette is dying of lung disease. When she overhears two Italian revolutionaries who are about to assassinate Ishmael as a traitor to socialism, she manages to interpose herself, and receives the dagger-thrust meant for him. Before she dies, Ishmael forgives her. He marries Lady Constance and resumes his family name. "Ishmael, the despised, the outcast, had redeemed the fortune of his race."

MEB had made the characters in *Ishmael* more than mere actors in the drama of their own lives: they are personages of the Second Empire. Amidst the splendors of 1867 Paris, she duly noted that "the diplomatists and statesmen who came to see the show . . . knew that the glory of the Empire had grown old." Taciturn and isolated, Napoleon III "reads little; he wrote no more. [He] was wrapped in his dream, and the dream was slowly darkening to the blackness of night." As *Ishmael* draws to a close, "trouble and confusion" are "in the minds of men . . . caught between an Empire . . . no longer Imperial in its policy, and a constitution" not yet created. Rumors circulate of explosives being manufactured in cellars, and of a secret society called the "Commune Révolutionnaire des Ouvriers de Paris." Persigny writes to his master, " 'The Empire crumbles on every side. Your enemies, under the pretext of founding a parliamentary *régime*, have sworn your ruin; your ministers truckle to your adversaries . . . your house is in flames.' "

Against this sombre background comes the final episode in the novel: Hector de Valnois one morning in 1867 is found dead, hanging from an iron bar of a window of a house in the rue de la Vieille Lanterne, an ancient street in a criminal neighborhood. Identified by a medical student as a brilliant talker who has been killing himself with absinthe, and mourned as a once-great poet, he is given a fine funeral, and a speech is made "by a young advocate called Rouméstan, who is going to be one of the greatest men in France." And within a week after the suicide, the fashionable poet who has been buying Valnois's verses all along publishes them as his own in his second volume, *Charniers et Sépulcres,* "the last development of the spasmodic school, *du Baudelaire poussé au vif* . . . bitter as absinthe; despairing; the death throes of a life's agony."[32]

In *Ishmael,* MEB had written not so much a novel influenced by Zola as a Zola novel. As if, like the master himself, she had traveled about the scenes of her story with a notebook, writing down precise information about the lives of Paris bricklayers, laundresses, *ébénistes,* cabaret-singers, engineers, and rag-pickers, she had made herself the master of the details of their daily existence, their houses, their conditions of labor, their earnings, their feelings. But the details did not obtrude: *Ishmael* is no sociological treatise, but a novel about real people presented naturalistically, in the critical as well as the literal sense of those terms. The achievement was the more remarkable because MEB had never lived in Paris; her spoken French retained an English accent to the end of her life; and she did not—because she could not—conduct a series of Zola-like inquiries *sur place*. Except for occasional impressions which as a tourist in Brittany or in Paris she had retained and written down, *Ishmael* came to her from reading.

She had read French fluently since childhood. As a girl, she had been a fanatical admirer of Napoleon I and she was only seventeen when his nephew became Emperor. When Napoleon III fell, she was thirty-five. Now in 1884, at forty-nine and at the height of her powers, she took a long retrospective look at the Empire whose whole life-span she had observed and about which she had been reading in newspapers and periodicals, in books of fiction and nonfiction, throughout its existence and during the dozen years since its fall. Twice in February 1884, for example, she noted that she was reading "Delord's Empire," which is surely Taxile Delord's *Histoire du Second Empire (1848–1869)*, published in six stout volumes between 1869 and 1875. Here, for example, she could have studied the history of Louis Napoleon's *coup d'état* of December 1851, of which she gave so vivid a picture in *Ishmael*.

When Ishmael mounts the barricades with the representative Baudin, "a group of blouses [workmen]" at the street-corner call out, " 'Down with the twenty-five francs,' " in scornful allusion to the daily salaries of the representatives, and Baudin replies, " 'You shall see how a man can die for twenty-five francs.' " This anecdote, together with a useful analysis of public opinion, MEB could have found in Delord. In his version, a workman to whom Baudin was handing a gun says sardonically, " 'Plus souvent que nous nous ferons tuer pour vous conserver vos vingt-cinq francs [Fat chance that we'll get ourselves killed to save you your twenty-five francs],' " to which Baudin then answers " 'Citoyen, tu vas voir comment on meurt pour vingt-cinq francs.' " Had she read Eugène Ténot's work on the *coup d'état*—and perhaps she had—she would have found a slightly different dialogue: "Est-ce que vous croyez que nous voulons nous faire tuer pour vous conserver vos vingt-cinq francs par jour?" "Demeurez là un instant, mon ami, . . . et vous allez voir comment on meurt pour vingt-cinq francs!" The story passed current at the time, though it is now regarded as legend.

Since in *Ishmael* MEB skipped the years between 1854 and 1867 and ended the novel in 1868, only the fifth volume of Delord's work would have been useful to her in addition to the first. In Volume V she could conveniently have found the text of Persigny's letter to Napoleon III, warning of the general decay, which she used effectively.[33] She probably took from Delord not only such details but some of the coloring for her comments on politics. Yet she did not adopt his unwavering hostility to Napoleon III, but recognized the Emperor's strengths as well as his weaknesses.

For the extraordinary series of pictures that MEB painted of various Parisian domiciles—from the rue de Sombreuil and the miserable house where Pâquerette grew up and Ishmael's workman's chamber, upward through Lisette's tidy apartment over the *charcuterie* and Ishmael's larger quarters as a foreman, to his house in the Place des Vosges and Lady Constance's villa in the Bois or the great *hôtel* of the Faubourg Saint-Germain where a ball is given, and down again to the squalor of the rag-pickers' City of the Sun—I have found no specific source in MEB's reading except for the last. Only a few months before she began to write *Ishmael,* the *Revue des Deux Mondes,* in an article by Othenin d'Haussonville, included an account of the rag-pickers' settlements. She often read the *Revue des Deux Mondes*; so quite possibly she read this article and transformed its rather colorless prose into the vivid account of the squalid place to which Pâquerette and her wretched grandmother had drifted.[34] The scenes at the *café-chantant,* with the text of Lisette's wonderful song, and at the Opéra, MEB may have taken from her own experience on trips to Paris.

Her political sophistication comes as a somewhat greater surprise: even after one has read *Under the Red Flag* and has appreciated how clearly she understood the forces at work during the Commune, one is still taken aback at her thorough awareness of the different shades of opinion during the years 1851–1854 and 1867–1868. By making Ishmael a "red" during the *coup* and expounding his political beliefs with sympathy, MEB naturally prepared the way for 1867, when she took her reader into his "Cercle du Prolo"—which had grown from the earlier "Société de la Loque"—and reported his entirely plausible views of the dangers of Marxism. Like the social life of all levels that is so much a part of *Ishmael,* the varieties of left-wing political belief formed an integral and necessary portion of the personalities of her characters and so were transmuted into fiction, although they were perfectly accurate historically.

Almost everything about the career of MEB's Hector de Valnois, down to the very name and character of the street where he is found hanging, she took from the career of Gérard de Nerval. It is true that Nerval committed suicide in the rue de la Vieille Lanterne in 1855, rather than in 1867, but it was necessary for MEB's plot to have Valnois live during the dozen years between those dates. Of course, Valnois's rescue of Ishmael

on the night of the *coup d'état* was pure fiction. Nor was the historic
Gérard de Nerval the sort of man who would have run off with Pâquerette. Highly neurotic, he had never known his mother and seems to
have preferred to worship women from afar. Pâquerette in any case was
no Jenny Colon or Marie Pleyel. But Nerval scholarship was hardly so
advanced in MEB's day, and it was fiction she was writing after all. She
would probably have read the two admiring essays that Théophile
Gautier wrote, twelve years apart, in 1855 and 1867, about his old friend.

Nerval's affection for old furniture and *objets* was one characteristic
with which MEB endowed her Valnois; but Nerval never enjoyed any
apartment half so luxurious as that in which she installed Valnois during
the days of his prosperity. The bibelots had to be there, however, for
Ishmael to smash in his wrath. Valnois's love for Germany and his visit
there with five hundred francs and a copy of *Faust* in his pocket were
perfectly in character with Nerval, the successful translator of *Faust*, who
was always deeply stirred by the land in which his mother had died in his
infancy. Perhaps unaware that "de Nerval" was a pseudonym that Gérard
Labrunie had adopted to ennoble himself, and that the ancestral estate in
Nîmes was just one of his fantasies, MEB gave a genuine noble ancestry
and inheritance to her fictional Valnois. Valnois's habits of writing were
Nerval's, and his *Mes Nuits blanches* a recognizably Nerval collection.
The poem "Gethsemane" which MEB called "blasphemous to audacity"
corresponds to Nerval's "Le Christ aux oliviers," from *Les Chimères*. The
"Cleopatra" which "ought to be burned by the public hangman" may
have been invented by MEB. She surely invented the funeral oration
given for Valnois, by the coming young lawyer, Rouméstan: Rouméstan
was the eponymous hero of Daudet's novel, *Numa Rouméstan*, and so not
a historic but a fictional personage. As for Nerval's mysticism and
madness, MEB made no effort to deal with them. Even without them,
Valnois—because she had created him so largely as a portrait of a real
poet—added still more realism to the realistic *Ishmael*.[35]

MEB did not entirely succeed in leaping the thirteen-year interval
between the earlier and the later portions of *Ishmael*. By the time the
reader meets Lady Constance, the love of Ishmael's life, it is too late to
know her as intimately as the other important personages. Nor is she
entirely credible or agreeable: would so appealing a woman have led so
futile a life, moving in ennui from one social event to the next, cushioned
by her great wealth, never as aware as the philanthropic Ishmael of the
misery about her or making any effort to alleviate it? And would Ishmael,
even in his new phase as a very rich man, have fallen in love with so

ordinary a woman? Perhaps she would have suited the stodginess in him. Perhaps MEB was adding a pinch of sardonic social commentary to what appeared to be a passionately romantic and eminently "suitable" love affair. In *Ishmael,* the fortunes of her personages—save of course for the vagaries of historic forces—arose directly from their own characters, solidly and convincingly drawn.

The *Spectator,* while admitting that it liked her "New Forest and Cornwall stories" better, declared that *Ishmael* was "by far the cleverest" of her novels. In "vigour, vivacity, and variety" it was MEB at her best. "There is exuberant life in the story, not a trace of fatigue, or distaste, or decline of fancy." It paid tribute to MEB's "diligent and extensive reading and assimilation of the history, memoirs, and newspaper literature of the period," and praised the character of Ishmael, but felt that MEB "fails to excite strong sympathy for Pâquerette." So richly did Pâquerette deserve her misery "that we cannot resist the conviction that Miss Braddon herself never cared at all about her," to which one might reply that MEB had effectively shown what would happen if an essentially empty-headed girl with a longing to go on the stage were condemned to sit with nothing but piano lessons and novels for amusement all day, and at night to watch a rather unsympathetic husband work on advanced engineering problems. When one puts Pâquerette's plight in these terms one realizes that Ishmael rather than Pâquerette was the instrument that revived the ancestral tradition of marital betrayal on both sides of the family, and made certain its continuation.

The *Spectator* critic also doubted that "such a man as Ishmael would . . . have smashed de Valnois's furniture." But Ishmael's father had been so determined to avenge his honor that he had traveled all the way out to the Indian Ocean to kill his friend for eloping with his wife. Finding family history repeating itself, Ishmael's resolve to kill his man was so frustrated that his explosion of rage amidst the bric-a-brac seems perfectly plausible behavior. But these (quite unjust) strictures did not prevent the critic from concluding that MEB's picture of the time was "altogether admirable," and "the rush, the flow, the animation . . . very remarkable."[36] Zola was still too little known in England to be recognized as a possible inspiration.

All that contributes to the interest of MEB's next novel, *Wyllard's Weird,*[37] is found in its French scenes, into which MEB apparently put some leftover bits she had been unable to use in *Ishmael.* The young French girl who fell to her death from the London train as it crossed the viaduct into Cornwall was pushed into the abyss by Julian Wyllard, a local landowner, because she alone could prove that in his youth in Paris he had committed a *crime passionel,* shooting his mistresss and her new lover. As the crime is investigated, the English sleuth meets a series of remarkable French personages.

There is the Paris detective, in his loose summer suit of white linen, relaxing with his cigars, his newspapers, and his poodle in his rooftop garden with its potted flowers and its nasturtium-vine, or expatiating in his neat salon downstairs upon his library of police reports or his collection of framed engravings of notorious murders. A kind of Braddonian Maigret, he derived perhaps from Gaboriau or Fortuné de Boisgobey rather than from Zola. There is the aged dressmaker almost starving in her dingy workrooms and pathetically eager for a glass of wine. There is the "paragraphist" for the press, who "knew the Paris of the Third Republic as well as Saint-Simon knew the Paris of the great Louis," a Bohemian, "a haunter of supper-tables and gambling-dens, a hanger-on of lorettes, steeped to the tips of his nails in the atmosphere of the *demi-monde,* a man who had known Gautier and Nerval and Gustave Planche, an *habitué* of the Boulevard theatres." There is the aged baroness, mother of the man murdered so long ago, solitary in her Norman château, with the parquet floors gleaming, reading nothing but her missal and Thomas à Kempis' *Imitation of Christ,* erect in her chair like Delaroche's portrait of Marie Antoinette. There is a painter now far gone in decay, but still a keen critic of English painting—" 'There are heads by Gainsborough and Reynolds which leave very little to be desired; though the treatment of the arms and hands is sometimes deplorably flimsy. . . . Your Millais has a Rubens-like *brio,* but he paints with a butter-knife. Your Leighton has grace, and a keen feeling for beauty, but he is cold and shadowy,' "[38]— in whose portfolio there lies the portrait drawing of the murderer that proves him to have been Julian Wyllard. Any of these might have walked out of the pages of *Ishmael* itself. In this respect, as a postscript to that great novel, the otherwise somewhat mechanical *Wyllard's Weird* retains an interest all its own. It is a measure of the curious insensitivity of contemporary English critics that the *Spectator* reviewer preferred it to *Ishmael,* although it was "not so clever," and lavished on its conventional cardboard English characters far more enthusiasm than on the full-bodied French creations of its predecessor.[39]

6. Epilogue: MEB on Zola, 1885

On February 12, 1885, MEB wrote in her diary "Began Zola article," and on March 17 "Despatched Zola article." Where she sent it I do not know, and apparently it remained unpublished. But the original manuscript survived among her papers, with her note on the outside leaf: "If accepted, proofs are to be sent to Mrs. Maxwell, Lichfield House, Richmond, Surrey." So the article had not been commissioned, and MEB was prepared for its rejection.[40]

Even now, Zola was little known and much denounced in England. As early as 1877, Swinburne—smacking his lips, however, over the details—had attacked *L'Assommoir* when its serial publication in France had been suspended, and in 1878 the first full-length criticism of the book in England proudly contrasted English reticence with French "ordure." Reade's highly dilute dramatic version—*Drink*—with Charles Warner playing Coupeau, DT's and all, outraged many critics. Andrew Lang in 1882 regretted the "unfortunate" English Puritanism that would prevent Zola from being understood in England, but he too thought *Thérèse Raquin* "repulsive" and *Nana* a gloating "appeal to the basest curiosities." *The Scottish Review* for 1883 expressed equal horror. It was late in 1884 that Henry Vizetelly (1820–1894)—who in 1858 had founded *The Welcome Guest* and more recently had published Longfellow, Harriet Beecher Stowe, and many French authors in England—brought out the first English translations of Zola: *Nana* and *L'Assommoir,* followed by other novels in the next year. In 1888, in a celebrated case, Vizetelly would be arrested and fined for "obscene libel"—"My dear Aurora," Edmund Yates wrote MEB on October 20, 1888, ". . . just summoned to go to the Old Bailey tomorrow and say all I can for poor old Viz"[41]—and in 1889 Vizetelly would be sent to prison.

In March 1885, then, Zola was becoming known and feared in England as an obscene writer. In her essay, "Émile Zola and the Naturalistic School, or Realism in French Literature," MEB indicated her own repugnance at much of what he had written. But she managed to set Zola in his proper place in the history of French literature, and to show herself a scholarly and independent literary critic.

Before Flaubert's *Madame Bovary* had appeared almost thirty years ago, she began, it was "popularly supposed" that Balzac "had gone as far in the analysis of vice" as genius could go. "But Balzac was not a realist in the modern sense of the word. He was an analyst, but not a naturalist.

The atmosphere of romance pervades all his books. . . . The love of the ugly had no place." No matter how low in the social scale Balzac descended, he always provided "the counterbalance of beauty, luxury, refinement."

Then came *Madame Bovary*, in which Flaubert, the "physiologist, the analytical student, the vivisectionist," left Balzac far behind. "In cold blood and with a passionless pen [he] traces the degradation of a selfish young woman . . . from dull provincial respectability . . . to the nethermost deep of infamy." Although there was "some touch of poetic feeling" in Emma Bovary's first liaison, her second was "gross and shameless." In Flaubert's telling of the story, "every sentence was the result of intense thought and study. . . . every line . . . true and clear as the lines of a marble figure, every phrase . . . instinct with life." There was much affinity between Emma Bovary and Hetty Sorrel, and between Flaubert and George Eliot, though she was more tender and reticent than he. Prosecuted for *Madame Bovary*, Flaubert had been acquitted. The novel had become a classic. And compared with later realistic novels, it was "the very mildest of improper stories, which seems to exhale an atmosphere of buttermilk or curds and whey as compared with the reeking odours of vitriol and *sang de boeuf* which pervade the novels of M. Émile Zola. *Plus avant* is M. Zola's motto."

As a critic, Zola had saluted the victory of Flaubert over the correctional tribunal, and welcomed "that wider license which has been given to himself . . . to depict all that is most horrible in modern Paris, from the open infamy roaming the *barrières* after dark to the occult vices of the boudoir." Zola felt himself entitled "to wallow in filthiness of every kind, from the drunken orgies of a party of courtesans to the grosser details of a difficult accouchement." He had praised the Goncourts' *Germinie Lacerteux*, "one of the most hideous stories ever written," and boldly claimed the right "to describe humanity upon every side and under every aspect, however revolting." And the Goncourts looked forward to the day when the "world of rank and fashion" would be subjected to the same sort of analysis that had "hitherto been exercised only upon the lower grades of society."

In *Nana* and in *La Curée* Zola had in fact done just that. MEB objected to Zola's "sounding the depths of sensuality and reducing womanhood to the level of brute beasts" in *La Fortune des Rougon*; she complained that he would not "spare us even the vicious propensities of a domestic cat," and had contrived "to be distinctly immoral in his description of the tropical plants and flowers in a conservatory." *La Curée* MEB thought a ghastly tale brilliantly presented—we have seen her adapting elements from it in *Phantom Fortune*. She now even translated the key conversations between Renée and her stepson, hitherto not known in English, all the while protesting that they exemplified "vice secret, vice obvious, and vice obscure, everywhere infamy and horror." Zola's detailed descriptions of vicious women at a Paris ball had "not one throb of real passion." In *La Curée*, in *Thérèse Raquin*, "It is all morbid anatomy: as one reads, one imagines M. Zola, cool as a cucumber, revelling in his demonstrations of humanity's vileness. . . . He delights in descriptions of diseases," and MEB rehearsed a long list of clinical descriptions of illness in his novels. Either he had a "morbid love of the horrible . . . or a perverse vanity which compels him to display his technical knowledge" of medical subjects. This "hankering after the loathsome, this rage for describing hideous sights and foul smells, vicious inclinations and unnatural passions" MEB thought "must indicate a morbid strain . . . such as that . . . in the writings of Jonathan Swift."

MEB explained the key importance of Adelaide Fouque, ancestress of the whole brood of Rougons and Macquarts, "M. Zola's Cybele," and called attention to the genealogical tree that Zola had published, showing each member's "heredity and natural predispositions." Then she retold in great detail and analyzed the story of Gervaise in *La Fortune des Rougon* and especially in *L'Assommoir*. Having shown her horror at many aspects of Zola, she now nonetheless found *L'Assommoir* his "cleverest" book, which fulfilled "the aims of Greek tragedy," and had deeply moved her by pity and terror: "It is almost as if he had lived with these people. . . . And by that potent faculty of mental imitation, *he has achieved the most wonderful book that was ever written about the working classes of any country* [italics mine]." Though MEB continued to voice her objections to gross details, this sentence represented the essence of her critical judgment—and very sound critical judgment it was, indeed extraordinary for an Englishwoman in 1885. The slow degeneration of a drunkard she had taken from *L'Assommoir* and had put into her own novel, *The Golden Calf*. Now she paid open tribute to the source of her inspiration. More than one-third of the essay she gave to *L'Assommoir*, translating some of the more pathetic passages; dwelling in admiration upon the character of Lantier, "an elaborate study of the genus scamp, sleek, plausible, and crafty, a hanger-on of foolish women, sensuous, self-indulgent, smart of exterior, filthy underneath . . . a past-master in the art of living upon other people"; and ending where Zola had ended, with the drunken undertaker, whose symbolic value throughout the novel she had thoroughly appreciated.

Having hidden her eloquent praise for Zola amidst her protestations of revulsion, MEB went on to denounce *Nana* ("There is no lesson, except that the more vicious a woman is, the more devoted are her admirers. . . . Nana is . . . vice incarnate . . . the avenging angel sent to wreak heaven's vengeance upon the corruptions of the great city. . . . an abominable book, serving no purpose, pointing no moral, but like all Zola's later novels . . . written by the hand of a master"), *Pot-Bouille* (". . . not one worthy character or agreeable episode . . ."), and *Une Page d'amour* ("There is . . . no reason why Helen should fall except that M. Zola wills it so"). *Au Bonheur des Dames* was "the most respectable and perhaps the best," and was not "immoral or filthy," yet MEB gave it less than a fifth of the space she devoted to *L'Assommoir*. And *La Joie de Vivre* was ". . . a most dreary and disgusting book." Zola, a great success in France, was, she concluded, ". . . a master of his art . . . the most imaginative writer in France. . . . a master of humour and . . . a master of pathos. . . . a consummate artist." He needed only "moderation and decency, the common self-restraint which good feeling should impose upon every writer of fiction."

MEB's 1885 essay on Zola marked the end of her own "Zola period." It is an example of advanced literary criticism in which an experienced Victorian woman of letters and of the world resourcefully faced up to a *nouvelle vague* in literature. It is an instructive example of the art of proclaiming what would certainly be an unpopular critical judgment, while hedging it about with what would certainly be popular reservations. It provides a model of MEB's own literary discrimination, taste, wisdom, and easy critical prose style. But it is also, after more than ninety years, a first-rate essay on Zola's writings before 1885. In 1890, she wrote in French an entertaining parody of Zola for *Punch*. And in 1897, reading Zola's new novel, *Rome*, MEB commented that he was "a wonderful genius in his power to enter into the minds and passions" of all sorts of men, from the pope himself to the driver of an engine, thus acutely singling out perhaps the chief merit of one of his least successful novels.[42]

CHAPTER IX

"It Is As Natural for Her to Write As It Is for a Mountain Torrent to Flow" (1885–1895)

The year 1885 provided us with a convenient landmark in MEB's professional life, as she turned away from her long preoccupation with France and French subjects. Over this watershed her private life continued as before. Ten years later in 1895 John Maxwell died, ending their thirty-four years of intimate association. And in that same year, she published her forty-eighth and last three-volume novel: *Sons of Fire*. Standard in England for about a century, the three-decker gave way in the late nineties to the one-volume novel, a drastic change, in effect ending the Victorian age for publishers, readers, and writers alike. Thus the decade 1885–1895 was at once the last decade of MEB's marriage and of her career as a Victorian novelist. When it ended, she had turned sixty. Ahead lay twenty years of widowhood and a new Edwardian and early Georgian career.

In the late eighties and early nineties MEB spent long periods of time in Europe with her family. She was always anxious about her husband's health. Her daughters married and had children; her sons were more or less certainly launched on professional careers: Gerald as an actor, Will as an editor and writer, Ted as a barrister-in-embryo. After 1891, with John Maxwell increasingly invalided, MEB's own horizons also perforce narrowed, and she devoted more and more time and energy to helping with his care and reading aloud to him.

Her writing reflected the vicissitudes of her life. She did not try her hand at a second Euripidean or Hardyesque classical tragedy like *Joshua Haggard's Daughter*, nor could she now give her work the single-minded attention necessary for a second novel like *Ishmael*. So the nine three-volume novels, the pair of two-volume novels, and the harvest of shorter fiction that she published included nothing that required the painstaking Zolaesque preliminary gathering of data, a vein which in any case she may have felt she had already exploited. Instead she reverted to her own specialties, sensation more or less laced with social satire, which—in *One*

Thing Needful (1886) —embraced also a more explicit personal political viewpoint than she had yet revealed.

In *The Fatal Three* (1888), she wrote the best sensation-novel of her entire career. It depended entirely upon psychological observation that displayed a new depth, perceptiveness, and certainty. But at least five novels of the decade—notably the last three—showed a marked falling-off in quality, written as they were in the shadow of worry about John Maxwell. One suspects that MEB kept on writing compulsively, as a means of forgetting her troubles. Even in novels that fell short of her highest level she found opportunity for picturesque and pungent social commentary, notably in *Gerard* (1891).

For business reasons MEB personally defied those who were hastening the death of the three-volume novel. But she was so well prepared for it that by 1895 she had already written three complete one-volume novels which were ready for publication once the fashion should change definitively. Inwardly she was probably reconciled—perhaps even not sorry—to see the three-decker die, to streamline her writing, to experiment with the shorter form, to embark—in due course—upon a wholly new phase as a writer. Her widowhood brought her instant grief and a difficult problem of readjustment. More than ever she would lean on Will's freely offered companionship and support, while as novelists they both began to ponder the relationships between sons and mothers.

1. "The Feast Is the Feast of Our Grandfathers"

"Amiable, kindly, introspective," MEB in 1887 seemed a "pleasant matron-like woman above the medium height," fair but "with a complexion suggesting more of horse exercise and open air than hard work in a library." She had, the observer continued, "a broad, firm compact forehead. Her eyes are small, and look a trifle tired; her mouth small, and full of character: firm lips, a small chin." Twenty-two years after Frith had painted her, she was at fifty-two quite recognizable still as the subject of that youthful portrait. The formal interview, invented in America, in England often seemed an invasion of privacy. But in this instance the interviewer was Joseph Hatton, novelist and reporter, who had been a personal friend of MEB's for twenty years; he assured his readers that his interests were literary rather than merely journalistic.

In his article, "Miss Braddon at Home," Hatton gave the public its first description of Lichfield House. The "noble" drawing-room with three bays, of which two were filled with "superb stained glass," had its walls "crowded" with works of art. There were cabinets full of bric-à-brac, easy chairs, a grand piano, a harmonium, and a table covered with current books and newspapers. Hatton noticed Frith's autobiography, which had just appeared, a volume of the *Life* of Darwin, a new edition of Rider Haggard's *King Solomon's Mines*, the issue of the *New York Tribune* containing a review of Henry Irving's opening American performance in *Faust*, a copy of MEB's *Mistletoe Bough*, and the current number of *Belgravia*, which she had not edited for eleven years. In the breakfast-room, Hatton was shown the little table on which the Duke of Wellington had written the despatch that told of the victory at Waterloo, "so con-structed that it is either a despatch-box, a card-table, a chess-table, or a writing-desk."

While MEB gave some orders to the servants, her husband, "Max . . . hale, hearty, and breezy despite his sixty-odd years," showed Hatton some newly acquired paintings: a David Cox, a Clarkson Stanfield, and two Linnells. And there in the breakfast-room, in a splendid English mar-quetry bookcase, was a collection of large volumes bound in red morocco. " 'The Braddon novels,' " Max exclaimed, " 'the original manuscripts.' " Here, he declared, was the evidence to confound any future doubter who might protest that no one person could possibly have written "so much and so well." When Hatton asked to see the manuscript of *Lady Audley's Secret*, Maxwell told him that it had been burnt in a fire at the publisher's office. At that moment, MEB rejoined them and added, " 'The truth is, Max did not think so much of my manuscripts in those days,' " and she herself had never thought of preserving them. Then lunch was announced.

In the "plain, comfortable" dining-room stood a sideboard which had been in the Crystal Palace Exhibition of 1851 and chairs designed by Inigo Jones. The fireplace was carved in black marble; and the paintings included the Frith portrait of MEB, a head by Alma Tadema, a Ruysdael, a pair of Stanfields, and "several" Gainsboroughs. The Maxwell hospital-ity was old-fashioned. "The feast is the feast of our grandfathers." Host and hostess and friends carved at table, and the "good old custom of 'tak-ing wine' " was maintained between the Maxwells and their guests. When Hatton complimented MEB on this, she answered that indeed she was a conservative in her taste " 'and if I am a politician, I am a Tory,' " perhaps not altogether "on strict principles," but "by birth and instinct. 'I love old things, old habits, old houses, old customs, old trees, old halls, old costumes.' "

After lunch, she showed Hatton her study, a large square room looking out on the garden. Here were her many books of reference, her large collection of French literature, including almost all of Tom Taylor's French library, which she had bought, and the works of Dickens, Scott, George Eliot, Lamb, and Madame de Stael, with "a host of old comedies." Everything was thoroughly businesslike, the bookcases plain and solid, a desk "that might have been made for a merchant's office," easy chairs and writing-chairs, no piano, no guitar, but a bright fire on the hearth. MEB allowed Hatton to examine one of her many "commonplace books," filled with extracts copied from books and newspapers. She chatted with him about her reading. She had, she maintained a bit disingenuously, read few contemporary English novelists and "more French stories than English."

And she openly avowed—as she would not have done in 1862—her debt to Wilkie Collins: " 'I always say that I owe "Lady Audley's Secret" to "The Woman in White." Wilkie Collins is assuredly my literary father.' " She had so greatly admired *The Woman in White* that it had inspired her with the idea for *Lady Audley's Secret* " 'as a novel of construction and character.' " She also told how generous Bulwer had been to her in her youth. Before Hatton left, Max handed him a stirrup cup of choice whiskey, with a little lemon juice and a dash of boiling water. The Maxwells were leaving next day to spend the winter in San Remo.[1]

The interview gave curious contemporaries, as it gives us still, a welcome glimpse of MEB, the mature and successful novelist, in her workshop, at her own fireside, in her luxurious eighteenth-century house packed with Victorian furniture, stained glass, pictures, bric-à-brac, and books, and with her husband at their hospitable board. Ever up-to-date, MEB must have realized the value of this new-fangled sort of publicity. She omitted certain matters which were none of Hatton's or the public's business. For example, in acknowledging her fondness for French literature and calling attention to her possession of Tom Taylor's French library, she said nothing of the use that both Taylor and she had made of French drama and fiction. Similarly, in proclaiming her Toryism, she said nothing about her radical version of the Tory creed, or about her deep-rooted dislike and distrust for the upper classes and their snobbery. These views she put into her novels, secure in her belief that most of her readers would not find them there.

Although John Maxwell seemed "hale, hearty, and breezy" in 1887, he had already retired from his publishing house on his doctor's orders.

Long ago he had missed a chance to grow rich when he had sold a half-interest in the *Standard* newspaper in order to make settlements on the five children of his first marriage. Had he held on, his income from the *Standard* alone during the seventies and later would have been forty-five thousand pounds a year. But the publishing house earned enough to pay all the family bills, and MEB saved her own earnings. In retirement Max fretted, walking about the house and murmuring to himself, " 'What have I got to think about next?' " And although MEB eagerly replied, " 'Dear Max, you have *nothing* to think about—only to rest and take things easily,' " it made no difference. It was too late for him to learn to relax.[2] Maxwell had illnesses every year—MEB noting laconically in her diaries his strained shoulder, his "incessant cough" necessitating consultations with the celebrated Morell MacKenzie, an accident to his leg, and his numerous "bilious attacks"—but he remained active until 1891.

During the late 1880's the family spent much time abroad. In January 1887, with Max, Will, Rosie, and Ted, MEB went off via Paris, Lyon, and Marseille, to Cannes, where they took a large fourth-floor apartment in a building called La Madeleine, with two bedrooms, a dressing-room, a salon, and a dining-room, and a large additional room for Will and Ted on the ground floor. The diary entry for February 23 is characteristically intrepid: "Earthquake 6:00 A.M. Walked morning with R[osie]. Bought ribbon. Wrote two and a half pages after *déjeuner*. Drove with M[ax] after four to post office. Villa Mezzomonte, left card Mrs. Frederick Walker," widow of the celebrated artist. Not even an earthquake could disrupt MEB's day. Lord Acton—a fellow-tenant of the Maxwells in La Madeleine—appeared at the height of the panic, a monumental figure in his nightshirt, and calmly took command.[3]

The Maxwells were welcomed at Cannes by M. Pilar, a perfume manufacturer and friend of their old London friend the perfumer, Eugène Rimmel. They were invited to meet the Prince of Wales. They went to Nice and Menton and to call on Mme. Paul Bourget. By April 9, 1887, after a visit to Avignon, they were back at Annesley Bank. In October 1887, they visited Dorset and Devonshire; and on November 21, the family party, this time including Gerald, was off to the Continent again. After Basel, Lucerne, Milan, and Genoa, they settled at San Remo on November 28, and stayed through the middle of February 1888. From San Remo on February 1, MEB wrote that Rosie—now nineteen—had been "elated" when she danced with Prince Henry of Battenberg, who was engaged to Queen Victoria's daughter, Beatrice. The "Royal party," said MEB, "tramp about all day, & positively pervade the place, but their simplicity of demeanour & unassuming air have made them very popular with everyone."[4] The Maxwells returned to Cannes for two months after Gerald recovered from a severe illness. In mid-April, MEB alone began a four-week tour in Italy, her first venture beyond Milan: to Pisa, Rome, Florence, Venice, and then via Milan, Basel, Laon, and Calais, home to England on May 14. Of the past seventeen months she had spent nine abroad. And on November 13, 1888, after less than six months at home in England, the family returned to Cannes for another prolonged stay. MEB visited Rome from March 31 to April 11, 1889, and went on to Florence, Venice, and the Lake of Como. She recorded in her notebooks her impressions of the Baths of Caracalla, Shelley's grave, the Certosa di Val d'Ema, the pictures in the Accademia in Venice, and Torcello.[5]

But these long and leisurely sojourns abroad had to be curtailed as John Maxwell's health grew worse. In January 1891 he was taken ill while on a visit to the Isle of Wight, and again in May. On May 20 MEB went to London "to select an invalid chair." Max did not leave his room until June 1 and could not go out in the garden in his chair until June 5. On July 20, 1891, MEB wrote, "Read to Max as usual, evening"; so by then it had become a regular practice. Soon a nurse became part of the household. Maxwell had to give up the meetings of the Corporation of the Borough of Richmond and of the Directors of the London and South Western Railway. As his life became more confined, so did MEB's. She allowed herself only an occasional short excursion in England itself. In 1893, she briefly visited her cousin Major Braddon at Skisdon and bought some land and a homestead called Trequite—the urge to own property near the beloved family place had apparently returned. With Max she passed most of July and August of 1893 and 1894 at Broadstairs and Ramsgate. Whichever of her two houses she was actually inhabiting, she frequently left it for a day or two and a night at the other, to make sure that things were in order and sometimes to give a party.

MEB's diaries do not suggest that Maxwell was ever ill-tempered; but Will Maxwell, who during the entire decade lived at home with his mother and father, remembered that, as the illness worsened, "Life under the same roof with him was often difficult. Trifles irritated him. . . . He had brief storms of unreasonable anger. He rated the servants for imagined faults. Sometimes all through a meal he made people uncomfortable." MEB was deeply disturbed at the signs of his mental deterioration and begged Will "never to forget that he was not always like this." She kept from Max any letters that might move him too much with "pathetical allusions." His intellect, she wrote in 1891, was "in most respects as powerful as ever. But he is highly *emotional*." The doctors said it was a symptom of his illness and that he must not be agitated.

But in the last year and a half of his life, another "almost miraculous" change came over Max: he became gentle and affectionate, "pathetically grateful for any service," and apologetic to his valet and nurse. His eyes followed MEB lovingly. "They looked dully at the door that she had closed behind her and did not brighten until she came back to him." She spent much of her day at his side. And in his last days he had a strange yearning to charter a yacht and go to sea, which he had always previously disliked. So, between the ages of fifty-six and sixty, while herself in excellent health and full of her usual energy, MEB added the role of nurse and comforter to all her other roles.[6] Her diaries record the long list of books, mostly novels by the old favorites, that she read aloud to her husband, occasionally noting that he had especially enjoyed one (Charles Lever's *Harry Lorrequer*) or "rejected" one (Thackeray's *Newcomes*), or found one "too dull" (Walter Besant's *Bells of St. Paul's*).[7]

MEB's children were now all grown up. After Gerald's single year at Cambridge, he spent two years in Germany at the Universities of Würzburg and Hannover. Soon, however, he followed in the footsteps of his mother in her youth and became an actor, often visiting his parents' house in the intervals between strenuous touring with dramatic companies. Early in February 1887, aged twenty-four, while on tour in the United States, he suffered a nervous collapse in Cincinnati. From Cannes, John Maxwell telegraphed his friend Tillotson to cable his American correspondent to pay all expenses, which Tillotson "promptly and kindly and considerately" did.

MEB was "sorely tried" at the bad news and for a day or two, Max wrote, had been "in dire peril herself, so fearful was the news to her sensitive nature and large heart." They prayed for the recovery of "our poor boy, so unexpectedly stricken when all around him seemed so bright and so full of promise, literary and dramatic." Anxious cables flew back and forth between Cannes and Cincinnati. Robert Maxwell went to America and, with the help of the American publisher, George Munro—who had issued many of MEB's novels in his cheap "Seaside Library"—in March brought Gerald home to Annesley Bank to recuperate. In July Gerald returned to the stage.[8]

MEB tried to advance his career. He had, she wrote in 1888 to her old friend Lady Monckton, a leading actress, been "upon the stroll" from town to town as the juvenile lead in three very important plays by Tom Robertson, pioneer among English Victorian dramatic realists: *Ours*

(1866), *Caste* (1867), and *School* (1869). Everywhere reviewers had found him "gentlemanly" and "manly." If "such a youth—tall, broad-shouldered—and in features and carriage very like Mr. Beerbohm Tree" should be needed, MEB asked Lady Monckton to keep him in mind. He was, she said, "a thoroughly good steady fellow—a good German scholar—and pretty good in French and Italian—fences, etc. etc." Then she asked, "Isn't this a selfish letter?" But Gerald was not coming abroad with the family this year, and his mother wanted to do everything she could for him.[9]

In January 1890 Gerald acted in *Cyril's Success*, a revival of the play by the prolific and successful H. J. Byron, first produced in 1868, which now seemed to one reviewer "insincere and hollow."[10] Three months later MEB saw Gerald in Ealing as Baron Hartfield, the sinister continental swindler and partner in crime of the forger in the popular melodrama, Sir Charles Young's *Jim the Penman*.[11] In July 1890, he was at Hull—where his mother had played forty-three years earlier—and on October 23 MEB and Max at Reading saw him play Levinson, an important part in *East Lynne*. In 1891 she and Rosie saw him at Southampton and Plymouth in MEB's own unpublished play *For Better For Worse*.[12] At the village Christmas festivities at Annesley Bank, Gerald was the Santa Claus. The next year he went to Russia briefly, perhaps on tour with some English theatrical company. In September 1893 he appeared in Richmond in Oscar Wilde's *Woman of No Importance*—which had only recently had its London *première*—and MEB took a large party. His autumn tour included Northampton, Cork, Hastings, Cambridge, Coventry, Leamington, Swansea, Bristol, Plymouth, Leicester, Portsmouth. On August 11, 1894, he sailed for an equally strenuous American tour, not to return to England until mid-1895, more than three months after his father had died. By then, at the age of thirty-three, Gerald was a hard-working professional actor, still a bachelor. He did not marry until late middle age, some years after MEB herself had died.

In 1885, MEB's second child, Fanny, became engaged at twenty-two to Edmund Selous, son of Frederick Lokes Selous, a wealthy man and chairman of the London Stock Exchange, who owned a country house at Wargrave-on-Thames and a London house in Gloucester Road, Regent's Park, which still stood in virtually open country. Of Huguenot origin, the family had moved to Jersey after the Revocation of the Edict of Nantes. Edmund's father, born in 1802, was also a "fine whist and chess player . . . and . . . the best amateur player of the clarionet. . . . a brilliant . . . talker." In 1843 he had translated Victor Hugo's tragedy, *Le Roi s'amuse*, as

Francis the First, or the Curse of St. Valier. His wife was an "advanced" woman, a poet, and lover of nature. One of Edmund's uncles, Henry, painted huge canvases of the lives of Hereward the Wake and Boadicea, and of Queen Victoria opening the Great Exhibition. Another, Angelo, wrote plays. When his *True to the Core, A Story of the Armada* opened at the Surrey Theatre (on September 9, 1866), the entire family crossed the river and "helped with our feet and umbrellas in the general enthusiasm." Edmund's older brother, Frederick Courtenay Selous, became a celebrated African explorer, big game hunter, and pioneer, who would be killed in the first World War. A barrister with no need to practice, Edmund was a lover of nature and a keen ornithologist. Between 1901 and 1933, he would write twenty-one books, some of them for children, on birds and bird-watching, animals and insects.

With Fanny and Edmund, MEB inspected the house they intended to take near Lichfield House in Sheen Park; she took Fanny to "Whiteley's to complete trousseau"; on January 12, 1886, "Pigott's men laid down crumb cloth, etc. drawing-room. Wine and plate to look out. Busy day"; and on the thirteenth came "Fanny's marriage. . . . Stormy morning, brightening as the bride drove up the hill. Bride and bridegroom left Lichfield House at 2:30. Arrived Bank at 7." The Maxwells had given them the Lyndhurst house for their honeymoon. One of Fanny's brides-maids remembered among the celebrities present at the reception "a plump, pasty, flabby round-faced preposterously garbed man" who came up to her pretty cousin, Rosie Maxwell, "kissed her hand and made an outrageously flattering speech, which produced in me a slight feeling of nausea." When he had moved on, Rosie "said in awed tones: 'That was Oscar Wilde.' " Within a month the young Selouses had moved in at Sheen Park and had begun what would be a lifetime of family dining back and forth with the Maxwells.

Fanny's son Gerald, often called "Gerald minor" in MEB's diaries, was born on July 14, 1887, and MEB shared in the anxiety and the nursing when her daughter became "seriously ill of a high fever" three days after the child's arrival. Fanny did not recover for a week. In October 1891, after Fanny and Edmund had moved to Barton's Mills, Mildenhall, Suffolk, she was again taken ill. MEB, Will, and Rosie all went to be with her and stayed ten days until—after three consultations with a specialist—her recovery seemed certain. Less than six months later, on April 8, 1892, MEB wrote in her diary, "Fanny's two girls born early morning"; so the illness had probably been some trouble connected with early pregnancy. MEB went to Mildenhall on the day the twins—Mary and Freda—were born, and the next diary entry for the ninth reads, "Much with Fanny, going on wonderfully well." With the three children and two nurses, the Selouses made a long visit in Richmond in spring 1893, and the next year they went to live in Belgium.[13]

MEB's third child, Will Maxwell, appears in her diaries almost every day. He accompanied his parents on all their travels and escorted his mother whenever she went to town without John Maxwell, even if only for a few hours. At fourteen in 1880, he had gone to Calderon's Art School in St. John's Wood, commuting daily by underground from Richmond. Doubtful of his gifts as an artist, he worked less and less. But at nineteen he moved on to "life" class at Ridley's school, and then "worked or pretended to work for a year or two by myself at the British Museum." One day he left his easel and drawing-board behind and never went back to claim them. On Will's twenty-first birthday (1887), his father made him a present of *The Mistletoe Bough*, last of the Maxwell magazines. Tired of managing it, Maxwell thought Will would find it easy and interesting. MEB continued to edit it and contributed a short story to every issue. Like everything she did, it was a success.

But Will Maxwell hated canvassing for ads and had trouble in filling the advertising pages. Sales began to fall off. He later thought he should more drastically have modernized the Annual's old-fashioned format and more actively have sought new contributors: "Except for my mother's," he remembered, "the stories had often seemed to me out of date." He energetically recruited talented new artists, notably Bernard Partridge, who drew a splendid Joan of Arc to illustrate MEB's story, "One Fatal Moment," in the issue of 1889. The illustrations suddenly took on a modish *art nouveau* quality. It was harder to enlist new writers, but Will Maxwell's close friend Leo Trevor, an intimate of the household since his schooldays, contributed a couple of short stories of regimental life, both of which later became successful London plays. Will also persuaded his sister Fanny Selous to become a contributor. When he advertised for contributions, he received such a flood that Gerald, Fanny, Rosie, and Leo Trevor all helped read them. Arthur Machen sent in *The Great God Pan*, which fascinated the entire family tribunal of editors, but which had to be rejected because it was too long. When it was published in 1894, it made Machen famous. Had Will Maxwell accepted it and used it to fill an entire number, it might have saved *The Mistletoe Bough*. But, he recalled, in 1893 a "queer sort of listlessness" seized him, and he delayed the preparation of the Annual so long that it simply did not appear. "I had allowed it to fade and die. If I felt any shame, I consoled myself with the joys of hunting."

Will Maxwell was not as listless as he pretended. With the "large aid" of his mother, he wrote a short story which her old friend Edmund Yates published in *The World,* and a second which Henry Labouchere—the famous "Labby," editor of *Truth* and another close friend of MEB—accepted but substantially rewrote. In 1886, MEB wrote to Wilkie Collins that she wanted to present Will to "the Master of my craft [who] is also my friend." Will, she said, was one of Collins' "most ardent admirers, as well as a devoted disciple of our dear Charles Reade." And Will had "fleshed his sword—written stories for the World and Truth." On MEB's introduction, George Bentley accepted a third story by Will for *Temple Bar.* In 1892 there appeared a collection of Will's short stories called *Tales of the Thames.* Yates, "Labby," Wilkie Collins, Bentley: MEB pushed Will with them all and doubtless with others. As Will later recalled ironically, "All the elders agreed that scarcely ever could a young man have had such good encouragement. I myself agreed; and, this being so, I stopped working, and never wrote another line for many years." He might, he obviously believed, have worked harder and written more had he had *less* encouragement from his famous and adoring mother, whose interventions made it difficult for him to assert himself in his own way.[14]

Shortly after her twenty-second birthday, in the spring of 1891, Rosie Maxwell became engaged to Robert Lachlan, just past thirty, a mathematician so able that he had come out ahead of Alfred North Whitehead in the first two parts of the mathematical tripos at Cambridge in 1883. A Fellow of Trinity, working for the degree of Doctor of Science, Lachlan in 1893 would publish *An Elementary Treatise on Modern Pure Geometry.* The young couple were to live in Cambridge, where MEB helped Rosie find a house. The wedding cake came from Greenfield, the trousseau from Whiteley's; on June 16, 1891, MEB wrote in her diary: "Wedding lovely weather, all things favorable, Max convalescent," and the Lachlans went off for two weeks in Paris. On September 8, 1892, their son Austin was born, and almost a month later Rosie was still "on sofa in drawing-room." In the midst of Maxwell's own recurring attacks in 1894, Rosie Lachlan was taken ill. MEB's diary records a visit to Cambridge to see her, a return visit by the Lachlans to Lichfield House, and their departure in September for a long sojourn in St. Malo. Rosie was apparently not recovering satisfactorily, and MEB was worried about her.[15]

Ted, the youngest Maxwell, went up to Trinity in March 1891. He was always subject to bronchitis and asthma, and MEB was often concerned about his health. When well, he rode, hunted, and traveled with his family. He was reading for the bar and ate his first dinner at the Inner Temple in May 1892, returning to Trinity in June. Now that Rosie and her husband were living in Cambridge, each of MEB's visits there took her to see Ted as well. "It must be a great comfort to you," wrote a friend to MEB sometime in 1892 when Ted was facing a difficult examination, "that your sweet *bouton de rose*—I always call your daughter thus—is there to look after him, and her *caro sposo* to tutor him." And no doubt it was. Ted took his B.A. in 1894 and in 1895 he was still reading for the bar.[16]

Of MEB's stepchildren, Nicholas and Elizabeth do not appear in her diaries, which record frequent visits from Polly and her husband and children. To John Maxwell, Jr. (Jack), and Robert Max turned over the publishing business. The former was as handsome as his father had been in his youth and very hard-working; the latter, according to his step-brother Will, was "distinctly an idle apprentice, but of a mild and blameless kind, never likely to sink low in the social scale . . . amiable and most amusing," and such good company that "even the sternest advocate of labour liked him." Jack Maxwell moved the firm out of its old cramped quarters into larger ones at Milton House, still in Shoe Lane.

Sometimes he drove a hard bargain, as in 1885, when he took over from another firm the right to reprint and keep two-thirds of the profits on the young H. Rider Haggard's first two novels—*Dawn* and *The Witch's Head*, neither one a great success—and bound the author in an "unnoticed" clause in the contract to give the Maxwells on the same usurious terms any other books he might write for the next five years. It took the threat of a lawsuit from Haggard's new literary agent, A. P. Watt, to persuade Jack Maxwell to compromise and extract only two new Haggard novels. On another occasion, in 1886, W. F. Tillotson took his own book publishing out of Jack's hands because of a disagreement that apparently arose when a clerk in the Maxwell office had drafted a letter badly and sent it off to Tillotson without Jack's having seen it. John Maxwell, Sr. wrote Tillotson that Jack "paddles his own canoe, and if he has dipped the blade of his paddle into dangerous waters, he must take the consequences."

Will Maxwell believed that Jack "literally worked himself to death." Certainly he became very ill in 1887, and his brother Robert was not the man to whom so important an industry as the publishing and marketing of their stepmother's fiction could be entrusted. *Mohawks* (1886) was the last of her novels to bear the Maxwell imprint—their eighteenth. For a single novel, *Like and Unlike* (1887), the firm of Spencer Blackett took over, acquiring also for one brief year the series of Braddon cheap reprints, now forty-eight in number. With *The Fatal Three* (1888), however, Simpkin, Marshall, Hamilton, and Kent became her publishers, not only for each successive novel of the next decade but for all the reprints as well. But since MEB herself bought the paper and had the sheets printed and bound, she was in many ways her own publisher, with Simpkin merely putting their imprint on her novels and distributing them. Poor Jack Maxwell died on April 10, 1889. His melancholy illness and early death brought MEB not only the natural grief at the loss of a young man whom she had mothered since he was a schoolboy, but also a certain business anxiety.[17]

Although retired, John Maxwell, Sr., still handled all negotiations for the newspaper publication of MEB's novels by Tillotson, who, after *Wyllard's Weird* was finished in the spring of 1885, asked for a Braddon novel for 1887. At first Maxwell believed that this must be a mistake for 1886. No, said Tillotson, he was filled up for 1886. After the usual initial sparring, twelve hundred pounds was agreed upon for the 1887 novel, including all serial, American, Tauchnitz, and translation rights for a period of seven years. "Be happy always getting own way from us, hence pleasantest relations," John Maxwell wired. The still unwritten novel in question would be *Like and Unlike*. But the 1887 date remained a worry; it was important to MEB to "fill in 1886." As Maxwell telegraphed, "Author refuses proposed idleness. Must write," but not—he hastily added—for any of Tillotson's competitors.

Yet new competition was now arising. William Leng, proprietor of a chain of newspapers in Sheffield and the first newspaper publisher to introduce linotype machines, had apparently been sounding out some fellow-publishers about forming their own syndicate to serialize a Braddon novel. John Maxwell reassured Tillotson: Leng's son had merely inquired what the price of a Braddon serial would be. When told that the figure was a minimum of one thousand pounds, he had said he would consult his father, and no more had been heard of it. Yet, added John Maxwell, obviously making the most of Tillotson's natural anxiety, "England is a free country, and Mr. Leng may feel himself free to make an offer to supply" something he had as yet no right to sell.

In October 1885, after having sold the serial rights of MEB's 1886 three-volume novel, *Mohawks*, to Chatto and Windus, Maxwell returned to the negotiations with Tillotson. He now wanted "to clear up our literary life for the next two years. . . . My wife must be occupied. It is as natural for her to write as it is for a mountain torrent to flow; and my gentle Willie ought to keep her pen going in his service." Additional competition was now coming from A. P. Watt, the literary agent, and, while Maxwell did not wish to "assist a 'parasite,' " he *did* need an outlet for the serialization of still another MEB novel—*One Thing Need-ful*—already completed and only two volumes in length. With some reluctance, Tillotson accepted this for 1886, paying five hundred pounds for it.

But the pressure now mounted. In 1887, Leng, who was knighted and became Sir William in Queen Victoria's Jubilee honors list, offered to publish a novel by MEB in each of the next three years and to pay more than Tillotson. As Maxwell told Tillotson, "Practically, this would take Miss Braddon out of your hands forever. Is this desirable?" Tillotson's adviser told him that to lose MEB would be "most unfortunate," but an annual Braddon novel "would be quite too much." Maxwell, he said, was "far too shrewd" to abandon their long-standing relationship.

Not at all. Maxwell accepted the Leng proposal. It "offered greater sequence of employment at higher prices." He reminded Tillotson that "Miss Braddon has the most perfect right to bestow her services wherever they are best remunerated." And early in 1888, when Tillotson regretted the loss of MEB's books, Maxwell replied that it had not been his fault; he had given Tillotson all the necessary information: "Our dearest Willie pronounced the decree of severance."

Leng—a staunch Tory, the model for Charles Reade's hero Mr. Holdfast in *Put Yourself in His Place*, who had resisted trades-union terrorism in Sheffield—paid MEB very well, at least a thousand pounds for the newspaper serial rights to each novel and probably more. While beginning her first story for him she wrote Lady Monckton: "Terms high, and my honour therefore engaged to do my best." The three Leng novels in the original arrangement were *The Fatal Three* (1888), *The Day Will Come* (1889), and *One Life One Love* (1890). Leng subsequently renewed the agreement for three additional years, and serialized *Gerard* (1891), *The Venetians* (1892), and *Thou Art the Man* (1894).

After a five-year hiatus, during which W. F. Tillotson died, his firm in 1892 once again approached MEB, who by then—with Maxwell an in-valid—was handling such matters herself. She sold Tillotson's serial rights to a two-volume novel, *All Along the River*, of which the last number was completed in February 1893, but had to decline their offer for another book because her commitments were so heavy. Moreover, she said, she was "bound, after an engagement extending over six consecutive years," to confer with Leng, "who, like the late Mr. Tillotson, has always been particularly considerate and courteous" in all his dealings. Then too, she had promised her sons "not to negotiate for any novel until the M.S. is complete, as their father's precarious health" made it impossible to accept obligations in advance. Otherwise, "home anxieties" might interfere with her writing.[18] So MEB once more had Tillotson's as her serial publisher, but for a single novel only.

Some time in 1889, MEB's brother Edward returned to England as agent-general for Tasmania in London, bringing his second wife Alice and their daughter May. They stayed about four years, often visiting at Richmond and at Lyndhurst. The bitter grievance MEB had felt against Edward in 1868 had somehow been dissipated with time. The terse entry in her diary for January 1, 1891, reveals her renewed pride in him: "Gazette announced E[dward] N[icholas] C[oventry] B[raddon]'s knighthood K.C.M.G. Walked to ice [the Braddons were staying with them at Lyndhurst and were skating at the time] with Will and told the news." Immediately she wrote off to Lord Lytton in Paris, and on January 8 he told her of his joy at the "grand news" and sent his congratulations. Thenceforth, MEB's diary usually refers to the Braddons as "Sir E. and Lady B."

When Edward's daughter by his first marriage, Amy Knyvett, wrote him from India a "loving and highly complimentary letter" congratulating him on the knighthood, he answered deprecatingly that it was "fortunately . . . conferred very much for political success," and so he supposed he was "as worthy of it as a lot of other men similarly rewarded." But he admitted that he rejoiced over the "wailing and gnashing of teeth" it would occasion his political enemies in Tasmania: "How they will have squirmed at the tidings. That is amiable on my part." His ambition was to become Governor of Tasmania, which he expected "in the fulness of time." After four years in London, Sir Edward Braddon was indeed summoned back to Tasmania, where he would become Premier. Will and Ted Maxwell attended the testimonial dinner given him at the St. George's Club on October 3, 1893, and three days later MEB saw all three Braddons off on the *Himalaya*. She greatly liked her new sister-in-law, and affectionate letters began to travel back and forth across the vast distances that separated them.[19]

During the year 1885 MEB lost three close friends. Madame Delepierre, an intimate of the Braddon family since the fifties, widow of the former Belgian Consul in London and mother of Madame Trübner—with whom MEB read French literature regularly—died in February, and MEB went to the funeral with Max, something she rarely did. In November 1885, Miss Elizabeth Philp, a frequent guest at Richmond and Lyndhurst, died. She was a composer and concert pianist, and MEB had written the words for at least two of her songs, "My Heart is Thine" and "The Song of the Galley Slave." Max went to the services alone. Early in December, Miss Browne, the family pensioner, was in a "terrible accident at Vauxhall," and Max, Gerald, and Will "followed the coffin." When Mrs. Sala died early in 1886, MEB wrote Sala affectionately that his wife had been "one of those privileged women whose superior charms never offended other women" and tried to console him and give him strength. In February 1892, Mrs. H. Nye Chart, MEB's friend and former manager of the Brighton Theatre Royal, died.

The Maxwells' old friend Edmund Yates had to go to jail in January 1885. Convicted of libel in 1884 in a suit brought against him by the Earl of Lonsdale, Yates lost his appeal and served seven weeks of a longer sentence. When she went to Holloway Prison on January 19, MEB was not allowed to see him. He wrote thanking Maxwell and "Aurora" for the "kind wish to see me," but found it "expedient to limit my visiting to members of my own family or persons on business" and added that he was "receiving every kindness and attention."[20] On May 13, "Max went to Yates dinner, Criterion," no doubt a celebration given for Yates after his release.

Before John Maxwell's illness, MEB's social life was as active as ever. On January 1, 1885, the Maxwells came home at four in the morning from Mrs. Labouchere's New Year's Eve party, and MEB was "very tired all day." But the diary adds "Letters, much work." The Laboucheres at Pope's Villa in Twickenham and the Whitings at Lavender Hill were perhaps MEB's most intimate friends; but now Lady Dorothy Nevill—born Lady Dorothy Walpole, daughter of the Earl of Orford, and a leading London hostess—began more and more often to invite MEB to lunch and to appear with her daughter at Lichfield House. During the "season"—June and July—the diaries for the years 1885–1891 include long lists of the people invited to Richmond or encountered elsewhere.

After "Mr. Whistler's conversazione" at the Suffolk Street Gallery on June 28, 1885, MEB went on to the Laboucheres', where she met Whistler again and Adelina Patti too. Augustus (Glossop) Harris—the successful theatrical entrepreneur, later knighted, whom MEB hoped to interest in a play she was writing—came to dinner (July 24, 1885). André Raffalovich and Oscar Wilde came often. So did the F. C. Burnands: he was editor of *Punch*; at his house MEB met artists such as Sir Frederick Leighton, Luke

Fildes, and Harry Furness, and stage people like the Bancrofts and the Moncktons. Lord and Lady Ardilaun, who gave many large parties, often included MEB and Maxwell. They were more than mere acquaintances. So were the Bram Stokers—he was manager for Sir Henry Irving and in 1887 still a decade away from writing his celebrated *Dracula*. Over one hundred people came to MEB's afternoon lawn party on June 30, 1888. A few days later she was presented to Lady Randolph Churchill at Lady Ellis's "principal fête." The single month of July 1890 included MEB's "own at home," the "Academy soirée," Mrs. Arthur Lewis's at home, Mrs. (Squire) Bancroft's dinner party, Mrs. Robson Roose's (her husband was a doctor) evening party, Mme. Castellani's concert, Lady Ellis's "evening party for royalties. Illuminations, Venetian fête, fireworks," Mrs. Labouchere's garden party, Lady Ardilaun's "evening party. Terrace illuminated," a performance of *Macbeth*, Lady Seton's "At Home" at Durham House, and a number of other festivities, among them a boating-picnic on the Thames that MEB gave for Rosie, now twenty-one, with a group of other girls as guests.

Even after Maxwell could no longer accompany her, MEB continued to get away from Annesley Bank to London for a day or two at a time, often timing her visit to coincide with a lunch party given by Lady Dorothy Nevill. At the Laboucheres' she several times encountered the Campbell-Bannermans. Mr. and Mrs. Dobson, who lived at Gentilshurst in Sussex, continued to exchange two- or three-day visits with her. In 1893 at a Mansion House dinner (given by the Lord Mayor of London) MEB found herself seated next to Sir John Millais, and two days later at Lady Ardilaun's she met not only the Wildes, the Stokers, and the Burnands, but the Pineros, the Hardys, and the Beerbohm Trees. In 1894, at lunch at Lady Dorothy's, she saw Mrs. Hodgson Burnett—*Little Lord Fauntleroy* now eight years behind her—and Lady Betty Balfour, daughter of MEB's friend, the Earl of Lytton, and granddaughter of her former idol and mentor, Bulwer. The Irvings, Ellen Terry, the Edmund Gosses, all appear and reappear.

It would of course—or so one romantically imagines—be interesting if MEB—or, indeed, any of her multitude of friends, many of whom wrote their memoirs—had reported what anybody said to anybody else on these occasions, especially those at which MEB was hostess, about which her diaries never say more than "everything satisfactory" or "successful." But no such record seems to exist. Lady Dorothy Nevill's own *Reminiscences*, for example, and her son Ralph's *Life* of his mother, together with the original letters she wrote to MEB, which MEB carefully preserved even when burning other correspondence, fail to convey any sense of that enormous charm which Lady Dorothy's friends all attributed to her, and which she herself was confident she possessed.[21]

But MEB's diaries do "place" the Maxwells in the London society of the late eighties and early nineties. They were active and admired members of a large circle of successful and self-confident writers, journalists, artists, and theatrical people. They had many intimates among upper-middle-class professional men and their wives. They enjoyed a close acquaintance, amounting in a few cases to real friendship, with those members of the aristocracy and persons important in political life who were bored by the stuffy atmosphere of purely upper-class social entertainment and enjoyed mingling with men and women who wrote books, painted pictures, managed theatres, edited newspapers, or acted in plays, especially those who were rich and secure enough to be able to return in kind the entertainment they were offered. MEB was a woman of precisely that sort.

2. Themes and Variations (1886–1892)

Between 1886 and 1892 MEB's best novels—*The Fatal Three* (1888), with *The Venetians* (1892) not far behind—represented her oldest stock in trade—sensation—but with the events now artfully deriving with total plausibility—even inevitability—from the characters of her personages. At times, as in *Like and Unlike* (1887) or *Gerard* (1891), a relatively mechanical plot screened incisive social commentary; or, as in *One Thing Needful* (1886), MEB's own political views; or, even when the story was implausible, as in *The Day Will Come* (1889), a satirical commentary on the fads of the moment.

Far more explicitly political than any of its predecessors, *One Thing Needful* (1886) showed MEB still strongly radical, but more obviously a Tory in politics than she had hitherto revealed herself. The workers' leader of "that centre of free-thinking and nihilism," Birmingham, is a "high priest of advanced radicalism" who believes in the "divine right of every man to lay hands upon any other man's possessions. . . . the old thesis, la propriété, c'est le vol." With Rousseau and Karl Marx as his gods, he wishes to "level all ranks, wage war against the privileged classes . . . do away with Monarchy and the House of Lords, and establish a

Republican Senate of working-men" with one intellectual or professional member for every two workers. Abroad, he would have England "turn her left cheek to be smitten by the hand" that had always smitten the right. He is also a gentleman, having rowed for Balliol. The local dowager Countess fiercely believes that " 'such a person . . . should not be allowed to exist,' " and condemns everything he says as " 'virulent nonsense' "; but her stepson, the Earl, a more tolerant Tory who engages in public debate with the radical, disagrees: " 'Virulent, sometimes, I grant, but not always nonsense. . . . The man's ideas are Utopian,' " but with " 'occasional flashes of common sense,' " and even " 'a strain of poetry.' "

It is understandable, then, that after the Earl rescues the radical's five-year-old daughter Stella from a fire in which her father has perished, the child is taken into the castle—like the waif in *Flower and Weed*—and lapped about with luxury and affection for five years until her benefactor dies. Then she is left to the tender mercies of the haughty Countess, who had always wanted to make a servant of her: " 'Our workhouses are now so well administered that I have not the least objection to take a servant from the pauper class.' " Demoted to the servants' hall, deprived of her books, even driven out of the library by the coarse new Earl, Stella nonetheless contrives to obtain a classical education and wins the love of a widowed retired Liberal Prime Minister, Mr. Nestorius, by showing him the manuscript of a brilliant novel she has written. But she rejects his proposal of marriage and—improbably enough—accepts the new Earl, who realizes that his past cruel treatment of her had all along stemmed from love, and whose vindictive mother—even more improbably—withdraws her opposition.

In Mr. Nestorius, classicist and Liberal politician, MEB was portraying Gladstone, the Nestor of the Liberals. His voice "had ruled in the senate . . . had touched the hearts of women . . . had been the most powerful influence in [his] career. He had that fine flow of language and those ever-musical tones which enable a man to talk nonsense unchallenged, nay, rather, to make nonsense appear logic, or wit." He was always in the company of attractive women, upon whom he exerted great magnetism. When he says of Stella, " 'I am deeply interested in her. I have not been so much interested in any woman since—,' " one of the ladies present "innocently" finishes his sentence: " 'Not since your dissolution,' " at which there came "an awkward pause," for at that time "it had been said that Mr. Nestorius was influenced by a feminine counsellor, and that if, as his admirers alleged, Nestorius was a prophet, there was also a prophetess—a sibyl behind the curtain giving forth mystic breathings, words of wisdom, but always just a little too far in advance of the time."

The "sibyl" can only be Mme. Olga Novikoff, a close friend of Gladstone in the critical years 1876 and 1877, and widely believed to have been responsible for what seemed his pro-Russian leanings, although he later certainly mistrusted her. Among the novelists who found her irresistible MEB's friend, the Australian-born Mrs. Campbell Praed, had unmistakably portrayed Madame Novikoff in her novel *Nadine* (1882), which had scored a *succès de scandale*. But MEB referred to the sibyl only briefly and offhand and tried the far more daring experiment of painting a recognizable portrait of Gladstone himself. If he ever noticed his likeness in *One Thing Needful,* he probably did not mind: he was on pleasant terms with MEB, whom he greatly admired.

So in *One Thing Needful* MEB disapproved simultaneously of the radicalism of the agitator, the reactionary views of the Countess, and the high-flown but empty liberalism of Mr. Nestorius, ranging herself with those Tories, like the kindly Earl, who wished to understand and help the working classes. When a young Marchioness, heiress to a huge ironworks in Birmingham, stubbornly refuses to yield to the entirely justified demands of her workers for higher wages, they burn down the plant, which costs her a million pounds to rebuild. Unfortunately she can well afford it.

The strongly political mood of *One Thing Needful* manifested itself also in a children's book called *The Good Hermione,* an elaborate parable of Queen Victoria's reign, which MEB was simultaneously writing, under the pseudonym of "Aunt Belinda," in preparation for the Jubilee Year of 1887. Here Victoria herself appears as the good Queen Hermione of Lyonesse, who comes into her heritage at eighteen upon the death of her uncle Clarentius (William IV, formerly Duke of Clarence). Lord Melbourne is "Lord Melliflous," Peel "Sir Spinning Jennins," Palmerston "Flam," Disraeli "Sligh Boote," Prince Albert "Pulcher," Napoleon III "Aquilon," and Gladstone "Woodman." The book escaped critical notice, and "Aunt Belinda" has never before been identified, even by the cataloguer of the British Museum. MEB did not mention *The Good Hermione* in her diary for 1886, and only the survival among her papers of the complete original manuscript in her hand proves that she wrote it. Having for several years pronounced both obliquely and directly on French politics, she had now turned to those of England.

At the same time, *One Thing Needful* obliquely provides unexpected insight into MEB's views of her own profession. Mr. Nestorius found Stella's novel admirable because she was so well educated: "The girl who had read Homer and Virgil, and Dante and Goethe, and Milton and Shakespeare from her childhood, had started with advantages rarely possessed by a writing young woman. Her style had never been vitiated by evil examples, her mental eye had never been dazzled by tinsel." So she wrote a clear and vigorous English, and was destined to make a fortune, " 'in an age when strong fiction is one of the necessities of life.' " Mr. Nestorius' views curiously echo those of John Gilby, who more than a quarter-century earlier had urged MEB to learn Latin and Greek in order to become a good novelist.

She had repudiated Gilby, of course, but could never rid her own mind of these opinions, so prevalent among Victorians. Bulwer always more than half believed that to be a novelist one needed a classical education like his own. Critics regularly took MEB to task for such minor details as having allowed "presumptious" to stand instead of correcting it to "presumptuous," or using a non-word such as "dilapitude." Contemporary adverse criticism of Dickens or praise of George Eliot often rested on such minutiae. MEB herself daily "did" some Cicero or Horace with Gerald on his holidays from Cambridge; she taught herself a little Greek; she read the classics in translation, partly from intellectual curiosity and an appreciation of good literature, but partly also to make up for what she had always felt to be a professional deficiency, and to turn herself into the kind of learned woman that Stella had become in her girlhood.

Certain modish literary trends she now satirized and deplored. " 'We leave plot,' " says a fashionable novelist, " 'to the men who write melodramas. . . . nothing of that kind for me. . . . My novel is a novel of character—my chief incidents, well—a little look at twilight—eyes meeting across the deck of a steamer or in a church at Venice—an angry word in the second volume—a fan dropped and picked up in the third.' " Those were the three central points: " 'for the rest, touch and go . . . all touch and go. Wit, satire, sentiment, introspection, self-communing, sparkle and play of words, lighter than thistledown.' " Perhaps MEB was thinking of the popular William Black, whose *Adventures of a Phaeton* she once called "bosh." In any case, a pleasant horsey girl answers the novelist on behalf of MEB, who may have been feeling beset by the new fashions, although always up with them, " 'I have sometimes thought that if you would—just for once in a way—make your heroine poison her father or your hero drown his wife, it would be nice.' " But then, this is a girl who does not "care a straw for any novel without murder, arson, or bigamy."[22]

After *Mohawks* (1886), her first venture in historical fiction since *Robert Ainsleigh,* an eighteenth-century costume piece,[23] MEB in *Like and Unlike* returned to contemporary social satire. Ostensibly it is her identical twins alone who are "like and unlike": Adrian, the elder—possessor of title, lands, and income—is bookish, gentle, and mild; Valentine, the younger, their widowed mother's favorite, is a headstrong inconsiderate athlete, who easily steals his brother's fiancée, neglects her after marriage, and kills her in a fit of temper when he discovers she is planning to elope with another man. His mother's spoiling in his youth has destroyed Valentine's character. She had loved him " 'foolishly, blindly, sinfully,' " making " 'an idol of poor humanity.' " Blandly presented as a flawed hero—in prison after his trial he becomes consumptive and his hair turns "silky white"—he is in fact a self-willed Braddonian upper-class brute, whose development has been frozen at a childish stage. Valentine has to have what he wants, but does not long care for it after he has got it. MEB had never before explicitly analyzed what happened to sons spoiled by their mothers, and only later would she recognize that they often became effete rather than aggressively masculine as a result. In *Like and Unlike,* it is the less beloved twin, Adrian, who is not man enough to hold his fiancée.

The contrast between the twins is explicit. Implicit is the contrast between the beautiful uneducated upper-class outdoor girl—with whom both brothers fall in love and who is about to run off with her lover when she is killed—and a girl of the most humble origin, granddaughter of a basket-weaver and daughter of a successful prostitute, who stoutly resists Valentine's determined efforts to seduce her and eventually allows him to try to expiate his crime by performing useful services in a refuge she has established for ex-prostitutes. This girl, "taught in the National School," Valentine later ironically reflects, knows more about all academic subjects than the girl he had married and murdered, whom he had chosen from his own rank of life, a "thoroughbred like himself." What would have happened, he wonders too late, if he had "flung conventionality to the winds" and married the poor girl? He is sure at least that she would never have betrayed him as his wife had done.

And, as if to underline her condemnation of the mindlessness and viciousness of the upper class and the strength and sobriety of the lowest,

MEB described in Zolaesque detail the flashy vacuity of the London social set in which Valentine's poor murdered wife had met her lover. The wife's elder sister Leonora, leading spirit of the group, had, in her younger married days in India, extracted a diamond necklace from a young officer, who later shot himself because of the debts he had incurred. Yet Leonora continues to wear the necklace afterwards. With her husband safe in India, she has many suitors, including a disagreeable man who pays her dressmaker's bills. When asked for kisses, she uses as a defense her poodle, "an artificial personage spoiled by London hours and high living, blasé, cynical," with shaven back and tail and three tufts of hair on each, with silver collar and bracelets. "Overeducated," he plays the piano, walks upstairs on his hind legs, and insults Mr. Gladstone in dumb show whenever a piece of sugar is offered to him: a poodle of whom a man in the Club smoking room is heard to say, " 'I back Mrs. Baddeley and her poodle against Lucretia and her dagger.' " But neither he nor MEB really believes that the poodle effectively enables Leonora to withhold her kisses or more important favors from her lovers.

Her behavior is clearly worse than that of the successful lower-class prostitute, who has remained loyal to the man she loves and, after he has deserted her, tells her daughter:

> "I have had my admirers by the dozen—I have had my victims too, and have wasted three or four fortunes in my time. . . . You would think I was lying, perhaps, if I were to tell you the chances I have had, and thrown away for his sake. You think, perhaps, that such as we don't have our chances. But we do, girl, and better chances than the women who are brought up in cotton-wool, and looked after by affectionate mothers and high-minded fathers. I might have married a man with half a million of money. I might have married a man with a handle to his name, and . . . been called my Lady and your ladyship."

For the first time MEB had introduced directly into her pages one of "ces dames." The daring and sophisticated, but wholly implicit, contrast between the superior values of the acknowledged lower-class whore and the cruder values of the unacknowledged upper-class almost-whore provides a third "like and unlike" pair to accompany the gentle, ineffectual elder brother and his heartless, brutal twin, and the erring, murdered upper-class wife and the unattainable lower-class woman. The subtle introduction of these barely audible social sub-themes as counterpoint to its melodramatic major theme transformed *Like and Unlike* into a virtuoso performance.[24]

Divided into three parts, one for each of the three fates and with each part corresponding exactly to a single volume of the published book, the tight and symmetrical physical structure of *The Fatal Three* reflects its extraordinary strength in plotting: MEB maintained her suspense by concealing from her readers the successive solutions to each of the story's mysteries until her personages themselves discover them. And all the characters behave precisely as they would have behaved in life, given their childhood circumstances and training, so that the reader eagerly accepts MEB's psychological analysis of their motives. If one of her critics of the sixties, who had complained with some justice that her novels were novels of pure incident, had read *The Fatal Three,* he would have had to concede that she had learned how to create believable people, even in a "sensational" situation.

Much to the distaste of his frivolous hypochondriacal wife, a rich London retired merchant introduces into his household an awkward, rather ill-tempered girl of fifteen called Fay, an heiress without relatives, who has only unhappy childhood memories. Everyone takes her for the master's illegitimate child, and since he offers no explanations even his wife believes the charge. Fay and the couple's seven-year-old daughter Mildred become devotedly attached to each other. But although she nurses Mildred through scarlet fever, Fay is sent away to finishing school in Brussels. Deeply grieved, Mildred at seven is too young to mourn her loss indefinitely.

Twenty-odd years later, long since happily married to George Greswold, a country squire, and the mother of a daughter of her own, Mildred—now orphaned—is aware that Fay had been her half-sister. She and George live a quiet idyllic life, dominated by her deep piety and marred only by his recurrent nightmare of being confined in a cage from which he cannot escape. When their daughter dies of typhoid, the grief that racks both parents begins to drive them apart, and George regards the death as somehow a judgment upon him.

Until a stranger casually remarks that he had known George's first wife, Mildred has never known that her husband had been married before. He will tell her nothing about it except that the memory is too tragic to discuss. But she goads him into showing her a photograph of his first wife: it was Fay, whom he had known under a different name. A devout churchwoman, Mildred believes that because she is his deceased wife's sister—or at least half-sister—in the eyes of the church and of the law her marriage to George is no marriage. Abetted by an ascetic bachelor parson who had been her religious instructor in her youth and who calls her marriage "unholy, immoral, accursed," Mildred insists upon leaving George, who had never previously suspected any connection between his first wife and his second and who naturally repudiates Mildred's actions as bigoted.

Having pushed like Bluebeard's wife at the door of her husband's secret chamber, Mildred is doomed to find what Bluebeard's wife found: the corpse of a former wife, one only, of course, but the one among all women who should not have been there. She discovers that George had been suspected of murdering Fay in Nice. Lacking self-confidence, bitter and jealous, Fay—pregnant—had, during a quarrel with George, thrown herself over a cliff into the sea. The police at first thought that George had pushed her; afterwards he suffered a temporary mental collapse and had been in an asylum. Now Mildred understands his recurring nightmare. Only after it is too late for a reconciliation with her husband does Mildred make her last discovery: that Fay was after all not the child of her father but of her aunt, her father's spinster sister, who has spent her life doing good works and whose brother had loyally kept her secret. Mildred has never been a deceased wife's sister and owes her misfortunes to her own narrow-mindedness and the law's cruelty.

Most modern readers will have forgotten or never have known what agony the law forbidding marriage to a deceased wife's sister aroused—until it was finally repealed in 1907—in the breasts of those who wanted to make such a marriage. As late as 1902, Vanessa Stephen could not marry Jack Hills, the man she loved, because he was the widower of her half-sister. Mildred's ordeal was genuine enough. MEB clearly agreed with George that a deceased wife's sister might well be the best possible wife for a widower. She skillfully portrayed Mildred's spiritual advisor as a medieval monk *manqué* who subconsciously objects to any marriage at all.

The pampered only daughter of a frivolous mother and loving father, deprived in childhood of her favorite playmate, trained in pious ways by a bigot, Mildred is a slave to duty real and imagined. Devastated emotionally by her daughter's death and by George's mysterious feeling that somehow it is a judgment upon him, unable to resume the affectionate relationship of a happy marriage immediately after the trauma of their loss, which George and she mourn separately, Mildred cannot avoid her fate.

As for Fay, whom the reader never sees directly after her expulsion from Mildred's parents' household, she is then a *farouche* girl of fifteen, whose disagreeable behavior reflects her yearning for emotional security. She has found the beginning of true affection in her fondness for Mildred and in her opportunity to nurse her through an illness, but suddenly and brutally she loses even this. What wonder if later she cannot believe that her husband truly loves her? Convinced that he has married her only out of pity, jealous of every look he casts at another woman, "soured, disappointed, barren, loveless," unfulfilled, she is prepared to make their lives a misery. MEB knew that children need love. In Fay she had drawn a woman who had been forced to grow up without it, who experienced nothing in her childhood except rejection and disappointment. Fay's passionate final quarrel with George and her suicide were also fated.

MEB portrayed George as not quite sporting enough to be a man's man, disliked by his father, the favorite of his mother, willing to wait for her death to inherit the manor and become a squire. He marries Fay out of pity rather than out of passion, and he is—as he would have been in life—quite unready to give up amiable harmless conversation with other women just because it makes a jealous wife more jealous. His first marriage grows desperately unhappy, and he is inwardly glad when it is over. But he feels such guilt at the thought of the harsh words that had led to Fay's suicide, and at the suicide itself, that he has a breakdown. His readiness to feel and assume guilt, whether deservedly or not, repeats itself when, through no fault of his—indeed, in spite of every possible effort—typhoid breaks out in his village and carries away not only his much pampered tenants but his beloved daughter. Of course he is certain that heaven has singled him out for punishment, a certainty only enhanced after Mildred insists upon leaving him.

Even Fay's unmarried mother is wholly genuine. Lively and talented as a girl, she is easily lured into a fraudulent marriage in Italy by her charming and unscrupulous singing-master. Once she has discovered the fraud and has borne an illegitimate daughter for whom she feels no love, she naturally finds that her most important need is to resume her place in the secure upper-middle-class English world. Her conscience impels her to settle money on Fay—paid through a trustworthy firm of solicitors—and to let nobody into the secret except her brother. And that brother, with true Victorian stoicism, suffers the suspicions even of his own wife rather than let his sister's story become known.

With all its characters—as the *Spectator* for a wonder realized— "standing well upon their feet," unmarred by the happy ending with which so many of MEB's contemporaries would have spoiled it, *The Fatal Three* is the best novel she ever wrote in the genre she had herself invented. There is no crime in the story, but the suspicion of crime and the lost identity of its tragic victim arouse pity and terror more effectively than an actual murder.[25]

The Day Will Come, MEB's second novel for Leng, was a less notable achievement: she now reverted to a real murder, to an investigation in the Wilkie Collins manner, and to a number of glaring improbabilities. But she had never been more vivid or up-to-the-minute in describing the behavior and belongings of her personages, this time mostly Dorset gentry and successful middle-class solicitors. Everybody, even in the countryside, reads treatises "on the deeper mysteries of Buddha." On their honeymoon, husband and wife discuss the writings of A. P. Sinnett, whose *Esoteric Buddhism* was half a dozen years old, and whom MEB knew. The wife hopes that the dead " 'will be better off in their next incarnation, and . . . won't get to that dreadful eighth world which leads nowhere.' " But the sensible young husband is a skeptic: " 'It is a very comforting theory, and it ought to be true; but by what authority is this gospel preached to us, and on what evidence are we to believe it?' " he asks; and he is even more doubtful about *Wider Horizons,* whose author wrote, " 'as if he had been there,' " about the future life that husband and wife would enjoy together in other planets, " 'climbing from star to star, and achieving a higher spirituality . . . with each new existence until we attain the everlasting perfection.' " With purposeful irony, MEB made this conversation the last between the young couple before the husband's murder. As one would expect, she had little use for the fashionable theories of reincarnation.[26]

Written too fast and with obvious fatigue, MEB's next novel, *One Life One Love,* was almost perfunctory.[27] As it neared completion in January 1890, she noted in her diary, "No disposition for new work of any kind." Yet she began a new historical novel, laid it aside after four months' work, and at the end of April reverted to the idea she had discussed in the sixties with both Sala and Bulwer: a tale based upon both Balzac's *La Peau de chagrin* and the Faust story, with a large element of the supernatural. In *Gerard* she combined the two plots and adapted their personages to the London of 1890. Her hero, Gerard, the jaded young man who inherits a fortune, is Faust and also Raphaël de Valentin; the woman he loves is Balzac's heartless tease, Foedora; Balzac's antique dealer who supplies the deadly talisman MEB combined with Mephistopheles in the person of a fashionable "thought-reader," who leads Gerard into dissipation and shows him his Marguerite, whom he seduces but marries on his deathbed. Repeatedly alluding to Balzac and Goethe, MEB kept reminding her readers of what she was trying to do, and making it difficult for them to ignore her inability to do it. The supernatural was, as she had thought in her youth, unsuited to her talents, and a mere "man without conscience and without passion"—even if he could do vanishing tricks—was no substitute for the devil himself.

Yet *Gerard* provided an extraordinarily colorful series of social vignettes. It also marked the beginning of MEB's lasting preoccupation with great wealth and its uses. The ostentation has now become overpowering. Edith, the woman Gerard loves, "tall, Juno-like," married to a stockbroker with "a palace in Surrey and a model house in Hertford Street," has splendid horses and a magnificent brown barouche. Her man-servants wear "dark brown coats, black velvet breeches, and silk stockings." The little octagon room at the back of her house, where she dines tête-à-tête with Gerard, is "upholstered like a tent, and furnished in so Oriental a fashion" that it seems "a solecism to be sitting upon chairs, and not to be eating pillau or kebobs with one's fingers." For the opera Edith is dressed "with that careless air which was her specialty, in some filmy fabric of daffodil colour . . . arranged in loose folds across her bust and shoulders, caught here and there, as if at random, with a diamond star. A great cluster of yellow orchids was fastened on one shoulder and there were yellow orchids pinned on her black lace fan, while big black gloves gave a touch of eccentricity to her toilette." And when she is ready to go to Hurlingham with Gerard, she teasingly asks him if she will " 'do,' " and stands up "before him in a cloud of muslin and lace, a gown so flowing and graceful in its draping over bust and hips that it might have been a cloud of spray clothing a nymph at a fountain." With this, all she needs is "a white Gainsborough hat and a pair of long suede gloves," and they are off.

But for conspicuous consumption, late-Victorian style, developed to its crassest limits, one must visit the house that Edith helps the newly rich Gerard select, rebuild, furnish, and staff: it must be " 'near the south side of Hyde Park, . . . in a walled garden. . . . In London, there is nothing like a garden. . . . The costliness of it always tells.' " Feeling that the Flemish and Jacobean styles have been "overdone," Gerard preserves its Italian façade in the wings he orders to be added. Inside, Edith wants " 'plenty of corners . . . quaint odd angles, don't you know—pretty little nooks that can be made Moorish, or Japanese, or Dutch, or Old English, just as one's fancy may suggest.' " But the architect protests that this idea " 'has now become the property of the restaurants,' " and Edith has to agree that "everything pretty and fantastical becomes common." So everything is sacrificed to grandeur. Even the breakfast room has one wall of glass "opening into a winter-garden, where a fountain plays in a low marble basin, encircled with camellias and palms. The shaded lamps give off a soft and tempered light." Here the walls are "the colour of a hedge-sparrow's egg, relieved by the warm sepia and Indian red of a few choice etchings. These, with a wonderful arrangement of peacock's feathers and celadon Sèvres vases over the chimney piece, were the only ornaments."

The cook whom Edith finds will not take the job

until assured of three underlings in his kitchen, a private sitting room, and the use of a brougham for his marketing. She had chosen butlers and footmen, and had devised a livery . . . darkest green, with black velvet collar and facings, black velvet small clothes, and black silk stockings. "It is a sombre livery," she wrote, "but the powder relieves it, and I think you will like the effect. Your men will wear silk stockings always, . . . and I have told your housekeeper to be very particular about their shoe-buckles. Their shoes will be made in Bond Street, and will cost thirty shillings a pair. . . . with your wealth, your only chance of distinction is by nicety in minor points. Your house will be simply perfect. I went through the reception-rooms yesterday. The ceilings are painted in the style of the Riccardi Palace—a banquet on Olympus. Cobalt predominates in the drapery of the goddesses, who although Rubenesque are quite unobjectionable. The effect . . . harmonises admirably with the subdued amber and russet of the brocade hangings and chair-covers. I engaged your major-domo yesterday. . . . He has a genius for organizing entertainment, and if he and your *chef* can only work harmoniously, your establishment will go on velvet. . . . I am not engaging many servants. Parton will be house-steward, groom of the chambers, and butler, with an under-butler and two footmen, a lad for cellar-work, and a house-manager, so that your stablemen need never be called away from their work. For a bachelor I think this personnel, with half a dozen women, quite sufficient. Anything further would mean display rather than usefulness, and I am sure you don't desire that."

At his parties, Gerard is assured, food will be the main point: " 'Your iced asparagus, ortolans, quails, plovers' eggs—those are the essentials.' "

When he protests that " '. . . as a reward for my hospitality my house will be called the Restaurant Hillersdon or the Café Gerard,' " he is reassured: " 'No, my dear fellow. You will not be laughed at. You have not made your money out of Russian hides or American manures. You do not come to us with inadequate aspirates fresh from the Australian backwoods. You are one of us. . . . You are only that nice boy, Gerard Hillersdon, plus two millions.' "

Son of a parson, Gerard is instantly reminded by his mother that he now has a duty to the poor: " 'Think of the thousands and tens of thousands who are almost starving.' " But he answers "irritably,"

> "I suppose everybody will tell me that. . . . Why should I think of the starving thousands? Why, just because I have the means of enjoying life, am I to make myself miserable by brooding upon the miseries of others? If it comes to that, a man ought never to be happy while there is a single ill-used cab-horse in the world. Just think of all the horses in London and Paris that are underfed and over-driven. . . . There is madness in it. Think of the ill-treated children, the little children, the gutter martyrs, whose lives are a burden. If we are to think of these things, our choicest luxuries, our most exalted pleasures, must turn to gall and wormwood. . . . Since we cannot heal all those gaping wounds . . . we must narrow our thoughts and hopes to the limits of home and family, and say 'Kismet, Allah is good.' "

Gerard refuses to enter Parliament: " 'I am not going to waste any portion of my scanty life in an ill-ventilated, malodorous, over-crowded bear-garden!' " But he is eager to give money to his brother-in-law, a philanthropic London parson who will accept only modest donations. And he even voices what were surely MEB's own views about the risk of "pauperising" the people by too much charity. If the state were to feed the school children even one meal a day, says Gerard, " 'we are told that we should be teaching the parents to look to State aid, and to squander their wages on drink. I dare say . . . but if . . . we could succeed in rearing a healthy race, the craving for drink might be lessened in the next generation.' " Although occasionally capable of such sound reasoning, Gerard is ostentatious, selfish (he objects to the death duties his lawyers must pay on his inheritance), and frivolous.

In describing his late-nights haunts, MEB showed herself knowledgeable. At "the Petunia, one of those after-midnight clubs, where the society is distinctly mixed and the champagne costs twice as much as at the Carlton or the Reform," or at "The Small Hours," where the music is good, and one can get "devilled bones or a lobster" for supper, the ladies are "mostly so intent upon being ladies that they forget to be amusing. The days were past of that fair *mauvaise langue* who charmed the peerage, and whose sturdy British bons mots were circulated over civilised Europe, plagiarised in Paris, and appropriated in Vienna." Gerard "had sought wild gaiety, and . . . had found decent dullness." And at Monte Carlo Gerard's partner is "a lovely German girl with a creamy complexion and innocent blue eyes, who . . . was said to have *rincé* (*Anglice*, beggared) one of the wealthiest Jew bankers in Frankfort." How shocked the censorious critics of MEB's novels of the mid-sixties would have been to read her explicit reference to the vice of the early nineties; how much opportunity she would have given them for cruel innuendo about her own probable morals. And how little notice such passages attracted now, only a quarter of a century later. World-weary and epigrammatical, her Mephistopheles declares, " 'There are women who elect to go through life with an unspotted reputation, just as an Indian fanatic will hold his arms above his head until they stiffen and wither. . . . But honour for honour's sake . . . where there is no one to praise, is beyond my belief.' "[28] *Gerard* introduces the problems posed by the coexistence of vast fortunes and extreme poverty that were to preoccupy MEB in her later years. Despite its obvious weaknesses, it is one of her most interesting novels.

The Venetians (1892) was the last novel for some years that MEB could write while comparatively free from worry about John Maxwell's health. Its immediate successors would show clear signs of hasty composition, eloquent testimony that her mind could not be on her work. After 1891, she wrote for the next four years only as a compulsive activity that provided release from her anxieties, and—in the very fatigue it caused her—a form of relaxation, even, perhaps, of therapy. But *The Venetians*—although another sensation-novel in MEB's earliest and least demanding genre—was almost as well-constructed as *The Fatal Three,* and even had similarities in theme.

Like Mildred, who discovers the secrets of George's past, the heroine of *The Venetians* discovers that her beloved husband has killed her brother in a stabbing affray over a woman at Venice. In each case, an agonizing separation follows, and the curious woman dies of her curiosity. In *The Fatal Three,* George is punished by death for sins he had never committed, while in *The Venetians* the guilty man's punishment is limited to

the death of his wife. A shallow hedonist, he reminds himself, upon learning that it is his wife's brother he has killed, that " 'Even Oedipus Rex had
a good time of it after he killed his father at the cross-roads. . . . It was not
till his daughters were grown up that the trouble began. He had a long
run of prosperity' "; and once he has lost his wife he will surely not
remain inconsolable, especially with a beautiful Venetian opera-singer
—whose lover he had killed—deeply in love with him.

Not far below the surface there lay fine Braddonian ironies. The "Venetians"—the opera-singer and her aunt and even her illegitimate son—who
might be assumed to be hot-blooded Italians with an appetite for
violence—are mild and honest, simple and decent. The girl had fled a life
of misery as a poor lacemaker and become an Englishman's mistress. She
is not ashamed of their illegitimate child. In her lover's absence she flirts
just as naturally with a second Englishman, and when he kills the first,
she falls in love with the killer, keeps his secret, makes an honorable and
successful career as a singer, is an affectionate and devoted mother, and
always rejects the advances of any man she does not love. Her aunt and
companion has the same high standards.

The two English gentlemen in Venice, each calling himself "John
Smith," provide a vivid contrast: one reaches for his new-bought souvenir
dagger and stabs the other (how unsporting, how un-English, how
Italian!), in answer to a low blow and a kick (how Italian, how
unsporting, how un-English!). Both are idlers, eager to take advantage of
a pretty Italian girl's poverty, one a gambler, the other virtually a
murderer. Moreover, although we are assured that the killer's relationship
with the girl remains pure all along, even after she has come to London
and he has secretly set her up in an apartment by way of compensation
for the death of her lover, we cannot help wondering why he visits her so
often even after his marriage.

If the two John Smiths are lecherous violent English gentlemen, the
English women are cruelly snobbish by contrast with the open-hearted
and simple Venetians. The killer's mother has been "born and bred in just
that stratum of English respectability which is narrowest in its sociology
and strongest in its prejudices . . . the county families," who think "the
word trade . . . an abomination." They regard the Church and the Army as
"established for the maintenance of their younger sons, . . . consider they
make a concession when they send a son to the Bar, and . . . shudder at the
notion of a doctor or a solicitor issuing from their superior circle." So she
naturally expects her son's bride to be "Pure as well as beautiful, sprung
from an honourable race, reared by a good and careful mother." And

among the minor characters is a gentleman who knows "more about a lady's dress and a lady's accomplishments and amusements than ninety nine women in a hundred," and admits that the ladies " '. . . like me because I can talk chiffons. I can tell them of the newest ladies' tailor . . . who . . . is going to take the town by storm next season. I can put them up to the newest shade of bronze or auburn hair, the Princess's shade.' " He takes as much interest in a girl's trousseau "as if he had been her maiden aunt," but protests "with a coquettish giggle" that he is not " 'a horrible effeminate little person.' "[29]

3. The End of an Era (1892–1895)

As John Maxwell's health declined, MEB altered her habits of work, writing regularly, but publishing only as opportunity offered. Simultaneously and alternatingly between late May 1891 and May 1893 she completed two three-volume novels and a two-volume novel. The last, *All Along the River*, after a serial run in the Tillotson newspapers, appeared as the first two volumes of a three-decker in 1893, with the third volume devoted to short stories. *Thou Art the Man* was published in three volumes in 1894 after having run serially in the Leng newspapers. And *Sons of Fire*, the first to have been begun and the last to have been completed, did not see the light in three volumes until 1895. It was MEB's last and feeblest three-decker, inspired by E.T.A. Hoffmann's tale of the Doppelgänger.[30] All of the last three, indeed, were the poorest of her fiction since *Fenton's Quest*, written in 1870 while she was still suffering from her nervous collapse after her mother's death.

During 1893, 1894, and 1895, she wrote three one-volume novels, which she would publish only in 1896, 1897, and 1898: *London Pride*—on which she had begun to work as early as 1890—, *Under Love's Rule*, and *Rough Justice*. Though written under even less propitious conditions, all were far superior to her last three-deckers. Were it not that MEB's diaries record the progress of the three one-volume novels, one would not have guessed that she wrote them so long in advance of publication. Because they belong in spirit to the final phase of her career, we reserve them for the next chapter. But their high quality and MEB's forehandedness in writing them suggest that as an artist and a business woman she had sensed, before even the first tremors shook the publishing world, that the day of the three-volume novel, sanctified by almost a century of tradition, was coming to an end. Although she would protest against the change when it came, she was simultaneously preparing to meet it with work of high quality. Her forehandedness would also mean that after John Maxwell's death in March 1895 she could for several years relax as she had never relaxed before in all her long professional life, and, for the first time since her breakdown and recovery of 1868–1869, would spend long weeks away from her writing-table.

Her writing of the last years before Maxwell died also included a four-act play, *A Life Interest*, never produced, although Madge Kendal showed much interest in it, and never published. An original typescript, much corrected in MEB's hand, survives and demonstrates that MEB's ear for dialogue was keen. The play conveys successfully the pathos of a woman's love for a child she cannot acknowledge,[31] a theme MEB would later transform and utilize in her novel *The White House* (1906). Into the earliest years of the new century, she continued to write plays, none of which was produced or published. She also wrote several short stories, and—in 1892–1893—a Christmas novelette, *The Christmas Hirelings*, a genuine, if minor, Braddonian gem.[32]

Here for the last time she took advantage of the "cover" provided by an ostensibly innocent and jolly Christmas story to deliver herself of a few home truths about good old British class distinction and the human tragedies it precipitated. Her readers at their own discretion might choose to savor them or to ignore them. Into the lonely Cornish castle of a "great landed proprietor and fine gentleman of the early Victorian school," who has disowned his daughter for eloping with a curate—only a grocer's son ("The landed gentry of Cornwall are a proud race. The roots of their family trees go down into the dark night of British history")—a whimsical bachelor friend proposes as a Christmas treat to introduce some children, whom he will hire for the occasion from their parents. He reassures his host: these will not be " 'poor children,' " who " 'don't know how to treat decent furniture' " and " 'scroop the heavy chairs on the oak floor, and leave prints of their horrid little thumbs' " on the books; these will be " 'poor relations,' " as he hints, of his own. The children, two little girls and a little boy, naturally conquer their crusty host; and when the youngest child, Moppet, becomes ill, her mother is sent for. She is of course the host's daughter, now a poor widow. Father and daughter are reconciled: the ruse of "hiring" the children has succeeded.

One cannot dismiss *The Christmas Hirelings* as a mere *fin-de-siècle* pastiche of warmed-over Dickens. Before their grandfather knows who they are, his grandchildren reveal that their mother—disowned and poor—is still as snobbish as he could wish. Mother and children live in France, but the children don't speak French, because, as Moppet explains, they are not allowed to learn it " 'from common people; so we only know the useful words. . . . food and clothes and such things, and how to ask our way, or to tell people where we live if we ever should be lost. . . . We can't help learning words on the sands when we hear the little French children . . . though mother won't let us play with them.' " How reassuring to the "fine gentleman of the early Victorian school," who all unwitting is listening to his own four-year-old granddaughter. And how alien to the Francophile MEB, who would have given much to have had as a child the opportunity to learn French at first hand that these children were being forced to throw away. To the Christmas Eve party given at the castle there come "all the little ladies and gentlemen of the neighbourhood, the pretty fair-haired girls from the Rectory, and the children of the only two gentlefolk's families within an easy drive." When Moppet regrets that there may be other children who have no Christmas tree, her grandfather tells her that she is a "little socialist." But on Christmas night, the village children, red-faced and in hobnailed boots—saying " 'Laws,' " and even " 'Crikey' "—have their own tree too.

Moppet and her brother and sister MEB drew as portraits of her own great-nieces and nephew, children of Edward Braddon's daughter Amy Knyvett, who had sent them to England while she was in Allahabad with her husband, Deputy Inspector-General of Indian Police in the Northwest Province. One of the reasons that the story manages to transcend its own sentimentality—skillfully administered to wring the hearts of the readers of *The Lady's Pictorial*—is that MEB was using as models living children of whom she was deeply fond. But the modern reader will be particularly grateful for her irony. Busily ladling the vinegar into the molasses, always innocent, she got away with a denunciation of the late Victorian social code that would have caused her trouble had it been detected.[33]

In mid-1894, soon after the appearance of *The Christmas Hirelings* in book form, the circulating libraries took the first steps that would eventually doom the three-volume novel and lead to its replacement by the novel in one volume. On June 27, Messrs. Mudie and Messrs. W. H. Smith & Sons issued a joint circular asking that, beginning with the year 1895, all publishers reduce the maximum wholesale price of fiction to four shillings per volume—a twenty percent cut from the prevailing price of five shillings—and at the same time undertake not to publish cheaper editions of their novels for a full year after the original publication date. *The*

Publisher's Circular, influential organ of the book-trade, commented editorially that if the publishers complied with these requests, they would no longer be able to pay authors at the going rates. It "would mean . . . a revolution in literature. . . . The occupation of two-thirds of our novelists would be destroyed at a blow, and the remaining third would be compelled to accept considerably lower terms than they now receive."

Did this mean the end of the three-volume novel? And if it did, would not that also mean the end of the circulating library? Yes, said *The Publisher's Circular*, "as soon as it becomes the practice to issue novels at once in cheap editions, the public will forsake the libraries and flock to the booksellers." This might not be a bad thing, and the trade could read-just itself after a time. The really popular novelist would have his public either way. But the less secure authors would go to the wall. R. B. Marston, of Sampson Low, a major publishing firm, was proposing that instead of the publishers reducing their prices to the libraries, the libraries should raise theirs to the readers, while Heinemann suggested four volumes as the proper length for very long novels and urged that the libraries charge less for "bad" novels than for "good." But who would decide what was good and what was bad? This would surely mean "invidious distinctions and consequent heartburnings." *The Publisher's Circular* supported Marston and urged the circulating libraries not to persist in their demands.[34]

During the summer of 1894, other correspondents pointed out that the public would be outraged at the discovery that the circulating libraries had all along been paying fifteen shillings—and now wanted to pay only twelve—for a three-volume novel that cost other purchasers thirty-one shillings and sixpence.[35] The London Booksellers' Society vigorously opposed the libraries' circular and declared themselves "unanimously in favour of . . . novels being published at once in a six shilling [one-volume] form."[36] The Incorporated Society of Authors, "after taking the opinion of several eminent novelists," concurred—suicidally, some thought—in calling for the abolition of the three-volume novel as an "artificial form of edition produced for a small body of readers only. . . . Publisher and author . . . would derive more profit from a single volume of 4,000 copies issued to the trade at 3s 8d each than from a three-volume edition of 750 copies issued at 14s."[37] *The Publisher's Circular* rejoined that the three-volume novel might be an artificial mode of publication "but then it would not be hard to prove that fiction itself is artificial, that libraries are artificial, and that . . . an artificial system has been followed to supply an artificial want." It was far too soon to "decide precipitately that the three-volume novel 'must go.' " Walter Besant predicted that the three-volume novel was not doomed to instant extinction, but would die a lingering death. Complaining that there were too many novels, Rider Haggard added that the purchase of a single copy of a novel by a circulating library stopped the sale of two other copies.[38]

With matters thus still in suspense, the controversy came temporarily to a halt in August 1894. As the autumn of the year turned into winter, the weather grew unusually severe. By January and February 1895, MEB was frequently noting in her diary how bitter cold it was at Annesley Bank. The Maxwells all suffered from illness; even MEB herself had a cold late in February and on the twenty-eighth she wrote, "M. feverish and ill." Across the empty spaces for the days between the first and fifth of March 1895, she drew two heavy lines. These were the days of John Maxwell's final illness—influenza—and death. Within a few hours after he died, MEB wrote to Juliette Whiting, daughter of her old friends and a particular favorite: "Your house and my brother's were the only thresholds he ever crossed as a guest after his helplessness came upon him—& those visits to you—so bright & gay—so restoring to him—were most precious to me—are as a remembrance most dear." She assured Juliette that the flowers she had sent would be on Maxwell's coffin.[39] On March 7, Father O'Connell, the local Richmond Catholic priest and a family friend of the Maxwells, read the funeral service. The next day, Will and Ted "left for Hendon, 7 A.M.," accompanying their father's corpse to its burial in Hendon Cemetery, where MEB's dead child and mother already lay. Gerald was in America, Fanny and Edmund Selous and Rosie and Rob Lachlan were abroad. Influenza continued to sweep through the household: Ted and the servants all had bouts of it that lasted for a good many days.

Restless in her bereavement, MEB went with Will and Ted to Weymouth for a few days in late March. On April 5, she paid her own first visit to Hendon since Max's death, "destroyed old letters" on April 26, and three days later went to Bond Court, the offices of the Maxwells' solicitors, Messrs. Addison and Walmsley, and "signed seven affidavits." Then she was off on a two-week visit to Cornwall in fine weather with Will. Her life as a widow had begun.

It was about thirty-four years since she had accepted John Maxwell as a lover and begun to take care of him and his children, and, soon, of their own. The powerful attraction he exercised over her had never lost its hold, although at times, amidst the social and personal frustrations of the 1860's and early 1870's, she had allowed herself to become skeptical, if not cynical, about romantic love. But Maxwell had "never shirked a domestic duty," he had always been "so good to" her, he had been a tower of strength through every family crisis: her mother's death, her brother's distressing behavior, Gerald's collapse in Cincinnati four thousand miles away. Bluster though he might—and his letters to Tillotson were full of emotional explosions—his "powerful business brain," MEB believed, had guided her professional career and had helped her capitalize fully on her talents, even if in the early days she had sometimes found him prosaic and less interested in great art than in driving a hard bargain and in the quick return of cash. She must have been sadly disappointed when their children did not love him as she thought he deserved; and long afterwards, when Will wrote his reminiscences, he reproached himself and his brothers and sisters for what he felt had been their impatience and even unkindness towards their father. To MEB, so long Maxwell's constant companion, his death was a stunning blow.

In Switzerland during the summer with Will and Ted, MEB was worried about Rosie, whom she had seen only for two brief visits at Lichfield House since Maxwell's death. On August 6, she wrote Fanny Selous a long letter about her. At St. Moritz on August 31, she wrote in her diary: "Alarming telegram from Cambridge." In stifling heat, MEB and her two sons rushed home to England. They left St. Moritz at three o'clock in the morning of September 1 by "special post," breakfasted at Mühlen, lunched at the station at Coire (Chur), dined at Basel, caught a train at 1:30 A.M. for Paris, arriving at seven that night, left Paris at nine, arrived at Dieppe at 1:00 A.M. for a "good but foggy" crossing of the Channel, and reached Lichfield House at 10:30 on the morning of September 3. Ted went to Cambridge that day, and on the next MEB "went to Cambridge with W[ill], brought Rosie and nurse back to Richmond. Read Clarissa Harlowe on journey." The diary now records a series of doctors' visits, and the engagement of a second nurse. By September 18, Rosie was going for a drive in Richmond Park.

During all of this, MEB made no mention of Rob Lachlan in her diary. But on September 29, she noted that he arrived from St. Malo (had he only returned there briefly to close a house or had he been there since September 1892?); on October 8 that he "left early for Cambridge"; on October 31 that he dined and stayed the night at Lichfield House; and on November 1 that she herself "Saw Rosie off with nurse on board Rodney." The doctors had apparently ordered Rosie to make the long sea voyage to Australia; on December 13, 1895, MEB "wrote to Rosie at Melbourne" and on the sixteenth "Rob Lachlan arrived on visit." Why did not Rob Lachlan accompany Rosie, since he was no longer attached to Trinity College? His reappearance at Lichfield House on a visit while Rosie was presumably still in Australia makes highly unlikely any hypothesis of a disagreement between husband and wife. Was Rosie's illness in part nervous, and had the doctors recommended a complete rest, away from her husband and her child and indeed from all of her family? MEB's breakdown of 1868 while she had been pregnant with Rosie had had some neurotic component. Will Maxwell was, he tells us himself, subject for some years in his youth to unaccountable periods of depression; in his later years, Gerald was distinctly "queer"; and all the family regarded Ted as unreasonable. Perhaps Rosie had had a miscarriage, which may have contributed to her illness. We can be sure only that late in 1895 she was voyaging toward Australia alone with a nurse.

On the very day of Rosie's first outing, September 18, MEB's *Sons of Fire* appeared. She and her publisher, Simpkin, Marshall, had decided to defy the libraries and have a test of strength. They published the three volumes at the traditional price of fifteen shillings wholesale and thirty-one shillings and sixpence retail. Mudie's counterattacked by printing a circular which they issued to all their subscribers who asked for a copy: "The publishers having decided to publish this book in three volumes, at a prohibitive price, the directors are compelled to wait for the production of the one-volume edition, which (judging from past experience) will be in a very few weeks." On September 20, MEB's diary has the entry, "Mr. Miles (Simpkin's) came down to discuss Mudie's circular." And on September 23, the *Times* published a letter from MEB, no doubt agreed upon between her and Miles at their conference. She pointed out that the allegedly "prohibitive price asked for 'Sons of Fire' " was the "same price paid by Mudie's Library for every one of the three-volume novels published for me during the thirty three years in which I have been known to the reading public," and added that the interval between three-volume publication and the first cheap edition of her novels had never been less than six months and in recent years had been eight. Now, in a rear-guard action against the libraries, MEB increased it to eleven: she was "happy to assure the West-end, suburban, and provincial librarians, who are freely circulating my new book, that no other or cheap edition of 'Sons of Fire' will appear until August, 1896."[40] Mournfully *The Publisher's Circular* declared that Miss Braddon's letter "probably marks the crisis in the fate of the three-volume novel." Readers who wanted to read their "old and very popular favourite" without waiting almost a year for the cheap edition would no doubt patronize not Mudie's but the circulating libraries which had bought the three-volume *Sons of Fire*. "What is one's loss will doubtless be another's gain."[41]

Although the three-decker lingered, as Besant had predicted it would, for two more years after 1895, the number published grew very small indeed, and MEB herself never published another. The novel in one volume would henceforth be standard. It was a major turning point. With three completed unpublished one-volume novels in manuscript ready in her desk, MEB might oppose the new fashion, but she had no need to fear it. So it was that a change which revolutionized not only the size but the very concept of the novel coincided almost exactly in time with John Maxwell's death. Grieving for her husband, and with her younger daughter under a nurse's care twelve thousand miles away, MEB's only entry in her diary for Christmas 1895 was "Burning M's letters afternoon." Her children and grandchildren would now have to try to fill the gap. But they could hardly become any closer to her than they already were. It was Will, of course, on whom she especially leaned, and Will in particular, mindful of his childhood vow never to abandon her, who now took the lead in rising to the emergency. Intense though their relationship was, both of them were sophisticated enough to perceive, if not always wholly to avoid, the dangers of it. In the two decades of widowhood that lay ahead of MEB, mother and son would reflect on these dangers in their hearts and portray them in the pages of their fiction.

CHAPTER X

From Victorian to Georgian:
the Final Decades (1895–1915)

1. The *Doyenne* of English Novelists at Home

During her last twenty years, the current of MEB's life flowed steadily except for the interruption caused by a severe illness beginning on November 22, 1907. Until January 6, 1908, when she went to church in an invalid chair, she wrote nothing in her diary. Although she afterwards referred to her attack as a nervous breakdown, it was in fact a slight stroke, which temporarily deprived her of the use of her limbs. Her left leg never fully recovered, and she walked with a cane. She was seventy-two, and for a time her days were more like those of other old women. But towards the end of her life, her activity had almost regained its former level. Except for this hiatus, her last two decades, then, were as crowded as ever.

Between 1895 and 1904, she went abroad each year. With Gerald and Will at the end of 1895 she passed three weeks in Cannes, one in Nice, and one in Menton. Drives, yachting expeditions, picnics, and parties culminated with the Battle of the Flowers. The French and Russian aristocrats were out in force. MEB met Richard Watson Gilder, editor of the *Century Magazine* in New York. Back in Richmond by February 10, 1896, she wrote on March 14, "Scarcely any work done this quarter year." For the first time since 1868–1869, she had slackened the pace.

After a month at Richmond—ordering a new border of flowers for John Maxwell's grave at Hendon, visiting Rhoda Broughton, Lady Monckton, and (on February 20 at Lady Dorothy Nevill's) meeting Henry James—she went off on March 12 to Lyndhurst, where Gerald and Will hunted. She herself had given up riding and hunting altogether after Maxwell's death: it was a severe deprivation. Friends and family thronged to Annesley Bank: the Laboucheres, Fanny and her children and two servants, Rob Lachlan with his little son Austin and Austin's nurse; Rosie had not yet returned from Australia. But on July 31 MEB and Will went to Cambridge by rail for the day and lunched with Rosie and Rob; so Rosie was at home again.

On August 14, MEB went with Will to Germany for a month, spent chiefly at Bad Homburg, where Gerald and Ted joined them. Excursions, the music of the band at the Kurhaus, a charity fête, where people were "expecting royalties, none came," made the days pass swiftly. On September 2, 1896, the Germans put on a great display of flags and garlands, and rang bells everywhere to celebrate the anniversary of their victory over the French at Sedan in 1870. Back in Richmond in mid-September, MEB saw a good deal of her neighbor and fellow-novelist, Miss Tuttiett, who wrote under the name of Maxwell Grey and whose new book, *The Last Sentence*, MEB was reading. On November 17, Ted Maxwell was called to the Bar, and on December 25 MEB wrote, "First happy Christmas day with sons all at home."

During the year 1896 she had read voraciously: in fiction, Stevenson's *Weir of Hermiston*, Stanley Weyman's *Minister of France*, H. S. Merriman (Hugh Seton Scott)'s *Sowers*, Mrs. Humphry Ward's *Marcella*, Hardy's *Jude the Obscure*, Gissing's *In the Year of Jubilee*, and "three melancholy short stories" by Henry James, *The Madonna of the Future*, *Longstaffe's Marriage*, and *Madame de Mauves*, as well as his *Portrait of a Lady*. In French she had been reading Hervieux, Bourget, Richepin, Coppée, Bassompierre, Dumas père. History and biography included Disraeli's *Charles I*, Masson's *Milton*, Gardiner, Michelet, Gibbon, Cornac's *Mazarin*, many of them useful for her historical novels. Dante, Hallam, Dorothy Wordsworth's letters, Tennyson and Browning, Sudermann's *Das Glück im Winkel*, A. P. Stanley's *Jewish Church*, Burton's *History of Scotland*, Huber's *Jesuiten*: it was an extraordinary range. She went to the opening nights of *Cymbeline*, of Mr. Hawtree's comedy *Mr. Martin*, of *Love in Idleness*, and of the famous *Sign of the Cross*, when she and Gerald and Fanny had the royal box and called at Wilson Barrett's dressing-room afterwards.

The year 1896 marked the completion of MEB's transition to her life as a widow. On her annual continental trip to a fashionable resort, she always did some sightseeing on the way out and back, but she spent her time abroad largely with the same English people whom she constantly saw socially at home. In 1897, she was in Cannes with Mrs. Whiting and Juliette, Gerald, and Will between January and the end of March; took excursions to Antibes and St. Raphael; passed three weeks in August at Ramsgate; and spent September at Cadenabbia. There on Lake Como were the Laboucheres and many others. In 1898, her winter holiday took her to Cornwall for three weeks in February and March, and she did not go to the Continent until August, when Will and Fanny joined her for two weeks in St. Moritz. Here MEB and Will read Browning together in the forest, and the young people played tennis. By the time MEB reached Cadenabbia in October for her second visit there, she found so many old friends among the English there that she called them in her diary "the gang." Philip Burne-Jones was one of their number. "The gang" boated on the lake, took tea at the same "latteria" almost daily, and went on picnics. In 1899, the pattern began as usual: MEB spent March and half of April on the Italian and French Rivieras, with a visit to Shelley's house at Lerici.

But the summer of 1899 brought a family tragedy. Rosie Lachlan died on July 21, at the age of thirty. MEB's diary shows a heavy double line drawn diagonally across the spaces for the days between July 20 and 25, and the only entry is for the twenty-fifth: "Drove to cemetery with W[ill] and in park afternoon." There is nothing to show that Rosie's death was expected or that MEB had been anxious about her. On the contrary, the diaries for 1897 and 1898 record the Lachlans' usual visits to Lichfield House and in January 1897 MEB had been greatly encouraged about Rosie's health.[1] Had she been ill, MEB would have been at her side. Indeed, were it not for the fact that Rosie's tombstone in Richmond bears the date July 21, 1899, we would not know from the diary alone who had died. Nor did Will Maxwell mention his sister's death in his autobiography, and the present generation of the Maxwell family knows nothing about its cause. As with Rosie's previous illness and her solitary trip to Australia, her sudden death remains a mystery.

On August 5, MEB "Walked to cemetery with W[ill] to carry fresh flowers" and on October 11 she "Drove alone to cemetery afternoon with Chrysanthemum cross, and to Russell's to order roses." In later years the diaries contain similar entries. Rob Lachlan continued to make frequent short visits to Lichfield House and by 1900 often brought Austin with him. At Christmas 1900, MEB took Austin to a Christmas party at Mme. Trübner's. She "went over" his preparatory school at Stevenage in November 1901, and during his years at Wellington he usually spent part of each holiday period with her. While he was still too young to travel by himself one of his uncles would meet him at the station and put him aboard the train for his return journey. MEB enjoyed taking him to the Natural History Museum in South Kensington. In her will she left him some of her property in Hampshire. His father remarried, but remained in touch with MEB, who wrote in her diary on October 28, 1913, "Mr. and Mrs. Lachlan to lunch with little girl, Mary," Austin's half-sister.

After Rosie's death, MEB's life resumed its former pattern. Then, as in each of the succeeding four years, she took a spring trip to Cornwall in April and a continental trip in the summer or autumn. In 1903, she revisited Skisdon, where the William Braddons received her with their elder son and five daughters; Will played croquet with his cousins. Four of the girls then came to tea with MEB at Tintagel, where she was staying. On the 1904 trip, MEB noted that she "Drove to Camelford, explored High Street. . . ." She saw the house of her uncle John Braddon, the bachelor lawyer of her childhood visit to Skisdon. She spent September and October 1900 in Cadenabbia. In 1901, the August–September trip was confined to Switzerland, where the rains were so persistent that the hotel guests at Beatenberg left and the dining-room closed. In Paris on the way home, MEB went up to the new Sacré Coeur on Montmartre and saw the panorama of the city. The 1902 continental holiday was spent in Homburg, with excursions to Constance; MEB returned there in 1903 and, for the last time, in 1904. Here as at home, her friends now included more members of the aristocracy than in earlier years. Lady Anna Chandos-Pole, daughter of Lord Harrington and still in occupation of Harrington House in Kensington Palace Gardens, Lord Ellenborough, the Leveson-Gowers: these were frequent companions. On each of these trips Will Maxwell accompanied his mother. But by 1904, he was falling in love, and quite possibly MEB's decision not to go to Europe in subsequent years sprang—consciously or not—from her reluctance to go without him.

The European trips were now replaced by frequent visits to English resorts: late in 1904 to Ramsgate, whence MEB was summoned back to Richmond by "bad news about dogs"; in August 1905 to Yorkshire and the Derbyshire Peak (MEB noted that the tea at Harrogate consisted of "stale bread, sloppy jelly, and no jam," but she read Charlotte Brontë's life, and walked on the moors, "explored" Haddon Hall, and finished the holiday at Whitby); in 1906 to Cornwall in the spring and back to Whitby and Matlock Bath in August, followed by three weeks at Ramsgate in December; in 1908, after her long illness, to Sidmouth and Bournemouth for most of February and March, and to Westgate for all of August (in Sidmouth MEB complained of an intolerably long sermon by an East-End curate; in Westgate she enjoyed a visit from Lady Bancroft [Marie], who entertained the assembled Maxwells by doing imitations for an hour and on another day played a gramophone). Brighton, Bexhill,

Exmouth, Ilfracombe, Folkestone—MEB returned repeatedly to each. In August 1914 she was at Bexhill during the days of mounting European crisis and of Great Britain's entry into the first World War—days that she left ominously blank in her diaries.

Before her illness of 1907, MEB's social life continued at its usual pace. The Laboucheres, the Bram Stokers, Lucy Clifford, Lady Dorothy Nevill, Rhoda Broughton, Miss Tuttiett appear and reappear. Mary Cholmondeley, now making her reputation as a novelist with *Red Pottage* (1899) and celebrated for her conversation and her charm, and Richard Pryce, by no means so successful a writer but equally distinguished, had become members of MEB's inner circle. Closest of all were the Whitings: when Mrs. Whiting was unwell in December 1901, MEB wrote to Juliette, "I have only one friend who occupies anything like the same place in my heart, my dear Mrs. Trübner, a friend of nearly forty years";[2] and on June 14, 1902, the diary recorded, "All ended at Lavender Hill, a peaceful end." MEB and Will attended the requiem High Mass for Mrs. Whiting at the Church of the Sacred Heart in Battersea. With Madame Trübner in her delightful house at Hampton—"Beveree"—MEB continued her weekly French reading sessions. To the list of novels and plays that they read, Maupassant, Rostand, Augier, Sardou, Labiche, Dumas père and fils, Feuillet, Ohnet, Anatole France all made major contributions.

At the Laboucheres' on June 22, 1898, Nordica and others sang, and MEB did not get home until 2:30 in the morning. On January 9, 1902, she stayed at the Friths only until midnight, but that may have been because it was the eighty-third birthday of her host, the great painter and her friend for almost forty years. Henry Irving, Conan Doyle, J. S. Tenniel, and F. C. Burnand and their wives were all at Sir Charles Scotter's dinner at the Carlton on July 2. MEB went to call on the widowed Lady Lytton in March 1900 and took with her one of the letters she had received from the late poet, Viceroy of India, her friend since his father's day. Lady Lytton made a copy of it for her son and returned it with an appreciative letter.[3] Having met Thomas Hardy and T. P. O'Connor at lunch one day in June 1903, MEB went on to meet Sir George Douglas, the Ranee of Sarawak, and Lucy Clifford at tea the same afternoon at Mary Cholmondely's.

On New Year's Day 1904 at Lady Dorothy's "everybody present [was] a protectionist"; at MEB's own party the next day everybody played the game of "how, when, and where." At Sir William and Lady Clayton's riverside place near Marlow, Ellensmede, on June 29, 1904, Radetsky's band played during a "recherché" luncheon, and the guests had a delightful time walking in the garden and inspecting the animals in the private zoo. Forgoing an opportunity ten days later to hear "pupil's music" at a music school attended by her great-niece, the younger Amy Knyvett (original of "Moppet" in *The Christmas Hirelings*), MEB instead lunched at Lady Humphrey's and met Lord Hugh Cecil, Maxine Elliott, Sir Charles Wyndham, the Bancrofts, Sir Gilbert Parker, and Mrs. Alec Tweedie.

"Tea in the drawing-room, and tea only" was served at Mary Cholmondely's on March 30, 1905, but MEB had a good talk with "Crackenthorpe, M.P., Nelson Hood, and Sidney Lee." Hilaire Belloc was at Mrs. Travers' lunch party on August 1, 1906. In September, MEB spent a weekend near Althorp, Northamptonshire, with Sir William and Lady Stables; Lord Spencer of Althorp and his daughter showed the house party the pictures in the great house. Gertrude Atherton, Elizabeth Robins, the Dowager Duchess of Bedford, Lady Jersey, Mrs. Humphry Ward, Lady Pollock, Violet Hunt, the Duchess of St. Alban's, Lord Doneraile, the Duc and Duchesse de Mandas, the Landgrave of Hesse, "Maarten Maartens" (Joost van der Poorten Swartz, the Dutch novelist): she met them all. She went to the private view at the Royal Academy, to a Fragonard exhibition with Fanny, to see "Spy's" *Vanity Fair* portraits on special show, to a Whistler exhibition. She watched croquet, races, polo at Aldershot between the Life-Guards, the Parthians, and Buenos Aires, and a hockey party at Beveree, at which the tea served was "sumptuous." She attended the massed military bands concert at Ranelagh, where the Duke of Connaught was present, Mischa Elman's concert, Patti's concert. In view of the cruel anonymous critical attack that Mrs. Oliphant had made upon her forty years before, it is ironical to find J. M. Barrie writing to MEB on January 4, 1907, asking her to sign a minute petitioning for a memorial tablet to be erected in Mrs. Oliphant's memory in Edinburgh Cathedral. What MEB answered we do not know, but she probably had never identified Mrs. Oliphant as her ancient enemy. And Mrs. Oliphant herself in 1892 had reversed her old position and publicly praised MEB in print as the "most complete Story-teller," with a "sense of life as a whole," amid the "froth of flirtation and folly" characteristic of the modern novel.[4]

In 1897, 1898, and 1899, MEB spent April and May at Lyndhurst. But the 1899 sojourn was interrupted by Gerald's serious illness, from which he took more than a month to recover: he was still unable to go out at the moment of Rosie's death. Thereafter, MEB went less and less often to Lyndhurst. In 1900 the visit had shrunk to only three days. MEB did not stay in the big house, but in one of her cottages. She catalogued books and gave orders for new planting in the garden. In 1901 and 1902, she did not go to Annesley Bank at all and in 1903 spent only a single night there in November, when she "looked over the house." A similar overnight visit "inspecting house, garden &c." sufficed for 1904, and was repeated only in 1906, when she "stayed in cottage, put away books, inspected shrubbery, and condemned forest trees." In 1907 she selected new wallpapers for the billiard-room, morning-room, and staircase, and on August 13 made her first prolonged visit to Lyndhurst in eight years, staying for two and a half months and, as in the old days, sending horses, dogs, coachman, and grooms ahead.

Only three weeks after her return from this sojourn she had her stroke. After her recovery, she decided that she should not maintain Annesley Bank as a residence. In early August 1909, she took an inventory of linen and in September sold the furniture. Sometime thereafter, she sold the big house, but kept some land and cottages. Lyndhurst disappears from her diary until October 13, 1913, when she and Fanny spent three nights in one of the cottages. A year later, she spent a final weekend there with Fanny, Gerald, and Will Maxwell's wife Sydney: by then the war had begun and Will was in the army.

MEB's sister-in-law, Alice Braddon, wrote her from Tasmania on February 14, 1897, reporting that Sir Edward wanted to accept "Mr. Chamberlain's invitation to the Colonial Premiers" on the occasion of the Queen's Diamond Jubilee, the "biggest festival of the century." But the Braddons were concerned lest the Tasmanian political opposition—not one of whom, Alice maintained, was "a gentleman at heart, whatever their birth," and all of whom had "been guilty at times of the meanest libels of Edward"—should be "nasty in his absence." Generous as always, MEB had made her sister-in-law a present of some money, which was spent on a mangle, a 750-gallon tank for the wash-house, and a fitted bath in the bathroom, "a great luxury" in Leith, on the northwest coast of Tasmania, where the Braddons were living. Alice was hoping to buy a boat with the remaining money, were it not for the anxiety she would feel when her daughter May was out in it. Meanwhile, she wrote, "it may be unromantic, but I think of you with gratitude when I am tubbing." Sir Edward overcame his political hesitation; in June 1897 the three Braddons from Tasmania came to England. MEB entertained them repeatedly and her children and stepchildren all rallied round to see their distinguished uncle. The visit lasted only three weeks.

It was the last time that MEB would see her brother. He wrote her from

Tasmania on August 14, 1898, that he was obeying her suggestion and enlisting the help of his son Ned—"manager of an important mining syndicate in New Zealand" and formerly "engaged in mining operations in Queensland and the West Coast of Tasmania"—in finding a post for Clode Braddon, great-grandson of MEB's uncle William, the retired Bengal merchant and judge, of whom she had been so fond as a little girl. Braddon family loyalty, as usual, was proving very strong: Clode's father was the present master of Skisdon, and MEB and Edward were doing all they could for the young man. If his own son Ned should not be able to help, Edward wrote, "you may depend upon my leaving no stone unturned . . . for I fully recognise the debt of gratitude our family, & I especially, owe to this young fellow's great grand-father," who had given Edward his first chance in India more than half a century before. Edward wrote that he himself was "a poor creature physically," with "little intermission to my pains, and none so far to my work. But I am able to conduct my administrative duties as Premier & my Parliamentary work as leader of my House and party without any absolute breakdown."[5]

Edward died on February 3, 1904. MEB wrote in her diary: "Bad news from Tasmania. Went with W[ill] to P[ost] O[ffice] to send cable to A[lice] B[raddon]." To a friend who had sent her a letter of condolence, MEB wrote that an election campaign involving two-hour speeches had shortened his life. "He loved the colony," she added, "and was keen in the strife of parties. . . . he had none of the attributes of age. He ought to have been spared for another decade."[6] Afterwards, Alice Braddon and her daughter May left Tasmania, visiting MEB in the spring of 1905 and again in the autumn, and in January 1906. MEB wrote of May as "young, *gentille*, and very fond of music."[7] For a time the Braddons lived in London, where MEB noted on January 26, 1906, that she had seen "presents and trousseau," presumably just before May's marriage to a Mr. Nicolay. Thereafter Lady Braddon visited relatives in India until October 1908, when she arrived from Bombay to stay at Lichfield House. At frequent intervals thereafter (as in April 1910, with "May and boy and nurse"), Alice Braddon and her affectionate sister-in-law met and each meeting was recorded in the diary.

Among the Maxwells, only Gerald went to the celebration of the Queen's Diamond Jubilee, watching from the roof of the Lyceum on June 22, 1897. He remained a bachelor throughout his mother's life and continued to live at Lichfield House but traveled widely. He often escorted his mother to the theatre: to a Paderewski concert, on June 15, 1897, and to see Sarah Bernhardt in *Lorenzaccio* two days later; to the Adelphi on

July 6, to see a play called *Spiritism* ("thin house," MEB noted); to the opening night of Lawrence Irving's *Peter the Great* on New Year's Day, 1898, when they went behind the scenes afterwards, and did not get home until 1:30 in the morning; to *Cyrano de Bergerac* on July 4 ("theatre full and hot"); to Anthony Hope's *Lady Ursula* at the Duke of York's on October 11, 1898; to *Lord and Lady Algy* on February 23, 1899. A diary entry of April 1899—"GM Her Majesty's Aberdeen"—suggests that Gerald had returned to the stage; but since he was about to become dramatic critic for the *Court Journal* and the *Daily Mail*, posts he held for many years, it may be that he had attended as a reviewer instead. In any case, he now suffered a severe illness, after which he accompanied his mother and Will to Eastbourne following Rosie's death. In 1900 he and his mother together saw *The Gay Lord Quex*, Sudermann's *Das Glück im Winkel*, Duse in *The Second Mrs. Tanqueray*, Mrs. Patrick Campbell in *Magda*, *Herod*, and *The Second in Command*.

On July 3, 1902, when the Lyceum Theatre was celebrating its fiftieth anniversary, MEB and Gerald went together to the festivities: "A magnificent assemblage & party superbly done. Indian princes in large numbers—gorgeously dressed. All the world and his wife. Theatre transformed into vast hall, with crimson-covered flights of stairs leading to stage," MEB noted in one of the longest single entries she ever made in her diary. Six months later she published a nostalgic article remembering that she had first gone to the Lyceum in the 1840's to see Mrs. Keeley as Cinderella and that her uncle, John Delane of the *Times*, had often given her mother free tickets. In Fechter's day, during the sixties, MEB had seen "Charles Dickens, standing up in his box, with his daughters at his side, to applaud his friend and *protégé* as the curtain fell upon the tragic story" of *Ruy Blas*. She recalled Herr Bandmann, Fechter's successor, in Bulwer's *Rightful Heir* (which she had seen in 1868, all unwitting, the night before her mother told her of Maggie's death) and how Bandmann had been supported by "his pretty and talented young wife, Miss Milly Palmer," who would become a close personal friend of the Maxwells. But of course MEB gave most of her article to the triumphs of Henry Irving—from Erckmann-Chatrian's *The Bells*, which Bulwer had called "a revelation," through *Hamlet* itself: a career which had for thirty years been "the most potent influence in the dramatic world."[8]

Aside from the theatre, Gerald's chief interest was freemasonry, and MEB's diaries often mentioned his attendance—sometimes with Will—at a Masonic or "rouge-croix" dinner. The purpose, she once noted, seemed to be the largest possible consumption of the most expensive champagne to be had for money. Gerald also wrote a novel, called *The Miracle-Worker*, in which a German doctor and his Afghan assistant discover a miracle-drug. It appeared in 1907, when his mother and Will both published novels of their own. MEB urged a friend to include "my eldest son's first novel" in any list she might be sending to a circulating library: "I venture to think the story & treatment . . . might interest you."⁹

In 1903, Ted Maxwell, who had joined the southwestern circuit in 1898, married Maud Hudson. Early in April MEB was busy with Maud: at Shoolbred's buying carpets and blinds, at Hampton's buying the furniture for the best bedroom, choosing wallpapers, blankets, and table-plate. The Ted Maxwells began their married life in a flat at Wellesley Mansions, and MEB was helping them settle in, doing so many things usually done by the mother of the bride that it seems likely that Maud had no mother. From April 1903 on, Maud often appears in the diary: it is clear that MEB liked her very much. In December 1903 Ted's and Maud's first child, Marjorie, was born; in October 1906 their second, Betty; in August 1909 their third, Georgina. Maud and her children often came to tea with MEB, and by the time the elder girls were five and three, their grandmother was taking them to the Victoria and Albert Museum: Betty's third birthday was celebrated with a nursery tea at Lichfield House. Like the Ted Maxwells, Fanny and Edmund Selous and their children, young Gerald and the twins, Mary and Freda, now growing up, visited Lichfield House regularly several times a year for long or short periods. MEB's diaries record the vicissitudes of their lives: their residence in Cheltenham, their illnesses and accidents, their long and repeated trips to France. After they came back to England, in the years immediately before the War, Fanny became prominent in the work of the Girl Guides.

With Will Maxwell MEB had an easy, unstrained relationship, seldom interrupted even for a day at a time, involving walks, excursions, and above all long conversations. Returning in the early years of the century to the profession of writing which he had tried but abandoned a decade earlier, he moved from strength to strength. A man of remarkable good looks and natural charm, he was a bachelor immensely popular in society. His *The Countess of Maybury* (1901) was a collection of witty episodes related by a fashionable noblewoman, not so young or so daring as E. F. Benson's famous *Dodo*, but an inhabitant of the same world. In *Fabulous Fancies* (1903) he brought together a collection of short fiction in a similar vein, including a particularly effective story in which a middle-class girl, briefly taken up by the British aristocracy in a continental watering-place, mistakes momentary popularity for true social acceptance, and is cruelly disillusioned when she gets back to London and finds that her fashionable friends no longer "know" her, while the people she has snubbed at home have in her absence been scoring exactly the social triumphs she would most have enjoyed.

These two witty ventures were well-received, but proved no notable financial success. Grant Richards, the publisher, prodded Maxwell into writing his first full-length novel, *The Ragged Messenger* (1904), an arresting story of an East End parson, with a dubious wife, a magnetic personality, and a passion for philanthropy, who obtains a vast fortune with which to realize his pet schemes. Suggesting what might happen if Christ were to return to earth, *The Ragged Messenger* was a timely novel on the interlinked social and religious questions which were preoccupying MEB at the same time, and about which she too would often write.

Mother and son discussed their work, and MEB gave Will good advice. In his second novel, *Vivien* (1905), he told a convincing twentieth-century Cinderella tale of the trials and temptations of a young woman who must go to work as a shop-girl. In its early stages, he recorded, he found himself stuck in his heroine's childhood and schooldays, elaborating detail upon detail. MEB advised him: *Let your girl grow up*, counsel which enabled him to see his heroine's early life in its just proportion to his story and to get on with the job of finishing it.

As Will Maxwell became more and more the assured professional writer, the bonds between him and his mother grew closer if possible than before. His third novel, *The Guarded Flame* (1906), brought him new self-confidence. Original in theme and skillful in execution, it centered upon an elderly scientist-philosopher, whose adoring but much younger wife has a brief love affair with his scientific assistant. Maxwell made credible the scientist's long series of pioneering books, and his discoveries about the nature of man. In writing this novel, Maxwell for the first time felt an

> intense joy. By it I seemed to be brought even closer to my mother; for I now understood much that had been puzzling in her absolute control of emotion, or power of escaping temporarily from a too long-continued distress of mind. I had always been begging her to spare herself, not to work too hard, and not to take up her pen in hours that should have been devoted to rest. Now I saw that she was not thus fatiguing herself but refreshing herself. Now I too could possess this other world into which I might retire, as she did, for solace and relief.[10]

To Lady Monckton on October 20 (1904), after MEB's European holiday—her last—had been cut short so that Will could substitute for Gerald as the *Court Journal*'s drama critic, while Gerald in turn could recover in Germany and Austria from a "sharp pneumatic-gouty attack," she wrote that she and Will—he was by now thirty-eight—were planning to go off for two weeks to quiet lodgings in Ramsgate, "where we can scribble to our hearts' content, & yet get plenty of air and ekker." The very use of the schoolboy slang for exercise and the picture of mother and son, each writing for long hours between walks in the sea air, make the companionship come to life. When her friend, the novelist Lucy Clifford, praised Will's *Ragged Messenger*, MEB was delighted and agreed proudly that "the book had strength and originality, . . . all he does is of a much higher quality than his poor mother's slap-dash invention. He writes much faster than I can, yet with infinitely more thought and care."[11]

Appreciative of his mother's devotion, W. B. Maxwell felt it at once a privilege, a pleasure, and a duty to repay it. One who knew them both well and who belongs to a generation schooled in modern psychology has acutely commented that W. B. Maxwell was "always MEB's *son*: never for a moment her substitute-husband." Since both mother and son were keen students and observers of mankind, however, we would expect to find in their novels an awareness of the dangers so often inherent in close relationships between mother and son. And we are not disappointed.

Though MEB far more often dealt with fathers and daughters, she had made uninhibited mother-love the central theme of *Like and Unlike* (1887), in which the "spoiled" son, who must have every thing and every woman he wants and who impulsively murders his wife, is the direct product of his mother's adulation. Twice in the novels of her later years, MEB turned to a similar theme. In *Dead Love Has Chains* (1907), completed on that very visit to Ramsgate in 1904 when MEB and Will were sharing their "air and ekker" as they scribbled, the protagonist is a handsome young man who can never hold a woman's love because his mother lives "only to worship him," and has in effect emasculated him by her adoration. And in *Our Adversary* (1909), MEB explicitly made her chief male character unable to satisfy a woman sexually. He is the somewhat effete son of a dead mother who in her "fervent imagination" has envisioned him as a Christian martyr, too good for this world, and has brought him up accordingly. Having always observed with interest men of doubtful masculinity, and having now lived in the world and seen the wrong sort of adoring mother, MEB—whether with Freud's prompting or without—had drawn twentieth-century conclusions about the relationship between the two phenomena. She took advantage of the new freedom accorded novelists in the early years of the twentieth century to make it a major theme in two important novels.[12]

Will Maxwell, as we might expect, never dealt with the subject directly. But one of his very best novels, *In Cotton Wool* (1912)—much admired by MEB—tells the story of a young man whose sole career is tactfully and affectionately looking after his widowed father, a rich man in whose house he lives, "in cotton wool," enjoying every luxury. He has a mistress, who slowly dries up through sexual frustration because of his infrequent attentions; he thinks he wants to go to fight in the Boer War but is quickly dissuaded. Even his loving father taunts him with being a "doctored tom-cat": he is not man enough to enlist. And after his father's death he breaks his engagement to a charming but sexually aggressive young widow because he fears he will not be able to satisfy her or will somehow be depleted of his energies or even killed if he tries to do so. After jilting her, he degenerates into hypochondria and eventual insanity.

Astonishingly explicit, though always without physiological detail, *In Cotton Wool*, Maxwell later wrote, was "really a tract to show the perils of shirking hard duties and living sheltered and completely selfish lives."[13] But surely it was also an exposition of the dangers threatening a man who renders such complete devotion to a parent that he wholly loses his masculinity. Maxwell's protagonist was "doctored" in the service of his father rather than of his mother. But one can hardly doubt that, before he married, Maxwell sometimes feared he might suffer the same fate, as the years went by while he remained a charming and devoted bachelor son, a prisoner—and, what was worse—enjoying his bondage, in the all-too-luxurious life of Lichfield House, Annesley Bank, and various delightful continental and English resorts. Whether he wanted to fight in South Africa and allowed himself to be dissuaded we cannot know. But when the Great War came, two years after the publication of *In Cotton Wool*, he acted with determination and energy: *he would go,* and go he did.

That every loving relationship brings with it its tensions and strains as well as its gratifications no man knew better than W. B. Maxwell. With his own wife and two children he always enjoyed and displayed affectionate understanding. Yet in 1933, the family, with both son and daughter grown up and unmarried, was temporarily scattered. Maxwell wrote in his autobiography: "For a long time I had nourished the theory that a family that is closely united, as ours was, full of mutual affection, should occasionally break up, in order that each member of it may learn

374 • THE YEARS OF FULFILLMENT

to banish anxieties and fears with regard to the other members, and be able to have quiet thought."[14] Though the scattering proved very brief, Maxwell's candid voicing of the theory that underlay it helps confirm our view of *In Cotton Wool*. The life of devotion to a parent that the hero of the novel and that Maxwell himself had led was indeed, as Maxwell had called it, "sheltered." But it was not, as he also called it, "completely selfish": it was rather too selfless, as the novel itself clearly revealed, and destructive of the essence of self. It destroyed his fictional protagonist. But it did not destroy W. B. Maxwell, perhaps in part because MEB was a more considerate parent than the fictional father and had three other attentive children, and in part because Maxwell himself was a man of balance, power, and perception.

In May 1901, MEB noted in her diary that she had had lunch with Will, Ted, and Miss Moore. During the next five years, Will and Miss Moore fell in love and eventually became engaged; on July 25, 1906, they were married, and she appeared in MEB's diaries for the first time under her first name: "Wedding at St. Simon's Will & Sydney. Drove alone to the Church. Then with Maud and Colonel Brabazon [Sydney's uncle] to Victoria Station. Then with Gerald and Maud to Army and Navy Stores. Home at 7." Sydney's mother was dead, and her father not on good terms with his family. Exactly two weeks later MEB "travelled by G[reat] N[orthern] Express to Whitby. . . . arrived at 5:30. W. & S. at station. Joined Will & Sydney after their Goathland honeymoon." After a mere fourteen days to themselves, the newly married couple were swept up in an MEB holiday: there were walks, drives, and teas; she read *Macbeth*, *Faust*, and Lewes's *History of Philosophy*; when they got to Matlock Bath, two close friends, Mrs. Hastings and Fanny Frith, daughter of the painter, were staying at the hotel. Fanny Frith joined them on their drive to Haddon Hall and visit to the house and garden and at tea at the Peacock—"fine old Inn, second-rate tea," MEB recorded. Afterwards—not surprisingly—Will felt "head-achy, not coming down to dinner."

Thereafter the Will Maxwells lived at Lichfield House. A daughter, Barbara, was born to them on March 25, 1907, and a son, Henry, on March 11, 1909. All the tensions inherent in any arrangement whereby three generations live under the same roof naturally came into play. MEB would surely have preferred Will not to marry at all, although perhaps she would not have admitted this even to herself. Will—who had known Sydney so long before actually proposing—felt that to some degree he was letting his mother down and at the age of forty might have remained a bachelor had he not felt committed to Sydney. Sydney had to live her married life in the house of a formidable, powerful, tireless seventy-year-old mother-in-law, a world-wide celebrity and a natural prima donna. MEB and Sydney Maxwell did not quarrel openly; the *convenances* were preserved even when Sydney insisted on discharging a cook whom MEB liked because she believed that her children's meals were not satisfactorily prepared. MEB yielded the domestic reins, but with much resentment. The realization that their mother and their grandmother were not "getting on" penetrated to Barbara's and Henry's nursery.

But open skirmishes were few; Sydney became part of MEB's extended family, often joining her on visits to relatives or friends and attending parties with her. On November 7, 1906, at the Lyceum Club, Mrs. Travers, daughter of MEB's old friend, the Bishop of Gloucester, asked her and Sydney to meet the Archbishop of York and gave them an *"excellent recherché lunch."* Before Barbara's christening on May 15, 1907, MEB gave a luncheon party for the Vicar and his wife, Fanny, and Sydney Maxwell's uncle and aunt, Major and Mrs. Moore. The Moores stayed to tea. At Ranelagh, a club of which MEB was one of the two woman honorary members, where she often watched polo, she and Will and Sydney and Fanny saw a balloon ascension on May 25. Thereafter, MEB noted, special arrangements had been made for Will, Sydney, the new baby and its nurse, and herself to occupy a through saloon carriage on most of the rail journeys from Richmond to their destination. On the 1907 visit to Lyndhurst the journey passed "in great comfort. Lunched on the way, S. making tea with her basket."

When MEB recovered from her stroke in January 1908, she had a resident nurse to take care of her and accompany her on some of her drives and during the long period of recuperation in Sidmouth, where every evening Will read *Pendennis* and Parkman's *Conspiracy of Pontiac* aloud to his wife and his mother. On her own, MEB was reading Carlyle and Heine and Dasent's biography of her cousin, John Delane of the *Times*. By April 1908, MEB was well again. But the end of the year brought a severe attack of neuralgia or sciatica, which kept her in pain and taking morphia to deaden it for six weeks in November and December. In the spring and summer of 1909, MEB's social calendar was looking more as it had before her stroke. She met Elinor Glyn and asked her to lunch: it was a success: *"sans faute:* everybody came." The next day at Lady Monckton's she dined with the Beerbohm Trees, Forbes-Robertson, the Bancrofts, and other leaders in the theatrical world. Elinor Glyn gave a party in June 1911: "sumptuous tea, ices, strawberries, and cream"; and in the same season MEB met Maurice Hewlett, Hugh Walpole, and "Yeats (poet)." She befriended Rosalind Travers, granddaughter of the Bishop of Gloucester, now at odds with her family because of her determination to marry the socialist leader, Hyndman, who was much older than she. Late in 1911, Katie Christmas (her father, Joe Christmas, husband of MEB's stepdaughter Polly, had died in October 1907) came to tea with her fiancé, Shelley Bysshe. In 1912 they sailed for Canada. MEB gave a luncheon party for fourteen at the Ritz and the next day a tea party for thirty at Lichfield House; Sydney—the diary entry notes—was "very ill" with colic. At family gatherings these days, when Gerald, Ted and Maud, and one or more of the Selouses, with Austin Lachlan and possibly Leo Trevor, joined MEB and the Will Maxwells for dinner, as they often did, Fanny Frith would read aloud from *Peter Ibbetson* or the *Life of Whistler*, which everybody greatly enjoyed.

Occasionally MEB would now refuse an invitation, as to a wedding which Sydney attended on January 16, 1912: "Did not go," she noted, "as I feared—or shirked—the fatigue. Sorry when I heard of the fine music and tea." Several times she mentioned "Hueffer"—later Ford Madox Ford: he came to a dinner party at Lichfield House in March 1912 and reappeared with his (first) wife in June; and on October 26, 1913, she complained—in the only such entry over the entire thirty-five years of her diaries—"Mr. and Mrs. Hueffer to supper, did not leave until 11 o'clock," by which it may be gathered that MEB found Ford less attractive than, as we have seen, he found her. At Brighton in 1912, she and Sir Arthur Conan Doyle read a play together on several successive days: probably one of her own unpublished and unproduced efforts. She went to see Bernard Shaw's *Fanny's First Play* at the Theatre Royal, where she herself had appeared as the Fairy Pineapple fifty-five years before.

At Mrs. Forbes's in Connaught Street, in November 1912, she found herself with Will at a "literary party really nice, full of clever talk. Mr. [A. E. W.] Mason, Mr. Cunninghame Graham." Her own luncheon party for the Moncktons, Richard Pryce, and General Sir Alfred Turner, married to MEB's dearly beloved young friend Juliette Whiting, was "all that could be wished," and Juliette, at home in Carlyle House, Chelsea, was "*plus affectueuse que jamais*" when MEB went to call with Will and Sydney and Fanny. In 1912, there was a new French teacher, Mlle. Daniel—". . . a nice little Française, juive je crois," MEB wrote to Juliette Turner, "who tries honestly to improve my pronunciation. One may learn just how the words should be pronounced—but accent is something much more subtle, and that I shall never achieve. It must always be the Stratford at Bow style."[15] On the other hand, few women to whom French had since childhood been a second language would still at seventy-seven be striving to improve it.

Ted and Maud were now living in Woking in a house called Stoneleigh, and MEB reported that Maud's party there in July 1913 was "a great success, all well done." In September, the circulating libraries tried to ban Will's new novel, *The Devil's Garden*, which they bracketed with Compton Mackenzie's *Sinister Street* as a "sex problem novel" that must be suppressed. Will, whom the far younger Mackenzie found a kind and helpful ally against the censors, brought him to tea at Lichfield House especially to see again "the famous Miss Braddon," whom he had first encountered in his teens in 1899. In October Fanny Frith took MEB to hear Kreisler. "If I live till he plays again," MEB wrote to Lady Monckton, "I must and will be there." A week before Christmas MEB gave a party for thirty-eight, from four to seven in the afternoon. It was what she called a "Richmond perpendicular . . . no music no nothing just let the people talk to each other—with plenty of cups and saucers, cakes etc. . . ."[16] In her diary she wrote: "Pleasant tea, after crowd had gone away, with F[anny] F[rith] etc. Everything put away before night."

Two entries from 1914—the crowded last full year of MEB's life—show her as indomitable as ever: March 1, "St. John's with Fanny Frith. Curate preached. After lunch in car to Molesey, found Wyatts at home, then to St. Albans, nice tea-party, met Hare architect, partner Scott, and others. Home soon after five, found General Roberts [Field-Marshal Lord Roberts, Sydney Maxwell's relative] and daughter, Mrs. Husband. Gerald, Fanny, Edmund, and Freda to supper." It had been just an ordinary Sunday. And on December 9, "Mrs. Wray's luncheon at the Berkeley. Lady Byron, Mrs. Turner, Mrs. Locke. Very lively party. Lady Byron delightful. Fanny came to tea and spent afternoon *pour me soigner et après pour m'amuser*. . . ." Less than three months later MEB was dead.

In these last years, her reading did not flag nor did her interest in the theatre. The death of Maupassant came as a blow; no French author seemed a worthy successor. Sudermann she greatly admired, as both playwright and novelist, and she wrote an essay on his work. She found Heinz Tovote's novel *Frau Agna* "a spirited and interesting story of blackmail." Among the Italians she told an interviewer that she liked d'Annunzio, Fogazzaro, and Matilda Serao. She enjoyed Hardy's *Far from the Madding Crowd*, *Tess*, and *Jude*, Gissing's *New Grub Street*, and some of the novels of Maurice Hewlett and Anthony Hope. Flora Annie Steel's novel of the Indian mutiny she thought "truly remarkable," with "vivid and brilliant" descriptions, but she felt that the fictional tragedy got in the way of the history of the mutiny, and preferred her "fact and fiction in separate volumes."[17] In 1905 she was "translating Hedda Gabler," perhaps from the German. She reread George Eliot and Flaubert, Tennyson and Browning, Balzac and Dumas. She read assiduously in Dante, in Tolstoy, in Carlyle. Of Arnold Bennett, she wrote, "I can't stick any novel . . . except *The Old Wives' Tale*, and that . . . only here and there. He pleases—he pleases—and waxes thin."[18] She read Ford Madox Hueffer's *Fifth Queen*, Gissing's *Emancipated*, Henry James's *Ambassadors*, and Thomas Mann's *Buddenbrooks* (January 5, 1911). She read Hooker and Pascal, Newman's *Sermons* and his novel of 1848, *Loss and Gain*, William James's *Will to Believe*, Froude's *Henry VIII*, Stubbs's *Plantagenets*, Maspéro on ancient Egypt and *The Book of the Dead*, Meredith, Molière, the novels of W. B. Maxwell, and Lord Rosebery's life of Pitt.

She went to the theatre less often now, but read a great many plays, especially French ones. But in the last three years of her life she saw *Macbeth, Othello*, and *Oedipus; The Fire Screen* by Alfred Sutro (in a private box at the Garrick with Will and Sydney: "very comfortable . . . amusing comedy. . . .") ; a matinée of *Joseph* ("Saw H. Tree in his official den") ; and in 1914 "Gala Performance *Peg Woffington*: Mrs. [Madge] Kendal and others brought home to tea after performance"; a play at Wyndham's theatre, with Will and Fanny ("Invited to G[erald] du Maurier's room between the acts"); Richard Pryce's new play *Helen* at the Vaudeville, with Will and Sydney ("W. treated us to tea at the Carlton afterwards . . . a most enjoyable treat all through") ; and several unnamed plays after the War had begun in August ("Home at 9 after dark *sans* searchlight," she noted during a blackout on October 21).

The years immediately before the War saw the speedy and insidious advance of technology, pushing the English people into the first phases of the age we now inhabit. As befitted a woman in her seventies, MEB looked with some alarm at the new-fangled devices. Of her first ride in a motor-car, she wrote to Lady Dorothy Nevill, "Well, it was very nice—car delightfully steered by the owner thereof—yet the pleasure of the new mode leaves me cold, and I felt none of the rapture that my friends describe . . . and shall ever share Frederic Harrison's opinions about motors as the enemies of the country-side."[19] On April 1, 1911, MEB noted in her diary that, on a carriage drive with Sydney to Putney, "a line of motors blocking the way" after the boat race made progress impossible, and they had to come home. But in June she went "in Mrs. Austin's small car" to the Claytons' at Ellensmede and noted that the journey each way took only an hour. Before long, MEB yielded to the inevitable and bought a car herself. On January 7, 1913, the diary noted, "Started for Woking 11:30; arrived at 1, pleasant day with Maud, Ted, and children. Home under an hour in car, wh. pleased us all." Sometimes, of course, things did not go so well, as on September 12, 1911, when MEB went with Will, Sydney, and Gerald for "motor car treat" from Bexhill to Alfriston. The car broke down near Battle Abbey on the Sussex Downs above Seaford. But the hardships were not insuperable: "Tea at Esplanade Hotel, Seaford, short walk on front, superb sunset. Russell brought car by 8 PM, home after night drive at 9:30."

On May 21, 1911, at Brighton, MEB "Walked on front after church and again before tea, seeing aeroplane in full flight, descending, and stationary." Although this is the only mention of flying machines in the diary, MEB had already made one of the characters in her novel of 1910, *Beyond These Voices*, a pleasure-seeker so jaded that fast cars no longer satisfied him and he had begun to fly dangerously in his own plane. In 1913, MEB went to the movies and sent the staff at Lichfield House also. It must have been an extraordinary occasion for her, although she made no comment on it in her diary. What they had all gone to see was the "picture show" of *Aurora Floyd*. After exactly half a century, Aurora lashed the Softy on the silver screen.

Except for the relief of Ladysmith and the Queen's Diamond Jubilee, MEB's diaries over the entire thirty-five years made no direct reference to public events or to social change. They were not intended to embody her views: those she put into her novels. But twice at least the diaries reveal, albeit laconically, her awareness of the profound ferment now at work beneath the surface of the luxurious and apparently serene world she inhabited. On the afternoon of August 21, 1911, at Bexhill, when MEB and her sons and daughter-in-law went to the colonnade to hear the band, no band was there. "Royal engineers expected, unable to come on account of railway strike," the diary noted. And on January 27, 1912, she wrote, "Bitter East wind, suffragettes marching through Richmond 'as to war.' "

Having observed her strong sympathy for the underdog, we may be reasonably certain that she accepted without rancor the absence of the band from the colonnade. As for the suffragettes, she saw them, in her own simile, as Christian Soldiers. Three years before, in a brief poignant essay, "The Woman I Remember," she had portrayed the "prim, pretty, nicely mannered, very shy" girl of 1859, as a "vigorous chicken in a shell of thick glass . . . seeing a wonderful world outside and hopeless of getting at it," who "could go nowhere, see no one, spend nothing, read nothing, think of nothing" without parental supervision and approval. "Hemmed round with conventionalities, stifled with respectability," she could escape only by becoming a governess or outrage propriety by going on the stage. She spent her "mornings in formal promenades with mamma, or in bad weather . . . writing to . . . aunts and cousins or working broderie anglaise" for her best petticoats. These contemporaries of her own she contrasted with the women of 1909, "who ride in a man's saddle across the desert of Gobi, take a South American President by the shoulders and tell him that he has to be interviewed, whether he likes it or not; . . . take degrees in mathematics," and in medicine and surgery "hold their own against all masculine Harley Street." Women, she concluded, "have everything now. Schools, University, cricket, freedom of speech, freedom of opinion. They can be Socialists, Deists, Buddhists, Theosophists, Bernard Shawists, just whatever they like. The world is theirs in a century that ought to be called the Golden Age of Womanhood."[20] But they did not have the vote, and one can hardly believe that MEB, whatever she thought of the suffragettes' tactics, would have disapproved of their obtaining it.

In his book, *The Strange Death of Liberal England*, George Dangerfield wrote a clever essay on the women and the workers, who, together with the Tories and their Ulster policies, were threatening in the years before the War to scuttle forever the England that MEB had inhabited for almost eight decades. With two of the three groups, workers and militant women, MEB was not unsympathetic, Tory though she was and often in agreement with the violent language of Lady Dorothy Nevill's letters to her inveighing against the super-tax, against Lloyd George, against the Liberals. But on Ulster, MEB was a Tory out and out: "Revolution is still seething in the land," she wrote on April 10, 1912, to Lady Monckton, "and agitators and syndicalists are doing all they can to make England an impossible place. . . . The Ulster scenes have been tremendous." Asquith's Home-Rule Bill she called "ill-advised" and Bonar Law's speech against it "fine."

Dangerfield remarks that "Society in the last pre-war years grew wildly plutocratic"; he provides his own economic explanations and expresses his regret that he could not have written a chapter on "fashion, furniture, manners and taste" in that plutocratic world.[21] Still the "doyenne" of English novelists, and still as little understood as ever, MEB, a keen-eyed inhabitant of the new plutocratic world, in effect wrote Dangerfield's chapter for him in the novels of her last years.

2. "The Novelist's Scope Has Widened Greatly": MEB's Last Novels and the Problems of the Plutocracy

Of the eighteen novels that MEB published during the last twenty years of her life, three were historical romances, all of them superior to *Robert Ainsleigh* or *Mohawks*, her earlier efforts in the genre. For many years she had steeped herself in the history of seventeenth- and eighteenth-century England and France, studying not only the standard secondary works like Gardiner and Michelet, but also the contemporary source materials: sermons, plays, memoirs: Jeremy Taylor, Andrew Marvell, Clarendon, Butler's *Hudibras*, La Rochefoucauld. Into her commonplace books she had been copying long extracts from them all and from such authorities as Disraeli's *Charles I* or Masson's *Milton* or Bussy Rabutin: on the Quakers, on George Villiers, Duke of Buckingham, on the Fronde, on Colbert, Fouquet, Mazarin.[22]

The first of the historical novels, *London Pride* (1896), was probably begun as early as 1889, certainly in 1890.[23] Following the advice that Bulwer had given her in 1864, MEB completed the beginning and the end before turning to the middle portion. She took her readers back to the London of the Restoration, the plague, and the fire, and found her inspiration in a text she had known since girlhood: the account in the State Trials of the trial of Lord Grey of Wark.[24] The central theme of the novel is the collapse of honest cavalier hopes and the degeneration of the old royalist idealism in the cynical new regime of Charles II. The heroine, brought up in a convent in Louvain during the Commonwealth and Protectorate, finds herself falling in love with the passionate and unhappily married husband of her fashionable elder sister: a "guileless but ill-starred" affair, said the *Spectator*; "illicit and innocent," said the *Athenaeum*.[25] Only the protagonists and their immediate circle were imaginary: all the chief historic personages of the 1660's appeared in the book. MEB had always been a conscientious student, able to "bone up" on a historic period, to set her scene accurately, and to describe the life of her characters convincingly. *London Pride*, however, was the first of her historical romances in which she managed to bring her people, and so the age itself, to life.

Unlike *London Pride, In High Places* (1898) presented no major moral issue that transcended in interest and importance the fate of its characters.[26] Best of the three novels was *The Infidel* (1900),[27] the story of a girl brought up from infancy as a skeptic by her father, a hack-writer of George II's London, who cynically proposes to sell her into concubinage with a rich and dissolute Irish peer. She refuses. But she consents to marry him despite his fatal illness. On his deathbed, her marriage unconsummated, she promises never to marry again and to be buried at his side in his ancestral Irish mausoleum. Alone, rich, widowed, beautiful, and an "infidel," she encounters a recent convert to Wesleyanism, who preaches with Wesley and Whitefield and whom she joins in his good works among the London poor. She rejects his love. Indifferent to the religious message of the Wesleyans, she prevails on Wesley himself to supervise her charitable activities. Constant listening to his sermons and reflections upon the Gospel does bring about her conversion: not to formal Christianity, but to the love of Christ and of his example. Wesley tells her former suitor that he may now "enjoy her society without peril to his soul."[28] She dies in Ireland of illness contracted in helping the poor.

Though MEB gave the novel the subtitle *A Story of the Great Revival*, she treated Whitefield and Wesley only peripherally, in order to focus upon the drama of a charming, talented, and passionate young woman doomed to lifelong celibacy because of the whim of a dying rake and her own deep sense of moral obligation. Could she have kept her head in the London of the 1750's and 1760's, as MEB assured us she did? In any case, MEB was exploring a new and daring theme: the relationship between riches, charitable work, and sexual sublimation. Her heroine not only spends her great fortune lavishly on good causes but throws herself into the problems of individuals among the poor, and somehow finds a substitute for the sexual fulfillment and children that her quixotism has denied her.

A fourth element—as important as money, frustrated sexuality, and fulfilled generosity—was religion. The sobriquet of "infidel" as applied to her protagonist was surely intended as ironical. Trained on the *philosophes*, she can never accept formal religion. But in the preaching of Wesley, in the Gospel, and in the example set by Christ, she finds inspiration for her life of self-sacrifice. So MEB told a plausible and even moving story about a woman's need to receive and to give love and to believe. In its commentary—never explicit—about faith, sex, money, and charity, *The Infidel* transcended the bounds of historical romance and became a novel. MEB wrote to her old friend W. P. Frith, who had praised it, "I like the book myself—I don't often like my books—so that such unstinted praise from so good a judge . . . is very sweet."[29]

It was in the interplay of the same human needs and drives, in many permutations, that MEB found the themes for most of her twentieth-century fiction. The "infidel's" money and the luxuries it could buy her did not play so important a part as does the wealth of the characters in many of MEB's other novels set in her own increasingly plutocratic England. With differing emphases these novels explore the various aspects of this same subject; collectively they not only enable us to understand MEB's own views in her old age about these highly important matters, but form almost a continuous and unified social commentary about the period from the last years of Victoria to the earliest years of George V.

A striking illustration of the relaxation of prudery since MEB's younger days is furnished by an episode that took place in 1901, the very year of Queen Victoria's death. C. Arthur Pearson, the publisher, had sued the author of *The Eternal City*, Hall Caine, on the ground that this novel was unsuitable for Pearson's *Ladies' Magazine*, for which it had been commissioned. Hall Caine's lawyers told him that he should obtain two authors, a man and a woman, to testify that there was "nothing . . . unsuitable" or "likely to corrupt" ladies who might read the novel, irrespective of their "age, class, or condition." The woman author Hall Caine selected was MEB, herself only a generation previously the target of such virulent accusations of immorality and sensuality. He had no doubt as to the outcome, Hall Caine wrote to MEB, but "it would be a pleasure . . . and no doubt a very material gain" if he could tell his counsel that MEB would testify.

With his letter, MEB kept the draft of her reply, declining to appear because "I have always avoided the ordeal of a public court even where my own interests [as in the case of the 1876 carriage accident] were at stake." She had read *The Eternal City* attentively, but

> . . . when it comes to the question of what kind of story is suited to a ladies' magazine, I find myself unable to pronounce an opinion. *The novelist's scope has widened greatly since I began to write, and subjects which I would not then have dared to approach have become the common stock of women writers* [Italics mine]. Your heroine . . . is grand and pure and the whole bent of your story makes for righteousness. Nowhere in the book do you expatiate upon the seamy side of life, and nowhere pander to the love of licentious description. The one terrible episode of the heroine's fall is treated with severe brevity, and with tragic power. So difficult,

so impossible I imagine would it be nowadays for even a jury of literary experts to decide where the line in fiction between the permissible and the unpermissible should be drawn, that I venture to hope this question of the fitness of your fine and immensely successful novel for the *Ladies Magazine* may be left open for literary argument in the future, and that you and Mr. Pearson may come to an amicable settlement even at the eleventh hour without recourse to law.

Though guarded, MEB's letter may perhaps have proved helpful to Hall Caine. Her keen sense of the ridiculous must have been touched when she found herself the acknowledged female authority on what was "permissible" in fiction. The pendulum had taken a long swing since 1867, and after 1901 would swing still further in the same direction.[30] What MEB called "the novelist's scope" would indeed be widened further, and in her social novels between 1897 and 1916 she took advantage of her new opportunities.

The first to be published was *Under Love's Rule* (1897), originally called *The Little Auntie*,[31] a brief sketch concentrating on the follies and false standards of the rich. A frivolous mother and her horsy husband, heir to an ironworks fortune, love their three little boys but neglect them. In their London house, everything has been sacrificed to the splendid suite of drawing-rooms. During the "season" in June and July, the children's stuffy gaslit bedrooms become dangerous, and the youngest child almost dies. His life is saved only through the devoted attention of his mother's younger unmarried sister, the loving aunt, who intervenes a second time to save the family when her brother-in-law loses his money and commits suicide. MEB brought home her attack on the rich by showing the impact upon the three children of their parents' false standards. She drew the three boys as individual characters: the eldest, wholly sporting in his tastes with a hatred for things of the intellect; the second, intellectual but overshrewd; and the youngest—hardly more than a baby—endowed with all the characteristics regarded by MEB's readers as lovable but which she quite obviously detested. Eustace ("Stacie"), the eldest, calls a cricket team from Camberwell a " 'cad eleven,' " and when his aunt tells him that " 'many of England's greatest men had begun their lives in just such seminaries,' " he calls her " 'a horrid little Rad.' " Her fiancé is Unionist in politics, and that, says Stacie, is " 'worse—so beastly middle-class.' " Paul, the middle boy, refers to the family servants as " 'beasts' "—" 'disgusting' " and " 'low' " and denounces the vegetable-maid to her face as an " 'incorrigible slut' " because she will not obey his order to bring him candles, which is not her job. And lovable little Fluff, after his family has lost their money, declares: " 'Now, we're cads. Cads. Now we're poor. It's the same thing, don't you know.' "[32] He has to be told that it is not the same thing at all, an answer MEB must have enjoyed putting into the mouth of a servant.

Rough Justice (1898), at first tentatively entitled *Shadowed*,[33] was the murder-mystery Arnold Bennett admired without appreciating its depth. The murderer, discovered after an ingeniously plotted search, proves to be a professional philanthropist, an eloquent radical socialist and atheist. He kills his cousin—who has disgraced herself in her girlhood and now lives in the London slums—because he knows (although she does not) that their common grandfather, a rich moneylender, has left most of his money to her and very little to him. He had wanted the money not for himself but to pursue his grandiose philanthropic plans. He kills, as he says himself, in " 'the belief that I was justified in suppressing a useless life, which blocked my way to a career of benevolence and usefulness, and in the interests of the many against the few.' " Nothing may be allowed to stand in the way of his advancing the cause of humanity.

The murderer hopes "to abolish everything that makes up old-fashioned people's idea of England, and to create a new England, without an established Church, or a House of Peers, or a great Capitalist, and possibly without a beer-shop along ten miles of dusty high-road." This would be "an over-educated and very uncomfortable England, in which Jack was to be not only as good as his master but a great deal better." Once the murderer has his grandfather's money, he founds a chain of "Magdalen homes" for reformed prostitutes—a culminating irony, since they are built with funds that properly belong to an individual Magdalen whom he has killed. The crime is brought home to him only because another suspect must clear his own name. In the London lodgings of the man who bought the gun used in the murder, Detective Faunce finds some shorthand notes containing passages from a fire-eating socialist speech; and soon, at a philanthropists' meeting, the murderer says these very words: his radical oratory literally leads to his undoing. But the evidence is too tenuous for prosecution. Left to the punishment of his own conscience, the murderer goes into a decline, but "everywhere, among people who try to leave the world better than they found it, his name commands admiration and respect."[34]

Despite her savage satirical touches, MEB's portrait of the megalomaniac philanthropist, the totalitarian liberal, was completely convincing, especially since, in the miserly grandfather, unscrupulous and harsh, who had brought him up, she took pains to give him a plausible childhood stimulus for his later beliefs and behavior. And in his fellow-philanthropists in *Rough Justice* MEB produced a gallery of late Victorian do-gooders—"Nineteenth-Century Crusaders," she called them ironically—some full of gentle impracticality and devotion, some full of righteousness and self-righteousness, some hypochondriac or neurotic, yet all perfectly recognizable types even after more than three-quarters of a century. Since the days of her unpublished poem about "Madeline" and of *Aurora Floyd* and *John Marchmont*, MEB had often let fall sharp *obiter dicta* about the characteristics of those who in Victorian society helped their fellow-man, but never before *Rough Justice* had she let the whole race of the charity-mongers receive such a blunderbuss all-purpose blast. For the first time in the thirty-eight years it had been reviewing her, the *Spectator* now noticed what we have come to accept as eternal Braddonian truth: "Although she has been writing novels for forty years . . . she has never failed to adapt her standpoint to that of the moment at which she happens to be writing. The latest fads, fashions, and foibles, are all alluded to in *Rough Justice*."[35]

In Detective Faunce MEB produced the first notable detective in the whole range of her crime stories. A devoted novel-reader, Faunce has studied Wilkie Collins, Gaboriau, and Boisgobey as well as Dumas, Scott, Dickens, and Balzac—whom he calls "a born detective." Under their impact he has become a writer himself, and he tells portions of *Rough Justice* in the first person, as Wilkie Collins would have made him do it. But the novel's social commentary was far more arresting than the mere unraveling of its mystery.

Faunce reappears in *His Darling Sin* (1899), first tentatively called "Lady Perivale,"[36] where his task is to disprove a libelous story set afoot by a shady Colonel to the effect that a beautiful rich young widow (who had three times refused to marry him) had been traveling abroad in his company. Most of her society friends, including the stuffy barrister-turned-novelist who loves her, seem to believe in her indiscretion. Faunce discovers the Colonel's actual companion, a run-down former actress, who is glad to admit her indiscretion in court for money. He plants a libel in a society paper; his client then sues the editor by prior arrangement. She clears her reputation in the lawsuit that follows. The murder of the actress by her ex-prizefighter husband and its solution only provides padding for a novelette too short even for one-volume publication without it. But in essence *His Darling Sin* is a sophisticated story of hard boiled society people. The cynical elderly Marchioness who alone sticks by the heroine when all her other friends have deserted her puts it in a nutshell:

> "They all swear that they thought of you as one of the nicest women in London—only they can't go on knowing you because of their daughters—their daughters, who read Zola, and Anatole France and Gabriele d'Annunzio, and talk about 'em to the men who take them in to dinner, and borrow money of their dressmakers. I have only one daughter, and I'm never afraid of shocking *her*. She has worked for a year in an East-end hospital, and she knows twice as much about human wickedness as I do.[37]

Riches, however, can buy redemption from slander: with enough money one can hire a detective, plant a libel, and then challenge and disprove it, thus obtaining rehabilitation and a happy marriage. Things have changed since the mid-Victorian era.

In *The Conflict* (1903),[38] MEB's first novel since 1900, published after a longer interval of quiescence than any since the years 1869-1870, she wove the themes that preoccupied her into a wholly new pattern. They were unobtrusively exhibited and examined behind the façade of a plot that—for the first time since *Gerard*, and with more skill and conviction—depended upon the supernatural. More than forty years before, in *A Strange Story*, Bulwer had exploited his own acquaintance with the occult to convey the inadequacy of the scientist's conviction that men have no souls, and to teach that belief in the soul and in the Christian message is the only way to peace and to surcease from spiritual malaise. In *The Conflict*, MEB restated the lesson. Bulwer's skeptical scientist, Fenwick—who had won through to faith and salvation in the end—she transformed into a bookish idler, Walter Arden, who "worships science" and scoffs at belief in "the invisible preserve of the dead . . . in forewarnings, in thought-transferences, in the subtle influence of one mind over another, in the . . . dominant force of the gifted soul." Arden makes a fortune in Alaska and marries a rich philanthropic woman, but becomes neurotically ill. Bulwer's literally soulless villain, Margrave, MEB transformed into a profligate seducer and duelist, whom Arden kills in a duel, and who—before he dies—curses and threatens to haunt him.

Seeking his revenge, the villain twice returns to life, each time occupying the body of a dying friend of Arden's. But MEB was less straightforward than Bulwer in her use of the supernatural. Deliberately she leaves her reader uncertain whether the "intense depression" tormenting Arden may not be only neurotic. It surely has psychological roots: Arden's mother died at his birth; his father held him in contempt; he shows no romantic interest in a beautiful girl whom he rescues—too late—from the villain; when he meets the woman he eventually marries, he "shrinks" from declaring his love for her: her "calm friendship" and companionship in charitable good works are enough for him; the malaise that strikes him after marriage becomes so intense that he cannot continue in their joint philanthropy but withdraws into his room, abandoning married life, fearful lest his wife think him a madman and lest he be put into an asylum. As if to emphasize his limited sexual drive, MEB on one occasion has him disguise himself as a monk. She was obviously trying her hand at a fictional case history. Perhaps it is Arden's swordsmanship that saves him: a superb fencer, he kills his man, and in the end rescues his marriage. But only his eventual conversion to Christianity dissipates the obsessions that have been haunting him.

Toward her philanthropists MEB was far kinder in *The Conflict* than she had been in *Rough Justice*. She made them generous men and women doing an essential job, rather than eccentrics capable of anything, even murder, in the name of charity. She did introduce a utopian socialist, like the murdering philanthropist of *Rough Justice*, who wants to abolish the British monarchy and all "rank and title"; but, like Arden, she was certain that any such ideal republic lay light-years in the future. And in *The Conflict*, her radical is the victim of notable social injustice; he is a reformed ex-convict and alcoholic who has killed his unfaithful wife. When "Mr. Jordan, the American novelist, who had long ago become entirely English," makes a brief appearance, he is recognizably Henry James: " 'His novels are always perfect. He chooses difficult problems; he sails very near the wind. But he touches things so delicately. And then there is the charm you know, the charm of style.' "[39]

Almost a historical novel, *A Lost Eden* (1904), first called "The Suburbans,"[40] we long ago found to be a gently gilded recollection of MEB's own girlhood in Camberwell, and of her début as an actress fifty years before. It constituted a break in the series of MEB's modern social commentaries. In *The Rose of Life*—at first tentatively called "Daniel"[41]—she returned to Edwardian wealth and its temptations. A triangle provides the structure: a rich and disappointed young widow; her former suitor whom she wants back; and her own "dog's governess," a beautiful young girl concealing a disastrous "marriage" in her teens to a man whose real wife was still alive. But the true interest of the novel centers upon Daniel Lester, poet, sybarite, and wit, who had once saved the "dog's governess" from suicide by drowning and who had got her her job with his old friend the rich widow.

Daniel is an exquisite: obese, epicurean, selfish about his own comforts, yet intensely kind in all his instincts and behavior, a celebrated host and a master of clever epigram. For his wife, who worships at his shrine, he cherishes a gentle affection, together with a slight objection to being embraced in warm weather. An authority on the arts, Daniel remarks that, in fiction, " 'the cultured minority ask for nothing but manner, a book that bristles with epigrams and paradox, in which the characters move dimly behind a mist of words . . . difficult to understand, and never quite understood' " (this, I would suggest, was MEB's view of Henry James's novels) ; while, as for the multitude, " 'Give them the nursery and the servants' hall, a runaway wife and a sick baby, or the mysteries of heaven and hell, the divine and the diabolical. Provided the showman clashes his cymbals loud enough, the unlettered millions are satisfied' " (this fairly represented MEB's opinion of her own books and her public).[42] Unable to keep up his luxurious style of life on his own substantial income, Daniel steals checks from his rich friend, makes them out to her dressmaker, and then cashes them by forging the dressmaker's signature, deluding himself that the fraud will not be detected, and that even if it should be, it would be regarded only as a good joke perpetrated by that *enfant terrible,* Daniel. But when the victim does discover Daniel's crime, she punishes him by turning the matter over to the bank—actually the defrauded party. Daniel will have to stand trial and go to prison for forgery. At first unable to believe that such a thing could happen to him, and then unable to face the prospect, Daniel commits suicide, but in such a way that it looks like a natural death.

MEB, it seems clear, had painted Daniel as a portrait of her own old friend Oscar Wilde, and in her account of Daniel's dilemma had set down her views of Wilde's case, some ten years after the scandal and five after his death. She endowed Daniel with many of Wilde's physical attributes and artistic and social talents, and with the *hubris*—the conviction that he could get away with anything, and that even if he were caught no evil consequences would befall him—that had characterized Wilde. She could not hint at homosexuality, nor did she need to do so. In making Daniel choose suicide as his only way out of his dilemma, MEB may well have been suggesting that this would have been a nobler course for Wilde to follow than to whine about his guilt in Reading Gaol and then to rot helplessly in exile until he died.

In *The Rose of Life,* MEB had clashed the cymbals, as she deprecatingly described the job of the ordinary novelist like herself, but the careful listener could hear an entire orchestra. The "dog's governess," ostensibly an appealing and sympathetic heroine, is actually a tough little adventuress. Unable to tolerate life with her dissipated and feather-brained mother, she first yields to a fascinating singer's sexual charms, next tries suicide and gets herself neatly rescued, then abandons her mother without a backward glance—though eventually she weeps crocodile tears over the deathbed—and finally steals her new employer's old lover without telling him about her past. This ostensibly heroic gallant is actually one of MEB's best-realized sentimental snobs. The ostensibly cold and mercenary rich widow actually deserves sympathy for having complied with the code in her marriage for money, and for her subsequent discovery that money cannot buy what she wants. Of little use to her, her money brings nemesis down upon Daniel.

Enormous wealth, philanthropy, love, and religion—the intertwined themes that had preoccupied MEB in *Rough Justice* and *The Conflict*—pervaded *The White House* (1906).[43] In *Rough Justice* the murderer had killed with a good conscience in order to obtain money for the poor; and in *The Conflict* husband and wife would have been successful and contented philanthropists had it not been for his neurosis. But in *The White House* the beliefs and behavior of Claudia, the heroine, and of her brother and their father force the reader to consider more analytically the whole question of philanthropy. Fearing that Claudia's children will manifest a hereditary madness, her father has left her a huge fortune on condition that she never marry. As with the heroine of MEB's unpublished play of 1893, "A Life Interest," she will lose her money if she does. And, similarly, she falls in love with a magnetic philanthropic preacher. Because he will not marry her secretly, Claudia contrives without his knowledge to spend a night under the same roof with him in Scotland, where the marriage laws automatically make them husband and wife as a result. But he will not allow her to evade the provisions of her father's will and goes off to Africa rather than lead a double life. She bears his child in secret, but is successfully blackmailed. Before she and her husband are reunited she discovers that her father's residuary legatee will not, despite her marriage, take over her fortune or even her important role in managing the family ironworks.

So she is able to have her cake and eat it too: she can live openly as a married woman with her husband and child and keep her father's money—which she will use for charitable purposes. Claudia enjoys not only the power to do good, but also the luxury that her wealth brings her.

She affects to despise money as such, but needs it so badly that she will not even acknowledge her marriage if it means she must give it up.

As for her brother, he interrupts a brilliant undergraduate career at Oxford to join "the Free Friars," mostly rich men, who "belonged to no denomination, were subject to no control, but had made their own rule of poverty and work. . . . They wore no habit," but the clothes of "a city clerk on a starvation salary. . . . a substitute for the brown woolen frock and rope girdle. . . . They would start on the longest journeys at an hour's notice. . . ." He joins them because he detests his parents' way of life: " 'Modern luxury suffocates me. . . . since I have seen the life-long agony of semi-starvation, the lean children, the haggard mothers. Think of it,' " he admonishes his father, " 'when you are kneeling in some toy church, a place of jewelled windows and costly vestments and salaried singers, think of it when you pray our Father for daily bread. Daily bread! Your chef at three hundred a year, your table with its hot-house flowers and old silver, your butler and powdered footman! Canvas-backed ducks from America, livers of tortured geese from Strasbourg. Champagne.' " That is all " 'scattered gold, wasted gold, while they are withering for want of bread.' " To which, predictably, his father reacts angrily: " 'Double-distilled fudge! If men who have made money don't spend it freely . . . what would become of trade?' " To him the Friars seem " 'fools who think they can put the calendar back five hundred years, and model themselves upon an ignorant mediaeval friar in the age of Darwin and Huxley, Spencer and [W. K.] Clifford.' " So the issue is joined, and the son, having consented to give up the Friars at his father's urging, eventually is killed while cleaning his pistol: everybody believes it suicide.

The crowning irony of *The White House* is that neither brother nor sister emerges as a truly successful philanthropist: neither the abandonment of a fortune nor its retention for philanthropic purposes really works. Only their father, the self-made ironmonger, had understood how simultaneously to do good and to eat his canvas-back ducks as well. In the village of Skepton, where the family ironworks are located, he has built comfortable housing for his workers and provided them with schools, a club, a library, and facilities of all kinds for recreation. In the two hospitals he has built, fresh flowers are provided daily for each patient. Hard-headed and hard-fisted, he helps those who are already helping themselves, already hard-working, already self-respecting. As a result, he is beloved in Skepton, which MEB portrays as a kind of paradise on earth, and after his death the working people transfer to Claudia their deep affection for him. Never explicit, MEB was suggesting that here lay at least one workable—if partial—solution to the problems posed by the coexistence of great fortunes, grinding poverty, and philanthropic urges.

In *The White House*, MEB frequently mentioned Wesley and Whitefield, and their zeal for helping the poor. And here, as in *The Infidel*, her novel of the Wesleyans, and again in *The Conflict*, she was making an explicit sexual comment about money and charity. In all three novels the money, or most of it, belongs to a woman. In *The Infidel*, the heroine has been condemned to lifelong celibacy by her vow to her dying husband, who had never consummated their marriage. In *The Conflict*, the wife finds her husband unable to function as a husband and haunted by a neurosis that must be exorcised before they can resume their married life and joint philanthropic activities. And in *The White House*, Claudia's possession of the money and her unwillingness to surrender it upon marriage in compliance with the will, threaten to transform her virile and active husband into what W. B. Maxwell in *In Cotton Wool* would outspokenly call "a doctored tom-cat." Only Claudia's husband's refusal to accept this kind of arrangement enables him to remain a man.

Money in a woman's hands is unsexing—MEB was saying—both of the woman herself, and of her husband. Extreme urges to throw it away in indiscriminate charity must be curbed. Well-planned philanthropic effort is not inconsistent with a comfortable personal life. Above all, charity is best directed toward people who are already at work. And the world is full of crackpot ideas: in passing, MEB levels a typical shaft at fashionable neo-feudalism when she makes a peer's daughter explain how her father had invented a livery for the old servants of his house, " 'green corduroy jackets and buff gaiters, and they keep the park roads and forest paths in order,' " to which a fatuous parson replies, " 'If all great people in the land would only do as much, England might be Merry England again, and we should see a May-pole on every village green.' "44

Sometime during 1904, MEB had completed a novel she called "Conrad," which she did not publish until 1907, under the title *Dead Love Has Chains*.45 Written when she was sixty-nine years old, it belongs with her very best novels: *The Lady's Mile, The Lovels of Arden, Joshua Haggard's Daughter, Ishmael*, and *The Fatal Three*. Altogether different from any of these and marking a new departure in its bold and delicate exploration of human psychology and in its economy of style, it won her no new critical attention then or since. It examined once more the theme of the under-sexed male, a subject that MEB turned about in her mind again and again as if seeking explanations for a phenomenon she saw all about her.

Conrad is the adored only son of an immensely rich widow, a duke's daughter who had married a shipbuilder. We are back among the plutocrats, where a supper party is " '*Gunter cum Gargantua*, an endless feast of peaches and asparagus and ortolans and quails, young turkeys stuffed with truffles, hams stewed in champagne, everything expensive that a greedy man could imagine,' " and after it is over Conrad is sad to see the tramps asleep in the park: "Everybody feels the same sharp pang, and forgets all about it three minutes afterward." But wealth and poverty merely provide the background. Conrad is "his mother's idol." She lives only "to worship him, and to maintain the dignity, the reserve, the aloofness from all unworthy people and paltry things, incumbent upon Conrad's mother." Behaving like "a Queen Regent," she regulates "every act of her life by Conrad's interests." She looks forward to his coming of age "as if it were to revolutionise the world." And Conrad himself is "like Absalom in his beauty—like Hamlet in his distinction. . . . a star at Eton and Christchurch, admired, followed, imitated, beloved, an easy first in those accomplishments that youth worships . . . an Oxford Blue, stroke of the Christchurch eight, captain of the Christchurch eleven." He must go into Parliament and "take the House by storm." His mother does not want him to marry until he is at least twenty-four, and would prefer twenty-six or twenty-seven, after he has seen the world. She knows of "half a dozen lovely girls, now in the nursery or school-room, born exactly as she would wish her future daughter-in-law to be born, in surroundings of unblemished respectability, fortified by blue blood."

But Conrad, still at Oxford, falls madly in love at first sight with a pub-keeper's daughter, "petted, overdressed, educated up to the highest all round smattering point, kept aloof from the bar and its vulgarities . . . very pretty." He never considers making her his mistress but wants to marry her. Though dazzled by the prospect, her father warns Conrad that she has been "a bit giddy." In her relationship with Conrad, she is moody: capricious, sometimes cold, sometimes weeping hysterically after their embraces. Her father wants to send her away to school for a year " 'to make her a lady and to get her away from people I don't like.' " But instead she runs off to America with a man who, Conrad learns, has been his rival all along, a prizefighter, "an olive-skinned gladiator, with close-cropped hair . . . a blue chin, a broken nose, and a drunken wife. . . .

muscular arms bare to the shoulder, supple form shining like pale bronze." Even her father calls her a "————— . . . a hideous epithet that was doubly horrible when linked with the name of his daughter." He had hoped vainly that she would have given up her lover and let Conrad make a lady of her.

Conrad now suffers a complete nervous collapse: he disappears for several weeks and when found he is mad. The doctors will not let his mother be his nurse and keeper. Conrad must go into a nursing home. His mother tells everybody that he is exploring in Central Africa. When he does recover—after seven years—she is told that a second such blow might be fatal. All these events have taken place before the novel opens, and are revealed to the reader gradually and retrospectively in skillfully-managed flash-backs.

About a year before Conrad's recovery, Conrad's mother meets on shipboard an inconsolably unhappy girl, whom she succeeds in befriending. Pregnant, the girl had never even been allowed to read *The Scarlet Letter*; it would have been better if she had. Her lover, who had not known of her condition, has deserted her and married the girl to whom he had been engaged all along. Having told her secret, she melodramatically makes Conrad's mother swear on the cross never to repeat it. And a year later, having had the baby and lost it, the girl appears in London society under her proper name, and Conrad falls in love with her.

His mother cannot tell him the girl's story because she is pledged to secrecy and also because a second disappointment might destroy his reason. So Conrad becomes engaged: he has thirty thousand pounds a year, and they go everywhere together "on" his Mercedes. The girl flatly refuses to release him. What if the former lover should return, Conrad's mother asks her, and resume his lovemaking?

"... how about your own feelings? You must have loved him desperately when you let him spoil your life."
"... What do you know of such tragedies— . . . with your smooth existence, hedged round with conventionalities, guarded on every side, you who could hardly have gone wrong if you had been the most vicious of women? What do you know about me? When I let him spoil my life! you say—When I let him! I was in the power of a profligate, intoxicated with sweet words, with flattered vanity, told for the first time that I was beautiful and that I

was beloved. What did I know of love but the sweetness of it. . . . You don't know—you can never, never, never understand!"

But then she does encounter her former lover, and Conrad's mother's prophecy, voiced in anger and despair, comes true. A handsome, brainless sportsman now at first repulsive to her, he presumes upon their earlier love. His wife has died, he is free, he proposes, insisting that their lost baby binds her to him. She feels hunted and helpless, but he embraces her the first moment he gets her alone, and "the old tyranny subjugated her, something . . . of the old magnetism, when the lightest touch of that strong hand, trembling as it stirred the lilies upon her breast, had thrilled her. . . . She knew that the battle was lost. . . . She knew that it was real love of its kind . . . violent, tyrannical, exacting, but real." And still protesting in a letter to Conrad that he is her true love, she runs off to marry the other man, leaving Conrad deserted—for the second time in his life—the day before their wedding was to have taken place. When he hears the news, Conrad says, with a sudden bitter laugh, " 'She was like the publican's daughter, I suppose. There was someone she liked better—some great coarse brute who knew how to master her.' " When a prostitute accosts him, Conrad gives her a handful of gold and says, " 'you never used any man as badly as I have been used.' " He hates the world and everybody in it except his mother.

In *Dead Love Has Chains*, MEB had sensitively and daringly told a simple but subtle story. Conrad, the handsome *preux chevalier*, though attracted to women, twice loses his girl. Each time she has every possible reason for marrying him. Each time she had preferred a "coarse brute," the prizefighter or the sportsman, "a creature of thews and sinews, a face flushed with high living." MEB had never touched so explicitly upon the physical aspects of love. Conrad, for all his beauty and charm, lacks virility. He is his mother's adored boy, who, in the heat of his second disappointment, hates all the world except her. In Conrad MEB not only portrayed an undersexed man with more sympathy and affection than ever before, but linked his troubles directly to his mother's adoration. She could not have told such a story earlier: even in the nineties it might have seemed shocking. In the first decade of the twentieth century it passed unnoticed.

After the emotional turbulence of Conrad's second lost love and threatened second madness, MEB ended the novel with a calm and matter-of-fact coda that resolved the dissonances in a last minor chord:

Conrad learns that his rival "had settled down in Yorkshire with his beautiful wife, who shone . . . in a society made up of land-owners in the neighbourhood, soldiers from York, and the men who came from afar for the big shoots. People talked of her as lovely, but with cold and unattractive manners" and liked her husband better. "They came to London for a short time in the season, but had no London house. They stayed at one of the smart hotels, and spent the greater part of their time at suburban race meetings and fashionable cricket or polo matches."[46]

MEB wrote seven more novels, but never again achieved anything like the distinguished portrayal of human emotions in the taut, tragic, controlled *Dead Love Has Chains*. *Her Convict* (1907) is a conventional Braddon story about the charming daughter of a Dartmoor vicar, who shelters a runaway from the nearby prison.[47] *During Her Majesty's Pleasure* (1908) deals with a woman who shoots her husband during a quarrel, is sentenced for life to an asylum, and later encounters her beloved daughter whom she had last seen as an infant.[48] *Our Adversary* (1909),[49] originally entitled "Old Iniquity," raises in even more daring form the themes of *Dead Love Has Chains*, but this time MEB lost control of them. The parson-hero, Julyan Danyell, seemed to his mother, now dead, a "radiant image, like the saints of old, only too eager for martyrdom." But he loses his pulpit after proclaiming in a sermon that there is no personal devil: evil is within each of us. And when he tries to play Pygmalion to a vicious slum girl's Galatea, she leaves him. We cannot doubt that she finds him effeminate: she even sings a mocking song to him about "Little Juli-uli-uli-ulier," who "Was so peculi-uli-uli-ulier. . . ." suggesting that he is Julia, not Julyan. He is so shattered at losing her that he begins to imagine that she is the devil incarnate. An un-English, effeminate youth also displays some fiendish characteristics and interferes in the upbringing of Julyan's wards, a boy and a girl. This gallery of homosexuals or near-homosexuals is completed by a feebleminded Earl, "epicene . . . in a velvet jacket and . . . red morocco shoes with old paste buckles,"[50] who has been brought up by three maiden aunts and an effete tutor to paint violets on white satin doilies and handkerchief sachets. The supernatural suggestions, like the moral problem posed by the question of evil, eventually peter out into thin air.

Hitherto MEB's fictional studies of the rich, though often damning, had usually exhibited—in the loving detail that chronicled their extravagance and lavishness in food, dress, and behavior—her own interest in the good things of life. But in *Beyond These Voices* (1910) she showed total disillusionment with fashionable splendor. The rich now take no active interest in philanthropy but simply write checks, so that they spin aimlessly in the whirlpool of ostentation and meaningless social activity of the Edwardian jet-set, without the devices for escape and stability provided by an active interest in the problems of the poor.

In this account of the marriage between an impoverished girl of good family and a much older, rich Italian international financier, MEB was explicitly once again telling the story of Othello, her first version of which dated back to *Aurora Floyd* in 1863. " 'At least,' " says one of her characters, the financier " 'is not black.' " Introduced by her rakish cousin to "the literature of decadence . . . Baudelaire, Verlaine, Nietzsche, the literature of pessimism and the literature of despair, that rebellion against law, human and divine, which Shelley began," the wife abandons her marriage, which ends in murder. Gossip crackles about her as she marries her cousin, who drives his Daimler and flies his private airplane too fast, and soon becomes entangled with another woman. Death and retribution lie ahead.

Two religious figures play a major part in *Beyond These Voices*. A fashionable Catholic priest offers the heroine "very little more than she had already in the ritual of her own church. The change did not seem worthwhile. . . ." Yet he makes a great impression when he preaches against the fashionable gods: " 'your substitutes for the church you have deserted, your Christian Science, Pragmatism, Humanism, your letters from the dead, your philanthropy—expressed in oranges and buns for workhouse children, and in fashionable bazaars; charities that overlap each other, and pauperise more than they relieve . . . your groves and high places, your Baal and Astarte . . . your Buddha, your Nietzsche, your Spinoza, your Comte. . . . You worship everywhere but in your church.' " There can be little doubt that these were MEB's own sentiments. Yet all that the priest can do in the end is hear the murderer's confession.

The spiritualist leader, the "high priest of the Transcendental," makes a more successful appeal to women. He publishes a quarterly called "The Unseen," whose articles " 'upon the spiritual life are adorable.' " Unlike Daniel Dunglas Home, the famous spiritualist of the fifties and sixties, he does not read thoughts or go in for slate-writing, materializations, or floating up to the ceiling: " 'He does nothing. . . . He talks. His disciples . . . believe in him as Orientals believe in Buddha. I have heard people say that he *is* Buddha. . . . There are no depths in the mysteries of occultism from ancient Egypt to modern India that he has not sounded.' " His group is called simply "Us," and its meetings are "like a Quaker meeting with the female members in Parisian frocks and hats. The congregation sits in melancholy silence until somebody . . . begins to say things that have been borne in upon her from Shakespeare or Browning, or Marlowe, or Schopenhauer; or her favourite bishop, if she is pious." One of "Us" is " 'strong upon politics and frankly socialistic; she has communications from Karl Marx and Fourier, George Eliot, and Comte.' " To belong to the group is " 'quite the smart thing to do. Its members give themselves no end of airs in a quiet way.' " Gossip reports that one member has gone to Paris to attend a Black Mass, and then told her young daughter about it: " 'and now the minx raves about the devil—says she would rather be initiated than presented next year.' " At one of his sessions the heroine hears a "passionate advocacy of Free Love"; adultery and murder soon follow. If the priest's conservative admonitions have failed, the spiritualist's radical nonsense has succeeded all too well.

Quite possibly MEB had in mind her old acquaintance, the theosophist A. P. Sinnett, whom she had slated more gently twenty years before in *The Day Will Come*. Perhaps Zolaesque laws of heredity had made the heroine what she became, since her father, a poet, had been "passionate, exalted, transcendental, more Swinburne than Swinburne, steeped in Dante and Victor Hugo, stuffed almost to choking with Musset, Baudelaire, and Verlaine; . . . too beautiful for a man,"[51] and his father the vicar had thought he was using his talents in the service of Satan. In this novel of fashionable *ennui*, MEB herself did not always avoid *ennui*. But one should emphasize instead the fact that she was now seventy-five and that this was her seventy-seventh novel and a book of outstanding interest with sharp contemporary social commentary at its core.

A special place in the long line of MEB's fiction is held by *The Green Curtain* (1911), last but two of her published novels, a leisurely biographical study of a great Shakespearian actor who scores his triumphant public successes in Regency London after a harsh apprenticeship in the provinces. To this extent the hero, George Godwin, was surely modeled upon Edmund Kean (1787–1833). Godwin's birth, like Kean's, is shrouded in mystery, although he has a noble lord in his ancestry. But otherwise MEB gave her hero quite a different life history. *The Green Curtain* was the final testimony to her lifelong fascination with the theatre. It has a mournful elegiac feeling appropriate to its title: the green curtain is the one that is finally rung down on the performance, and MEB intended it to be symbolic: "The audience would vanish. The lights would go out. The green curtain must fall. Death must come. Nothing matters." In her last years, this reflected her own misgivings as she viewed her own long literary career. Thanking Lady Monckton for "kind . . . words" about *The Green Curtain*, MEB referred to herself as "an ancient story-spinner who has passed into the stage where years are a labour in sorrow, and is naturally inclined to feel written out and despondent." Yet, she added, "I really enjoyed writing that book."[52]

Miranda (1913) and *Mary* (1916), her last two novels, as the work of a woman nearing eighty, cannot be judged by the ordinary standards. No reader can miss the fatigue that permeates the writing, the failure to revise and tighten, the occasional careless loose thread; *Mary*, indeed, was not quite completed at her death, and MEB would probably have improved it had she had the opportunity.

In *Miranda*, the two men in the heroine's life are the fastidious philanthropic bachelor high-church priest, who keeps his late mother's portrait (in white, by Whistler) "as in a shrine" on the wall between an icon and a crucifix; and the sensual author of an immoral but fashionable Faust poem now embarked on an even more "hideous" work, which " 'good women must not read.' " Naturally Miranda chooses the poet—who assures her that his work is no worse than the tragedy of Oedipus—but he seduces her, initiating her into sexual passion at a moment of great grief. They marry because she is pregnant, but she feels revolted by him and indeed by sex: " 'You ought never to have married a *man*,' " he says to her one day "when she had shown disgust at some particularly masculine trait in his character, 'Another woman would have been a better partner for you. A she-poet, *par exemple*. You would have sat on an Italian hill, and talked philosophy. Two Sapphos.' " Unsexed now, as he cruelly reminds her, she is ready, after his suicide, for marriage to the tame-cat parson and a life of good works. Full of mechanical melodrama, *Miranda* was nonetheless a powerful modern novel for 1913. A few days before it was published, MEB wrote Lady Monckton that it was "very mild, namby pamby stuff—still it is an *experiment* in a way."[53]

MEB's last novel, *Mary*, had been largely typed and revised at the moment of her death, but the very end was still in manuscript.[54] Alone and penniless, Mary "Smith," the orphan daughter of an unloving scholarly recluse in Cornwall, has been abandoned by her lover, who had tricked her into running away with him by a promise of marriage. Her baby is dead; she has eluded a London bawd; and she tries to drown herself. A lymphatic young philanthropist rescues her from the river, finds shelter for her in a refuge for unfortunate women, and gets her a job as companion to his own enormously rich invalid uncle, a connoisseur and former sportsman, crippled for life in an accident. A cantankerous man, the invalid soon becomes devoted to Mary, whose gentle voice, quiet manners, and unselfish service please him greatly, despite the grumbling of his other servants and of his relatives. The rescuer and his cousin, a hard-working barrister, both fall in love with Mary. MEB kept her reader guessing which of the two cousins Mary might prefer and what she would do after her employer has died, leaving her independently wealthy; and after her former lover returns to London with a fortune made in South America, is ruined, and kills himself. Though always well-written, the story was not tense and tightly woven but leisurely and even rambling.

Mary Smith's real name is Tremayne, the name that MEB in 1880 had first chosen for the Trevornock family in *The Story of Barbara*, whose father, like Henry Braddon, was his own worst enemy and cruelly neglectful of his wife and two daughters. For some reason MEB had changed "Tremayne" to "Trevornock" in the manuscript of *The Story of Barbara* before it went to the printer. It is plausible that in 1915 as in 1880 "Tremayne" was for her the equivalent of "Braddon" and that Mary Tremayne was the fictional counterpart of Mary Braddon. Mary Tremayne's father had never loved her; so in those weeks just before MEB's death, when she was writing *Before the Knowledge of Evil* and deliberately recalling her childhood, she was simultaneously putting into her last novel a girl of her own name whose father had disliked her and who had even been responsible for her ruin.

Cultivated, quiet, interesting rather than pretty, the young Mary Tremayne—victim of the swaggering seducer "Argentine Jack"—attracts the love not only of the elderly millionaire invalid but also of his two nephews, the virile barrister and the more epicene philanthropist. In the light of Mary Braddon's letters to Bulwer soon after her liaison with Maxwell had begun, referring to her own "wasted sufferings," viewing young love cynically, calling her own circle "matter-of-fact" hard-headed people, in the light of her absorbing interest in jealousy and bigamy, one cannot help speculating how much of herself MEB put into Mary Tremayne. In addition to Gilby and Maxwell, had there been another man in MEB's life, met perhaps while she was on the stage, a seducer who had promised her marriage, swept her off her feet and abandoned her? Was it possible that Maxwell had rescued her and given her a husband's love even though he could not marry her legally for thirteen years? Could this or something like it have been the "everything" that she had always told her mother?

Were all the mothers in MEB's fiction who suffer because they have children they cannot acknowledge (as in *A Life Interest*, or *The White House*, or *During Her Majesty's Pleasure*), or who grieve all their lives because of a child lost in infancy (as in *Mary*) only figures of romance? Or could MEB perhaps have had a comparable episode in her own life? Did she bear and lose an infant in her girlhood after a love affair? Were it not for the fact that Gerald—her eldest known child—looked so much like John Maxwell that he was instantly recognizable as his father's son, one might even be tempted to ask whether in taking her under his protection Maxwell might not have also given a father's care to her child by some other man. But Gerald was surely a Maxwell. And MEB, we know, did indeed lose an infant son by Maxwell—younger than Fanny, older than Will, and greatly mourned. Probably these known experiences account sufficiently for the themes in *Mary*, for the emotion in which she clad them.

Yet the more startling hypothesis—that she had a lover before Maxwell—still retains a certain attraction. If it were true, for example, it would help account for MEB's unswerving loyalty to Maxwell, no matter how trying she found him. Of all the people who ever knew him, including his own children, she seems to have been the only one who had a true affection for him: an affection explicable if he had indeed saved her from wretchedness and not so easily explicable on any other grounds. "Mary Tremayne of Warburton House [the millionaire's mansion she inherited]," wrote MEB, "had the world and all that it could give—could go where she liked, do what she liked. But she could not mend the Past; there would always be the memory of disgrace, of bitter experiences, and of one abiding sorrow."[55] Were not these things all true also of Mary Braddon of Lichfield House? The query can lead only to speculation. And yet it has arisen, perhaps inevitably, as the natural outcome of this long investigation, in the course of which we have so often found one or another of MEB's eighty novels shedding light upon her life. So we try without success to ask questions of the very last and perhaps the most enigmatic novel of them all, the one that bears her own first name.

3. "A Little Tired After Exciting Days"

When the news of Great Britain's entry into the World War reached the Maxwells in Bexhill in early August 1914, Will—now forty-eight years old and without any military training—at once went to London to

402 • THE YEARS OF FULFILLMENT

volunteer. He helped raise a battalion in the City of London, went into camp at Colchester, Essex, and received a lieutenant's commission on September 3, 1914, becoming Regimental Transport Officer.[56] Of these devastating events, MEB's diary says only, on August 6, 1914, "W. in London"; on August 21, "Saw the territorials and their wagons coming into Richmond for the night"; and on September 17, "Will left for Colchester in uniform."

But a letter to Lady Monckton shows what a blow it all had been:

> You know what Will is to his wife and children who adore him, and how he loves his home—his quiet evenings with books—and his own literary work—well, he has left us all to be Military Secretary to the Tenth Battalion Royal Fusiliers, the battalion he helped to raise, with a lieutenant's commission, and where that battalion goes I suppose he will have to—or want to—go, till this accursed war is over. I won't plague you with any more scribble, my kind friend, for I should only howl about the war. S[ydney] and I and most of our friends talk of nothing else, think of nothing else—I read nothing but battle-histories. I go about with "Creasy's Decisive Battles" under my arm, as if it were the Bible, and am always telling my friends that the "brunt of the battle" at Ramillies was over in an hour and a half, and it crumpled up France.

MEB sadly permitted herself a touch of vindictiveness in the post-script: "Think of those poor fellows day in, day out, and in the dreary night—facing the German guns. I shall be glad when after a little the Ghurkas come, with their crooked knives, which I am told are useful."[57]

Since young womanhood and the family friendship with Octave Delepierre, Belgian Consul and father of her intimate friend who became Madame Trübner, MEB had had a particular affection for Belgium. To A. P. Watt, now her literary agent, she sent off sample pages of a short essay in which she proposed to reminisce about a trip taken in Belgium in 1866: John Maxwell, whom she called only "masterful John," had been with her, and his jollity and resourcefulness gave the female travelers— MEB and her mother—a splendid time. MEB instructed Watt that all the proceeds from the sale of this manuscript—which she never finished—were to go to Belgian relief.[58] And she also supplied a contribution to a large volume called *King Albert's Book*, containing tributes to the Belgian king and people from men and women prominent in the world's affairs and in

33. Exterior view of Lichfield House.

34. Lichfield House, another view.

35. ". . . a lady clad in riding-dress of the severest order; the sable habit is relieved only by a tiny patch of colour at the throat, and the orthodox 'chimney pot' completes the costume." Edmund Yates describing MEB in 1877.

Copyright. MISS BRADDON'S HOUSE. ANNESLEY, BANK, LYNDHURST, NEW FOREST. F.R.H.&S. 238.

36. Annesley Bank.

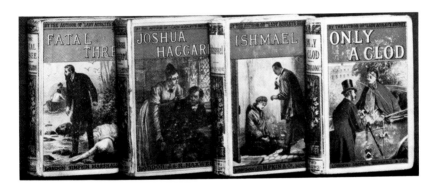

37. Braddon yellowbacks.

38. *Joshua Haggard's Daughter*: latter portion of the original manuscript.

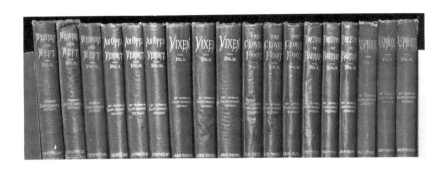

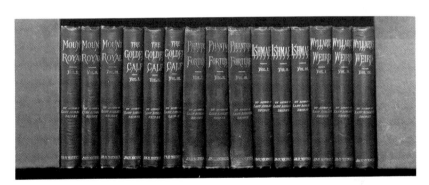

39. Braddon novels, 1877–1885.

MISS M. E. BRADDON.

"JUST AS I AM!"

40. "Just As I Am," *Punch* caricatures MEB, March 5, 1881.

ONE SHILLING

CHE

MISLETOE

BOUGH

UNDER THE RED FLAG

A Complete Story
By M. E. BRADDON

LONDON: J & R. MAXWELL,

41. *Under the Red Flag*, the *Mistletoe Bough* for 1883.

Emile Zola & the Naturalistic School.   (1.

Nearly thirty years ago there appeared a novel which inaugurated a revolution in the art of novel-writing & a new departure in morals. Before Gustave Flaubert leapt into renown by the literary success of his first novel & by the public prosecution of that work as an outrage against morality & religion Balzac stood alone as the high priest of the naturalistic school, & it was popularly supposed that in La Cousine Bette or in Splendeurs et Misères des Courtisanes that philosophic & laborious writer had gone as far in the analysis of vice as it was possible for the audacity of genius to go. But Balzac was not a realist in the modern sense of the word. He was an analyst but not a naturalist. The atmosphere of romance pervades all his books; there is in all the same flavour of the ideal a tropical splendour a mixture of mille-fleurs in the ink with which he wrote, a Ouida-esque suggestion of velvet dressing gowns & eau-de-cologne baths. His women of fashion are lovelier than in life, his young heroes Rastignac de Rubempré, & the rest of them, have all the same excess of gifts. They are veritable princes of fairy-land on whom all potential godmothers have showered graces & talent. They are of a stronger fibre than the heroes of Disraeli: but they too have an oriental flavour, curled, perfumed, sleek, silken, the beloved of Duchesses the destroyers of marital honour. Balzac was essentially the novelist of society. He himself declared that the first duty of a writer of fiction is to see as much as possible of the great world. All other things he may evolve out of his inner consciousness or find in books, science, art, philosophy: but manners & fashion must be studied from the life. And Balzac worshipped that great world & its elegant surroundings. The love of the ugly had no place in his art-gospel. Let him descend never so deeply into the gloomy basement of the social fabric there is always the counterbalance of beauty, luxury, refinement somewhere in the picture. There is always something to gladden the eye & soothe the senses.

The appearance of Madame Bovary opened new vistas & revealed wider horizons. The novelist of the old school was left a long way behind by the physiologist, the analytical student, the vivisectionist of the present. In cold blood & with a passionless pen Gustave Flaubert traces the degradation of a selfish & vain young woman, mated with a husband of coarser clay for whom her only feeling is indifference. Step by step he follows her in the progress from dull provincial respectability — a young wife solitary in a shabby-genteel home, nursing vague yearnings for all the beauty & luxury, the pomps & pleasures of this world — to the nethermost deep of infamy. Her fall is inevitable from the outset. There is no ballast of religion or morality to steady this linnet's head. But in the first of her two intrigues there is, on her side, some touch of poetic feeling, tho' the lover is almost as commonplace as the husband: his superiority a question of externals, the work of the tailor & the boot-maker.

42. MEB's essay on Zola. The original manuscript, 1885.

43. MEB in the eighties.

44. Drawing room at Lichfield House. (Original in the possession of Henry Maxwell, Esq.)

45. Ante-room at Lichfield House. (Original in the possession of Henry Maxwell, Esq.)

46. Breakfast room at Lichfield House with the bookcase containing MEB's
manuscripts: *Birds of Prey* on the table. (Original in the possession of Henry
Maxwell, Esq.)

47. MEB's library-workroom.

48. Will Maxwell's first book, 1892.

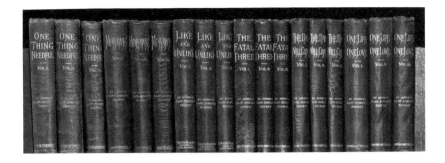

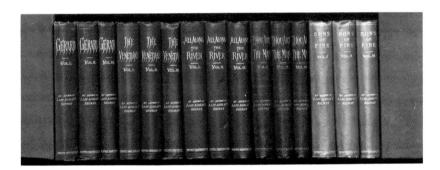

49. Braddon novels, 1886–1895.

50. Original manuscript of *The Good Hermione*: top and bottom lines in John Maxwell's hand.

51. *The Christmas Hirelings*: in the *Lady's Pictorial* for Christmas 1893.

52. *The Christmas Hirelings*: in its original dust jacket, 1894.

53. MEB about 1895.

54. MEB about 1905.

55. Sir Edward Braddon, shortly before his death. (By kind permission of Mrs. Clifton, Hungarton, Leicestershire, Sir Edward's granddaughter)

56. W. B. Maxwell, 1909.

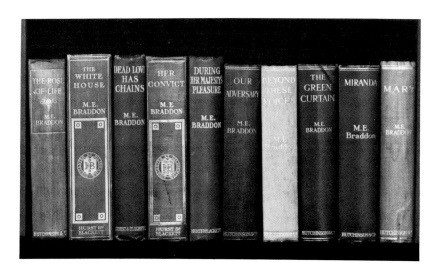

57. Braddon novels, 1896–1916.

NEWNES' SIXPENNY NOVELS ILLUSTRATED.

THE TRAIL
OF THE SERPENT

BY M.E. BRADDON.

ILLUSTRATED BY H·M·BROCK·

58. MEB's first novel of 1860, the "chartered libertine" in Edwardian dress, about 1905.

59. *The White House* (1906). First page of the original manuscript.

Continuation of Chap XXXI.

Mary who had waited, like Damocles, in a mockery of splendour for the suspended sword to fall, heard nothing of what was going on in that mystery-land — the city. Austin came to see her occasionally; but then he did not read the financial newspapers, in which some far-from-complimentary "open letters" to Mr John Rayner had appeared. The engineering supplement of "The Times" was more in his line, as it concerned the Yard whose interests were so dear to him. And the "Labour Leader" had to be studied carefully, much as it shocked his ideas of universal

60. *Mary* (1916), the final portion, left in manuscript when MEB died.

61. W. B. Maxwell during the first World War.

FRIDAY, 25th.

CHRISTMAS DAY.

S. Johns. with W. & S. Vicar preached fine sermon.

SATURDAY, 26th.

ST. STEPHEN, MARTYR.

BANK HOLIDAY.

To Criterion with W. & S. then to tea in the C. tea room. Splendid?

SUNDAY, 27th.

ST. JOHN, EVANGELIST.

1ST SUNDAY AFTER CHRISTMAS.

No church — a little tired after exciting days. Walk in garden with Will.

62. "A Little Tired after Exciting Days": Final pages of MEB's Diaries.

63. MEB's tombstone in Richmond cemetery.

SACRED·TO·THE·MEMORY·OF
"MISS·BRADDON"
(MARY·ELIZABETH·MAXWELL)
A·WRITER·OF·RARE·AND·REFINED·SCHOLARSHIP
WHO·GAVE·PROFITABLE·AND·PLEASURABLE
LITERATURE·TO·COUNTLESS·READERS·IN·HER
LIBRARY·OF·THREESCORE·&·TEN·WORKS·OF·FICTION
BORN·4·OCT·1837 · DEPARTED·THIS·LIFE·4·FEB·1915
"THE·LORD·PRESERVETH·THE·SOULS·OF·HIS·SAINTS"

64. Bronze memorial tablet to MEB in Richmond Parish Church (St. Mary's).
Close by is the tablet to Edmund Kean, the protagonist of her novel *The Green
Curtain*.

the arts, English and continental alike: Winston Churchill, Rudyard Kipling, Edmond Rostand, Blasco Ibañez, Elgar and Debussy, Galsworthy, Rider Haggard, and others, edited by Hall Caine with a preface dated Christmas 1914 and published by several English newspapers early in 1915.[59] With the other Maxwell women, she also visited the wounded in the hospitals. It was typical of MEB, old though she was, that she should have done her own war work promptly and effectively. And her rueful common sense never deserted her. To Juliette Whiting she wrote on October 14, 1914, that Will "tells his wife and me that he is broken-hearted at being away from us, but I rather suspect that he is having the time of his life! . . . I think, talk, & dream of nothing but the War."[60]

"I have been a little pulled down," she wrote to Lady Monckton (perhaps about November 15, 1914) by a sudden faint while undressing for the night. Her doctor, of whom she was very fond, ordered her to bed and she submitted, but she was quite indignant to have been "treated as an invalid for a fortnight." But the real question was: when would the War be over?

> All who come straight from the front, the wounded soldiers whom we talk with in our hospitals, seem to think it can't go on much longer. A man who fought at Lille . . . told Fanny it would be over by Christmas, but what do these know, poor lambs, who go to die more meekly than sheep to the slaughter-house. Will comforts me when he sees me down-hearted by saying that the war will be over before his Battalion is ready to go to France. He "feels it in his bones," but he is . . . happy in his work, tho' I know he hates leaving us and his . . . novel-spinning. He has more than enough of penwork where he is—poor dear—& fifteen horses to look after—& 14 grooms . . . & if the order comes he will go to the danger zone in the best spirits—but every minute of his absence will be misery for me.

MEB, who had once written Lady Monckton, when Will was in Ireland on a brief visit, that she was missing him " 'every day in the hour,' " was putting a brave face upon it now, but she declared as she ended her letter that, "in a sleepness night . . . morbid imaginings take hold of me & fear sits on my pillow,"[61] and she was preoccupied with the tragic news of sons lost, and families left without their natural heirs and mothers bereft.

Lady Monckton wrote promptly, in alarm at the news that MEB had fainted, and MEB replied at once that it was only a "trifling upset. There is nothing really the matter with me except A.D., & I have been moun-ching [sic] plenteously of late, and taking a glass of Sauterne with my dinner."[62] Whenever he could, Will did come home on leave: MEB recorded these all-important days in her diary: November 7, November 21, December 5, and again at Christmas. Colchester was not very far, and Will himself wrote that he "took leave on any excuse, and would boldly make excuses for it. To refresh myself with a sight of London, to be alone with my mother in her quiet library at Lichfield House. I was anxious about her health. The War had shaken her."[63]

On Christmas, MEB went to St. John's Church in Richmond with Will and Sydney: "Vicar preached a fine sermon." The day after Christmas, Will took his mother and his wife to the theatre, the Criterion, and to tea in the Carlton tea-room: "Splendid," MEB noted. The next day was Sunday, December 27, 1914. MEB wrote in her diary: "No church. A little tired after exciting days. Walk in the garden with Will." It was the last time she would write in her diary, and Will's name was the last word that appeared in it. Early in the New Year MEB received almost impassively, her daughter-in-law remembered, the news that Will Maxwell's regiment would soon be going to France. Her final illness—apparently the gradual breaking of a number of minor blood-vessels in the brain—had now begun. On February 4, 1915, she died.

As one would have expected, Will reproached himself bitterly: for "abandoning her" when she was old and weak, for having joined the army as a soldier, although at the time it had seemed the only right thing to do, and in accordance with the "teaching" that he "had tried to inculcate" in his books. Reflecting in his grief that perhaps there had been an element of "vainglory, a desire for novelty, a grasping at the chance of adventure" in his decision, he now thought he "should not have run off to regimental duties that anyone could perform, but have remained in London with my pen and tongue at the service of the government."[64] And these doubts were compounded by his growing conviction that the war itself was a tragic mistake and the war years "wasted years."

But while Maxwell's feelings of guilt toward MEB in her last days were natural enough and enhance for us the pathos of her death, we may at this distance—forty years after he recorded his emotions of twenty-two years earlier still—and at the end of our own journey through the more than seventy-nine years of MEB's long life—feel some assurance that Maxwell had indeed done the only thing his mother would have understood and respected. Despite her anguish at the thought of los-ing him, she would—as the war crept on—never have been content to have him "in cotton wool," well overage for active service though he was. His behavior was true not only to his own teachings but to his mother's standards. Had he convinced himself that he should not have abandoned her physically, Maxwell paradoxically would have been abandoning what she stood for. By leaving her, he paid her the ultimate tribute of remaining true to her principles. And if there was an element of joyous seeking for adventure in his enlistment, who would have understood it better or applauded it more vigorously than she?

Her own life as a woman exemplified at every turn a passionate loyalty to principles and to persons, combined with sound common sense, a self-deprecatory appreciation of the ridiculous, a sensitivity to human suffering, and a tough capacity to bear suffering herself. MEB's love for her own mother had been not unlike the love that Will Maxwell in his turn felt for MEB. As a romantic schoolgirl, she braved the social disapproval and the knowing sneers that would follow her for decades, when she determined to become an actress and make enough money to keep her mother from poverty. And of course, as her own heroine of *A Lost Eden* stoutly confessed, what Will Maxwell called "a desire for novelty, a grasping at the chance of adventure" had played its part in her decision. She seized the opportunity that the success of *The Loves of Arcadia* and Gilby's patronage gave her to abandon the stage and embark upon her true career as a novelist. When she and John Maxwell had fallen in love, she deliberately flouted the conventions even more bravely; she bore her children and gave his family and theirs constant tenderness and support; she made her astonishing successes as a writer in spite of her critics' savagery and meanness; and she emerged victorious if scarred into the calmer waters of middle life.

Her sense of duty never left her. She reserved her keenest scorn for "his own enemy," her father, Henry Braddon, who had neglected wife, children, and duty. In grieving over John Maxwell's death she wrote, "he never shirked a domestic duty" as the highest praise. Had she been a man in wartime, who can doubt what her decision would have been?

Her loyalty to mother, husband, children, stepchildren, grandchildren extended to all who deserved it. Bulwer, who had so greatly encouraged her, received not only her heartiest thanks, but—in the flattery, quite sincere, that she lavished upon him—the sort of tribute he craved most. And after he died—his popularity already well past—MEB published her appreciation of his achievements for the world to read. Her close friends—Mrs. Whiting and Juliette, Mme. Trübner, Lady Monckton—were decade after decade irradiated by the warmth and light of her affection for them. Distant Braddons or Maxwells (or Basdens or Cowlands or Rumbles or other part-Braddons or part-Whites or part-Maxwells) could command her purse from the first moment it held an extra shilling to the opulent end of her days. Her kindness and consideration for her servants became a legend among their descendants. Her charities were often private: school bills or other fees paid, summer holidays provided, and the like; sometimes public, as in the supplying of hot lunches to poor children, or in any subscription for the prevention of cruelty to animals.

The fruits of success were sweet: at first in the mere absence of money worries and the secure knowledge that no dun would ever again appear, and then in the enjoyment of the things that money could buy: Lichfield House, Skisdon—saved for the family—Annesley Bank; horses and hunting, old silver and china, pictures and books; and travel, in luxurious comfort, to France and Italy, Germany and Switzerland. It all "came out of her own head," and she took proper pride in that. And entertainment and being entertained—the great houses that opened wide, the clubs— Ranelagh, Sheen House, the Lyceum—the delicious food, the clever people, the good "nabble"—her word for a long quiet gossip-session—the long walk on the front at a seaside resort; the theatre, music, reading—these made the intervals between laborious days agreeable indeed.

Better still had been the work itself: that absorbed creative passing of the long long hours which, as Will Maxwell had shrewdly recognized, brought MEB not exhaustion but exhilaration. She called it "copy-spinning" or "novel-spinning," and sometimes it had been no more than that, though always—even in the *Halfpenny Journal* days—performed with a conscientious determination to please her readers. But often—far oftener than she had realized—she had caught and held on to that eel-like "archetype" that so often eludes the artist. At every stage in her career she had risen above the merely workmanlike, the merely entertaining. A master of plot-weaving from *Lady Audley's Secret* on, she had written a better book almost simultaneously in *Aurora Floyd*. No sooner had she become Wilkie Collins's disciple than she had challenged him successfully. With *The Doctor's Wife* only a year later, she had made action flow from character, taking all the help she could from Flaubert; and this she would hereafter strive to repeat in each successive book, though the speed with which she had to work would prevent her from fulfilling her ambition. As early as 1866, with *The Lady's Mile*, she had already shown that she did not need murder or bigamy and had found what the baffled critics called her "second manner," the ability to tell a story about "a parcel of people."

After the interim of the illness of the late sixties and her recovery, she had gone from strength to strength in the face of cruel social discrimination, and in *Joshua Haggard's Daughter* (1876) had told a classic story with classic restraint. Socially secure after her marriage, she had for a time allowed Zola to influence her more than Balzac or Flaubert had ever done, and in the early eighties had mastered this new influence and made it her instrument in *Under the Red Flag* and *Ishmael*. Before the decade was out, she wrote her best novel in her old vein: *The Fatal Three*, where every turn of the plot unfolded with the inevitability predetermined by the childhood experience and personal qualities of each of her characters. Though distracted by John Maxwell's long illness of the early nineties, she came close to repeating this success with *The Venetians*. And with the three-volume novel a thing of the past and her marriage ended by Maxwell's death in 1895, she had gone on to use the new freedoms of the new plutocratic era to reflect in fiction upon its problems—economic, social, religious, and sexual—in a series of novels closely knit together in theme, of which the best was *Dead Love Has Chains*.

Throughout, she was resilient and full of surprises. In her novels she drew with candor and affection full-length portraits of George Augustus Sala (*Dead Sea Fruit*), Zola (*Under the Red Flag*), Gérard de Nerval (*Ishmael*), Mr. Gladstone (*One Thing Needful*), Oscar Wilde (*The Rose of Life*), and others. But she did this so rarely that the reader stumbles upon them unsuspecting. She was a camera, her eye recording inside and out the dwellings of her personages of all classes and all the periods of her life, their gardens, their food and drink, their paintings, bric-à-brac, dress, amusements. The lost world of the Victorian theatre lives again in her pages in all its rich variety.

Her ostensible heroes were often lovingly painted as vicious cads, her ostensible heroines as calculating chits, her ostensible villains as men with foibles that might be understood and even forgiven. Having been accused of sensuality and immorality—ridiculous charges, both of them—she became an adept at working within the framework of Victorian censorship: assuring her blindly devoted readers that no irregularity was taking place, yet enabling her more sophisticated contemporaries and all posterity to realize that she and they knew better. In retrospect, perhaps one may call her especially effective in dealing in this way with evangelical cant, in those novels of the late seventies and early eighties in which even murder may be forgiven a regular church-goer. But though she was always a realist, and often sardonic—even cynical—recognizing the pettiness of human actions and their mercenary motives, she was seldom bitter and never despairing.

Lucy Clifford told MEB that she had written too much and that only a few of her novels would survive. But even this proved too sanguine a prediction. If her contemporaries had been too hasty in "typing" her as a sensation novelist and too complacent to notice that she had grown and developed and changed, those who have come after her have allowed her to become completely forgotten. When in *The Green Curtain* she asked what difference an actor's performance on the stage could make in the long run, after that final curtain had fallen, she was probably half-predicting this future neglect for herself. Yet those who neglect her, even in the full tide of a Victorian revival, are the losers: they have missed the pleasure that even her least successful novels provide, and above all the astonishment and exhilaration aroused by her very best.

When MEB was a little girl, she heard the tinkle of the muffinman's bell in Soho. She remembered *Vanity Fair* appearing in its monthly yellow-covered paper parts. It took two days to go from London to Cornwall. Toward the end of her life she owned a motor-car, watched an airplane, transcribed an article on atomic energy, saw *Aurora Floyd* in the picture show, and read Thomas Mann. It had been a long life, and she had always taken change in her stride. Forbidden in her youth to describe a chaste embrace or to suggest that a man and woman who had contrived to be alone together on a yacht might be interested in something other than sailing, she lived long enough to write with twentieth-century frankness, though never without restraint, about human sexual drives and their psychological foundations. Although there were—as there must always be—elements of sadness about her death, she had bestowed and received much love, and had enjoyed—deservedly—a sensational success. It had been a triumphant career, and its close early in 1915—enabling her to escape the heartache of the next three years of war and what would surely have been severe physical infirmity—came not as tragedy but as fulfillment.

NOTE ON SOURCES,
AND
ACKNOWLEDGMENTS

The author's own collection (Wolff Collection) includes the following unpublished materials: the typescript of Mary Elizabeth Braddon's autobiographical memoir of her girlhood, *Before the Knowledge of Evil*, prepared in 1914 just before her death; her manuscript diaries for the years 1890–1914 inclusive; seven of her seventeen known surviving manuscript notebooks; the corrected original typescript of her unpublished play, *A Life Interest* (1893); and the manuscript of her unpublished (?) essay on Zola (1885); more than two hundred holograph letters to Miss Braddon—all that she saved—from members of her family, from friends, and from admirers, among them Henry James, Thomas Hardy, and W. E. Gladstone; and well over one hundred of her own holograph letters to others. It also includes the complete original manuscripts of two novels and large portions (all that survives) of several others. Also present are playbills, privately printed plays and verse, proof-sheets of certain fiction, and printed ephemera, some of signal importance in establishing the facts of Miss Braddon's life. This part of the Braddon collection—amounting to a Braddon archive—was largely acquired in five separate purchases in the 1960's: three of materials discovered at intervals in abandoned boxes in storage warehouses, and two of the Braddon collection formed by the late Rex Sercombe-Smith, who had contemplated writing a biography but died in 1964 before he had begun it. I should like to thank R. A. Brimmell, C. D. Massey, and A. D. Miller, and the other book- and autograph-dealers who have helped me form my collection.

In 1961 Henry Maxwell, Miss Braddon's grandson, approved my plan to write this book and has since done everything in his power to make it possible. He gave and loaned me and allowed me free use of manuscripts and photographic material in his possession (Maxwell Collection). This includes Miss Braddon's earliest surviving diaries, from 1880 to 1888 inclusive (the year 1889 is missing), one of the seventeen surviving notebooks, and the manuscripts of several important unpublished early short stories, plays, and never-completed novels. Mr. Maxwell waited patiently during the years when my work on this book moved slowly or not at all. Eventually he read and commented most helpfully upon it in typescript. He and his sister, Miss Barbara Maxwell, kindly shared with me their memories of their grandmother. Their cousins, Miss Helen Nethersole and Mrs. Amy Clifton, graciously loaned me letters and photographs.

Of capital importance also are: a notebook of Charles Reade ("Antiqua-Wreck," 1874) including a four-page manuscript account of Miss Braddon, for the free use of which I thank the London Library, always so hospitable; the thirty-seven letters written between 1862 and 1873 by Miss Braddon to Sir Edward Bulwer-Lytton, first Lord Lytton, and his two surviving replies, a correspondence I have published in the *Harvard Library Bulletin* 22 (1974), 5–35, 129–161, with the kind permission of Lady Hermione Cobbold and the Honourable David Lytton-Cobbold, and with the assistance of Peter Walne, Esq., County Archivist of Hertfordshire, to whom I express renewed thanks here; the approximately two hundred letters and telegrams from Miss Braddon's husband and business adviser, John Maxwell, to W. F. Tillotson, newspaper publisher of Bolton, Lancashire, together with examples of prospectuses for MEB's novels and memoranda of various kinds dating from 1879 to 1887, and two letters from Miss Braddon herself to Tillotson's firm, from 1892 and 1894, all in the files of Tillotson Newspapers Ltd., Mealhouse Lane, Bolton, for whose use I am indebted to the courtesy of the St. Regis Paper Company, proprietors of the *Bolton Evening News*, and to the kindness of J. Wilmot, Esq., Managing Director.

In the Houghton Library at Harvard are nine of the seventeen surviving Braddon manuscript notebooks, including those in which she drafted some of her earliest efforts at verse and prose; two complete manuscripts of Braddon novels; and two important letters. These materials Harvard acquired at my prompting from one of the storage warehouse boxes mentioned above. I should like to thank the late Professor W. A. Jackson and Professor William Bond for many courtesies. The Parrish Collection in the Princeton University Library, the Beinecke Library at Yale, the Lilly Library at Indiana University, and the Library of the University of Illinois also have important letters. My thanks go to Alexander Wainwright, Curator of the Parrish Collection at Princeton; Miss Marjorie Wynne of the Beinecke Library at Yale; the late Professor David

Randall, Lilly Librarian at Indiana; and Dr. Gordon Ray, formerly Vice President of the University of Illinois. For the use of various valuable collections of playbills, I should like to thank Miss Helen Willard of the Houghton Library; Donald Roy, Esq., of the Department of Drama, University of Hull; Messrs. W. H. Southern and James Mason of Wilberforce House, Hull; the Victoria and Albert Museum; and the curators of the Enthoven Collection. G. P. Rye, Librarian of Weston-Super-Mare, kindly responded to inquiries. John S. R. James gave permission to quote from unpublished letters of Henry James, as did Christopher Dilke for quotation from the letters of his grandmother, Lucy Clifford.

By far the most important single published source for this book has been the large body of Miss Braddon's own work. All of her books are in the Wolff Collection, as are the issues of all the periodicals without which this book could not have been written: the *Welcome Guest*, the *Halfpenny Journal*, the *London Journal*, Ward & Lock's *Sixpenny Magazine*, *Once A Week, Temple Bar, Belgravia*, and the *Mistletoe Bough*. Because Miss Braddon wrote so much and because her books, especially in first edition, are hard to come by, I append herewith a chronological checklist of her most important writings with place and date of publication and a reference to the chapter or chapters in this book where each is discussed.

The secondary literature about Miss Braddon consists mostly of reviews and criticism by contemporaries and others, to which full reference is made in the notes. Modern scholarship has hardly touched upon her. Professor C. Heywood's articles are referred to in Chapter V, note 32, and in the Appendix, Section 5. Benjamin Matthew Nyberg, *The Novels of Mary Elizabeth Braddon* (Ann Arbor, Michigan: University Microfilms, Inc., 1965) is a University of Colorado Ph.D. thesis, in which Dr. Nyberg skillfully shows that Miss Braddon was far more than a mere "sensation" novelist. He does not deal with her life or its relationship to her work, and he had no access to a good many of her novels. It is hoped that this book will answer some of the questions that Dr. Nyberg himself shrewdly asks at the conclusion of his study.

For pursuing several leads for me in the British Museum's newspaper collections, I should like to thank Professor Angeliki Laiou. My daughter and son-in-law, Rosamond and Dennis Purcell, expertly and generously took most of the photographs. Mrs. Madeline Gleason helped me clear up several stubborn mysteries. My colleagues John Clive and Howard Mumford Jones and my friend Mark Saxton read the book in an early draft and suggested many improvements. Mrs. Elizabeth Flavin patiently and supportively associated herself with the project from its beginnings and uncomplainingly typed transcripts of the manuscript sources and the now uncountable drafts of the book itself.

For the second time in two years it has been my privilege to publish a long book under the Garland imprint. My special thanks go to Carol Irelan for supervising its progress from typescript to completed volume, to Barbara Bergeron for eagle-eyed proofreading, and to Katy Homans for the handsome design.

Chronological Checklist of MEB's Important Writing

(See index for alphabetical entries)

Short Title	Book Publication (London except as noted) * = 3 vols.	Discussed in Chapter
Loves of Arcadia ("Comedietta")	Unpublished 1860	II
Three Times Dead	London: W. & M. Clark and Beverley: Empson (1860) Republished 1861 and later as *Trail of the Serpent*	III, IV
Garibaldi (verse)	Bosworth & Harrison 1861	III, IV
The Black Band	*Halfpenny Journal* 1861 Vickers, as book 1877	IV (with other penny-novels)
The Lady Lisle	Ward, Lock & Tyler 1862	IV
*Lady Audley's Secret	Tinsley 1862	Prologue, IV, VI
Captain of the Vulture	Ward, Lock & Tyler 1863	IV, Note 1
*Aurora Floyd	Tinsley 1863	V, VII
*Eleanor's Victory	Tinsley 1863	II, V
*John Marchmont's Legacy	Tinsley 1863	II, V
*Henry Dunbar	Maxwell 1864	V
*The Doctor's Wife	Maxwell 1864	I, II, IV, V
*Only a Clod	Maxwell 1865	V
*Sir Jasper's Tenant	Maxwell 1865	V
*The Lady's Mile	Ward, Lock & Tyler 1866	V
Ralph the Bailiff &c.	Ward, Lock & Tyler (1867)	IV
Circe (2 vols.) as by "Babington White"	Ward, Lock & Tyler 1867	VI
*Rupert Godwin	Ward, Lock & Tyler 1867	IV, VI
*Birds of Prey	Ward, Lock & Tyler 1867	V
*Charlotte's Inheritance	Ward, Lock & Tyler 1868	V
*Run to Earth	Ward, Lock & Tyler 1868	IV, VI
*Dead Sea Fruit	Ward, Lock & Tyler 1868	V
*Fenton's Quest	Ward, Lock & Tyler 1871	VII
*The Lovels of Arden	Maxwell 1871	VII

Short Title	Book Publication (London except as noted) * = 3 vols.	Discussed in Chapter
*Robert Ainsleigh	Maxwell 1872	VII
*To the Bitter End	Maxwell 1872	VII
*Milly Darrell &c.	Maxwell 1873	VII
Griselda (drama)	Unpublished 1873	VII
*Strangers & Pilgrims	Maxwell 1873	VII
*Lucius Davoren	Maxwell 1873	VII
*Taken at the Flood	Maxwell 1874	VII
*Lost for Love	Chatto & Windus 1874	VII
*A Strange World	Maxwell 1875	II, VII
*Hostages to Fortune	Maxwell 1875	II, VII
*Dead Men's Shoes	Maxwell 1876	III, VII
*Joshua Haggard's Daughter	Maxwell 1876	VIII
*Weavers and Weft &c.	Maxwell 1877	VIII
*An Open Verdict	Maxwell 1878	VIII
*Vixen	Maxwell (J & R) 1879	VIII
*The Cloven Foot	Maxwell (J & R) (1879)	VIII
Aladdin &c. (juvenile)	Maxwell (J & R) (1880)	
The Missing Witness (drama)	Maxwell (J & R) (1880)	VII
*The Story of Barbara	Maxwell (J & R) (1880)	I, II, VIII
*Just As I Am	Maxwell (J & R) (1880)	VIII
*Asphodel	Maxwell (J & R) 1881	VIII
*Mount Royal	Maxwell (J & R) 1882	VIII
Flower & Weed (with other stories) :	*Mistletoe Bough* 1882 Maxwell (J & R) (1884)	VIII
*The Golden Calf	Maxwell (J & R) 1883	VIII
*Phantom Fortune	Maxwell (J & R) 1883	VIII
Under the Red Flag (with other stories) :	*Mistletoe Bough* 1883 Maxwell (J & R) (1886)	VIII
*Ishmael	Maxwell (J & R) (1884)	VIII
*Wyllard's Weird	Maxwell (J & R) (1885)	VIII
The Good Hermione (juvenile) by "Aunt Belinda"	Maxwell (J & R) 1886	IX
*One Thing Needful	Maxwell (J & R) 1886	IX
Cut by the County	Maxwell (J & R) (1886)	IX

Short Title	Book Publication (London except as noted) * = 3 vols.	Discussed in Chapter
*Mohawks	Maxwell (J & R) (1886)	IX
*Like and Unlike	Spencer Blackett (1887)	IX
*The Fatal Three	Simpkin, Marshall (1888)	IX
*The Day Will Come	Simpkin, Marshall (1889)	IX
*One Life, One Love	Simpkin, Marshall 1890	IX
*Gerard	Simpkin, Marshall 1891	IX
*The Venetians	Simpkin, Marshall 1892	IX
A Life Interest (drama)	Unpublished 1893	IX
*All Along the River	Simpkin, Marshall 1893	IX
The Christmas Hirelings (juvenile)	Simpkin, Marshall 1894	IX
*Thou Art the Man	Simpkin, Marshall (1894)	IX
*Sons of Fire	Simpkin, Marshall (1895)	IX
London Pride	Simpkin, Marshall 1896	X
Under Love's Rule	Simpkin, Marshall 1897	X
In High Places	Hutchinson 1898	X
Rough Justice	Simpkin, Marshall 1898	X
His Darling Sin	Simpkin, Marshall (1899)	X
The Infidel	Simpkin, Marshall 1900	X
The Conflict	Simpkin, Marshall 1903	X
A Lost Eden	Hutchinson 1904	I, II, X
The Rose of Life	Hutchinson 1905	X
The White House	Hurst & Blackett 1906	X
Dead Love Has Chains	Hurst & Blackett 1907	X
Her Convict	Hurst & Blackett 1907	X
During Her Majesty's Pleasure	Hurst & Blackett 1908	X
Our Adversary	Hutchinson 1909	X
Beyond These Voices	Hutchinson 1910	X
The Green Curtain	Hutchinson 1911	X
Miranda	Hutchinson 1913	X
Mary	Hutchinson 1916	X

ABBREVIATIONS

BKE = *Before the Knowledge of Evil*, MEB's unpublished autobiographical memoir of her early childhood.

Braddon Notebook I = Houghton Library MS Eng 1122.2. See chapter II, note 9; chapter IV, note 7.

Braddon Notebook VI = Wolff Collection. See chapter II, note 31.

Diary (with date) = MEB's diaries; the years 1880–1888 are in the Maxwell Collection, the years 1890–1914 in the Wolff Collection. 1889 is lost.

ENCD = Allardyce Nicoll, *A History of Early Nineteenth-Century Drama, 1800–1850* (2 vols., Cambridge, England: University Press, 1930).

HLB 1 = R. L. Wolff, "Devoted Disciple: The Letters of Mary Elizabeth Braddon to Sir Edward Bulwer-Lytton, 1862–1873," *Harvard Library Bulletin* 22, 1 (January 1974), 1–35.

HLB 2 = the same, 22, 2 (April 1974), 129–161.

LNCD = Allardyce Nicoll, *A History of Later Nineteenth-Century Drama, 1850–1900* (2 vols., Cambridge, England: University Press, 1946).

"Schedule" = MEB's manuscript "Schedule of Work" for the years 1874–1885. See Appendix, Section 7.

TG = W. B. Maxwell, *Time Gathered* (London: Hutchinson, 1937), the autobiography of MEB's son.

Tillotson File: see Note on Sources and Acknowledgments.

Tillotson Memo: in the Tillotson file. See chapter VII, note 37.

NOTES

PROLOGUE

1. E. A[rnold] Bennett, "Miss Braddon," *Fame and Fiction, An Enquiry into Certain Popularities* (London: Grant Richards, 1901), pp. 23–33; M. E. Braddon, *Lady Audley's Secret* (3 vols., London: Tinsley Brothers, 1862), quotation in text from I, p. 173. MEB to Bulwer, No. 3, April 13, 1863; *HLB* 1, p. 12. Michael Sadleir, *XIX-Century Fiction* (London: Constable and Berkeley, Los Angeles: University of California Press, 1951), I, no. 306, discusses the publication of *Lady Audley's Secret*. Ward & Lock's *Sixpenny Magazine* 2 (1862), 278, in the opening number of the second serialization, refers to Miss Braddon as "The Author of 'Lady Lisle,' 'Aurora Floyd,' &c." *Lady Lisle* had appeared in book form earlier in 1862; see below, chapter IV. *Aurora Floyd* began its serial run in *Temple Bar* in January 1862. "A Novel of unsurpassed domestic interest and unrivalled narrative power," said Ward & Lock's introductory blurb for *Lady Audley*, designed to satisfy the "disappointed subscribers to *Robin Goodfellow*" as well as their own readers. For an account of the financial aspects of its publication, see below, chapter IV.

2. *Spectator*, No. 1791, October 25, 1862, p. 1196.

3. *Times*, November 18, 1862, p. 4.

4. *Lady Audley's Secret*, I, pp. 58–59; II, pp. 284–285.

5. Percy Fitzgerald, *Memoirs of an Author* (2 vols., London: Bentley, 1895), I, p. 279.

6. See especially chapters IV and VI below.

7. For the controversy, see below, chapter VI.

8. Lady Ritchie [Anne Thackeray], "A Discourse on Modern Sibyls," *Cornhill Magazine*, n.s., 34 (March 1913), 311. Reginald Smith of Smith & Elder, publishers of the *Cornhill*, sent MEB (then seventy-seven) a copy of the article, and she wrote thanking Lady Ritchie. Lady Ritchie replied: "How glad I am you have so kindly liked the little message! I was telling Mrs. Perugini [Dickens' daughter Kate, first married to Charles Allston Collins] one day of my small discourse [on the Sibyls] and we began talking of those who had

been read and who counted in our youth, and she said how very much her father had admired the *Doctor's Wife,* and I said how my father delighted in *Lady Audley's Secret.* And so between us we concocted the little paragraph. How kindly you have responded and sympathised, and what pleasure you have given me. . . . I am sending your note on to her. . . ." Lady Ritchie to MEB (Mrs. Maxwell), Folkestone, March 9 [1913], Wolff Collection. For the story of Thackeray going to the railway station, see *TG,* p. 284. Since it was a three-volume Braddon novel Thackeray triumphantly waved at his daughter, it must have been *Aurora Floyd, Eleanor's Victory,* or *John Marchmont's Legacy,* the only Braddon three-deckers besides *Lady Audley's Secret* to appear before he died on December 24, 1863. John Coleman, *Charles Reade as I Knew Him* (New York: Dutton, 1903), p. 265.

9.   Robert Louis Stevenson to MEB (Mrs. Maxwell), quoted in *TG,* pp. 284–285.

10.   George Moore, *Confessions of a Young Man* (New York: Brentano's, 1917), pp. 2–3. For *The Doctor's Wife,* see chapters I–V *passim,* and chapter V, note 32, for its influence on Moore.

11.   "Rita," *Saba Macdonald* (London: Hurst & Blackett, 1906), p. 16.

12.   For Henry James's published criticism of *Aurora Floyd,* see chapter V, text, and note 4 below. Henry James to MEB (Mrs. Maxwell), Theydon Hill, Epping, August 2, 1911, and Lamb House, Rye, October 1, 1911, Wolff Collection.

13.   Ford Madox Ford, *It Was the Nightingale* (Philadelphia and London: Lippincott, 1933), pp. 88–90. Ford thought that MEB had written *East Lynne,* which was actually by Mrs. Henry Wood. He did say of Miss Braddon: "Few novelists of her day had her workmanlike knowledge or could write such good English, like Cobbett's." Ford was inventing details about MEB's drawing room: she had no Taj Mahal, no Turkey carpet.

14.   Charles Tennyson, *Alfred Tennyson* (London: Macmillan, 1950), p. 377. W. E. Gladstone to MEB (Mrs. Maxwell), Hawarden, October 24, 1891, Wolff Collection.

15.   Dr. Robert Treadwell to MEB, Via Republica 12, primo piano, Bologna, Italy, November 7, 1888, Wolff Collection.

16.   *Loc. cit.,* note 1 above.

17.   Lucy Clifford (Mrs. W. K. Clifford) to MEB (Mrs. Maxwell), Chilworth Street, July 25 [1911], Wolff Collection.

CHAPTER I

1. W. B. Maxwell, MEB's son, found the MS of *BKE* and gives a few brief quotations from it (*TG,* p. 270). The original typescript of 185 pages is now in the Wolff Collection. MEB's diary for 1914, also in the Wolff Collection, includes under March 2 the entry, "Wrote a little 'Rem.' after tea," which confirms Maxwell's belief that *BKE* was actually written in the last year of MEB's life. Unless otherwise attributed, all quotations in this chapter are derived from it; but since it remains unpublished, there seems no need to give page references.

2. Birth and baptismal dates in Baptismal Register of St. Anne's Church, Soho. The *DNB* account gives 1837. Skisdon came into the Braddon family in 1807, when its owner, Major William Clode of the East India Company, died unmarried, leaving it to his sister, Sarah, wife of Henry Braddon, also of the East India Company. Sarah Clode Braddon and Henry Braddon were MEB's paternal grandparents. C. S. Gilbert, *An Historical Survey of the County of Cornwall* (2 vols. in 3, Plymouth Dock: J. Congdon; London: Longman, etc., 1820), II, Part 2, p. 610.

3. Henry Braddon is listed in an Emanuel College, Cambridge, manuscript as having been admitted as a pensioner in 1822, but "he did not reside." J. A. Venn, comp., *Alumni Cantabrigiensis* . . . Part 2 (1752–1900), I (Cambridge: University Press, 1940), p. 354. He is called "student at law" in 1820 (Gilbert, *Cornwall*, II, Part 2, p. 38). Of his "Gilbert Forester" sketches, none is particularly noteworthy except the final instalment of a report on a trip to the West Country (*Sporting Magazine* 79, No. 22 [February 1832], pp. 306–307), in which he rides from North Devon into Cornwall to inspect the harriers of Mr. Braddon of Treglith (parish of Treneglos, between Launceston and Camelford). This was John Braddon, a cousin. The Braddons of Skisdon were immediately descended from Henry Braddon of Treworgy (Parish of St. Gennys), who died in 1711. He is buried with his Braddon ancestors in the parish church, with the epitaph, "In Peace I lived, and in peace did die,/And now translated am to peace on high;/Where I in peace perpetual shall remain,/Until the Prince of Peace return again" (Gilbert, *Cornwall*, II, Part 2, p. 572). This was MEB's great-great-grandfather.

4. (MEB) "Author of Lady Audley's Secret," *The Story of Barbara* (3 vols., London: John & Robert Maxwell, n.d. [1880, preface dated 1880; and see chapter II and chapter VIII, note 18, below]). The original manuscript is in the Houghton Library MS Eng 1122.1, of 301 ff., each numbered and lettered "Bab." MEB originally called the Trevornock family "Tremaine," but later changed the name. Otherwise there are only insignificant differences between the manuscript and the printed version. Quotations in text from I, pp. 22, 61–67; see also pp. 157–159.

5.   *Ibid.*, pp. 68–69, 97–104, 110–111.

6.   Fuller discussions of *The Doctor's Wife* in chapters II, IV, and VI. The career of Sleaford owed something to MEB's personal acquaintance with the son of an actual forger.

7.   Fuller discussion of *A Lost Eden* in chapter II.

8.   MEB's Braddon grandmother was born Sarah Phillis Clode, of a family originating in Dorset; in 1782 she married Henry Braddon, third and youngest son of John Braddon (d. 1788) and Mary Martyn of Melford, Devon. In 1807 Sarah Clode Braddon inherited Skisdon from her bachelor brother. She and Henry Braddon had five sons and two daughters: Richard, a major in the Bengal Army, who died unmarried in 1837 in India; William, whom MEB first met on her childhood visit to Skisdon, who had three sons and five daughters, although MEB met only two daughters; John, the bachelor solicitor of Camelford; Henry, MEB's father; Edward Nicholas Coventry, Vicar of St. Mary's, Sandwich, Kent, for whom MEB's brother was named; Sarah Phillis Clode Braddon (MEB's "Aunt Cowland"), whose first husband, Captain Kelly, died in 1831 and who later married the Reverend William Cowland, Rector of Werrington, Devon; and Mary, who married Admiral Basden. Sir Bernard Burke, *A Genealogical and Heraldic History of the Colonial Gentry* (London: Harrison, 1891), I, pp. 331–332, under "Braddon of Treglith." Grandmamma Braddon would die in 1846; Uncle John in 1850; and Uncle William in 1858, murdered. See chapter V, text, and note 29 below.

9.   Edward Braddon to Mrs. Braddon: "Dear Mama" and "My very own dearest Mamma," November 29 and December 6, 1842, Wolff Collection.

10.   Manuscript autobiographical fragment, four pages long, perhaps a false start for *BKE*, Maxwell Collection.

11.   This clue suggests that the following papers, all signed "Mrs. White" (Mrs. Braddon's maiden name), were probably by her: "Wanted a Governess," *Ainsworth's Magazine* 6 (1844), pp. 226–231; "The Rebels: A Tale of Emmett's Days," *ibid.*, pp. 313–319 and pp. 407–443; "A Night in a Fog," *ibid.*, pp. 533–537; "Mary Drewitt," *ibid.* 7 (1845), pp. 44–48 and 168–173; and "The Separate Purse," *ibid.* 8 (1846), pp. 524–531.

12.   Julia Pardoe (1806–1862) wrote many travel books and novels. MEB may have been reading her fictional *Romance of the Harem* (3 vols., London: Colburn, 1837). Miss Pardoe's celebrated *Beauties of the Bosphorus* (London: Virtue, 1839), magnificently illustrated with steel-engravings, and her *City of*

the Sultan and Domestic Manners of the Turks (2 vols., London: Colburn, 1837) were popular books for the drawing room table.

13.   M. E. Braddon, "My First Novel," *The Idler* 3 (February 1893), p. 20; reprinted in *My First Book,* with an introduction by Jerome K. Jerome (London: Chatto and Windus, 1894), p. 110.

14.   Manuscript of "The Old Arm Chair," in the Maxwell Collection.

CHAPTER II

1.   For Edward Braddon, see the *DNB* and the *Times* obituary, February 3, 1904. Six letters from Maggie Braddon Cartighoni (see chapter VII): Georgina Braddon to Fanny White Braddon, September 16, n.y. [1863], Wolff Collection. Georgie mentions reading MEB's novel *Eleanor's Victory* as it was appearing in *Once A Week,* where it ran serially from March 7 to October 3, 1863.

2.   (MEB) "Author of Lady Audley's Secret," *The Story of Barbara* (3 vols., London: John and Robert Maxwell, n.d. [1880]), I, pp. 3–4, 4–5, 10–11, 1–2, 18, 31–32. Aunt Sarah Cowland to Fanny White Braddon, June 18, 1848, Wolff Collection. When *Barbara* was published, the *Athenaeum* critic commented (No. 2530, February 21, 1880, p. 244) that MEB had

> probably never written anything better than the opening chapters. . . .
> The two pretty sisters and their pretty mother, living humbly but in
> refinement in an obscure suburban home, their troubles about money,
> their advertisement for a "partial boarder," his arrival, and the love-
> making which naturally follows, are all described in a manner which is
> at once lifelike and fascinating, showing a delicacy of touch for which
> most readers would hardly have given the author credit and a
> brightness, gaiety, and good sense, which could only be equalled by
> Miss Flossie herself.

Since "Miss Flossie herself" *was* MEB, the critic had neatly hit upon the truth.

3.   M. E. Braddon, *A Lost Eden* (London: Hutchinson, 1904), pp. 5–6, 29, 74.

4.   (MEB) "Author of Lady Audley's Secret," *The Doctor's Wife* (3 vols., London: John Maxwell & Co., 1864), I, pp. 28, 29, 30, 34, 42–43. In his

Victorian Suburb. A Study of the Growth of Camberwell (Leicester: University Press, 1961), H. J. Dyos gives the sober record of the ways in which the region was built up, echoing for the economic and social historian the notes that MEB had struck in her three reminiscent novels. The street plan in the pocket at the back of Dyos' book enables the reader to locate within a few streets the homes of the Trevornocks, Sandfords, Sleafords, and Braddons.

5.   *The Doctor's Wife*, I, pp. 53–54, 54–55, 160–161.

6.   M. E. Braddon, "My First Novel" (as above, chapter I, note 13) : *Idler*, pp. 23–24, and *My First Book,* pp. 114–115.

7.   Quotations from *The Doctor's Wife*, I, pp. 164–165, 175–176.

8.   M. E. Braddon, "The Woman I Remember," *The Press Album* (London: John Murray, 1909), p. 5.

9.   *TG,* pp. 274–275. MS note, to Miss Seyton, Wolff Collection. "Islam" pasted into Braddon Notebook I (see chapter IV, note 7, below), Houghton Library MS Eng 1122.2, on verso of p. 117. The poem, signed "Brighton, Nov. 21, Mary Seyton," was contributed to the "Poet's Corner" of an unidentified newspaper, probably the *Brighton Herald*, in 1858 or 1859. It reads:

Cease, oh my soul, thy prison-house to rend
   With agitating doubt or daring dream,
To vain results thy futile struggles tend,
   Await the light, and bless each transient beam;
Nor can'st anticipate thy future home.
   Thou art all powerless in the Maker's hand.
Seek not to learn thy fate.
   The gate will open to the unseen Land;
That gate is Death—Await!

The secrets thy dull powers cannot conceive
   He who died yesterday could tell to thee.
Thy poor material nature can believe
   In that alone thy mortal eye can see.
Thy wildest hopes are wiser than thy fears:
   Accept thy yearning for more radiant spheres,
Thy deep desire to reach the far unknown.
   As prophets of thy fate.
The grave is the true Oedipus alone.
   Cry, "Islam!" and wait!

Address: "Miss Seyton, at Mrs. Robinson's, 13 Marischal Street, Aberdeen"

NOTES TO PAGES 46–49 • 423

on verso of last sheet of MEB's MS draft of Act II of an unpublished play called "The Revenge of the Dead," Maxwell Collection.

10.   The Beverley playbill for May 1, 1857, Wolff Collection. On Taylor, see Winton Tolles, *Tom Taylor and the Victorian Drama* (New York: Columbia University Press, 1940). See also Thomas Hughes, "In Memoriam," *Macmillan's Magazine* 42 (1880), 298–301; John Sheehan, "Tom Taylor," *Dublin University Magazine* 90 (1877), 142–158. For a charge of plagiarism and Taylor's mild rebuttal, see "Q" (Thomas Purnell), *Dramatists of the Present Day* (London: Chapman and Hall, 1871), pp. 94–140. The "handlists" in Allardyce Nicoll, *LNCD*, are indispensable. For *Still Waters Run Deep*: *LNCD*, I, pp. 100–101; Tom Taylor, *Still Waters Run Deep, An Original Comedy in Three Acts* (London: Thomas Hailes Lacy, n.d.), pp. 5, 23, 49. For Wybert Rousby, see Thomas Sheppard, *Evolution of the Theatre in Hull and District* (Hull: A. Brown Ltd., and at London and York, 1907), pp. 96, 158; no mention of MEB. On Charles Dance, *ENCD*, I, pp. 125-126. Charles Dance, *A Wonderful Woman. A Comic Drama in Two Acts* (London: Thomas Hailes Lacy, n. d.).

11.   Playbill collections in Hull, discussed in Donald Roy, "Theatre Royal Hull; or, The Vanishing Circuit," *Essays on Nineteenth-Century British Theatre,* ed. Kenneth Richards and Peter Thomson (London: Methuen, 1971), pp. 25–38. The collections are divided between the Hull Central Library, the Municipal Museum in Wilberforce House, and the Department of Drama at the University. Professor Roy kindly consulted the University's collections and reported no trace of MEB. In August 1973 I examined the collections in the Hull Central Library and in the Museum at Wilberforce House. The May 11, 1857, Queen's Theatre playbill is in Wilberforce House. On Sheil, *ENCD*, I, p. 166, and the *DNB.* Richard Sheil, *Evadne; or, the Statue,* ed. Epes Sargent, *Modern Standard Drama,* no. LII (New York: Breford and Company, 1847), II, i, p. 17. More about *The Lady of Lyons* below.

12.   Brighton playbill in Harvard Theatre Collection. On Buckstone, see *ENCD, passim,* and II, pp. 262–265, and for *Leap-Year, LNCD,* I, pp. 106–107, and II, p. 287. J. B. Buckstone, *Leap-Year; or, The Ladies' Privilege* (New York and London: French's Standard Drama, n.d.). For *The Era's* advertisement, see Peter Davey, *The Chronicles of the Old Country Theatres in the South of England,* manuscript compilation in the Enthoven Collection of the Victoria and Albert Museum.

13.   The Hull Theatre Royal playbills are distributed as follows: May 30, 1859, announcing the Brighton Company, and June 1, Hull Central Library; June 6, June 7 (two copies), June 8, Wilberforce House; June 9 and June 10, Hull Central Library with duplicate in Wilberforce House.

14.   Samuel Lover, *Rory O'More, A Comic Drama*, ed. Benjamin Webster, Comedian; The Acting National Drama, Vol. II (London: National Drama Office, n.d.), II, ii, pp. 25–26, and III, i, p. 39. J. Sterling Coyne, *The Man of Many Friends, An Original Comedy in Three Acts* (New York: A. O. Roorbach, 1855), I, i, p. 5.

15.   J. B. Buckstone, *Rural Felicity, an Operatic Comedy in Two Acts*, had opened at the Theatre Royal, Haymarket, on June 9, 1834, with Buckstone as Simon Sly. Version used here published in London by William Strange in 1834. Charles Selby, *The Last of the Pigtails. An Original Petite Comedy in One Act* (New York: Samuel French and Sons, n.d.), p. 16. J[oachim] H[ayward] Stocqueler, *An Object of Interest. A Farce, in One Act* (New York: Samuel French, n.d.). Tom Taylor, *Victims. An Original Comedy in Three Acts* (London: T. H. Lacy, n.d.), pp. 4, 20; see Tolles, *Tom Taylor* (cited in note 10 above), pp. 158–161.

16.   John Maddison Morton, *Lend Me Five Shillings. A Farce in One Act* and *Slasher and Crasher, A Farce in One Act* (New York: William H. Taylor, n.d.), p. 9. All details of opening dates from Nicoll, *ENCD* and *LNCD*. MEB had already played Dinah Blowhard at the Theatre Royal, Coventry, on Friday, April 23, 1858, in the second part of a double bill with Shakespeare's *Henry IV, Part I*, in which she appeared as the Earl of Westmoreland. Nye Chart's Brighton company had licensed the theatre. Playbill in Harvard Theatre Collection.

17.   *Daily Telegraph*, February 5, 1915, p. 6. The paper listed the actors and actresses who had appeared with MEB in Brighton. J. R. Planché, *The Prince of Happy Land: or, The Fawn in the Forest, a New and Original Grand Comic Extravaganza, in Two Acts (founded upon the Countess d'Aulnoy's popular story, "La Biche au Bois")* (London: Lacy's Acting Edition, n.d.), song on p. 21. Thomas Egerton Wilks (1812–1854) was author of at least fifty-six plays (*ENCD*, II, pp. 410–411, and *LNCD*, II, p. 623). For Mark Lemon (1809–1870), celebrated editor of *Punch* and man of letters, see Arthur A. Adrian, *Mark Lemon* (London and New York: Oxford University Press, 1966). Without playbills we cannot know which Wilks or Lemon plays MEB adorned. *Dame Madge Kendal by Herself* (London: John Murray, 1933), pp. 86–87, has a few words about the famous "African Roscius," Ira Aldridge. In Murphy's *All in the Wrong*, MEB played Clarissa, one of two indistinguishable young women loved by two indistinguishable young men. Barnabas F. Rayner wrote *The Dumb Man of Manchester, a Melo-Drama in Two Acts* (London: Thomas Hailes Lacy, n.d.), which, so the published version states, was first presented at Astley's Amphitheatre in 1838 (not in *ENCD*). William Thomas Moncrieff (1794–1857) wrote a play called *Perourou the Bellows Mender; or, the Beauty of*

Lyons (London: J. Duncombe, 18___), produced on February 14, 1842, at the Sadler's Wells Theatre: *ENCD,* II, p. 351. *Phoebe Hessell; or, Eighty Years of a Woman's Life* is probably the same play listed in *ENCD,* II, p. 509, as *Phoebe Hepell; or, the Struggle of Seventy Years,* by an unknown author, first produced in Brighton on November 11, 1847.

18.   *Weekly Register and Catholic Standard,* August 19, 1876. On Charles Dance (1794–1863), see *ENCD,* I, pp. 125–126. *Delicate Ground* was published by Thomas Hailes Lacy (London, n.d.). MEB may also have acted in Liverpool. William Tinsley, in *Random Recollections of an Old Publisher* (2 vols., London: Simpkin Marshall, 1900), II, p. 92, says that Charles Milward, a member of London Bohemian circles and a "very noted monumental stonemason," wrote in the *Liverpool Porcupine* that he had seen MEB as Cinderella in a Liverpool pantomime.

19.   "Address Written by Miss M. E. Braddon, (Author of 'Lady Audley's Secret,' &c) Delivered by Miss Woolgar (Mrs. Alfred Mellon,) at the St. James's Hall Concert for the Benefit of the Widow and Children of the late Mr. Sam Cowell, On Tuesday, June 7, 1864. Already Subscribed £150 7s. 3d. . . . Perfumed by Eugene Rimmell. . . ." Four-page leaflet, 4½ x 7 inches, with MEB's "Address" in blank verse on the two inner pages and Rimmell's perfume advertisement on the fourth page, Wolff Collection, still fragrant. Affectionate letters from Buckstone to MEB in later years are in the Wolff Collection. For *Griselda,* see Chapter VII.

20.   Quotations from *A Lost Eden,* as cited in note 3 above, pp. 20, 28, 137, 138, 140, 157, 158, 159, 160, 162, 164, 165, 171, 277, 293. "Across the Footlights," *Mistletoe Bough Annual* for 1884, pp. 112, 113, 114, 115; reprinted in M. E. Braddon, *Under the Red Flag and Other Tales* (London: John and Robert Maxwell, n.d. [1886, as shown by a printer's datemark at the foot of p. 352]), pp. 285–316. "Too Bright to Last" here quoted from *Weavers and Weft* (3 vols., London: John Maxwell, 1877), III, pp. 61, 64–65. First publication in *Belgravia Christmas Annual* for 1871.

21.   M. E. Braddon, *Eleanor's Victory* (3 vols., London: Tinsley, 1863), I, pp. 97, 107–108, 116, 118–119, 119–120, 121–124, 125. For an appreciation of the London melodramatic theatre, see H. S. Leigh, "Over the Water," *Carols of Cockayne* (London: Chatto and Windus, 1888), pp. 41–43: "Look always on the Surrey side/For true dramatic art./The road is long, the river wide,/But frequent busses start/From Charing Cross and Greenchurch Street,/(An inexpensive ride;)/So, if you want an evening's treat,/O seek the Surrey side.//. . . . I gape in Covent Garden's walls;/I doze in Drury Lane;/I strive in the Lyceum stalls/To keep awake—in vain./There's naught in the dramatic way/That I can

quite abide,/Except the pieces that they play/Upon the Surrey side." For a description of the way in which the London stage of the early sixties was "deluged with adaptations from the French," see Clement Scott, *Drama of Yesterday and Today* (2 vols., London: Macmillan, 1899), I, pp. 474–475.

22.   (MEB) "Author of Lady Audley's Secret," *John Marchmont's Legacy* (3 vols., London: Tinsley, 1863), I, pp. 23–24.

23.   For MEB's resurrection of *Rupert Godwin*, a potboiler, see chapter IV. (MEB) "Author of Lady Audley's Secret," *Rupert Godwin* (3 vols., London: Ward, Lock & Tyler, 1867), I, pp. 291–300, 302, 307–310, 316–317, 319.

24.   In a short story called "At Daggers Drawn," published under her pseudonym "Babington White," MEB told of the rivalry between two "low-comedy" actors, Tayte and Munford. Tayte hates Munford until Munford falls ill, and the manager, though generous, is forced to discontinue Munford's salary. Tayte secretly pays it out of his own pocket down to the moment of Munford's death. " 'Come back to the theatre,' " says Tayte to Munford on his sickbed, " 'and I'll hate you again,' " a remark that saves the story from being a mere Victorian sentimental trifle. *Belgravia*, 1, No. 3 (January 1867), 335–345; reprinted in M. E. Braddon, *Under the Red Flag and Other Tales* (as in note 20, above), pp. 239–252. Quotation from p. 250. Original manuscript in the Wolff Collection.

25.   (MEB) "Author of Lady Audley's Secret," *Dead Sea Fruit* (3 vols., Ward, Lock & Tyler, 1868), I, pp. 268–269, 277–278, 278–279, 296–297, 298–299, 300–301, 305–306, 310–311, 313, 314; II, pp. 52–53, 57, 59, 60–61, 68, 97, 122.

26.   (MEB) "Author of Lady Audley's Secret," *A Strange World* (3 vols., London: John Maxwell and Co., 1875), I, pp. 5–7, 8–10, 18–21, 37–40, 40–41, 41; III, pp. 112–121; II, pp. 145–147, 148, 237.

27.   (MEB) "Author of Lady Audley's Secret," *Hostages to Fortune* (3 vols., London: John Maxwell and Co., 1875), I, pp. 15, 138–144; II, p. 4; III, pp. 277–280, 281; II, pp. 9–10, 12. Like the Frivolity of *Hostages to Fortune,* the Kaleidoscope of *Mount Royal* (1882) is a bonbonnière which looks "as if it ought to be filled with glacé chestnuts or crystallized violets rather than with substantial flesh and blood." Its décor consists of dove-colored poplin and velvet and cream-white satin, with occasional flashes of crimson, gold-monogrammed, slender pilasters and moldings, "all airy, light, graceful." Here there is playing "a dreamy classical compound, made up of reminiscences of Mozart, Beethoven, and Weber" called *Overture,* in which the actress in the leading role of Psyche wears a diamond necklace and an emerald butterfly on

her shoulder. She had been taken off the stage when she had been in the back row of the ballet at Drury Lane at seventeen and sixpence a week, and her lover "gave her a house in St. John's Wood, squandered his money on her, had her educated, . . . and would have married her, if she had only behaved herself." (MEB) "Author of Lady Audley's Secret," *Mount Royal* (3 vols., London: John and Robert Maxwell, 1882), I, pp. 215–216, 216, 239–240.

28.　M. E. Braddon, *His Darling Sin* (London: Simpkin, Marshall, Hamilton, Kent, n.d. [1899]), p. 200.

29.　"Circumambulatory," in the Maxwell Collection, is written on the rectos of twenty-nine leaves of white paper, folded into three. The title used here is pasted over an earlier title, "Our Sussex Circuit, being some account of the brief dramatic tour of those distinguished Messrs ___ and ___ and ___ and Mrs. ___ , known familiarly and among their personal friends as Volage, the Dougal, the Zoophyte, and Hypatia."

30.　The obituary in the *Morning Post* of February 5, 1915, noted that "Her maiden efforts . . . which took the form of verses, parodies, and political squibs, appeared in a paper published at Brighton, to which she gained access through the influence of her friend, the late William Sawyer, who was then engaged on the editorial staff. . . . at that time nothing more than a beginner." Sawyer's paper was the *Brighton Herald*.

31.　In the Harvard University Theatre Collection are three Strand Theatre playbills: that for March 5, 1860 announces that on the 12th *The Loves of Arcadia*, "a New and Original Comedietta, written expressly for this Theatre by Miss M. E. Braddon" would "positively be produced," with Miss Swanborough in her first appearance of the season, the announcement coming at the end of the list of attractions scheduled for the week of March 5–12. The playbill for the week of March 12 shows that on opening night the comedietta shared billing with *Frightful Accident*, a "new and original farce," and *Sisterly Service*, also a comedietta. By the 26th, MEB's comedietta was billed as "immensely successful," and the bill noted, "The Free List is entirely suspended, the Public Press excepted." Date of the first production is also given in *LNCD*, II, p. 273. The clipping of the review is in Braddon Notebook I (see note 9, above) pasted on the verso of p. 120. In the Wolff Collection is another notebook (brown morocco cover, spine missing, size 4 x 6 inches), hereafter Notebook VI, belonging to the mid- and late-1890's and early years of the twentieth century, which includes four pages containing a draft of dialogue labeled "Loves of Arcadia," including a song and some witticisms. MEB may have been planning a musical version of her very first success about forty years after it had taken place.

32.   The Sawyer letters to MEB in the Wolff Collection.

33.   The *Morning Post* and the *Times*, issues of February 5, 1915.

CHAPTER III

1.   Malcolm Elwin, *Charles Reade* (London: Jonathan Cape, 1931), pp. 266–267; *TG*, pp. 23–24. Maxwell omitted the last two sentences: the "task-master" was his father, MEB's husband and publisher, John Maxwell. See above, Prologue and note 8 for Reade's opinion of MEB. In conversation, too, he called her "quiet . . . modest . . . as unassuming as she is accomplished."

2.   Reade Notebook, "no. IV, 15, Antiqua-Wreck of 1874," alphabetized, now in the London Library. E. G. Sutcliffe, "Charles Reade's Notebooks," *Studies in Philology* 27, No. 1 (January 1930), 102, noted that "the most interesting item" in this notebook was "a fairly extended sketch of the life and character of M. E. Braddon, imputing bigamy to her husband, John Maxwell." But he did not transcribe the entry, and this is the only published reference that suggests what might be in the portion of the entry not quoted by Elwin or W. B. Maxwell. Wayne Burns, in "More Reade Notebooks," *Studies in Philology* 42, No. 4 (October 1945), 831, notes that Reade regarded himself as an authority on women.

3.   *TG*, p. 162. Founded in 1858 by Henry Vizetelly, who was tempted by the fantastic sum of £24,000 recently paid for the copyright of the *London Journal,* another penny weekly, the *Welcome Guest* began with a circulation of 120,000 copies. But Vizetelly lost money and sold the paper to Maxwell, who in turn lost "another couple of thousand pounds" before he let the paper die. Henry Vizetelly, *Glances Back through Seventy Years* (2 vols., London: Kegan Paul, 1893), II, pp. 9–10.

4.   M. E. Braddon, "My First Novel" (as cited above, chapter I, note 13), pp. 24–25, 25, 27–30, 29, and *My First Book*, pp. 115–116, 116, 119–122, 121.

5.   For discussion of the date of *Three Times Dead* see below, Appendix, Section 1.

6.   Maxwell Collection, written on the rectos of twenty-five sheets of "patented straw paper." MEB later put it into a long blue envelope and docketed it "Unpublished MS Kingdom of Boredom." See chapter IV.

7.   Letter and envelope in the Wolff Collection. Clement Scott, in *The Drama of Yesterday and Today* (2 vols., London: Macmillan, 1899), II, pp. 194 ff., remembered Miss Swanborough as "a charming and graceful actress" and printed still another Strand playbill for February 27, 1860, promising Miss Swanborough's approaching appearance in MEB's *Loves of Arcadia*.

8.   (MEB) "Author of Lady Audley's Secret," *Dead Men's Shoes* (3 vols., London: Maxwell, 1876), I, pp. 94–102; II, p. 7. For further discussion of this novel see chapter VII; it was completed on December 20, 1875, and published the next year. Bulwer's description of the town he calls L--- in *A Strange Story* (1862), where society is stratified in much the same way as in "Redcastle" and is similarly ruled by a colonel's wife, may have stimulated MEB to recall Beverley. For the notebook, see chapter II, note 9, above, and chapter IV, note 7, below.

9.   All Gilby letters and the Halliday/Swanborough and Swanborough/ Braddon notes in the Wolff Collection.

10.   The *Welcome Guest* is rare; there is a complete set in the Wolff Collection. The individual weekly numbers of the "New Series," beginning with No. 1 on September 24, 1859, were not dated. MEB's "Captain Thomas," in No. 50, would have appeared on September 1, 1860, pp. 471–475. It was republished as one of the short stories in MEB's *Ralph the Bailiff and Other Tales* (London: Ward, Lock & Tyler, 1862), not available to me, and in the edition of 1867, pp. 55–68. "The Cold Embrace" appeared in No. 54 of the *Welcome Guest,* pp. 25–28, and was reprinted in the 1867 edition of *Ralph the Bailiff*, pp. 69–78; "My Daughters" appeared in No. 56, pp. 79–81, not reprinted. The original manuscript of this is preserved on the versos of pp. 10, 9, 8, 7, and 6 in Braddon Notebook I.

11.   Sawyer and Gilby letters and letter from William Sawyer's sister in the Wolff Collection.

12.   *DNB,* "Wraxall."

13.   Sawyer letter in Wolff Collection.

14.   Gilby letters in Wolff Collection.

15.   For information on the Gilbys, see Appendix, Section 2.

16.   "London on Four Feet" in the *Welcome Guest,* No. 64, pp. 277–278, not

afterwards reprinted; "My First Happy Christmas" in No. 65, pp. 312–315, reprinted in *Ralph the Bailiff* (1867), pp. 200–212; see below, chapter IV, note 21, for the story's re-use in the *Halfpenny Journal* for December 29, 1862.

17. *Edmund Yates: His Recollections and Experiences* (2 vols., London: Bentley, 1884), II, pp. 63–64. The story was first entitled "Christmas at Rilston Kagstar."

18. *Under a Cloud* ran from September 11, 1858, through January 22, 1859. Its authors were identified in the issue of April 9, 1859, when *Looking Back* was announced as about to begin in the next number. It ran through August 6, 1859. Frederick Greenwood also contributed a story to the *Welcome Guest*'s Christmas issue for 1858. He would serve as editor of the *Queen* in 1861–1863 and would move on to the *Cornhill* in 1862, where he served as joint editor with George Lewes in 1862–1864 and alone from 1864 to 1868. In February 1865 he became the founding editor of the new daily *Pall Mall Gazette*.

19. Gilby letter in the Wolff Collection.

20. MEB's diary for 1895 and the three letters from Maxwell to MEB in the Wolff Collection. For an interesting letter showing that Empson, the Beverley printer of the first edition, protested against Maxwell's republication of the book, see Michael Sadleir, *XIX-Century Fiction*, I, p. 53. See chapter IV, text and note 11 below.

21. Harriett Jay, *Robert Buchanan, Some Account of His Life, His Life's Work, and His Literary Friendships* (London: T. Fisher Unwin, 1903), pp. 93–95. Isabella Fyvie Mayo, a minor novelist who sometimes wrote under the name "Edward Garrett," had heard of Maxwell's having treated Buchanan "with an inconsideration that amounted almost to brutality," and her informant and friend, Mrs. Hall, had claimed that her own intervention had mollified Maxwell's manner. See Isabella Fyvie Mayo, *Recollections of Fifty Years* (London: Murray, 1910), p. 217.

22. Quotations from *TG*, p. 157; Mayo, *Recollections*, p. 221; *TG*, pp. 157, 159. Private information.

23. MEB to Mrs. Jeaffreson, March 30, 1875, in the Wolff Collection; MEB to Lady Monckton in the Parrish Collection, Princeton University.

24. The late Rex Sercombe-Smith in 1956 interviewed Mrs. Blanche Howell, daughter of the Maxwells' former servant, Eliza Mary Pryke—later

NOTES TO PAGES 103–108 · 431

Mrs. Gilkey—and recorded the below-stairs anecdote summarized here. Gerald
Maxwell's birth date in *Admissions to Trinity College, Cambridge,* ed. W. W.
Rouse Ball and J. A. Venn, V, 1851 to 1950 (London: Macmillan, 1913),
p. 649. I. F. Mayo, *Recollections,* p. 220.

25.   The obituary notice for Fanny Maxwell (Mrs. Edmund Selous) in the
Daily Telegraph for September 15, 1955, indicated that she was in her 93rd
year, which puts her birth date in 1863. MEB to Bulwer, No. 23, August 9
[1866], refers to a "great domestic sorrow," and No. 30, November 3 [1868],
said that Mrs. Braddon had "two and a half years earlier"—i.e., in the summer
of 1866—chosen the grave for the "sweetest babe that was ever laid in earth to
rise an angel in heaven." *HLB* 2, pp. 136, 147. These passages fix the date of
the infant's death.

26.   *Court Journal,* 17, No. 1826, January 16, 1864, p. 56, under
"Metropolitan on-dits"; *Public Opinion,* 5, No. 122, January 23, 1864, p. 107,
carried the report, giving the *Court Journal* as the source. In the very next issue,
No. 123 (January 30, 1864), p. 125, Knowles published his denial. Similarly the
report appeared in the *Guardian,* 19, No. 946, January 20, 1864, p. 54, and was
denied in the next issue, No. 947, January 27, 1864, p. 95, under "Table-Talk."
The *London Review,* 8, January 30, 1864, p. 130, paraphrased the denial, concluding: "it is therefore impossible for the authoress of *Lady Audley's Secret* to
have become Mr. Maxwell's wife." The *Court Journal* announced Knowles's
denial in 17, No. 1829, February 6, 1864, p. 128. Among the daily newspapers,
the *Sun* for Monday, January 18, 1864, p. 2, carried the original announcement
a day earlier than the *Morning Advertiser,* and Knowles's denial, paraphrased,
on February 1, 1864, p. 3. See text, and note 2 above, for reference to Charles
Reade's "Antiqua-Wreck" notebook.

27.   Charles J. Mathews to John Maxwell, and Maggie Braddon Cartighoni
to Mrs. Fanny Braddon, Wolff Collection.

28.   W. B. Maxwell's birth date supplied by his son, Henry Maxwell. MEB
to Bulwer; quotations from No. 25 [September 1866]; No. 29, October 10
[1867]; No. 30, November 3 [1868], for "the older faith." For the school at
Totteridge: No. 17 [April 1865]. *HLB* 2, pp. 140, 145, and notes 151, 147; *HLB*
1, p. 33.

29.   MEB to Bulwer, No. 3, April 13, 1863; *HLB* 1, p. 12.

30.   Michael Sadleir, "Mary Elizabeth Braddon," *Things Past* (London:
Constable, 1944), pp. 71–72 and p. 72, note 1.

CHAPTER IV

1.   In addition to *Lady Audley's Secret,* 1862 saw the publication in one volume of *Lady Lisle* by Ward & Lock. In 1863 the same publishers issued in one volume MEB's *The Captain of the Vulture,* which had run serially in their *Sixpenny Magazine* from September 1861 through March 1862. This was a melodramatic costume-romance, set in the mid-eighteenth century, complete with highwaymen, smugglers, identical twins, and murder, wooden as to construction and character drawing, but sprightly as to dialogue.

2.   M. E. Braddon, *Garibaldi and Other Poems* (London: Bosworth and Harrison, 1861), p. 82. Maggie Braddon Cartighoni wrote MEB from Naples on August 10, 1864, that some "Garibaldini" had told her that Garibaldi would surely have written had he received the book. Letter in the Wolff Collection.

3.   William Sawyer to MEB, November 29 and December 3, 1860, Wolff Collection. Sawyer had read the proofs in advance of publication. Sawyer later published an article (place and date unknown but photostat in the Wolff Collection) entitled "Miss Braddon as a Poetess," and saying of "Olivia": "Owen Meredith has not surpassed it. . . . Had she devoted herself to poetry she must have taken rank with the boldest and sweetest of our female singers." In the late sixties and early seventies, Sawyer occasionally contributed his own verse to MEB's *Belgravia.* In the early seventies, he became editor of the *Mirror,* "a high-class weekly journal," according to J. E. P. Muddock, a sub-editor, in *Pages from an Adventurous Life* (New York: Kennerly, 1907), p. 119. It may be that Sawyer's article on MEB as poetess appeared in the *Mirror.*

4.   *Garibaldi and Other Poems,* p. 169.

5.   *Athenaeum,* No. 1739, February 23, 1861, p. 259. MEB pasted into one of her notebooks, now MS Eng 1122.7 in the Houghton Library, a number of reviews of *Garibaldi*: one from an unidentified newspaper praised "Mr. Braddon" for having made "Olivia . . . a life drama of rare excellence," and concluded that he could be no tyro. The *Illustrated Times* said that the author was "occasionally . . . not inferior to any living singer . . . sometimes indifferent, more rarely bad. . . . ," while the *Times* said, "Miss Braddon has been good enough to run our Italian correspondence upon the wheels of the Spenserian stanza. . . . failure was inevitable and is no disgrace. . . ."

6.   The poem on the death of Prince Albert is "In Memoriam," signed M. E. B. in *Temple Bar* 4 (January 1862), 180.

7. Braddon Notebook I (see above, chapter II, note 9), bound in green morocco and stamped in gold on the front cover "Beverley Archery Society," consists of 128 leaves, counting both endpapers, paged 1 to 127 on the rectos only. MEB wrote in it from front to back, from back to front, and sometimes sidewise. The manuscript of "Garibaldi," on the versos of ff. 77–47, is virtually complete, lacking only a few stanzas of the published version. "Olivia" occupies the versos of ff. 103–78; on f. 14 verso is "Gabriel" (*Garibaldi and Other Poems,* pp. 299–300); on f. 44 verso are two untitled poems later published as "Farewell" and "Waking" (*ibid.,* pp. 301, 302–303); on ff. 111 and 110 verso is a manuscript draft of "Waiting" (*ibid.,* pp. 289–291). On f. 46 verso are some draft lines that appeared in "Under the Sycamores" (*ibid.,* pp. 205–209, 214).

8. The poem about De Grammont and the Marchioness includes 206 stanzas and appears on the versos of ff. 36–17 and on the rectos of ff. 21–28 and 39–41. The two stanzas quoted are numbered 11 and 72, and appear respectively on ff. 35 verso and 24 verso.

9. In Braddon Notebook I, the poem about Madeline was originally written on ff. 124 verso to 204 verso. It is largely covered by pasted clippings, but the numbers of the 126 stanzas are visible. A fair copy, with stanzas unnumbered, is in Houghton Library MS Eng 1122.5, on ff. 42 verso to 22 verso. This notebook, with green leather spine and corners and board sides, consists of forty-two leaves numbered in pencil in the lower left-hand corners of rectos. Between ff. 21 and 22, five leaves have been cut out and their stubs remain. Stanzas quoted are on f. 31 verso and were numbered 72 and 73 in the first draft.

10. Manuscript in the Maxwell Collection. See above, chapter III, note 6. Quotations from pp. 1–2, 4, 13, 16, 18, 20, 23.

11. "My First Novel" (as cited above, chapter I, note 13), pp. 25 and 27, and *My First Book,* pp. 116–117. Maxwell's letter quoted by Michael Sadleir in *XIX-Century Fiction,* I, p. 53. I do not think that Sadleir was right in conjecturing that Empson succeeded in getting the reprinted novel temporarily suppressed.

12. M. E. Braddon, *Three Times Dead; or, The Secret of the Heath* (London: W. and M. Clark, Warwick Lane; Beverley: C. H. Empson, Toll-Gavel, n.d. [1860]), pp. 1–2, v.

13. William Sawyer wrote MEB on February 11, 1861, that Sala had asked this question of a mutual friend. Letter in Wolff Collection.

14. MEB to George Augustus Sala, probably March 1861, in the Beinecke Library at Yale University. For further details, see Appendix, Section 3.

15. MEB to George Augustus Sala, probably April 1861, in the collection of the University of Illinois at Urbana. Portions of an original manuscript draft of *Ralph the Bailiff* survive in Braddon Notebook I, ff. 18 verso, 22, 23, and 25–31 recto, and include a version of the very beginning of the story and Chapter VI of the text as later printed in *Ralph the Bailiff and Other Tales* (London: Ward, Lock & Tyler, n.d. [1867]), pp. 35–54. The story ran serially in *St. James's Magazine* during April, May, and June, 1861. The villain was allowed to get away and prosper in Australia.

16. "Tommy and Harry," manuscript of seventeen folios in the Maxwell Collection, is preserved in an envelope inscribed by MEB: "Unpublished M.S. Tommy and Harry, folios 1–16 consecutive opening to novel." She had posted this direct to Sala. The seventeenth leaf is blank save for Sala's address on the verso and the postmarks of June 14 and June 15, 1861.

17. Sala to John Maxwell, Wolff Collection. Undated and preserved in its original envelope, marked "Delivered by Hand," the letter was written from the Reform Club to Maxwell at the office of *Temple Bar*. If Sala still had three installments of *Captain Dangerous* to write—those for November and December 1862, and January 1863—the letter can be attributed to October 1862. In fact, he had to wind up his clockwork mouse himself. MEB's *Gerard; or, The World, the Flesh, and the Devil* (3 vols., London: Simpkin, Marshall, 1891) combined Balzac's *Peau de Chagrin* with *Faust* (see below, chapter IX); Sala, *Margaret Forster. A Dream within a Dream* (London: Fisher Unwin, 1897), published posthumously, is by far his best novel. In his *Life and Adventures of George Augustus Sala* (2 vols., London: Cassell, 1895), II, pp. 33 ff., Sala recalled MEB's early days as a writer, but without special reference to these particular exchanges between them. (MEB) "'The Mystery at Fernwood,' by the Author of 'Lady Audley's Secret,' etc.," *Temple Bar* 3 (November 1861), 552–563; 4 (December 1861), 63–74.

18. M. E. Braddon, "Samuel Lowgood's Revenge," *Welcome Guest,* 2nd ser., 3, No. 74 [February 23, 1861], 583–588; "The Lawyer's Secret," *ibid.,* Nos. 75, 76, 77 [March 2, 9, 16, 1861], 603–609, 631–638, 677-683. "Margrave," the name MEB gave her rascally lawyer, was also the name of the soulless villain in Bulwer's *A Strange Story,* which appeared serially in *All the Year Round* during 1861. See R. L. Wolff, *Strange Stories* (Boston: Gambit, 1971), pp. 265–322. Both "Samuel Lowgood's Revenge" and "The Lawyer's

Secret" were reprinted by MEB in *Ralph the Bailiff and Other Tales* (London: Ward & Lock, 1862).

19.   Quotations from *The Lady Lisle* in the *Welcome Guest*, 2nd ser., 4 [April 6–August 24, 1861], 44, 71, 73, 100, 325. These were the final twenty-one numbers of the magazine.

20.   Preface (unpaged) to the final volume as cited in note 19 above.

21.   Montague Summers, "The Black Band Scandal," *Times Literary Supplement*, No. 2246, February 17, 1945, p. 84, identified MEB's contributions to the *Halfpenny Journal* but did not mention *Woman's Revenge* as possibly by her. The only reason for conjecturing that she may have written it is that she was always especially interested in Restoration England. Summers noted that the *Halfpenny Journal* had "well-nigh disappeared." There is a set in the Wolff Collection. The following was the publication schedule of MEB's novels: *The Black Band*, July 1, 1861–June 23, 1862; *The Octoroon*, November 18, 1861–March 17, 1862; *Woman's Revenge*, March 24, 1862–August 4, 1862; *The White Phantom*, May 26, 1862–January 12, 1863; *The Factory Girl*, January 12, 1863–October 26, 1863; *Oscar Bertrand*, November 2, 1863–June 13, 1864; *Three Times Dead; or, The Trail of the Serpent*, August 1, 1864–November 28, 1864; *The Banker's Secret*, November 21, 1864–June 5, 1865. In addition, MEB reprinted in the issue for December 29, 1862, her successful Christmas story "My First Happy Christmas," from the *Welcome Guest* of two years before.

22.   First in penny numbers and then as a lurid "yellowback" octavo, Montague Summers, "Miss Braddon's 'Black Band,'" *Times Literary Supplement*, No. 2151, April 24, 1943, p. 204, referring to this volume as "of the last rarity," recorded that he had examined a copy belonging to Dr. H. J. Norman. This copy appeared unrecognized in a lot with other books in a London book auction in July 1963, and is now in the Wolff Collection.

23.   M. E. Braddon, *The Black Band; or, The Mysteries of Midnight* (London: George Vickers, 1877), t.p. and pp. 42, 47. The leaf, $5^5/_{16}$ x $8\frac{1}{2}$ inches, written on recto only, in the Wolff Collection, found in the MS of *Run to Earth* (see note 35, below), corresponds to the opening paragraphs of Part II, Chapter VI, of *Oscar Bertrand*, as printed in the *Halfpenny Journal* 3, No. 149 (May 2, 1864), 357.

24.   (MEB) "Author of Lady Audley's Secret," *Rupert Godwin* (3 vols., London: Ward, Lock & Tyler, 1867), I, p. (v).

25.   The *Halfpenny Journal* having ceased publication, *Diavola* ran in the *London Journal* 44, No. 1133 (October 27, 1866), to 46, No. 1171 (July 20, 1867). A set is in the Wolff Collection. *Athenaeum,* No. 2051, February 16, 1867, pp. 221–222.

26.   *Athenaeum,* No. 2052, February 23, 1867, p. 254.

27.   *Ibid.,* No. 2053, March 2, 1867, p. 290.

28.   *Ibid.,* No. 2054, March 9, 1867, p. 323.

29.   *Ibid.,* No. 2055, March 16, 1867, p. 354.

30.   *Ibid.,* No. 2056, March 23, 1867, p. 387.

31.   *Ibid.,* No. 2063, May 11, 1867, p. 634.

32.   *Ibid.,* No. 2064, May 18, 1867, p. 635.

33.   (MEB) "Author of Lady Audley's Secret," *Run to Earth* (3 vols., London: Ward, Lock & Tyler, 1868).

34.   *Athenaeum,* No. 2130, October 31, 1868, p. 528.

35.   See chapter III, text, and notes 1 and 2, above. Manuscript of *Run to Earth,* as far as I, p. 201, on 102 numbered sheets of pale mauve paper, 5⅜ x 8¼ inches, written on rectos only, Wolff Collection.

36.   MEB to Bulwer, No. 1 [December 1862], postscript; *HLB* 1, p. 11.

37.   (MEB) "Author of Lady Audley's Secret," *The Doctor's Wife* (3 vols., London: Maxwell, 1864), I, pp. 18, 16–17, 20, 20–21, 21, 22, 23, 94–96.

38.   Bulwer to MEB, December 13, 1864, Wolff Collection; MEB to Bulwer, No. 14 [December 1864]; *HLB* 1, pp. 29, 30. For Soulié, see Harold March, *Frédéric Soulié, Novelist and Dramatist of the Romantic Period,* Yale Romanic Studies (New Haven: Yale University Press, 1931), pp. 163, 179, 270. See also Max Milner, *Le Diable dans la littérature française de Cazotte à Baudelaire* (2 vols., Paris: José Corti, 1960).

39.   *The Doctor's Wife,* I, pp. 96–98, 99, 97, 99–100, 100–102, 102–105.

40.   *Ibid.,* pp. 106-109; Percy Fitzgerald, *Memoirs of an Author* (2 vols., London: Bentley, 1895), II, pp. 280–281. It was during the summer of 1861 that MEB had the conversation that she first attributed to Sigismund Smith in *The Doctor's Wife* three years later and in 1891 reported to Percy Fitzgerald as an actual episode. Strong local tradition at Ingatestone, Essex, identifies the celebrated family house of the Petre family there—now the Essex County Records office—with MEB's Audley Court. And indeed, its clock with one hand over the stables and its avenue of limes make the identification entirely plausible. An additional scrap of evidence strengthens the plausibility. On the manuscript of "Tommy and Harry" mailed by MEB to Sala on June 14, 1861 (above, note 16), the postmark is "Ingatestone," clear evidence that MEB was indeed there at precisely the right moment for the conversation about "peopling it with fiends" to have taken place. In *The Doctor's Wife* she told the story as happening to Sigismund, and in the letter to Percy Fitzgerald she related it as autobiography.

41.   *The Doctor's Wife,* II, pp. 114, 130, 131.

42.   (MEB) "Author of Lady Audley's Secret," *Like and Unlike* (3 vols., London: Spencer Blackett, n.d. [1887]). See chapter IX.

43.   *The Doctor's Wife,* III, pp. 302, 303–304.

44.   (MEB) "Author of Lady Audley's Secret," *The Lady's Mile* (3 vols., London: Ward, Lock & Tyler, 1866), I, p. 8; II, pp. 137–138.

45.   *The Doctor's Wife,* I, p. 16.

46.   MEB to Bulwer, No. 1 [December 1862]; *HLB* 1, p. 10.

47.   H. Sutherland Edwards, *Personal Reflections* (London: Cassell, 1900), said (pp. 136–138) that Edward Tinsley had got credit from the papermakers and printers and borrowed £1,000 to pay MEB for *Lady Audley's Secret.* In a letter to the *Athenaeum,* dated June 5, 1900, and republished in his *Random Recollections* (cited above, chapter II, note 18), II, pp. 343–344, William Tinsley, the surviving brother, set the record straight. The original price had been £250. Tinsley also challenged Edwards' statement that his firm "had no standing as publishers" before publishing MEB. They had, he pointed out, been in business for four years and had published "quite a score of new books and new editions." He did not deny having to borrow the money.

48.   Edward Tinsley to MEB, Maxwell Collection. *Times,* November 18, 1862, p. 4. See Prologue, text and note 3, above.

49.   Original contract in the Wolff Collection.

50.   Edward Tinsley to MEB and MEB's draft reply in the Wolff Collection.

51.   MEB to Bulwer, No. 3, April 13, 1863; *HLB* 1, p. 13. *Eleanor's Victory,* illustrated by George du Maurier, ran serially in *Once A Week* from March 7 to October 3, 1863; *John Marchmont's Legacy* in *Temple Bar* from December 1862 through January 1864.

52.   MEB to Edward Tinsley, Princeton University Library. *The Outcasts,* later *Henry Dunbar,* appeared serially in the *London Journal,* from September 12, 1863, to March 26, 1864.

53.   Tinsley, *Random Recollections,* I, p. 57. Tinsley remembered "a very good profit" on *Lady Audley's Secret* and that "we also did very well out of" *Aurora Floyd.* He recalled that the publisher Charles Skeet had advertised *Lady Audley's Secret* as about to appear under his imprint before the Tinsleys had taken it away from him. I have found such an advertisement at the end of Volume III of W. H. Marshall, *Old Vauxhall* (3 vols., London: Charles Skeet, 1862), which says that *Lady Audley's Secret: A Novel* will appear in November. Poor Skeet: he lost his great chance and never had another.

54.   In *Ralph the Bailiff and Other Tales* (London: Ward, Lock & Tyler, n.d. [1867]), pp. 213–382.

55.   MEB to Bulwer, No. 6, n.d. [c. September 19, 1863]; *HLB* 1, pp. 17–18.

56.   See Wolff, *Strange Stories,* pp. 185 ff.

57.   Yates, *Recollections* (as in chapter III, note 17, above), II, pp. 171 ff.

58.   MEB to Bulwer, No. 7, January 17, 1864; *HLB* 1, p. 19.

59.   MEB to Bulwer, No. 8, June 24 [1864]; *HLB* 1, p. 20.

60.   MEB to Bulwer, No. 12 [November or December 1864]; *HLB* 1, pp. 2, 7. In August 1864, Maggie Braddon Cartighoni, who had been urging MEB to visit her and her husband in Naples, wrote that she hoped it would not be long "ere you consider yourself rich eno' to leave off writing for a few months." Wolff Collection.

61. MEB to Bulwer, No. 13, December 9, 1864; *HLB* 1, p. 28.

62. MEB to Bulwer, No. 15 [January 1865]; *HLB* 1, p. 32.

63. MEB to Bulwer, No. 18 [late in 1865]; *HLB* 1, p. 34.

64. MEB to Bulwer, No. 19, January 16, 1866; *HLB* 2, p. 130. For Bentley, see chapter VI, note 54 below.

65. MEB to Bulwer, No. 20 [mid-March 1866]; *HLB* 2, p. 131.

66. MEB to Bulwer, Nos. 19 and 20, as above.

67. MEB to Bulwer, No. 21 [mid-March 1866]; *HLB* 2, p. 133.

68. MEB to Bulwer, No. 22 [March 1866]; *HLB* 2, p. 135.

69. MEB to Bulwer, No. 26, September 24, 1866; *HLB* 2, p. 141.

70. For further discussion, see below, Appendix, Section 4.

71. MEB to Bulwer, No. 23, August 9 [1866]; *HLB* 2, pp. 136–137.

72. MEB to Bulwer, No. 29, October 10 [1867]; *HLB* 2, p. 145.

73. MEB to Bulwer, No. 27 [early 1867]; *HLB* 2, pp. 141–142.

74. *A Complete Parochial History of the County of Cornwall, Compiled from the Best Authorities.* . . . (4 vols., Truro: William Lake; London: John Camden Hotten, 1867–1872), II, p. 362, says discreetly: "The representatives of the late Mrs. Braddon [MEB's grandmother, who died in 1846] have recently sold Skisdon Lodge to a gentleman named Maxwell, who, however, does not reside there." In *BKE* (1914), MEB wrote that ". . . for a few years" Skisdon was her own property. "To think that that dear place was mine, and that I had no use for it, and was glad to part with it, when my cousin the East India merchant and head of the family [William Braddon, Jr.] wanted it for his son's marriage settlement. I thank God that a Braddon still owns the dear old place, and that the gardens are still cherished and kept in all their old beauty. . . ."

75. MEB to Bulwer, No. 36 [December 1872]; *HLB* 2, p. 156.

76. *The Grievances between Authors and Publishers* (London: Field and Tuer and Simpkin Marshall, 1887), pp. 88, 105.

77.   MEB to unnamed correspondent, but surely "George Roberts," January 14, 1863, Houghton Library. Matthews was manager of the St. James's Theatre between December 1862 and December 1863. See Diana Howard, *London Theatres and Music Halls, 1850–1950* (London: The Library Association, 1970), pp. 210–211. In *Lady Audley's Secret* he played Luke Marks, the brutal blackmailing husband of Lady Audley's maid. The cast is listed in the published version: George Roberts, *Lady Audley's Secret. A Drama in Two Acts, founded on and in part adapted from Miss Braddon's novel of that name* (London: W. S. Johnson & Co., 1864), copy in Wolff Collection.

78.   MEB to unnamed correspondent, but surely "George Roberts," a few days later than the letter cited above, Houghton Library.

79.   MEB to Bulwer, No. 4 [May 1863]; *HLB* 1, p. 15.

80.   George Roberts, *Lady Audley's Secret. The Original Version* (London: privately printed, not published, n.d.), copy in Wolff Collection.

81.   Hazlewood version in Michael Sadleir, *XIX-Century Fiction* (see above, note 11), I, p. 49, no. 302a. Suter version in the Wolff Collection: William E. Suter, *Lady Audley's Secret*, Lacy's Acting Editions, No. 849 (London: Thomas Hailes Lacy, n.d.).

82.   I do not know who was responsible for the "adaptation" in which George Belmore appeared, or whether it was ever printed. The Webster version was published: B. Webster, Jun., Esq., *Aurora Floyd: or The Banker's Daughter. A Drama, in a Prologue and Three Acts,* "as performed at the New Theatre Royal, Adelphi," Webster's Acting National Drama, No. 204 (London: Webster and Co. etc., n.d.), Webster's "To the Public" on p. [3], leaf A2 recto. The original cast is listed on the verso. Copy in the Harvard College Library. The acting time was supposed to be three and a half hours, but obviously ran far over that on opening night. Henry Morley, *The Journal of a London Playgoer from 1861 to 1866* (London: Routledge, 1891), pp. 243–244. For George Belmore see also Erroll Sherson, *London's Lost Theatres of the Nineteenth Century* (London: John Lane, 1925), p. 190. William E. Suter, *Aurora Floyd. A Drama, in Two Acts* (London: Thomas Hailes Lacy, n.d.), copy in the Wolff Collection. Michael Sadleir (*XIX-Century Fiction*, I, p. 44, no. 269b) describes a copy of the Hazlewood version in his collection. *LCND*, II, p. 412, which does not mention the Hazlewood version of *Lady Audley's Secret*, gives the date of the production of his version of *Aurora Floyd*.

83.   Tinsley, *Random Recollections*, I, p. 60.

84.   This copy of *Lady Audley's Secret* in the Lilly Library of Indiana University at Bloomington.

85.   *The English Reports*, vol. 71, Vice Chancellor's Court, 16, containing Hemming & Miller, vols. 1 and 2 (Edinburgh: William Green & Sons; London: Stevens & Sons Ltd, 1907), pp. 327–330, a reprint of George W. Hemming and Alexander Edward Miller, *Reports of Cases Adjudged in the High Court of Chancery before Sir William Page Wood, Kn., Vice-Chancellor*, I, 1862–1864, pp. 747–754: Tinsley v. Lacy. For references to the case with respect to the law of copyright in general, see The Earl of Halsbury and Others, *The Laws of England* (London: Butterworth, 1909), VIII, pp. 146 (no. 354), 166 (no. 395), 183 (no. 427).

86.   John Maxwell to W. F. Tillotson, March 23, 1885:

> A novel can be dramatised; but if it contains in drama extracts, the D. version can be played without concurrence of Novelist; but it cannot be printed and published as a drama. See Tinsley v. Lacy. A Drama may be novelised without consent of dramatist unless Author of Drama has based drama upon a previously published story in which the Copyright—i.e. first publication—really is. See Reade v. Conquest [the case involving *Gold*, and *Put Yourself in His Place*]. (Tillotson File)

Tom Taylor, *Henry Dunbar; or, A Daughter's Trial. A Drama in Four Acts Founded on Miss Braddon's Novel of the Same Name* (London: Thomas Hailes Lacy, n.d.), copy in the Wolff Collection. For *L'ouvrière de Londres*, see Tolles, *Tom Taylor* (cited in chapter II, note 10), p. 209. *LNCD*, II, p. 643, records a fifth adaptation of *Aurora Floyd*, by an unknown author, played at the Effingham Saloon in Whitechapel on April 20, 1863, and (pp. 672, 700, 751) the following performances adapted from MEB's other early novels: *Eleanor's Victory* at the Victoria, March 4, 1864; *John Marchmont's Legacy* at the Prince of Wales Theatre in Birmingham on April 23, 1864; and *Sir Jasper's Tenant* at the Sadler's Wells Theatre on November 22, 1865.

CHAPTER V

1.   M. E. Braddon, *Aurora Floyd* (3 vols., London: Tinsley, 1863), II, pp. 241–242; I, pp. 61, 35, 273–274.

2.   *Ibid.,* III, pp. 92–93; II, pp. 66, 64; I, pp. 166-167.

3.   *Saturday Review* 15, No. 379 (January 31, 1863), 149. She wrote to Edmund Yates:

> Do you see what the [*Saturday Review*] says about *Aurora Floyd* and my philosophy in the matter of beer, brandy, cigars, and tobacco? It is all Mr. Tinsley's fault for advertising me as 'Mary Elizabeth.' I used to be called *Mr.* Braddon, and provincial critics were wont to regret that my experience of women had been so bitter as to make me an implacable foe of the fair sex. They thought I had . . . learned in the Divorce Court what I taught in three-volume novels. (*Yates: Recollections* [cited in chapter III, note 17, above], II, p. 171.)

The *Spectator,* No. 1805, January 31, 1863, pp. 1586–1587, criticized MEB for imitating Thackeray in those passages where as author she spoke directly to the reader. She had a talent for melodrama, the critic said, and should cultivate that exclusively. He also objected that the murder case prolonged the novel unnecessarily.

4.   Henry James, "Aurora Floyd," *Notes and Reviews,* ed. Pierre de Chaignon La Rose (Cambridge, Massachusetts: Dunster House, 1921), pp. 108–116; reprinted from the *Nation* of November 9, 1865.

5.   MEB to Bulwer, No. 1 [December 1862]; *HLB* 1, p. 10.

6.   MEB to Bulwer, No. 3, April 13, 1863; *HLB* 1, p. 12.

7.   MEB to Bulwer, No. 4 [May 1863]; *HLB* 1, pp. 13–14.

8.   MEB to Bulwer, No. 5 [May 1863]; *HLB* 1, pp. 15–17.

9.   MEB to Bulwer, No. 6 [September 1863]; *HLB* 1, p. 17.

10.   MEB to Bulwer, No. 8, June 24 [1864]; *HLB* 1, p. 20.

11.   MEB to Bulwer, No. 12 [November or December 1864]; *HLB* 1, p. 27.

12. In *Only a Clod,* which the *St. James's Magazine* published serially during 1865, Francis Tredethlyn, a young Cornishman in Tasmania as servant to an impoverished young officer, inherits thirty thousand pounds a year, returns to England, and marries his former master's former fiancée. Outraged, the master, Harcourt Lowther, tries to destroy the marriage and to kill him by drink and debauchery. Tredethlyn takes far too long to discover the plot against his happiness, and one cannot understand his wife's utter passivity in the face of it.

13. *Saturday Review* 16, No. 412 (September 19, 1863), 396–397.

14. *BKE.*

15. *Spectator,* No. 1838, September 19, 1863, 252–253, hostile as usual, said of *Eleanor's Victory,* "Forbid her bigamy and Miss Braddon has little to tell the world." *Henry Dunbar,* oddly enough, it regarded as MEB's best book (No. 1875, June 4, 1864, p. 656) and it maintained this wrongheaded view for twenty years.

16. MEB to Bulwer, No. 7, January 17, 1864; *HLB* 1, p. 19.

17. (MEB) "Author of Lady Audley's Secret," *John Marchmont's Legacy* (3 vols., London: Tinsley, 1863), I, pp. 132–134, 279; II, p. 161; I, pp. 312, 105.

18. MEB to Bulwer, No. 6 [September 19, 1863]; *HLB* 1, p. 18.

19. MEB to Bulwer, No. 7, January 17, 1864; *HLB* 1, pp. 20, 19.

20. MEB to Bulwer, No. 8, June 24 [1864]; *HLB* 1, p. 21.

21. MEB to Bulwer, No. 9 [Summer 1864]; *HLB* 1, pp. 21–22.

22. MEB to Bulwer, No. 7, January 17, 1864, and No. 9 [Summer 1864]; *HLB* 1, pp. 20, 22.

23. MEB to Bulwer, No. 10 [Summer 1864]; *HLB* 1, pp. 22–23.

24. *Ibid.,* p. 23.

25. *Temple Bar* 12 (August 1864), 11–12; *The Doctor's Wife,* II, p. 312.

26. Letter to MEB, Wolff Collection.

27. MEB to Bulwer, No. 10 [Summer 1864]; *HLB* 1, p. 23.

28. MEB to Bulwer, No. 11, September 7, 1864; *HLB* 1, p. 25.

29. MEB to Bulwer, No. 12 [November or December 1864]; *HLB* 1, pp. 25–26. Although Bulwer's letter of advice is not preserved, we infer his suggestion from MEB's reply, and thirty-three years later she told some details to an interviewer for a popular magazine: see Mary Angela Dickens, "Miss Braddon at Home," *Windsor Magazine* 6, No. 33 (September 1897), 418.

30. *Saturday Review* 18, No. 471 (November 5, 1864), 571–572.

31. *Spectator,* No. 1895, October 22, 1864, pp. 1214–1215.

32. For Professor C. Heywood's studies of *The Doctor's Wife,* see below, Appendix, Section 5.

33. It ran serially in *Temple Bar* from February through December 1865.

34. MEB to Bulwer, No. 12 [November or December 1864]; *HLB* 1, pp. 26–27.

35. MEB to Bulwer, No. 13, December 9, 1864; *HLB* 1, p. 28.

36. MEB to Bulwer, No. 14 [December 1864, after the 13th), and No. 15 [January 1865]; *HLB* 1, pp. 30 and 31.

37. MEB to Bulwer, Nos. 14 and 15, as in note 36 above, and (on Balzac) No. 12, as in note 34 above. Letters No. 16 and No. 17 of February 28, 1865, and [April 1865] are unfortunately not preserved complete. MEB probably mentioned *Sir Jasper's Tenant* in the missing portions. By the time it was next mentioned in the correspondence, it was almost if not altogether completed.

38. *Spectator,* No. 1947, October 21, 1865, pp. 1174–1175.

39. MEB to Bulwer, No. 18 [mid-October 1865]; *HLB* 1, p. 34.

40. *Ibid.*

41. MEB to Bulwer, No. 19, January 16, 1866; *HLB* 2, p. 130.

42. (MEB) "Author of Lady Audley's Secret," *The Lady's Mile* (3 vols., London: Ward, Lock & Tyler, 1866), I, pp. 13–14.

43. For authentic details about a barrister's life MEB consulted F. W. James,

Q.C., who read the proofs of *The Lady's Mile*. On January 20, 1866, he wrote her a long and friendly letter:

> A Queen's Counsel in good practice, as your Irish hero is represented to be, would not be likely to devote all his mind and energies to one case in particular, and therefore I have added another (to which you may add more if you like) to his favorite "Giddles and Clithery." . . . It is usual to place the letters Q.C. after the name of a Queen's Counsel instead of the words at length. . . . Blue bags are not now in vogue for Queen's Counsel. They are sort of dark crimson or "Alecampane" colour. . . . You are rather hard upon the lawyers, but my wife fully sympathises with your Lady Cecil, and says it is exactly her own case with reference to me. However, I can bear this . . . for "sufferance is the badge of all our tribe." . . . We are afraid you are working too hard for your health, but we are always glad to hear of you and whatever concerns you, and shall be most happy to see you. (Letter in the Wolff Collection)

44.   (MEB) "Author of Lady Audley's Secret," *The Lady's Mile* (3 vols., London: Ward, Lock, and Tyler, 1866), II, pp. 258–259; I, p. 297; II, pp. 88–89.

45.   M. E. Braddon, *Eleanor's Victory* (3 vols., London: Tinsley, 1863), II, pp. 309–310. The villain is a painter, as is the wicked Paul Marchmont in *John Marchmont's Legacy,* where his art collection is inventoried: III, pp. 135–136.

46.   (MEB) "Author of Lady Audley's Secret," *Henry Dunbar* (London: John Maxwell, 1864), III, pp. 20–22.

47.   (MEB) "Author of Lady Audley's Secret," *Sir Jasper's Tenant* (3 vols., London: John Maxwell, 1865), II, pp. 106, 110–245, 166–167; I, pp. 198–199.

48.   W. P. Frith to MEB, March 25, 1865, Wolff Collection; *John Marchmont's Legacy,* III, p. 262; "Babington White" (MEB), *Circe, Belgravia* 2, 1 (March 1867), 125. *The Lady's Mile* (as above, note 44), I, p. (v).

49.   *The Lady's Mile,* I, pp. 135, 136–138, 142, 143, 134–135, 218, 148–149; II, pp. 158–160.

50.   MEB to Bulwer, No. 22 [March 1866]; *HLB* 2, pp. 134–135. MEB must have asked her old friend Buckstone about dramatizing *The Lady's Mile;* he wrote her: "I have read a good many chapters of *The Lady's Mile,* and I am delighted with it. O'Boyneville [the barrister] is a capital character; also the artist's daughter Flo. I do not yet see that I could make a comedy of it for the

Haymarket, although the title is very suggestive." J. B. Buckstone to MEB, March 12, 1866, Wolff Collection.

51.   For the sale of *Temple Bar,* see below, chapter VI, note 54. MEB to Bulwer, No. 23, August 9 [1866]; *HLB* 2, pp. 136, 138. Swinburne to Watts, March 31, 1876. C. Y. Lang, ed., *The Swinburne Letters* (New Haven: Yale University Press, 1963), III, p. 163, letter no. 726. MEB was about to relinquish the editorship of *Belgravia,* sold to Chatto and Windus. They had bought Swinburne's poem "A Ballad of Dreamland," which appeared in the issue for September 1876. He comforted himself by adding "Still, pecunia non olet"; profanely and obscenely he declined to have his poem accompanied by a picture: "No sanguinary aboriginal of Bulgaria [bloody bugger], whether (as now) in a state of insurrection [this was the moment of the Bulgarian Revolution of 1876–1877] or quiescence, shall illustrate me." MEB had hoped to secure Trollope as a contributor until she discovered that Smith and Elder had paid him £1800 for the serial rights to *The Claverings* for *Cornhill,* leaving him free to realize another £1800 for the book rights. "Pretty good for that easy-going common-sense kind of writing," she commented to Bulwer.

52.   MEB to Bulwer, No. 24 [c. August 20, 1866]; *HLB* 2, pp. 138–139.

53.   *Birds of Prey* ran in *Belgravia* from the opening number of November 1866 through the next twelve monthly numbers, and was published in three volumes by Ward, Lock, and Tyler in October 1867. *Charlotte's Inheritance* ran in *Belgravia* from April 1868 through February 1869, but appeared in three volumes published by Ward, Lock, and Tyler well before the end of 1868.

54.   MEB to Bulwer, No. 24 [c. August 20, 1866]; *HLB* 2, p. 138.

55.   (MEB) "Author of Lady Audley's Secret," *Birds of Prey* (3 vols., London: Ward, Lock, and Tyler, 1866), I, pp. 31, 169. Reade met his friend MEB at the opening night of Wilkie Collins' play *The Frozen Deep,* October 27, 1866 (*LNCD,* II, p. 318.); Charles L. Reade and Compton Reade, *Charles Reade, A Memoir* (London: Chapman & Hall, 1887), II, pp. 267–268.

56.   MEB to Bulwer, No. 12 [November or December 1864]; *HLB* 1, p. 27.

57.   MEB to Bulwer, No. 13, December 9, 1864; Bulwer to MEB, dated from the Queen's Hotel, Naseby, December 12, 1864, Wolff Collection; *HLB* 1, pp. 27–28, 29.

58. (MEB) "Author of Lady Audley's Secret," *Birds of Prey,* as above in note 55, I, pp. 238–240; II, pp. 49–50.

59. MEB to Bulwer, No. 9 [Summer 1864]; *HLB* 1, p. 22.

60. MEB to Bulwer, No. 10 [Summer 1864, before August 1], and No. 11, September 7, 1864; *HLB* 1, p. 24.

61. MEB to Bulwer, No. 19 [January 16, 1866], see chapter VIII for MEB and Gérard de Nerval; No. 20 [late January or early February 1866]; No. 21 [February 1866]; and No. 35, September [1872], quoted in chapter VII. Bulwer's response of September 28, 1872, in the Wolff Collection, quoted and illustrated in R. L. Wolff, *Strange Stories* (Boston: Gambit, 1971), pp. 305–306; MEB to Bulwer, No. 36 [December 1872]; *HLB* 2, pp. 130, 132–133, 134, 154, 155–156.

62. Serial publication in *Belgravia* from August 1867 through September 1868. It began while *Birds of Prey* was still appearing and was completed after *Charlotte's Inheritance* had begun. See above, note 53.

63. MEB to Bulwer, No. 22 [March 1866]; *HLB* 2, p. 135.

64. (MEB) "Author of Lady Audley's Secret," *Dead Sea Fruit* (3 vols., London: Ward, Lock, and Tyler, 1868), I, pp. 73, 75-76, 49–52, 78–79.

65. *Belgravia* 4, 1 (November 1867), 55; see chapter VI.

66. W. P. Frith to MEB, Wolff Collection, as cited in note 48 above. Sala was very near-sighted and had written jocularly to Frith, who had asked his opinion of MEB's portrait, that he didn't think he would recognize MEB if he met her " 'promiscuous,' " and so "does not consider himself a good authority as to *likeness.*"

67. MEB to Bulwer, No. 24 [c. August 20, 1866]; *HLB* 2, p. 139.

68. *TG,* p. 82.

69. *Life and Adventures of George Augustus Sala* (2 vols., London: Cassell, 1895), II, pp. 33, 376.

CHAPTER VI

1.   *Standard,* March 25, 1863, p. 5, and March 26, 1863, p. 4.

2.   S. W. Fullom, *The Man of the World; or, Vanities of the Day* (3 vols., London: Charles Joseph Skeet, 1856). In the Wolff Collection is an undated holograph letter from MEB to Edmund Yates, in which she thanked him effusively for writing a letter on her behalf. She added, "I have just got the book. It *looks* a regular London J[ournal] story: with shoals of characters, chartists, rioters, & goodness knows what." Probably this refers to Fullom's novel, and Yates had somewhere defended MEB's originality against Fullom. Fullom, who died in 1872, wrote a good many other novels, a work on *The Marvels of Science and Their Testimony in Holy Writ,* and another on *The History of Woman.* In his letters to the *Standard,* Fullom said his novel had appeared five years earlier; it had in fact been published *seven* years earlier.

3.   *Standard,* March 27, 1863, p. 4.

4.   MEB to Bulwer, No. 2, March 30, 1863; *HLB* 1, p. 11. There rose to MEB's defense against Fullom a journalist named Folkestone Williams. Months later, on November 7, 1863, she wrote him apologizing for delaying her "most sincere & grateful acknowledgements for the able and hearty manner in which you defended me against Mr. Fullom's unwarrantable attack. Forgive me for this long delay. . . ." But Folkestone Williams' "excellent defence" had remained unpublished: "Mr. Maxwell told me that his motive for withholding it was the desire to give no new publicity to Mr. Fullom's manoeuvre." Maxwell had placed five guineas to Williams' account, double what his article "would have realised if published in [Ward & Lock's] 'Sixpenny Magazine.' But although he may thus wipe out his debt as a publisher, I shall always remain your debtor." On the 20th, MEB wrote again to Williams, who may have been disgruntled, sending him a case of champagne, "In order that we may drown the recollection of Mr. Fullom's attack and any unpleasantness connected therewith." MEB to Folkestone Williams, November 7 and 20, 1863, Wolff Collection.

5.   *Quarterly Review* 113 (April 1863), 481–514. Author identified in W. E. Houghton, ed., *The Wellesley Index to Victorian Periodicals* (Toronto: University of Toronto Press, 1966), I, p. 745, no. 1419. The article was reprinted under Mansel's name in his *Letters, Lectures and Reviews,* ed. H. W. Chandler (London: John Murray, 1873), pp. 215–251. Among the other novels Mansel discussed were Wilkie Collins' *No Name,* Mrs. Henry Wood's first book, *Danesbury House,* Winwood Reade's *Liberty Hall, Oxon.,* and Lascelles Wraxall's *Only a Woman.*

6.   *Quarterly Review* 113 (April 1863), 482–483, 483, 484, 485, 486, 487, 488, 490–491, 491, 492, 505.

7.   *Medical Critic and Psychological Journal* 12 (October 1863), 585–604; quotations from pp. 589, 591–592.

8.   *New Review* 8 (December 1863), 564–575; quotations from pp. 565, 565–566, 566, 567, 574.

9.   "Four Illustrated Sensation Novels," *Beeton's Christmas Annual,* Fifth Season (1864), 77–81; the other two were "Prinvilliers the Poisoner; or, The Live Coal and the Deadly Cup," and " 'Arry the 'Eartless; or, a Bad Brother's Name and End."

10.   (MEB) "Author of Lady Audley's Secret," *Henry Dunbar, The Story of an Outcast* (3 vols., London: John Maxwell, 1864), I, p. iv.

11.   *North British Review,* 43 (n.s. 4), no. 85 (September 1865), 180–205. For identification of Rae as author, see *Wellesley Index* (cited in note 5 above), I, p. 690, no. 793.

12.   *North British Review,* 43 (n.s. 4), no. 85 (September 1865), 180, 181, 182, 185, 186, 187–188, 190, 193, 195, 196, 197, 199, 201, 202–203, 203–204.

13.   *Sun,* September 12, 1865, column on unnumbered editorial page, headed "Literature."

14.   MEB to Charles Kent, September 13, 1865, Wolff Collection.

15.   For Greenwood's novel and his personality, see below, Appendix, Section 6.

16.   *Sun,* October 17, 1865, column on unnumbered editorial page, headed "Literature."

17.   MEB to Charles Kent, letters of October 4, 1865; October 11 and November 26, 1866; February 28, 1867; February 25, 1878; in the Wolff Collection, which includes sixteen of her letters to him. The *DNB* article on Kent provides a good sketch of his career.

18.   MEB to "Mr. Reynolds," n.d., a draft of a letter, laid into one of her manuscript notebooks (Houghton Library MS Eng 1122.8). I found this letter in 1962 and was able to identify N.B.R. as the *North British Review.* But what

was "S.N.L."? Not until 1966, when I acquired MEB's letters to Charles Kent, could I identify S.N.L. as *Saunders's News Letter*. Then, much to my pleasure, I found her writing to him on September 4, 1866 after he had in the *Sun* gently expressed his "not altogether favorable opinion" of the (newly reprinted) *Trail of the Serpent,* which she cheerfully called "my earliest atrocity." Just to show him that there were some reviewers who liked even that "first attempt," she enclosed "a copy of Saunders's News Letter." So there I had my explanation for "S.N.L." The response to the *North British Review* for which MEB thanked Mr. Reynolds is in *Saunders's News Letter and Daily Advertiser* for October 24, 1865, p. 3. The favorable review of *The Trail of the Serpent* that she sent to Charles Kent appeared August 29, 1866, p. 3.

19. *Blackwood's Magazine* 102, No. 623 (September 1867), 257-280; quotations from pp. 257, 258–259. 260. For identification of Mrs. Oliphant as the author see *Wellesley Index* (note 5 above), I, p. 127, no. 1197. On Mrs. Oliphant, see Vineta and Robert Colby, *The Equivocal Virtue. Mrs. Oliphant and the Victorian Literary Market Place* (Hamden, Connecticut: Archon Books, 1969), which does not entirely supersede *The Autobiography and Letters of Mrs. M. O. W. Oliphant,* ed. Mrs. Harry Coghill (Edinburgh and London: Blackwood, 1899). The Colbys do not refer to the *Blackwood's* article of 1867.

20. Tinsley, in *Random Recollections* (cited in chapter II, note 14 above), II, pp. 248–249, remembered that Annie Thomas could write a three-volume novel in six weeks. She was courted by W. S. Gilbert, but married a curate named Pender Cudlip. It was, inevitably, the dissolute painter Simeon Solomon who made in "Gampese" the obvious pun in a letter to Swinburne: "I have been staying with . . . Miss Annie Thomas, now Mrs. Pender Cudlip (I beg to state that I did not pend her cudlip, I would scorn the action)." *The Swinburne Letters,* ed. C. Y. Lang (New Haven: Yale University Press, 1959), II, p. 142, no. 385, c. May 1, 1871.

21. *Blackwood's Magazine* 102 (as cited in note 19 above), 260, 261, 263, 263–264, 264.

22. MEB to Bulwer, No. 28 [early September 1867]; *HLB* 2, pp. 142–143. On Bulwer and phrenology see Wolff, *Strange Stories,* p. 241. Bulwer had occasionally published in *Blackwood's Magazine,* notably "The Haunters and the Haunted," a celebrated ghost story, in 1859, and Wm. Blackwood & Sons had published *A Strange Story* (1862) and *Caxtoniana* (1863), his two most recent books.

23. MEB to Bulwer, No. 29, October 10 [1867]; *HLB* 2, pp. 144–145.

24. *Ibid.,* pp. 145–146.

25. George Augustus Sala, "The Cant of Modern Criticism," *Belgravia* 4, No. 1 (November 1867), 45–55; quotations from pp. 46, 47, 47–48, 49, 50, 50–51, 52–53, 53, 54, 55. Wolff, *Strange Stories,* pp. 23 ff., includes a discussion of the Newgate novel, with especial reference to *Rookwood.*

26. MEB to Bulwer, No. 29, October 10 [1867]; *HLB* 2, p. 144.

27. Babington White, *Circe: Three Acts in the Life of an Artist, Belgravia* 2, No. 1 (March 1867), 113–130; No. 2 (April 1867), 236–256; No. 3 (May 1867), 361–382; No. 4 (June 1867), 480–503; *ibid.* 3, No. 1 (July 1867), 108–130; No. 2 (August 1867), 240–256; No. 3 (September 1867), 302–326; and in book form (2 vols., London: Ward, Lock & Tyler, 1867). Octave Feuillet, *Dalila* (Paris: Michel Lévy Frères, 1857), p. 63, for the line about artists spitting blood; cf. *Circe* in *Belgravia* 2, No. 4 (June 1867), 495. *Dalila,* pp. 70–71, for the line mentioning Circe as an enchantress. *Dalila* was first published as a novel in 1853, but without success. On Feuillet's theme and purpose, A. Borreson, *La Théatre d'Octave Feuillet (1821–1890)* (Paris: Editions Spes, 1929), pp. 86 ff.; for the success of the play, p. 186. Mme. Octave Feuillet remembered that on opening night the actor playing the musician insisted on biting his tongue to produce genuine blood on the handkerchief. Mme. Octave Feuillet, *Quelques Années de ma vie* (Paris: Calmann Lévy, 1894), p. 180. Montague Summers, in "Mr. Babington White," *Times Literary Supplement,* No. 2226 (September 30, 1944), p. 480, summarized the *Pall Mall Gazette* affair both inadequately and inaccurately. He said, for example, that MEB had taken only "the merest hint" from *Dalila.*

28. *Pall Mall Gazette,* September 16, 1867, p. 9.

29. *Ibid.,* September 17, 1867, p. 3.

30. *Ibid.,* September 18, 1867, p. 4.

31. *Ibid.,* September 20, 1867, p. 2.

32. *Ibid.,* September 21, 1867, p. 4.

33. *Ibid.,* September 23, 1867, p. 8.

34. *Morning Star,* September 26, 1867, p. 3; *Pall Mall Gazette,* September 26, 1867, p. 8.

35. *Morning Star,* September 27, 1867, p. 5; *Pall Mall Gazette,* September 27, 1867, p. 8.

36.   *Pall Mall Gazette*, September 28, 1867, p. 5.

37.   *Ibid.,* September 30, 1867, p. 8; *Morning Star,* October 1, 1867, p. 4.

38.   *Saturday Review* 24, No. 622 (September 28, 1867), 399–400; *Spectator*, No. 2048, September 28, 1867, pp. 1083–1084.

39.   *Pall Mall Gazette,* October 3, 1867, p. 9.

40.   *Spectator*, No. 2049, October 5, 1867, p. 1103.

41.   *Pall Mall Gazette*, October 5, 1867, p. 5.

42.   *Ibid.*, October 9, 1867, p. 9; *Morning Star,* October 3, 1867, p. 3.

43.   MEB to Bulwer, No. 29, October 10 [1867]; *HLB* 2, p. 144.

44.   Scott, *Drama of Yesterday and Today,* I, p. 474.

45.   W. M. Thackeray, *Pendennis,* Chapter XXXII; see also Chapters XXXIV and XXXV. Thackeray reintroduced the paper into *The Adventures of Philip* in 1862.

46.   *Belgravia* 4, No. 1 (November 1867), 80–86.

47.   Robertson Scott, *Pall Mall Gazette* (cited in note 15 above), p. 198, refers to the episode briefly without noting MEB's reply as Shandon, and generally maintaining even in 1950 the sneering tone of Greenwood in 1867.

48.   George Augustus Sala, "The Sensational in Literature and Art," *Belgravia* 4, No. 4 (February 1868), 448–458; quotations from pp. 456, 457, 458.

49.   MEB to Bulwer, No. 35, September 27 [1872]; *HLB* 2, p. 155.

50.   *Belgravia* 5, No. 1 (March 1868), 41–50, and No. 2 (April 1868), 162–175. In addition to *Circe,* "At Daggers Drawn" (above, Chapter II, note 24), and "The Mudie Classics," MEB used the pseudonym "Babington White" for the following: "Dorothy's Rival," *Belgravia Christmas Annual,* 1868; "The True Story of Don Juan," *ibid.,* 1869; "Sir Philip's Wooing," *ibid.,* 1870 (the first and third reprinted in *Under the Red Flag and Other Tales,* discussed in chapter VIII); and "Violets," verses in *Belgravia* 11, 2nd ser., No. 1 (April 1870), 260.

51.   *Lucretia . . . etc.* (London: Joseph Masters, 1868), pp. 11, 11–12, 298, 301, 302. This is a very rare book. No library in the United States reports a copy. There is one in the Wolff Collection. Paget and his friend, the Reverend William Gresley, were the "acknowledged fathers" of Tractarian fiction. See R. L. Wolff, *Gains and Losses* (New York: Garland, 1977), pp. 114–116.

52.   *Spectator,* No. 2093, August 8, 1868, p. 931.

53.   *The Mask: A Humorous and Fantastic Review of the Month,* ed. Alfred Thompson and Leopold Lewis, 1, No. 5 (June 1868), 137–139: "The Mask's Album, No. IV." Copy in the Wolff Collection.

54.   In an article published anonymously in *Temple Bar* (29, No. 3 [June 1870], 410–424) Alfred Austin—who was to become poet laureate in 1896—ridiculed sensation novels. Without giving their titles he summarized and protested against *Lady Audley's Secret* and *Aurora Floyd.* But he never named MEB, much less attacked her personally, and he was equally scornful of Wilkie Collins' *Moonstone* and Sheridan Le Fanu's *Uncle Silas.* The very mildness of the tone is the best indication that all heat had gone out of the great issue of three years earlier. It seems surprising that the periodical in which *Aurora Floyd* (and *John Marchmont's Legacy, The Doctor's Wife,* and *Sir Jasper's Tenant*) had first appeared should now disapprove of sensation novels. But Richard Bentley and Son had bought *Temple Bar* from Maxwell in January 1866 (for £2,750); Yates resigned as editor in July 1867, and a stuffier, less Bohemian regime took over with George Bentley himself as editor. See *A List of the Principal Publications Issued from New Burlington Street During the Year 1866* (London: Bentley, 1910) under January 27; issues for 1867 (1910) and 1870 (1912) unpaged, at the end. All contributors are identified, including Austin. This limited publication is usually known as the "Bentley Private Catalogue"; only fifty copies were printed, and each issue was inscribed "For Official Use Only." A copy is in the Wolff Collection.

CHAPTER VII

1.   Maggie Braddon Cartighoni to her mother, Fanny White Braddon, letters of August 10, 1864; April 3, 1866; January 3 and May 31, 1867; July 6 and 17, 1868; Wolff Collection. Also in the collection are the other family letters from the nephew whom MEB rescued and from the aunts in Devonshire alluded to in the text.

2.   MEB to Bulwer, No. 30, November 3 [1868]; *HLB* 2, p. 146. *LNCD*, II, p. 460, gives the date of the opening of *The Rightful Heir* as October 3, 1868.

3.   Maggie Cartighoni to Mrs. Braddon, July 17, 1868, as in note 1 above.

4.   MEB to Bulwer, No. 30, November 3 [1868]; *HLB* 2, pp. 146–148.

5.   Rosie Maxwell's birth date from her tombstone in Richmond cemetery.

6.   MEB to Bulwer, No. 31, June 13 [1872]; *HLB* 2, pp. 148–149 and note 100.

7.   *TG,* p. 280.

8.   MEB to Bulwer, No. 31, June 13 [1872]; *HLB* 2, p. 148.

9.   MEB to Bulwer, No. 33, July 2 [1872]; *HLB* 2, p. 150.

10.   In February 1870 *Belgravia* published her "Mr. and Mrs. de Fontenoy," about a couple claiming to be related to a noble family, who rent a seaside house. When the local tradesmen discover that the de Fontenoys have no aristocratic connections, they force them to pay their bills in gold coin, which proves false; the de Fontenoys are professional counterfeiters, their money as spurious as contemporary social values. Another trifle, "The Splendid Stranger" (March 1870), told of a gentleman who beguiles and jilts the daughter of a farmer in whose house he has taken lodgings, and who returns many years later to be recognized and to die in wretchedness. *Fenton's Quest* ran in *Belgravia* from April 1870 through April 1871, and was published in three volumes by Ward, Lock & Tyler before the serial publication was complete. Mechanical in plot, uninteresting as to character, lacking MEB's usual pungent social commentary, the novel must have seemed an incomprehensible falling off to her perceptive readers.

11.   MEB to Bulwer, No. 31, June 13 [1872]; *HLB* 2, p. 150. "On the

Brink," *Belgravia* 12, 2nd ser., No. 2 (September 1870), 324–350; "The Sins of the Fathers," *ibid.* (October 1870), 485–507.

12.   In 1873, MEB published *Milly Darrell and Other Tales* (3 vols., London: John Maxwell, 1873), which included not only the title story and the three other short stories we have mentioned but eight additional straightforward tales, all but one of which she had contributed to *Belgravia* or its *Christmas Annual* in 1871, 1872, and 1873. The eighth, "The Zoophyte's Revenge," first appeared in a paperbound compilation she edited in 1871, called *The Summer Tourist*, published by Ward, Lock & Tyler.

13.   Edward Henry Harrington (Ted) Maxwell's birth date in *Admissions to Trinity College, Cambridge* (cited in chapter III, note 24, above), p. 913. On June 21, 1872, MEB invited Bulwer to come and see "a fat young Hercules with big blue eyes who bears yr name—which is also the name of my uncle, brother, & first & second cousins without number." MEB to Bulwer, No. 32; *HLB* 2, p. 150. The name was of course Edward.

14.   *The Lovels of Arden* ran in *Belgravia* from February 1871 through February 1872, but achieved three-volume publication well before the end of 1871. (MEB) "Author of Lady Audley's Secret," *The Lovels of Arden* (3 vols., London: John Maxwell & Co., 1871), I, pp. 75–76; II, pp. 111, 71; III, pp. 88, 170; I, pp. 9, 85; II, pp. 177–178.

15.   MEB to Bulwer, No. 35, September 27 [1872]; *HLB* 2, p. 153. *To the Bitter End* ran in *Belgravia* from February through December 1872. Quotations from (MEB) "Author of Lady Audley's Secret," *To the Bitter End* (3 vols., London: John Maxwell & Co., 1872), I, pp. 173–175; II, p. 74.

16.   *Athenaeum,* No. 2343, September 21, 1872, p. 357.

17.   MEB to Bulwer, No. 33, July 2 [1872]; *HLB* 2, p. 151.

18.   MEB to Bulwer, No. 35, September 27 [1872]; *HLB* 2, p. 155.

19.   Bulwer to MEB, September 28, 1872; *HLB* 2, p. 156, and note 190.

20.   MEB to Bulwer, No. 34, July 20 [1872]; *HLB* 2, p. 153.

21.   MEB to Bulwer, No. 33, July 2 [1872], and No. 34, July 20 [1872]; *HLB* 2, pp. 152–153. In Rhoda Broughton's *Good-bye Sweetheart* (3 vols., London: Bentley, 1872), a beautiful "fast" young English girl disguises herself

as a Breton peasant in order to force a young traveling Englishman who dislikes women to make her acquaintance. Naturally, he falls in love with her. But her incurable flirtatiousness leads to tragedy. All the literature about Rhoda Broughton reports her pun, usually incorrectly. Even Leon Edel, *Henry James, The Master: 1901–1916* (Philadelphia & New York: Lippincott, 1972), p. 32, gets it wrong. The Yonge was of course Charlotte M., the gentlest and least improper of authors, and to make the sentence sound right one must slur together the words "was" and "Zola" so that they sound like "was older."

22.   MEB to Bulwer, No. 34, July 20 [1872]; *HLB* 2, p. 153. No. 32, June 21 [1872]; *HLB* 2, p. 150. No. 36 [December 1872]; *HLB* 2, p. 137. Nos. 20 and 21 [mid-March 1866]; *HLB* 2, pp. 131–134.

23.   MEB to Bulwer, Nos. 23, 24, 25: August 9, August, and early September [1866]; *HLB* 2, pp. 136–140.

24.   MEB to Bulwer, Nos. 25 and 26: [early September] and September 24 [1866]; *HLB* 2, pp. 140, 141.

25.   Bulwer to MEB, December 13, 1864, Wolff Collection; *HLB* 1, pp. 29–30 and notes 73, 74. MEB to Bulwer, No. 14 [December 1864, after the 13th]; *HLB* 1, pp. 32–33 and note 84. For the review, comparing Bulwer to Victor Hugo, Lamartine, Schiller, Goethe, and Voltaire, see *St. James's Magazine* 13, No. 1 (April 1865), 25–36.

26.   MEB to Bulwer, No. 35, September 27 [1872]. Bulwer to MEB, September 28, 1872; see above, note 19. MEB long afterwards took the theme of *A Strange Story* for her novel *The Conflict* (1903); see chapter X.

27.   MEB to Bulwer, No. 23, August 9 [1866]; *HLB* 2, p. 136.

28.   MEB to Bulwer, No. 19, January 16 [1866]; No. 8, June 24 [1864]; No. 33, July 2 [1872]; No. 27 [early 1867]; Bulwer to MEB, No. 35-A, September 28, 1872; MEB to Bulwer, No. 36 [December 1872]; *HLB* 2, p. 129; 1, p. 21; 2, pp. 151, 142, 156, 157.

29.   MEB to Bulwer, No. 36, undated, but written in December 1872; *HLB* 2, p. 157. Julian Young to MEB, January 28, 1873, Wolff Collection; *HLB* 2, No. 37-A, p. 159. Young himself died only a few months later, on July 3, 1873; see *Last Leaves from the Journal of Julian Young M.A.*(Edinburgh: Edmiston & Douglas, 1875). Description of Young from W. H. Mallock, *Memoirs of Life and Literature* (London: Chapman and Hall, 1920), pp. 40–41.

30.   MEB, "Lord Lytton," *Belgravia* 20 (March 1873), 73–88.

31.   The second Lord Lytton (Robert) to MEB, Paris, December 12, 1873, published by W. B. Maxwell in *TG,* pp. 86–88; MEB to the second Lord Lytton, unpublished letter in Robert Lytton MSS in the Hertfordshire County Record Office, without index number. Undated but written in reply to his letter immediately after its receipt, so about December 14, 1873. For further information on Bulwer's *The House of Darnley,* see *HLB* 2, pp. 160–161. (MEB) "Author of Lady Audley's Secret," *Weavers and Weft* (London: John Maxwell, 1877), I, p. 201. MEB to Charles Kent, n.d. but 1881, Wolff Collection.

32.   MEB to Bulwer, No. 33, July 2 [1872]; *HLB* 2, p. 151.

33.   Lord Lytton to MEB and MEB to Lord Lytton as in note 31 above.

34.   For Mrs. Rousby, see Tolles, *Tom Taylor,* pp. 234–235. *'Twixt Axe and Crown* was an adaptation of Charlotte von Birch-Pfeiffer's six-act German drama, *Die Prinzessin Elisabeth von England.* Thomas Sheppard, *Evolution of the Drama in Hull and District* (Hull: A. Brown, 1927), p. 158, mentions Mrs. Rousby's sad fate more briefly. See also Erroll Sherson, *London's Lost Theatres of the Nineteenth Century* (London: John Lane, The Bodley Head, 1925), pp. 163, 206–207; Raymond Mander and Joe Mitchenson, *The Lost Theatres of London* (London: Rupert Hart-Davis, 1968), p. 378. E. B. Walford, editor of the *Gentleman's Magazine,* sent *Griselda,* with a letter from MEB, to William Longman, who found it *"perfectly charming. . . . my children will read it one after the other. When Christmas is over—say during the 2d or 3d week of January 1874—I shall be glad to see you in order to consider whether it can be utilized in combination with other compositions of the same writer."* But apparently nothing came of Mr. Longman's enthusiasm. William Longman to E. B. Walford, December 23, 1873, Wolff Collection.

35.   *LNCD,* II, p. 273, lists "Genevieve" as having been produced at Liverpool on April 6, 1874, and "The Missing Witness" as a separate play published in 1880. However, they are the same play. MEB's own copy of the printed version (M. E. Braddon, *The Missing Witness. An Original Drama in Four Acts* [London: John and Robert Maxwell, n.d., but 1880 given by the British Museum Catalogue of Books as well as by *LNCD,* II]) is in the Wolff Collection. A fifty-four–page pamphlet bound in yellow paper wrappers, size 4¾ x 6¹⁵/₁₆ inches, it includes much rewriting in MEB's hand in the margins and on additional sheets taped to the text, as well as a pen-and-ink drawing of the stage set of the climactic avalanche scene. Genevieve *is* the missing witness: she has seen the villain throw the hero off a bridge into the raging torrent, and is then locked into a nearby hut, which is buried by the falling ice and snow. But she is rescued in time. The villainy is exposed, the villain kills himself, and his victim then turns up alive, having landed safely on a ledge.

36.   Frank Singleton, *Tillotsons, 1850–1950. Centenary of a Family Business* (Bolton and London: Tillotson and Son Ltd., 1950), pp. 8, 16, 17–18; quotations from pp. 41-42 and 47.

37.   (MEB) "Author of Lady Audley's Secret," *Taken at the Flood* (3 vols., London: Maxwell, 1874), I, p. (v). In the Tillotson file is a memorandum of Tillotson's, hereafter referred to as "Tillotson Memo," drawn up in 1880, which shows that *Taken at the Flood* began publication in the *Bolton Journal* on August 30, 1873.

38.   (MEB) "Author of Lady Audley's Secret," *Lucius Davoren* (3 vols., London: Maxwell, 1873), I, pp. 109-110, 195–197. Gustave Doré and Blanchard Jerrold, *London: A Pilgrimage* (London: Grant & Co., 1872). For a house like it, still standing in Rotherhithe, see Nikolaus Pevsner, *London, Except the Cities of London and Westminster*, The Buildings of England, BE 6 (London: Penguin Books, 1952), pp. 63–64. The Arctic portion of *Lucius Davoren* was inspired by *The Northwest Passage Overland* (1865) by William Fitzwilliam Milton, Viscount Milton, and Dr. W. B. Cheadle. Perhaps warned by past storms over plagiarism, MEB dedicated *Lucius Davoren* to Viscount Milton (with no mention of Cheadle), "in acknowledgement of the aid derived from his admirable book of travels, 'The North-West Passage Overland', to which the author is indebted for the scenery in the prologue."

39.   *Athenaeum*, No. 2427, May 2, 1874, p. 592.

40.   *Athenaeum*, No. 2387, July 26, 1873, p. 170.

41.   *Strangers and Pilgrims* appeared serially in *Belgravia* from January through October 1873 and appeared in three volumes toward the end of July. Quotations from (MEB) "Author of Lady Audley's Secret," *Strangers and Pilgrims* (3 vols., London: Maxwell, 1873), II, pp. 150, 73–74; I, pp. 241, 206, 224–225.

42.   For MEB's "schedule," beginning with these two books, see Appendix, Section 7.

43.   (MEB) "Author of Lady Audley's Secret," *A Strange World* (3 vols., London: Maxwell, 1875), II, pp. 169–170; III, pp. 162–163.

44.   (MEB) "Author of Lady Audley's Secret," *Lost for Love* (3 vols., London: Chatto & Windus, 1874), I, p. 178; II, pp. 139–140; III, p. 278. Why Chatto & Windus were allowed to publish this single novel I do not know. The Maxwell firm resumed publication of MEB's books with the very next one, and

Chatto & Windus never published her again. That this was part of the bargain when they bought *Belgravia* seems unlikely because that sale was not completed until two years later.

45.   *Spectator,* No. 2416, October 17, 1874, pp. 1303–1304. Mrs. Henry Wood (née Ellen Price, 1814–1887) was, like MEB, enormously popular. Her *East Lynne* (3 vols., London: Bentley, 1861) was as famous as *Lady Audley's Secret.* Like MEB, she edited her own magazine, *The Argosy.* But unlike MEB, she was stuffy, pompous, and of extremely limited talents. She did not improve with age. Her son, Charles Wood, wrote an adoring life of her: *Memories of Mrs. Henry Wood* (London: Bentley, 1894).

46.   (MEB) "Author of Lady Audley's Secret," *Hostages to Fortune* (3 vols., London: Maxwell, 1875), I, pp. 204–205.

47.   "Ireland for Tourists. A Reminiscence of a Recent Excursion," by the Editor, *Belgravia* 24, 3rd ser., No. 4 (July and August 1874), 76–88 and 177–190; quotations from pp. 85–86 and 182. For Griffin and John Maxwell, see *TG,* p. 161; and for a bibliographical description of the edition of Griffin's works that Maxwell published, see Michael Sadleir, *XIX-Century Fiction,* I, pp. 157–159, no. 1075.

48.   For Reade's notebook, see chapter III, text, and notes 2 and 26, above.

49.   "Counter-Notice" in Wolff Collection. See also chapter III, text, and note 26, above.

50.   For the source of this anecdote, see above, chapter III, note 24.

51.   Date and place of marriage taken from G. C. Boase and W. P. Courtney, *Biblioteca Cornubiensis. A Catalogue of Writings . . . of Cornishmen. . . .* (London: Longmans, etc., 1882), III, p. 1092. When it reported MEB's death on February 5, 1815, the *Daily Telegraph* said: "At 37, she married her publisher, John Maxwell." Since the newspaper, like everyone else, believed 1837 to be the year of her birth, this would date the marriage in 1874. Of course the *Daily Telegraph* gave no dates for the births of MEB's children or any hint that the marriage was in any way belated. For the move to Chelsea, see *TG,* p. 127.

52.   The "schedule" (see Appendix, Section 7) says "Began Hostages to Fortune, September 25, 1874," and "Finished Hostages May 31, 1875." It ran in *Belgravia* from November 1874 through November 1875 and appeared in three volumes in early September 1875. The "schedule" says "Began Dead Men's Shoes, February 18, 1875" and "Finished Dead Men's Shoes, December 20,

1875." In its turn a Tillotson novel, *Dead Men's Shoes* ran serially in the *Bolton Journal* for six months beginning on July 31, 1875, and appeared in three volumes late in February 1876. Tillotson paid £450 for the serial rights. Dates of serialization and price paid from "Tillotson Memo."

53.   *Athenaeum,* No. 2522, February 26, 1876, p. 295.

54.   *Hostages to Fortune,* II, pp. 192–193, 276, 146, 99.

CHAPTER VIII

1.   *TG*, pp. 10–11, 11, 13, 128–129, 134, 133, 12, 21–22, 280, 281. John Maxwell to W. F. Tillotson, October 7, 1882, in Tillotson File.

2.   MEB to Charles Kent, October 27 [1876], and to Mr. Venables, December 23, 1876, Wolff Collection; MEB to Mrs. Sala, June 28, 1877, Yale University Library. The episode of the runaway horses she would use a decade later in her novel *One Thing Needful* (1886). Edmund Yates, "Miss M. E. Braddon (Mrs. Maxwell) at Richmond," *Celebrities at Home*, First Series (London: Office of 'The World,' 1877), pp. 317–324.

3.   The diaries from 1880 through 1888, octavo notebooks bound in stiff green paper, are in the Maxwell Collection. Those from 1890 through 1914, duodecimo volumes neatly and uniformly bound in steel-blue cloth, with the year stamped in gold at the foot of each spine, are in the Wolff Collection.

4.   Diary, April 8, 1882; Florence Hardy, *The Early Life of Thomas Hardy* (New York: Macmillan, 1928), p. 172; Diary, August 19, 1883.

5.   MEB to Bulwer, No. 5 [May 1863]; *HLB* 1, p. 16. Charles L. Reade and the Rev. Compton Reade, *Charles Reade . . . A Memoir* (London: Chapman and Hall, 1887), II, pp. 279–284.

6.   Diaries: January 3, March 31, January 29, January 28, January 31, March 23, January 10, 1880; April 25, 1881; various dates for books read; for theatrical performances, January 3, 1881, February 2, 1880, June 10, 1881, January 13, 1880. John Maxwell to W. F. Tillotson, in Tillotson File, three letters about *The Golden Calf*: March 6, 17, and April 17, 1882, and thirty-three letters and telegrams about *Phantom Fortune* between October 7, 1882, and September 7, 1883. Quotations from those of October 7 and March 17, 1882,

and January 5, 16, February 17, and September 7, 1883. Printed circular included in the file, dated December 30, 1882.

7.   The "schedule" says of *Joshua Haggard's Daughter*: "Began Joshua Hag-
gard, August 20, 1875," and "Finished Joshua Haggard, September 26, 1876."
So the novel took more than a year to write. Work on completing *Dead Men's
Shoes* overlapped for the first four months, but thereafter the only in-
terruptions were brief: for a short story, for an article on Brittany, and for occasional intermittent work on a short novel. *Joshua Haggard's Daughter* was
MEB's last *Belgravia* novel, running serially from December 1875 through
December 1876. In the Wolff Collection is the original manuscript of the last
portion of the novel, slightly more than half, representing numbers seven
through thirteen of the original installments in *Belgravia*, manuscript pages
numbered 183-A through 349. The Collection also includes MEB's manuscript
revisions of the opening scene, made between magazine and book publication,
which amount to a six-fold expansion and complete rewriting. She dedicated
the book to Captain the Hon. John Carnegie, R.N., who had helped her with
this scene.

8.   (MEB) "Author of Lady Audley's Secret," *Joshua Haggard's Daughter* (3
vols., London: Maxwell, 1876), I, pp. 13, 35, 32–33, 40, 89, 108–111; III, pp.
24–25; I, pp. 40, 42, 38, 89, 184, 198; II, pp. 172, 43, 55, 222, 267; III, pp. 17,
38.

9.   *Ibid.*, III, pp. 225, 245, 253.

10.   *Athenaeum*, No. 2558, November 4, 1876, p. 591.

11.   *Spectator*, No. 2526, November 25, 1876, pp. 1479–1480.

12.   *Joshua Haggard's Daughter*, I, p. 290; III, pp. 41–42; I, pp. 29–31; III,
pp. 24–25.

13.   *Weekly Register and Catholic Standard*, December 2, 1876, p. 362;
MEB to Charles Kent, December 3, 1876, Wolff Collection. In the Collection
also are the copy of the novel MEB sent to Kent, with a presentation inscription
dated October 30, 1876, and a letter to him of October 27, telling him that it
was her thirty-first and that she hoped he would "find some slight improvement since the old days when you were so hearty a champion of my
literary claims."

14.   The "schedule" (which begins in August 1874) says, "Took up Weavers

and Weft at p. 62 February 76. finished No. 14, April 21st 76," and "Finished Weavers and Weft November 1, 76," five weeks after the completion of *Joshua Haggard's Daughter*. The "Tillotson Memo" shows that Tillotson published it in the *Bolton Journal* beginning August 27, 1876. It was less than half as long as a three-volume novel, and Tillotson paid MEB £300 for the serial rights. Maxwell published it as the longest and most important in a series of shorter pieces of fiction: (MEB) "Author of Lady Audley's Secret," *Weavers and Weft* (3 vols., London: John Maxwell, 1877), I, p. 40; II, p. 15. For the short stories, see below, Appendix, Section 8.

15.   The "schedule" says, "Began An Open Verdict November 10, 76," and "Finished An Open Verdict Oct. 17, 77." The "Tillotson Memo" shows that it began in the *Bolton Journal* on May 5, 1877, and that MEB received £500 for the serial rights. Maxwell published it in three volumes early in 1878: (MEB) "Author of Lady Audley's Secret," *An Open Verdict* (3 vols., London: John Maxwell and Co., 1878), II, pp. 91–92. *Athenaeum*, No. 2626, February 23, 1878, p. 250; Charles Kent, in the *Weekly Register and Catholic Standard*, February 23, 1878, pp. 122–123; MEB to Charles Kent, February 25 [1878], Wolff Collection.

16.   Description of *Vixen* in MEB's letter to Charles Kent, as in note 15 above. *TG*, p. 280. The "schedule" says, "Began Vixen, December 15, 76," and "Finished Vixen March 30, 78"; so the writing of the first half overlapped with the writing of the last half of *An Open Verdict*. MEB wrote the last half of *Vixen* uninterrupted by other work. I have not been able to trace its first serial appearance, but it was probably not a Tillotson novel. This was MEB's first book to appear under the new imprint of "John and Robert Maxwell," Maxwell's two sons, who had taken over many duties of the publishing firm. (MEB) "Author of Lady Audley's Secret," *Vixen* (3 vols., London: John and Robert Maxwell, 1879), I, pp. 230–231; II, pp. 196–197, 99–101, 18–19; I, pp. 248, 302–304. Mrs. W. K. (Lucy) Clifford to MEB [1911], Wolff Collection.

17.   The "schedule" says, "Began J. Treverton. April 1, 78. Cloven Foot." John Treverton is the hero of the novel, and this was its first, tentative title. The "schedule" adds, "Finished J. Treverton Feb. 10. 79. Cloven Foot." The "Tillotson Memo" indicates that the novel ran serially in the *Bolton Journal* beginning October 7, 1878, and that MEB received £400 for the serial rights. (MEB) "Author of Lady Audley's Secret," *The Cloven Foot. A Novel* (3 vols., London: John and Robert Maxwell, n.d. [1879]), II, p. 135.

18.   The "schedule" says, "Began Barbara, Feb 14. 79," and "Finished Barbara December 24, '79." *Barbara* was not a Tillotson novel, but was serialized in Edmund Yates's newspaper, the *World*. *Barbara* is the first of MEB's

novels to appear in her surviving diaries. On January 26, 1880, she notes, "Max subscribed Barbara"; on January 28, "Barbara published"; on February 4, "Filed for registration in France of Barbara"; on April 29, "Filed on February 4 French authority to register Barbara, and today forwarded to Madame Bongy, 33 rue St. André des Arts, Paris." On August 16, 1880, the diary notes, "First subscription Barbara 19,100, 1200 cloth [the three-volume edition]; Reprint 10,000 ordered by Jack [John Maxwell, Jr.]." For additional information on its publishing history, see below, Appendix, Section 9.

19.   The "schedule" says, "Began (Just As I Am) The Old Adam [a tentative title] December 18, 79," and "Finished Just As I Am July 9th. 80." The "Tillotson Memo," in its last entry, shows that the novel began publication in the *Bolton Journal* for February 2, 1880, and that MEB received £500 for it. The diaries enable one to follow MEB's progress week by week during 1880. (MEB) "Author of Lady Audley's Secret," *Just As I Am* (3 vols., London: John and Robert Maxwell, n.d. [1880]), I, p. 139; II, pp. 4–7.

20.   MEB to Charles Kent, October 6, 1879, Wolff Collection. *Asphodel* was first called "Daphne," the name of the younger half sister. The "schedule" says, "Began Daphne Jan'y 24, 80," and "Finished Daphne, December 31, 80." The diary for 1880 provides fuller details. The *Athenaeum* (No. 2783, February 26, 1881, p. 295) said *Asphodel* was "written in Miss Braddon's later manner. It does not depend upon crime or upon mystery; it is as simple a tale as could be contrived, with its interest centered upon one character. The style is wonderfully easy and fluent; the conversations are brilliant, pointed, and vigorous; and the description . . . is always vivid. . . . Here and there a masterly touch is obvious." But the critic made nothing of the implicit social commentary. MEB dedicated it to Lady Londesborough, a Countess and New Forest friend and neighbor, as if further to disarm suspicion.

21.   For information on these and other miscellaneous writings by MEB in the period before 1885, see below, Appendix, Section 10.

22.   The "schedule" says, "Began Novel Mount Royal, October 24, 81," and "Finished Mount Royal, March 15, 82." I do not think that *Mount Royal* was a Tillotson novel, but I have not been able to trace its preliminary serial publication. Diary entries show that MEB tentatively entitled it "Celia" and "Christabel." (MEB) "Author of Lady Audley's Secret," *Mount Royal* (3 vols., London: John and Robert Maxwell, 1882), II, pp. 267, 268; III, pp. 192–193, 194.

23.   The "schedule" says, "Began Xmas Story Flower and Weed March 30, 82. Finished June 10, 82." The 1882 diary gives details. Quotations from

Flower and Weed as published in *Mistletoe Bough* [1882], pp. 12, 15, 20, 21, 34, 35, 36, 54, 50, 77, 103, 104. In 1884 it was reprinted in a volume with short stories. See below, Appendix, Section 10c.

24.   *The Cloven Foot* (see above, note 17), I, pp. 71–72, 75–76, 77, 78–79, 82.

25.   The "schedule" says, "Began Golden Calf Feb 26, 79. 50 pp. finished April 8th." Then MEB laid it aside for more than three years. The "schedule" adds, "Resumed Golden Calf at p. 63, July 21st, 82. Finished Jan. 13th, 83." The diary shows that the tentative title was "Ida." Tillotson paid £750 for the novel, a new high price. Maxwell originally asked £1,000, but came down. It was published late in February 1883. (MEB) "Author of Lady Audley's Secret," *The Golden Calf. A Novel* (3 vols., London: John and Robert Maxwell, 1883), III, pp. 39, 41, 29, 51, 52, 54, 56, 75–76, 77, 79, 81, 82, 82–83, 83, 85, 151, 221. The *Athenaeum* (No. 2888, March 3, 1883, p. 276), finding the first two volumes "as good as anything" MEB had "ever written," felt that in the third volume, which described Brian's degeneration, "the interest flags." The critic was not ready for naturalism. For *Drink*, see *LNCD*, II, p. 536.

26.   The "schedule" says of *Phantom Fortune*: "Resumed Phantom Fortune Jan. 15th, 83 at p. 28," without indicating when MEB had written the first twenty-eight pages. It adds, "Finished Phantom Fortune July 25th 83." The diary supplies additional details. Tillotson again paid £750 for the serial rights, as he had for *The Golden Calf*. It appeared in three volumes in September. (MEB) "Author of Lady Audley's Secret," *Phantom Fortune* (3 vols., London: John and Robert Maxwell, 1883), II, pp. 217, 242; III, p. 77; II, p. 301; I, pp. 138, 248–249; II, pp. 164, 170–171, 292–293, 245, 212–213, 215–216, 217–220, 221–222; III, pp. 167–168. For Zola's indebtedness to Dr. Prosper Lucas with regard to the theory of heredity, see F. W. J. Hemmings, *Émile Zola*, 2nd ed. (Oxford: Clarendon Press, 1966), pp. 56–59; on Zola's French, see Harry Levin, *The Gates of Horn. A Study of Five French Realists* (New York: Oxford University Press, 1963), p. 348: ". . . it is still a salutary shock to open the book [*L'Assommoir*] and listen at once to the vivid phraseology of the concierge's lodge and the neighborhood *bistro*." *Athenaeum*, No. 2918, September 29, 1883, p. 398.

27.   The diary entry for June 20, 1883, reports that MEB was reading *Criquette*, and she mentions the novel in *Ishmael* (as cited below, note 30), II, p. 95.

28.   The "schedule" says, "Began Xmas Story Red Flag March 10 83. Finished June 20 83"; so it was begun and completed while *Phantom Fortune* was being written. The diary refers to it as "Commune Story" and "Girt with

Fire," and records (June 24 and July 15, 1883) the visits of a Mr. Weiner, who helped revise it. Quotations from *Under the Red Flag* as published in the *Mistletoe Bough* [1883], pp. 19, 18, 32, 4, 41, 40, 42, 43, 39–40, 44, 45, 53, 61, 67–68, 96, 103, 104. Reprinted in book form in *Under the Red Flag and Other Tales* (London: John and Robert Maxwell, n.d. [1886]). For the "other tales" see below, Appendix, Section 11. (Édouard Ferdinand de la Bonninière) Vicomte de Beaumont-Vassy, *Histoire Authentique de la commune de Paris en 1871, Ses Origines, Son Règne, Sa Chute* (Paris: Garnier, 1871).

29.   The "schedule" says, "Began *Ishmael* on September 6th, '83," and "Finished with the exception of some introductory passages March 27, 1884." The diaries provide additional details. It appeared serially in the *Whitehall Review* and in three volumes in September 1884. For Maxwell's negotiations with Tillotson at this period, see below, Appendix, Section 12.

30.   (MEB) "Author of Lady Audley's Secret," *Ishmael* (3 vols., London: John and Robert Maxwell, n.d. [1884]); quotations from I, pp. 106, 109, 103–104, 225, 237–238, 243, 299–300, 302, 315–316, 316–317, 318–319, 323.

31.   *Ibid.*, II, pp. 27, 44, 46–47, 51, 54, 72–73, 81, 86, 86–87, 87–88, 115, 119–120, 121, 124, 127–128, 126–127, 129–130, 143, 144, 161–162, 162, 149–150, 151, 164, 216, 217, 227.

32.   *Ibid.*, II, pp. 244, 248, 248–249, 250–251, 252; III, pp. 7, 31, 35, 34, 36; II, pp. 256, 264–265; III, pp. 213, 214, 215, 218, 295, 102, 104, 296, 297, 301, 302.

33.   *Ibid.*, I, p. 253. Taxile Delord, *Histoire du Second Empire* (6 vols., Paris: Germer Baillière, 1869–1875), I, p. 346; Eugène Ténot, *Paris en Décembre 1851, Étude Historique sur le coup d'état* (Paris: Armand Le Chevalier, 1868), p. 194. Delord, *Histoire*, V, pp. 263–264.

34.   Othenin d'Haussonville, "La Vie et les salaires à Paris," *Revue des Deux Mondes,* Troisième Période, 56 (April 15, 1883), 815–867; ragpickers and their village on pp. 844 ff.

35.   Théophile Gautier, "Mort de Gérard de Nerval," appeared first in *la Presse* for January 25, 1855; his "Gèrard de Nerval" in *l'Univers Illustré* for November and December 1867; reprinted the next year as the preface to Nerval's *Oeuvres Complètes* published by Michel Lévy; and again in T. Gautier, *Portraits et Souvenirs littéraires* (Paris: Levy, 1875), pp. 3–68. Any of these would have been available to MEB before she wrote *Ishmael*. Both of Gautier's articles conveniently reprinted in his *Souvenirs Romantiques,* ed. A.

Boschot (Paris: Garbier, 1929), pp. 244–249. MEB copied a portion of "Le Christ aux Oliviers" into the same notebook that contains the "schedule" (Wolff Collection).

36. *Spectator,* No. 2935, September 27, 1884, pp. 1273–1274; see also *Athenaeum,* No. 2967, September 6, 1884, p. 303. In 1885, MEB sent Lord and Lady Lytton a copy of *Ishmael* which was temporarily mislaid. After it had been found, the Lyttons read it in Switzerland, and Lady Lytton wrote to MEB that she thought it one of her best books and "the scenes in Paris and the French life give it a special attraction." But she was "rather irritated" when Ishmael had to marry Pâquerette. Lord Lytton to MEB, July 28, 1885, and Lady Lytton to MEB, September 29, 1885, both in the Wolff Collection.

37. The "schedule" says, "Began A Double Life [the tentative title, crossed out] Wyllard's Weird June 10th 84," and "Finished Wyllard's Weird, January 23rd 85." The diaries provide additional details. For the Maxwell-Tillotson correspondence over this novel, see below, Appendix, Section 13.

38. (MEB) "Author of Lady Audley's Secret," *Wyllard's Weird* (3 vols., London: John and Robert Maxwell, n.d. [1885]), II, pp. 53, 57; III, pp. 175–176. Apparently *Wyllard's Weird* had in some way been suggested to MEB by Lord Lytton. He wrote to MEB on August 28, 1885, from Brigue that he was "delighted with" the book:

> The plot is most ingenious and original—leading naturally to a very powerful conclusion. Although I began the book with an inkling (from your letter) of what the dénouement was bound to be, I was throughout the first volume completely the dupe of your narrative skill and thrown by it quite off the scent. If the conception of this story was indeed suggested by any chance word of mine, it is a curious proof of the facility with which you can light your torch at the tiniest spark.

Lord Lytton to MEB, August 28, 1885, Wolff Collection.

39. *Spectator,* No. 2966, May 2, 1885, pp. 581–582; cf. *Athenaeum,* No. 2995, March 21, 1885, pp. 371–372.

40. Manuscript in the Wolff Collection, written on the rectos of twenty-two plain white sheets, size 7½ x 10⅛ inches, numbered on rectos as follows: pp. 1, 1A, 2, 3, 4, 5, 6, 7, insertion 7A, 8, 8A, 8B, 8C, 8D, 8E, 8F, 8G, 9, 10, 11, 12, 13. Numerous additional inserts written on versos. Two preliminary leaves.

41. Clarence R. Decker, "Zola's Literary Reception in England," *Publica-*

tions of the Modern Language Association of America 49 (December 1934), 1140–1153, does not mention MEB's article, which helps confirm my conjecture that it probably remained unpublished. Raymond Mander and Joe Mitchenson, *The Lost Theatres of London* (London: Rupert Hart-Davis, 1968), pp. 348–349. Edmund Yates to MEB, October 20, 1888, Wolff Collection.

42.   MEB called her parody "Gorgonzola" when she sent it off to F. C. Burnand, the editor, on November 30, 1890; it appeared as "Le Pétrolium; ou, les Saloperies Parisiennes," No. 14 of "Mr. Punch's Prize Novels," *Punch* 100 (February 28, 1891), 100–101, as by Zorgon-Gola. Anonymous and wholly in French, it was a witty piece. She had already "done" Daudet similarly in "Jonnie," No. 8 of "Mr. Punch's Prize Novels," *Punch* 99 (November 29, 1890), 253. On *Rome*, see MEB, Cannes, January 30, 1897, to her niece Amy Knyvett, then in India, daughter of Sir Edward Braddon. Letter in the possession of Mrs. Clifton, Hungarton, Leicester, daughter of the recipient.

CHAPTER IX

1.   Joseph Hatton, "Miss Braddon at Home," *London Society* (January 1888), 22–29; reprinted with a few editorial changes in his *Old Lamps and New* (London: Hutchinson, n.d. [1889]), pp. 199–215. Exact date of the interview: November 20, 1887, when MEB's diary notes that Mr. and Mrs. Hatton came to tea. Hatton's substitution of lunch for tea was admissible journalistic license, since he had in fact often lunched at Lichfield House. In *Melia's Magazine* (February 1888), 48–50, a hostile critic of MEB quoted passages from Hatton's interview, adding, "Her novels glitter on the surface, but the substance is base metal" and plagiarizing some of the most hostile remarks in the *North British Review* article by W. Fraser Rae written more than twenty years before.

2.   *TG*, pp. 162–163.

3.   The earthquake was severer on the Italian Riviera. For George MacDonald's novel *A Rough Shaking*, inspired by the disaster at Bordighera, see R. L. Wolff, *The Golden Key. A Study of the Fiction of George MacDonald* (New Haven: Yale University Press, 1961), pp. 313–315. *TG*, pp. 169–170.

4.   MEB, Hôtel des Anglais, San Remo, February 1, 1888, to Lady Monckton, Princeton University Library.

5.   The 1889 diary is lost, but MEB's MS notes on 1889 travel and her Italian sojourn survive in a small octavo notebook, bound in blue vertically

ribbed cloth, red leather spine-label, lettered in gold "Mss. Vol IV," pp. 6–29, Wolff Collection.

6.   *TG,* pp. 163–164; MEB to a Mr. Lake, August 13, 1891, Wolff Collection.

7.   For the incredibly long list of books read by MEB to Max, see below, Appendix, Section 14.

8.   Gerald Maxwell, *The Old-World Germany of Today* (New York: Dodd Mead & Co., 1929), pp. 7, 93. John Maxwell to W. F. Tillotson, telegram of February 5, and letters of February 6 and March 10, 1887, Tillotson File. Munro, said John Maxwell, had "acted like a most considerate friend." All other information from MEB's diary.

9.   MEB, Annesley Bank, Lyndhurst, November 2, 1888, to Lady Monckton; Princeton University Library. On Robertson, see *LNCD,* II, p. 546; I, pp. 120 ff. and the bibliography there given. His youngest sister, Madge Kendal, was a close friend of MEB.

10.   For the first production, see *LNCD,* II, p. 197, and I, pp. 110 ff.; *Athenaeum,* No. 3249, February 1, 1890, pp. 157–158.

11.   When *Jim the Penman* was first performed at the Haymarket in 1886, Lady Monckton played the feminine lead, and MEB wrote her that the play was "the finest melodrama that I have seen or read for many years, not excepting the very best French plays. . . . The construction of the third and fourth acts seemed to me faultless, and the rehabilitation of Jim in the last scene really a stroke of genius." MEB to Lady Monckton, n.d. [c. May 23, 1886: her diary shows that she saw the play on May 22], Princeton University Library.

12.   Diary, November 1, 1890, reads, "Finished front scene For Better for Worse, and so far finish of the play." *LNCD,* II, p. 273, says it was performed at Whitby on June 9, 1890, and at Brighton on June 4, 1891, but does not mention a published edition. I have never seen one. It was based upon MEB's novel *Like and Unlike* (1887) and was written in 1890.

13.   For Frederick Lokes Selous' translation of Victor Hugo, see *ENCD,* II, p. 392. J. G. Millais' *Life of Frederick Courtenay Selous, D.S.O.* (New York: Longmans Green, 1919) includes on pp. 3 ff. some notes on his family by Edmund Selous and by his sister Ann, from which I have taken the remainder of the information about the family. Henry Courtney Selous' painting of the 1851 Exhibition in the Victoria and Albert Museum. Reminiscence of Oscar Wilde at the wedding reception from Mrs. Claude Beddington (Ethel Mulock), *All That I*

Have Lost (London: Cassell, 1929), p. 63. Other information from MEB's diaries.

14. *TG*, pp. 56, 119. Will Maxwell came to know well the Miles family, owners of Simpkin, Marshall, which now published and distributed the *Mistletoe Bough*; Wrigley's, the papermakers; Ryders and Clowes, the printers; Leighton, Son & Hodge, the binders; and Evans, the engravers. His new artists included Frederick Townsend, Fred Pegram, A. J. Finberg, Ronald Gray, and William Parkinson. Actually (*TG*, p. 122), he wrongly remembered that the story Partridge illustrated was entitled "Joan of Arc," but one cannot doubt that he had in mind the drawing on page 1 of the number for 1889, illustrating "One Fatal Moment." Leo Trevor's stories: "Cophetua of 'Ours,'" 1891 issue (pp. 1–14); "Common Clay," 1892 issue (pp. 96–112). "Cophetua" was dramatized by Sir Seymour Hicks as *The New Sub* (Court Theatre, April 27, 1892) and "Common Clay" by Trevor himself as *Brother Officers* (Garrick, October 10, 1898). Maxwell (*TG*, p. 125) had forgotten the original title of "Cophetua" and wrote of it under the title it eventually had as a play. *LNCD*, II, pp. 420, 604. Fanny's story not surely identifiable. For Yates, Labouchere, and Bentley, see *TG*, p. 124. In two letters to his "dear Aurora" (December 18, 1884, and December 3, 1885; Wolff Collection), Yates indicated that he was treating Will's contributions with special consideration. Maxwell does not mention his own *Tales of the Thames* (London: Simpkin, Marshall, 1892). A copy of this rare book is in the Wolff Collection. MEB to Wilkie Collins, Lichfield House, n.d. [1886], Princeton University Library. Final quotation, *TG*, p. 64.

15. Robert Lachlan's birth date in *Admissions to Trinity College* (cited in Chapter III, note 23, above), p. 605. He was the son of George Lachlan of Dry Hill Park, Tonbridge, Kent; for his academic distinctions see *The First Register of the University of Cambridge* (Cambridge: Cambridge University Press, 1917), pp. 543, 546. He entered Trinity in 1879, became a Scholar in 1880, was Third Wrangler in Parts I and II of the mathematical tripos in 1880 (Whitehead was bracketed for fourth), passed Part III (in which the successful candidates are not ranked but listed alphabetically) in 1884, and took his B.A. He won the second Smith's Prize for mathematics, became a Fellow of Trinity in 1885, and took his M.A. in 1887. His book was published by Macmillan in 1893, by which time he had resigned his fellowship. For many years he produced editions of Euclid and other works on geometry and algebra. During World War I, when Gerald Maxwell published a book called *The Military Map: Elements of Modern Topography (French School of War)* (London: Macmillan, 1916), Robert Lachlan supplied a long Introduction on maps and map making which, Gerald acknowledged, did "much to make what follows complete, concise, and clear." Remainder of information from MEB's diaries.

16.   Letter to MEB, signature indecipherable, Wolff Collection.

17.   *TG*, p. 163. For the Haggard episode, J. E. Scott, *A Bibliography of the Works of Sir Henry Rider Haggard* (Takeley, Bishop's Stortford, Herts.: Elkin Mathews Ltd, 1947), p. 33. Hurst and Blackett had printed Haggard's first two novels in three volumes, *Dawn* in 1884 and *The Witch's Head* in 1885, but declined to publish one-volume reprints. Of course, Haggard should have read his contract. But had the Maxwells not insisted on the two-thirds-of-the-profits clause, they might have published *She* and made a killing. As it was, after Watt's intervention and the settlement, they got only *Mr. Meeson's Will* (1888) and *Allan's Wife* (1889). For the disagreement with Tillotson, John Maxwell, Jr., to W. F. Tillotson, letters of January 27, January 30, and February 4, 1886 (quoted), Tillotson File. It is plain that Tillotson was very angry, and John Maxwell, Sr., sought to soothe him ("the fullest consideration, each for the other, should govern your relations *at all times*. Any other state of business between you would be a serious grief to me"), but he accepted the break as final and dissociated himself completely from it ("I am very seldom at Milton House. I only see my son occasionally"). MEB's diary notes on August 1, 1887, "Telegram from Alice. Jack very ill"; on July 19, 1888, "Called on Alice and Jack. Jack very ill"; on July 25, 1888, "Drove in rain to see Jack." The diary for 1889, when Jack died on April 10, is missing.

18.   Tillotson File: exchange of telegrams and letters on May 21 and 22, 1885, and a memorandum in the Tillotson File headed "Braddon Novel Negotiations, May 1885" give the substance of the discussions over the price for the 1887 novel, *Like and Unlike*. John Maxwell to Tillotson, June 9, 1885, reported the initial feeler from Leng. Maxwell to Tillotson, October 14, 1885, made the original offer of the two-volume *One Thing Needful* for 1886. When Tillotson stalled, Maxwell wrote on October 29, 1885: "The risk you run in taking a short novel by Miss Braddon for £500 payable by acceptances at long dates is so very small, I must ask you to accept or reject by return post. The author feels a little degraded by your hesitation; and I know I can very easily dispose of the work, if it does not suit you to take it," and within a few days, Tillotson capitulated. On the eventual break: letters of April 16 and September 16, 1886; March 8, 10, 22, and 26, 1887; and January 24, 1888. Tillotson's adviser was R. E. Leader, editor of the *Sheffield and Rotherham Independent*; his letter to Tillotson quoted in the text is dated March 25, 1887. MEB to Lady Monckton, n.d. [Summer 1887], Princeton University Library. See also Hatton interview (p. 29 of *London Society*, cited in note 1 above). MEB to the Messrs. Tillotson, November 4, 1892, Tillotson File, and Diary, December 27, 1892, and February 6, 1893.

19.   Lord Lytton to MEB, Paris, January 8, 1891, Wolff Collection. Sir

Edward Braddon to Amy Knyvett, n.p., n.d., but obviously from London in early 1891 to Mrs. Knyvett in Allahabad. Letter in the possession of Mrs. Clifton of Hungarton, Leicester, Amy Knyvett's daughter. Sir Edward also remarked that if he entered the British Parliament and made himself "sufficiently obnoxious," he would only be, "like Pope-Hennessey . . . kicked upstairs into the viceroyalty of the Leeward Islands or Mauritius." See James Pope-Hennessey, *Verandah* (London: Allen & Unwin, 1964), for an account of his grandfather. A program of the testimonial dinner is in the Wolff Collection.

20.   Diary entries. MEB to George Augustus Sala, January 28, 1886, Yale University. Edmund Yates to John Maxwell, January 21, 1886, Wolff Collection. Miss Philp's songs: "My Heart is Thine," produced as a valentine by E. Rimmell, February 1876, listed as with words by MEB in Boase and Courtney, *Biblioteca Cornubiensis* (as cited in Chapter VII, note 51, above), III, p. 1313; and "The Song of the Galley Slaves," dedicated to the Duchess of Wellington, published by Mills and Sons, December 1884, listed in G. C. Boase, *Collectanea Cornubiensia* (Truro: Netherton and Worth, 1890), p. 735.

21.   Ralph Nevill, ed., *The Reminiscences of Lady Dorothy Nevill* (London: Edwin Arnold, 1906) and *The Life and Letters of Lady Dorothy Nevill* (London: Methuen, 1919). The Squire Bancrofts' books are equally disappointing for our purposes: Marie Bancroft, Squire Bancroft, *The Bancrofts. Recollections of Sixty Years* (London: John Murray, 1909); Squire Bancroft, *Empty Chairs* (London: John Murray, 1925).

22.   *One Thing Needful* ran in the Tillotson newspapers from March 27 to July 24, 1886, before book publication in August; the diary preserves no full details of its composition. (MEB) "Author of Lady Audley's Secret," *One Thing Needful* (3 vols., London: John and Robert Maxwell, 1886), the title story occupying volumes I and II, and a novelette, *Cut by the County,* volume III. Quotations in text from I, pp. 21, 23, 72, 292–293; II, p. 43. For *Cut by the County,* see below, Appendix, Section 15, and for Madame Novikoff, Gladstone, and the novelists, see Section 16. "Aunt Belinda," *The Good Hermione, A Story for the Jubilee Year* (London: John and Robert Maxwell, 1887). Original holograph manuscript in the Wolff Collection, consisting of eighty-two numbered sheets of plain white paper, size 7⅜ x 9¾ inches, and twelve additional pages of inserted matter lettered A–H, Z-1–Z-5. The Preface is dated October 25, 1886, and the book was presumably published in time for Christmas sales in that year, despite the date of 1887 on the title page. *One Thing Needful,* II, pp. 36–38, 76–77; I, p. 290. MEB's diary for August 13, 1895, refers to Black's novel as "bosh."

23.   *Mohawks* began in 1708, the year of Malplaquet, and ended in 1727,

the year of George II's coronation. The plot centered upon that antique device, a confusion of infants—girls, this time. The characters include an alchemist, already more than a century old and feverishly in pursuit of the elixir of life, obviously drawn both from Bulwer's Zanoni and Balzac's Balthasar Claës in La Recherche de l'absolu. His death at the age of 111, with "the elixir of life, the universal panacea, simmering in the crucible beside him . . . ," MEB cribbed from the death of Margrave in Bulwer's Strange Story. Pope, Swift, Sir Robert Walpole, Lady Mary Wortley Montagu, Bolingbroke, and the first two Georges appear, conscientiously behaving the way the contemporary sources had told MEB they had behaved. (MEB) "Author of Lady Audley's Secret," Mohawks (3 vols., London: John and Robert Maxwell, n.d. [1886, begun (diary) on August 10, 1885, and almost completed by late July 1886, when the diary for that year breaks off]). Mohawks appeared serially in Belgravia. The Wolff Collection includes the original report to John Maxwell, Sr., from the firm of John and Robert Maxwell on the costs and receipts of the original 1,500-copy three-volume first edition of Mohawks from its publication in October 1886 to November 30, together with a statement of the accounts rendered to MEB. Maxwell turned over to Tillotson the job of selling American book rights to Mohawks. Although he pressed for a larger sum than the £25 or £30—which was all Harper's would pay for advance sheets, to be published forty-eight hours after English production—there is no evidence that he got more. John Maxwell to Tillotson, letters of November 23, 1885, and June 10, 1886, Tillotson File.

24.   The writing of Like and Unlike was underway on May 26, 1886, and completed on May 25, 1887. (MEB) "Author of Lady Audley's Secret," Like and Unlike (3 vols., London: Spencer Blackett, n.d. [1887]), I, p. 95; III, pp. 42–43; II, pp. 92–93, 197; II, p. 14.

25.   MEB began The Fatal Three on May 17, 1887, and finished it on December 30. (MEB) "Author of Lady Audley's Secret," The Fatal Three (3 vols., London: Simpkin, Marshall, n.d. [1888]), I, p . 262; III, p. 49. For Vanessa Stephen and Jack Hills, see Quentin Bell, Virginia Woolf (London: Hogarth Press, 1972), pp. 70–72. Spectator, No. 3148, October 27, 1888, p. 1475.

26.   The Day Will Come was begun on October 12, 1887, and finished on March 28, 1889. (MEB) "Author of Lady Audley's Secret," The Day Will Come (3 vols., London: Simpkin, Marshall, n.d. [1889]), I, pp. 90, 51–52, 74, 72. A. P. Sinnett, Esoteric Buddhism (London: Trübner, 1883). He wrote many other books, but the most important before 1889 were Incidents in the Life of Madame Blavatsky (London: G. Redway, 1886), and two occult novels, Karma (2 vols., London: Chapman and Hall, 1885) and United (2 vols., London: G. Redway, 1886). Sinnett was president of the Simla Eclectic Philosophical Society.

27.   (MEB) "Author of Lady Audley's Secret," *One Life One Love* (3 vols., London: Simpkin, Marshall, 1890). Lack of the 1889 diary makes it impossible to give exact dates for its composition. It was first entitled "Whose Was the Hand?" and MEB revised it in late January and early February 1890.

28.   *Gerard,* begun on April 28, 1890, was completed at the very end of that year, and revised for book publication during 1891, chiefly in August. (MEB) "Author of Lady Audley's Secret," *Gerard* (3 vols., London: Simpkin, Marshall, 1891), III, p. 236; I, pp. 25, 27, 5, 31, 201–202, 34–35, 93, 156–157, 176, 208–209, 229–230, 222–224, 240, 240–241, 128–129, 226, 236–237, 105; III, pp. 59, 60; II, pp. 76, 70.

29.   *The Venetians,* begun on January 8, 1891, had reached 150 manuscript pages by June 23, was completed in August, revised for book publication at intervals until May 1892, and published in three volumes early in June 1892. (MEB) "Author of Lady Audley's Secret," *The Venetians* (3 vols., London: Simpkin, Marshall, 1892), II, p. 19; I, pp. 170–171, 200, 107, 200; II, p. 164.

30.   The terse diary entries indicate that MEB began *Sons of Fire* on December 22, 1891, laid it aside, and went back to it on September 28, 1892; on March 7, 1893, she "resumed" work on it (206 pages long by then), and sent it to the printer for periodical appearance (untraced) on May 8, 1893. *Thou Art the Man* (first tentatively entitled *In After Days*), which she began on February 19, 1892, had finished its seventh Leng newspaper number on April 26; MEB had virtually completed it by August 12 and by December had proofs and "revises" in hand, finishing them late in January 1893. *All Along the River* was already being revised in part late in March and early in April 1892; on December 27, 1892, she was sending a revised Part VII to Tillotson, and on February 6, 1893, she was revising the last number; by April 4, 1893, she had finished the final revise of the two-volume novel for book publication, and on May 9, that of the third volume, containing the short stories. So the last of the longer fiction to be completed was the first to be published in book form: (MEB) "Author of Lady Audley's Secret," *All Along the River* (3 vols., London: Simpkin, Marshall, 1893). The two-volume novel tells the tragic story of Isola Disney, who succumbs to a seducer, and wins her husband's forgiveness, only to die. For the eight short stories in Vol. III of *All Along the River,* see below, Appendix, Section 17. *Thou Art the Man* (3 vols., London: Simpkin, Marshall, n.d. [1894]) is an unsuccessful variation on the theme of *The Fatal Three*: the orphan is truly the illegitimate daughter of the heroine's father, and so her true half sister. In MEB's manuscript notebook (Houghton MS Eng 1122.8), pp. 1-2 of Part II, appears a brief scenario of *Thou Art the Man,* with a list of characters and a few words of description beside each. Some names were changed in the published version. A second scenario, showing the story in a much more finished form, is

on pp. 49–61 of another one of MEB's notebooks, a small leatherette-bound volume of 112 lined pages, Maxwell Collection.

In *Sons of Fire* (3 vols., London: Simpkin, Marshall, n.d. [1895]), MEB for the only time in the entire range of her fiction deceives the reader: a striking resemblance between two men proves to be only a coincidence, and the story peters out. A brief scenario of what would become *Sons of Fire* appears on pp. 60–65 in Houghton MS Eng 1122.8, headed "Idea from Hoffman [*sic*]." MEB was then planning to call the novel "One of Two."

31., The diary entry for October 27, 1892, which reads "Began play," is probably the first reference to *A Life Interest*. On January 30, 1893, MEB sent a portion of it to Madge Kendal; by February 10, she was well into Act IV, and discussed it with Mrs. Kendal, who said she could produce it in three weeks. After more discussions and more revisions, MEB noted on August 16, 1893, "Finished fair copy Life Interest." This was its final appearance in the diary. It was never produced or published. The typescript of *A Life Interest* is in the Wolff Collection, each of the four acts bound separately in heavy brown-paper wrappers, size 8⅛ x 11 inches, with a paper label on the front covers showing title and act number. Besides the eighty-three typed pages there are many penciled additions and corrections to the dialogue on the blank versos, and numerous inserted pages of new dialogue. The entire typed version of Act IV is penciled out and twenty substitute longhand pages are inserted and dated August 16, 1893.

32.   For the plays and short stories see Appendix, Section 18. *The Christmas Hirelings* was begun on January 25, 1892, continued in March, laid down, and "resumed" in August. It became the entire Christmas number of the *Lady's Pictorial* for 1893 and was published in a single volume by Simpkin, Marshall, in 1894. MEB also wrote in July 1892 what the diary calls "squib" for *Punch,* which I identify as "Racine with the Chill Off," *Punch* 102 (July 16, 1892), a brief, clever, and rather daring skit in French, in which Oscar Wilde is made to rewrite some lines of Racine's *Phèdre* for Sarah Bernhardt in the "school of Baudelaire and Valles"; and a "dramatic sketch" called "Drifting," finished on April 18, 1893; publication not traced, if it was in fact published.

33.   Quotations from pp. 19, 243, 31, 134, 142. Mrs. Clifton of Hungarton, Leicester, younger daughter of Amy Knyvett, and herself named Amy, informs me that she was the original of Moppet; her brother Leycester and her sister Beatrice were the two older children. MEB was particularly fond of these children and of their mother.

34.   *Publisher's Circular*, No. 1462, July 7, 1894, pp. 5, 7–8.

35. *Ibid.*, No. 1463, July 14, 1894, p. 34.

36. *Ibid.*, No. 1464, July 21, 1894, p. 57.

37. *Ibid.*, No. 1465, July 28, 1894, p. 80.

38. *Ibid.*, No. 1466, August 4, 1894, pp. 104, 101.

39. MEB to Juliette Whiting, March 5, 1895, Wolff Collection.

40. *Times,* Monday, September 23, 1895, p. 4.

41. *Publisher's Circular,* No. 1526, September 28, 1895, p. 334.

CHAPTER X

1. MEB, Hôtel Montfleuri, Cannes, January 30, 1897, to her niece, Amy Knyvett, in India: "Rosie seemed so much better in health when she and Rob spent a long day with us [at Lichfield House] at the beginning of the year [on January 5, 1897, according to the diary]. She had a good appetite and did not once talk of her ailments, which I thought a cheering sign." Letter in the possession of Mrs. Clifton, Amy Knyvett's daughter, of Hungarton, Leicester.

2. MEB to Juliette Whiting, December 6, 1901, Wolff Collection.

3. Lady Lytton to MEB, March 28, 1900, Wolff Collection.

4. J. M. Barrie to MEB, January 4, 1907, Wolff Collection. Mrs. Oliphant, *The Victorian Age of English Literature* (London: Macmillan, 1892), pp. 494-495.

5. Lady Braddon to MEB, February 14, 1897, Wolff Collection; Sir Edward Braddon to MEB, August 14, 1898, Wolff Collection.

6. MEB to Mrs. Guyon, n.d., Yale University Library.

7. MEB to Lady Monckton, May 8 [1905], Princeton University Library.

8. M. E. Braddon, "Fifty Years of the Lyceum Theatre," *Strand Magazine* 24 (January 1903), 36–40.

9.   MEB to Lady Campbell Clarke, n.d. [1907], Wolff Collection.

10.   *TG*, pp. 153–154.

11.   MEB to Lady Monckton, October 20 [no year, but both the diary and letter mention the removal of Mary Selous' adenoids, which the former dates on October 19, 1904], Princeton University Library. MEB to Lucy Clifford, December 24 [no year, but 1904, since Ted Maxwell's daughter Marjorie is just a year old], Clifford Papers, in the possession of Christopher Dilke, Esq.

12.   Both MEB's novels discussed in Section 2 of this chapter.

13.   *TG,* p. 334.

14.   *TG,* p. 322.

15.   MEB to Lady Turner (née Juliette Whiting), November 17, 1912, Wolff Collection.

16.   Compton Mackenzie, *My Life and Times: Octave Four: 1907–1915* (London: Chatto & Windus, 1965), pp. 195–196; and *Octave Two: 1891–1900* (London: Chatto & Windus, 1963), pp. 265–266. MEB to Lady Monckton, October 23, 1913, and no date, Princeton University Library.

17.   Clive Holland, "Fifty Years of Novel Writing. Miss Braddon at Home. A Chat with the *Doyenne* of English Novelists," *Pall Mall Magazine* [48, No. 223] (November 1911), 697–709 (a shortened version published in the *Bookman* 42, No. 250 [July 1912], 149–157), reported all these opinions but the last, which MEB wrote from Cannes, January 30, 1897, to Amy Knyvett, in India. M. E. Braddon, "Hermann Sudermann," *National Review* 21 (August 1893), 751–770. It is curious that the plot of Sudermann's play, *Sodom's Ende,* to which MEB devoted most of her essay, is almost identical with Feuillet's *Dalila,* which she had pirated as *Circe* a generation earlier.

18.   MEB to Lady Monckton, October 23, 1913, Princeton University Library.

19.   Ralph Nevill, *The Life and Letters of Lady Dorothy Nevill* (London: Methuen, 1919), pp. 209–210.

20.   M. E. Braddon, "The Woman I Remember," *The Press Album* (London: John Murray, 1909), pp. 3–6.

21.   MEB to Lady Monckton, April 10, 1912, Princeton University Library. George Dangerfield, *The Strange Death of Liberal England* (reprint, London: Paladin, 1970), pp. 199, 14.

22.   Such excerpts are to be found in Houghton Library MS Eng 1122.10, a "dummy" volume in the green cloth binding that Maxwell used for all her three-deckers between 1872 and 1887, and that Spencer Blackett and Simpkin, Marshall used for them through 1894, but with pages blank and no cover-lettering; MS Eng 1122.9, a dummy volume of *Belgravia* with blank pages; and MS Eng 1122.8, in navy morocco cloth sides with morocco leather spine, lettered "17th-Century M.S. Notes," containing 360 leaves paged twice from 1–180.

23.   For the growth of *London Pride*, see Appendix, Section 19.

24.   For MEB's method of work and source of inspiration for *London Pride*, see Mary Angela Dickens, "Miss Braddon at Home," *Windsor Magazine* 6, No. 33 (September 1897), 418. This was an interview granted a year after *London Pride* had been published. MEB also told Miss Dickens that she usually wrote about 1,500 words an hour, or three "closely written pages of manuscript." In a letter to J. Cordy Jeaffreson, of July 23, 1894, returning a copy of one of his own books, which he had loaned her while she was writing *London Pride*, she wrote "The sensational Berkeley Trial . . . suggested my story. It comes next in the volume to my ancestor Laurence Braddon's trial for treason, & I read it & built the idea of a story upon it more than 30 years ago" (Wolff Collection). Simpkin, Marshall published *London Pride* in one volume in October 1896.

25.   *Spectator*, No. 3556, October 31, 1896, p. 595; *Athenaeum*, No. 3599, October 17, 1896, p. 521.

26.   For the development of *In High Places*, see Appendix, Section 20.

27.   MEB "planned" *The Infidel* on January 17, 1898, and began it the next day. She wrote it on the 24th, and on February 2, 18, 21, 23, 25, 27, and 28, by which time it was 107 pages long. Although she mentioned working on it further only on March 24 and 31, and on April 13 and 26, by April 30 it had reached page 216; and by May 31 (with no further diary references), page 274. She resumed it on June 27, and revised it on July 27, August 8, October 25, and December 8. She did not mention it again after that date.

28.   M. E. Braddon, *The Infidel. A Story of the Great Revival* (London: Simpkin, Marshall, copyright 1900), p. 322.

29.   MEB to W. P. Frith, November 10 [1900], Wolff Collection.

30.   Hall Caine to MEB, November 11, 1901, and MEB's draft reply, un-dated, Wolff Collection. Does not the following appreciation by a fellow mid-Victorian novelist enhance the irony? "One secret of such enormous and world-wide popularity is doubtless the cleanness and wholesomeness of Miss Braddon's stories. No page, no sentence, tempts youthful readers to lift the forbidden veil, by hook or crook to attain the knowledge that is as the poison of asps, 'a stumbling block before the children.' Can any writer desire a nobler epitaph?" M. E. Betham-Edwards, *Mid-Victorian Memories* (London: John Murray, 1919), p. 123.

31.   Braddon Notebook VI, pp. 17–22, contains a preliminary list of characters for *The Little Auntie* and a few notes for the plot. This was one of the three one-volume novels that MEB completed in manuscript before the demise of the three-decker. For its development, see Appendix, Section 21.

32.   M. E. Braddon, *Under Love's Rule* (London: Simpkin, Marshall, 1897), pp. 176–177, 73–77, 276.

33.   Braddon Notebook VI, pp. 61–84, includes a preliminary sketch of this novel, including drafts of several of its key scenes. For its development, see Appendix, Section 21.

34.   M. E. Braddon, *Rough Justice* (London: Simpkin, Marshall, 1898), pp. 382, 307, 392. For Arnold Bennett's inadequate criticism of this novel, see above, Prologue.

35.   *Spectator,* No. 3635, February 26, 1898, p. 310.

36.   For its development, see Appendix, Section 21.

37.   M. E. Braddon, *His Darling Sin* (London: Simpkin, Marshall, n.d. [1899]), p. 79.

38.   For its development, see Appendix, Section 21.

39.   M. E. Braddon, *The Conflict* (London: Simpkin, Marshall, 1903), pp. 9–10, 81, 130, 100–101, 144, 110. On Bulwer's novel, see my *Strange Stories,* frequently cited.

40.   *A Lost Eden*, discussed in Prologue and in Chapters I and II above. For its development, see Appendix, Section 21.

41.   For its development, see Appendix, Section 21.

42.   M. E. Braddon, *The Rose of Life* (London: Hutchinson, 1905), p. 71.

43.   For its development, see Appendix, Section 21.

44.   M. E. Braddon, *The White House* (London: Hurst & Blackett, 1906), pp. 29–30, 35, 39, 35, 107–108.

45.   The only mentions of this novel in the diary are on a memorandum page at the back of the volume for 1894, where MEB wrote, "Finished Conrad, 133 pp," and on January 11, 1906, where she wrote, "Finished Revise Dead Love." Only the fact that the hero's name is Conrad enables us to be certain that the two are the same.

46.   M. E. Braddon, *Dead Love Has Chains* (London: Hurst & Blackett, 1907), pp. 123, 47, 46, 50, 56–57, 62, 64, 71, 70–71, 163–164, 239–240, 251, 262, 252, 269–270.

47.   M. E. Braddon, *Her Convict* (London: Hurst & Blackett, 1907). The diaries make no recognizable mention of this novel. In it MEB referred (p. 362) to radium and "new atomic theories." She transcribed an article on this subject in Houghton MS Eng 1122.10, pp. 4–5.

48.   Braddon notebook VI, pp. 99–106, contains a draft of this story in an earlier form as a play. The diary first mentions it on August 16, 1897: "Wrote a little 'Her Majesty's &c.'" The same words reappear on January 6, 1898. On October 21, 1899, she "resumed story His [sic] Majesty's Pleasure," which shows that by then it was no longer cast in dramatic form. She wrote more on October 26, November 20, 29, and, 30, December 5, 11, and on December 27: "Revising Her M. P. all this week." Thereafter it does not appear. Apparently MEB kept it unpublished for nine years, until Hurst & Blackett published it in 1908.

49.   The diary for November 30, 1906, says, "Old Iniquity 63 pp." This was *Our Adversary*, as shown by the hero's remark, "on the question of a personal devil, the Old Iniquity of the Middle Ages, he had been made to turn his gaze inward." M. E. Braddon, *Our Adversary* (London: Hutchinson, 1909), p. 10. The diary makes no further mention of the novel under either of these titles, but it seems likely that the entry for May 7, 1908, "Finished His House in Order," refers to it. "His House in Order" appears only this once, and would have been a plausible second-thought as the title for this novel. If it is not *Our Adversary*, I do not know what it is.

50.   Quotations from pp. 109, 173.

51.   Unless the entry in the diary for December 17, 1909, "Finished Smart Sets," is a reference to *Beyond These Voices*—and "Smart Sets" would have been a plausible title for the novel—there is no mention of it in the diary. M. E. Braddon, *Beyond These Voices* (London: Hutchinson, 1910), pp. 76, 120–121, 83, 88, 252, 83–85, 108, 110, 111, 145, 2–3.

52.   Diary entry of June 23, 1910, says, "Wrote . . . a little Godwin." This is surely *The Green Curtain*. It reappears on July 13, 1911, when she was "Revising G.C." and on August 7 and September 16, the latter mention giving the full title. M. E. Braddon, *The Green Curtain* (London: Hutchinson, 1911), p. 294. MEB to Lady Monckton, October 10 [1911], Princeton University Library.

53.   *Miranda* appears in the diary entry for February 5, 1912, "Engaged all day on revising 20 p.p. Miranda"; and on May 30, 1913, "A little revision Miranda." But that is all. M. E. Braddon, *Miranda* (London: Hutchinson, 1913); quotations from pp. 65, 75, 283, 141, 288, 351, 352, 384. MEB to Lady Monckton, September 27 [1913], Princeton University Library.

54.   In the Wolff Collection is the entire original typed portion of *Mary*: 455 pages, with many corrections in ink in MEB's hand, and several manuscript inserts, plus thirty-nine numbered half-quarto sheets of lined paper in her hand, completing the novel. Also in the collection is an envelope inscribed in MEB's hand, "Notes for 'Mary,'" the contents of which include a time schedule for the events of the novel and a list of characters with a few words after each name. The first diary reference to *Mary* is that of December 16, 1911: "2 or 3 pp Mary." On June 6, 1912, she said, "Wrote a little Mary. Very little. Difficult to get back to work after interval." She worked on *Mary* all morning on October 10, and all day on October 14 and 15. This is all the diary tells us.

55.   M. E. Braddon, *Mary* (London: Hutchinson, 1916), p. 221.

56.   *TG*, pp. 214–233.

57.   MEB to Lady Monckton, n.d. [early September 1914], Princeton University Library.

58.   MEB to A. P. Watt, n.d.; original typed pages of the Belgian essay, Wolff Collection.

59.   *King Albert's Book* (London: The *Daily Telegraph* in conjunction with the *Daily Sketch,* the *Glasgow Herald,* and Hodder & Stoughton, n.d. [1915]). MEB's contribution on p. 112. Copy in the Wolff Collection.

60.   MEB to Lady Turner (Juliette Whiting), October 11, 1914, Wolff Collection.

61.   MEB to Lady Monckton, n.d. [c. November 15, 1914], Princeton University Library.

62.   Same to the same, a few days later, Princeton University Library.

63.   *TG,* p. 224.

64.   *Ibid.,* p. 225.

APPENDIX

1. The date of the first publication of *Three Times Dead* (Chapter III, note 5)

2. The Gilbys (Chapter III, note 15)

3. MEB's March 1861 (?) letter to Sala: text and commentary (Chapter IV, note 14)

4. MEB's financial position, 1866–1871, and Michael Sadleir (Chapter IV, note 70)

5. C. Heywood's studies of *The Doctor's Wife* (Chapter V, note 32)

6. Frederick Greenwood's novel and personality (Chapter VI, note 15)

7. MEB's "schedule of work," *Lost for Love* and *A Strange World* (Chapter VII, note 42)

8. MEB's short stories in *Weavers and Weft* (Chapter VIII, note 14)

9. The lawsuit over *The Story of Barbara* (Chapter VIII, note 18)

10. MEB's chores of 1880–1881 (Chapter VIII, note 21)

    (a) The *Figaro* novel
    (b) Abridging Scott
    (c) The "other tales" in *Flower and Weed and Other Tales* [1884]
    (d) Plays
    (e) "Revising" other people's novels; essays

11. The short stories in *Under the Red Flag and Other Tales* (Chapter VIII, note 28)

12. Maxwell's negotiations with Tillotson about *Ishmael* (Chapter VIII, note 29)

13. Maxwell's negotiations with Tillotson for *Wyllard's Weird* (Chapter VIII, note 37)

APPENDIX

1. *The date of the first publication of* Three Times Dead
(Chapter III, note 5)

Montague Summers (*Times Literary Supplement*, No. 2117, August 29, 1942, p. 432), one of the few who had ever seen a copy of the extremely rare first edition of *Three Times Dead,* simply asserted that the book belonged to 1854, as if there had been a printed date in the copy he saw. Even then, Sir Ian MacAlister (*ibid.,* No. 2121, September 26, 1942, p. 480) rightly pointed out that Miss Braddon's poem on Garibaldi's campaign (composed simultaneously with *Three Times Dead*) could not have been written in 1854, because the campaign itself did not take place until 1860. On the same page Summers replied, without adducing any evidence, that Miss Braddon had wrongly remembered that she had worked on both books simultaneously and flatly reasserted that *Three Times Dead* had been published in 1854. Michael Sadleir (*XIX-Century Fiction,* I, p. 53) accepted the date of 1854. His own copy of *Three Times Dead* was incomplete, and he may have thought that a complete copy would bear a date. There are two complete copies in original board binding in the Wolff Collection. *The first edition was undated.* Since *Three Times Dead* was published without a date, since it was written during the same summer as *Garibaldi,* and since *Garibaldi* was perforce written during 1860, while the campaign was going on, and published in February 1861, *Three Times Dead* must have been written during the same months in 1860.

Writing to an unnamed correspondent on November 2, 1906, MEB herself wrote: "The following is the chronology of my earlier books: 'The Trail of the Serpent,' published in serial form as 'Three Times Dead' 1860 . . ." (Princeton University Library). In a letter of March 13, 1904 to Malcolm C. Paton, MEB wrote: " 'Three Times Dead' or 'The Trail of the Serpent' was my first novel, and it appeared in the [Beverley] newspaper, with no circulation in London, and, I believe, very little at Beverley. The volume you possess [now in the Wolff Collection] is no doubt composed of the original unsold numbers, with the dreadful illustrations which I well remember. The story first appeared in book form under the title of 'The Trail of the Serpent,' " (Wolff Collection). Clearly either MEB had forgotten that the penny numbers had been assembled, bound in boards, and published in book form under the original title, or else she had never seen a copy, which—given her relations with Empson—is quite possible. In any case, she twice affirmed the date of 1860, which is also indicated by the date of Garibaldi's campaign. 1854 must be abandoned as without foundation.

2. *The Gilbys* (Chapter III, note 15)

For William Robinson Gilby and his son William Gilby, see J. A. Venn, comp., *Alumni Cantabrigiensis* . . . Part II (1752–1900), (Cambridge: University Press, 1947), III, p. 48. Gilby Sr. was B.A. 1809 and M.A. 1812, and was ordained in Durham in 1818. He was the son of John Gilby, Rector of Barmston, Yorkshire, whose family came originally from Winterton, Lincolnshire. For our John Gilby's house and its street, see J. J. Sheahan and T. Whellan, *History and Topography of the City of York; The East Riding of Yorkshire* (2 vols., Beverley: John Green, 1857), II, pp. 227-228; p. 401 for Gilby's putative grandfather and some property he owned. For Newbegin, today, "a very pleasant backwater," see N. Pevsner, *Yorkshire: York and the East Riding* (London: Penguin, 1972), p. 187. For Gilby's horse Flash in the Pan, see *Sporting Magazine* 134 (1859), 56. For his paralysis, see J. Fairfax-Blakeborough, *Yorkshire East Riding* (London: Robert Hale Ltd., 1951), p. 86.

Fairfax-Blakeborough also says, "the wealthy Mr. Gilby" had been so greatly impressed by MEB's poetry printed in the local newspaper that he had offered to "be financial sponsor" for a book of poems, and he quotes MEB directly (without indicating his source) as having advised Gilby to publish *Lady Audley's Secret* instead (chronologically impossible and obviously a Beverley myth). She is also supposed to have said that she "learnt all" she "ever knew about racing stables and racing, not only from Mr. Gilby" but from "everyone else in the neighbourhood." The quotation may be from a paragraph MEB sent to the *Beverley Recorder* or to a Hull paper at the time of its centennial in the 1880's or 1890's. In any case, as "Gilbert Forester" 's daughter, she had no need to wait until she met Gilby to learn about horses. She was often disingenuous about recalling her past when there was nobody likely to read her who could remember the actual facts.

3. *MEB's March 1861 (?) letter to Sala: text and commentary* (Chapter IV, note 14)

MEB wrote: "You write 'The Seven Sons of Mammon,' and you tell me not to 'have the honour to be!' You are the author of 'Hogarth,' 'Twice Around the Clock,' 'Mrs. Cruiser,' (Mr. Mayhew's finest girl is at least a cousin of that lady), 'The Baddington Peerage,' etc. etc. etc., and you desire me to be other than obedient! What can I be but obedient? How can I ever feel that unspeakable honour for which I have so long hoped?" Sala's novel *The Seven Sons of Mammon* ran in *Temple Bar* from the third number, February 1861, to December. Tinsley published it in three volumes with an 1862 date on the title page. "Hogarth" was Sala's *William Hogarth, Painter, Engraver, and Philosopher,* which had appeared during 1860 in Thackeray's newly launched *Cornhill Magazine* and was eventually published as a book by the *Cornhill's* publishers, Smith, Elder and Company, in 1866. *Twice Around the Clock,* perhaps Sala's most remarkable book, a series of twenty-four sketches of London, one for each hour of the day, had appeared first in Maxwell's *Welcome Guest* between May 1 and November 27, 1858, and then in book form, published in October 1859 by Houlston and Wright. "Mrs. Cruiser" was *How I Tamed Mrs. Cruiser,* which ran in the *Welcome Guest* for six weeks, between July 31 and September 4, 1858, and was published as a book by James Blackwood, undated but late in 1858 or early in 1859. *The Baddington Peerage,* Sala's first novel, had appeared in the *Illustrated Times* in 1859 before achieving publication in three volumes by Charles Skeet in 1860. Ralph Straus, *Sala. The Portrait of an Eminent Victorian* (London: Constable, 1942), is incomplete or incorrect about some of these dates. "Mr. Mayhew's finest girl" who "is at least a cousin" of Mrs. Cruiser refers to Augustus Mayhew's novel *The Finest Girl in Bloomsbury. A Tale of Ambitious Love,* which appeared serially in the *Welcome Guest* from August 2, 1860 (n.s., No. 42), to February 14, 1861 (n.s., No. 68), and was published as a book by W. Kent in 1861. Among the MEB manuscripts in the Maxwell Collection is an unpublished bit of doggerel verse written at Beverley in 1860 and entitled "The Lay of the Little Ones, addressed in all humility to Mr. Augustus Mayhew," in which MEB humorously took up the cudgel on behalf of small men, who were ridiculed in Mayhew's story, adjuring him not to be "quite so hard upon the 'fine girl's' small-sized lover." The "nine leaders" means Sala's various "leading articles" for numerous periodicals. His "immense and varied labour" had indeed made him the most prolific and versatile writer of 1861, and one of the best known.

MEB's letter continued:

> So you have a Strawberry Hill [GAS's new house in the country, Upton Court near Slough, rented in 1861] and you will be soon setting up your printing press and pulling a copy of Mammon in Black Letter [since he had a Gothic house, like Horace Walpole's Strawberry Hill, he would soon be printing his latest book, *The Seven Sons of Mammon,* in Gothic type]. I am glad you are in Buckinghamshire, and not at that Upton where Susan Hopley lived and everybody murdered each other. To a person of my theatrical experience there is always something rather awful in the sound of "Upton." I am sure you must have "my murdered brother, Andrew," walled up in your bedroom. Some day, when you are shaving or hanging up your coat, you will touch a secret spring in the wainscoat, and he will come out with a back-fall, green and festering.

The references are to the popular melodrama *Susan Hopley; or, The Trials and Vicissitudes of a Servant-Girl,* based on a penny-number novel by T. P. Prest, 1842. Susan Hopley lived in Upton, Norfolk; Sala's house was in Upton, Buckinghamshire. The servant's name was pirated from Caroline Crowe's novel of 1841, *Adventures of Susan Hopley; or, Circumstantial Evidence.*

4. *MEB's financial position, 1866–1871, and Michael Sadleir*
(Chapter IV, note 70)

Michael Sadleir, in "Mary Elizabeth Braddon," *Things Past* (London: Constable, 1944), p. 75, on the strength of these letters of MEB to Bulwer, which he read but left unpublished, argued that it was the publishing house of Ward, Lock & Tyler to which Maxwell had owed money. Ward, Lock & Tyler, he imagined, had moved to secure a lien on MEB's earnings and were able to force her to write her next group of seven novels for them, until she had worked off Maxwell's debt. "Whatever the details of the affair," he wrote, "her frantic productivity during the next years [1866–1871] is proof enough of a need for money beyond the ordinary, and the most likely explanation is that Ward and Lock, sore with themselves for missing a best-seller, and now furious at the acumen of their former employé [John Maxwell] contrived, on contractual or other grounds, to trip him up and, in effect, to foreclose on a mortgage." But Sadleir was wrong on all counts.

MEB's letters to Bulwer—now published—show that she did not find herself without financial resources or in a position where she had to comply with anybody's demands upon her. She experienced only "serious inconvenience" by having been at least temporarily denied a mere £1000 (or £1100) that she had expected to be paid and that were owing to her; and the inconvenience had meant only that in order to pay for Lichfield House, she had to sell—disadvantageously—some consols.

Sadleir's opinion that in the years from 1866 to 1871 MEB showed "frantic productivity" until she had worked out her imagined obligations to Ward and Lock was also mistaken. These very years were, in fact, by far the *least* productive of her career so far. Of her eight novels that Ward, Lock & Tyler published, two, *Rupert Godwin* (1867) and *Run to Earth* (1868), were reprints of penny fiction, and only six were new: *The Lady's Mile* (1866), *Birds of Prey* (1867), *Dead Sea Fruit* (1868), *Charlotte's Inheritance* (1868), *Fenton's Quest* (1871), and *The Lovels of Arden* (1871). Moreover, at precisely the beginning of the six-year period, MEB gave up altogether the lucrative writing of penny fiction. The period further included two consecutive calendar years, 1869 and 1870, in which she published *no books at all,* the only time in her writing career until the years 1901 and 1902 when so long a period elapsed without a new novel from her pen. There were good reasons for her silence, but they were not financial.

MEB's freedom to choose Ward, Lock & Tyler in preference to Chapman & Hall shows that Ward, Lock & Tyler cannot have been hostile to Maxwell, as Sadleir imagined. In all probability, it was Bentley, who acquired *Temple Bar* in

January 1866, who was "hostile" (see chapter IV, n. 64 and chapter VI, n. 54).

Sadleir's picture of MEB's life between 1866 and 1871 as frenziedly active and cursed by debt vanishes into thin air when one reads with care the very sources on which he based it. On the contrary, these were years notable for less work and for constantly increasing wealth.

5 . C. Heywood's studies of The Doctor's Wife
(Chapter V, note 32)

The Doctor's Wife is MEB's only novel so far to have engaged the interest of a professional scholar of English literature. In "Flaubert, Miss Braddon, and George Moore," Comparative Literature 12, No. 2 (Spring 1960), 151–158, C. Heywood worked out in some detail the resemblances between it and Madame Bovary: he did not know the MEB letters to Bulwer in which she so fully discussed her indebtedness to Flaubert and the problems it caused her, so he said (p. 156) that there is "no external evidence" of her knowledge of Flaubert. The letters to Bulwer provide the evidence he lacked. Heywood satisfactorily showed that George Moore drew directly from The Doctor's Wife as well as from Flaubert. In "The Return of the Native and Miss Braddon's The Doctor's Wife: A Probable Source," Nineteenth-Century Fiction 18, No. 1 (June 1963), 91–94, and in "Miss Braddon's The Doctor's Wife: An Intermediary between Madame Bovary and The Return of the Native," Revue de Littérature Comparée 38 (1964), 255–261, Heywood called attention to Hardy's possible borrowings. Heywood was wrong in thinking that MEB was still editing Belgravia when The Return of the Native appeared there (she gave it up in 1876). Also, the resemblances between Eustacia and Isabel might be those between any two romantic heroines. On the other hand, as Hardy and MEB were on good personal terms, he may well have been influenced by The Doctor's Wife. Returning to the novel a third time ("A Source for Middlemarch: Miss Braddon's The Doctor's Wife and Madame Bovary," Revue de Littérature Comparée 44 [1970], 184–194), Heywood made a strong case for its influence upon George Eliot, but sometimes went to extremes in a dogged search for parallels (Sigismund Smith he derived from Flaubert's Léon, without realizing how much more Sigismund owed to MEB's own hack-writing). Heywood's assumption that Isabel's marriage with George Gilbert was "probably unconsummated" can hardly be substantiated. No doubt George Eliot too was adapting Madame Bovary; no doubt she had read The Doctor's Wife as well. But each reader will have to make up his own mind how much more of Heywood's case he wishes to accept.

He was clearly right in identifying Mr. Raymond, Isabel Sleaford's employer when she turns governess, as Charles Bray, the Coventry phrenologist-philosopher whom George Eliot eight years later took as the model for Mr.

Brooke in *Middlemarch*. How MEB had come to know Charles Bray I have no idea. Heywood refers to George Eliot (p. 18) as "ambiguously placed" by her liaison with Lewes, but did not know that MEB was far more so by hers with Maxwell, which had given her children.

6. *Frederick Greenwood's novel and personality*
(Chapter VI, note 15)

[Frederick Greenwood], *Margaret Denzil's History. Annotated by her Husband* (2 vols., London: Smith, Elder and Co., 1864), was reprinted from the *Cornhill Magazine*, where it had run from November 1863 through October 1864. It contains many elements of a Braddon novel or of other melodramas: a heroine whose identity is a mystery to her, a crime or crimes committed long before the story opens, a duel, a pretended suicide, and subsequent bigamy. But the construction is so inept that one cannot cheerfully accept, as one usually can with MEB, the improbabilities of the plot. Moreover, Greenwood dwells so lovingly upon the sufferings of his heroine that the story takes on an unpleasantness quite foreign to MEB. As a child, Margaret is entertained by her foster father with the story "how . . . a young lady was bound to a tree by wicked men who slew her lover before her eyes, and wrote his name across her bare bosom with his blood. And how the blood could never be washed from it; only whenever any of the cruel murderers came to his dying hour the letters faded from her bosom for the time and came out all wet on his [Vol. I, p. 7]." Margaret tells this tale as proof of her foster father's kindness! It is typical of the farrago of horrors that characterize the book. Despite his eminence as a man of affairs and his reputation as "a man of tender heart" and exemplary family life, marked especially by kindness toward his daughters (see J. W. Robertson Scott, *The Story of the Pall Mall Gazette, and of its First Editor Frederick Greenwood* . . . [London: Oxford University Press, 1950], pp. 342–343), Greenwood must have had quite a nasty streak. The *Saturday Review* (18, No. 475 [December 31, 1864], 819–821) assumed that the author of *Margaret Denzil's History* was a woman and criticized it as badly constructed and executed, but showing a certain talent.

7. *MEB's "schedule of work,"* Lost for Love *and* A Strange World
(Chapter VII, note 42)

For eleven years, between 1874 and 1885, MEB kept a kind of schedule of her work, listing each of her novels and many of her short stories, usually with the date at which she had begun to write and the date of completion. This schedule occupies the verso of one leaf and the recto and verso of the next, immediately preceding the final leaf of a duodecimo notebook in the Wolff Collection, bound in navy blue, vertically ribbed cloth, with a dark red label on the spine lettered in gold "M.S.S./Vol. V." It consists of several hundred unnumbered pages of plain white paper, the top edge gilt, and contains chiefly miscellaneous notes and extracts from MEB's reading. This "schedule" is particularly helpful for the years 1874 through 1879 before MEB's diaries begin. The first two entries are:

Finished Lost for Love, August 22, 1874.
Finished Strange World, October 20, 1874.

We do not have the dates at which MEB began these novels. But she usually took from eight months to a year to complete a novel; we may assume that she began *Lost for Love* after she had completed *Lucius Davoren* in 1873 but well before she had finished *Taken at the Flood*; and that she began *A Strange World* sometime before the end of 1873 after finishing *Taken at the Flood*. *Lost for Love* ran in *Belgravia* from November 1873 through November 1874 and was published in three volumes in mid-September. *A Strange World* was a Tillotson novel: its run in the *Bolton Journal* began on April 18, 1874, and it appeared in three volumes in mid-February 1875. But the "schedule" shows that they were completed within two months of each other.

8. *MEB's short stories in* Weavers and Weft
(Chapter VIII, note 14)

The short stories that occupied the remainder of the three volumes of *Weavers and Weft* are: "In Great Waters" (originally published anonymously in *Belgravia* 15, 2nd series, No. 5 (August 1871), 229–248, set in Normandy. It retells the old folklore tale of the "two sisters." The elder sister loves a man who loves the younger sister, but the younger sister lets her head be turned by a smooth-talking fop from Paris. When the fop is drowned, she becomes so distressed that she eventually enters a convent, and the elder sister gets the man in the end. "Sebastian" (written, according to the "schedule," between May 29 and June 10, 1876, and originally published in the "Holiday [i.e., Summer] Number" of *Belgravia* for 1876) is a quiet sketch of a young eighteenth-century squire saved from a murderous Italian valet by a faithful Saint Bernard. "Levison's Victim" (originally published anonymously in *Belgravia* 10 [January 1870], 329–341) deals with a forced marriage and a murder in the Tyrol. "Christmas in Possession" (first publication not traced) is a comic anecdote of a young woman married to a reckless scapegrace, so deep in debt that the bailiffs take over the house while he has gone off to Scotland. The bailiff's man, far from being a brutal intruder, is an elderly grandfather who does the chores, takes care of the baby, and proves a friend to his involuntary hostess until her husband returns, having come into his inheritance. "John

Granger" (originally published in the *Belgravia Christmas Annual* for 1871) is the story of a decent farmer whose money is stolen and who is killed as he attempts to go to America after a disappointment in love. "Prince Ramji Rowdedow" (first published anonymously in the *Belgravia Christmas Annual* for 1874) is a farce about a comedian made up as a Hindu prince in order to attract an audience in an out-of-the-way town where audiences usually are disappointing. "Too Bright to Last" (see Chapter II, text and note 20, above) is a sentimental story of an actress who falls in love with a married actor. She marries her kind manager, but always wishes that she had kissed her real love goodbye. "The Scene-Painter's Wife" (previously printed in the yellowback edition of *Ralph the Bailiff* and in the *Belgravia Christmas Annual* for 1870) tells of a beautiful tiger-tamer, married to the scene-painter and cruelly punished for an innocent flirtation. In "Sir Luke's Return" (originally published in the *Belgravia Christmas Annual* for 1876), a man who has made a fortune as a youth in Australia returns to England in late middle age to confront two possible heirs to his money, a toady and a decent man, neither of whom has known him previously. After playing up to the pompous Sir Luke and bullying his gentle, humorous steward, the toady discovers to his horror that the two had changed roles before leaving Australia and that the man he has snubbed is after all the millionaire, who has discovered what he wanted to know: which heir to favor. This would have made an effective one-act play, and may have originally been intended for the stage. "Her Last Appearance" (original publication not traced) is the story of an eighteenth-century actress, her unhappy marriage, her true lover, and her death. "Sir Hanbury's Bequest" (originally published in the *Belgravia Christmas Annual* for 1875) has more substance than most of these frothy Christmas tales. Loomborough, in which it is set, is certainly Manchester, and the library it describes, left to the city by a wealthy Elizabethan, is an actual Manchester institution. A nineteenth-century descendant of the founder appears in the library, and through his dream the reader learns that an ancient injustice to his father will be righted. The story, apparently based on a historic case and dealing with ancient documents and a lost heir, is in some ways trite, but MEB told it well, probably under the inspiration of Harrison Ainsworth, whose *Mervyn Clitheroe* (1852) touches upon many of the same Manchester themes. "A Very Narrow Escape" (original publication not traced) deals with a foolish, neglected young wife, who is saved from being talked into a fatal indiscretion by her husband's loyal confidential clerk. "My Unlucky Friend" (original publication not traced) tells of a rich bachelor, jilted long ago, who later suffers the same fate at the hands of his first love's daughter.

9. *The lawsuit over* The Story of Barbara
(Chapter VIII, note 18)

After publication of *Barbara* had begun under the title *Splendid Misery*, which Yates had chosen from several submitted by MEB, John Dicks, proprietor of the weekly magazine *Every Week,* brought action against Yates in the Court of Chancery. In 1874, Dicks had published a serial story by C. H. Hazlewood (since deceased) under the same title. MEB and Yates changed the title to *The Story of Barbara; Her Splendid Misery and Her Gilded Cage,* and in court their counsel argued that in 1801 T. S. Surr had used the title *Splendid Misery* for a three-volume novel, so that Hazlewood had no proprietary right in it, adding that MEB's novel was wholly different from Hazlewood's. But Vice-Chancellor Bacon found that Yates should pay the costs of the suit. On appeal, the Master of the Rolls accepted the views of MEB's and Yates's counsel, reversed the decision, and not only awarded costs to Yates, but declared that Dicks's copyright claim to the title was invalid. The *Times,* Wednesday November 10, 1880, p. 4, reported the Chancery Court's decision; the *Bookseller,* No. 283, June 3, 1881, p. 512, summarized the Master of the Rolls' reversal, which it called "of very great importance in the trade." Full texts of the Chancery case can be found in the *Law Times Reports* n.s., 43 (September 1880–February 1881), 470–472; and of the appeal in *ibid.* n.s., 44 (March–August 1881), 660–667.

10. *MEB's chores of 1880–1881* (Chapter VIII, note 21)

(a) The *Figaro* novel.

Neither the "schedule" nor the diaries mention the novel in French. But W. B. Maxwell recorded (*TG,* pp. 281–282) that MEB "wrote in French a novel that was published in the Paris *Figaro.*" He gave no date and said no more about it. The *Figaro* files reveal that this was *Le Pasteur de Marston,* which was the *feuilleton* of the *Figaro* appearing in the eight issues of November 26, 27, 28, 29, and 30; and December 3, 4, and 5, 1881: Monday through Friday of an entire week, and Monday, Tuesday, and Wednesday of the next (*Le Figaro,* 27e Année, 3e Série, Nos. 330–334 and 337–339 inclusive, p. 2 of each issue).

For an MEB addict, *The Pastor of Marston* comes as a thorough disappointment. Its protagonist is an ex-convict, an embezzler, who takes refuge under a false name in an English provincial manufacturing town. By rigorous self-denial and prolonged hypocritical demonstrations of piety he becomes the much-admired minister of the Dissenters' chapel and wins the love of a rich and beautiful orphan girl. But he is already married, and blackmail intervenes: he is tracked down by his brother-in-law, who threatens to report his whereabouts to his wife. The minister gives the blackmailer money, but, for security, murders his wife and is about to marry his fiancée when he is unmasked through the detective work of a young lawyer who loves the same girl. The "respectability" that is the fetish of the small town is scathingly lampooned, and the suggestion that a criminal who readily murders an innocent, hard-working young woman would find his proper place in a dissenting pulpit is a crude restatement of MEB's hostility to cant.

But even Sigismund Smith or MEB in her own *Halfpenny Journal* days took more trouble with the plot machinery and made crime and detection more plausible. The minister allows himself to be followed while buying his false beard and old clothes in the London slums, and after he has killed his wife throws away his disguise where it is easily found. It is almost as if MEB were taking revenge on the French for their reams of similar penny-dreadfuls that she had read and cheerfully plagiarized in the sixties and had satirized through Sigismund: " 'Philip Launay, what doest thou do there with the corpse of thy victim?' " Some of the names she chose—Deuzil for the minister, Huret for the young lawyer—were as preposterous as her story. If this had been the sort of fare that the *Figaro* regularly served up in its *feuilletons,* one might understand; but Loti, Maupassant, Tolstoy, Kipling, Bret Harte, and other distinguished writers appeared in its pages. Moreover, one would have expected that in view of MEB's love of French and her preoccupation in the early eighties with French writers and subjects, she would have tried to give French readers a sample of her best work. Not so. *Le Pasteur de Marston* was probably an old French exercise dating from the sixties.

(b) Abridging Scott.

The abridgment of Scott's novels began with *Rob Roy* on October 12 and 13, 1880, and the diaries record progress on it throughout that year and the next. In a publisher's catalogue (p. ix) at the end of (MEB) "Author of Lady Audley's Secret," *Flower and Weed and Other Tales* (London: John and Robert Maxwell, n.d. [1884]), is an advertisement for "Miss Braddon's Penny Edition of Sir Walter Scott's Novels," which declares that "Whatever scruple may have been felt hitherto by the Cleric and the Layman to placing fiction before children of tender years, it is hoped that the New Penny Editions of Sir Walter Scott will be found to satisfy every scruple and to realise every requirement." The whole set of sixteen volumes bound in a single paper volume sold for one shilling and in cloth for a shilling and sixpence. MEB's diary for September 21, 1881, records that 21,000 copies of the abridged *Quentin Durward* alone had been sold in advance of publication.

(c) The "other tales" in *Flower and Weed and Other Tales* [1884].

While *Vixen* was in progress, the "schedule" shows that MEB completed on November 10, 1877, two short stories, "Thou Art the Man," and "The Clown's Quest." Where they appeared originally I do not know, but both were republished in *Flower and Weed and Other Tales* (London: John and Robert Maxwell, n.d. [1884]). The former (pp. 310–337) tells of a brilliant actor in the years right after Waterloo, when the theatre was a passion of the London populace. Matthew Elyard is, in externals at least and in his extraordinary dramatic skill, drawn as a portrait of Edmund Kean, whom MEB would make the hero of *The Green Curtain* (1911). Elyard's electrifying performance as a murderer in a play called "The Venetian Husband" proves his undoing: a spectator in the theatre, just returned from five years at sea, learns that the girl he had been in love with in England has disappeared, and is convinced that she has been murdered. Under another name, Elyard had been in the house at the time as secretary to her grandfather, and now the murder is brought home to him. In "The Clown's Quest" (pp. 166–194), John Groman (otherwise Grumani, a successful clown in pantomime, whose name echoes that of the famous Grimaldi) had restored to a firm of jewelers that had employed his scapegrace brother the price of a diamond bracelet the brother had stolen. In due course, the brother too refunds the money, and the jewelers return it to Groman. Ten years later, just as Groman concludes that his brother has died, he appears, a rich man from investing in diamonds, and they all have a happy reunion during the intermission of a pantomime. But when Groman's act is over, his brother and the bags of diamonds have vanished. Helped by a friendly police constable, Groman finds the missing man, who has been robbed but is still alive and well. The constable is an able detective and an avid fan of Groman, telling him " 'That trick of yours with the old woman and the umbrella is the finest thing that has ever been done in the British drama. There's nothing in Skakespeare to beat it' " (p. 178).

The diary for May 9, 1881, records that MEB "began tale for M[istletoe] B[ough]." Called "Boscobel" in the "schedule," this actually appeared as "His Secret" and was later reprinted in *Flower and Weed and Other Tales* (pp. 278–309). It is a lively story of eighteenth-century Cornwall. The volume also contains four other short stories: "George Caulfield's Journey" (pp. 132–165, written, according to the "schedule," in July 1879, and first published in the *Mistletoe Bough* for 1879, pp. 5–21), in which a reserved young curate accedes to a stranger's request to escort an invalid lady on a train journey, only to find soon after the train's departure that his charge is dead, and to be arrested on suspicion of murder; "Dr. Carrick" (pp. 195–217, first published in the Extra Summer Number of *All the Year Round* for 1878), in which mesmerism is used for both good and evil purposes; "If She Be Not Fair to Me" (pp. 228–258, first published in the *Mistletoe Bough* for 1880, pp. 114–128), a more conventional story about a debutante who twice rejects a young officer, only to fall in love with him after he has transferred his affections to her younger sister, who wins him; and "The Shadow in the Corner" (pp. 259–277, first called "Wildheath Grange" and, according to the "schedule," written between May 28 and June 3, 1879, originally published in the Extra Summer Number of *All the Year Round* for 1879), a grim, tragic little story of a haunted room.

(d) Plays.

During July and most of August 1881, MEB wrote the comedy *Married beneath Him*, at first entitled *Polly*, and three essays, entitled "The Children," "The

Observant," and "A Little Hunting," none of which I have seen. Two other plays, *Dross* (first entitled *The Root of Evil*) and *Margery Daw,* were also written during July and August 1881.

Dross, in four acts, was more a farce than a comedy, showing the terrible change that comes over a thoroughly decent man when he unexpectedly inherits money, and his equally incredible recovery of decency when he loses it. MEB hoped that it would reach the stage. As late as 1884, her diary shows that on February 12 she worked on *Dross* all morning and that in the afternoon "Mr. James" and Clement Scott, the drama critic, came to Lichfield House to hear *Dross* read and to "suggest improvements." On February 23, she "revised and improved *Dross* all day," and sent it to "Clement Scott by night post." In the interim John Maxwell had tried to secure a "retaining fee" from David James, who on February 20, 1884, refused, calling Maxwell's request "a little premature":

> I have not yet been asked to pay a *retaining fee* by such authors as H. J. Byron, F. C. Burnand, Robert F. Reece, James Abbey, and others, not even on *completion* and *acceptance* of their works. Our custom is to pay a nightly fee on production, no length of run being guaranteed, and in each case having the refusal of American and Colonial rights. This we all thought a fair and equitable arrangement; when Mrs. Maxwell's play is completed and approved I think I shall be able to meet you in a satisfactory manner. I trust for *all* our sakes you will see this matter in the same light as I do. You know how anxious I am to get a good new play, and what with Mrs. Maxwell's name in conjunction with our good friend Clement Scott and the few suggestions I gave, which were fully approved by Mrs. Maxwell and Scott I think I may venture to predict a big success for us all. (Wolff Collection)

Whether Maxwell dropped his demand or whether MEB never wrote a version satisfactory to Scott and Davis is uncertain, but *Dross* was never produced.

Margery Daw, suggested by a story of Thomas Bailey Aldrich, is a two-act "Household Idyl," in which a devoted young woman catches the interest of her fretful male cousin, a painter, while he awaits an operation on his eyes, by inventing a family that—so she says—has just moved in next door with a beautiful daughter. What happens after he has fallen in love with the imaginary girl, and then, when he recovers and learns that she has never existed, forms the substance of the play. Both *Dross* and *Margery Daw* were published in *Under the Red Flag and Other Tales* (London: John and Robert Maxwell, n.d. [1886]) on pp. 148–206 and pp. 332–352 respectively. Clement Scott (1841–1904) in his youth was on the staff of *Fun* with W. S. Gilbert and F. C. Burnand, later editor of *Punch* and a great friend of MEB. Scott had some success in adapting the plays of Sardou for the English stage. Taking some of the liveliness of his style from his colleague on the *Telegraph*, Sala, he was a much feared critic. His first wife was George du Maurier's sister, Isabelle.

(e) "Revising" other people's novels; essays.

During 1882 and 1883 the diaries show that MEB revised several novels by other authors for publication by Maxwell. The entries are always abbreviated and sometimes cryptic. But "Sphinx" (September 1 and 2, 1882) is probably Major E. Rogers, *A Modern Sphinx* (3 vols., London: Maxwell, 1881), dealing with an army surgeon who is actually a woman in male disguise, and based on the true case of Dr. Barry James, Inspector-General of the Army Medical Department, whose true sex was not discovered until her death. Copies of the three-volume original edition and of MEB's "edited" one-volume revision (undated) entitled *Madeline's Mystery* are in the Wolff Collection. MEB also "revised" for Maxwell a novel called *Married in Haste* (Diary, September 6, 1882), of which an American edition (Popular Novels, vol. I, No. 346, New York: Norman L. Munro, 1885) is in the Wolff Collection; published anonymously and sometimes attributed to MEB, it is surely not by her. She also "revised" *Put to the Test* by Ada Buisson; *Only a Woman*, anon.; *On Her Majesty's Secret Service*, for which see the advertisements at the back of Mayne Reid, *The Pierced Heart* (London: John Maxwell, 1884), a yellowback first edition; and a novel by Lascelles Wraxall (Diary, October 25, 1882), one by somebody named Williams (Diary, October 27, 1882), and one that MEB called simply "R.M." (Diary, November 4, 1882). Revisions in 1883 included "Irish novel" (Diary, January 24, 1883); "Tales of English Peasantry" (Diary, February 28, 1883); and—most interesting—Victorien Sardou's play *Fédora* (Diary, May 10, 11, 14, 17, 1883). The play opened at the Gaiety Theatre in London, with Sarah Bernhardt in the lead, on July 10, and received an unfavorable notice in the *Athenaeum* (No. 2907, July 14, 1883, p. 58). See also Squire and Marie Bancroft, *The Bancrofts, Recollections of Sixty Years* (London: John Murray, 1909), pp. 233 ff.

The diary for January 4, 1884, records that MEB wrote an essay for the *Whitehall Review* entitled "People who Write to the *Times*," and another entitled "A Friendly Moment."

11. *The short stories in* Under the Red Flag and Other Tales
(Chapter VIII, note 28)

The volume also included "Across the Footlights," first published in the *Mistletoe Bough* for 1884 (see Chapter II, text and note 20, above), "At Daggers Drawn" (see Chapter II, text and note 24, above), and five other stories. Three of these dated back to *Belgravia* days, and two had originally been published under the "Babington White" pseudonym: in "Dorothy's Rival," pp. 224–238 (originally published in the *Belgravia Christmas Annual* for 1867), an

eighteenth-century curate engaged to the vicar's daughter is suspected of keeping a secret mistress. She is only a blind, deaf, and dumb girl he has rescued
from misery. In "Sir Philip's Wooing," pp. 207–223 (originally published in the
Belgravia Christmas Annual for 1870), set in the time of Charles II, a wicked
rake seduces his cousin's wife and murders his cousin, but is brought to book
for his crimes. "My Wife's Promise," pp. 317–331 (originally published in the
Belgravia Christmas Annual for 1869), tells of an Arctic explorer and the ghost
of his beloved wife, which appears to him in the icy northern wastes, a tale
surely suggested by the loss of Sir John Franklin and the various expeditions
that searched for him. "A Great Ball and a Great Bear, " pp. 253–266 (first
publication untraced but early in MEB's career), is about a girl of fifteen, whose
cousin and suitor keeps his promise to return from his travels for her twenty-first
birthday. "The Little Woman in Black," pp. 266–284, was the last written,
between June 22 and June 30, 1885, according to the diary for that year. The
original manuscript of twelve holograph pages is in the Wolff Collection. First
published in the *Mistletoe Bough* for Christmas 1885, the story tells of a
beautiful actress of the Covent Garden Theatre in 1753, formerly in love with a
dashing rake and now engaged to a great nobleman, who is saved from disgrace
when her former lover's wife, the little woman in black, returns the indiscreet
letters she had written him.

12. *Maxwell's negotiations with Tillotson about* Ishmael
(Chapter VIII, note 29)

On June 9, 1883, as *Phantom Fortune* was nearing completion, Maxwell asked
Tillotson, "What say you to next year? The dose then to be repeated as
before?" But Tillotson apparently had other plans for the first nine months of
1884. On July 11, 1883, Maxwell asked incredulously: "Am I right in inferring
that October 1884 will be your next opening for another novel from my wife? I
am not certain that she will write another *at any time,*" a suggestion—perhaps
only partly serious—that MEB was considering giving full time to the drama.
Tillotson had Wilkie Collins and several other popular novelists on his string
and was presumably not prepared to use more than one Braddon novel every
nine or ten months, while Maxwell always pushed her writings. Perhaps
Tillotson also wanted a holiday from Maxwell's hectoring correspondence. On
October 29, Maxwell wrote that the *Whitehall Review* wanted MEB's next
novel—*Ishmael*—(to begin in its issue of January 16, 1884) and asked if Tillotson would "help to plant it out elsewhere for ¼ share of [serial] profits,"
"elsewhere" meaning America, New Zealand, and Australia, since the *Whitehall
Review* would possess exclusive rights in England, Scotland, and Ireland. But
there intervened in November 1883 a brief but heated controversy about Tillotson's allegedly improper reprinting of Mary Cecil Hay's novel *Missing*, the
copyright of which Maxwell—while asserting that he hated "argumentative
correspondence"—insisted was his alone.

By early December, the question of Tillotson's role in selling newspaper serial rights to *Ishmael* abroad had become entangled with the question of his undertaking to publish MEB's next novel, for which he apparently offered Maxwell less than he had paid for *Phantom Fortune*. On December 11, Maxwell wrote, "The negotiation for another new Braddon novel is ended. . . . The probabilities are that Miss Braddon will drift into drama, her first love." But on December 26, Maxwell accepted £75 for the Australian newspaper rights to *Ishmael,* and after a flurry of telegrams, just as publication in the *Whitehall Review* was about to begin, Tillotson produced £150 more for the American newspaper rights, in spite of Maxwell's apparent inability to convince him that ten days advance possession of the proofs would be ample to satisfy the American subscribers to the "côterie," while any longer time would endanger copyright. On January 2, 1884, even though his own newspapers were not publishing *Ishmael* in England, Tillotson issued for American newspapers a circular like that for *Phantom Fortune,* offering serial rights for £25. When the whole matter had been settled, Maxwell was still disappointed that Harper's had not been brought into the fold: "It would be a great relief to me," he wrote, "if you could lose your temper and damn and blast as I should like to do at this moment, but not at you, my gentle Willie!" And before *Ishmael* was completed, there was another brief spat in July 1884, when Tillotson objected that the date Maxwell had fixed for three-volume publication—August 9, 1884, six weeks before *Whitehall Review* serial publication was to terminate on September 18—was too early. Maxwell reluctantly put book publication off four weeks to accommodate Tillotson, though objecting that "Since you have crossed the big pond you appear to think that I have a fiendish delight in trying to damage you. . . . Please get any such notion out of the way. It should never have got in to your very clever head." (John Maxwell to W. F. Tillotson, thirty letters and telegrams between June 9, 1883, and July 25, 1884; quotations from letters of June 9, July 11, October 29, November 2, December 11, December 26, 1883, and January 16, July 19, 1884 [Tillotson File].)

13. *Maxwell's negotiations with Tillotson for* Wyllard's Weird
(Chapter VIII, note 37)

In spite of John Maxwell's decision in December 1883 to terminate all negotiations with Tillotson for MEB's late 1884 novel (see above, Appendix, Section 12), by February 15, 1884 he was offering a new novel to begin the first week in October, on the same terms as *Phantom Fortune* (see Chapter VIII, text and note 26). By February 19, the agreement was completed, and on the 21st, Maxwell told Tillotson that the title would be *Wild Miss Wyllards,* "and a ripping good one too." In March, he referred to Tillotson two inquiries from newspaper proprietors, with instructions to "nail" them. On July 8, he told Tillotson that the novel's title would be changed and asked whether Tillotson "could contrive an opening for a short novel—say one volume story," presumably *Cut by the*

County (see below, Appendix, Section 15). On July 10, he notified Tillotson that Harper's would pay £175 for the use of the new novel and £100 for the shorter story, for which he was asking Tillotson £200. *"Wyllard's Weird* for ever!," he proclaimed on August 9, after the first copy had been sent in, and euphorically invited Tillotson to visit in the New Forest, "Bed and Board are ready: scenery superb: welcome certain!" But once more, differences arose over the times of payment and details of the contract, which Maxwell declared should be identical with those of 1882 for *Phantom Fortune.* Then an American named Caldwell, publisher of the Sea-side Library in New York, who had paid £150 for the sheets of *Ishmael,* twice complained because the novel had been published in London six weeks before it was finished in his newspaper. Caldwell, said Maxwell, had no case, and moreover he had "used Miss Braddon's good name as author of literary rubbish that she never saw." By September 17, Tillotson had received the first seven numbers of *Wyllard's Weird,* and Maxwell was demanding to know when and where it would begin publication in England, and asking a fortnight's hiatus in exporting proofs and in corresponding with MEB *"who needs rest and must take it."* As the time for book publication drew nearer, Maxwell grew more and more nervous about protecting the English copyright: "The publication of W.W. in Sunday Mercury [New York] is both dangerously and unnecessarily close," he wrote on January 19, 1885, "You must undertake to defend me or to indemnify me from loss of copyright." He was planning to publish it in three volumes on March 10. As late as March 5, he was agonized about the possibility that Caldwell in New York, publisher of the *Sunday Mercury,* was issuing *Wyllard's Weird* installments prior to their appearance in Tillotson's *Newcastle Weekly Journal* in England, and so jeopardizing the copyright. (John Maxwell to W. F. Tillotson, twenty-five letters between February 15, 1884, and March 5, 1885; quotations from those dated February 19, 21, July 8, August 9, September 16 and 17, 1884; January 19, March 5, 1885 [Tillotson File].)

14. *The books MEB read to Max, 1892–1895* (Chapter IX, note 7)

In 1892: Scott's *Woodstock,* Bulwer's *Last Days of Pompeii,* Scott's *Ivanhoe* and *The Fortunes of Nigel,* Bulwer's *The Disowned,* Dickens' *Great Expectations,* Bulwer's *My Novel,* Trollope's *Phineas Finn,* Thackeray's *Esmond,* W. E. Norris' *Miss Shafto,* Scott's *Fair Maid of Perth,* G. J. Whyte-Melville's *Good for Nothing;* in 1893, Scott's *Quentin Durward,* Rider Haggard's *She,* Conan Doyle's *Micah Clarke,* Scott's *Pirate,* Walter Besant's *Bells of St. Paul's* (which was "discarded; too dull"), F. Anstey [T. Anstey Guthrie]'s *Pariah,* Bulwer's *Pelham,* Charles Lever's *Harry Lorrequer* (about which MEB noted "M. much enjoying it"), Lever's *Charles O'Malley,* Dickens' *Little Dorrit,* Lever's *The O'Donoghue,* the *Life* of Benjamin Robert Haydon, Dumas' *Count of Monte-Cristo,* Charlotte Brontë's *Jane Eyre,* Hall Caine's *Scapegoat,* Dickens' *Tale of Two Cities,* Trollope's *Last Chronicle of Barset,* Lever's *Tom*

Burke of Ours, Trollope's *Framley Parsonage,* Lever's *Knight of Gwynne,* Quiller-Couch's *Splendid Spur,* W. D. Howells' *Rise of Silas Lapham,* Thackeray's *Philip,* Stevenson's *Catriona* (i.e., *David Balfour*), Scott's *Talisman* and *Anne of Geierstein;* in 1894, Scott's *St. Ronan's Well* and *Guy Mannering,* Lever's *One of Them,* Wilkie Collins' *Armadale,* Dickens' *David Copperfield,* Scott's *Heart of Midlothian,* Blackmore's *Lorna Doone,* Bulwer's *Last of the Barons,* Scott's *Montrose,* Menella Bute Smedley's *Twice Lost,* Dickens' *Our Mutual Friend,* Charles Reade's *Griffith Gaunt* and *Put Yourself in His Place,* Dickens' *Bleak House,* Richard Henry Savage's *My Official Wife,* S. Baring-Gould's *Cheap Jack Zita,* Wilkie Collins' *Mrs. or Miss,* Conan Doyle's *Raffles Haw,* Trollope's *He Knew He Was Right,* Dickens' *Barnaby Rudge,* Trollope's *Can You Forgive Her?,* Stanley Weyman's *In the House of the Wolf,* Thackeray's *Newcomes* (which Max "rejected"), Albany de Fonblanque's *Tangled Skein,* Scott's *Black Dwarf,* Goldsmith's *Vicar of Wakefield,* Stevenson and Lloyd Osbourne's *Wrong Box,* Weyman's *Memoirs of Francis Cludde,* Haggard's *Allan's Wife* and *Beatrice,* Conan Doyle's *Round the Red Lamp* and *Sign of Four,* "Rita" [Mrs. Desmond Humphries]'s *Naughty Mrs. Gordon,* Stevenson's *Kidnapped,* Hall Caine's *Manxman,* Wilkie Collins' *Poor Miss Finch* and *The Black Robe.* In the first two months of 1895, before Maxwell died, MEB managed to read to him: Weyman's *My Lady Rotha,* du Maurier's *Trilby,* Grant Allen's *Bred in the Bone,* Kate Douglas Wiggin's *Timothy's Quest,* Spinola's *Johanna Trail,* Haggard's *People of the Mist,* Anstey's *Vice Versa,* Haggard's *Cleopatra,* Sir John Astley's *Memoirs (Fifty Years of My Life in the World of Sport* [London: Hurst & Blackett, 1894]), Mrs. Henry Wood's *East Lynne,* Hall Caine's *Bondman,* Anstey's *Giant's Robe* and *Black Poodle.* At the moment of Max's death she was reading him Wilkie Collins' *Legacy of Cain.*

15. Cut by the County (Chapter IX, note 22)

The novelette *Cut by the County,* a melodramatic story of robbery, hereditary alcoholism, and murder, MEB originally intended as a three-act play—as yet untitled—for Lady Monckton, for whom she wrote a long preliminary synopsis of the plot from St. Malo on August 13 [1883] (letter in the Princeton University Library). Perhaps Lady Monckton did not like it, because on April 9, 1884, MEB began to write it as a Christmas story. By May 14 it was finished. Tillotson handled its sale to the *People* for weekly serial publication and the sale of American serial rights. There was a fearful uproar from Maxwell about Harper's and the Messrs. Lovell in America, who would not realize that the novel was only as "long as the Vicar of Wakefield and may become equally popular," denounced the Lovells as "humbugs," declared himself in "a terrible funk," and fumed over possible loss of copyright. (Twenty-five letters and telegrams from John Maxwell to W. F. Tillotson between November 8, 1884, and March 21, 1885, in the Tillotson File.) In the end, *Cut by the County* did not appear in any of Harper's publications. After serial publication in the *People,* it was first published in book form as the third volume of MEB's three-decker of 1886, the first two forming *One Thing Needful.*

16. *Madame Novikoff, Gladstone, and the Novelists*
(Chapter IX, note 22)

On the intimacy between Madame Novikoff and Gladstone in 1876–1877, enthusiastically endorsed, with copious quotations from the letters they exchanged, see W. T. Stead, *The M. P. for Russia. Reminiscences and Correspondence of Madame Olga Novikoff* (2 vols., London: Andrew Melrose, 1909), I, pp. 274 ff. and especially 292 ff. and 294, note 1. When asked by his private secretary on May 12, 1885, how far he trusted Madame Novikoff, however, Gladstone replied, " 'About as far as I would trust an R.C. Church dignitary like Manning. She would be truthful enough so long as her end could be gained by adherence to truth. After that she would probably not be very scrupulous as to means.' " (*The Diary of Sir Edward Walter Hamilton,* ed. Dudley W. R. Bahlman [Oxford: Clarendon Press, 1972], II, p. 862.) For Madame Novikoff see also Wilfred Scawen Blunt, *My Diaries* (London: Martin Secker, 1920), II, p. 250. She appears in Mrs. Campbell Praed, *Nadine* (2 vols., London: Chapman & Hall, 1882); see Colin Roderick, *In Mortal Bondage. The Strange Life of Rosa Praed* (Sydney and London: Angus and Robertson, 1948), pp. 88–92. Mrs. Praed also put Madame Novikoff into *Zéro* (2 vols., London: Chapman & Hall, 1884). She appears also in W. E. Norris, *Misadventure* (3 vols., London: Spencer Blackett, 1890), and Grant Allen, *Under Sealed Orders* (3 vols., London: Chatto & Windus, 1895).

17. *The short stories in* All Along the River, *vol. III*
(Chapter IX, note 30)

The stories are: "One Fatal Moment" (first published in *Mistletoe Bough* for 1889, pp. 1–16), in which bored young officers stationed in Lowford (Lincoln) entertain the ladies of a theatrical company at dinner, and a magnificent Irish equestrienne is so outraged by a drunken young officer's denunciation of Ireland that she stabs him fatally: she escapes, but in later years her victim's elder brother falls in love with her (a switch in sexes of the plot of *The Venetians*), and she is prevented from marrying him when the Colonel, who had witnessed the stabbing, forces her to confess to her fiancé. This is her punishment, and years later the Colonel himself marries her. In "It Is Easier for a Camel" (first published in the *Mistletoe Bough* for 1888, pp. 88–98), MEB shows with much irony how a man who has unexpectedly inherited £3,000,000 dies without having been able to decide how to spend it. In "The Ghost's Name" (first published in the *Mistletoe Bough* for 1891, pp. 115–132) a sinister apparition that kills all those who have slept in a certain room proves to be typhoid fever. "Stapylton's Plot" (first published in the *Mistletoe Bough* for 1887, pp. 67–73) tells of a rich young man who has a plot for a novel that he never can write, dealing with the rescue of a woman from suicide. Stapylton does, however, *live* the plot, and the girl, saved once, succeeds in killing herself before he can discover anything about her. The best of this collection, this story would serve as the basis for *Mary*, MEB's last (posthumously published) novel (1916); see chapter X. "His Oldest Friends" (first published in the *Mistletoe Bough* for 1890, pp. 1–15) tells of a ghostly tradition in a French noble family, and how it repeats itself. In "If There Be Any of You" (first published in the *Mistletoe Bough* for 1889, pp. 110–114), a woman who has grown to hate her dull country-squire husband, and so abstains from communion, is persuaded by the vicar to repent. The narrator of "The Island of Old Faces" (first published in the *Mistletoe Bough* for 1892, pp. 1–8) tells of his visions on a tropical island: he meets the dead he has loved, yet the island is uninhabited. "My Dream" (previous publication untraced) tells of a girl who has all too true a vision of her lover being killed on a shooting party; her will is so powerful that she summons his spirit back to see her for a brief moment.

MEB never again published a collection of short stories after this third volume of *All Along the River,* which helps explain why some titles appearing in her diaries for the nineties have proved untraceable. See below, Appendix, Section 18b.

18. *Plays and Short Stories in the final years* (Chapter IX, note 32)

(a) Plays.

When MEB died, W. B. Maxwell found in her desk seven unpublished plays, which he does not identify (*TG,* p. 281). Those referred to by name in her diaries are as follows:

Nero (May 30, June 6, 1890).
Free Lances (September 23, 25, 27, 30; October 2, 4, 5, 9, 1893; June 21, 1895).
Worldlings (November 11, 13, 1893).
The Garreteers (September 24, 1894; January 10, February 12, August 23, 1895; May 12, 1899). Braddon Notebook VI, pp. 113–124, contains a preliminary sketch, set in 1750.
Breadwinner (October 21, 1895, "Sketch and experiment in Robertsonian comedy"; July 13, 16, 17, 1896).
Sigismund (March 31, May 26, 1904).

The celebrated dramatist Arthur Wing Pinero wrote MEB on December 29, 1895 (Wolff Collection), agreeing to read "either of the two plays, and tell you what I think of it." He probably was referring to *Free Lances* and *The Gar-reteers*. But he struck a discouraging note: "I wonder why you, with your great and assured gifts, should trouble about the wretched theatre, but you *will* do it—so there's an end to that. And as you are so intent upon it, everyone would like to see you triumph. I wish I could think I could help you in such a direction, but at any rate my counsel is at your service."

On December 8, 1896, MEB wrote to Edward Terry that she was sending him two acts of a play, on which he had offered to collaborate if he liked it. "I have plenty of material"—she wrote—"for what I venture to think will be a third act of strong human interest. . . . If you don't like the play, or don't see your way to wanting it this side of eternity, please let me have the M.S. at your earliest convenience [Wolff Collection]." Three days later he politely rejected it, finding the leading characters "so uncongenial that they leave a most unpleasant taste in the mouth [Wolff Collection.]" This was probably *The Breadwinner*. A year later, Beerbohm Tree found one of her "costume plays" unsuitable; this was probably *The Garreteers*. And on May 24, 1902, Lionel Brough, the actor, whom she had known in Brighton more than forty years before, when she was an actress and he a journalist, wrote her that he had been reading two of her plays and would be giving her his "(candid) opinion on both" before long (Wolff Collection). This is all the information that the record seems to provide.

(b) MEB's late short stories.

MEB never published a collected volume of short stories after 1893. The diaries mention several, but do not tell where they appeared. Others are never mentioned. The following are the diary references together with additional comment:

"Sweet Simplicity" (December 13, 15, 27, 1892; February 17, 1894): untraced.

"Venetian Glass" (December 27, 1892): untraced.

"Herself" (January 2, 1893): untraced.

"The Fly from the George" (January 17, 21, 1893): untraced.

"Does Anything Matter" (February 7, 1893): untraced.

"Dean or Devil" (February 24, 27, 1893) is surely "The Dulminster Dynamiter," *Pall Mall Magazine* 1, No. 4 (August 1893), 469–482, which tells of the Dean of a Cathedral obsessed with his belief in a personal devil.

"A Modern Confessor" (not mentioned in the diary proper, but noted on a separate leaf headed "Journal of Work" as written with "The Dean" during February 1893), a playlet, appeared in the *Pall Mall Magazine* 1, No. 2 (June 1893), 140–146. The "modern confessor" is the physician to a fashionable woman, who tells him of her distress at the discovery of her husband's infidelity.

"Good Lady Ducayne" (December 4, 1893; September 18, 19, 1895), *Strand Magazine* 11 (1896), 185–199, is about a young girl, eager for a job, who finds one in the service of a female vampire. At the same time, MEB's close friend Bram Stoker was writing *Dracula,* published in 1897. A study of possible influence either way would perhaps be of interest.

"Uncle Jacob" (December 11, 1893): untraced.

"The Higher Life" (February 20, 1894): publication untraced, but signed galley proofs in the Wolff Collection; a tale of the deathbed of a wicked rich man.

"His Good Fairy" (February 21, 1894: "suggested by W[ill]"; February 22, 26): untraced.

"The Doll's Tragedy" (March 19, 22, 1894): untraced.

"Where Many Footsteps Pass" (August 12, 19, 26, 1895): untraced.

"The Winning Card" (October 17, 1895): untraced.

"The Honourable Jack" (sometimes called "Jack") (September 23, 25, 28; October 1, 3, 5, 15, 31; November 2, 1895): untraced; this may have been a novelette or even a play.

"Jane" (November 31: "novelette"; December 3, 19, 1895). This was the same as "Naomi" (July 12, 13, 15, 21, 27, 31: "Finished Naomi 78 pp.," 1897): publication untraced. Houghton Library MS Eng 1122.9 (pp. 22–25) includes a scenario for "Jane," a Cornish murder story in which conscience kills the murderess. A second, more developed version is in Braddon Notebook VI (pp. 140–143) headed "Naomi," although the protagonist's name is still Jane. MEB noted that she had finished the story on July 31, 1897, the same day on which the diary noted that *Naomi* had been completed. "Jane" and "Naomi" were surely the same. I have not been able to find its subsequent appearance in print.

"In the Nick of Time" (February 25, 1897): untraced.

After 1897 the diaries mention no further short stories, but MEB surely wrote some, for example, "The Cock of Bowker's," *London Magazine* 16, No. 9 (April–May 1906), 287–295, a copy of which is in the Wolff Collection, but of which no mention is made in the diaries. It tells of an ineffectual man, down and out and a member of the middle class, whose only sense of importance derives from his position as the oracle of a lower-class London pub; and of what happens when he marries and tries to conceal his innocent pastime from his wife.

A search of popular periodicals and newspapers for 1892–1915 would probably turn up published versions of the stories named in the diaries and as yet untraced, and also of an uncertain number of others unnamed in the diaries but surely written and published.

19. *The growth of* London Pride (Chapter X, note 23)

On pp. 10, 11, 12–16, and 17 of the second portion of Houghton MS Eng 1122.8 is a preliminary sketch of characters in *London Pride*. Braddon Notebook VI, pp. 22–54, comprises a detailed series of jottings for it, including some drafts of dialogue. The diary entries that show the progress of the writing are as follows: July 13, 1885, "Reading for R[estoration] novel"; July 15, 1885, "Began R[estoration] novel"; January 22, 1890 (after almost five years), "Wrote a little *Caroline* story"; further references in February and March and on April 18. After a hiatus of more than three years, it reappears as follows: December 25, 1893, "No Work, reading for L[ondon] P[ride]"; January 1, 1894, "Revising and writing L. Pride"; January 8, "Reading Shadwell and making extracts [for *London Pride*]"; January 10, "Working at L. P. Reading Ruigh's 'London' "; January 22, "Writing and reading for L. P."; January 25, "Revised 2d time, 15 folios L. P. sent to E. Dickens [the typist]"; February 6, "Wrote morning"; February 15, "Writing L. P. Letters morning"; February 17, "Wrote L. P."; February 20, "Revised The Higher Life [a short story, see Appendix, section 18]," "A little L. P."; March 5 and 12, "Writing L. P."; March 13, "Writing and revising L. P."; there are similar entries for April 13, 16, 17, 18, 24, 30; May 1; June 6; July 25, 26, 30; then August 7, "Finished L. P."

But the various revisions of *London Pride* began at once, and continued at intervals for more than a year, until December 11, 1895. The diary entries show that MEB worked on revisions on August 13, 20, 21, 22, 27, 28, 30, and 31; on September 4, she noted, "Finished revise, L. P." On September 26 and 29 and October 3, 1894, she was "revising proofs L. P." Then she did other work until March 11, 1895. On that date and March 18, 20, 21, and April 8, 9, 15, and 16, she was again working on "Revises L. P." On May 8, she "revised sheets L. P. morning"; and on May 18, 20, 21, she continued, until on May 22 she wrote, "Finished 3d revision of L. P." On October 10 and 14, and November 16 she was "revising London Pride for St. James's," the magazine that published it serially.

20. *The growth of* In High Places (Chapter X, note 26)

What would be *In High Places* made its first appearance in the diary on October 5, 1895: "Began novel (Felton) [i.e., the assassin in 1728 of the Duke of Buckingham]." She returned to it on March 18, 1896, after she had done no work for three months following Maxwell's death. (The diary of March 14 says "Scarcely any work done this quarter year.") She wrote it on March 31, April 6. and May 30. By June 16 it was called "George." On June 30, July 29, August 10 and 12, she was revising what she had written for the typist. On September 24 she was "working on George but very slowly." On October 1, 15, 20, 24, and 29; November 11, 13, 20, 24, 25, 26, and 27; December 14, 23, and 28, 1896, she was either writing or revising it. In 1897, she worked on it on March 5 and

6; April 5, 20, 21, 24; May 5, 14, 27; June 16. She revised again on October 15 and on the 18th noted, "Engaged on proofs 'George,' whole novel in hand"; on November 2, she "began extra chapter, George." And on December 7, 11, 14, 15, and 27 she continued to revise. Not until June 16 did it make its next and last appearance, its only one under its final name: "Revising In High Places. Sheets of Vol." *In High Places* was serialized in the *Lady's Realm* beginning in November 1897, and was published in one volume by Hutchinson in the autumn of 1898. There is a preliminary manuscript outline in Houghton MS Eng 1122.9, with many excerpts from sources for the book.

The novel begins at the moment of the assassination in 1728 of the Duke of Buckingham and tells of the hero's adventurous life through the next three decades. Many of its most important scenes were set in the court of the young Louis XIV, still dominated by Anne of Austria and Mazarin. This was Dumas territory—as indeed was Felton's crime. It is no longer possible, as it was for MEB's readers of 1898, to care who was the father of the protagonist.

21. *The development of some late novels*
(Chapter X, notes 31, 33, 36, 38, 40, 41, 43)

(a) *Under Love's Rule.*

The diaries show that she began it on August 23, 1893; wrote it on August 24 and 25, September 2, 12, and 18, October 11, November 2, 10, 14, and 15. She revised it on September 5, 6, 7, and 12 of 1894, almost a year later. Thereafter it disappeared from the diary until January 6, 1897, when she wrote, "Working on proofs, Under Love's Rule." This is the first and only time the story appears under its eventual title. It appeared serially under its first title, but I have not traced its periodical publication.

(b) *Rough Justice.*

In the diaries the first mention is under January 7, 1895. MEB wrote it on January 9, 12, 25, 28, 29, 30, and 31; February 1, 13, 14, 16, and 19. On the 25th she had a bad cold, and the quinine she took for it interfered with working; the first week in March was the week of Maxwell's last illness and death. She resumed "Shadowed" on April 22, wrote it again on May 3, 29, 30, and 31; June 3, 6, 20, 22, 27, and 28; July 3, 8, 9, 10, 11, 13, 16, 17, 19, 20, and 24; on August 8 she "posted proof"; writing resumed on August 27, and on September 17, she "finished Shadowed." For more than a year the diaries make no further mention of the novel, which was probably being serialized: where, I do not know. On December 7, 1896, she was "busy on revise of Shadowed." There is no further mention until a final note on June 29, 1897, when the novel has its final name for the first and only time: "Finished revision Rough Justice for book form."

(c) *His Darling Sin.*

The first appearance of this novel in the diaries is on February 1, 1899: "*Lady Perivale,* 51 pp."; so it was already well underway. MEB wrote it on March 23, "despatched proofs 2 & 3 on March 30" (but where was it being published serially?); worked on it on April 27, and finished it on May 5. The serial version had been short; for book publication expansion was necessary: the diaries show that MEB worked on this on August 25 and 31 ("40th p. revised, + 18 pp. written"), and on September 12, 13, and 15: "Finished editing and expanding novel His Darling Sin—Lady P." There was more revision on September 26. The completed novel—with no date on its title page—was published during November 1899, and reviewed in the *Athenaeum* on November 25.

(d) *The Conflict* and *A Lost Eden.*

The diary for 1900, kept with all the usual meticulousness, makes no mention of writing throughout the year, except on June 11, when MEB said, "At home all morning, too hot for work," implying that when it was cooler she *did* work. But she had now begun *not* to mention in her diaries the progress of her writing. From now on, they become less helpful. During 1901, she noted on January 29 that she had "finished play," but gave no clue as to what it might have been. On August 8, she was "writing new story, Suburbans," which would become *A Lost Eden,* but it did not reappear until March 31, 1902. *The Conflict* made its first appearance only on April 3, 1902, when she was already revising it. It appeared only twice more: on August 27 she was "Dividing 'Conflict,'" perhaps into new chapters after serial publication; on September 6, she "revised it." This is all we know about the growth of the novel. The diaries mention "The Suburbans" as having begun on August 8, 1901, and work on it was going forward on March 31 and October 9, 1902, and on January 10, 12, and 13, 1903, when MEB was revising it. She simply omitted to mention it most of the time that she was in fact working on it. It never appears in the diary under its final title, *A Lost Eden,* but there can be no doubt that the family in Camberwell were "suburban," and the villainous seducer refers (p. 51) to Marion's "suburban" prejudices that must be overcome before he can make her his mistress.

(e) *The Rose of Life.*

Braddon Notebook VI, pp. 125–139 and 170–176, contains a full preliminary sketch of the story that would become *The Rose of Life,* called "Viola" and then "Marion," after its heroine, whose name MEB eventually changed to Helen. The sketch includes a discussion of the central character Daniel and passages of dialogue for key scenes. The scanty diary entries with regard to its composition show that on May 6 and August 3, 1903, she ". . . wrote a little Daniel"; on August 19 and September 23 she was revising it. A note on a separate page of memoranda says, "Daniel, August 31, p. 139," which suggests that it was nearly if not entirely complete.

(f) *The White House.*

The first portion of the original manuscript of *The White House,* written in
purple ink on the rectos of seventy-two numbered lined pages, and corresponding to the firest eighty-five pages of the printed book, is in the Wolff
Collection. Here the name of the heroine is Helena, which MEB eventually
changed to Claudia before publication. Without the manuscript, one would be
unable to identify as *The White House* the novel that appears in the diary as
"Helena." The diaries have now grown increasingly cryptic and laconic about
MEB's writing. On September 9, 1905, the entry "Began new story" refers, I
believe, to the beginning of "Helena," otherwise *The White House.* On November 30, the entry is "Helena 127"; so the story was well advanced by then. On
January 31, 1906, "187. Story" probably means "Helena" again. And this is all.
One should note that the novel next published after *The White House—Dead
Love Has Chains* (originally entitled "Conrad")—had actually been completed
in 1904, before *The White House* was begun, and three years before its publication in 1907.

INDEX

Novikoff (Novikov), Mme. Olga, Gladstone's Russian friend: in MEB's *One Thing Needful*, 339–340, 501; in other novelists' fiction, 340, 501

Nyberg, B. M., 411

"Observant, The" (MEB), essay, 494–495

O'Connor, T. P., 365

Octoroon, The (MEB), halfpenny fiction, based on Boucicault's play, 119

O'Donnell, Mrs., John Maxwell's sister, 259

Ohnet, Georges, 365

"Old Arm Chair, The" (MEB), her earliest story, written at age ten, survives, 38–39

Oliphant, Mrs. Margaret Oliphant Wilson, novelist, 366; author of fierce anonymous attack on MEB in *Blackwood's Magazine*, 200–207, 208, 218, 366; answered by G. A. Sala, q.v., 207–209

"Olivia" (MEB), long poem published in *Garibaldi*, q.v., 83, 110–111

"On the Brink" (MEB), short story, 229–230

Once A Week: *Eleanor's Victory* serialized in, 438 n. 51

"One Fatal Moment" (MEB), short story, 330, 501

One Life, One Love (MEB), 334, 347

One Thing Needful (MEB), 321–322, 334, 338–342, 400 n. 2; portrait of Gladstone in, 339–341, 407, 501

O'Neill, Eliza, actress, 44–45, 48, 55, 64, 70

O'Neill, Eugene, 277

Only a Clod (MEB), 109, 137, 138, 139, 158, 167, 168, 195–196

Only a Woman, novel "edited" by MEB, 496

Open Verdict, An (MEB), 277–278

Oscar Bertrand; or, The Idiot of the Mountain (MEB): serialized in *The Halfpenny Journal*, 119, 122

Ouida, see Ramée, Louise de la

Our Adversary (MEB), 372, 396

Outcasts, The (MEB), title under which *Henry Dunbar* was serialized, 136

Ouvrière de Londres, La, French dramatic version of *Henry Dunbar*, 147

Paderewski, Ignace, 368

Paget, the Reverend F. E.: *Lucretia*, satirical anti-sensationalist novel, 218–219

Pall Mall Gazette: attacks on MEB in, 188, 210–216

Palmerston, Lord, 340

Pardoe, Julia, writer, 38, 420 n. 12

Paris Commune of 1871: and MEB, 257; in *Under the Red Flag*, 301–304, 313

Parker, Sir Gilbert, 366

Parkman, Francis: *The Conspiracy of Pontiac*, 375

Partridge, Bernard, artist, 330

Pascal, Blaise, 267, 378

Pasteur de Marston, Le (MEB), novelette written in French for *Le Figaro*, 285, 492–493

Patti, Adelina, 336, 366

Pearson, C. Arthur, publisher, 383–384

Peel, Sir Robert, 340

People, The: MEB's *Cut by the County* serialized in, 501

"People Who Write for the Times" (MEB), essay, 496

Perugini, Mrs. (Kate Dickens), 9

"Pétrolium, Le . . ." (MEB), parody of Zola in French in *Punch*, 320, 467 n. 42

Phantom Fortune (MEB): Zola's influence on, 295–299, 319, 497

Philp, Elizabeth, composer: MEB writes lyrics for, 336

Pinero, Sir Arthur Wing, playwright, 73, 337, 501–502; *The Second Mrs. Tanqueray*, 369

Pixérécourt, René Charles Guilbert de, French melodramatic playwright, 130

Planché, J. R., playwright: *The Prince of Happy Land*, 53